Dordogne & Lot

with Bordeaux & Toulouse

the Bradt Guide

Dana Facaros & Michael Pauls

www.bradtguides.com

Bradt Guides Ltd, UK
The Globe Pequot Press Inc, USA

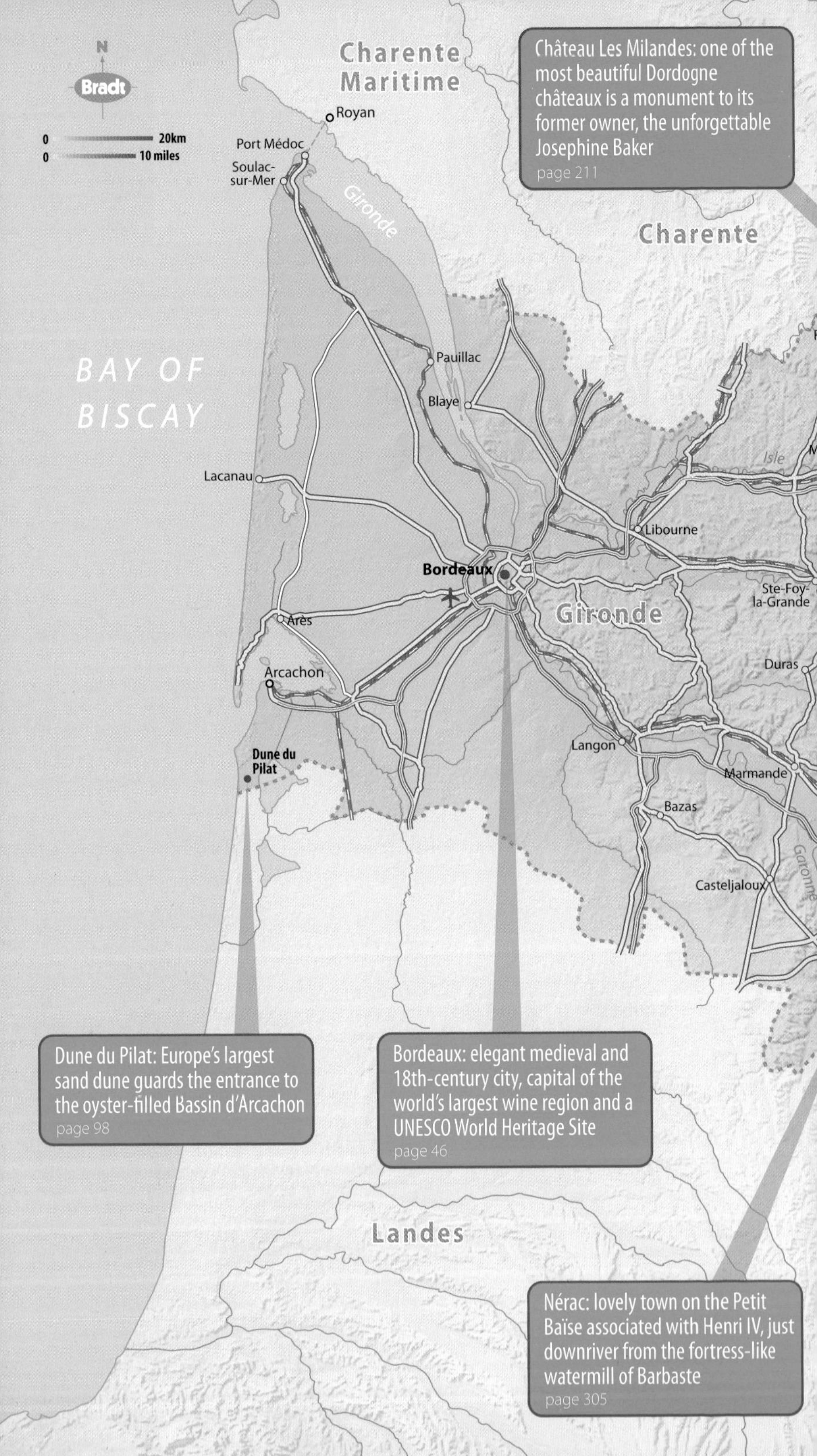

N
Bradt
0 20km
0 10 miles
Charente Maritime
Royan
Port Médoc
Soulac-sur-Mer
Gironde
Château Les Milandes: one of the most beautiful Dordogne châteaux is a monument to its former owner, the unforgettable Josephine Baker
page 211
Charente
BAY OF BISCAY
Pauillac
Blaye
Lacanau
Isle
Libourne
Bordeaux
Ste-Foy-la-Grande
Gironde
Arès
Arcachon
Duras
Dune du Pilat
Langon
Marmande
Bazas
Casteljaloux
Garonne
Dune du Pilat: Europe's largest sand dune guards the entrance to the oyster-filled Bassin d'Arcachon
page 98
Bordeaux: elegant medieval and 18th-century city, capital of the world's largest wine region and a UNESCO World Heritage Site
page 46
Landes
Nérac: lovely town on the Petit Baïse associated with Henri IV, just downriver from the fortress-like watermill of Barbaste
page 305

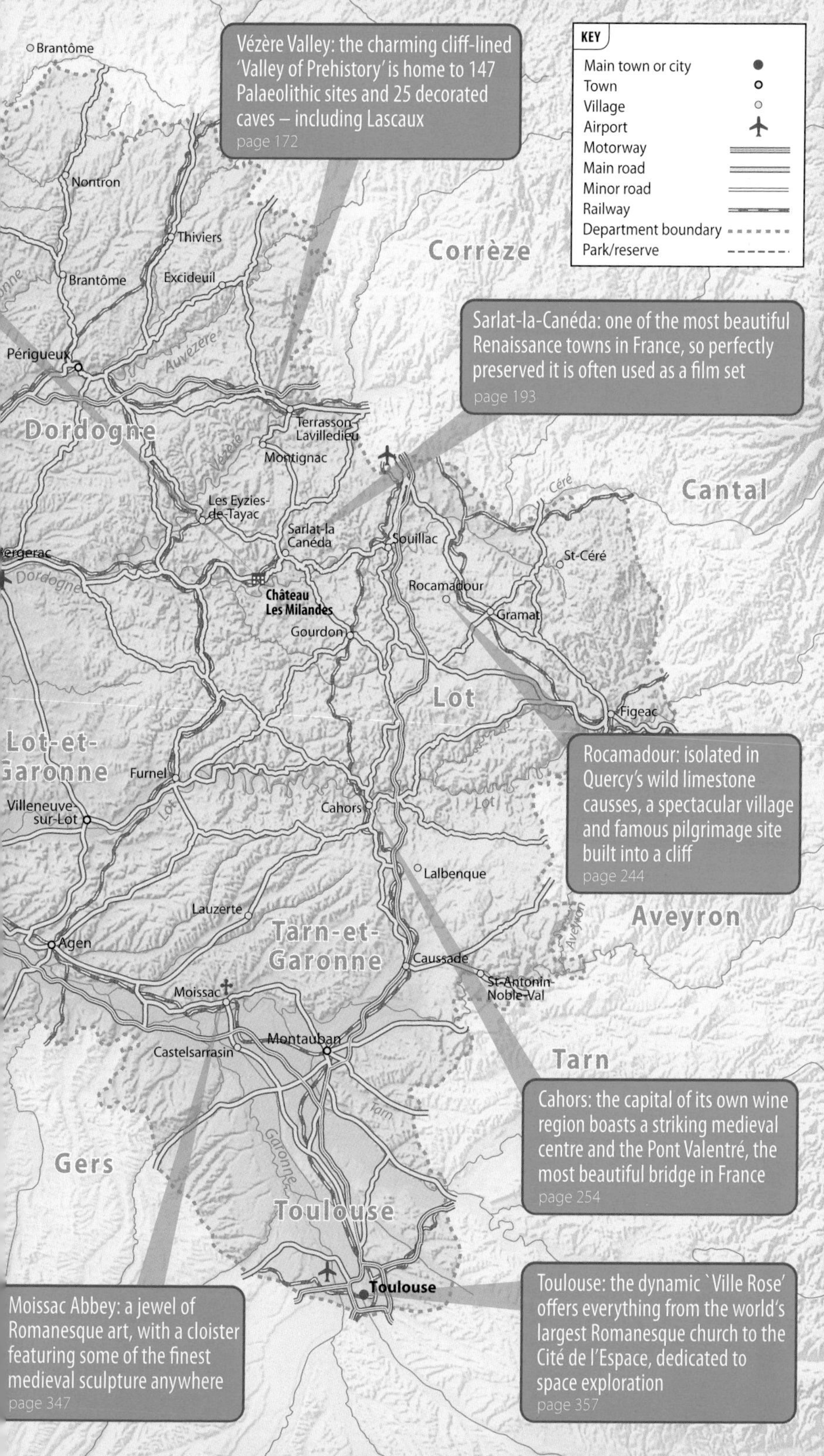
Vézère Valley: the charming cliff-lined 'Valley of Prehistory' is home to 147 Palaeolithic sites and 25 decorated caves – including Lascaux
page 172
KEY
Main town or city
Town
Village
Airport
Motorway
Main road
Minor road
Railway
Department boundary
Park/reserve
Sarlat-la-Canéda: one of the most beautiful Renaissance towns in France, so perfectly preserved it is often used as a film set
page 193
Rocamadour: isolated in Quercy's wild limestone causses, a spectacular village and famous pilgrimage site built into a cliff
page 244
Cahors: the capital of its own wine region boasts a striking medieval centre and the Pont Valentré, the most beautiful bridge in France
page 254
Moissac Abbey: a jewel of Romanesque art, with a cloister featuring some of the finest medieval sculpture anywhere
page 347
Toulouse: the dynamic `Ville Rose' offers everything from the world's largest Romanesque church to the Cité de l'Espace, dedicated to space exploration
page 357
Brantôme
Nontron
Thiviers
Brantôme
Excideuil
Périgueux
Auvézère
Corrèze
Dordogne
Terrasson-Lavilledieu
Montignac
Vézère
Les Eyzies-de-Tayac
Sarlat-la Canéda
Souillac
Cère
Cantal
Bergerac
Dordogne
St-Céré
Rocamadour
Château Les Milandes
Gramat
Gourdon
Lot
Figeac
Lot-et-Garonne
Furnel
Villeneuve-sur-Lot
Lot
Cahors
Lot
Lalbenque
Aveyron
Lauzerte
Agen
Tarn-et-Garonne
Caussade
Aveyron
St-Antonin-Noble-Val
Moissac
Montauban
Castelsarrasin
Tarn
Tarn
Garonne
Gers
Toulouse
Toulouse

Dordogne & Lot Don't miss...

Castles

More than 1,000 castles dot this land, some built for defence and some, like the fairy-tale Château de Jumilhac (pictured), for sheer beauty and prestige

(IW/S) page 165

Bordeaux

Bordeaux has more listed buildings than any French city outside Paris, including the majestic Palais de la Bourse (pictured)

(En/S) page 69

Landscapes
Bucolic landscapes of meadows and woodlands, winding rivers, rolling fields of sunflowers and vines are key to the region's charm. Pictured: Périgord Noir's Dordogne Valley (csp/S) page 193

Villages
Beynac-et-Cazenac, home to the mighty Château de Beynac, is just one of innumerable villages le changed since the Hundred Years' War (B944/S) page 210

Wine
Although Bordeaux is the greatest wine region in the world, there are many river wines waiting to be discovered. Pictured: Malbec vines near Cahors (MP) page 284

Dordogne & Lot in colour

top left The beloved frog fountain in the Manoir d'Eyrignac's White Garden (w/S) page 203

left Lascaux, the 'Sistine Chapel of Prehistory', is the star of the UNESCO World Heritage-listed Vézère Valley (th/S) page 180

below Château Les Milandes is filled with memories of its former chatelaine, Josephine Baker (OFC/S) page 211

above **The Cathédrale St-Étienne in Toulouse was built in three periods that didn't get along with each other** (SD/S) page 385

below **Bordeaux's new Cité du Vin is dedicated to wines and wine culture around the world** (KV/S) page 76

AUTHORS

Dana Facaros wrote her first travel guide to the Greek Islands in 1977, then married her college sweetheart **Michael Pauls** and dragged him into the fray. Ever since, they have been writing guides and apps and contributing to a number of UK publications, including the *Sunday Times, Sunday Times Travel Magazine, Daily Telegraph, Wanderlust* and *Which*? Over the past decades they have lived in Greece, Spain, Italy, Ireland and southwest France where they are currently based.

AUTHORS' STORY

Dana Facaros and **Michael Pauls** have lived in the Lot Valley since 1989, and over the decades have uncovered all the ins and outs (and quirks) of the region. Their children went to school here and they have even picked up the local twangy accent and know how to make garlic *tourain* soup, *pommes de terre sarladaises* and *cassoulet* with the best of them. They've been to nearly all of the festivals, climbed the Dune du Pilat, and poked around every single Romanesque church at least once. After all these years, what they don't know about the region isn't worth knowing.

FEEDBACK REQUEST

At Bradt Guides we're aware that guidebooks start to go out of date on the day they're published – and that you, our readers, are out there in the field doing research of your own. You'll find out before us when a fine new family-run hotel opens or a favourite restaurant changes hands and goes downhill. So why not tell us about your experiences? Contact us on ☎ 01753 893444 or **e** info@bradtguides.com. We will forward emails to the author who may post updates on the Bradt website at **w** bradtguides.com/updates. Alternatively, you can add a review of the book to Amazon, or share your adventures with us on Facebook, Twitter or Instagram (@BradtGuides).

COVID-19

Please note that research for this guide was carried out during the Covid-19 pandemic. Because of the impact of the crisis on tourism, some businesses or services listed in the text may no longer operate. We will post any information we have about these on **w** bradtguides.com/updates. And we'd of course be grateful for any updates you can send us during your own travels, which we will add to that page for the benefit of future travellers.

Published July 2022
Bradt Guides Ltd
31a High Street, Chesham, Buckinghamshire, HP5 1BW, England
www.bradtguides.com
Print edition published in the USA by The Globe Pequot Press Inc,
PO Box 480, Guilford, Connecticut 06437-0480

Project Manager: Susannah Lord
Cover research: Ian Spick

ISBN: 9781784779009

British Library Cataloguing in Publication Data
A catalogue record for this book is available from the British Library

Photographs Michael Pauls (MP); Pays de Bergerac: Joffrey Revoy (JR/PdB); Saint-Emilion Tourisme: Ferme du Cabestan (FdC/SET), Steve Le Clech (SLC/SET); Shutterstock.com: arcachonphoto.com (ap/S), BearFotos (BF/S), Gordon Bell (GB/S), Belt944 (B944/S), Borisb17 (B17/S), Jon Chica (JC/S), csp (csp/S), dvoevnore (d/S), Sergey Dzyuba (SD/S), Eo naya (En/S), Carlos Gandiaga (CG/S), JeanLucIchard (JL/S), Kiev.Victor (KV/S), Fabien Monteil (FM/S), OSTILL is Franck Camhi (OFC/S), Philippe 1 bo (P1b/S), Stanislav Simonyan (SS/S), SpiritProd33 (SP33/S), thipjang (th/S), travellight (tr/S), vouvraysan (v/S), Ivonne Wicrink (IW/S), wjarek (w/S), Bernd Zillich (BZ/S); Tourisme Tarn-et-Garonne (ADT82)

Front cover Puy L'Eveque on the River Lot (GB/S)
Back cover Château Palmer, Bordeaux (FM/S); River Domme, Périgord (CG/S)
Title page The Lomagne in southwest Tarn-et-Garonne (ADT82), Grosse Cloche, Bordeaux (B17/S), Malbec grapes on the vine (MP)

Maps David McCutcheon FBCart.S, assisted by RedGeographics, Daniella Levin and Liezel Bohdanowicz; colour map relief base by Digital Maps/Alamy Stock Photo.

Typeset by Ian Spick, Bradt Guides and www.dataworks.co.in
Production managed by Jellyfish Print Solutions; printed in India
Digital conversion by www.dataworks.co.in

Acknowledgements

Our friends around the region have been a huge help in compiling this book, especially in helping us keep up with the restaurants and bars as places re-opened and closed after Covid-19. We'd like especially to thank Samson Collier, Carmel Crawford, Karina and Phil Knight-Spencer, Victoria Hayman, Linda and Tom Ryall and Pam Sullivan. Also a big thank you as ever to Susannah Lord, editor extraordinaire, and David McCutcheon and colleagues for all their hard work on the maps.

UNRAVELLING THE NAMES

Perhaps the biggest source of confusion for newcomers here is that underneath the tidy names and numbers of its *départements* bestowed by the French Revolution, older regional names have survived – like peeling circus posters, one atop the other. 'Aquitaine' sufficed for most of the region from Roman times until the Middle Ages, when things began to get confusing and new names appeared: Gascony, for the lands west of the Garonne, and Languedoc, for those to the east, while everything owned by the English crown after the marriage of Eleanor of Aquitaine and Henry II became known as Guyenne, from the English inability to pronounce 'Aquitaine', a name that survives today whenever anyone feels like using it.

Within Guyenne, what is now the département of the Dordogne was the county of Périgord until the Revolution, and the name is still synonymous with the Dordogne département. The Lot, and most of the Tarn-et-Garonne were, and still are, known as Quercy, Haut and Bas. The Lot-et-Garonne and the Gironde were always the heartland of Aquitaine/Guyenne, although their southern reaches belong to Gascony. Toulouse was the medieval capital of the Languedoc, but in the division of French regions in the 1970s the name Languedoc migrated to the southeast half of the territory (to foil any attempts to undo the 13th-century Albigensian Crusade that annexed the once nearly independent County of Toulouse to France and left the rest with the now obsolete name of Midi-Pyrénées). Paris made amends in 2016 when creating the *grands régions* when Toulouse, once again, was made the capital of its old county – but now it has been renamed Occitanie or Occitania. This encompasses the Lot and Tarn-et-Garonne in this book while the *grand région* of Nouvelle-Aquitaine includes the Dordogne, Gironde and Lot-et-Garonne with Bordeaux as the capital. Got it?

Contents

LIST OF MAPS

Introduction

If southwest France could croon a tune, it would have to be that old Inkspots hit 'I Don't Want to Set the World on Fire'. Endowed with the soft, gentle beauty of rolling vine-clad hills and valleys and oak and chestnut forests, the region rarely demands your awe and homage. But, like all true lovers, it magically opens your eyes to the grace and charm in little things, in everyday life.

Of course, like any place it has its superlatives, its bragging rights. This is river country par excellence, where waterways born in the Pyrenees and Massif Central – the Dordogne, Lot, Aveyron, Tarn, Garonne and their countless tributaries – put on their brakes to weave gracefully down to the broad estuary of the Gironde and the Atlantic, flowing past a thousand châteaux and as many medieval villages, the world's foremost wine region and some of its very first great art in the cave paintings of Lascaux, Font-de-Gaume, Pech Merle and a score of others.

Apart from Bordeaux and Toulouse, the two great cities that form the limits of this book, nothing much has happened here since the Hundred Years' War. Out of history, out of mind, this region retains something that most of the industrialised world has lost in its mad rush towards modernity. The Occitan word is *èime*, similar to the Catalan *seny* – the intangible spirit of the nation, its good sense, its spirit of measure and moderation, homeland of France's most reasonable thinkers, of Montaigne, Fénelon, La Boétie and Montesquieu.

For if nothing else, southwest France is indeed a fine place to hear yourself think. The great wine helps, of course, and the delicious regional cuisine puts your digestion in harmony with the universe. The pace of life is slow, and there's time to contemplate that old stone farm on the next hill, blending into the environment naturally and effortlessly. The sun-soaked wall by your chair is covered with eglantine and honeysuckle; the fragrance, the flitting butterflies and the blackbirds trilling away make you delightfully drowsy and once again all plans and outings are postponed. You can't put it off forever, of course – there's a full whack of sights and surprises for you in this book – but the true purpose of this corner of the world is in teaching us all to pause and regain a bit of perspective. Or, as in the words of Michel de Montaigne:

> The value of life lies not in the length of days, but in the use we make of them; a man may live long, yet get little from life. Whether you find satisfaction in life depends not on your tale of years, but on your will.

HOW TO USE THIS GUIDE

ADMISSION PRICES In this guide prices to museums and other attractions are often expressed eg: €5/€3, where the first price is the adult entry free and the second a concessionary rate. Other prices are specified.

PRICE CODES Throughout this guide we have used price codes to indicate the cost of those places to stay and eat listed in the guide. For a key to these price codes, see page 34 for accommodation and page 35 for restaurants; also the inside front cover.

MAPS

Keys and symbols Maps include alphabetical keys covering the locations of those places to stay, eat or drink that are featured in the book. Note that regional maps may not show all hotels and restaurants in the area: other establishments may be located in towns shown on the map.

Grids and grid references Several maps use gridlines to allow easy location of sites. Map grid references are listed in square brackets after the name of the place or site of interest in the text, with page number followed by grid number, eg: [54 C3].

Part One

GENERAL INFORMATION

DORDOGNE & LOT AT A GLANCE

Location Southwest France (departments of the Gironde, Dordogne, Lot, Lot-et-Garonne and Tarn-et-Garonne, and Toulouse city)
Size 34,319km^2 total
GDP per capita €40,521 (France, 2020)
Population Gironde 1,654,372; Dordogne 410,786; Lot 174,232; Lot-et-Garonne 329,960; Tarn-et-Garonne 262,265; Toulouse metropolitan area 1,037,000 (2021; estimates)
Life expectancy 82.9 years (France, 2021; estimate)
Climate Bordeaux and the Gironde are in a maritime zone, with mild winters and hot summers. Inland regions are generally similar. There is moderate, regular rainfall throughout, though inland departments can have very dry summers. Cooler in the Lot, which borders the Massif Central. Average temps: (winter) 5–6ºC in January; (summer) 20–21ºC in July.
Regional capitals Bordeaux (Nouvelle Aquitaine) and Toulouse (Occitanie)
Other main towns Montauban, Agen, Périgueux, Bergerac, Villeneuve-sur-Lot, Cahors, Sarlat
Main airports Bordeaux-Mérignac, Toulouse-Blagnac; many low-cost airlines operate out of Bergerac and Brive-Souillac Airport in the Corrèze.
Language French
Religion Roman Catholic (41%), Muslim (5%), other Christian (4%), other and non-religious (50%)
Currency Euro (€)
Exchange rate £1 = €1.19, US$1 = €0.92 (April 2022)
International telephone code +33
Time GMT +1
Electrical voltage 220V/50H, two-pin or three-pin round plugs
Public holidays 1 January, 6 January, Easter Sunday, Easter Monday, 1 May, 8 May, Ascension Day, Pentecost, 14 July, 15 August, 1 November, 11 November, 25 December, 26 December

1

Background Information

GEOGRAPHY

Important rivers – the Dordogne, Lot, Aveyron Tarn and Garonne – and their many tributaries define the geography here, making a leisurely descent down to the broad estuary of the Gironde, the biggest in Europe, constantly in flux from the vast amounts of sediment in the rivers Garonne and Dordogne (hence its normal light brown colour). The Gironde is also the name of the biggest department in France, roughly half of it supporting the world's most acclaimed wine region. Much of the rest is forested, once-swampy ground that has been reclaimed since the 18th century. The tidal oyster-filled Bassin d'Arcachon – the only feature to interrupt the die-straight Atlantic coast – has, at its entrance, the Dune du Pilat, Europe's tallest sand dune and mini-Sahara, which began to form 4,000 years ago and is still relentlessly marching inland like the Blob in the eponymous horror movie, gobbling up pine trees, roads and campsites.

The river valleys upstream make up the most fertile and productive parts of the region, growing grains, fruit, walnuts, sunflowers and, above all, vines, notably around Bergerac and Cahors.

This corner of France is also a land of caves, mostly famously along the Vézère Valley, lined with limestone cliffs that hold the densest concentration of prehistoric art on the planet. Much of the eastern Quercy is made up of *causses*, sparsely populated limestone plateaux. These are classic examples of karst topography, dry land with very poor soil where most of the rainfall disappears underground to create caves, sinkholes, chasms (including the spectacular Gouffre de Padirac) and subterranean lakes and rivers. The valleys and some parts of the *causses* are just fertile enough for sheep raising. Quercy's other department, the Tarn-et-Garonne, is a green and flourishing place, embellished with roads lined with plane trees dating from the 18th and 19th centuries. It has prosperous agriculture in the valleys of the Tarn, Garonne and Aveyron, and dramatic scenery to the east in the Gorges d'Aveyron.

The Lot-et-Garonne, like many departments of France, is a mishmash of lovely bits and pieces with no particular identity, cobbled together out of parts of five different pre-Revolutionary regions. One thing they have in common is fruit. The largest portion grows in the hinterland of the capital, Agen – the Agenais, famous for prunes.

CLIMATE

The Aquitaine Basin, shielded from intemperate Continental influences by the Massif Central, has a fairly balmy, humid Atlantic climate, with long hot summers broken by heavy thunderstorms. Early spring and late autumn usually get the most rainfall – and it can rain for weeks at a time. Winters are fairly mild, with only

20–40 days of frost a year, although every 30 years (on average) killer frosts descend: the one in 1956 killed off 95% of the vines.

Of late the weather has been capricious and strange, so it's impossible to predict what you might get: after five years of drought, which produced some of the greatest wine of the 20th century, the autumns of 1992 and '93 saw endless rain and floods. December 1999 saw some of the strongest and most destructive storms in France's recent history, and then 2003 produced a summer of relentless, unforgiving heat. Extreme April frosts have troubled the vineyards again in recent years, most recently in 2021.

NATURAL HISTORY AND CONSERVATION

The Gironde is one of Europe's last natural and relatively unspoiled estuaries, its banks lined with wetlands, reeds, alders, orchids, and the rare endemic *Angelica heterocarpa*, with its distinctive white ball flowers, that grows only in France's western estuaries. As part of the East Atlantic flyway, it sees thousands of raptors, waterfowl, doves, swallows, swifts, orioles, skylarks, nightingales and other songbirds from mid-March to May. Mink and green turtles live along the Gironde, while the waters host 75 species of fish, including commercially important ones such as mullet, salmon, sea trout, flounder, shad, smelt, sturgeon (page 152), eels, and sea and river lampreys. Serious conservation efforts and planning for sea level rises are underway especially after the devastating storm in late 1999 that swamped the polders of the Médoc and the Gironde's formerly inhabited Île Nouvelle.

The lakes, lagoons, wetlands, dunes and salt marshes along the Côte d'Argent are also prime (and protected) bird habitat, especially the pristine Réserve Naturelle de l'Étang de Cousseau. The Bassin d'Arcachon and nearby islets are now in marine and land parks, notably La Teich's Réserve Ornithologique, where thousands of cranes spend the winter.

The Dordogne is the only UNESCO biosphere reserve river in France, designated for its unique human heritage and array of migratory fish, otters, muskrats, bats, newts, frogs and salamanders. The deeper river, Lot, is known for its pike, pikeperch and carp, with several 'no kill' zones to preserve stocks. Wels catfish (*silures*) introduced from the Danube can reach 5m and haunt the depths of the rivers Garonne, Lot, Tarn and Aveyron, surfacing now and then to grab an unsuspecting duck.

There are four regional national parks here, in the least populated areas: the Landes de Gascogne, Périgord Limousin, Causses de Quercy, and Médoc, dedicated to preserving local resources, farming and biodiversity and to promoting local heritage and culture to visitors. Because of rural abandonment, nearly half the Dordogne and Lot, and eastern Tarn-et-Garonne are covered in trees – oak, chestnut, hornbeam and, deep in old woodlands, beech – the last remnants of the forests that covered the entire region after the last ice age. They are often covered in lichen, a sign of clean air; mistletoe is common in the Dordogne and Tarn-et-Garonne. Dozens of species of wild orchids grow in its meadows.

Most of the insects are temperate zone familiars, except for the praying mantises, those tigers of the insect world, and the hummingbird hawk moth, which can fool the unsuspecting into thinking they are indeed tiny birds. Larger fauna include foxes, roe deer, red squirrels, bats, hares, badgers, cat-like nocturnal genets in the trees (you'll be lucky to see one, though), hedgehogs and coypus by the rivers (imported in the 19th century from South America for fur and pâté, only no-one liked either). There are far too many wild boar, who damage crops and dig up more than their fair share of truffles. Green and yellow grass snakes, toads, frogs and green lizards are common, as are swifts, swallows, doves, magpies, blackbirds, finches, titmice, woodpeckers, buzzards, kites, hawks, eagles, Peregrine falcons, and little, barn, scops, eagle and tawny owls. Cormorants, kingfishers, mallards, egrets, herons and swans live by the rivers. In rural areas, nightingales sing so loudly at night in June it can be hard to sleep.

HISTORY

400,000–600BC *The southwest gets off to an extremely precocious start, and humanity comes to the Dordogne for its first summer art course*

A mere 400,000 years ago, somebody was poking around Périgord and other parts of the southwest, laboriously making flint tools and managing to get a fire lit. The crossing from the Lower to the Middle Palaeolithic occurred in this area about 75,000 years ago; the newcomer was Neanderthal man (presumably accompanied by Neanderthal woman). These come across as thick-skulled brutes in popular culture, but were really rather clever, inventing better tools and techniques and developing the first rituals and burials, and even architecture (page 341): the elements of the 'Mousterian culture' in the southwest. The Neanderthals get pushed off the stage at about 40,000–35,000BC by Cro-Magnon man, or *Homo sapiens sapiens* – us, more or less; books on Cro-Magnon man usually mention with a touch of whimsy that, if one of them got on the bus today in a business suit, nobody would notice.

The creations of the Cro-Magnon (named after the hamlet in Périgord where their bones were first discovered) are varied enough for scholars to define distinct Upper Palaeolithic cultures. The Périgordian and Aurignacian (35,000–20,000BC) left jewellery, finely crafted spear points and some of the world's first painting and sculpture. In the Solutrean culture (20,000–15,000BC), people brought their stone tools – axes, spear points, arrowheads, knives, even sewing needles – to a point of perfection. The Upper Palaeolithic reached its height when the Magdalenian culture (15,000–9000BC), produced the paintings in the caves at Lascaux and elsewhere. This period was the slow end of an ice age, and it is possible that the people who made Magdalenian art gradually migrated northwards, following the herds of reindeer and other animals they hunted. The Mesolithic cultures that followed them (9000–4000BC) did not paint, nor do much of anything else that was interesting.

Neolithic culture reached the area about 4000BC, either by migrations or by transmission of ideas – a lot of ideas: better tools, the first pottery, sedentary agricultural life, the domestication of animals and a complex religion. The Neolithic peoples made Europe's first great civilisation. Their dolmens, menhirs, stone circles and tumuli are common all along the continent's coasts, but the Lot and the Dordogne have the greatest inland concentration of them anywhere. The Neolithic age was peaceful, probably matriarchal; they lived in unfortified villages, and evidence of warfare is singularly lacking. Lost so far back in time, hard facts are few, and Neolithic culture leaves us with a tangle of fascinating riddles: the purposes of their megalithic monuments and their siting of them, their considerable achievements in astronomy, and above all the vision of an extremely sophisticated culture, living in close harmony with nature and living well, without metals or technology.

This world lasted for more than three millennia in many areas. But the unity of Neolithic civilisation was broken c2000BC, with the arrival of new peoples like the metalworking Artenac civilisation, around Bordeaux. Then the picture grows increasingly confused, as ever more peoples and cultures pass through. The first to have a name, courtesy of later Roman writers, are the Aquitanii; they arrived in the 7th century BC (or much earlier, according to some), and they may have been related to the various tribes of Celts who followed them.

600BC–AD507 *In which Celts and the Romans first bash swords, and later clink glasses*

In the 6th to 4th centuries BC, new waves of Celtic peoples slowly spread over what came to be called Gaul: the Petrocorii north of the Duranus, or Dordogne, and south of it the Eleuteti and the fierce Cadurcii, who gave their name to Divona Cadurcorum (Cahors) on the Oltis, or Lot. In what is now the lower Lot-et-Garonne lived the Nitiobroges; while the plains around Toulouse were home to the Tolosates and Volcae Tectosages. The region around Bordeaux was occupied by the Biturges Vibiscii, who called themselves the 'Kings of the World'. A culturally complex people who nevertheless preferred pretty jewellery to the less mobile trappings of civilisation – like temples and cities – the Celts, or Gauls, did settle a number of small towns, or *oppida*, which often served as trading stations. Even in this remote age, the 'Gallic isthmus' between the Atlantic and Mediterranean was a busy trade route; tin from Cornwall went one way, and back the other came imports from the Greek world including wine, of which the Gauls were very fond.

Rome's conquest of Gaul was hardly an overnight affair. Julius Caesar, who arrived in 59BC, gets credit for the job, but Roman influence in the south at least was already strong – a Roman garrison was installed at Tolosa (Toulouse) around the middle of the 2nd century BC. Caesar's invasion came in response to revolts among Gauls who already found Roman control a little too heavy for their tastes. The last Gaulish redoubt to fall, Uxellodunum, was near Martel in the Lot. The southwest, from the Loire to the Pyrenees, was organised into the Roman province of Gallia Aquitania.

Under direct Roman rule, southern Gaul became completely integrated into the Mediterranean economy. The new rulers apportioned out much of the land to Roman investors and veterans of the legions. Among the many new crops they introduced to the area was the grape, and soon the new Gallo-Roman Aquitania was not only meeting its own considerable demand for wine, but actually exporting it to Italy. Some of the oppida became towns – Tolosa, Burdigala and Divona Cadurcorum, among many others. Others naturally declined and died, and their ruins can be seen at such places as Mursens and Luzech. Mines and quarries were exploited, and many towns made a good living on manufactures. By the 1st century AD, the larger towns were looking quite opulent, with forums, temples, public baths and amphitheatres imitating the cities of Italy.

Despite all this, life in Aquitania would not have looked so rosy to the average inhabitant. As elsewhere in the western Empire, Roman Gaul was a profoundly sick society, a pyramid with a few fantastically wealthy landowning families at the top, their estates tilled by vast armies of slaves. Things got progressively worse. The small middle class in the towns was ground into poverty, as taxes rose and trade declined. Like the equally small class of free farmers, the middle class found itself gradually pushed into serfdom by debt.

The Germanic raids of the mid 3rd century AD were an omen of troubles to come, as the Franks and the Alemanni broke through the Rhine frontier. Though the legions eventually recovered and drove them out, things would never be the same. The towns suffered most: Tolosa and Vesunna (Périgueux) contracted to a fraction of their former size, huddling inside circuits of hastily built walls. By this time the elite had already given up on urban life, and in the 4th century AD their sumptuous villas grew into towns in themselves; well defended and self-supporting, these were the centres of what economic life remained in the last days. The fatal invasions came after AD407; both Vandals and Visigoths passed through, and after AD420 the region found itself part of the new Visigothic kingdom, with its capital at Tolosa. Barbarian Franks replaced the barbarian Goths in AD507, after the Battle of Vouillé, but this meant little to a part of Gaul that had effectively dropped out of history altogether.

AD507–1000 *In which Aquitania is Frankly demoralised*

Christianity had come to the region in the 4th century, as it was being established everywhere as the state religion of the Empire. The Church strengthened its power in the 6th century under the newly Christianised Franks. The Frankish Merovingian kings held only a tenuous control over most of Gaul; the day-to-day government was usually in the hands of landowners and their younger brothers in the Church. One bright light in the Dark Ages was Cahors. Controlled by a long line of powerful bishops beginning with the legendary Didier, the city survived and somehow prospered through the troubles; Cahors's aqueduct and baths were even restored in the grim 7th century.

Under the Merovingians, Frankish and Roman landowners gradually fused through intermarriage into a new ruling class much like the old one. Over generations their villas metamorphosed into castles, while the landowners themselves gradually made their logical transformation into feudal barons. The Merovingians created the duchy of Aquitaine in the 7th century; for seven centuries the largely independent dukes would be in control of all the western coast from Poitou to the Pyrenees. In this poor backwater, they weren't always up to the task. The Arabs roared through from Spain in the early AD700s, seizing Bordeaux and dominating the area until Charles Martel beat them at Poitiers in AD732. Soon afterwards, the Frankish kingdom under its new Carolingian dynasty – headed by Charles Martel's son Pepin the Short – tried to seize the duchy, while the duke, Waiofer, sheltered refugee lords who had been dispossessed by the Carolingians and led the southern resistance to the ambitious new power descending from the north. The result was a bloody war of three decades; Aquitaine was not completely brought under control until AD774.

Pepin's son Charlemagne found a compromise solution: raising the duchy of Aquitaine into a kingdom, the first 'king' of which was his son Louis; this title lasted only until AD877. The height of Frankish power under the Carolingians was a peaceful time for most of France, although it was short-lived. Charlemagne was still warm in his grave when his empire started to disintegrate, and the western shores suffered the visits of the worst barbarians ever: the Normans, or Vikings. In AD848 they sacked Bordeaux, and throughout the century their regular raids brought terror and destruction to all the river valleys as far as Toulouse. Many people in the 9th century, looking forward to the millennium, were convinced that the end of the world was at hand, when in fact the ground was only being swept clean for something new and better.

1000–1271 *The southwest creates a civilisation, and the French and English come down to make nuisances of themselves*

If the 9th century was the low point for the southwest and many other parts of Europe, the sudden strong impulse of cultural achievement and economic power that followed – the dawning of the Middle Ages – is all the more surprising. The Vikings' settling down in Normandy marked an end to foreign invasions, and in a period of relative tranquillity (marked by constant but not-too-serious feudal warfare) the feudal system in the southwest reached its perfection. The crazy quilt of *comtés*, *vicomtés*, *sénéchaussées* and *duchés*, interspersed with huge areas where local barons were free to do what they liked within the limits of their feudal oaths, made for a finely balanced anarchy that somehow managed to permit a rapid rebirth of towns, trade, wealth and culture.

In the brilliant 12th century, great abbey complexes appeared under the patronage of local rulers and the mighty Compostela-pilgrimage-promoting abbey of Cluny. New churches in the Romanesque style were under way in every town and village – the biggest one in Europe, St-Sernin, went up under the wealthy and enlightened counts of Toulouse, the strongest lords of the southwest, who tended all to be named Raymond. Along the coast lived their near-equals, the dukes of Aquitaine; all these were Guillaumes, and the list included Guillaume IX (1086–1127), who besides his capable political leadership was one of the first of the troubadours, heralding the rebirth of poetry in Europe. That poetry was written in Occitan, the *langue d'oc*, and it was the pride of an Occitan nation, stretching from the Atlantic to the Alps.

Guillaume had a granddaughter, a beautiful and wilful woman whose life would be the stuff of romances, and whose career would change history: Eleanor of Aquitaine. She was sole heir to the rich duchy, and when she married Louis VII in 1137, the French crowed for having plucked the biggest feudal plum imaginable. Eleanor did her best with the cold, pious Louis, and even accompanied him on a crusade. Her manifest discontent led inevitably to a divorce, in 1152, and two years later she found a more convivial marriage with Louis's mortal enemy: Henry Plantagenet, Duke of Anjou, soon to be Henry II, King of England.

Along with Eleanor came the land, and for the next three centuries Aquitaine would be a possession of the English crown. The English proved good rulers, usually sympathetic to local concerns, and they gained a high degree of loyalty from the people of Aquitaine. (One sour note at the beginning came with the depredations of Henry and Eleanor's sons – worst of all Richard the Lionheart, a fellow who gets off all too easily in history and legend. Richard battled and pillaged across the region more to line his pockets than to solidify English rule, and in Aquitaine, as elsewhere, he gained a well-deserved reputation as a bloody-minded thug.) Under English control, Bordeaux grew into a city of 30,000 with a new prosperity based on wine; at the height of the trade with England, in 1308, Aquitaine exported almost as much of the stuff as it does today.

Toulouse, under its counts, grew even bigger and richer than Bordeaux. The city that might have been a natural capital of a nation of Languedoc instead itself became a victim of imperialism from the north. The French would have made their play for Toulouse in any case, but in the early 1200s fortune provided them with a cause: the presence of the Cathars. This heretical sect, which came from the Balkans by way of north Italy, found a perfect haven in the sophisticated, tolerant atmosphere of Languedoc. In 1209, a sordid deal between Pope Innocent III and the French King Philippe-Auguste paved the way for the Albigensian crusade, supposedly directed against the heretics but in reality a naked grab at the lands of the counts of Toulouse. The troops were provided from Paris, a force under the cruel, lucky and always victorious Simon de Montfort. The total subjection of the south was clinched by de Montfort's victory at the Battle of Muret, near Toulouse, in 1213; resistance continued, though, giving Louis VIII an excuse to bring down another army to finish the job in 1226.

In 1271, the French crown inherited Toulouse by a forced marriage; long before that, fiefs and offices had been handed out to northerners, and the Inquisition was introduced, not only to incinerate the few surviving Cathars but to ensure that the free culture that made heresy possible would be extinguished forever.

1271–1453 *In which the French and the English continue their quarrels and mischief*
Despite the vicious way the French had gone about their conquest, with plenty of bloody massacres *pour encourager les autres*, recovery was rapid. The surest sign of the continuing economic boom was the founding everywhere of bastides, planned new towns, usually built on lands that had gone back to forest or swamp during the late Empire and Dark Ages. Bastides had their political aspect too. Over a score were founded by Alphonse de Poitiers, the first (and last) French Count of Toulouse, King Louis IX's brother and the man in charge of establishing French control over the new conquests. The English in response founded scores of their own bastides in Aquitaine.

The older towns also continued to thrive, notably Cahors, which attracted Italian banking families fleeing the disruptions of the Albigensian crusade. The little city on the Lot soon grew into a major financial centre with its own university, and even supplied a pope, John XXII.

England and France, now the only two powers in the region, battled fitfully for a century after the marriage of Eleanor and Henry II, until Louis IX (St Louis) agreed to the Treaty of Paris in 1259, formally ceding Périgord and Quercy to the English. From then on the two parties suspiciously eyed one another, in an uneasy truce that occasionally broke out into open hostilities; the French even succeeded in occupying Bordeaux for a decade, until a revolt of the Bordelais threw them out in 1303.

But for all the politeness generally shown by both sides, it was a situation that could not last. In an age when nation-states were dawning, feudal logic no longer worked: as dukes of Guyenne (from the English mispronunciation of Aquitaine), the English kings owed homage to the kings of France – a fine position to be in whenever the two nations' interests were in conflict. The inevitable final showdown began in 1337 and went into the books as the Hundred Years' War.

The first decades of the war saw Aquitaine as the major battlefield, without major results until the arrival of Edward of Woodstock, son of Edward III, in 1355. The Black Prince, as he came to be known, ended the war's first round decisively with the Battle of Poitiers (1356), capturing French King Jean II among many others. Now in undisputed control of the southwest, England declared its lands a principality free of any claims of French allegiance; the Black Prince ruled it from Bordeaux until his death in 1376.

The next round went to the French, under Bertrand du Guesclin, who recaptured Quercy and most of Périgord by 1369. As the war dragged on, the exhausted combatants found it increasingly hard to maintain control of events. Both sides hired mercenary companies; these got out of hand, and, combined with the other desperados shaken loose from society by constant warfare, they formed the *routiers* ('highwaymen'), armed bands loyal to nothing but their own profit who reduced much of the southwest to anarchy. Coming on the heels of the Black Death (1348–50), which reduced the population by a third in many areas, it caused a time of troubles the region had not known since the days of the Vikings.

In the early 1400s, it seemed that France was coming apart once and for all. The English regained all they had lost, and even took Paris in 1420, a time that coincides with the worst ravages of the *routiers*. Thanks to Joan of Arc, of course, the French soon recovered and prevailed. They blockaded Bordeaux in 1451, and two years later the climactic Battle of Castillon, near Bordeaux, put an end to the wars and to England's continental empire forever.

1453–1594 *In which the lobotomised southwest starts arguing with itself over religion*

The French moved quickly to consolidate their new possessions. Bordeaux got a big new fortress to watch the citizens, and a *parlement* to scrutinise their morals and political opinions; the city's wine trade with England was ended by royal decree, sending it – along with most of Aquitaine – into economic decline.

The 1539 decree of Villars-Cotterets mandated the French language in law and government, the first step along the road to the eradication of the *langue d'oc*. Southwesterners, when able to build, sculpt or write at all, found themselves forced to ape the fashions imported by their governors from the north, and over the generations it became a habit.

The French grip was strong, and with political opposition impossible, the next wave of southern rebelliousness came in the form of religious dissent. Protestantism first seeped into the southwest from Calvin's Geneva, and it found its most attentive audience among the industrious middle classes and some of the more enlightened courts. The first Protestant communities appeared in Ste-Foy-la-Grande and Agen about 1532. Soon after, the court at Nérac of the Albrets, a powerful noble family of the Agenais, became a centre of humanistic learning and religious heresy (Calvin came to visit). This happened in the reign of the learned Marguerite d'Albret – or rather Marguerite of Navarre, for this ambitious family had, with French help, worked its way to the kingship of that small and woebegone Pyrenean realm. Protestantism swept across the south, bringing the good news that there was more to life than abject submission to Rome and Paris.

With the spirit of the time, civil war was inevitable – the Wars of Religion. Towns and regions chose sides. Cahors, with its powerful bishops, remained steadfastly Catholic and fought a continuous battle with Protestant Montauban and Figeac; Protestant Bergerac stomped on Catholic Périgueux as early and as often as possible. The religious rebels found a firm pillar of support in Jeanne d'Albret, daughter of Marguerite and a grisly bigot for the new cause, as Protestant and Catholic armies recaptured the spirit of the Hundred Years' War, prowling the region and looking for enemy towns and souls to burn.

In much of the rest of France it was the same story; now, however, for the first time, the southwest stepped up to centre stage in France's history, thanks to the Albrets and Jeanne's son Henri, who by a complicated set of circumstances just happened to be the heir to the French throne. Henri of Navarre was a good Protestant and a hardy warrior. In two decades of campaigning to win his rightful crown, the Protestant lands of the southwest were his solid base. In the end, though, Henri's good sense and goodwill made him the man to finally put an end to the Wars of Religion – by the conversion of convenience that finally made him acceptable to the Catholics who were controlling Paris. As Henri IV, he ruled well, proclaiming religious tolerance with the Edict of Nantes (1598), and earned a secure place for himself as a national hero in the southwest.

1594–1789 *In which the French do their best to make everyone miserable, and the southwest fights back and loses*

Riots and popular revolts had been common enough in the 1500s, usually over oppressive taxes like the *gabelle*, or salt tax. In the sympathetic Henri's reign, the first of a century-long series of peasant uprisings occurred. The movement of the 'Croquants', in Périgord and Quercy, was more directed at the grasping nobles and their high rents. In 1594 the Croquants formed a peasant army in Périgord; the barons organised and beat them, and punished the survivors with memorable ferocity. Henri's successors in Paris heaped more woes on the common folk: more taxes, more forced labour, and lots of revenue agents and troops to enforce them. The early 17th century would have been rough enough without them. High rents and prices, combined with bad harvests, recurring outbreaks of plague (1629 and 1652) and a climate of hatred and everyday violence, the heritage of the religious wars, made further revolts inevitable. In Languedoc, in 1629, things were so bad that even the royal governor, Montmorency, joined the rebels, and Louis XIII had to lead a big army down from Paris to crush them.

From 1637 to 1642 the Croquants were back in business again. This time they nearly captured Périgueux, though once again the arms of the king and the nobles had the last say. This would be the last revolt on a large scale, though smaller outbreaks were regular features of rural life up until the Revolution. For the nobles, times were never better, as witnessed by the large number of grand châteaux built in this period. At the same time, a lot of the old-style castles were disappearing – pulled down on the orders of Louis XIII's minister Cardinal Richelieu, who didn't want any strong places left that could possibly shelter resistance to the national state.

If the countryside was in despair, the two large cities weren't doing too badly. Bordeaux found a new prosperity in the late 17th and 18th centuries, based not only on wine but also on the slave trade with the Americas; the city grew enough to become the third-largest in France. Toulouse in the 16th century was enjoying a boom from the export of pastel, dyer's woad, and the building by local initiative of the Canal du Midi (inaugurated in 1681) made the city the centre of a new trade route that crossed the French isthmus. The pastel business dwindled in the face of foreign competition, though, and, despite its natural advantages, Toulouse generally continued its long slide into cultural and economic torpor.

Hard times continued through the 1700s. The Americas offered many poorer folk a way out: tens of thousands emigrated to Canada and the West Indies. Most of the Protestants had already gone to Prussia, Britain and elsewhere, after Louis XIV revoked the Edict of Nantes in 1685. For those who remained, the century was a drowsy era, at least when the peasants weren't revolting. Intendants (administrators) from Paris ran everything and made a few lasting contributions, notably an excellent network of roads (usually embellished with pretty rows of plane trees, still seen in many places today). The intendants also dressed up Bordeaux, remodelling the city into what would be the template for Baron Haussmann's Paris.

1789–1940 *The southwest helps make a revolution, learns to regret it, and then takes a long nap*

In 1789, no people in France were more cheerfully assiduous than the southwesterners in smashing up churches and châteaux and burning the tax records and rent rolls. But at the same time, at the National Assembly in Paris, Bordeaux's merchants and southwesterners in general were providing most of the voices of moderation and good sense. Their faction, the Girondists, stood for liberal reforms and political decentralisation. When the radical, Paris-dominated Jacobin faction gained control in 1792, the Terror began; the Girondists and their federalist hopes became its first victims. A 1793 federalist counter-revolt in the southwest failed, largely because Toulouse and Montauban wouldn't have anything to do with it; stoutly conservative areas like the Lot were against the Revolution from the start.

The Lot, ironically, loved Napoleon and contributed more than any part of France to his Grande Armée, including fine soldiers like Joachim Murat, the son of a village innkeeper, who ended up King of Naples. Jean-Baptiste Bessières of Prayssac, who was in charge of the occupation of Moscow, briefly claimed the title of Duke of Istria. At the end, though, people here were as tired of Napoleon as anybody else. The Duke of Wellington marched through in 1814, on his way up from Spain. In Toulouse, the people hailed him as a liberator.

If the Revolution had been a disappointment, nothing in the century that followed it would be any improvement. Paris-appointed prefects replaced Paris-appointed intendants, and the old regional distinctions and boundaries were destroyed in favour of dividing France into départements, but through all the shifts of the Gallic banana republic/monarchy/empire in the 19th century, no-one lifted a hand to help the southwest; nor did the region ever show much energy of its own. It had become the most sluggish and listless of all French provincial backwaters, and anyone with any spunk or talent was off to Paris as soon as possible.

The railway arrived in Bordeaux in 1850; seven years later the line from there to Toulouse and the Mediterranean was finished. Instead of catalysing trade and industry, however, this merely made it easier to leave, and easier for imported goods to flow in and ruin the already hard-pressed southwestern farmers and manufacturers. The farmers did their best, introducing new crops such as tobacco and types of corn, and they managed just barely to survive the 1868 phylloxera epidemic that killed off their vineyards, but prices stayed low and business stayed bad. And all across the southwest, the villages began to dwindle.

Undoubtedly the biggest event of the last century was one that happened elsewhere – World War I. Of the millions who died pointlessly for the glory of France, the southwest contributed more than its share. Many towns and villages lost a third, or even half, of their young men; in every one you will see a pathetic war memorial or plaque in the church to remind you of France's greatest catastrophe since the Black Death. Between the war and rural abandonment, the southwest declined in population by almost 25% from 1850 to 1950; in some places, the figure was as high as 60%.

1940 TO THE PRESENT *A Nazi interlude, followed by the unexpected return of the English*

Though World War II was less costly and destructive, it was still a miserable and dangerous time for the people of the southwest, however far removed they were from the actual fighting. From the beginning, the Germans seized the entire Atlantic coast. The 'border' between the occupied zone and Vichy-controlled territory was heavily patrolled, and locals needed special papers to cross it – many were killed trying to visit their cousins, or sneaking produce over the line to the market. Deportation of men to forced labour in Germany was a terrible burden and not all who went returned (many would join the maquis to avoid it). Another strain was supporting the wave of refugees from Belgium and northern France who arrived in 1940, but this one the people handled ungrudgingly.

The Resistance was not much of a force until 1943 but from then on it operated effectively in the lonely *causses* of Quercy. In retaliation for their acts of sabotage, the Germans sent the SS Das Reich division on a tour of the southwest in May 1944; these distinguished themselves with massacres of civilians at Mussidan, Frayssinet-le-Gélat and Montpezat-de-Quercy. Liberation came for most of the southwest in August 1944; Bordeaux's story was much like that of Paris. Colonel Kühnemann, the German commander, was in civilian life a wine merchant with many friends in the city. He had orders to blow up nearly everything on his way out, but instead he spent a delicate week dodging the Nazi spooks while successfully negotiating with the Resistance for a peaceful exit.

Since the war, the big news has been the unexpected awakening of Toulouse. With considerable assistance from the government planners, the city followed up its early prominence in aviation by becoming France's forward-looking City of the Air, home of Aérospatiale and the French space agency, a manufacturer of satellites and supersonic jets. Striving to become the European 'technopole' of the 21st century, Toulouse has also fixed up its historic centre. Once grubby, snobby Bordeaux meanwhile has upped its game with a remarkable facelift, promoting wine tourism as never before and basking in its recent UNESCO World Heritage status.

The British invasion of the Dordogne began in earnest after World War II, led by retired veterans of the foreign service and military, when lovely country homes in that delightful region could be had for a song. That particular song is ended, but the département today has one of the largest British expat colonies in France. The locals joke that the English are trying to buy back what they lost in the Hundred Years' War; so far, though, relations are generally good. Until Brexit, many villages even elected British expats to their municipal councils.

GOVERNMENT AND POLITICS

Politics is generally peaceful and nicely balanced in most of the region; all of France's many factions have their adherents, and in the departmental and regional councils right and left groups alternate periods in power. The Lot and Dordogne traditionally lean towards the left, although in the last election Dordogne voted three of its four seats in the Assemblée Nationale to President Macron's LREM party.

In Toulouse, despite rapid growth and change politics remains generally quiet and sensible, with the left usually in the advantage. Though the Gironde too shows a balance of alternating right and left, its capital, Bordeaux, is traditionally one of the few French cities to favour the right. A string of 73 years of conservative rule included the long, brilliant mayoral reign of Alain Juppé (1995–2004 and 2006–19) which transformed the face of the city. That string finally ended in 2020 with the surprise victory of the Green Pierre Hurmic as mayor.

The Rassemblement National (RN), latest reincarnation of the far-right Front National, always wins a few seats in some regional and departmental councils. The party usually gets its best returns in the Tarn-et-Garonne and Lot-et-Garonne.

Politically, the biggest change of the post-war era was the socialist government's 1981 decentralisation plan, creating the regions of Aquitaine and Midi-Pyrénées, which have since been expanded by another reform into Nouvelle Aquitaine and Occitanie. So far the regions have only limited powers, but it brings at least a hope that the southwest and the rest may someday finally regain from Paris some degree of control over their destinies.

Since 2000, government reform has extended to the creation of *métropoles* for the major cities, including Bordeaux and Toulouse. *Métropoles* are a form of metropolitan government with limited powers, designed to promote economic development and equality. In a similar vein, the state has been consolidating small rural *communes* to reduce government costs – some now have three or even four names strung together like beads on a wire.

ECONOMY

There are really two distinct economies: Bordeaux and Toulouse, and all the rest. The two big cities are modern and high-tech, at once industrial and post-industrial, thoroughly integrated into contemporary Europe. The rest of the region gets by almost entirely on agriculture, tourism and increasingly on state subsidies.

Toulouse has for decades been one of the most prosperous and fastest-growing cities in France, owing largely to its aviation industry, which goes back to 1917. Bordeaux is big in these industries too, though less known for it. Together, the two cities are the poles of France's 'Aerospace Valley' with some 120,000 jobs in the field between them. Beyond aerospace, both cities possess modern, diversified economies, where service industries, government and tourism are important. Toulouse is a major centre for education, with over 100,000 university students. Bordeaux has France's seventh-largest port, and a large sector of older industries – some in decline, such as the automotive sector, while others are booming.

Surrounded by great vineyards, with more than 14,000 producers, Bordeaux and the Gironde still count wine as an important part of their economy. But these are only part of the story for the lands beyond the two great cities. Aquitaine and Occitanie are the two most important agricultural regions in France, a feat they manage without a lot of the highly mechanised farming common in the north. Over the centuries, they have learned to specialise.

The ducks, geese and other poultry of the southwest are prized all over France and beyond. The great garden of the Lot-et-Garonne supplies most of France's prunes, along with the famous tomatoes of Marmande, apples and pears, and more raspberries, kiwis and hazelnuts than any other department. The Tarn-et-Garonne is known for fruit trees too, along with other treats such as the Chasselas table grapes of Moissac. Though no-one wants it anymore, malodorous French tobacco was a boom crop for much of the 19th and 20th centuries; old wooden drying barns still dot the countryside.

Tourism can mean many different things: cultural touring and weekend trips, nature holidays, rural chill-out *gîte* holidays. Our regions are uniquely blessed for all of them. Once you get here you'll begin to understand how important tourism really is to rural areas. Across the region 6% of all building units are holiday homes. The presence of visitors and retirees from the north, and from Britain, Belgium and the Netherlands, will often make the difference between a thriving village and one that is sad and empty.

PEOPLE

Human settlement here goes back to the end of the last ice age, when Cro-Magnon people were painting horses and bison on the cave walls. Since their day, countless others have passed through: Neolithic and Bronze Age tribes, Celts, Romans, Germans, even a few Arabs and Vikings. All of them contributed something to the southwesterners of today. They have a distinctive look to them, shorter and darker than the French up north.

And that is only the beginning of a split that colours the history through the ages. The south of France grew up in the early Middle Ages a nation unto itself, with its own culture and language, the *langue d'oc* or Occitan – the language of the troubadours. By the late 19th century, however, it was derided as a *patois*, and children were being punished for speaking it in the schoolyard. At the same time, however, as in so many other forgotten regions of Europe, the southwest began to revive its traditional language and culture before they were lost forever. You will see street signs in Occitan dialects, books are published, and songs are sung, but hardly anyone grows up speaking it.

Also in the last 200 years, while economic hard times were forcing many among the native population to move out, some newcomers were finding opportunities they couldn't get at home, and the southwest became a land of immigration. In the 20th century, large numbers of Portuguese moved in. Many of them found work in the building trades, and their families carry on today. Poles and Spaniards came too, including a large wave of refugees in 1939 after the Civil War. North Africans, predominantly Moroccans, came first to the big cities and have been gradually diffusing across the region. Some 20,000 *pied-noirs* (French colonists forced to flee Algeria after its independence in 1962) settled the region; their modern outlook and entrepreneurship have made valuable economic contributions here.

Other refugees, washed up here from the storms of post-war decolonialisation, turn up in surprising places. Two in particular suffered some scandalous treatment at the hands of the French government. A few thousand *harkis*, native Algerians who had been loyal to France, came after 1962, and some Indo-Chinese still live in the camp in Ste-Livrade where their families were brought in 1954.

CULTURE

ART AND ARCHITECTURE

Prehistory and ancient The southwest's artistic career begins with a bang, in the world-renowned Palaeolithic painted caves of Périgord. Two-thirds of the 115 or so prehistoric decorated caves known in the world are in southwest France, the best of them in the Vézère Valley (see box, page 172). The Musée National de Préhistoire in Les Eyzies provides a good introduction, and most of the main sights are not far away: Lascaux, with the most compelling paintings, though only in reproductions; the Grotte de Font-de-Gaume, the best original art we're still allowed to see, along with Pech Merle in the Lot; the caves of Roffignac and Combarelles are also exceptional.

For 10,000 years after the age of the cave artists, not much at all happened in our corner of the world. At least Périgord and Quercy (c2000BC) participated in the late stages of the Neolithic era, when agriculture, architecture and astronomy first came to Europe. Neolithic people liked to live close to the water, on the sea coasts or around major rivers, and in fact the Lot department has the greatest concentration of Neolithic remains of any inland region in Europe. Don't expect anything like Stonehenge; the sites are generally simple menhirs (standing stones) and dolmens (collective tombs made from a large flat stone balanced on two or more others).

After the Neolithic, the Gauls held sway here for centuries, but despite their cultural sophistication, artistic remains here are rare. Similarly, the southwest was a busy, prosperous place for two centuries after the Roman conquest, without a lot to show for it. The best collections of Roman-era finds are in the Musée Saint-Raymond in Toulouse, and the Vesunna Museum in Périgueux, laid out among ruins of the ancient city, near the southwest's only surviving Gallo-Roman temple, the cylindrical Tour de Vésone.

In the troubled late Roman centuries, the southwest settled in for another long hibernation. With no economy to speak of, the region produced almost no art and architecture. In some churches you will find fragments of sculpture, re-employed from older churches of Merovingian and Carolingian times, but they will usually be rough and primitive, as if they were carved by children.

Romanesque In the long economic boom that began in the 11th century, the rebirth of art was sudden and explosive. New churches in the Romanesque style sprang up everywhere, often decorated with stone carving the equal of anything

THE ROMANESQUE BUG

The Romanesque is a bug that bites unexpectedly; no other art and architecture in the West has the same inexplicable capacity to enchant. As Ralph Glaber, an 11th-century English chronicler wrote: 'So it was as though the world had shaken herself and cast off her old age, and were clothing herself everywhere in a white garment of churches.' At first sight, especially if you've been indoctrinated in school, you might think that these products of modern Europe's first artistic urge are mere 'primitives', child steps on the way to the Gothic and Renaissance.

A closer look reveals an immensely sophisticated art that seems to have sprung, fully formed, out of nothing at the dawn of the Middle Ages. In fact, the ideas of Romanesque had been around for a while, breaking out occasionally in unexpected places like Syria, or Armenia, or Asturias in northern Spain. Only in the huge economic upsurge of the 11th century did anyone in Europe really have a chance to build. When they got the chance, they built for the ages. At first sight their works may seem heavy, with the little light that filters through the narrow windows in the afternoon. But let your eyes adjust to the shadows for a minute, and you'll see wonders.

'Romanesque', for such a momentous and varied movement in architecture, is as misleading a term as 'Gothic'. Among the few things it has in common with ancient Rome are round arches and the frequent basilica plan for churches. But Romanesque has nothing to do with the classical Orders of ancient buildings; rather it depends on a new system of sacred geometry, which probably began with 6th-century Hagia Sophia in Constantinople. Anyone with a mathematical bent will enjoy looking over the churches or their plans; every point in the ground plans and elevations can be proved with a compass and straight edge, the same way the master masons designed them.

In the springtime of the medieval world, nearly every large region of Western Europe developed its own distinctive style. Freedom and fancy were in the air in the 11th and 12th centuries; standards were high and rules few. Along with the architecture goes its sculptural decoration – the first great age of sculpture since classical Greece. Early medieval society found the resources not only to raise all these buildings, but to decorate their portals and columns with a wealth of detail, even in some village churches. The southwest contributed more than its share; many consider Moissac's portal to be the greatest masterpiece of all medieval sculpture.

And what have the French done with this heritage? From the Renaissance Italians, the French first learned a rationale for contempt for their greatest buildings, and set off on a path of slavish imitation of the Romans and a submission to academies and rules. In the philistine 17th and 18th centuries,

in Europe. Toulouse's Basilica of St-Sernin (begun 1070) is the biggest of all Romanesque churches; the city was also the centre for a remarkable school of sculptors, creating heavily stylised, expressive masterpieces at Souillac, Moissac, Cahors and Carennac.

Périgord has more than a hundred Romanesque churches, in a wealth of differing styles, while the Gironde offers a curiosity, the Église Monolithique in St-Émilion, carved out of the rock. Domed churches are a particularity of the Dordogne and Lot, an idea brought home by Crusaders, inspired by the great Greek churches of Constantinople. These include St-Front and St-Étienne in Périgueux, Cahors cathedral, and the abbey church at Souillac.

the tastemakers in the academies considered anything medieval the artistic equivalent of *patois*. They spoilt the interiors of thousands of churches, plastering them over with gaudy Baroque frippery (most of that has been cleared away in the last few decades). There was more to the world of the Romanesque than the Enlightenment ever dreamt of in its philosophy, and in the first days of the Revolution uncomprehending mobs gleefully smashed exquisite medieval sculpture. Casualties included Toulouse's magnificent cloisters of St-Sernin and St-Étienne; you can see the surviving fragments in the Musée des Augustins.

After the Revolution, scores of churches and monasteries saw duty as barns, warehouses and barracks; many more were simply torn down for their stone. When the first attempts at restoration were made, the result was often just as unfortunate – the classic example being Paul Abadie's supremely arrogant job on St-Front in Périgueux. France, surprisingly one of the most backward nations of Europe in historic preservation, only got its act together in the 1960s.

Wandering among the fragments of the early Middle Ages you often feel like an archaeologist, exploring the enigmatic survivals of a lost civilisation. The architecture speaks for itself, an inexhaustible vernacular of simple arches, barrel vaulting, pilasters and apses recombined in a thousand different ways. The sculpture is more of a problem; its imagery often reflects concepts that have nothing to do with orthodox religion. Why is the Prophet Isaiah dancing at Souillac, and what made the seemingly obscure episode of Daniel in the lions' den the most copied and most significant image in the sculpture of the southwest? And what about the mermaids?

The sculpture is the key, although you'll always have to look carefully to find it. When you visit a Romanesque church, scrutinise every corner, inside and out. The great themes of the Life of Christ and the Apocalypse are portrayed for all to see, but the esoteric bits are in places you wouldn't expect. The faces are everywhere, especially on the modillions, or corbel-stones around the roofline: hundreds of faces, grimacing, smiling, interspersed with monsters, cats, dogs, boars, unicorns and all the other inhabitants of the medieval imagination. There may be a giant with a club, a dim memory of ancient Hercules, or a fine lady in a small boat who symbolises Desire.

The meaning, and even the identity of the characters is often lost to us, though if you could go back to the 1100s, a troubadour, or a street singer, or a monk with a little Latin might have explained them all. But you can't, and unless you're willing to spend the rest of your life at it, travelling, reading and looking, you'll never know.

Gothic This was a foreign style never completely at home in the southwest, and wherever it appears it is almost always an imposition of foreign rulers, whether French or English. Not surprisingly the architecture is dependent on northern inspirations too, as in the two great Flamboyant Gothic churches of Bordeaux, St-Michel and St-André, or the lavishly decorated cathedral of Bazas, and the romantically ruined Abbaye de la Sauve-Majeure. Cahors Cathedral has a lovely Gothic façade that rises high above the older parts of the building; this is perhaps the grandest example of the *clocher mur* so common in the southwest churches, where the façade takes the place of a bell tower, and was sometimes designed to aid in the defence of the town.

The biggest building projects in this period were the bastides, planned new towns built to make homes for a burgeoning population. Most appeared in the 13th century, as a tool for repopulating empty lands, founded by the French king, the English or the Counts of Toulouse, lined up against each other like the start of a chess match. Bastides are the first work of conscious urban planning in Europe since the Romans, and they have a very modern air. Their grid of straight streets is a Chicago on a village scale. The central market square, often surrounded by Gothic-arched arcades, made a handsome civic centre. And bastides were a civic and commercial enterprise (being permitted to hold a market was a key attraction), not a community under the wing of religion. Bastide churches never had pride of place on the squares, but were tucked off in a corner.

The Dordogne, a land of endless feudal battles, is also the land of castles. At one place along the Dordogne river you can see five of them at once. Other rare secular survivors are the town halls at La Réole and St-Antonin-Noble-Val. Urban palaces appeared wherever there was money. Up in the Lot, there was a surprising Italian influence, especially in Cahors and Figeac, home to colonies of Italian merchants. Here, the private palaces with their arcades of pointed arches and top-floor loggias give these cities a look reminiscent of Tuscany. Cahors's golden age also left us perhaps the most beautiful of all medieval bridges, the Pont Valentré.

Renaissance The Renaissance came to France largely through nobles and court officials who had accompanied French kings to the long Wars of Italy (1494–1559). These often brought home Italian artists and architects, to create wonderful things like the Château de Montal (begun 1510), a piece of quattrocento Tuscany lost in the Lot. Dozens of Italianate châteaux were soon to follow. Most popped up in Périgord, where predatory barons had all the money and spent it all on themselves. The Château de Biron, with its delightful pavilion and chapel, is an epitome of the French Early Renaissance. From about the same time is Jumilhac, with its magical skyline of conical turrets and chimney pots and wrought iron finials expressing alchemical allegories.

The châteaux of Périgord's barons rival the contemporaneous, but more famous châteaux of the Loire valley. Sometimes these were built from scratch, but often they simply expanded older medieval castles such as Bourdeilles and Gramont.

The southwest's cities shared in the Renaissance, too. In Toulouse the era began with the charming Donjon du Capitole, a demonstration of the transition between Gothic and Renaissance styles. In the 16th century profits from the pastel (woad) trade funded the supremely elegant *hôtels particuliers* of the merchants, such as the Hôtel de Bernuy and the Hôtel d'Assézat. With their pleasing contrast of white limestone and pink brick, finely carved Italianate windows and lavish courtyards, often embellished with a decorative tower, these palaces form an architectural genre of their own, and they rank among the finest works of the French Renaissance.

Périgord too has a city that is an open-air museum of this era: Sarlat. With an unmatched collection of buildings from the 15th to 17th centuries, Sarlat is often pressed into service as a film set.

Surprisingly, one thing the French did not bring home from Italy was the Italian love of painting. In the southwest, you are likely to see only indifferent portraiture and religious painting, some of it utterly primitive, like the 15th-century processions of the *Seven Deadly Sins* that decorate so many country churches. There is some fine sculptural work in the churches and châteaux, though seldom any name to attach them to. The southwest's most notable artist in this period may have been the ceramicist Bernard Palissy, extremely popular at the royal courts for wildly colourful platters decorated with snakes and shellfish.

18th–21st centuries The 18th century was an important period for architecture in Bordeaux. Enlightened intendants such as Claude Boucher and Louis-Urbain Aubert, de Tourny, transformed the city. Under their direction excellent architects created the grand panorama of the quays of the Garonne and laid out the Jardin Public and a system of boulevards that would later inspire Haussmann in Paris. Ange-Jacques Gabriel, the architect who perhaps best expressed the elegance and grace of the French Enlightenment, came to Bordeaux in 1729 to give the city its landmark and symbol, the Place de la Bourse. Another Parisian, Victor Louis, contributed the superb Grand Théâtre.

In Toulouse, the rebuilding of the Capitole (1760) provided a symbol for the city's transformation into a modern metropolis over the next century. For decades, redevelopment was under the direction of Jacques-Pascal Virebent (d1831), who planned the grand Place du Capitole, Place Wilson and many other squares and boulevards. His son Auguste Virebent and his brothers would grace these new streets with façades in interlaced brick and pink stone that carried on the city's Renaissance traditions.

In a country whose cultural life continued to be dominated by Paris, the southwest gave little to art in the 19th and 20th centuries. Montauban produced the 19th-century academic painter Dominique Ingres, Rodin's follower Antoine Bourdelle, and the undefinable Marcel Lenoir. Bordeaux's pride is the painter and printmaker Odilon Redon, whose dreamlike images made him a precursor of surrealism. Other talented local painters did their best to keep up with the trends set in Paris, including the Fauvist Albert Marquet and the Cubist André Lhote. Toulouse's greatest contribution to modern art was Henri Martin, symbolist and later pointillist, who painted grand murals in the public buildings of Paris and in his home city's Capitole, before spending half the year at his home in a Lotois village, the idyllic Labastide-du-Vert, scenes of which provided the subjects for many of his finest works.

He wasn't the only one to discover the pleasures of country life. Russian sculptor Osip Zadkine brought avant-garde flash to the Lotois village of Les Arques; Jean Luçat, who revived the art of tapestry, worked for the Resistance in the Lot and later made his home in a castle at St-Céré.

Of the great architectural heritage of Bordeaux and Toulouse, almost nothing found its way into the buildings of the 20th century. Both cities became devoted to the most soulless brand of Modernism, and both spent a bomb creating megaproject showpieces that have turned out to be civic embarrassments. Bordeaux's was Meriadeck, just east of the city centre, where an entire working-class neighbourhood was destroyed for a gruesome expanse of grey concrete with second-floor connecting walkways that suck all life off the streets. In Toulouse, it was Le Mirail, a gargantuan concrete project that soon made its reputation as one of the worst slums of Europe. The only grace note in the Modernist assault was Le Corbusier's model housing project, the Cité Frugès in Pessac (page 105); its colourful, geometrical but charming buildings have had an enormous influence on architecture since.

The bad habits of Bordeaux and Toulouse have not spread much into the smaller cities and towns, but architecture in the southwest remains in a sorry state, with a few exceptions such as Jean Nouvel (b1945), from Fumel and perhaps France's most innovative architect, who designed Périgord's Vesunna museum and the Hotel

Saint-James in Bordeaux. Bordeaux's Cité du Vin (2016) by Anouk Legendre and Nicholas Desmazières has laid down the gauntlet for the 21st-century showcases, which Toulouse may someday trump with its first skyscraper, the Tour Occitanie by Daniel Libeskind and Kardham Cardete et Huet (that is, if building permission ever gets out of the courts).

MUSIC The oldest songs to survive from our regions were the Occitan lays sung by the troubadours (from *trobar*, Occitan for compose or invent), starting in the early 12th century with the often bawdy compositions of Aquitaine's Duke Guillaume IX. Like him, many of the troubadours who followed were noblemen and women (*trobairitz*). They sang songs of courtly (often unrequited) love, although they also wrote humorous, satirical and war songs in intricate meter and rhyme that bedevil translators. While some 2,000 troubadour songs have survived, there are only 315 extant melodies, jotted down minimally in the manuscripts, open to improvisation.

The Albigensian Crusade in the early 13th century was the day the music died in this part of France, but several medieval songs in Occitan have survived in the region's traditional songbook, including the 12th-century haunting and esoteric Cathar hymn 'Lo Boièr' ('the Oxherd'). Toulouse radio played it as a song of resistance during World War I. Another one everyone knows, 'Se Canta' ('If It Is Sung') was composed in the 14th century by Count Gaston Phoebus of Foix and sung at weddings and at rugby or football matches in Toulouse.

As for modern troubadours, there's Toulouse's *chanson française* singer-songwriter Claude Nougaro (1929–2004), and an adopted Lotois, Léo Ferré (1916–93), who lived in a partly ruined château near Gourdon with his menagerie of animals. And there are the two 20th-century international stars linked to the region: the 'King of Tango' Carlos Gardel (1890–1935), who was born in Toulouse and left as a baby for Argentina; and the inimitable Josephine Baker (1906–75), who for three decades made the Dordogne her home (page 211).

LITERATURE Aside from the 4th-century AD Latin poet Ausonius from Bordeaux, literature began here with the troubadours, who inspired Dante among others. They were so missed in Toulouse that in 1323 the locals created a poetry contest, the Jeux Floraux, in the hopes of restoring their beloved poetry – and along the way founded the world's oldest literary academy. But the first post-troubadour poets to make waves were from Quercy: Hugues Salel of Cazals (1504–53), translator of the *Iliad*, and Clément Marot of Cahors (1495–1544), a royal favourite (page 258) who wrote some of the first sonnets in French and is best known these days for his praises of female anatomy. The next writer to make the big time nationally was his polar opposite – the indelicate tell-all gossip Brantôme (1540–1614; page 161).

Most of all this corner of France is renowned as a land of deep thinkers, starting in the 16th century with the humanist poet Étienne de la Boétie of Sarlat (page 201), whose untimely demise inspired his dear friend and fellow Périgourdin Michel de Montaigne to invent the essay (page 230) – and whose wise, humanist views influenced every philosopher and writer who read him, including Shakespeare. In the next century another Périgourdin, François Fénelon, wrote for the heir of Louis XIV the *Aventures de Télémaque*, a fable decrying the absolute monarchy and expansionist wars, which didn't go down well with the king – but then became one of the most read books of the time (page 241). In 1748, Montesquieu from the Gironde wrote his masterful *The Spirit of the Laws*, based on the idea that 'government should be set up so that no man need be afraid of another' and advocated the division of powers that became a bedrock of the US Constitution.

Jasmin (Jacques Boé; 1798–1864) of Agen was one of the first poets in the modern era to write in Occitan, renewing the language when it was on the verge of dying out. Périgord's Eugène Le Roy (1836–1907) was born in Hautefort into a family of château labourers – a background that inspired his classic, *Jacquou le Croquant* (1899), describing the abject poverty of Périgord's peasants and their rebellions. He was offered the Légion d'Honneur in 1904…and refused.

Bordeaux produced two major 20th-century writers: novelist François Mauriac (1885–1970), winner of the 1952 Nobel Prize for Literature (page 120), and one of France's greatest playwrights, Jean Anouilh (1910–87). Other literati associated with our area include Marguerite Duras (1914–96), who set her earliest novels in and around her father's native Lot-et-Garonne (page 320), and the high priest of Surrealism, André Breton, who spent his summers in St-Cirq-Lapopie.

CINEMA You may already have seen the cities, castles and villages in this book without knowing it, especially those of the Dordogne: Claude Chabrol's thriller *Le Boucher* (1970) was filmed in Trémolat; Ridley Scott used Sarlat in *The Duellists* (1977) and Beynac in his *Jeanne D'Arc* (1998), then returned just before the Covid lockdown to film *The Last Duel* (2021) in Monpazier and the mighty Château de Beynac.

Elegant 18th-century Bordeaux stood in for Paris in Robert Hossein's classic version of *Les Misérables* (1982), then played itself in the Spanish film *Goya in Bordeaux* (1998). André Téchiné's 1993 classic, *Ma Saison Préférée* with Catherine Deneuve and Daniel Auteuil, was set in Toulouse.

The Tarn-et-Garonne is another favourite location. The 1963 cult crime comedy *Les Tontons flingueurs* ('Pistol-toting Uncles', or *Crooks in Clover* in English) is so famous in Montauban because of the line in the film 'I should have stayed in Montauban' that there's a roundabout named after the film, although all the action takes place in Paris. Parts of Louis Malle's controversial *Lacombe Lucien* (1974) were shot in Tarn-et-Garonne; *Charlotte Gray* starring Cate Blanchett (2001) and *The Hundred Foot Journey* (2013) with Helen Mirren were filmed in St-Antonin-Noble-Val.

SPORTS AND ACTIVITIES

BEACHES Besides the endless sands and dunes along the Atlantic's Côte d'Argent, nearly all the rivers here are exceptionally clean, with beaches and lifeguards in the summer. If there's not a river nearby, rural France is well endowed with lakes or artificial *plans d'eau*, some with elaborate water parks attached.

CANOEING AND KAYAKING The Leyre ('the little Amazon') south of the Bassin d'Arcachon, shaded by a canopy of trees, is a magical place to paddle a canoe. But the Ciron, Dordogne, Vézère, Dronne, Dropt, Lot, Isle, Célé and Aveyron are all pretty wonderful too. Outfitters hire out canoes or kayaks by the hour, half-day or longer, and will fetch you back to your starting point when you're done.

CYCLING With lovely scenery, quiet rural roads and new traffic-free *voie verte* routes opening all the time, cycling is more popular than ever, and if you haven't brought a bike, local tourist offices can help you find one to hire. Worth a special mention are the 290km bike path along the banks of the Canal Latéral à la Garonne from Bordeaux to Toulouse, and the 160km Véloroute de la Vallée du Lot between Cahors and Aiguillon along quiet roads (**w** cahorsvalleedulot.com), or the more challenging 85km Véloroute Vallée et Gorges de l'Aveyron departing from Montauban. Velo Tourism (w en.francevelotourisme.com) has an overview of routes in English; holiday firms (page 26) can arrange accommodation.

FISHING You can fish in the sea without a permit as long as your catch is for local consumption; the Arcachon tourist office can help arrange an ocean-fishing excursion by the day and half-day. Freshwater fishing is extremely popular in this region of rivers, where the big sport fish is the *silure* (Wels catfish); in 2021 a local bagged one weighing 265kg using chicken guts. It requires an easily obtained permit from a local club – a day license costs around €14, a weekly license €35; tourist offices can help you find them.

GOLF There are some gorgeous courses to play here. To find courses in the Gironde, Dordogne or Lot-et-Garonne, see w ligue-golf-nouvelle-aquitaine.fr; in the Lot, Tarn-et-Garonne and around Toulouse see w liguegolfoccitanie.fr.

HIKING A network of long-distance paths, the **Grandes Randonnées** (GR), criss-cross the land, including many blazed by pilgrims in the Middle Ages. Each GR is described in a Topoguide, with maps and details about camping sites, refuges and *rando-étapes* (inexpensive shelters) and so on, available in area bookshops, or at w ignrando.fr. You can also download the maps via their app (IGN rando).

Among the most scenic paths are the GR36/6, the Traversée du Périgord, beginning at Angoulême and passing down the Vézère Valley to Cahors; the pilgrims' GR65 Sentier de St-Jacques Cahors–Roncevaux; or the GR652 alternative, from Rocamadour and the Atlantic coast's GR8. For less daunting pilgrimages, there's the historic 180km path from Bergerac to Rocamadour by way of Cadouin (w compostelle-limousin-perigord.fr) or the walk from Agen to Moissac along the 107km Chemin Clunisien de Guyenne, taking in four Cluny foundations (w cheminclunisienguyennegascogne.com). Also see the list of holiday companies on page 26.

Shorter paths are often maintained by local walking groups. Many are circular (including day and half-day Petites Randonnées, or PRs) – many are listed at w visorando.com or w sentiers-en-france.eu. For the Gironde, see w gironde-tourisme.fr/sur-place/balades; for Dordogne, w rando.dordogne.fr; for the Lot, w tourisme-lot.com/balades-et-randonnees; for Lot-et-Garonne, w rando.tourisme-lotetgaronne.com; and for Tarn-et-Garonne, w tourisme-tarnetgaronne.fr/a-voir-a-faire/bouger/balades-et-randonnees.

HORSERIDING Local tourist offices have lists of *centres équestres* to get you on a horse. Some offer group excursions and treks year-round, at weekends or during the week, with vans to take your luggage and overnight stabling. Also see the riding holidays on page 26.

PARAGLIDING/HANG-GLIDING The Dune du Pilat (page 98) is a perfect launching pad for hang-gliding. Other spots are the cliffs along the Dordogne and Lot: see Parapente Périgord (w parapente-perigord.fr), Parapente Valley (w parapentevalley.com) and Rêve Parapente (w parapente-lot.com) and the Gorges de l'Aveyron (w atgparapente82.com). Or go up in a glider at Castelsarrasin (w planeur-tarn-et-garonne.com).

PÉTANQUE Also known as *boules*, pétanque is an essential ingredient of daily life here: even the smallest village has a *boulodrome* for its practitioners. Tournaments (with big prize money!) are frequent and well attended.

ROCK CLIMBING There are a number of sites in the Lot (for details, see **w** escalade-dans-le-lot.com) and on the Rocher d'Anglars at St-Antonin-Noble-Val in the Gorges de l'Aveyron (**w** tarn-escalade.fr).

RUGBY Since 1900, rugby, perfectly adapted to the Gascon temperament and physique, has been the national sport of southwest France, the cradle of most of the players on the national team. Stade Toulousain is one of the top teams in Europe; they have won the Coupe d'Europe five times, most recently in 2021.

SURFING Lacanau is the main centre for riding the waves on this stretch of the Côte d'Argent with a number of schools and rentals.

2

Practical Information

WHEN TO VISIT

Winter can be a bleak time to visit outside of Bordeaux and Toulouse, which are always lively and full of things to see and do. Elsewhere hotels, restaurants and sights (including most caves and châteaux) simply close down, and the skies are often cloudy all day. The first crocuses often show up in January (which is also peak truffle season) but, whatever the weather, things are pretty sleepy until March. Spring-term school holidays and Easter week bring the first tourist rush of the year, but nothing too dramatic. May and June, usually warm and not too crowded, are among the best times to visit.

Hot July and August are French school holidays, when the countryside comes to life with thousands of holidaymakers. Towns and attractions are crowded, prices rise and there are scores of festivals, village fêtes, fairs, concerts and more. In late September/early October, when the tourists have gone and everyone is concentrating on the wine harvest, the vineyards turn golden and red in romantic mists. November and December can be dismal and wet, but wild mushrooms, truffles, walnuts and game dishes offer some consolation, along with the Christmas concerts and fairs.

HIGHLIGHTS

Start with magnificent 18th-century Bordeaux, capital of the Gironde, a département chock-full of superlatives – it's the largest in France, with 116km of Atlantic coast lined with fine silver sand, with calm lakes just inland if you're not ready to ride the waves. The great rivers of the Garonne and Dordogne meet here to form Europe's largest estuary, winding through arguably the best wine region in the world, while to the south there's the Dune du Pilat, Europe's highest sand dune and the oyster-filled Bassin d'Arcachon. Inland wait bucolic landscapes of hills, woodlands and river valleys, historic art cities and towns – St-Émilion, Périgueux, Sarlat, Rocamadour, Cahors, Figeac, Moissac (to name just a few) – some of the most beautiful villages in France, and literally hundreds of medieval and Renaissance châteaux. Lascaux, Font-de-Gaume and Pech Merle are only the most famous of the unique array of palaeolithic decorated caves. Toulouse, the 'Ville Rose' has a stunning historic centre and high-tech attractions along the edges. The surfing, canoeing and kayaking, hiking and cycling are exceptional – and the local cuisine fantastic, the perfect foil for all that wine.

SUGGESTED ITINERARIES

THE REGION'S TOP SIGHTS IN 18 DAYS

Days 1–2 Begin in Toulouse – visit its historic centre and museums.

Day 3 Head up to Moissac for the abbey, then Agen for its art museum and a look at the fine towns of La Réole, St-Macaire and Bazas.

Day 4 Visit a château in the Graves or Sauternes in the morning, then Bordeaux and the Cité du Vin – don't miss the Miroir d'Eau by night.
Day 5 Bordeaux and its Musée des Beaux-Arts; overnight in St-Émilion.
Day 6 Spend the morning in St-Émilion; then head to Brantôme in the afternoon.
Day 7 Take in Roman and medieval Périgueux.
Days 8–9 Visit Lascaux IV, then drive down the Vézère Valley to Les Eyzies; explore a cave, the Musée de la Préhistoire, and Roque St-Christophe.
Day 10 La Roque-Gageac, Château de Beynac and Les Milandes, followed by evening in Sarlat.
Day 11 Stop in Souillac for the Abbaye de Ste-Marie, then the pretty villages of Martel, Carennac and Beaulieu-sur-Dordogne; overnight in St-Céré.
Day 12 Château de Montal, then the Gouffre de Padirac; overnight in Rocamadour.
Day 13 Rocamadour; in the afternoon drive to Figeac.
Day 14 Figeac; then in the afternoon Grotte du Pech Merle and St-Cirq-Lapopie.
Day 15 Cahors; then drive west to Château de Bonaguil, Château de Biron and Monpazier.
Day 16 A bastide tour – Issigeac, Villeréal, Monflanquin, Tournon d'Agenais and Lauzerte.
Day 17 Tapestries in Monpezat-de-Quercy; then the Gorges de l'Aveyron – St-Antonin-Noble-Val, Penne and Bruniquel.
Day 18 Montauban and its art museum, then back to Toulouse.

TEN DAYS WITH THE KIDS

Days 1–2 Start in Toulouse – visit the Cité de l'Espace, Halle de la Machine and Natural History Museum, then drive to Cahors; walk across the Pont Valentré and stay overnight.
Day 3 Visit the Grotte du Pech Merle and the Écomusée de Cuzals, then head north to Rocamadour.
Day 4 Meet the Barbary apes at Rocamadour and take in the Rocher des Aigles bird show.
Day 5 Take a gondola into the Gouffre de Padirac and spend the afternoon in the Parc Animalier in Gramat; afterwards drive to Montignac.
Day 6 Visit Lascaux IV and the Roque St Christophe.
Day 7 Kayak down the Dordogne, past half a dozen medieval castles.
Day 8 Tour Castelnaud and its museum of medieval warfare and the Parc Le Bournat.
Day 9 Bordeaux – including the Miroir d'Eau and Bassins des Lumières, then Arcachon.
Days 10–12 Explore Dune du Pilat and play on the beach; take a boat to the Îles aux Oiseaux. It's 2½ hours back to Toulouse.

TOURIST INFORMATION

Every city and town (and important villages) will have an Office du Tourisme or Syndicat d'Initiative. Many are open year-round and have very useful websites, often covering a fairly wide area (the Lot valley, say, instead of each village), and nearly all are in English, as well as French, offering extensive listings of accommodation, campsites, sports and activities, etc. The regional tourist boards are a good place to start: Nouvelle Aquitaine (**w** nouvelle-aquitaine-tourisme.com) and Occitanie (**w** tourisme-occitanie.com).

TOUR OPERATORS

FRANCE

Aquitaine Bike w aquitainebike.com; see ad, 2nd coour sec. Self-guided cycling tour of Périgord Noir.
Aquitaine Navigation w aquitaine-navigation.com. Canal boat hire on the Baïse & the Canal Latéral à la Garonne.
Babou Marine w baboumarine.com. Houseboat cruising on the Lot from Cahors or Canal Latéral à la Garonne.
Dordogne Riding w dordogneriding.com. Week-long riding holidays based near Bergerac.
France Just for You w france-justforyou.com. Self-guided driving tours in the Gironde.
French Bike Tours w french-biketours.com. Along the Canal Latéral à la Garonne.
Greeter France w greeters.fr. Initiative offering a chance to take a 2hr walk with a local volunteer (in English or French) who can tell you all about whatever interest you share; book at least a week in advance – & it's free.
PeriGourmet w perigourmet.com. Gourmet excursions in Périgord Noir in a Citroën 2CV.
Ride in France w rideinfrance.com. Horseriding holidays in the Gironde & the Lot.

UK

Arblaster & Clarke w arblasterandclarke.com. Wine tours of Bordeaux.
ATG w atg-oxford.co.uk. Walking & cycling in the Dordogne & Lot.
Explore Worldwide w exploreworldwide.com. Cycling the Canal Latéral à la Garonne.
Far and Ride w farandride.com. Horseriding holidays in the Gironde, Dordogne & Lot.
Headwater Holidays w headwater.com. Cycling, walking & canoeing in the Dordogne & Lot.
Hooked on Cycling w hookedoncycling.co.uk. Boating, biking & hiking.
Inntravel w inntravel.co.uk. Walking in the Dordogne & cycling in Bordeaux & St-Émilion.
Le Boat w leboat.com. Houseboats on the Lot, Canal Latéral & Baïse.
Locaboat w locaboat.com. Boat hire with bases in Agen & Valence-sur-Baïse.
Lot Explore w lotexplore.com; see ad, page 43. Cycling in the Parc Naturel Régional des Causses du Quercy.
Nicols w boat-renting-nicols.co.uk. Canal boats on the Lot, Canal Latéral & Baïse.
Travel Local w travellocal.com. A UK-based website where you can book direct with selected local travel companies, allowing you to communicate with an expert ground operator without having to go through a 3rd-party travel operator or agent. Your booking with the local company has full financial protection, but note that travel to the destination is not included. Member of ABTA, ASTA.
Unicorn Trails w unicorntrails.com. Atlantic coast & Bordeaux wine region riding holidays.
Walkers Britain w walkersbritain.co.uk. Dordogne on foot or by bike.

USA

Audley Travel w audleytravel.com. Guided Bordeaux & wine tours.
Du Vine w duvine.com. Luxury bike & wine tours around Bordeaux & the Dordogne.
Go Away w goway.com. Packages & experiences in Bordeaux.
Macs Adventure w macsadventure.com. Dordogne walking & cycling tours.

RED TAPE

Citizens of EU member states and holders of passports from some 50 nations do not need a **visa** for stays of 90 days or less. These include Australia, Canada, Hong Kong, Israel, Japan, Malaysia, Mexico, New Zealand, Singapore, South Korea, Switzerland, the UK and the USA. If you intend staying longer than three months, the law says you need a *carte de séjour*. Non-EU citizens should kick off the process months in advance by applying for an extended visa at their French consulate before leaving home, a complicated procedure requiring proof of income, etc. You can't get a carte de séjour without this visa, a trial run for the ennui you'll undergo in applying for a carte de séjour at your local prefecture. See w france-visas.gouv.fr/en/web/france-visas/long-stay-visa.

EMBASSIES

The UK and the USA have consulates in Bordeaux. Check **w** embassypages.com/france for a constantly updated list of other options, including French consulates and embassies abroad.

E **UK (consulate)** [54 B3] 353 Bd du Président Wilson; 05 57 22 21 10

E **USA (consulate)** [54 E2] 89 Quai des Chartrons; 01 43 12 48 65

GETTING THERE AND AWAY

BY AIR The major international airports in the region are at Bordeaux and Toulouse, both of which have direct connections with numerous airports in the UK and Ireland and around Europe. There's also a small-scale international airport at Bergerac, and a smaller one at Brive-Souillac. Others in the vicinity are in Limoges (90mins from Périgueux by train or car) and Rodez (an hour's drive from Figeac). Destinations and airlines keep changing, though, so it is always worth browsing Skyscanner (**w** skyscanner.net).

From North America, the only direct flights to southwest France are from Montreal on Air-Transat (**w** airtransat.com), which fly direct to Bordeaux and Toulouse from May to September. Otherwise, your best option may be to find a cheap flight to a European hub then continue from there to Bordeaux or Toulouse. If you fly into Charles-de-Gaulle (Roissy), there are direct fast LGV trains to Libourne and Bordeaux from the airport.

BY RAIL From the UK, travelling from London St Pancras to Bordeaux can take as little as 6 hours with **Eurostar** (**w** eurostar.com), changing in Paris (Gare du Nord to Gare de Montparnasse; see **w** thetrainline.com for options). You'll save money if you purchase tickets in advance (up to 180 days before your return date). There are discounts on the Eurostar for children aged 4–11; under 4s travel for free.

For the Dordogne or Lot, an Intercity train from Paris Austerlitz to Périgueux (via Limoges) or Cahors might be quickest. Another option is the overnight sleeper (*intercité de nuit*), leaving Paris Austerlitz at 22.00 and arriving in Toulouse at 06.00. Check out options on the French SNCF rail website (**w** sncf-connect.com), which now includes BlaBlaCar car sharing and Hiflow vehicle transport options.

BY ROAD It's 1,028km (an 11hr drive) from London to Bordeaux by way of the Eurotunnel and *autoroutes* (toll motorways), and at the time of writing this costs around €220 in tolls and fuel. The Michelin website (**w** viamichelin.com) is useful for calculating routes, times, traffic conditions, and petrol and toll prices in France.

Drivers with a valid permit from an EU country, the UK, Canada, the USA or Australia don't need an international licence. A car entering France must have its registration and insurance papers. If you're coming from the UK or Ireland, the dip of the headlights must be adjusted to the right. Carrying a warning triangle and yellow vest inside the car is mandatory; the triangle should be placed 50m behind the car if you have a breakdown.

BY SEA The Dover–Calais ferries offer the most frequent crossings, although ferries from Portsmouth to Caen (plus 603km/5½hrs onward drive to Bordeaux) may be a good option, depending on where you live.

Dover–Calais
DFDS w dfds.com
P&O w poferries.com

Portsmouth–Caen
Brittany Ferries w brittany-ferries.co.uk

HEALTH AND SAFETY *with Felicity Nicholson*

Research for this guide was completed during the Covid-19 pandemic. Check the Foreign Commonwealth and Development Office travel advice (w gov.uk/government/organisations/foreign-commonwealth-development-office), including the country-specific pages, to get the latest information on travel restrictions, testing and quarantine requirements. Do this on a regular basis as changes can occur where there are rapid increases in case numbers.

You can insure yourself for almost any possible mishap – cancelled flights, stolen or lost baggage and ill health. Check any current policies you hold to see if they cover all the activities you plan to do.

HEALTH EU citizens with an EHIC (European Health Insurance Card) are entitled to care in France from the national health system (which in practice means you are covered for 75–80% of your treatment). As the UK is no longer a member of the European Union, requirements for UK citizens may differ – check before travelling. All travellers should consider comprehensive travel insurance that includes 24/7 medical assistance, medical expenses and emergency evacuation; accidental death and permanent total disability, baggage loss or delay, money and passport, trip cost cancellation and personal liability.

Travel clinics and health information A full list of current travel clinic websites worldwide is available on w istm.org. For other journey preparation information, consult w travelhealthpro.org.uk (UK) or w wwwnc.cdc.gov/travel (USA). Information about various medications may be found on w netdoctor.co.uk/travel. All advice found online should be used in conjunction with expert advice received prior to or during travel.

Health risks On the whole, health risks are no different from those in other Westernised countries. In summer, aside from the danger posed by over-exposure

TICK REMOVAL

Ticks should ideally be removed complete, and as soon as possible, to reduce the chance of infection. You can use special tick tweezers, which can be bought in good travel shops; or failing this with your fingernails, grasping the tick as close to your body as possible, and pulling it away steadily and firmly at right angles to your skin without jerking or twisting. Applying irritants (eg: Olbas oil) or lit cigarettes is to be discouraged as a means of removal since they can cause the ticks to regurgitate and therefore increase the risk of disease. Once the tick is removed, if possible douse the wound with alcohol (any spirit will do), soap and water, or iodine. If you are travelling with small children, remember to check their heads, and particularly behind the ears, for ticks. Spreading redness around the bite and/or fever and/or aching joints after a tick bite imply that you have an infection that requires antibiotic treatment. In this case seek medical advice.

to the sun, there's the nuisance of mosquitoes, and the rare possibility of being bitten by a tiger mosquito carrying dengue, chikungunya or even West Nile Virus. The latter disease typically occurs from May to November. Using an insect repellent containing 50% DEET or 20% Picaridin and applying according to the manufacturer's instructions can help. Apply sunscreen first, ideally about 20 minutes before applying the insect repellent. Similarly, if you are walking in areas where mosquitoes are prevalent, consider pre-soaking or spraying your outer layers of clothing with permethrin to kill the mosquitoes on contact.

More common now is Lyme's disease from ticks. Wear light colours when walking in the woods, making it easier to spot a tick in case one lands on you. It is also worth checking yourself at the end of the day, particularly behind the ears, in the groin and under the armpits. If you do find a tick, then follow the guidance in the box on the opposite page.

Medical services The local hospital is the place to go in an emergency (*urgence*). If it's not an emergency, pharmacies have addresses of local doctors (including those who speak English), or the nearest outpatient clinic. A shortage of doctors in rural areas (especially in August!) can mean a long wait for an appointment. After consulting and paying the doctor, you will be given a *feuille de soins* (medical treatment form) with your *ordonnance* (prescription). The pharmacy will stick the prices on the forms so you can be reimbursed by your insurer.

Pharmacists are trained to administer first aid and dispense free advice for minor problems. In cities pharmacies open outside normal hours (*pharmacie de garde*) on a rota basis; addresses are posted in their window. You can ring the doorbell of many rural pharmacies after hours (although they prefer that you telephone first).

For a serious accident or illness or any **emergency**, dial 112 (someone will speak English) from a mobile or fixed phone (if you can't phone, send a text to 114). In urban areas this will summon the SAMU (*paramedics*), while in rural areas you will get the *pompiers* (fire brigade), who have ambulances too and are trained in first aid and medical emergencies. From a mobile, the 112 operator should be able to discern your position.

SAFETY If you take the same precautions you do at home, you should be fine.

Holiday homes that look empty are a prime target for burglars. Report any thefts to the nearest gendarmerie – the reward is the bit of paper you need for an insurance claim. If your passport is stolen, contact the police and your nearest consulate for emergency travel documents. By law, the police in France can stop anyone anywhere and demand ID; in practice, they only tend to do it to harass minorities, the homeless and scruffy.

Drug use is illegal in France but in practice the police only make an issue of victimless crime when it suits them, and there's not much your consulate can do about it.

In recent years, terrorists have hit France and it is now common to see armed police at airports and popular holiday areas. You can download the SAIP app which gives alerts to any major incident.

Swimming If you aren't used to the Atlantic currents, stick to beaches with lifeguards (all listed under 'supervised beaches' at w medoc-atlantique.co.uk) and heed the warnings: green flags mean safe, orange be careful, and red stay out of the water.

INFORMATION FOR TRAVELLERS WITH A DISABILITY

Hotels, bed and breakfasts, many gîtes, bars and restaurants, and the most important museums and churches are nearly all accessible to wheelchair users, but steep hill villages less so, although there are often specially designated parking spots near the top; disabled parking is also clearly marked at tourist attractions, supermarkets and elsewhere. The new trams in Bordeaux and Toulouse are wheelchair accessible. Airports offer free assistance, although it's important to let them know 48 hours in advance of your needs. Some Côte d'Argent beaches have ramps leading down to the sea. During July and August, several resorts provide free loan of beach-buggy-style wheelchairs at their lifeguard stations.

Gov.uk (w gov.uk/guidance/foreign-travel-for-disabled-people), provides advice and practical information for travellers with disabilities preparing for overseas travel.

Holiday firms can take care of the nitty gritty, such as **Seable** (w seable.co.uk) for travellers with vision impairment, or the US-based **Travel for All** (w travel-for-all.com). In France, the national **Association Tourisme & Handicaps** (w tourisme-handicaps.org) label sights by their accessibility for those with hearing, visual, intellectual and mobility disabilities; **Jaccede** (w jaccede.com) lists accessible places all around France, put together by users. For listings in Bordeaux, see w bordeaux-tourism.co.uk/accessibility; for Toulouse see w toulouse.fr/-/handicap-and-accessibility.

WOMEN TRAVELLERS

Women travelling alone should not encounter any problems, although try to avoid arriving or leaving big city train stations alone late at night, where you might attract unwanted attention. If you are hesitant about travelling alone, download an app such as Find My Phone, Noonlight, bSafe and Life360 which can be used to check in with family or alert the police to your location.

LGBTQ+ TRAVELLERS

France is a very tolerant country, but in remote villages a certain amount of discretion may be called for as you may encounter confusion, especially among elderly residents. A list of LGBTQ+ friendly hotels, bed and breakfasts, bars, and more, in France is available in English at w travelgay.com and w dailyxtratravel.com.

TRAVELLING WITH KIDS

With its ocean and river beaches, castles, canoeing, caves, animal parks, theme and adventure parks and village fêtes, this corner of France is an exceptionally welcoming place for families (see *Ten days with the kids*; page 25). Reptiland in Martel (page 243), the Toy Museum in Montauban (page 336) and the Automaton Museum (page 252) in Souillac are other kid-pleasers. Even gourmet temples will have a children's menu, and almost every garden and castle has an 'escape game' of some sort to keep young travellers amused; if your gang likes treasure hunts, download the free Terra Aventura app (in English; w terra-aventura.fr) – which has some 400 geocaching adventure trails to follow.

WHAT TO TAKE

Pack sufficient amounts of any medications you need to take regularly. Layers of warm clothing are a good idea for winter and at least a light jacket for summer evenings. Hats, sunscreen, sunglasses and mosquito repellent (containing 50% DEET or 20% Picaridin) are summer essentials.

As in the rest of the continent, France uses **electricity** at a current of 220 volts at 50 cycles per second (50Hz). If you don't have the necessary plug adaptors and converters, they are easy to find at international airports before you leave, but very hard to find once you arrive.

MONEY AND BUDGETING

MONEY France's currency is the euro (€). Credit cards are accepted at most major points of sale, although not always at bed and breakfasts and Ferme Auberges. **ATMs** are widely available and will spout cash with your bank card and PIN for the price of a significant commission; check with your bank if it has an agreement with any banks in France which will allow you to withdraw cash without paying international ATM access fees. Americans using credit cards without the right chip may find that ticket machines, toll booth machines and self-serve petrol pumps won't work, so, again, check with your bank before leaving and see what you can do to avoid excess surcharges. You might check out pre-paid bank cards such as Visa's Netspend (**w** netspend.com) or use WISE (**w** wise.com) to transfer currencies at optimum rates and top up as you go along.

BUDGETING On a shoestring, excluding accommodation, you could get by on around €30–€40 per person a day for food, drink and the occasional bus or admission fee, including a €3 breakfast (a café au lait and a croissant), a €5 sandwich lunch and a €20 dinner at an inexpensive restaurant. If your budget is mid-range, then you can expect to do well on around €50–€80 per person, again not including accommodation. This will allow for better meals at a good restaurant. Around €80–€100 per person per day will get you excellent meals and even a taxi here and there.

GETTING AROUND

BY RAIL Southwest France has a decent network of fast TGVs and LGVs, long-distance intercity and regional (TER) trains, although smaller lines may have only two or three connections a day, and may use buses to replace the rail service. Many trains will transport bicycles (look for the logo on the timetable and book a ticket (€10 or €5) for your bike; on TERs use of the special bike car is free, operating on a first come, first served basis). Fares are still reasonable, and discounts are available, especially if you book early and travel off-peak; see **w** sncf-connect.com, which now also lists available BlaBlaCar car-shares.

BY BUS AND OTHER PUBLIC TRANSPORT Do not count on seeing much of rural France by bus. The network is barely adequate between major cities and towns and rotten in rural areas. However, to make finding routes and schedules easier, all have been put under regional umbrellas: for the Gironde, Dordogne and Lot-et-Garonne, see **w** transports.nouvelle-aquitaine.fr; for the Lot, Tarn-et-Garonne and Toulouse, see **w** lio.laregion.fr. Cities will have a *gare routière* (coach station), which is usually just a small parking area near the train station. To help get around the public transport systems of Bordeaux and Toulouse, download the Citymapper app.

BY CAR Unless you stick to the major towns, cycle or walk, a car is the only way to see the area. Roads are generally excellently maintained, but don't blindly rely on GPS for 'the shortest route' as it can take you down some very narrow hilly back roads and take twice as long as it should.

The price of **petrol** (*sans plomb*, unleaded; *gasoil*, diesel) varies considerably, with motorways always more expensive and supermarkets always the cheapest; all are nearly always open 24/7 with self-service – if you have a debit or credit card with the right chip and a four-digit code. Otherwise try to buy your fuel during working hours; the big supermarkets will have someone in the booth to take your cash or credit card. Drivers of **electric vehicles** will find fast-chargers along the autoroutes and others in village car parks, by supermarkets and hotels. Download one of the European apps, Chargemap or Plug Share, to find them; also check out advice from the AA (w theaa.com). Not all charging stations in rural France work well with just the app but there is always a number to ring for help.

Watch out for the *cédez le passage* (give way) signs; generally, as you'd expect, give priority to the main road, and to the left on roundabouts. If you are new to France, think of every intersection as a new and perilous experience. Watch out for Byzantine street-parking rules (which would take pages to explain: do as the natives do, and be careful about village centres on market days). Increasingly towns have pay and display (*horodateur*) parking meters which are unduly complex and rely on you typing in your license plate number and probably your grandmother's year of birth! Most take cards as well as coins.

Speed limits are 130km/80mph on the autoroutes, 110km/68mph on dual carriageways, 80km/50mph on other roads and 50km/30mph (but in many places 30km/18mph) in an 'urbanised area', ie: as soon as you pass a white sign with a town's name on it and until you pass another sign with the town's name barred. Speed cameras are more sophisticated (and vandal proof) than ever. Fines for speeding begin at about €60, but rise rapidly depending on the circumstances, place and speed, and start at €135 if you flunk the breathalyser (anything more than an apéro and a couple of small glasses of wine may take you over; the legal limit is 50mg/100ml of blood – lower than most of the UK's 80mg/100ml).

If you have a minor accident, the procedure is to fill out and sign a statement (*constat à l'amiable*). If your French isn't sufficient to deal with this, hold off until you find someone to translate for you. If it's serious, the emergency number to summon an ambulance and the police is ☎ 112. Ring the French branch of your insurance provider in case of a breakdown. Use one of the emergency orange phones, located every 2km, for accidents and breakdowns on the autoroutes (w autoroutes.fr) or ring the emergency number (if possible avoid getting out of your car on the autoroute; it's extremely dangerous).

Car hire Major companies have branches at airports and larger train stations; most domestic one-way rentals carry no surcharge. You must be at least 18 (age may vary by car category) and have held your licence for at least a year. Some companies will rent only to drivers aged 21 and over; drivers under 25 may incur a surcharge. There is no maximum age.

BY BICYCLE French drivers, not always courteous to fellow motorists, usually give cyclists a wide berth. Getting your bike to France is fairly easy: most airlines will carry them as long as they're boxed and are included in your total baggage weight. Ferries accept foot passengers with bikes and cars with bike carriers for free or a minimum charge; check conditions when you book. For more on cycling, see page 21.

Main towns and holiday centres have at least one shop that **hires** out mountain bikes (VTT), touring bikes and e-bikes by the day, week or longer; some will even deliver the bike to your hotel. Be prepared to pay a fairly hefty deposit on a good bike.

ACCOMMODATION

Hotels, bed and breakfasts, farm stays, camping...whichever you choose, book ahead, especially for stays from May to October. July and August are the only really impossible months; otherwise it usually isn't too difficult to find something. Nearly every kind of lodging offers free internet access, although in some places it may only be in a public room.

HOTELS These range from exquisite châteaux to independent family-run hotels although it's becoming harder and harder to find the latter. Don't confuse chains with the Logis de France (**w** logishotels.com) or the prestigious Relais et Châteaux (**w** relaischateaux.com) organisation which promote and guarantee the quality of independently owned hotels and their restaurants.

Many hotel restaurants are superb and non-guests are welcome. Often seasonal seaside hotels with restaurants will require that you take half-board (*demi-pension* – breakfast and a set lunch or dinner). In the off-season, board requirements vanish. Otherwise, in French hotels breakfast is always extra and prices in smart hotels can be eyewatering; in bed and breakfasts it's usually included.

SELF-CATERING Self-catering is extremely popular, and Airbnb has made great inroads here as elsewhere. An advantage of booking with one of the few surviving holiday firms often means ferry discounts, quality control, insurance and help on the ground. Both Bordeaux and (especially) Toulouse are full of apartment hotels (or *hôtel-résidences* or *apparthotels*, among their many names) for urban stays; many are fine with one- or two-night stays and are cheaper than hotels. Adagio City (**w** adagio-city.com) is a big chain; for the Bordeaux area try All Suites (**w** en.allsuites-apparthotel.com).

France

Abritel **w** abritel.fr. Holiday homes, villas & apts by the week, listed by owners.
Clevacances **w** clevacances.com. All kinds of holiday rentals & rooms in B&Bs.
Gîtes de France **w** gites-de-france.com. Huge selection of self-catering properties & B&Bs, plus green-friendly ecogîtes.
Papvacances **w** papvacances.fr. Listings by owners; especially good for Arcachon.
Pure France **w** purefrance.com. Holiday villas & châteaux with pools.

UK

French Cottage Holidays **w** french-cottage-holidays.co.uk. Cottages in the Lot valley.
Holiday France Direct **w** holidayfrancedirect.co.uk. Villas, gîtes, beach holidays & B&Bs.
Oliver's Travels **w** oliverstravels.com. Luxury villas with pools in the Dordogne & St-Émilion.
Simpson **w** simpsontravel.com. Upmarket villas with pools.

USA

Owner Direct **w** ownerdirect.com. Condo, apt & villa rentals.
Vrbo **w** vrbo.com. Vast range of properties, listed by owners.

ACCOMMODATION PRICE CODES

Prices are based on a double room; expect to pay about 75% for single occupancy.

€€€€€	Luxury	€200+
€€€€	Upmarket	€150–€200
€€€	Mid-range	€100–€150
€€	Budget	€75–€100
€	Shoestring	less than €75

AGRITOURISM AND FARM STAYS Many farmers in France supplement their income by offering *gîtes*, bed-and-breakfast rooms, *camping à la ferme*, restaurants (*ferme-auberges*) and riding stables. Check listings at Bienvenue à la Ferme (**w** bienvenue-a-la-ferme.com) with brochures you can download for each department and Gîtes de France (**w** gites-de-france.com).

BED AND BREAKFAST (Aka *chambres-d'hôtes*) These can be anything from glam and romantic to basic; see **w** chambres-hotes.fr, **w** gites-de-france.com or **w** clevacances.com for listings.

CAMPING This is extremely popular especially along the coast, lake shores and riverbanks. Increasingly these offer bungalows, mobile homes, yurts or other accommodation by the week, as well as pitches for tents and camping cars. Camping Qualite (**w** campingqualite.com) lists sites that meet criteria of cleanliness and welcome. Also check the listings at Camping France (**w** campingfrance.com) and Eurocampings (**w** eurocampings.co.uk). Le French Time (**w** lefrenchtime.com) focuses on campsites offering family-oriented nature experiences – or in the grounds of châteaux (see 'Les Castels Camping' on the same website).

GÎTES D'ÉTAPE A *gîte d'étape* or *refuge* is a simple shelter set up by a community with bunk beds (usually four to a room) and a rudimentary kitchen along a long-distance (GR) or pilgrimage trail or scenic bike route. See **w** gites-refuges.com/www for a complete directory. Sometimes sheets and towels are not included, but can be rented on site.

EATING AND DRINKING

RESTAURANTS They can also be called *auberges*, *relais*, *cafés*, *hostelleries*, *brasseries*, *bistrots* or *restaurants bistronomiques* (combining bistro informality with gastronomy) or *guinguettes* (informal 'huts' usually on riverbanks). All tend to keep pretty strict hours – lunch (*déjeuner*) between noon and 14.00 and in the evening (*dîner*) from 19.00 to 21.00, with later summer hours. If possible always ring ahead and book, even if you don't speak a word of French; the person on the other end of the phone will manage in English. Some smart restaurants allow you to book online. Brasseries and some bistrots double as bars and are open all day.

A full-on French meal takes at least 2 hours and begins with an *apéritif*, *hors d'œuvres* (or *amuse-bouches*), a starter (*entrée*), a fish course (*poisson*), a main course (*plat*), cheese, dessert, coffee and chocolates or petits fours, and perhaps a *digestif* to round things off. For most that only happens at a special meal in a special restaurant, and even Michelin-starred restaurants are increasingly fine with you just ordering a starter and a main course, or a main course and a dessert. Nearly all offer a good-value lunch with two or more choices on a set-price menu or no choices at all (*formule*) or even just a *plat du jour* on the blackboard. Eating *à la carte* will always be much more expensive – if it's even offered. Gastronomic restaurants offer a set-price *menu dégustation* – a tasting menu of the chef's specialities. All restaurants post menus outside the door; many now post them on their websites or Facebook, especially if they frequently change.

Escoffier would roll over in his grave, but the sad truth is that many cheaper French restaurants buy frozen food and reheat it, which is why you may see some advertise *fait maison* – food prepared from scratch.

Increasingly, restaurants offer **gluten-free, vegetarian** and even **vegan** choices (fancy restaurants often request you warn them a day in advance about any dietary requirements or allergens).

Set-price menus sometimes include the house wine (*vin compris*); in *fermes-auberges* as often as not the bottles or carafes will just keep reappearing until you pass out. If you choose a better wine anywhere, expect a big mark-up; otherwise, in informal places, you can order a quarter, half or litre *pichet* or carafe of *blanc*, *rosé* or *rouge*. More and more, restaurants offer a few wines (often dessert wines) by the glass as well. Tap water (*eau de robinet*) is always free, although you may have to ask for it.

If **service** is included, the bill (*l'addition*) will say *service compris* (*sc*); if not, *service non compris* or *snc*, although the latter is rare. **Tipping** is optional but appreciated, and it's common to add something extra for good service.

SPECIALITIES OF THE BORDELAIS The cuisine of the Bordelais starts with seafood: the oysters of Arcachon and mussels; from the Gironde estuary come prawns, eels, salmon, salmon trout and, perhaps a bit shocking to the uninitiated, lamprey, a dish so prized that the canons of St-Seurin in Bordeaux gave up all their rights to property in the city in 1170 in exchange for 12 good fat lampreys a year (page 134).

Shallots are just as essential to the Bordelais, attaining a kind of epiphany on the famous *entrecôte à la Bordelaise* with a sauce of butter, shallots, thyme and red wine. Much passion is reserved for cèpes: the true *cèpe bordelais* (*cèpe de chêne* or penny bun) and less tasty *cèpe des pins*. Asparagus, both green and white, is one of the joys of spring in the region.

A speciality revived in the past few decades is milk-fed lamb, or *agneau de Pauillac*, which holds pride of place among meat dishes along with the beef from Bazas. Among the sweets, try a *canelé*, a little caramelised pastry said to have been invented by people living around the port of Bordeaux from the flour and sugar left over in the holds of ships.

RESTAURANT PRICE CODES

Prices are based on the average price of a main course.

€€€€€	Expensive	€25+
€€€€	Above average	€20–€25
€€€	Moderate	€15–€20
€€	Cheap & cheerful	€10–€15
€	Rock bottom	less than €10

SPECIALITIES OF PÉRIGORD AND QUERCY For all the blah blah about tradition, the dishes that bring hungry Parisians down here en masse only became popular fare after the Revolution; before then, local barons were so rapacious that the peasants' diet was based on cabbage, chestnuts, turnips, fruit, and fish if they lived near the river. These days, perhaps to make up for the past, meat is liable to appear in every course except dessert. The calorie- and cholesterol-conscious can take courage from recent studies showing that the basic southwest diet, with all its duck and goose fat ('*sans beurre et sans reproche*', as the great gastronome Curnonsky described it), garlic and red wine, is actually good for you and your heart; many natives live well into their 90s.

The best place to tuck into a traditional meal is the *ferme-auberge*, where most of the food has been raised on the spot. A typical meal here or in a good traditional restaurant may start with an apéritif, perhaps a *fénelon* (a cocktail of walnut liqueur, cassis and Cahors wine). Then comes the *tourain* (or *tourin*), a garlic soup cooked with duck or goose fat, ladled over slices of country bread and cheese. The proper way to finish up the dregs is *faire chabrol*: pour in a dash of red wine, swish it around, and drink it directly from the bowl.

The next dish is generally a *pâté*, often duck or goose, or *rillettes* (the meat left over after preparation of foie gras and confits, mixed with a bit of fat to make a smooth paste) or *foie gras*, the enlarged liver of either a goose or duck. Foie gras usually comes prepared in a terrine or half-cooked (*mi-cuit*) or fresh and quickly fried (*pôelée)* with apples or other fruit or chutney. Other popular starters include a warm salad of *gésiers*, or gizzards, preserved in fat (it tastes much better than it sounds!), cooked and sliced with lettuce, walnuts and croutons, or a plate of charcuterie.

Main courses often feature yet more duck in the form of confits. Confits are the southwest's traditional way of keeping meat: unless otherwise listed, a *confit de canard* will be the thigh and legs of the duck cooked in tins or jars with their own fat, and reheated until crispy and golden. The other option is usually a *magret,* steak-like fillets of duck breast, usually simply grilled, or a fat chunk of duck sausage. *Cou d'oie*, goose neck stuffed with truffled minced pork and foie gras, and *demoiselles*, carcasses of fattened ducks grilled on a wood fire, are traditional rural favourites. Duck or goose fat is the essential ingredient for preparing the accompanying *pommes de terre sarladaise* – sliced potatoes sautéed in fat, with garlic and parsley, and sometimes cèpes in the autumn, a combination that lifts the humble spud to culinary heaven.

Some restaurants and ferme-auberges serve *mique*, a (often very heavy) dumpling cooked in chicken bouillon, with cabbage, carrots and salted pork which was long a staple in old Quercy and Périgord.

Game dishes appear in season – venison, pheasant, hare, rabbit, boar and *marcassin* (young boar, served in a *civet* or red wine stew). Rabbit and lamb, especially *agneau de causse*, grazed on Quercy's limestone plateaux, are very popular, but often served too rare for Anglo-Saxon tastes. Pork appears in sausages – the omnipresent fat *saucisse de Toulouse*, or thinner chipolatas; another favourite, spicy merguez, is made with lamb or cooked with prunes and wine in a delicious sweet and savoury combination.

Walnuts are serious business here. The classic salad is made of curly lettuce and walnuts, seasoned with walnut oil, the perfect accompaniment to the famous goat's cheese of the region, little roundlets of AOP (Appellation d'Origine Protégée) Rocamadour or *cabécou*, which is often served grilled, sometimes with honey, as a starter.

Traditional southwest desserts are *tarte aux noix* (walnut tart) and *tourtière* (apples topped with a pile of crispy layers of a paper-thin pastry called *pastis*).

MARKETS In most villages, market day is the event of the week. In cities they take place every day, while smaller towns and villages have markets once or twice a week, which double as social occasions for the locals. Most finish up around noon. In July and August look out for *marchés nocturnes* or *marchés gourmands* which take place in the evening: local producers set up stands selling everything from soup to dessert and wine. Often there is music, and the kids can run around, and it's all good fun.

DRINKS Cafés serve drinks, but they are also a home away from home, places to read the papers, play cards, meet friends and just unwind, sit back and watch the world go by. Prices are listed on the *tarif des consommations*: note they are based on whether you're served at the bar (*au comptoir*), at a table (*dans la salle*) or outside (*à la terrasse*).

If you order *un café* you'll get a small black espresso; if you want milk, order *un crème*. If you want more than a few drops of caffeine, ask them to make it *grand*. For decaffeinated, the word is *déca*. The French only order *café au lait* (large cup with milk) when they stop in for breakfast; many now offer cappuccinos but they are rarely as good as the ones in Italy. Many have baskets of croissants and pastries to make up a quick, cheap breakfast. *Chocolat chaud* (hot chocolate) is usually good; if you order *thé* (tea), you'll nearly always get an ordinary bag in a little pot unless you go to a special *salon du thé*. An *infusion* or *tisane* is a herbal tea – *camomille*, *menthe* (mint), *tilleul* (lime or linden blossom) or *verveine* (verbena). These are kind to the *foie*, or liver, after you've overindulged at table.

Mineral water (*eau minérale*) comes either sparkling (*gazeuse*) or still (*non-gazeuse* or *plate*). Apart from bottled fruit juices (*jus de fruits*), some bars also do freshly squeezed lemon and orange with a jug of water (*citron pressé* or *orange pressée*). The French are also fond of fruit syrups – red *grenadine* and ghastly green *diabolo menthe*.

Beer (*bière*) no longer means the big national brands but a full range of locally made craft beers to try. Draught (*à la pression*) is cheaper than bottled beer. Smarter bars and cafés in the cities are rightly proud of their cocktails.

Wine One of the joys of travelling (especially here!) is discovering new wines and drinking them for a fraction of what you'd pay at home. Visiting the wine châteaux and *vignerons* is half the fun (and a good way to save money). Don't pass up a *fête du vin* – these usually mean buying a glass and tasting your way around the stands until you discover the ones you like best. Then you can buy a bottle or a carton or more.

Bordeaux Bordeaux, the largest wine region in the world, covers 113,000ha and annually produces on average 486 million litres (650 million bottles), enough to launch a battleship. Bordeaux wines come from four main regions: **Médoc**, along the south bank of the Gironde estuary; **Graves/Sauternes**, south of the Garonne; **Entre-Deux-Mers**, between the Dordogne and Garonne; the **Right Bank** of the Dordogne and Gironde. These are subdivided into 57 appellations, including some of the most prestigious in France – Pomerol, Sauternes, St-Émilion, Pauillac and Margaux. Each *cru*, or growth, results from a unique combination of the soil, climate, location – the famous, ineffable *terroir* that the French are always talking about.

By the 18th century, much of the best land for growing grapes in the Gironde was consolidated into the hands of Bordeaux's movers and shakers, the *noblesse de robe*, who built splendid manor houses by their properties. These became the basis for Bordeaux's château system.

Bordeaux and claret (similar to modern rosés) were always popular in Britain. In 1853, with the construction of the railway to Paris, the market began to expand in France as well, especially after the 1855 Paris Exhibition, which saw the famous classifications of Bordeaux wines – without tasting a single one! – and the establishment of stringent rules governing their growing and vinification. Bankers (most famously, the Rothschilds) and investors, both French and foreign, bought up estates just in time for the outbreak of phylloxera in 1878.

Vines were quickly replanted, grafted on phylloxera-resistant American roots, and good wine was produced again by 1893. Even so, bad weather, war, the Great Depression, and more war took their toll. In the increasingly confident 1960s and 70s, innovations crept into the wine-making in spite of the *règlements* – the use of sprays against rot, mechanical harvesters that can pluck grapes at their moment of perfect ripeness, and adjustments in the temperature of fermentation to an even coolness for white wines.

In the roaring 1980s and 90s, as more and more people around the world began to drink wine, investors moved in once again to buy up vineyards, even Château d'Yquem. And many who bought small châteaux are sorry now. Not because their wine was bad (in fact, 1995–2003 saw a rare consecutive string of superb years, with 2000 considered one of the very best ever), but because the triumph of world wines has simply knocked the stuffing out of once-unrivalled Bordeaux.

In response, Bordeaux, after decades of aloofness, has discovered wine tourism in a big way, with its wine festival and sparkling new showcase, the Cité du Vin. Many châteaux now offer visits and tastings (although the prices can be eye-popping), some have opened restaurants, guest rooms and spas, and offer picnics and other wine experiences; tour operators offer a huge variety of half-day to week-long tours by car, tuk-tuk, e-bike, horseback, etc (especially in St-Émilion, where the landscapes are especially beautiful).

But there are many other wines waiting to be discovered – Bergerac, Cahors, Buzet, Duras, etc. In the Middle Ages, some were preferred to Bordeaux, but because they were upriver they were held hostage – by the Bordelais, of course, who insisted on selling theirs first. If you like to visit wineries or *chais* (a Gascon word meaning the buildings where the wine is stored in oak barrels, before being bottled and laid in the *cave*, or cellar), visits and tastings in these upriver estates are often free. Don't neglect the wines labelled IGN (Indication Géographique Protégée), formerly known as *vin de pays* or *vin de table*, which may not send you to seventh heaven, but at least they're usually quite quaffable and cheap.

If you're buying direct from the vigneron, you'll be offered glasses to taste from various bottles, each older than the previous one, until you are feeling quite jolly and ready to buy the last (and most expensive) vintage. Many producers (outside of Bordeaux, that is!) sell loose wine (*en vrac*), often good AOP stuff that you can take home and bottle yourself (or just drink). Invest in an inexpensive *cubivin*, a plastic flexible container with a tap in a cardboard box, which preserves the wine for a few weeks. They come in various sizes, from 5 to 33 litres; if they're not available in the vineyards, they can tell you where to get one.

FESTIVALS AND ANNUAL EVENTS

The French know how to throw a party. Every village celebrates at least once a year: up go the fairy lights and flags, the big tables and folding chairs for a feast (you must book ahead and look for your name scrawled on the paper tablecloth) and a platform for the band – larger towns can afford both a *bal musette* (accordion waltzes, tangos and French songs) and a local pop band that might just play until dawn. In larger villages, a travelling funfair and/or circus pulls into town; there will be fireworks if the *mairie* has the money to spare.

PUBLIC HOLIDAYS

1 January	New Year's Day	**14 July**	Bastille Day
6 January	Epiphany	**15 August**	Assumption
March/April	Easter Monday	**1 November**	All Saints' Day
1 May	Labour Day	**11 November**	Armistice Day
8 May	VE Day	**25 December**	Christmas Day
Mid May	Ascension	**26 December**	St Stephen's Day
Late May/ early June	Pentecost		

One of the oldest festivals, the century-plus-old **La Félibrée** takes place in a different town in the Dordogne every year, with traditional music, dance and food, organised by **Lo Bornat dau Perigòrd** (f lobornat). In 2021, the Dordogne and Lot-et-Garonne combined to create a new event, the **Châteaux en Fête** (w chateauxenfete.com), with all kinds of day and night activities from late May to mid-June. On or around 21 June it's time for the national **Fête de la Musique**, with free concerts in hundreds of places. The third weekend in September sees the **Journées du Patrimoine** (w journeesdupatrimoine.culture.gouv.fr), when usually closed châteaux and other historic sites open their doors.

In June, each department publishes a guide to its summer events, but check with the relevant tourist offices before setting out as dates can change. Also see listings under Bordeaux (page 52) and Toulouse (page 371).

JANUARY

Lalbenque — **Truffle festival** and **market** (w truffesnoires-lalbenque.com); every Tuesday at 14.00 until mid-March.

Sarlat — **Truffle festival** (w sarlat-tourisme.com); mid month.

FEBRUARY

Bazas — **Fête des Bœufs Gras** (w boeufsgrastradisud.fr): with plenty of folklore; Thursday before Carnival. 2023 will be its 740th year.

Bordeaux — **Le Carnaval des 2 Rives** (page 52).

MARCH

Sarlat — **Fest'Oie** (w sarlatadugout.fr): goose festival, with lots of geese and lots of foie gras; early March.

APRIL

Blaye — **Spring Wine Festival** (w bordeauxvillageblaye.com); mid month.

MAY

Beaulieu — **Fête de la Fraise** (w fraisedebeaulieu.fr): record-breaking strawberry fête; second weekend.

Bertric Burée — **Fête d'Escargot** (w perigordriberacois.fr): snail festival in the Dordogne; first weekend.

Bussière-Badil — **Marché Céramique** (w bussiereceramique.com): France's oldest pottery fair; Ascension weekend.

La Réole — **Festival Millesime** (f millesimefestival): big electronic-music festival; end of the month.

Marmande	**Fête des Fleurs et des Saveurs** (w valdegaronne.com): flowers and food; third weekend.
Rocamadour	**Fête des Fromages Fermiers** (w vallee-dordogne.com): goat cheese competition; Pentecost.
St-Aulaye	**Foire de la Latière** (w saint-aulaye.com): traditional rural fair; 1 May.
St-Jean-de-Côle	**Floralies** (w floralies-saintjean.fr): massive flower festival; closest weekend to 8 May.
Sarlat	**La Ringueta** (w sarlat-tourisme.com): traditional games; Pentecost (even numbered years).
Vergt	**Fête des Fraises et des Fleurs** (w vergt-perigord.fr); third weekend.

JUNE

Arcachon	**Les Escapades Musicales** (w lesescapadesmusicales.com): concerts around the Bassin and Val de l'Eyre; mid-June to mid-July.
Bazas	**St John's Day**: bonfires, homage to the bull; third week.
Marmande	**Garorock** (w garorock.com/le-festival): massive rock festival; late month.
Périgord	**New Orleans Music Festival** (w mnop.fr); June to August.
St-Émilion	**Jazz festival** (w saint-emilion-tourisme.com); late June to early July.

JULY

Andernos	**Jazz Festival** (w andernos-jazz-festival.fr); end July.
Arcachon	**Arcachon en Scène** (w arcachon.fr): music festival (pop, soul, rock, rap, electro); July and August.
	Fêtes de la Mer: oysters and more, all around the Bassin; July and August.
Cahors	**Blues Festival** (w cahorsbluesfestival.com); second week.
Cajarc	**Africajarc** (w africajarc.com): celebrating African music and culture; third week.
Cap Ferret	**Music festival** (w capferretmusicfestival.com): with chamber music and piano recitals; second week.
Castillon	**Re-enactment of the 1453 Battle of Castillon** (w batailledecastillon.com); mid-July to mid-August.
Duras	**Fêtes de la Madeleine** (w tourismeduras.com): lively festival, with wine and a funfair; third weekend.
Gignac	**Ecaussystème** (w ecaussysteme.com): major new music festival over three nights; end of July.
Le Teich	**Music O Teich** (w comitedesfetesleteich.fr): over three days, ending with fireworks; 14 July.
Médoc	**Les Estivales de Musique** (w estivales-musique-medoc.com): festival in the châteaux and other venues featuring young classical musicians who have won major competitions; first two weeks of the month.
Montauban	**Jazz à Montauban** (w montauban.com); all month into early August.
Montignac	**International folklore festival** (w festivaldemontignac.fr); last week.
Périgord	**Itineraire Baroque** (w itinerairebaroque.com): Baroque music in Romanesque churches; July and August.
Périgueux	**Mimos International Mime festival** (w mimos.fr); late July.
St-Céré	**Festival of opera and classical music** (w festival-saint-cere.com); July to mid-August.

Sarlat	**Festival des Jeux du Théâtre** (w festival-theatre-sarlat.com); mid-month to early August.
Souillac	**Souillac en Jazz** (w souillacenjazz.fr); third week.

AUGUST

Bergerac	**L'été musical en Bergerac/Festival du Périgord Pourpre** (w festivalbergerac.com): classical music, opera, etc in venues throughout the region; first half of August.
Gindou	**Rencontres Cinéma de Gindou** (w gindoucinema.org); late August.
Moncrabeau	**International Festival of Liars** (page 308); first Sunday.
Montignac	**Festival du Périgord Noir** (w festivalmusiqueperigordnoir.com): all kinds of music through the region; first half of August.
Nontron	**Fête du Couteau** (w nontron.fr): knife festival, with displays from around the world, and other events; first weekend.
Rocamadour	**Sacred Music Festival** (w rocamadourfestival.com); a week mid month.
Vertheuil	**Sun Ska Music Festival** (w sunska.fr): reggae and ska in Médoc; early August.

SEPTEMBER

Arcachon	**Festival Cadences** (f cadencesarcachon): dance festival; third week.
Bergerac	**Festival Jazz Pourpre** (w jazzpourpre.com); mid-September to mid-October.
Médoc	**Médoc Marathon** (w marathondumedoc.com): run in silly costumes, drink wine at the châteaux, eat lovely food; second weekend.
Moissac	**Fête du Chasselas** (w chasselas-de-moissac.com): all about table grapes; mid-September.
Périgueux	**Vintage Days** (w perigueuxvintagedays.com); first weekend.
Rocamadour	**Mongolfiades** (w rocamadouraerostat.fr): two-day hot-air balloon festival; last weekend.
St-Aulaye	**Foire de la Latière** (w saint-aulaye.com); 800-year-old rural fair; last weekend.

OCTOBER

Anglars-Juillac	**Wine and cheese festival** (w cahorsvalleedulot.com) in the Lot valley; last weekend.
Nontron	**Rue des Métiers d'Art** (w metiersdartperigord.fr): crafts fair; late October or early November.

NOVEMBER

La Réole	**Foire de la Toussant** (w lareole.fr): 1,000-year-old street market along the Garonne; 1 November.
Périgueux	**Gourmet book festival** (w livre-gourmand.com); mid month.
Sarlat	**Festival du Film** (w festivaldufilmdesarlat.com); all month.
Varaignes	**Foire aux Dindons** (w varaignes.fr): 16th-century turkey fair, with costumes; 11 November.

DECEMBER

Andernos	**Cabanes en Fête** (w andernos-tourisme.fr): oyster and wine tasting; early December.
Sarlat	**Christmas market** (w sarlat-tourisme.com); lasts three weeks.

SHOPPING

You can find scores of interesting boutiques in Bordeaux and Toulouse, and occasionally elsewhere, but on the whole the best buys in the area are wine and food. From May to October many a summer Sunday is dedicated to seeking out treasures in a village *vide grenier* ('attic emptiers') – the French equivalent of a car boot sale. The website **w** vide-greniers.org publishes a full listing.

ARTS AND ENTERTAINMENT

CINEMA The French love films. In the cities and even some small towns you'll find a cinema that occasionally shows a film in VO (*version originale*, usually English) or VOST (with subtitles). Toulouse, Bordeaux, Sarlat and the little Lot village of Gindou hold annual film festivals.

MUSEUMS There are museums for all interests and ages, from the spectacular new Cité du Vin in Bordeaux and the Cité d'Espace and Halle de la Machine in Toulouse to the whacky Musée d'Insolite (Museum of the Unusual) in the Lot. Most are closed on either Monday or Tuesday, and many in rural areas close down in the winter. Although we've done our best to update their times and opening hours, it's always best to check on their websites or ring before setting out.

MUSIC Bordeaux and Toulouse, with their orchestras, opera and dance companies and music bars, host live music year-round. In summer there is music everywhere in the region, but out of season it tends to be slim pickings.

MEDIA AND COMMUNICATIONS

INTERNET Hotels, restaurants, bars, tourist offices and even taxis offer free Wi-Fi these days, so you can spend your whole holiday staring at your phone. Beware that hackers often use free hotspots, so don't log on to your bank, etc unless you use a VPN.

POST Post offices (Bureaux de Poste) are marked by a kind of blue bird on a yellow background. In the cities, main office hours are 08.00–19.00 Monday to Friday and 08.00–noon on Saturdays. In villages offices close for lunch and shut around 16.30; they may not open every day.

PRINT AND ONLINE MEDIA Bordeaux's *Sud-Ouest* (**w** sudouest.fr) is the main newspaper for Nouvelle-Aquitaine and Toulouse's *La Dépêche du Midi* (**w** ladepeche.fr) is the largest paper covering Occitanie. *Le Petit Journal* (**w** lepetitjournal.net) also offers local news. For French news in English, there's *The Local* (**w** thelocal.fr) and *The Connexion* (**w** connexionfrance.com).

TELEPHONES France's international dialling code is +33; when dialling from outside the country, omit the initial 0 of the telephone number. Mobile numbers start with 06 or 07, and increasingly you'll find numbers starting with 09 that go through the internet. To make an international call from France, dial 00, then the country code, followed by the area code (omitting any initial 0) and the number.

Non-EU **mobile phone** users can get walloped with roaming charges. Many UK mobile network providers who initially didn't charge post-Brexit now do. Check before you travel.

New model smartphones, tablets and computers come with e-SIM cards; using them with a company like Ubigi (**w** ubigi.com) can save you money. Another option is a pre-paid French SIM that gives you a French number and includes free EU roaming, which you order before you go. See offers from Orange (**w** boutique.orange.fr), Bouygues (**w** bouyguestelecom.fr) and FreeMobile (**w** mobile.free.fr).

TELEVISION AND RADIO Now that French television has gone to satellite, there are scores of free channels and even more payable ones. Many hotels offer BBC World and CNN, and some offer France 24, the country's 24-hour news service, in English. France Inter (public service culture station, the equivalent of the American NPR) is the most listened-to station in France, followed by RTL and NRJ for the latest hits, which is your chance to catch up on the French music scene as 40% of their content by law must be made in France. Classique and France Culture play a lot of classical music (but expect a lot of chat); Swing FM is good for jazz and very little talking.

TRAVELLING POSITIVELY

Supporting local farmers and producers at markets, *ferme-auberges*, *marchés nocturnes*, etc (page 37) and restaurants that source local ingredients are a great (and healthy) way to give back to the local area.

Part Two

THE GUIDE

3

Bordeaux

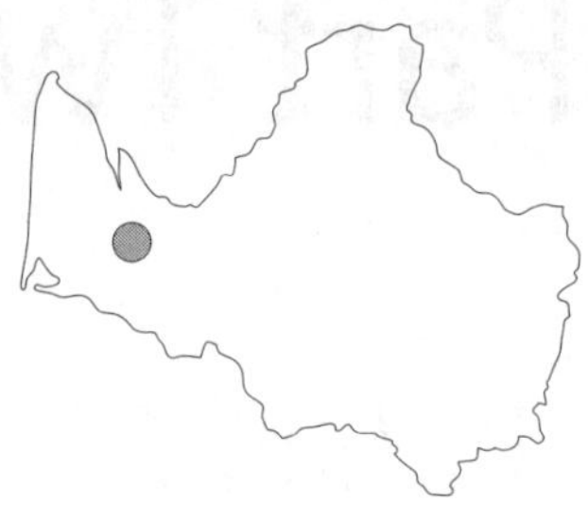

Bordeaux, that warm, magic, generous name on the bottle, the capital of Nouvelle Aquitaine, and 'undoubtedly the most beautiful city in France', as Stendhal called it in 1838, has, after a long slump, recreated itself to make Stendhal's words ring true once more. In 2007, it was designated a UNESCO World Heritage Site as 'Bordeaux, Port of the Moon', with 362 listed buildings. In France, only Paris has more. With its fabulous new wine museum, the Cité du Vin, its array of new boutique hotels and great restaurants and festivals, Bordeaux has never been a happier or more delightful place to visit than right now.

HISTORY

The Greek geographer Strabo was the first to mention the future Bordeaux: in the 3rd century BC, he wrote that a Celtic tribe from Bourges called the Bituriges Vibisci was 'the only foreign people to settle among the Aquitains'. Bituriges translates as the 'kings of the world', a big bold title for a band of tin-traders; their crescent-shaped city, Burdigala, was the 'Port of the Moon' – reflecting not only its shape but also the lunar influence over the Gironde estuary. Besides tin, Burdigala helped initiate the barley-beer-swilling Gauls into the joys of wine – imported from southern Italy and the Mediterranean colonies of Greece and Rome by way of Toulouse.

Burdigala knew on which side its bread was buttered and posed no objection to being captured in 56BC by the Roman general Crassus. Quickly Latinised, the Bituriges soon tidied up their trading centre to conform to the basic Roman town grid, with a north–south *cardo* (Rue Ste-Catherine) and east–west *decumanus* (Cours de l'Intendance). One of the most annoying problems was the fact that they had to import their wine. Every year, ever hopeful, they planted new varieties of grapes, but none could cope with the climate and soil – until around AD20, when the Biturige druids came across vines called Basilica, with wide-grained wood and fairly loose fruit that the Greeks in Marseille had imported from Epirus. The druids planted the grapes around what is now St-Émilion, where they took so well that the Bituriges, never known for their modesty, renamed the vines Biturica.

Burdigala had hardly begun to make a name for itself when it was severely mutilated in the barbarian invasion of AD276 and retreated into a more defensible castrum. It was rebuilt mainly by Christians, devoted to the cult of St Seurin (Severinus), bishop of Bordeaux (d AD420). The first monks, needing wine for the Mass, rescued the Biturica grape from oblivion.

MEDIEVAL BORDEAUX The city once again became the capital of Aquitaine in the 7th century AD under Merovingian King Dagobert. The son of one of his dukes, Huon de Bordeaux, shares a *chanson de geste* with Charlemagne and the 'Elf Oberon'; he was followed by a string of ten dukes all named Guillaume. The most famous was

Guillaume IX (1071–1126), who became France's first troubadour after his marriage to Philippa, young widow of the King of Aragon, who brought along with her Arabian dancers and court that patronised poetry, song and pleasure. He was the grandfather of the great Eleanor, who ended the streak of Guillaumes by being the only child of the tenth one. She inherited the duchy and gave Bordeaux first to France when she wed Louis VII (1137), then to Anjou and England when she divorced the pious and dour Louis to marry the far more amusing Henry Plantagenet.

Bordeaux blossomed under the English and grew so much that the walls had to be rebuilt twice; for the Bordelais, English rule meant paying fewer taxes and a thirsty market for their wine. Their beloved duchess Eleanor granted the wine-growers special privileges that were confirmed by her son King John Lackland in 1206, after Bordeaux was besieged by his brother-in-law, the King of Castille. The siege revealed John's inability to defend the city, so to keep it loyal he granted it considerable municipal powers – a mayor and councillors, the *jurats* – and in 1214 he went even further with letters of patent that gave the bourgeoisie the right to sell wine and other goods duty-free. Another plus for Bordeaux was the powerful English fleet, able to protect the city's vital sea trade.

Medieval Bordeaux was a tough town that produced some tough hombres. One was its archbishop Bertrand de Got, who was elected Pope Clement V in 1305 after an 11-month conclave. Clement V stirred the pot like few popes before or since. He earned the everlasting hatred of Rome by never setting foot there, but keeping the papacy in France – eventually in Avignon. He colluded with Philip IV to put an end to the powerful and wealthy order of the Knights Templars (Philip was broke and wanted their possessions, and Clement gave him the justification for annihilating the Templars by declaring them heretics). He loaded the Curia with 11 Gascon cardinals, who if nothing else kept right on electing popes from southwest France.

Philip IV's grandson, Edward III, opened the Pandora's box that became known as the Hundred Years' War by claiming the French throne. After English victories in Crécy and Calais, Edward III's eldest son, Edward of Woodstock (known as the Black Prince for his fashionable black armour), won the first round of the war at Poitiers (1356), capturing the French King Jean II and his greatest captain, Bertrand du Guesclin, as well as a bouquet of the 'flowers of French chivalry'. In 1360, Jean signed the Treaty of Calais, giving Edward III, in exchange for his claims on France, a sure title to the independent Duchy of Aquitaine.

The Black Prince, as Duke of Aquitaine, made Bordeaux his capital. For the French, however, the prince in black armour was definitely the bad guy: not satisfied with Aquitaine, he campaigned to recapture the rest of the 'old duchy of the Plantagenets'. But cash, or rather the lack of it, stymied his ambitions; in spite of his victories, the financing he needed to continue his campaigns was withheld by the jurats and nobility of Aquitaine – especially the Armagnacs and the Albrets who, rather than pay the Black Prince's high taxes, turned to France and Charles V. With their encouragement, King Charles began another round of the Hundred Years' War in 1369; the Black Prince, disillusioned, ill and exhausted, died in 1376.

Throughout this period, English rule meant that Jews expulsed by the French kings in 1284, 1305 and 1310 were safe in Aquitaine, and remained so after 1492; many Spanish and Portuguese Jews ended up in southwest France. By 1753 Bordeaux had seven synagogues.

FRENCH RULE The French finally took Bordeaux in June 1451, an event known in the city as the Male Jornade, the Rotten Day – 10,000 Bordelais were massacred

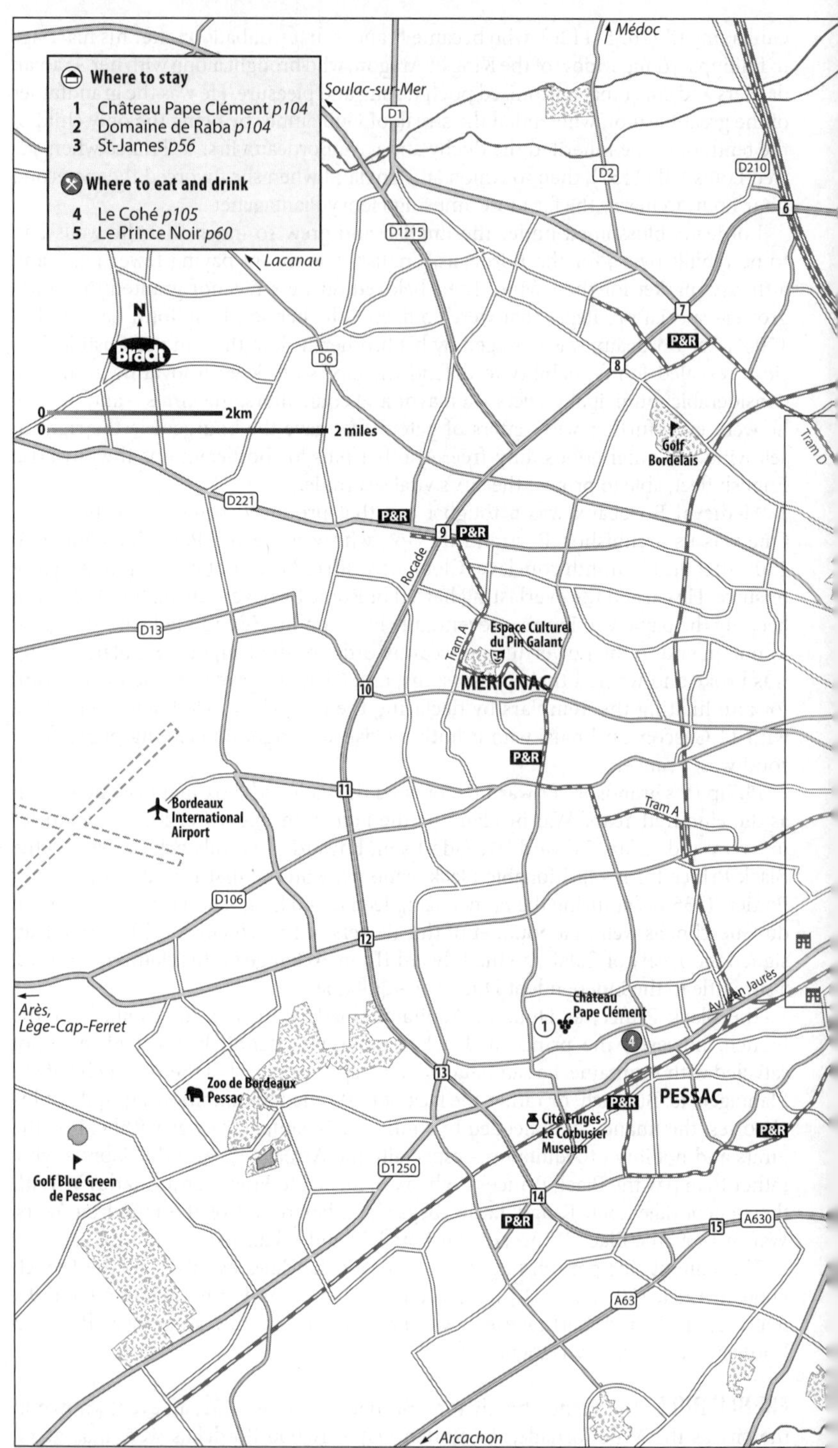
Where to stay
1 Château Pape Clément p104
2 Domaine de Raba p104
3 St-James p56
Where to eat and drink
4 Le Cohé p105
5 Le Prince Noir p60
N
Bradt
0 2km
0 2 miles
Médoc
Soulac-sur-Mer
Lacanau
D1
D2
D210
D1215
D6
D221
D13
D106
D1250
A630
A63
P&R
Rocade
Golf Bordelais
Tram D
Tram A
Espace Culturel du Pin Galant
MÉRIGNAC
Bordeaux International Airport
Arès, Lège-Cap-Ferret
Château Pape Clément
Av Jean Jaurès
PESSAC
Zoo de Bordeaux Pessac
Cité Frugès-Le Corbusier Museum
Golf Blue Green de Pessac
Arcachon

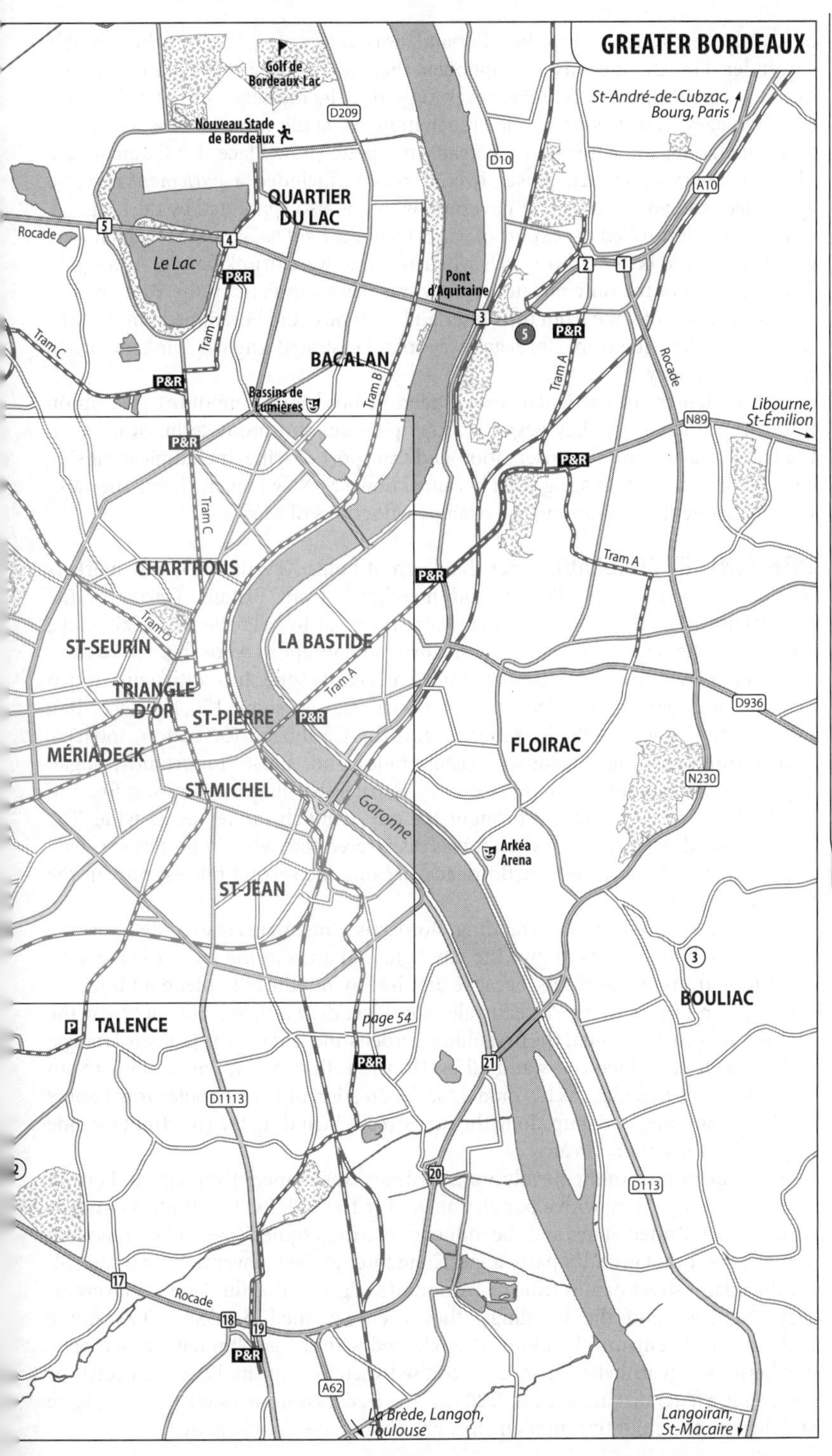
GREATER BORDEAUX
Golf de Bordeaux-Lac
Nouveau Stade de Bordeaux
QUARTIER DU LAC
Le Lac
Rocade
Pont d'Aquitaine
BACALAN
Bassins de Lumières
Tram A
Tram B
Tram C
Tram D
St-André-de-Cubzac, Bourg, Paris
Libourne, St-Émilion
CHARTRONS
ST-SEURIN
LA BASTIDE
TRIANGLE D'OR
ST-PIERRE
MÉRIADECK
ST-MICHEL
FLOIRAC
Garonne
Arkéa Arena
ST-JEAN
BOULIAC
TALENCE
page 54
La Brède, Langon, Toulouse
Langoiran, St-Macaire
P&R
D209
D10
A10
N89
D936
N230
D1113
D113
A62

before the city's archbishop, Pey Berland, was able to negotiate an honourable surrender. French rule was so unpopular that the Bordelais rebelled off and on until the end of the 17th century, never forgetting the massacre, or their old rights and privileges. The unsympathetic French monarchy built three fortresses to police them, including the enormous Château Trompette (now Place des Quinconces). The machinery of French power over Bordeaux included a *parlement* of royal appointees and an intendant, or governor, who was also appointed by the king.

Bordeaux controlled the export of wines from the *haut pays*, many of which were greatly preferred back in those days when all wines were drunk young. As a sop to Bordeaux (about the only one, too), a law was passed in Paris in the 16th century to block the sale of wine from the hinterlands – none could be shipped down to the sea until all the wine from Bordeaux was sold. Frustrated English drinkers turned to port and sherry.

But the Dutch, in particular, who traded in Bordeaux wine didn't give up on it. In the 17th century they began to buy up estates and promote innovations in the vineyards and in the conservation and transport of wine, including sterilising barrels with sulphur, creating what became known as New French claret. They also were instrumental in draining the swampy wilderness of Médoc.

18TH-CENTURY BORDEAUX After the death of Louis XIV in 1715, new markets opened up in the New World, and merchants from Britain, Germany, the Netherlands, Portugal and elsewhere were on hand to help the Bordelais make fortunes in the triangular trade: glass, fabrics and weapons were shipped to slave counters in West Africa in exchange for human cargo (one ship, with a nice touch of irony, was named the *Contrat Social*). The slaves (some 150,000 according to the records) were sold in America and the Caribbean for cotton, tobacco, indigo (undermining Toulouse's pastel trade) and, most importantly, sugar. Sugar was so fashionable in 18th-century Europe that, imported raw, refined in Bordeaux and re-exported, it brought the city as much money as its wine. The local glass industry took off when it was discovered that wine in bottles survived the journey to America better. Bordeaux became the second busiest port in the world after London.

To create a city equal to its standing, Bordeaux's intendants started demolishing its poky medieval streets to give the city light and air – in the face of fierce local opposition from the Bordelais, because they had to foot the bill. Intendant Boucher got the ball rolling with the Place Royale (now Place de la Bourse). His successor, the Marquis de Tourny planted the first public gardens and laid out the Golden Triangle with its wide tree-lined *cours* and *allées*. (In the 19th-century, Baron Haussmann would use Tourny's ideas as his model for the creation of Paris's boulevards.) Some 5,000 new buildings went up along the new streets, including the riverfront Grande Façade and the Grand Théâtre.

By the beginning of the Revolution, Bordeaux was France's third city and one of its most cosmopolitan, with a population of over 100,000. Its close trading contacts with the new United States and the influence of Montesquieu (page 104) combined to make the local Girondin party a moderate force at the Convention. You can still see the quaint street names (Rue de l'Amour de l'Égalité, Rue du Peuple Souverain) they engraved into the buildings; they even renamed Bordeaux 'Commune Franklin' after Benjamin Franklin. They clashed with the Jacobin fanatics – mostly northerners – who believed in a centralised dictatorship; in 1793, suspected of fomenting a federalist insurrection, 20 Girodin leaders were arrested by Robespierre and died on the guillotine after an all-night fling in the Conciergerie.

19TH AND 20TH CENTURIES During and immediately after the Napoleonic wars, Bordeaux hit one of its lowest ebbs. The continental blockade had destroyed the city's commerce, the slave trade was abolished in 1815 and the competition from sugar beets undercut its sugar refineries. The grand urban plans of the intendants ground to a halt, although the city did build its first ever bridge over the Garonne (1822). It was only with Louis XVIII (and the demolition of the hated Château Trompette) that Bordeaux began to get on its feet again. Although it had one of the first railways in France (1841), little new industry came its way. Inexorably, port traffic moved to the north, although new trade with France's African colonies kept Bordeaux ticking along.

Even the wine business was suffering; after disastrous bouts of mildew (finally cured by treating the vines with sulphur), microscopic, sap-sucking phylloxera lice arrived from the USA – accidentally introduced by Victorian botanists in England – which wiped out most of France's vines in 1878.

Bordeaux finally bestirred itself in the late 19th century. At least it began to spread into single-storey terraced houses (*échoppes*) after the installation of the first tramlines in the 1900s; today the Bordelais have the dubious honour of taking up more room per capita than other city dwellers in France.

Meanwhile the heart of Bordeaux, so grandly moulded to fit the French idea of a capital, actually served as one three times, all in circumstances France would prefer to forget: in 1870, 1914 and 1940. Bordeaux remembers 1914 most fondly, when it hosted *tout Paris*, while June 1940 leaves the bitter memory of First World War hero Philippe Pétain, announcing to France over the radio from Bordeaux '*Je fais don de ma personne à la France*', before moving the government to Vichy, because Germany and Italy wanted the Atlantic ports for themselves. But there were heroes in Bordeaux, too, especially the Portuguese consul-general, Aristides de Sousa Mendes, who in May and June 1940 illegally granted thousands of Portuguese visas to Jews, allowing them to cross into Spain and escape the Nazis.

Another was a German officer named Heinz Stahlschmidt, who was stationed in Bordeaux in 1941, and fell in love with the city and his future wife. He had the key to the blockhouse where the keys to detonating all the explosives placed around Bordeaux's bridges and port were stored, and when the order came to blow everything up (21 August 1944), he blew up the blockhouse instead.

Bordeaux's post-war years were dominated by Jacques Chaban-Delmas, a 31-year-old Resistance general when De Gaulle sent him to sort out Bordeaux in 1946. Pragmatic, dynamic, foxy and a brilliant manipulator of his own image, Mayor Chaban was an updated intendant, radically changing the face of Bordeaux with the mostly unloved urban-renewal project of Mériadeck and the more successful Quartier du Lac, a congress and leisure complex north of the centre. His more useful successor as mayor, former Prime Minister Alain Juppé (1995–2004 and 2006–19) proved to be just the intelligent, arrogant product of the *classe politique* system Bordeaux needed.

Under Juppé, the new tram system – rather uncannily elegant, high-tech streetcars – have by themselves changed the look of centre; the lovely pale golden stone of the city's monuments has been liberated from a century of grime and, under the direction of landscaper Michel Corajoud and his team, Bordeaux's once junky waterfront has become a delight. And Bordeaux has learned to have fun, holding its first ever wine festival in 1998; some of the best Bordeaux wines in decades were produced in 1990, 2000, 2005, 2009, 2015 and 2018.

Today, the sixth largest city in France, Bordeaux hosts 70,000 students at its university as well as the lion's share of France's air defence industries and associated research facilities. In 2020, when Juppé retired, the city elected ecologist/left-wing

FESTIVALS AND EVENTS

Bordeaux's busy calendar of festivals kicks off in late January with the **Bordeaux Rock Festival** (w bordeauxrock.com) in venues around town. Then there's **Le Carnaval des 2 Rives** (w carnavaldesdeuxrives.fr), the biggest Carnival celebration in the region. In July there's the enormous **Fête le Vin** (held in even-numbered years; w bordeaux-fete-le-vin.com) or the **Fête le Fleuve** (odd-numbered years; w bordeaux-fete-le-fleuve.com), both involving tall ships and plenty of wine, food and music. **Bordeaux Open Air** (w bordeauxopenair.fr) features free electronic music in the parks on summer Sundays; the **Relache Festival** (f relachefestival) either free or charging €5–€10) brings music – reggae, Afro, Cuban, etc – into the city squares throughout the summer. The alternative **Climax Festival** (w climaxfestival.fr) takes the first week in September in the Darwin Eco-System, with conferences, sports, music and dance; the second week of September sees the **Festival Musical Écran** (w bordeauxrock.com), dedicated to music documentaries, with the October **Festival International du Film Indépendant** (w fifib.com) close on its heels. **L'esprit du Piano** (w espritdupiano.fr) featuring jazz and classical piano concerts runs from November to early December.

mayor Pierre Hurmic, while the urban regenerators have honed in on the formerly slummy area around the train station with its new LGV (Ligne à Grande Vitesse) links to Paris in just over 2 hours.

GETTING THERE AND AWAY

BY AIR Bordeaux International Airport (05 56 34 50 50; w bordeaux.aeroport.fr) is 12km west of the centre at Mérignac. A shuttle bus (w 30direct.com) links the airport to the St-Jean train station every 30 minutes from 06.00 during the week, and about every 45 minutes from 08.45 at weekends (runs start at 05.30 from the station to the airport; €8, ages 5–26 €7, under 5 free). A taxi into the centre costs around €30, or €45 at night.

Airport car hire

- **Avis** 08 20 61 16 73; w avis.fr
- **Budget** 08 21 23 04 98; w budget.fr
- **Enterprise** 05 56 34 20 68; w enterprise.fr
- **Europcar** 08 25 74 00 40; w europcar.fr
- **Hertz** 08 25 00 24 00; w hertz.fr
- **Sixt** 05 56 34 08 15; w sixt.fr

BY TRAIN All trains arrive and depart from Bordeaux St-Jean station [55 F6] in Rue Charles Domerq, including the LGV from Paris-Montparnasse and the not-quite-so-fast TGV that goes on through Agen, Montauban and Toulouse. Other regional (RER) connections are Périgueux (2hrs), Sarlat (3hrs) by way of Libourne, St-Émilion (1½hrs) and Bergerac (2hrs); other RER trains make stops in Langon, Marmande, Agen and Moissac (2½hrs). There are also local lines to Médoc's Pointe-de-Grave and, roughly once an hour, to Arcachon.

BY BUS The Gironde has integrated Bordeaux's tram and the RER trains with its buses, serving most towns and villages. For information and schedules, call 09 70 87 08 70 or visit w transports.nouvelle-aquitaine.fr.

BY CAR Bordeaux has a great ring road or *rocade*, which sucks up all the autoroutes and national roads and spins them around the city, making it sometimes easier to circumvent rather than to penetrate to its centre. Exit 21 will take you along the Garonne, offering the finest introduction to the Grand Façade along the Port of the Moon.

GETTING AROUND

Bordeaux has ever more cycle lanes and tram lines, and ever fewer streets for cars. On the first Sunday of each month, cars are not allowed in the city at all.

BY BUS AND TRAM The city's bus network TBM (05 57 57 88 88; **w** infotbm.com) is integrated in the four tram lines, converging at the city centre. Tickets cost €1.70 (or €3 for two, €13.70 for ten), each offering an hour's transport by bus, tram or boat – the same tickets are valid for all services. You can order contactless tickets on their website and top them up as necessary. There are information kiosks at the train station, in Place des Quinconces and at St-Michel.

BY BOAT Integrated into the TMB network, Bat3 catamarans link the right bank near the Stalingrad tram stop [54 E4] and Pont de Pierre with Place de la Bourse, Cours de Médoc in the Chartrons, the Cité du Vin and Pont d'Aquitaine, with room for 65 passengers and six bikes.

BY CAR You'll want to park as soon as possible. Only a few hotels have their own parking; others in the city centre (Place des Grands Hommes etc) can be booked online (**w** fr.parkindigo.com). A cheaper option is to leave your car in a **Parc Relais** (park and ride) along the tram routes – download a map and instructions in English on the TBM website. For €5 per person you can park and have unlimited access to the TBM network the day, or pay for €14.20 per person for seven days.

For visiting the wine châteaux, check out the car-sharing scheme Citiz (05 56 31 10 66; **w** bordeaux.citiz.coop; from €2/hr plus €0.37/km).

BY BIKE Flat Bordeaux is made for bikes. VClub (05 57 57 88 88; **w** infotbm.com), the bike-share scheme run by TBM, has 184 stations and more than 2,000 bikes, including 1,000 e-bikes. A 24-hour subscription costs €1.70; the first 30 minutes are free, and then it's €2 per hour. There are instructions in English at **w** portail.cykleo.fr/V3?l=en.

BY TAXI Download the Taxis Couleurs Bordeaux app or call 05 56 21 33 33.

BORDEAUX CITY PASS

The Bordeaux City Pass includes entry to the Cité du Vin (if you go before noon) and more than 20 museums, unlimited access to the TMB transport network, parking at a Parc Relais, and an app which shows current exhibitions and opening hours. Purchase your pass via the TBM website (**w** boutique.infotbm.com/pass-tourisme/12-tourisme-city-pass.html; 24hrs for €29, 48hrs €39, 72hrs €46; there's also a City Pass Junior €17/€25/€30 for ages 6–17) and collect it either at the tourist office or a TBM kiosk. (There are plans to replace the ticket with a QR code.)

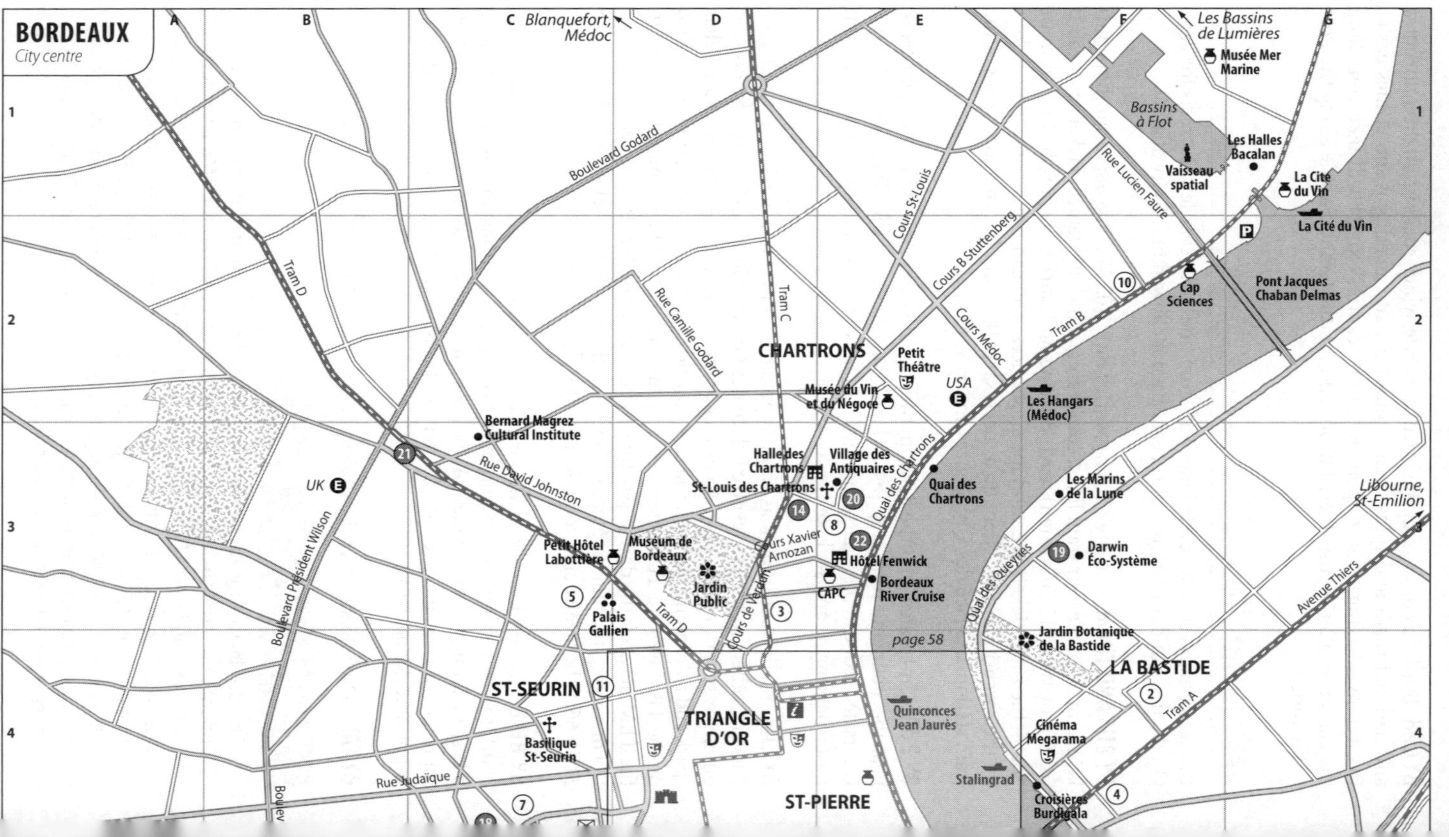
BORDEAUX
City centre
Blanquefort, Médoc
Les Bassins de Lumières
Musée Mer Marine
Bassins à Flot
Les Halles Bacalan
Vaisseau spatial
La Cité du Vin
La Cité du Vin
Boulevard Godard
Rue Lucien Faure
Cours St-Louis
Cours B Stuttenberg
Tram D
Tram C
Rue Camille Godard
Cap Sciences
Pont Jacques Chaban Delmas
Cours Médoc
Tram B
CHARTRONS
Petit Théâtre
USA
Musée du Vin et du Négoce
Les Hangars (Médoc)
Bernard Magrez Cultural Institute
Halle des Chartrons
Village des Antiquaires
Quai des Chartrons
Quai des Chartrons
Les Marins de la Lune
UK
Rue David Johnston
St-Louis des Chartrons
Libourne, St-Emilion
Cours Xavier Arnozan
Petit Hôtel Labottière
Muséum de Bordeaux
Jardin Public
Hôtel Fenwick
Darwin Éco-Système
Bordeaux River Cruise
CAPC
Quai des Queyries
Avenue Thiers
Boulevard Président Wilson
Palais Gallien
Tram D
Cours de Verdun
Jardin Botanique de la Bastide
page 58
LA BASTIDE
ST-SEURIN
TRIANGLE D'OR
Quinconces Jean Jaurès
Tram A
Basilique St-Seurin
Cinéma Megarama
Rue Judaïque
Stalingrad
ST-PIERRE
Croisières Burdigala
Boulev

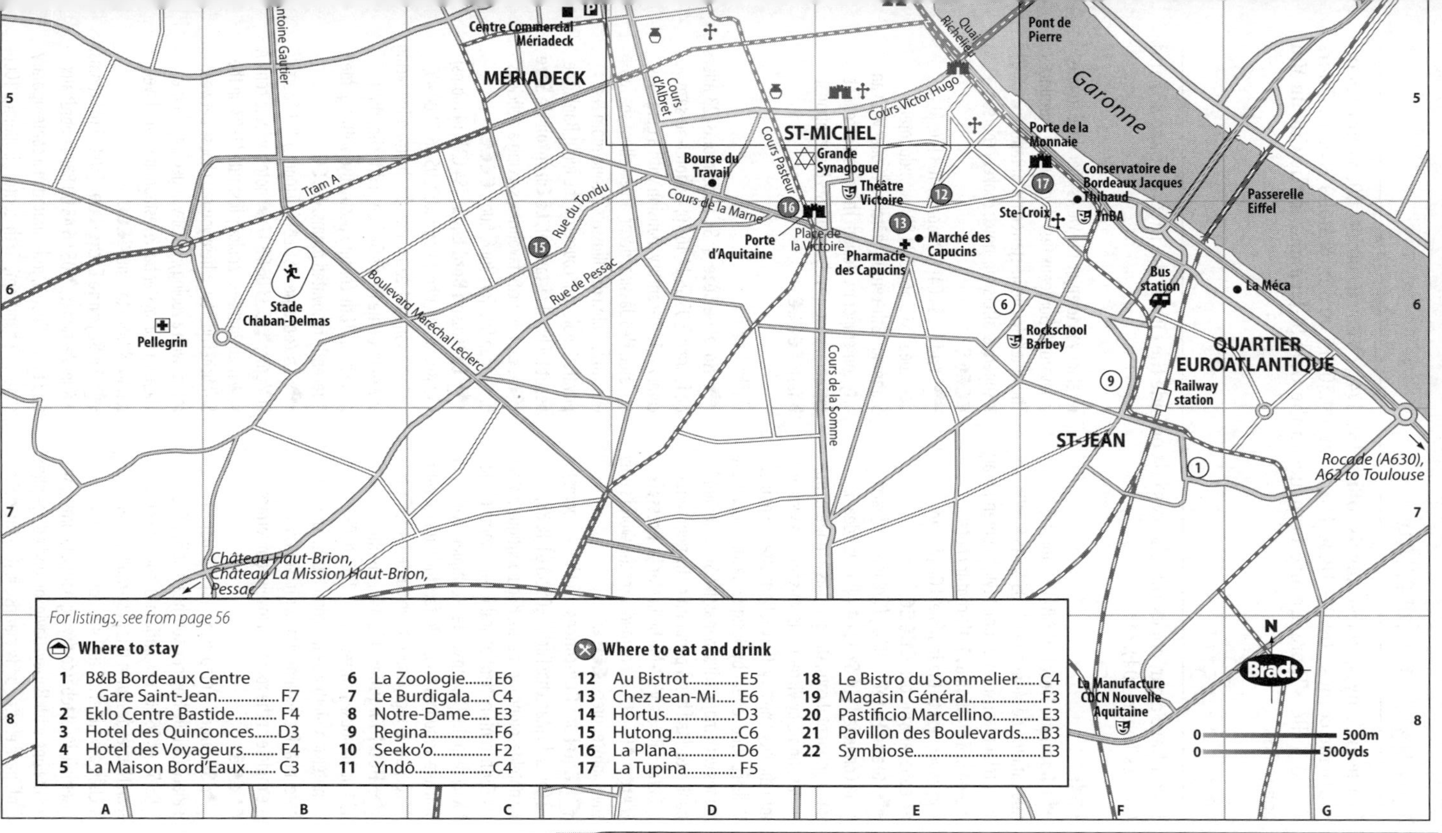
Centre Commercial Mériadeck
MÉRIADECK
ST-MICHEL
Cours d'Albret
Cours Victor Hugo
Quai Richelieu
Pont de Pierre
Garonne
Porte de la Monnaie
Conservatoire de Bordeaux Jacques Thibaud
Passerelle Eiffel
Grande Synagogue
Bourse du Travail
Cours Pasteur
Théâtre Victoire
Tram A
Rue du Tondu
Cours de la Marne
Porte d'Aquitaine
Place de la Victoire
Pharmacie des Capucins
Marché des Capucins
Ste-Croix
TnBA
Rue de Pessac
Boulevard Maréchal Leclerc
Stade Chaban-Delmas
Pellegrin
Bus station
La Méca
Rockschool Barbey
QUARTIER EUROATLANTIQUE
Railway station
Cours de la Somme
ST-JEAN
Rocade (A630), A62 to Toulouse
Château Haut-Brion, Château La Mission Haut-Brion, Pessac
La Manufacture CDCN Nouvelle Aquitaine
Bradt
N
0 500m
0 500yds
For listings, see from page 56
Where to stay
1 B&B Bordeaux Centre Gare Saint-Jean F7
2 Eklo Centre Bastide F4
3 Hotel des Quinconces D3
4 Hotel des Voyageurs F4
5 La Maison Bord'Eaux C3
6 La Zoologie E6
7 Le Burdigala C4
8 Notre-Dame E3
9 Regina F6
10 Seeko'o F2
11 Yndô C4
Where to eat and drink
12 Au Bistrot E5
13 Chez Jean-Mi E6
14 Hortus D3
15 Hutong C6
16 La Plana D6
17 La Tupina F5
18 Le Bistro du Sommelier C4
19 Magasin Général F3
20 Pastificio Marcellino E3
21 Pavillon des Boulevards B3
22 Symbiose E3

TOURIST INFORMATION

Bordeaux's hyperactive **tourist office** [54 D4] (05 56 00 66 00; w bordeaux-tourisme.com; 09.00–18.30 Mon–Sat, 09.30–17.00 Sun & hols) is at 12 Cours du 30 Juillet. There are also branches in the **Gare St-Jean** and in the **Cité du Vin** (page 76).

WHERE TO STAY

If you have a car, check out choices just outside the city in the Médoc (page 83) and Graves (page 104).

LUXURY

Boutique Hotel [58 B2] (27 rooms) 3 Rue Lafaurie de Monbadon; 05 56 48 80 40; w hotelbordeauxcentre.com. Stylish contemporary design in a prestigious 18th-century *hôtel particulier* next to the Triangle d'Or, plus an exceptional wine bar. **€€€€€**

Grand Hotel [58 D2] (130 rooms) Place de la Comédie; 05 57 30 44 44; w bordeaux.intercontinental.com. Designed as a monumental private home by Victor Louis, this hotel is woven into the city's history. Now reborn after an opulent Belle Époque retreat by designer Jacques Garcia, it comes with major frills: a massive Spa Guerlain & pool, a cocktail bar & panoramic 7th-floor terrace, & Gordon Ramsay's 2-Michelin star **Le Pressoir D'Argent** (€€€€€) named after the world's only silver lobster press. **€€€€€**

Hotel des Quinconces [54 D3] (9 rooms) 22 Cours du Maréchal Foch; 05 56 01 18 88; w hoteldesquinconces.com. Bijou boutique hotel in the 19th-century Neoclassical former home of the UK, & then the US, consulate – complete with Cold War-era armoured doors. Perfect for couples, with its cocktail lounge & secret Zen garden. **€€€€€**

Hôtel Singulier [58 A4] (8 rooms) 12 Rue Toulouse Lautrec; 05 57 60 20 03; w hotelsingulierbordeaux.com. Plush, romantic hotel near Place Gambetta, with bathtubs in the middle of the room & a lovely roof terrace. **€€€€€**

St-James [map, page 48] (18 rooms) 3 Place Camille Hostein, southeast at Bouliac; 05 57 97 06 00; w saintjames-bouliac.com. Jean Nouvel designed this post-modern Relais & Châteaux hotel in steel intended to rust to resemble local tobacco drying barns. Rooms (ask for the one with Harley-Davidson parked, for photo fun!) have electric beds that rise just to the right level for you to enjoy the views over the Garonne, vineyards & Bordeaux first thing in the morning. The hotel's Michelin-starred restaurant (€€€€€) is superb & offers top-notch cookery courses. **€€€€€**

Yndô [54 C4] (12 rooms) 108 Rue Abbé-de-l'Epée; 05 56 23 88 88; w yndohotel.fr. Stunning 18th-century *hôtel particulier* with an arty contemporary design. There's an excellent restaurant exclusively for guests & exceptional b/fast. **€€€€€**

UPMARKET

Hotel de Sèze [58 C1] (55 rooms) 23 Allées de Tourny; 05 56 14 16 16; w hotel-de-seze.com. An 18th-century mansion with a gorgeous updated Neoclassical décor, an excellent spa, an evocative 'Salon des Illustres' sitting room & a private 6-hole golf course on the Right Bank. The beautiful hotel restaurant, **Le Comptoir de Sèze** (€€€€€), is a city favourite, serving a delicious brunch on Sun (exc Jul & Aug). **€€€€**

La Maison Bord'Eaux [54 C3] (14 rooms) 113 Rue du Dr Albert Barraud; 05 56 44 00 45; w lamaisonbord-eaux.com. On the tramline facing the ruins of the Palais Gallien, a little boutique hotel in an 18th-century posthouse with a garden & recently renovated rooms. **€€€€**

La Zoologie [55 E6] (40 rooms) 151 Cours de la Marne; 05 33 06 99 17; w hotelzoologie.com. A new hotel in the ex-Zoology Institute (1903) in the St-Michel quarter, where you can choose between rooms with a zoology, botany or geology theme. There's a spa, oyster bar & restaurant with a lovely terrace & bikes to rent. **€€€€**

Le Bayonne Etche-Ona [58 C3] (61 rooms) 4 Rue Martignac; 05 56 48 00 88; w bordeaux-hotel.com. Rooms, redecorated in a contemporary style, in 2 handsome 18th-century buildings 100m from the Grand Théâtre. Public parking 50m away. **€€€€**

Le Burdigala [54 C4] (82 rooms) 115 Rue Georges Bonnac; 05 56 90 16 16; w burdigala.com. Just west of the Musée des Beaux-Arts, this is an elegant hotel with a great restaurant €€€€ & Art Deco bar; it's also one of the few hotels in the city with an underground car park. **€€€€**

MID-RANGE

Bleu de Mer [59 E3] (20 rooms) 12–14 Rue St-Rémi; 05 56 81 66 58; w hotel-bleudemer.com. In Quartier St-Pierre, the former Acanthe was purchased by local wine baron Bernard Magrez & has been completely remodelled; guests are offered visits at his Château Pape-Clément (page 104) & other goodies. **€€€**

Hotel Konti [58 B3] (51 rooms) 10 Rue Montesquieu; 05 56 52 66 00; w hotel-konti.com. Comfy rooms & friendly staff in a former *hôtel particulier* in the Golden Triangle in a pleasing retro-contemporary style. **€€€**

Le Majestic [58 D2] (47 rooms) 2 Rue de Condé; 05 56 52 60 44; w hotel-majestic.com. Central, with trpl & quad rooms, an inner garden, parking, but no restaurant. **€€€**

Mama Shelter [58 C4] (97 rooms) 19 Rue Poquelin Moliere; 05 57 30 45 45; w mamashelter.com/bordeaux. Buzzy chain hotel in the former gas tower offering rooms in a dozen sizes, & a cocktail bar with DJ sessions & pizzas on the 6th-floor roof terrace. **€€€**

Seeko'o [54 F2] (44 rooms) 54 Quai de Bacalan; 05 56 39 07 07; w seekoo-hotel.com. Near the Cité du Vin, this 4-star futuristic hotel resembles an iceberg – hence its Inuit name. Rooms are big, immaculate white & filled with light. **€€€**

BUDGET

Hôtel des Voyageurs [54 F4] (11 rooms) 3 bis Avenue Thiers; 05 56 81 18 00; w hotel-voyageurs-bordeaux.com. Over on the Right Bank, a charming bright hotel built in 1850, 100m from the Pont de Pierre & a short walk from Place de la Bourse. **€€**

Hôtel de la Presse [58 D3] (27 rooms) 6–8 Rue Porte Dijeaux; 05 56 48 53 88; w hoteldelapresse.com. One of the very last family-run hotels in Bordeaux; central, with good sound proofing & parking nearby. Organic b/fast available. **€€–€**

SHOESTRING

B&B Bordeaux Centre Gare Saint-Jean [55 F7] (126 rooms) Gare Armagnac, 7 Allée du Corail; 02 98 33 75 29; w hotelbb-bordeaux.fr. Tidy bargain near the station & airport shuttle, with family rooms; parking nearby. **€**

Eklo Centre Bastide [54 F4] (127 rooms) 10 Rue de la Gare d'Orléans; 05 35 54 52 54; w eklohotels.com/Bordeaux. In the up-&-coming Right Bank Bastide quarter, a cheap & cheerful choice, with dbls & family rooms sleeping 4, affordable buffet b/fast & restaurant € & live music Fri nights. **€**

Notre-Dame [54 E3] (22 rooms) 36 Rue Notre-Dame; 05 56 52 88 24; w hotelbordeauxchartrons.com. Pleasant no-frills rooms in the Chartrons, 20m from an underground car park. **€**

Regina [55 F6] (39 rooms) 34 Rue Charles Domercq; 05 56 91 66 07; w hotelreginabordeaux.com. Historic hotel with vintage flourishes opposite the station. **€**

WHERE TO EAT AND DRINK

The city has some exceptional Asian restaurants, even before the influx of Chinese wine lovers (and châteaux buyers). Always book ahead, especially in August when many restaurants close for all or part of the month.

EXPENSIVE

Garopapilles [58 A3] 62 Rue de l'Abbé de l'Épée; 09 72 45 55 36; w garopapilles.com; lunch Tue–Fri, dinner Mon–Thu. A wine shop/restaurant offering elegant uncomplicated modern cuisine. Tanguey Laviale was one of the first of the young, exciting chefs who have taken Bordeaux by storm. *Lunch from €45 for 3 courses, dinner from €65.* **€€€€€**

La Tupina [55 F5] 6 Rue Porte-de-la-Monnaie; 05 56 91 56 37; w latupina.com; closed lunch Mon. The high temple of traditional Bordelaise cuisine, founded in 1964 by Jean-Pierre Xiradakis & now in the good hands of

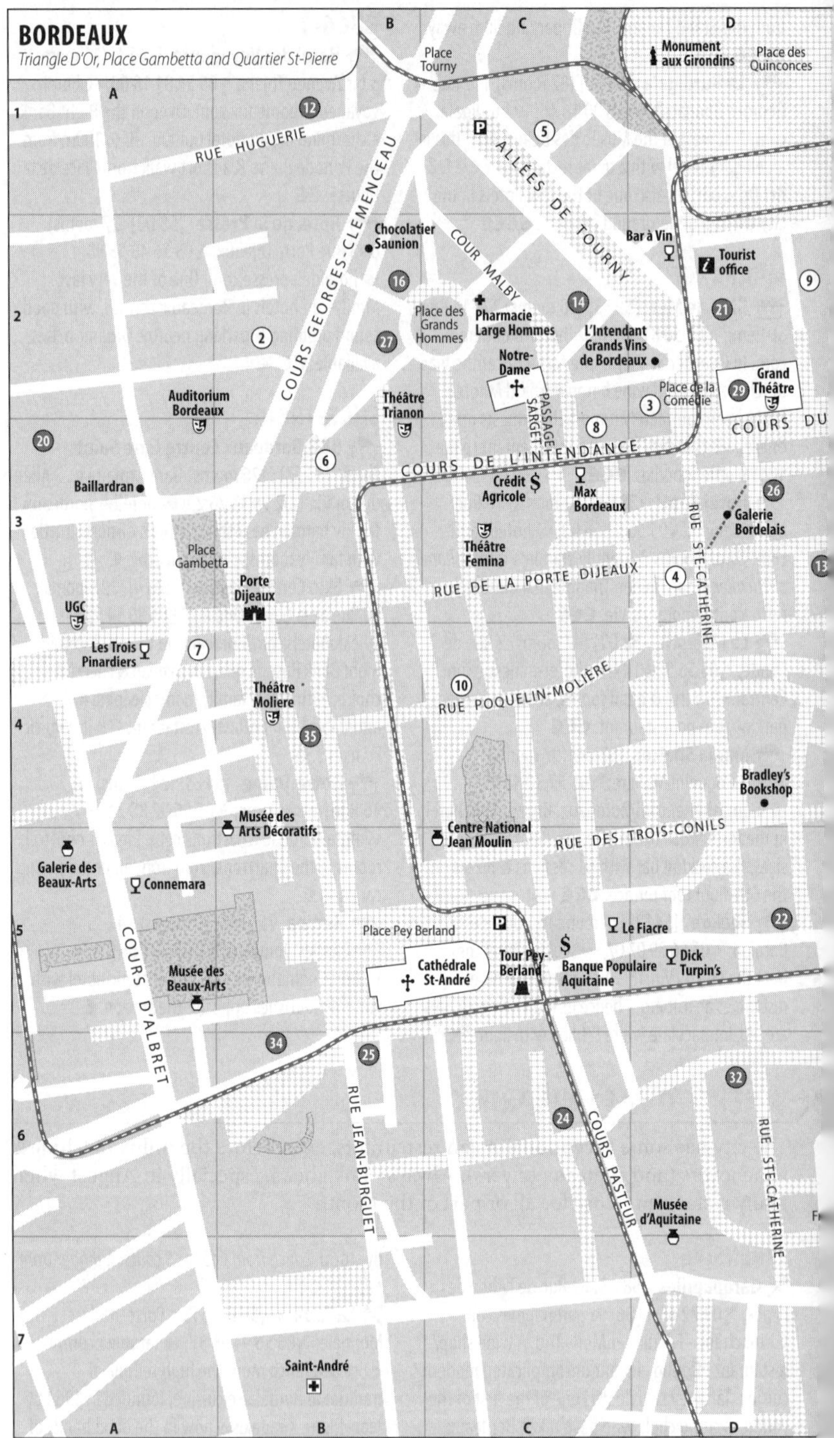
BORDEAUX
Triangle D'Or, Place Gambetta and Quartier St-Pierre
Place Tourny
Monument aux Girondins
Place des Quinconces
Rue Huguerie
Cours Georges-Clemenceau
Allées de Tourny
Cour Malby
Chocolatier Saunion
Bar à Vin
Tourist office
Place des Grands Hommes
Pharmacie Large Hommes
L'Intendant Grands Vins de Bordeaux
Notre-Dame
Passage Sarget
Place de la Comédie
Grand Théâtre
Cours du
Auditorium Bordeaux
Théâtre Trianon
Cours de l'Intendance
Baillardran
Crédit Agricole
Max Bordeaux
Galerie Bordelais
Théâtre Femina
Place Gambetta
Porte Dijeaux
Rue de la Porte Dijeaux
Rue Ste-Catherine
UGC
Les Trois Pinardiers
Théâtre Moliere
Rue Poquelin-Molière
Bradley's Bookshop
Musée des Arts Décoratifs
Centre National Jean Moulin
Rue des Trois-Conils
Galerie des Beaux-Arts
Connemara
Place Pey Berland
Le Fiacre
Cours d'Albret
Musée des Beaux-Arts
Cathédrale St-André
Tour Pey-Berland
Banque Populaire Aquitaine
Dick Turpin's
Rue Jean-Burguet
Cours Pasteur
Musée d'Aquitaine
Rue Ste-Catherine
Saint-André

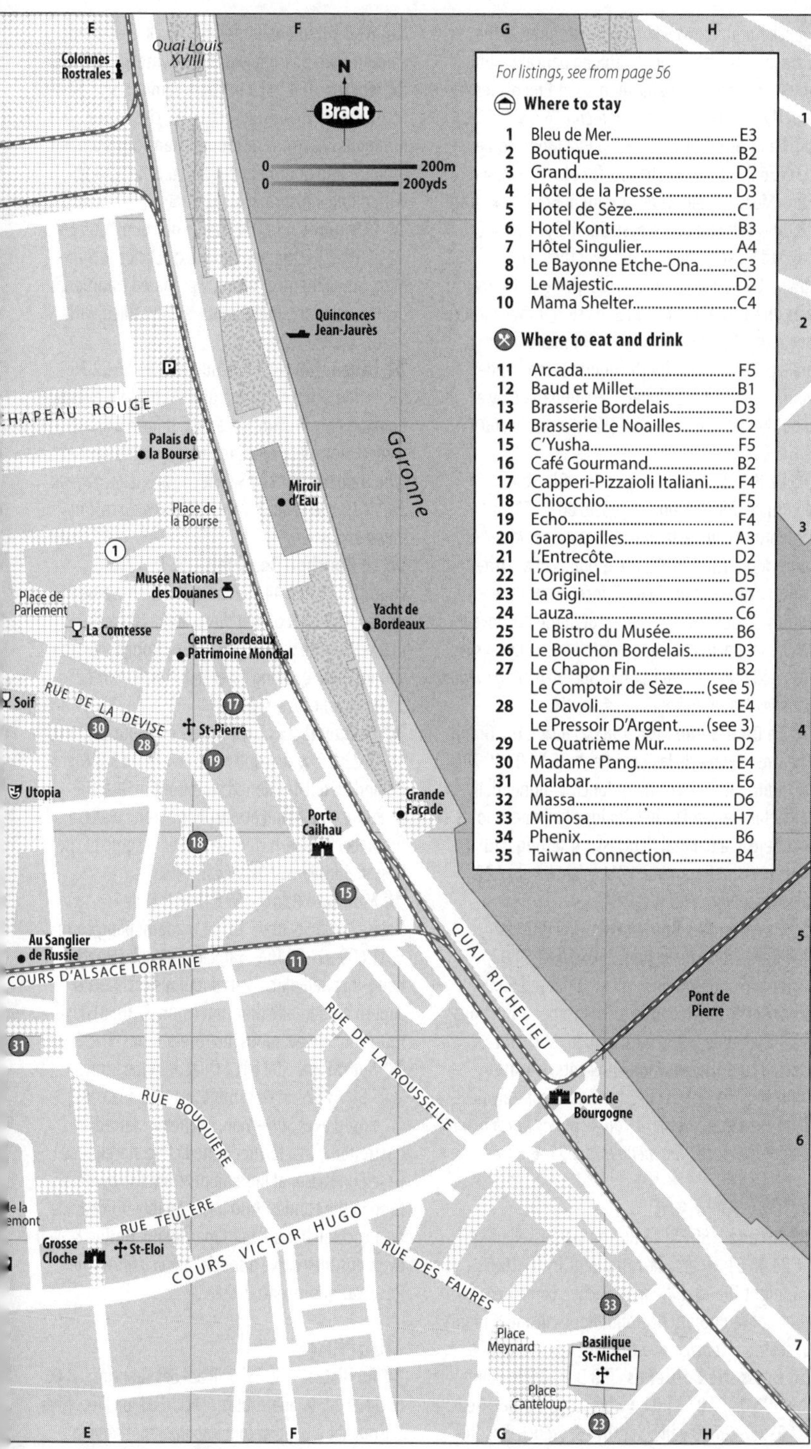
For listings, see from page 56
Where to stay
1 Bleu de Mer E3
2 Boutique B2
3 Grand D2
4 Hôtel de la Presse D3
5 Hotel de Sèze C1
6 Hotel Konti B3
7 Hôtel Singulier A4
8 Le Bayonne Etche-Ona C3
9 Le Majestic D2
10 Mama Shelter C4
Where to eat and drink
11 Arcada F5
12 Baud et Millet B1
13 Brasserie Bordelais D3
14 Brasserie Le Noailles C2
15 C'Yusha F5
16 Café Gourmand B2
17 Capperi-Pizzaioli Italiani F4
18 Chiocchio F5
19 Echo F4
20 Garopapilles A3
21 L'Entrecôte D2
22 L'Originel D5
23 La Gigi G7
24 Lauza C6
25 Le Bistro du Musée B6
26 Le Bouchon Bordelais D3
27 Le Chapon Fin B2
Le Comptoir de Sèze (see 5)
28 Le Davoli E4
Le Pressoir D'Argent (see 3)
29 Le Quatrième Mur D2
30 Madame Pang E4
31 Malabar E6
32 Massa D6
33 Mimosa H7
34 Phenix B6
35 Taiwan Connection B4
Bradt
0 200m
0 200yds
Colonnes Rostrales
Quai Louis XVIIII
Quinconces Jean-Jaurès
Chapeau Rouge
Palais de la Bourse
Place de la Bourse
Miroir d'Eau
Garonne
Musée National des Douanes
Place de Parlement
La Comtesse
Yacht de Bordeaux
Centre Bordeaux Patrimoine Mondial
Soif
Rue de la Devise
St-Pierre
Utopia
Porte Cailhau
Grande Façade
Au Sanglier de Russie
Cours d'Alsace Lorraine
Quai Richelieu
Rue de la Rousselle
Pont de Pierre
Rue Bouquière
Porte de Bourgogne
Rue Teulère
Cours Victor Hugo
Grosse Cloche
St-Eloi
Rue des Faures
Place Meynard
Basilique St-Michel
Place Canteloup

Franck Audu. It's well known for lamprey, & the ultra-traditional *sanguette* (blood pancake), but you'll find many less alarming-sounding dishes too. *W/day lunch €18, classic menu €64.* €€€€€

Le Chapon Fin [58 B2] 5 Rue Montesquieu; 05 56 79 10 10; w chapon-fin.com; closed Sun–Mon. The oldest restaurant in Bordeaux (since 1825) is still one of the best. Sarah Bernhardt & Edward VII stopped by whenever they were in town, & when Michelin started giving out stars it was one of the first to bag 3. Its sumptuous rockery décor (unchanged since 1901) & inner garden are a perfect match for the gourmet food under young chef Cédric Bobinet – accompanied by a fabulous list of *grands crus. W/day lunch menu €40.* €€€€€

Le Prince Noir [map, page 48] 1 Rue du Prince Noir, Lormont; 05 56 06 12 52; w leprincenoir-restaurant.fr; dinner Mon–Fri, lunch Mon, Thu–Fri. On the grounds of a 14th-century castle of the Black Prince, & later the summer house of the bishops of Bordeaux, lovely Michelin-starred, environmentally friendly cuisine from jolly chef Vivien Durand. *Superb tasting menu: 6 dishes €95, 8 dishes €125.* €€€€€

Le Quatrième Mur [58 D2] Inside the Grand Théâtre at Place de la Comédie; 05 56 02 49 70; w quatrieme-mur.com; lunch & dinner daily. Michelin-starred TV chef Philippe Etchebest holds fort here in a palatial Neoclassical setting with a weekly changing menu. *W/day lunch from €29, set-price dinner €52.* €€€€€

Pavillon des Boulevards [54 B3] 120 Rue de la Croix-de-Seguey; 05 56 81 51 02; w lepavillondesboulevards.fr; closed Sun–Mon. At the north end of town in a beautiful house with a veranda in the back garden, Michelin-starred chef Thomas Morel presents delicate, sophisticated dishes based on the absolutely best & freshest ingredients. *4-course w/day lunch menu €45, 9-course tasting menu from €95.* €€€€€

ABOVE AVERAGE

Arcada [59 F5] 13 Rue de la Rousselle; 05 56 23 08 61; w arcada-restaurant.fr; 10.00–midnight Tue–Sat. Near St-Michel. Come here for cool, contemporary bistronomique cuisine & plenty of seafood. *Lunch menu €26, dinner €43.* €€€€

Brasserie Bordelais [58 D3] 50 Rue Saint-Rémi; 05 57 87 11 01; w brasserie-bordelaise.fr; 09.00–23.00 daily. Southwest French-Basque cuisine & succulent hams, beef, duck, free-range chicken from Gascony plus huge wine list. €€€€

Hortus [54 D3] 114 Cours Verdun; 05 57 59 90 63; w hortus-restaurant.fr; closed Sun. This luminous Chartrons restaurant transforms organic produce into gourmet delights (try the scallops with girolle mushrooms). €€€€

L'Originel [58 D5] 35 Rue du Loup; 05 56 44 21 19; f LOriginelBordeaux; closed Sun–Mon. Small menu of lovingly prepared traditional dishes, using top ingredients; always filled with locals. €€€€

Lauza [58 C6] 5 Rue du Hâ; 05 56 52 76 59; w lauza.fr; closed lunch Sat–Mon, eves by booking only. Delights in a chic, informal stone-walled room & terrace prepared by a young chef who trained with Guy Savoie in Paris. *Lunch menu from €19, menu découverte €52, evening tasting menu €65.* €€€€

Le Bouchon Bordelais [58 D3] 2 Rue Courbin; 05 56 44 33 00; w bouchon-bordelais.com; lunch & dinner daily. Smiles & fresh market cuisine wait in this bistrot from a dynamic young team; booking essential. *Lunch from €23, dinner from €41.* €€€€

Le Davoli [59 E4] 13 Rue des Bahutiers; 05 56 48 22 19; w ledavoli.com; closed Sat & Sun. Behind an old-fashioned storefront in Quartier St-Pierre, you'll find atmospheric stone walls, a fireplace, & superb creative dishes – some of the best in Bordeaux. *Menu €44.* €€€€

Madame Pang [59 E4] 16 Rue de la Devise; 05 56 38 47 13; w madamepang.com; 19.00–01.00 Tue–Sat. Elegant, silky Hong Kong-inspired place, with fabulous cocktails & superb homemade dim sum (from €7 for 3). Live music on Sun evenings; no reservations. €€€€

Symbiose [54 E3] 4 Quai des Chartrons; 05 56 23 67 15; w symbiose-bordeaux.com; closed eves Sun–Mon. Michelin-starred gastronomy in a former Benedictine storehouse based on seasonal ingredients from the owners' farm in the Landes. Also has arguably Bordeaux's best cocktail bar & a bar tapas menu. On Tue & Wed evenings they serve a special *menu dégustation*. Reservations essential. €€€€

MODERATE

Au Bistrot [55 E5] 61 Place des Capucins; m 06 63 54 21 14; w aubistrot.fr; closed Mon–Tue. Near the market, a popular contemporary spot serving *cuisine du marché à l'ancienne* with some rarely seen dishes, plus an extraordinary wine list. €€€

Brasserie Le Noailles [58 C2] 12 Allées de Tourny; 05 56 81 94 45; w lenoailles.fr; lunch & dinner daily. A very French place where you can pretend you've walked into a Renoir painting with mirrors, murals & waiters dressed *comme il faut*. Nobel novelist François Mauriac used to hold court here. Serves equally classic dishes: oysters, scallops, lamprey, confits, etc. €€€

C'Yusha [59 F5] 12 Rue Ausone; 05 56 69 89 70; w cyusha.com; closed Sun–Mon, & lunch Fri–Sat. Only a few tables & an open kitchen where Pierreck Célibert whips up delicious surprises, sometimes with Vietnamese coriander & jalepeños. *Lunch menu €20, dinner €43*. €€€

Chiocchio [59 F5] 20 Place du Palais; 05 57 99 21 12; Chiocchio; lunch & dinner daily. Same owners as Echo (see below), named after their native Italian village, here serving delicious Italian dishes prepared in an open kitchen. Try the crispy fried artichokes if they're on the menu. €€€

Echo [59 F4] 18 Rue de la Cour des Aides; 05 56 81 69 95; echo.caveamanger; closed lunch Mon–Fri. Trendy little wine & food bar, with unusual dishes that match the unusual bottles from France & beyond. *3 courses €35, plus €15 for wine & coffee*. €€€

La Plana [55 D6] Place de la Victoire; 05 56 91 73 23; w laplana.fr; 08.00–02.00 daily. Old favourite, serving generous high-quality bistro classics with a Spanish touch, & platters of tapas to share; excellent *magret de canard. Menus €20 & €30*. €€€

Le Bistro du Musée [58 B6] 37 Place Pey-Berland; 05 56 52 99 69; w lebistrodumusee.com; closed Sun. Near the cathedral, bustling place renowned for its *souris d'agneau* (braised lamb shank with preserved lemons). €€€

Le Bistro du Sommelier [54 C4] 163 Rue Georges Bonnac; 05 56 96 71 78; w bistrodusommelier.com; closed Sat–Sun. Stylish spot serving meaty classics (grilled meats, *tartare de boeuf*, duck, *andouillette*), but also seafood & daily specials, all designed to enhance its wide selection of wines. Every 2nd Mon in the month they host an evening of Havana cigars. *3 courses €29.50*. €€€

Pastificio Marcellino [54 E3] 11 Rue Sicard, Chartrons; 05 54 78 69 64; w pastificio-marcellino-bordeaux.eatbu.com; lunch only, closed Wed & Sun. Prepares & serves the best homemade pasta in Bordeaux, along with other Italian favourites. €€€

CHEAP AND CHEERFUL

Baud et Millet [58 B1] 19 Rue Huguerie; 05 56 79 05 77; w baudetmillet.com; closed Sun. A paradise for mice & other cheese lovers, offering hundreds of wines from all around the world to go with a hundred types of farm cheese, raclette, fondue & tapas. €€

Capperi-Pizzaioli Italiani [58 F4] 3 Rue de la Cour des Aides; 05 56 90 93 05; w capperi.fr; 18.00–23.00 Thu–Sun. Superb pizzas, made by the pros. €€

Hutong [55 C6] 137 Rue du Tondu; 09 87 74 45 86; w restauranthutong.weebly.com; eves only Wed–Sun. Here the delectable cuisine will transport you to Singapore. €€

La Gigi [59 G7] 32 Rue des Allamandiers; 09 80 73 20 69; w lagigi.fr; eves only. Cocktails, wine & tasty 'street food' burgers, truffled frites & vegetarian choices. €€

Mimosa [59 H7] 7 Rue des Faures; 05 56 94 62 86; w mimosa-restaurant.fr; lunch Fri–Mon, dinner Thu–Mon. Very young & talented chef Violette who worked in 3-star Michelin restaurants prepares organic dishes to share. Try the *oeuf mimosa* (devilled eggs, with truffle cream), homemade focaccia & divine desserts. In the afternoon it turns into a tearoom. €€

Phenix [58 B6] 17 Rue des Frères Bonie; 05 56 81 74 59; w phenixdor.fr; closed Sat–Sun. Since 1984, one of the best Vietnamese restaurants in Bordeaux. €€

Taiwan Connection [58 B4] 32 Rue des Remparts; 05 56 38 44 39; w taiwanconnection.fr; lunch Mon–Sat, teatime (with Taiwanese snacks) 14.30–17.30 Wed–Sat. Always packed. Try the excellent *canard laqué au curry rouge*. €€

ROCK BOTTOM

Café Gourmand [58 B2] 3 Rue Buffon; 05 56 79 23 85; noon–midnight Mon–Sat. Bistro with a turn-of-the-century feel, energetic young staff & a family-friendly menu of tasty burgers & salads. €

Chez Jean-Mi [55 E6] In the Marché des Capucins; w marchedescapucins.com; 05.30–14.00 Tue–Sun. Bordeaux's favourite oyster bar for a white wine & oyster pick-me-up. €

L'Entrecôte [58 D2] 4 Cours du 30 Juillet; 05 56 81 76 10; w entrecote.fr; noon–14.00 & 19.00–22.30 daily. Always queues for this branch of the Toulouse institution (page 370). €

Magasin Général [54 F3] Darwin Caserne Niel-87; 05 56 77 88 35; w magasingeneral.camp; 08.00–20.00 daily. Hip all-organic food court & the locally brewed Darwin beer in the Darwin Éco-Système (page 77). €

Malabar [59 E6] 7 Rue des Ayres, 05 56 52 18 19; closed Sun–Tue. Bordeaux's best Indian restaurant, with a wide choice of vegetarian dishes. Excellent value. €

Massa [58 D6] 36 Rue des Ayres; 05 47 47 89 42; w massabordeaux.com; noon–14.30 Tue–Sat. Hummus, falafel & other Israeli treats, prepared fresh every day. €

ENTERTAINMENT AND NIGHTLIFE

BARS

Bar à Vin [58 D2] 3 Cours du 30 Juillet; 05 56 00 43 47; w baravin.bordeaux.com; 11.00–22.00 Mon–Sat. By the tourist office, in the elegant prow-shaped Hôtel Gobineau, taste 30 different Bordeaux wines by the glass. Prices are reasonable even for *grand crus*, served by knowledgeable young wine students. Get there by 16.00 to grab a table.

Connemara [58 A5] 18 Cours d'Albret; 05 56 52 82 57; 11.30–02.00 Tue–Sat, 16.00–midnight Sun, 17.00–02.00 Mon. Irish bar with a Fri-night trad session, & much more.

Dick Turpin's [58 D5] 72 Rue du Loup; 05 56 48 07 52; f Dick-Turpins; 16.00–23.00 daily, until 02.00 Sat. A traditional convivial English pub.

La Comtesse [59 E4] 25 Rue Parlement Saint-Pierre; 05 56 51 03 07; f laccomtesse; 17.45–02.00 daily. Shabby chic, lively, friendly venue with sublime cocktails.

Le Fiacre [58 C5] 42 Rue de Cheverus; 09 51 53 12 77; f fiacrebordeaux; 16.00–02.00 Mon–Sat. Classic rock bar with Belgian beers & cocktails.

Les Trois Pinardiers [58 A4] 2 Rue Georges Bonnac, just off Place Gambetta; 05 54 52 21 52; w les3pinardiers.com; 14.00–21.00 Wed–Sun. Cool, contemporary & woodsy, with great wines & platters of goodies.

Max Bordeaux [58 C3] 14 Cours de l'Intendance; 05 57 29 23 81; w maxbordeaux.com; 11.00–20.00 Mon–Sat. Wine workshops & *grands crus* by the glass.

Soif [59 E4] 35 Rue du Cancera; 09 86 10 42 40; w soif-bordeaux.com; 19.00–midnight Mon, Wed–Sat, noon–14.00 Sun. Atmospheric, great choice of wines, & divine little plates – a lovely place to while away the evening.

CINEMAS

Cinéma Megarama [54 F4] 7 Quai de Queyries; 05 56 40 66 70; w bordeaux.megarama.fr. The former Gare d'Orléans on the Right Bank has been restored as an enormous multiplex cinema, with some films in original language (VO).

UGC [58 A3] 13–15 Rue Georges Bonnac; 08 92 70 00 00; w ugc.fr. Often shows films in VO.

Utopia [59 E4] 5 Place Camille-Jullian; 05 56 52 00 03; w cinemas-utopia.org/bordeaux. Art cinema in a former church, showing films in VO.

THEATRE, OPERA AND MUSIC

Arkéa Arena [map, page 48] 48–50 Av Jean Alfonséa, Floirac; w arkeaarena.com. The biggest venue in the region, part of the Quartier Euroatlantique project (page 72) built in 2018 & capable of seating 11,000 for major concerts & sporting events.

Auditorium Bordeaux [58 A3] 8–13 Cours Clemenceau; 05 57 78 41 19; w opera-bordeaux.com. The Opéra National de Bordeaux's modern auditorium, with great acoustics.

Espace Culturel du Pin Galant [map, page 48] Cnr avs de la Libération & de l'Yser, Mérignac; 05 56 97 82 82; w lepingalant.com. A full calendar of opera, musicals, concerts, jazz, dance & theatre from around the world, from the dancing monks of Tibet to Offenbach operettas.

Grand Théâtre [58 D2] Place de la Comédie; 05 56 00 85 95; w opera-bordeaux.com. Operas, ballets, symphonic concerts & more performed by the Opéra National & the Orchestre National de Bordeaux. See also page 65.

La Manufacture CDCN Nouvelle Aquitaine [55 F8] 226 Bd Albert 1er; 05 57 54 10 40; w lamanufacture-cdcn.org. A former shoe factory, now the centre of contemporary dance & theatre.

Petit Théâtre à Bordeaux [54 E2] 10 Rue du Faubourg des Arts; 05 56 51 04 73; lepetittheatrebordeaux. Charming little theatre; do check their page to see what's on.
Rockschool Barbey [55 E6] 18 Cours Barbey; 05 56 33 66 00; w rockschool-barbey.com. Big music complex with workshops & stage for local new & old bands.
Théâtre Femina [58 C3] 10 Rue de Grassi; 05 33 49 13 00; w theatrefemina.com. Major concert & drama venue.
Théâtre Moliere [58 B4] 33 Rue du Temple; 05 56 20 13 20; w bordeauxtheatres.com. This theatre puts on plays, comedies & musicals as do 2 other neighbourhood venues, **Théâtre Trianon** [58 B3] (6 Rue Franklin) & **Théâtre Victoire** [55 E5] (18 Rue des Augustins) all sharing the same phone & website.
Théâtre National de Bordeaux en Aquitaine (TnBA) [55 F6] 3 Place Pierre Renaudel; 05 56 33 36 80; w tnba.org. Converted into a theatre from an 18th-century sugar refinery near St-Michel, now a major venue for drama & dance.

SHOPPING

Rue Ste-Catherine is the longest pedestrian street in France, and lined on both sides with shops: big names and chains are clustered at the north end, gradually evolving into the cheap, quirky and cheerful shopping on the south end.

Bordeaux has exceptional **food markets**: the **Marché des Capucins** [59 E6] (Place des Capucins; w marchedescapucins.com; 05.30–14.00 Tue–Sun) is the biggest and liveliest. Also **St Michel** [59 G7] (Places Meynard & Canteloup; 07.00–13.00 Sat) and **Les Halles Bacalan** (10 Quai de Bacalan, by the Cité du Vin; 05 35 54 44 82; w biltoki.com/hallesbacalan; 09.00–14.30 & 16.30–21.00 Tue–Wed, 08.00–23.00 Thu–Sat, 08.00–16.00 Sun), where farmers, artisans and regional chefs sell enough ready-to-eat food to make a meal. The Sunday morning market along the **Quai des Chartrons** [54 E3] also offers alfresco dining with tables in a fun atmosphere.

The city's liveliest **flea market** takes place Sunday morning by St Michel, in Places Meynard and Canteloup. On Monday it turns into a clothes market.

BOOKS

Bradley's Bookshop [58 D4] 1 Rue de la Merci; 05 56 52 10 57; w bradleys-bookshop.com; 10.00–18.00 Tue–Sat. Books in English.

FOOD AND WINE

Baillardran [58 A3] 36 Place Gambetta (& many other locales); w baillardran.com. One of the best-known makers of *canelés*, Bordeaux's cute, fluted & caramelised pastries flavoured with vanilla & rum, with a soft custardy inside. Other *pâtissiers* in Bordeaux produce them as well, in traditional & avant-garde flavours.
Chocolatier Saunion [58 B2] 56 Cours Georges Clemenceau; w saunion.fr. An essential stocking-up point for chocolate-lovers, where Thierry Lalet makes 40-plus fresh chocolates; the house speciality is the *guinette*, a cherry soaked in alcohol & covered in dark chocolate.
L'Intendant Grands Vins de Bordeaux [58 D2] 2 Allées de Tourney; 05 56 48 10 29; w intendant.com. Very smart, unique wine shop, with bottles lining a spiral staircase.

OTHER

Au Sanglier de Russie [59 E5] 67 Cours d'Alsace et Lorraine; w ausanglierderussie.com. One of the last remaining shops of its kind in France, the 'Russian boar' was founded in 1814, selling brushes for absolutely any imaginable household or personal use.
Village des Antiquaires [54 E3] 61 Rue Notre Dame, in the Chartrons; 05 56 52 66 13; 10.00–19.00 Tue–Sun. Since 1982, this has been the home of 35 antiques dealers; others line Rue Notre-Dame around the Protestant Temple.

SPORTS AND ACTIVITIES

BOAT TOURS

Bordeaux River Cruise [54 E3] Quai des Chartrons; ☎05 56 39 27 66; **w** croisiere-bordeaux.com. Offers a variety of cruises, including wine tasting, a UNESCO cruise, & aperitif & dinner cruises.

Croisières Burdigala [54 F4] 7 Quai de Queyries; ☎05 56 49 36 88; **w** croisieresburdigala.fr. Offers a UNESCO cruise but also longer excursions to Blaye, Bourg or Cadillac.

Yacht de Bordeaux [59 F3] Ponton d'Honneur, Passerelle Gironde (near the Place de la Bourse); ☎05 57 91 60 11; **w** yachtdebordeaux.com. Runs cruises between the Pont de Pierre & the Pont d'Aquitaine.

CANOEING AND KAYAKING See Bordeaux and its Port de la Lune from an entirely different angle on a 90-minute guided canoe or kayak excursion organised by Les Marins de la Lune Bordeaux Canoë [54 F3] (21 Parc d'Activités des Queyries; **w** bordeauxcanoe.com; book online).

FOOTBALL AND RUGBY The Girondins de Bordeaux, in the football First Division at the time of writing, play in the Nouveau Stade de Bordeaux (currently known as MatMut) in the Cours Jules-Ladoumègue (**w** girodins.com), which will be used in the 2023 Rugby World Cup and 2024 Summer Olympics. Bordeaux's beloved rugby team, Union Bordeaux Bègles (**w** ubbrugby.com), plays in the Art Deco Stade Chaban-Delmas (1938) [55 B6] in Boulevard du Maréchal Leclerc. Purchase tickets via their websites.

GOLF There are three courses on the outskirts of town [map, page 48]: the 27-hole Golf Blue Green de Pessac (5 Rue de la Princesse; ☎05 57 26 03 33; **w** bluegreen.fr/Pessac), the 18-hole Golf Bordelais (Rue de Kater, at Caudéran; ☎05 56 28 56 04; **w** golf-bordelais.fr) and the 36-hole Golf de Bordeaux-Lac (Av de Pernon; ☎05 56 50 92 72; **w** asgolfbordeauxlac.com).

ZOO DE BORDEAUX PESSAC [map, page 48] (Bus 23 then 1km on foot; 3 Chemin du Transvaal, Pessac; ☎05 57 89 28 10; **w** zoo-bordeaux-pessac.com; ⏲ Jul–Aug 09.30–19.00 daily, other months check the complicated online calendar; €17.50, ages 3–11 €12) Just outside Bordeaux, this is a well-maintained little zoo with free-flying parrots, a pair of jaguars who love to swim, giant chickens and more.

OTHER PRACTICALITIES

$ **Banque Populaire Aquitaine** [58 C5] 2 Rue Dufour Dubergier

$ **Crédit Agricole** [58 C3] 8 Cours de l'Intendance

➕ **Pellegrin** [55 A6] Rue de la Pelouse de Douet; ☎05 56 79 56 79; **w** chu-bordeaux.fr. Has A&E.

➕ **Saint-André** [58 B7] 1 Rue Jean Burguet; ☎05 56 79 56 79; **w** chu-bordeaux.fr. A&E.

✚ **Pharmacie des Capucins** [55 E6] 30 Place des Capucins; ⏲ 24hrs.

✚ **Pharmacie Large Hommes** [58 C2] 1 Place des Grands Hommes

✉ **Post office** [54 C4] 52 Rue Georges Bonnac

WHAT TO SEE AND DO

THE TRIANGLE D'OR 'Bordeaux being one of the cities in the kingdom where one meets the most foreigners,' wrote the Intendant Marquis de Tourny, 'it is fitting to try to give them a favourable opinion of France… I will make you the most beautiful city in the realm.' His elegant Golden Triangle of good taste is formed by Cours de l'Intendance, Cours Georges-Clemenceau and Allées de Tourny. In the centre is the iron-and-glass boutique mall and useful car park, the **Marché des Grands-Hommes** [58 C2] (Place des Grands Hommes), rebuilt in 1991 and quickly dubbed the *bouchon de carafe* ('carafe stopper'). The Place de la Comédie occupies the most important corner of the Triangle, with the tourist office, Victor Louis's Grand Hotel (page 56) and Grand Théâtre.

Notre-Dame [58 C2] (Place du Chapelet; w notredamedebordeaux.fr; ⌚ 08.30–19.00) Bordeaux's chief Baroque church was a Dominican convent church (1684–1707), directly inspired by the Gesù in Rome. Its luxurious altar, 18th-century organ and paintings show a marked change in Dominican taste since the days of Les Jacobins in Toulouse (page 378). Next door, the former cloister, **Cour Malby** (3 Rue Malby), is used for special events.

From Place du Chapelet you can reach elegant Cours de l'Intendance via the glass-covered **Passage Sarget** (1878), a fashionable arcade lined with shops and cafés.

Grand Théâtre [58 D2] (Place de la Comédie; ☎ 05 56 00 85 95; w opera-bordeaux.com; ⌚ 14.30–18.30 Wed & Sat (exc hols) for 90min guided tours; from €6; phone first) Place de la Comédie once contained 300 houses, a church and a remarkable Gallo-Roman palace called the Piliers de Tutelle – all demolished by order of Louis XIV, who, after the uprising of the nobility against him in the Fronde (1648–53), wanted nothing to stand in the way of his cannons pointed at the city from the Château Trompette (now Place des Quinconces).

In 1773, the Maréchal-Duc de Richelieu, great nephew of the famous cardinal, governor of Guyenne and a famous libertine (at one of his parties the only guests were the 29 most beautiful ladies of Bordeaux, masked to permit every indiscretion), felt he wasn't being properly entertained and rectified the matter by commissioning an opera house from Neoclassical architect Victor Louis and making the jurats pay for it.

From the outside it resembles a Greek temple, crowned with statues of goddesses and muses. Louis came up with a number of innovations in its construction, especially the great metal tie-beam (the 'clou de M. Louis') that supports the entablature of the peristyle (France's 18th-century architects had a hard time making their monumental stone confections stand up, and by necessity became innovators in the use of iron – a habit that culminated in the Eiffel Tower). His bold grand stair was copied by Garnier for the Paris Opéra; the auditorium, seating 1,100, has golden columns and a domed ceiling (repainted in 1919) hung with a 860kg crystal chandelier. From the day it opened, this high temple of illusion answered a deep-felt need in business-oriented Bordeaux; every single night it thronged with merchants who paid a king's ransom to bring down the best players and dancers from Paris.

Galerie Bordelaise [3A D3] (12 Rue Ste-Catherine) Long, long pedestrian Rue Ste-Catherine begins just south of the theatre, with chic boutiques and Bordeaux's older, once very fashionable *passage* (shopping arcade), a rare one built at an angle in 1834 by four wealthy wine négociants who moved to the city from South America after the Mexican War.

Monument aux Girondins [58 D1] North of Place de la Comédie, the Cours du 30 Juillet leads to this irresistible overblown 19th-century monument to Bordeaux's moderate but doomed revolutionaries. It boasts a lofty column crowned by Liberty over a fountain mobbed by Happiness, Eloquence, Security and a host of other attractive allegories. Originally statues of the Girondins themselves were planned, but lack of funds kept them from coming to their own party, as it were. In the fountain basin, two stupendous quadrigas of bronze horses violently rear sea-monster paws to the sky while Falsehood (holding a mask), Vice (with pig ears) and shameful Ignorance cower under the vacuous gaze of the Republic.

Place des Quinconces [58 D1] The Monument aux Girondins stands at the head of Europe's largest, and least interesting, squares, although redeemed by the fact that there's nearly always an event happening in its huge space. When speculators purchased the hated Château Trompette and began dismantling it just before the Revolution, their intention was to lay out new streets and build 1,800 houses – only it never happened. You're hard put to find any quincunxes at all. (What's a quincunx, you ask? A pattern like the five on a dice; all French farmers plant their trees in rows like this. Supposedly the fashion was started by the granddad of all gardeners, King Cyrus of Persia.) At the river end, the massive square is closed by two columns, the **Colonnes Rostrales**, erected in 1829, decorated with sculptures of ancient Roman ships' prows and topped by allegories of Commerce and Navigation.

PLACE GAMBETTA AND AROUND Originally Place Dauphine, this handsome square was laid out with uniform façades by Tourny in 1743; a simple gateway, **Porte Dijeaux** [58 B3], was added shortly after. All distances in the city are measured from the 0km marker, at no. 10.

During the Terror in the autumn of 1793, the guillotine here parted the heads from the trunks of 300 Bordelais. The chief of the revolutionaries in Bordeaux was the fiery redhead Tallien, editor of the *Ami du Citoyen*. Tallien would have given many more Bordelais the chop had it not been for the gentle pleadings of his beloved, soft-hearted Spanish mistress, Teresa Cabarus. When Tallien was recalled to Paris and Teresa was imprisoned by Robespierre, he freed her – by toppling Robespierre himself on the 9th of Thermidor. Legend has it that Tallien's name was on a list that an acquaintance accidentally found while rifling through Robespierre's famous sea-green coat, looking for a piece of paper to answer to a bodily need. Tallien and the others on the list joined forces and acted first, so it was Robespierre's head that rolled instead of theirs.

Cathédrale St-André [58 B5] (Place Pey-Berland; ☎05 56 44 67 29; **w** cathedrale-bordeaux.fr; ⏲ 15.00–19.00 Mon, 10.30–13.30 & 15.00–19.00 Tue–Sat, 09.30–13.30 & 15.00–20.15 Sun) Bordeaux's Gothic cathedral is the successor of the church where the 15-year-old Eleanor of Aquitaine married the future Louis VII in 1137. It would witness another royal wedding in 1615 when Anne of Austria married Louis XIII. Neither marriage was very happy.

What you see today, a church in the form of a Latin cross and supported by an intricate web of buttresses, was built under English rule between the 13th and 15th centuries, and given a huge boost after 1305, when Archbishop Bertrand de Got was elected Pope Clement V. A fine 14th-century tympanum crowns the **north transept** door, carved with the *Last Supper, Ascension of Christ* and *Triumph of the Redeemer*. The nearby **Porte Royale** (used by visiting kings and dignitaries) has another, decorated with a throng of saints and a serene 13th-century *Last Judgement*, in which the lids of the open tombs on the lintel add a nice rhythmic touch. The west front, which originally formed part of the city wall, is strikingly bare. The **south portal**, dedicated to the Virgin, lost its tympanum to make room for carts when the church was converted into a feed store during the Revolution, but carvings of the Wise and Foolish Virgins, angels and apostles have survived; these doors are usually open, as in the Middle Ages, admitting both worshippers and pedestrians taking a shortcut.

The single nave is nearly as long and wide as Notre Dame in Paris (124 by 18m) and was the only place large enough to hold the tremendous pageant on 6 April 1364 when 1,447 nobles came to pay homage to the Black Prince, 'the most magnificent lord of his time'. The wrought-iron grille in the choir is 18th-century, and there are fine statues in the seven chapels radiating from the ambulatory, especially the 16th-century alabaster Notre Dame de la Nef.

Tour Pey-Berland [58 C5] (w pey-berland.fr; ⌚ 10.00–13.15 & 14.00–18.00 daily; €6, under 18 & EU residents under 26 free) In 1440, the cathedral's architects were reluctant to add the weight of a tower to the church building because of its marshy ground, and instead gave it this detached bell tower, a Flamboyant Gothic masterpiece named after the archbishop who built it. The tower was used as a lead ball factory from 1793 until 1850, when it was repurchased by the archbishop, truncated (today it stands 66m) and crowned with a shiny statue of Notre-Dame-de-l'Aquitaine. Climb the 233 steps for the view over Bordeaux.

Centre National Jean Moulin [58 C5] (48 Rue Vital Carles; ☎ 05 56 10 19 90; ⌚ reopening sometime in 2022) In 1967 Mayor Chaban-Delmas founded this collection devoted to the Occupation, Resistance and Deportation ranging from posters to an ingenious folding motorcycle used in a parachute drop to the Resistance. Upstairs, the office of famous Resistance leader Jean Moulin has been reconstructed, containing a collection of his drawings – his cover was running an art gallery in Nice.

Musée des Arts Décoratifs et du Design [58 B4] (39 Rue Bouffard; ☎ 05 56 10 14 00; w madd-bordeaux.fr; ⌚ 11.00–18.00 Wed–Mon; €5/€3) This museum has a perfect home in a Neoclassical *hôtel particulier* of 1779. The 35,000 items in its collection include furniture, wallpaper, ceramics, French tin-glazed ware, wrought iron, paintings, gold- and silverwork, glass and jewellery and costumes which evoke the good life in the 18th and 19th centuries up to the Art Nouveau and Art Deco periods. There are fine engravings of Bordeaux, back when its port and quays were bustling; there are also period documents, famous signatures, and more. The design branch, added in 2013, carries on from the 1980s to the present.

Musée des Beaux-Arts (MUSBA) [58 A5] (20 Cours d'Albret; ☎ 05 56 10 20 56; w musba-bordeaux.fr; ⌚ 11.00–18.00 Wed–Mon; €5/€3, under 18 free) Bordeaux keeps its cache of art in two wings of the luxurious Palais Rohan, built in the 1770s by the Prince Archbishop Mériadeck de Rohan to replace the insufficiently princely medieval archbishop's palace. To make space for his ecclesiastical bachelor's pad, Rohan got permission from the king to knock over several acres of medieval Bordeaux. Since 1835, most of the palace has been Bordeaux's city hall.

The rest contains the Musée des Beaux-Arts. It has paintings by artists rarely seen in French provincial museums: works by Titian and Perugino; a portrait of a senator by Lavinia Fontana (1552–1602), a rare female painter from Bologna; a chubby *Magdalen* and equally chubby *Marie dei Medici* by Van Dyck; Rubens' *Martyrdom of St George*; and the jolly *Fête de la Roserie* by Jan Brueghel de Velours. Amid a room of 17th-century rosy-cheeked portraits and mythologies are a pair of paintings of the cruel world of galley slaves by the Genoese artist Alessandro

GOYA IN BORDEAUX

In 1824 Spain's greatest living artist and official painter of the Spanish court asked permission of Ferdinand VII to settle in Bordeaux. At the time Goya was suffering from serious illnesses, deafness and political disillusionment. In his last four years in Bordeaux, in the company of his fellow exiles, he turned to a new medium, lithography (*The Bulls of Bordeaux* and *La Laitière*) and evolved a nearly Impressionistic freedom in his handling of paint. He died suddenly in 1828, age 82; his house at 57 Cours de l'Intendance is now the Institute Cervantes, dedicated to Spanish language and culture. But if you want to see his paintings in the area, you'll have to go to Agen (page 301).

Magnasco (1667–1749), that singular 'painter of phantasmagorias' completely out of synch with his time, both in his choice of subject matter (you wonder who would have commissioned these disturbing scenes) and in his technique of quick, nervous, impromptu brush strokes that lend his works their strange light, and his often tormented figures their peculiar phantom-like unreality.

Later paintings from the 18th century include Reynolds' *Portrait of Baron Rockeby*, Dutch landscapes by Ruysdael and co (favourites of Bordeaux's nouveau riche merchants), and a *Nature Morte* by the inimitable Chardin. The next room has representatives of all the 19th-century grand-isms, from the antiquating Neoclassical (Guérin's *Hippolytus and Phaedra*, the funniest painting in the collection: the protagonists have identical features and Phaedra looks as if she's just sucked a lemon) to the highly charged Romanticism of Delacroix (*Grèce sur les ruines de Missolonghi*) and Isabey (*Incendie du Steamer Austria*).

There are several glossy snigger-nudge-nudge nudes that first became popular in the decorously pornographic Second Empire, including Henri Gervex's notorious *Rolla*, a painting inspired by a poem by Alfred de Musset and the source of a tremendous scandal at the 1878 salon (the fact that the naked girl on the bed was neither a goddess nor an allegory was considered indecent according to the magnificently hypocritical taste of the time). There are paintings by proto-Impressionist Boudin and proto-Surrealist Bordeaux native Odilon Redon, and the unforgettable *Chacun sa Chimère* by Henri Martin, based on Baudelaire's prose-poem.

Along with Redon, Bordeaux produced two other influential artists, whose paintings are displayed in the last room: Albert Marquet (1875–1947), who was a fellow student of Matisse and co-founder of Fauvism before going on to paint his simple landscapes, and André Lhote (1885–1962), represented by his hallmark colourful, geometric compositions on various planes. A lesser-known Bordelais is Impressionist Alfred Smith, whose best works resemble early Monets. Temporary exhibitions are held nearby in the **Galerie des Beaux-Arts** [58 A5] in Place du Colonel Raynal (🕘 same hours).

Mériadeck [55 C5] Behind this, and on one of the axes so beloved of French urban planners (in this case, aligned with the Palais de Rohan), is the new quarter named after the aforementioned Cardinal de Rohan. Mériadeck was a fragrant slum before it was flattened in 1954 by Mayor Chaban-Delmas, clearing 30ha to create the largest single urban renovation scheme in France. Some 7ha were set aside for greenery and fountains, and the buildings facing this central strip were designed by planner J Willerval, to spare pedestrians the sight of Mériadeck's plain-Jane skyscraper. As corporate bosses haven't been beating down the doors for office space here, most of Mériadeck is occupied by government bureaucracies. It did, however, earn a gold star as the first major project in Europe to make large-scale use of geothermal heating (1981), and a tram stop has helped revive its shopping mall, the **Centre Commercial Mériadeck** [55 C5].

QUARTIER ST-PIERRE Up until the 12th century, St-Pierre was a walled quarter, built around the Palais de l'Ombrière, home of the French and English dukes of Aquitaine and, later under French rule, the Parlement of Bordeaux. In the Middle Ages the parish of St-Pierre was inhabited by English merchants and craftsmen remembered only in the street names – Rue des Bahutiers (cabinet-makers), Rue des Argentiers (silversmiths) and Rue Maucoudinat ('badly cooked', the address of the tripe butchers).

Place de la Bourse [59 E3] Jacques Gabriel's Neoclassical showcase was commissioned by Intendant Boucher in 1735, who wanted to give the city a touch of class. Originally called the Place Royale, it had for a centrepiece a bronze equestrian statue of Louis XV that was gleefully pulled down and melted into cannons to fire at other kings during the Revolution; today a **fountain of the Three Graces** (1864) holds pride of place, the Graces in this case representing the Empress Eugénie, the Queen of Spain and Queen Victoria. On one side stands the **Palais de la Bourse**, or stock exchange (now the Chamber of Commerce), enlarged in 1862 and 1925, and repaired after bomb damage in 1940.

Miroir d'Eau [59 F3] Bordeaux's spectacular water mirror is nothing less than the world's largest reflecting pool (3,450m^2). Designed by Michel Corajoud, this inch-deep pool has the best loved (and certainly the most photographed) set piece in the Port de la Lune project. Every 15 minutes in summer the pool shoots out clouds of mist, much to the delight of splashing children; at night, when the Place de la Bourse is bathed in golden light, it's simply magical.

Musée National des Douanes [59 F3] (1 Place de la Bourse; ☎ 09 70 27 57 66; **w** musee-douanes.fr; ⏲ 10.00–18.00 Tue–Sun; €4/€2, under 18 free) Installed in the magnificent vaulted clearance halls of the former Fermes du Roy (ie: the king's tax farms), this museum is devoted to a subject that annoys people to this day – French customs. It traces the history of taxes on imports from the days of the Gauls to more recent uniforms, weapons, weights and measures (including a grand 200-year-old scale) of France's redoubtable *douaniers* and examples of the forgeries and contraband they've nabbed. Among the originals: Monet's *La cabane des douaniers, effet d'après-midi* (1882).

Centre Bordeaux Patrimoine Mondial [59 E4] (2–8 Place de la Bourse; ☎ 05 56 48 04 24; ⏲ 10.00–13.00 & 14.00–18.00 daily, until 17.00 Sun; free) This exhibition space is dedicated to the city's UNESCO World Heritage-listed architecture; occasionally the staff offer tours.

St-Pierre [59 E4] (Place St Pierre; ☎ 05 56 94 30 50; ⏲ 09.00–17.00 Mon–Fri, 10.00–17.00 Sat–Sun) This 14th-century Gothic church that stood next to the Palais de l'Ombrière, replaces a much earlier one that served Bordeaux's port – St Peter being one of the patron saints of boatmen. It was substantially rebuilt in 1882 and has a rather mysterious stained-glass window by Joseph Villiet with a sorrowing white queen and a black slave from 1860.

Porte Cailhau [59 F5] (🕘 10.00–13.00 & 14.00–18.00 daily; €5/€3.50, under 12 free) Although the Palais de l'Ombrière was destroyed in 1800, its fairy-tale 35m gate still overlooks the river with its asymmetrical turrets and tower. One of only two surviving city gates (the Grande Cloche is the other), it was begun in 1493 to celebrate the Battle of Fornovo, where Charles VIII and the French fought to a draw against the united Italian republics; the nobility of Guyenne played a prominent role. Inside is a museum of stonework and masonry, a film and a fine view of the Pont de Pierre.

On either side of the gate along Quai Richelieu stretches the 18th-century riverfront **Grande Façade** [59 F4], conceived by Jacques Gabriel and the Intendants Boucher and Tourny to create a homogenous kilometre of architecture – creamy white stone houses, all the same height, with two floors of large windows, slate mansard roofs with stone dormers, fronted by arcades, each arch with a mascaron at its key, many of them framed in the interlocking triple moon symbol of Bordeaux.

Quartier St-Pierre boasts stately 18th-century *hôtels particuliers*, many of which were built by members of Bordeaux's Parlement. You can see the best of them by walking straight through Porte Cailhau to Rue du Loup (note especially no. 71, and the 200-year-old wisteria in the courtyard in the Hôtel des Archives). Cross busy Rue Ste-Catherine, turn right in Rue de Cheverus and from here turn up Rue Poquelin-Molière. In 1656 Molière and his troupe performed at no. 9, then a *jeu-de-paume*, a court for real tennis, although after a fire in 1728 it was replaced by a handsome *hôtel particulier*.

ST-MICHEL This once run-down, slightly dangerous neighbourhood has evolved into one of the most interesting, multicultural, young and happening parts of the city.

Porte de Bourgogne [59 G6] (Place de Bir Hakeim) This Roman-style arch was built by Tourny in 1755 to honour a visit by the Duke de Bourgogne. It marks the ceremonial entrance to the city, where visitors from Paris were wont to cross the Garonne, although money ran out before it could be festooned with statuary. In 1842 the Garonne ferry was replaced with the **Pont de Pierre**, the oldest of Bordeaux's bridges, and prettily lit at night by a necklace of streetlamps. The arch itself is bathed in coloured light.

Basilique St-Michel [59 G7] (Place Maynard; 📞 05 56 94 30 50; 🕘 closed for restoration until 2026) Rue de la Fusterie, once lined with coopers' shops, leads from Porte Bourgogne to this Flamboyant Gothic church, a product of Bordeaux's medieval prosperity, largely built by the city's guilds on the docks where wood and other goods were unloaded from the flat-bottomed *gabarres*. Inside, the chapels furnished by the guilds contain the best art: the Chapelle Ste-Ursule in the right aisle has a rare 15th-century sculpture of St Ursula and the 11,000 Virgins (she also shelters a pope, emperor and several prelates under her cloak); in the left aisle, the Chapelle de St-Sépulchre contains a beautiful *Descent from the Cross* (1492); the Chapelle Notre-Dame has a Flemish painting of the *Annunciation* (1500); and the Chapelle St-Joseph has nine Renaissance alabaster bas-reliefs. In 1994 these, much to Bordeaux's surprise and embarrassment, were discovered for sale at an auction in New York; ten years earlier, thieves had made off with them, unnoticed after replacing them with shoddy plaster copies. Its hexagonal bell tower, the 'arrow' or **Flèche** (1472–92), shoots up 114m, the second-highest in France. It was financed in part by Louis XI, a devotee of the archangel Michael, and over-restored in the 19th century by Abadie. Beneath the tower lies a once-celebrated crypt where Victor

Hugo and other tourists came to gape at the 70 naturally mummified bodies ('the family poisoned by mushrooms' and so on) put on display until 1990.

Grosse Cloche [59 E7] (1 Rue St-James; 05 56 00 66 00) Rue St-James has been bustling since the Middle Ages – this was the road to Compostela – and the 14th-century gate that straddles it is hung with an 18th-century bell named Armande-Louise, which weighs 7.8 tonnes and chimes out deep reverberations through the streets at noon on the first Sunday of each month and at 11.00 on Bastille Day. Built next to and dwarfing the little Romanesque chapel of **St-Eloi** [59 E7], this gate was part of the second wall built by the English (hence the golden leopard); once adorned with six towers, it figures on the city's coat of arms.

Musée d'Aquitaine [58 D7] (20 Cours Pasteur; 05 56 01 51 00; w musee-aquitaine-bordeaux.fr; 11.00–18.00 Tue–Sun; €5/€3, under 18 free; free 1st Sun of each month exc Jul–Aug) Although from the outside it looks like a hard slog, don't be deterred: this is one of the most compelling museums in southwest France. Its subject is the history of Aquitaine, and one of its first works is the unique, 25,000-year-old bas-relief of the *Venus with a Horn* from Laussel in the Dordogne. The horn she holds curves like the moon, her hair is coiffed in 'corn rows' and her outline, even after all the millennia, still bears traces of red ochre. Another evocative, if less clearly defined, relief has two figures holding hands, one above the other, their arms forming the shape of an egg.

The excellent Gallo-Roman section has a Celtic treasure of old coins and a torque from Tayac and 4,000 coins from the time of Claudius found in the Garonne, as well as mosaics, sculptures (note the fragment of a highly stylised relief of horses pounding through water) and a fascinating set of reliefs from everyday life in ancient Burdigala. Ironically, it's the funerary steles that really bring the dead to life: thin-faced Tatiana gazing at eternity with a wry look and wrinkled brow, and the delightful child Laetus, clutching a kitten the way toddlers do, while a rooster at his feet nips at the kitten's dangling tail.

Further on is a legless but still impressive life-size bronze Hercules, and a room dedicated to finds from a Mithraeum discovered under Cours Victor-Hugo. In the 2nd and 3rd centuries AD Mithraism, an all-male, monotheistic religion from the East, posed serious competition to Christianity. A small statue shows the birth of Mithras, rising from earth with the cosmic globe in one hand and a knife to slay bulls in the other; there are statues of Cautes and Cautopatès, his two companions, in Persian costumes, and a rare Leontocéphale, a lion-headed man holding keys, his legs entwined with chicken-headed snakes.

Beyond the Early Christian sarcophagi and mosaics are a few strange 11th-century capitals from the Abbaye de La Sauve-Majeure and from La Brède, along with English alabasters, which the Bordelais traded for wine. Montaigne's cenotaph with its Greek inscription stands among the section devoted to French rule. Upstairs are rooms devoted to Aquitaine's last 300 years: its agriculture, industries, port and wine, with the copy of a letter from Thomas Jefferson to the Count of Lur-Saluces praising his Sauternes – and a letter from Ronald Reagan to the count's descendant, thanking him for hosting a banquet celebrating the bicentennial of the Battle of Yorktown. A new permanent exhibit covers the city's shameful role in the triangular slave trade – Bordeaux's merchants sent more than 480 expeditions to Africa.

One branch of the building holds the **Musée Goupil** (05 56 01 69 42; by appt only) with photos and engravings from the archives (1827–1920) of the Parisian printer and editor Goupil.

Grande Synagogue de Bordeaux [55 D5] (6 Rue du Grand Rabin Joseph Cohen; ☎ 05 56 91 79 39; w communautejuiveaquitaine.fr; ⊕ 14.00–17.00 Mon–Thu, book a guided tour 72hrs in advance online; €5/€3) This is one of the most beautiful synagogues in France, built in 1882 in an eclectic neo-Gothic style; the Nazis converted it into a prison, but two decades of renovations have returned it to its former glory.

Place de la Victoire One of the liveliest squares in Bordeaux occupies the south end of busy, pedestrian-only Rue Ste-Catherine, Bordeaux's main shopping street since Roman times. The gate, the **Porte d'Aquitaine** [55 D6] (1753), guarded by a pair of sea gods, now has a second monument to keep it company – a 16m obelisk made of blocks of red marble dedicated to wine and winemakers. Fans of Art Deco might like to stroll briefly from Place de la Victoire up Cours Aristide Briand to see the **Bourse du Travail** (1934–38) [55 D5], commissioned by Bordeaux's socialist mayor later turned collaborator Adrien Marquet.

Ste-Croix [55 F6] (Place Pierre Renaudel; ☎ 05 56 94 30 50; ⊕ 10.00–18.00 Mon–Fri) In Merovingian times, a Benedictine abbey was built by a stream called the Eau Bourde. Destroyed by the Arabs in AD730 and then by the Vikings, Ste-Croix was rebuilt beginning in the 10th century. Its exuberant Old Curiosity Shop of a façade was entrusted in 1860 to Paul Abadie (page 147) who added a new north tower. The south tower, portal, figures of Avarice, Lust and Luxury and some carved capitals in the transept survived the Abadie touch; the relics in the parish chapel were reputed in the Middle Ages to cure madness. Note the unusual 15th-century crucifix with a 'bald Christ', and the curious Last Supper on the altar. The monastery of 1672 now houses the École des Beaux Arts, while nearby along the Quai Ste-Croix, a monster bunker from the 1980s housing the Jacques Thibaud music conservatory proves that Abadie had no patent on dubious taste.

Passerelle Eiffel and around [55 G5] This metal railway bridge (1858–60) made the reputation of its 26-year-old chief engineer, Gustave Eiffel, who came up with the idea of using the Triger Process (invented in 1840 by Jacques Triger for mines) for sinking the piles for the bridge. He would later use the same process for the tower that bears his name. Replaced by a wider bridge for TGVs in 2008, plans are to make it accessible to pedestrians and cyclists as part of the **Quartier Euroatlantique** project to revitalise the 738ha around the station. First to be completed here is the bright white **Méca** [55 G6] (Quai de Paludate; ☎ 05 47 30 34 67; w la-meca.com; ⊕ 13.00–18.30 Tue–Sat), an arch-shaped cultural centre designed by BIG of Copenhagen, dedicated to cinema, literature, contemporary art and spectacles; it also has a café-restaurant (**€€**).

ST-SEURIN AND THE GARDENS This is a peaceful and prosperous residential neighbourhood, where Christianity began in Bordeaux. The atmosphere was rather different in the past; Flaubert described the hanky-panky that used to go on, even in his time, in front of the basilica in the Allées d'Amour (renamed Place des Martyrs-de-la-Résistance in 1946).

Basilique St-Seurin [54 C4] (⊕ 08.00–noon & 14.00–18.30 daily) Bordeaux's oldest church, dedicated to its 4th-century bishop Severinus (Seurin), still stands, although often rebuilt, notably after the Vikings destroyed it in the 9th century. The site of a famous Gallo-Roman-Merovingian cemetery, it is full of wonderfully

AUSONIUS

Near St-Seurin was the Pagus Novarus, city address of Decimus Magnus Ausonius (circa AD310–94), scion of one of Burdigala's noblest families. After his studies in Toulouse, Ausonius returned to Bordeaux as a professor of rhetoric, with such a reputation that he was appointed tutor of Gratian, son of Emperor Valentinian; Emperor Gratian in turn appointed him prefect of Gaul (AD377). A familiar of St Ambrose of Milan and Emperor Theodosius, Ausonius managed to live blithely through the golden twilight of the Roman Empire, in a choice of villas sprinkled across the Gironde, where he could hunt, fish, make wine and write elaborate, exceedingly bland poetry. His surviving letters to his disciple, the poet-saint Paulinus de Nola, are more illuminating than his verse; the two broke their long friendship towards the end of Ausonius's life, when Paulinus rejected his master's conviction that the new religion could be reconciled with the Olympian muses and the sweet, soft, worldly life he loved. It's perhaps fitting that his greatest claim to fame these days is in the name of St-Émilion's top wines, produced on one of his old estates (page 132).

murky stories: they say two even earlier churches stood here, one built by Martial, a follower of St Peter, apostle of Gaul and patron saint of Aquitaine, and one founded by St Veronica (page 91). She was buried here, along with her convert Benedicta and St Martial, whose miraculous staff would be carried in a procession around Bordeaux every year.

That's not all. They say some of Roland's paladins slain at Roncesvalles were buried here (Roland himself was buried at Blaye; page 138). The great medieval poem *Chanson de Roland* records how Charlemagne laid on the altar Roland's great horn Oliphant (the same one that the hero blew so hard he blew out his brains), and filled it full of gold coins. For Compostela pilgrims from Britain, all these relics made St-Seurin their first stop after Soulac. The Dukes of Aquitaine would come here for their investiture, and come to pray and receive their weapons before going to war.

Although Oliphant sadly went missing in the 17th century, there are other things to see. Some original capitals on the west front are original, as is the Chapel of Notre-Dame-de-Bonne Nouvelle. A 7th-century sarcophagus does duty as an altar in the Chapelle St-Étienne, and there are beautiful 15th-century alabaster works: the *retable* in the Chapel of Notre-Dame-de-la-Rose with scenes on the life of the Virgin, and 14 marble panels in the choir on the lives of St Severinus and St Martial. There's a magnificent 15th-century episcopal throne, the Gothic pulpit and the sculpted choir stalls: try to find the fat man pushing his stomach in a wheelbarrow, and the man grilling tongues.

The 11th-century crypt has a fine collection of 6th- and 7th-century sarcophagi, medieval tiles, Merovingian plaques and the tomb of St Fort ('Saint Strong'), supposedly the first bishop of Bordeaux. Of all the famous saints buried here, he was believed to have the most sway: the Bordelais would bring their children to his tomb, circle it nine times and then sit them on top to make them strong by mystic osmosis; the mayors of Bordeaux, even Michel de Montaigne, came here to swear their oaths of office. Some say the key to the sea was down here next to the tomb, and in bad weather one could supposedly hear the cries of drowning mariners. Excavations underneath in 1910 revealed the 4th-century AD **necropolis** (€3.50), which goes back to the very origins of Christianity in Bordeaux.

Palais Gallien [54 C3] (Rue du Docteur Albert Barraud; ⌚ always) A monumental entrance and a few arches is all that remains of Burdigala's 20,000-seat amphitheatre which was built in the 3rd century AD. Its name comes from a tangled tale that Charlemagne built it as a palace for his wife, Galliene. Old engravings show that the arena remained fairly intact until the 18th century, a haunt of thieves and prostitutes and, supposedly, witches; during the Revolution it was used as a quarry and its walls were incorporated into the surrounding buildings which still trace its oval shape. It is especially romantic at night when the ruins are illuminated.

Muséum de Bordeaux [54 D3] (5 Place Bardineau; 05 56 48 29 86, **w** museum-bordeaux.fr; ⌚ Apr–Sep 10.30–18.00 Tue–Sun, Oct–Mar until 17.30; €5 or €7 with special exhibitions, ages 6–18 €3, free 1st Sun of the month) After years of restoration, this natural history museum in a *hôtel particulier* of 1778 has reopened, with the skeleton of a blue whale hanging from the ceiling plus stuffed animals from around the world, an important collection of Quaternary fossils, and plenty of things for young children to do and see.

Jardin Public [54 D3] (⌚ 07.00–21.00 daily, winter until 18.00) In 1745, Tourny laid out a promenade, now the Allées de Tourny, to give the Bordelais a place to stroll under the lindens; the houses were limited to two storeys to allow cannonballs from Château Trompette to fly over them. In 1756, Tourny added the city's first park: 'In a commercial city,' he explained, 'one must look at such public gardens as very useful, where merchants, often meeting one another there, transact much business. It is like having a second Exchange.' Originally laid out by Jacques-Ange Gabriel with all the perspectives of a *jardin à la française*, it was destroyed by Napoleon's troops. When replanted in 1856, the garden was redesigned in the romantic *style anglais* popularised by Napoleon III, who spent his early years in exile in London. It makes for a delightful wander: on sunny Sundays, expect to see half of Bordeaux here. It has everything a French garden should have: a Jardin Botanique, Grand Guignol at the marionette theatre, a historic merry-go-round, and the chance to take a boat ride on the lake.

Petit Hôtel Labottière [54 C3] (13 Rue St-Laurent; 05 56 94 12 56; **w** hotellabottiere.com; ⌚ guided tours only (see website for times) with a glass of wine or champagne at the end; €10/€5) This is your chance to get inside a beautiful listed *hôtel particulier* from the 1780s and check out its contemporary art exhibits.

Bernard Magrez Cultural Institute [3x C3] (16 Rue de Tivoli; **m** 06 72 40 50 02; **w** institut-bernard-magrez.com; ⌚ 13.00–18.00 Fri–Sun; €8/€6, under 12 free) A 15-minute walk northwest of the Jardin Public, this extremely grand 18th-century *hôtel particulier* is owned by wine magnate Bernard Magrez and hosts both artists in residence and exhibitions three times a year, as well as concerts and other events.

THE CHARTRONS AND BACALAN In 1383, Carthusians chased out of Périgord found refuge in the swamp north of Bordeaux's walls and drained the land, then went home in 1446, leaving behind a few monks and their name. For centuries afterwards the presence of the massive Château Trompette kept the Chartrons apart from the rest of Bordeaux, and in the 17th century Flemish wine merchants (then known as *courtiers*), feeling discriminated against by the pro-English *jurats*, set up their own business and quay here. They were soon followed by German,

Dutch and Irish traders, and then the English, creating an independent town of foreign *negociants*, or wine merchants, where they stored and loaded barrels of wine on ships.

The most successful of these merchants, brokers and shippers bought their own vineyards, founding fabulously wealthy wine dynasties, the *aristocratie de bouchon*. Their closed social circle – the source of Bordeaux's old reputation for snobbery and affected mannerisms – first suffered in 1685 with the Revocation of the Edict of Nantes. This sent the Protestants among them abroad, although many of them kept up their commercial ties with Bordeaux and helped enlarge the market for Bordeaux wine wherever they went.

The decline of the Chartrons began with the Revolution, when most of the lucky wine barons who were not guillotined moved abroad. Under Napoleon, commerce came to a standstill – for 30 years the Chartrons lived only by fitting out corsairs. Although its commerce revived, it was never the same. If in the 1950s the brokers still had their offices along the quay, by the 1960s the switch to land transport of wine made even this vestige of the past irrelevant. Today the Chartrons is one of the city's smartest addresses, with a charming village atmosphere, while downriver in Bacalan you'll find the Bassin à Flots, the 19th-century port and new attractions, including the city's pride and joy, the Cité du Vin.

CAPC (Centre d'Arts Plastiques Contemporains) [54 E3] (7 Rue Ferrère; 05 56 00 81 50; w capc-bordeaux.fr; 11.00–18.00 Mon–Tue, Thu–Sun, 11.00–20.00 Wed; €7/€4) Founded in 1973, Bordeaux's contemporary art museum occupies the Entrepôt Lainé (1824), where spices and other goods imported from the colonies were unloaded. Its vast spaces are used for the giant-scale exhibitions and installations, but only four pieces – by Christian Boltanski, Keith Haring, Richard Long and Max Neuhaus – are on permanent display. The same building contains the **Arc en Rêve Centre d'Architecture** (05 56 52 78 36; w arcenreve.eu; same hours; €5/€3, under 18 free, free 1st Sun of month exc Jul–Aug), dedicated to architecture, landscape, design and urban development.

The snobbiest of the Chartrons' nobility lived just north of here on the Pavé des Chartrons (now **Cours Xavier Arnozan**), paved (one of the first in Bordeaux) by Tourny and planted with trees to draw in the élite. Where it meets the quay stands the **Hôtel Fenwick** [54 E3], built in 1790 for Joseph Fenwick, who combined his duties as the first American consul in Bordeaux with his mercantile activities – represented in the ship's-prow decoration.

St-Louis des Chartrons [54 E3] (51 Rue Notre-Dame; w saintlouisdebordeaux.fr; 09.00–19.00 daily) This neo-Gothic church of 1879 with its many Irish and Flemish parishioners was nicknamed the 'Foreigners' Church' by the Bordelais; its Wenner & Gotty organ of 1881 is said to be the finest in the region. Behind the church, in Place du Marché des Chartrons, the handsome octagonal **Halle des Chartrons** (1869) is now a cultural centre.

Musée du Vin et du Négoce [54 E2] (41 Rue Borie; 05 56 90 19 13; w museeduvinbordeaux.com; 10.00–18.00 Fri–Wed; €10 with tasting of 2 wines, students €5, under 18 free) The old wine trade is remembered in the *hôtel particulier* of Irish broker Francis Burke (1720), with a collection of lithographed wine labels and bottles going back to the 1600s. You can also learn about the once renowned '*retour des îles*' wines – in the old days, brokers would load Caribbean-bound ships with 900-litre casks of the finest *crus*, accompanied by a vintner to keep an eye on the evaporation and top up the casks when necessary. This precious cargo was not for the colonies, however; when the ship arrived in the Antilles, wine and vintner stayed on board, and sailed straight back to Bordeaux. The journey improved the wine so much that *Bordeaux retour des îles* commanded a premium price in Parisian restaurants. When steamers took over the route, it was found that the wine didn't improve at all; the secret had been the gentle rolling motion of a sailing ship, and *retour*, as it was known by its lovers, went the way of the dodo – although Château le Puy (w chateau-le-puy.com) has restarted the tradition.

Cap Sciences [54 F2] (Hangar 20, Quai Bacalan; 05 56 01 07 07; w cap-sciences.net; 14.00–18.00 Tue–Fri, 14.00–19.00 Sat–Sun; €9/€6.50, under 5 free, planetarium and other experiences are extra) This exhibition centre aims to bring scientific subjects home to the public and introduce new scientific innovations and techniques, through a changing programme of exhibitions and themes. It's great for even three- to five-year-olds, but probably best if you or they can speak some French.

Bassins de Lumières [map, page 48] (Impasse Brown de Colstoun (Tram C to Ravezies, then bus 9; in summer there's a shuttle from the tourist office); 05 35 00 00 90; w bassins-lumieres.com; daily, book a time slot online; €13.50, over 65 €12.50, ages 5–25 €9, under 5 free) Since the war, the docks along Boulevard Alfred Daney in the Bassins à Flot port were disfigured by the German and Italian submarine base, the southernmost of the five they built along France's Atlantic Wall: a vast indestructible concrete bunker with 5m-thick walls, with 11 pens for U-Boats and Italian submarines, each 100m long, built by Spanish, French, Russian and Vietnamese prisoners of war. Since it would take forever to remove the monster, Bordeaux has converted it into the world's largest digital art museum, offering a mesmerising 3D full immersion into art, featuring annually changing exhibitions.

Vaisseau spatial [54 F1] (In the middle of the Bassins à Flot) Yes, it's what it looks like: a flying saucer, a 9.9-tonne sculpture made from two World War II shipwrecks by British artist Suzanne Treister that arrived in 2018 and seems ready to plunge into the drink.

Musée Mer Marine [54 F1] (89 Rue des Étrangers; 05 57 19 77 73; w mmmbordeaux.com; 10.30–19.00 Sat–Sun & hols; €14, students €11, ages 6–17 €10). This vast new museum, dedicated to ships, sailors and their art sits on the edge of the Bassins à Flot: there are all kinds of ship models, displays on the history of navigation and real ships (including the *Défi Français* yacht from the America's Cup, which was later bought by China) plus a section on oceanography and current ocean explorations and special exhibitions.

La Cité du Vin [54 G1] (134 Quai Bacalan; 05 56 16 20 20; w laciteduvin.com; Apr–Jun 09.30–19.00, Jul–Aug 09.30–19.30 daily, Sep–Mar 10.00–18.00 Mon–Fri, 10.00–19.00 Sat–Sun; €21, under 17 with their family €9, under 6 free) Opened in June 2016, the city's latest marvel features 3,000m^2 dedicated to the world's wine regions. Designed by XTU architects Anouk Legendre and Nicolas Desmazières, it's an architectural *tour de force* that swirls like a taster's glass of wine, packed full of clever, high-tech interactive experiences, from 3D films of the world's winemaking techniques to a tasting room that engages four of your five senses in the wine-drinking experience so that by the time you reach the eighth-floor Belvédère, your complimentary glass of the real stuff will taste extra good. There's grape juice for the kids.

The bridge here, the **Pont Jacques Chaban Delmas** [54 G2] (built in 2013) with its four tall towers, is one of the largest vertical-lift bridges in Europe – if a cruise ship is drawing near, stay to watch it lift the road high overhead in only 10 minutes.

Quartier du Lac [map, page 48] To the west the last swamps of the Chartrons were drained in 1960 into a lake, where Bordeaux's fair buildings, congress centre, casino, golf courses and recreational facilities await, all in easy reach of the A630.

BORDEAUX'S RIGHT BANK Not so long ago the only real reason for crossing over the Garonne into the Bastide district was to see the views back towards the famous façade.

Darwin Éco-Système [54 F3] (87 Quais de Queyries; w darwin.camp) 'Coming here is like coming to the future' according to its founder, Philippe Barre. This mini village in a military barracks abandoned in 2015 is an experiment in sustainable development, with co-working spaces designed to nourish entrepreneurs in a new green economy. Everything is recuperated, recycled and greener than green. The main hall is covered with a sculpture of wood and neon called the *Vortex*. Admire the street art, listen to a concert, watch the kids fly in the skate park, and shop and eat organically at the Magasin Général (page 62), part of Europe's largest organic store.

Jardin Botanique de la Bastide [54 F4] (Esplanade Linné; 05 56 52 18 77; w jardin-botanique-bordeaux.fr; 11.00–18.00 Tue–Sun; free) This new branch of Bordeaux's botanical gardens was created in 1997 in the Bastide quarter, with lovely views back across to Place de la Bourse. There are several different environments, including water plants, orchards, an arboretum, a vertical garden, greenhouses and special exhibitions.

4

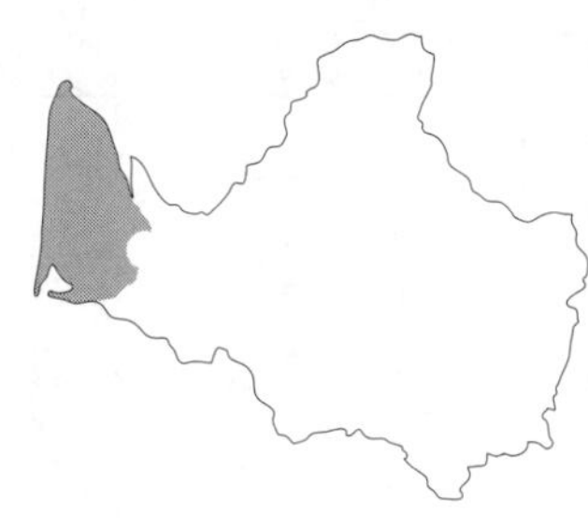

The Médoc, Côte d'Argent and Bassin d'Arcachon

The Médoc today is synonymous with some of the world's finest and priciest wines, but this triangle of land north of Bordeaux, between Europe's largest estuary and the Atlantic was the back of beyond for centuries, '*solitaire et sauvage*' in the words of the poet La Boétie, after a visit in the mid 16th century. The fortress towns Bourg and Blaye grew up on the right bank (page 135) but not here on the left bank, where much of the land was covered in pines and salt marshes. In the late 17th century, however, canny Dutch merchants, wanting to compete with the port, Madeira and malmsey that the wealthy English were buying, recognised the Médoc's wine-growing potential and had the technology to drain the marshes.

The west side of the Médoc triangle is Bordeaux's playground. From the mouth of the Gironde down to the Bassin d'Arcachon, the Côte d'Argent boasts beaches, dunes and lakes where you can surf, paraglide, sail and practise just about every watersport imaginable, and visit some of France's most important wetlands, landscapes still as *solitaire et sauvage* as they were in La Boétie's day. In 2019 this unique environment of lakes, estuary, islands, coast, marshes, pines and vines became the Parc Naturel Régional du Médoc, dedicated to promoting eco-friendly development. And it has its World Heritage Sites: Cordouan, the last inhabited lighthouse in France, and Soulac-sur-Mer's Notre-Dame at the World's End, traditional first stop for British pilgrims to Compostela.

But at the very southern tip of the Gironde, the coast surrenders to the oyster-filled mini-inland sea of the Bassin d'Arcachon, where wild nature and French seaside resort chic have been happily married for a century – sheltered by Europe's largest sand dune.

THE MÉDOC, ITS WINES AND CHÂTEAUX

When it comes to wine, Médoc means a flat ridge running along the left bank of Gironde, where the unusual depth of the gravel forces the vine roots to go deep in search of water and nourishment. The older the vine (ten years is the minimum age for a Médoc *cru*), the stronger and deeper the roots, and the greater its ability to withstand drought. Equally, in soggy years the perfect drainage of the gravel keeps the roots from getting waterlogged. Because the gravel absorbs heat during the day, damage from spring frosts can generally be avoided.

Climate, as always, is another important factor. The vast Gironde estuary regulates the temperature, protecting the Médoc from extremes (the great estates all 'see the water'), while the rains and winds off the Atlantic are tempered by the

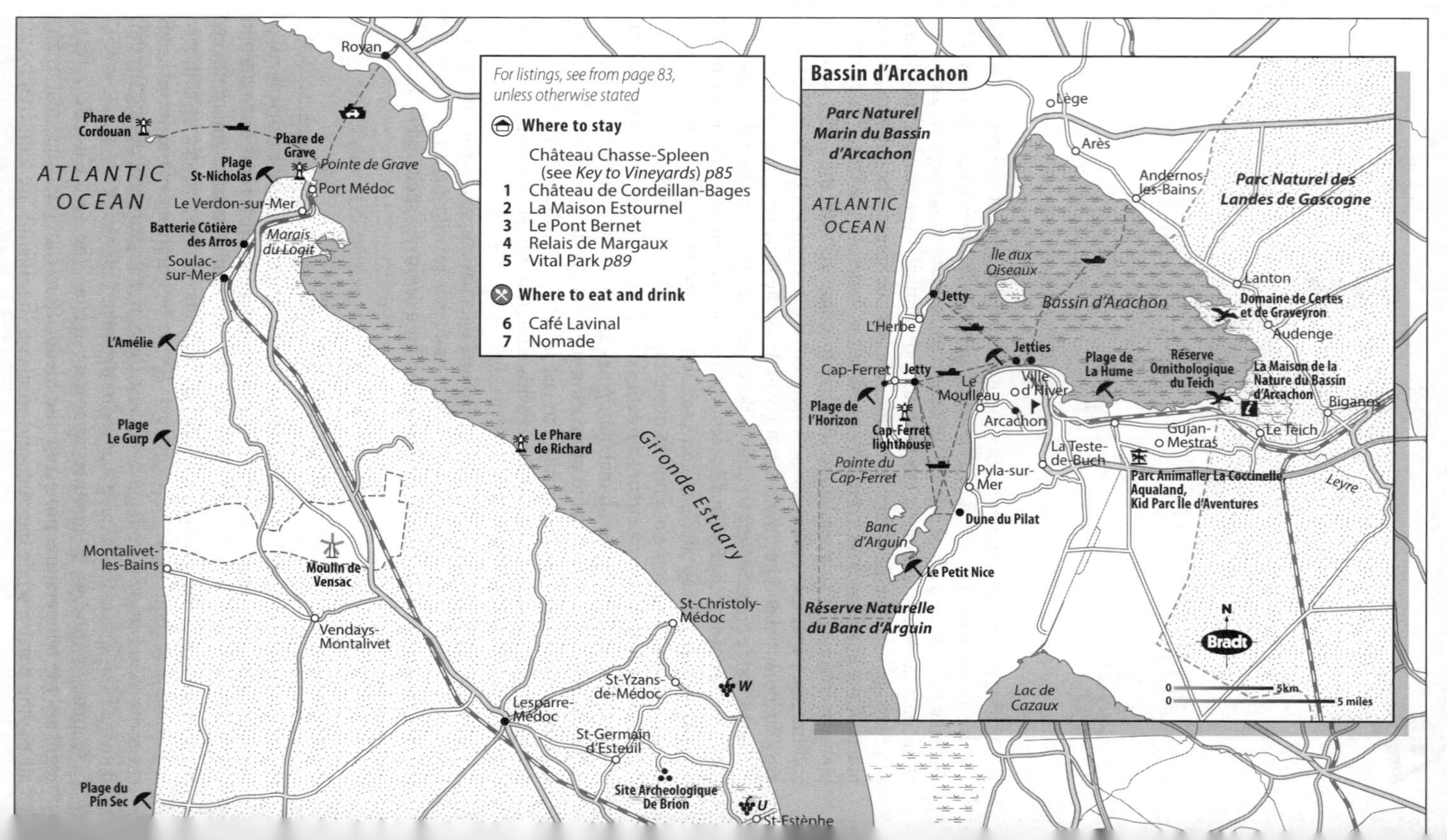

For listings, see from page 83, unless otherwise stated
Where to stay
Château Chasse-Spleen (see Key to Vineyards) p85
1 Château de Cordeillan-Bages
2 La Maison Estournel
3 Le Pont Bernet
4 Relais de Margaux
5 Vital Park p89
Where to eat and drink
6 Café Lavinal
7 Nomade
ATLANTIC OCEAN
Phare de Cordouan
Phare de Grave
Plage St-Nicholas
Pointe de Grave
Royan
Port Médoc
Le Verdon-sur-Mer
Batterie Côtière des Arros
Marais du Logit
Soulac-sur-Mer
L'Amélie
Plage Le Gurp
Le Phare de Richard
Gironde Estuary
Montalivet-les-Bains
Moulin de Vensac
Vendays-Montalivet
St-Christoly-Médoc
St-Yzans-de-Médoc
W
Lesparre-Médoc
St-Germain d'Esteuil
Site Archeologique De Brion
Plage du Pin Sec
U
St-Estèphe
Bassin d'Arcachon
Parc Naturel Marin du Bassin d'Arcachon
ATLANTIC OCEAN
Lège
Arès
Andernos-les-Bains
Parc Naturel des Landes de Gascogne
Île aux Oiseaux
Bassin d'Arachon
Lanton
Domaine de Certes et de Graveyron
Audenge
Jetty
L'Herbe
Jetties
Cap-Ferret
Jetty
Le Moulleau
Ville d'Hiver
Plage de La Hume
Réserve Ornithologique du Teich
La Maison de la Nature du Bassin d'Arcachon
Biganos
Plage de l'Horizon
Cap-Ferret lighthouse
Arcachon
Gujan-Mestras
Le Teich
La Teste-de-Buch
Pointe du Cap-Ferret
Pyla-sur-Mer
Parc Animalier La Coccinelle, Aqualand, Kid Parc Île d'Aventures
Leyre
Dune du Pilat
Banc d'Arguin
Le Petit Nice
Réserve Naturelle du Banc d'Arguin
N
Bradt
Lac de Cazaux
0 5km
0 5 miles

THE MÉDOC, COTE D'ARGENT AND BASSIN D'ARCACHON

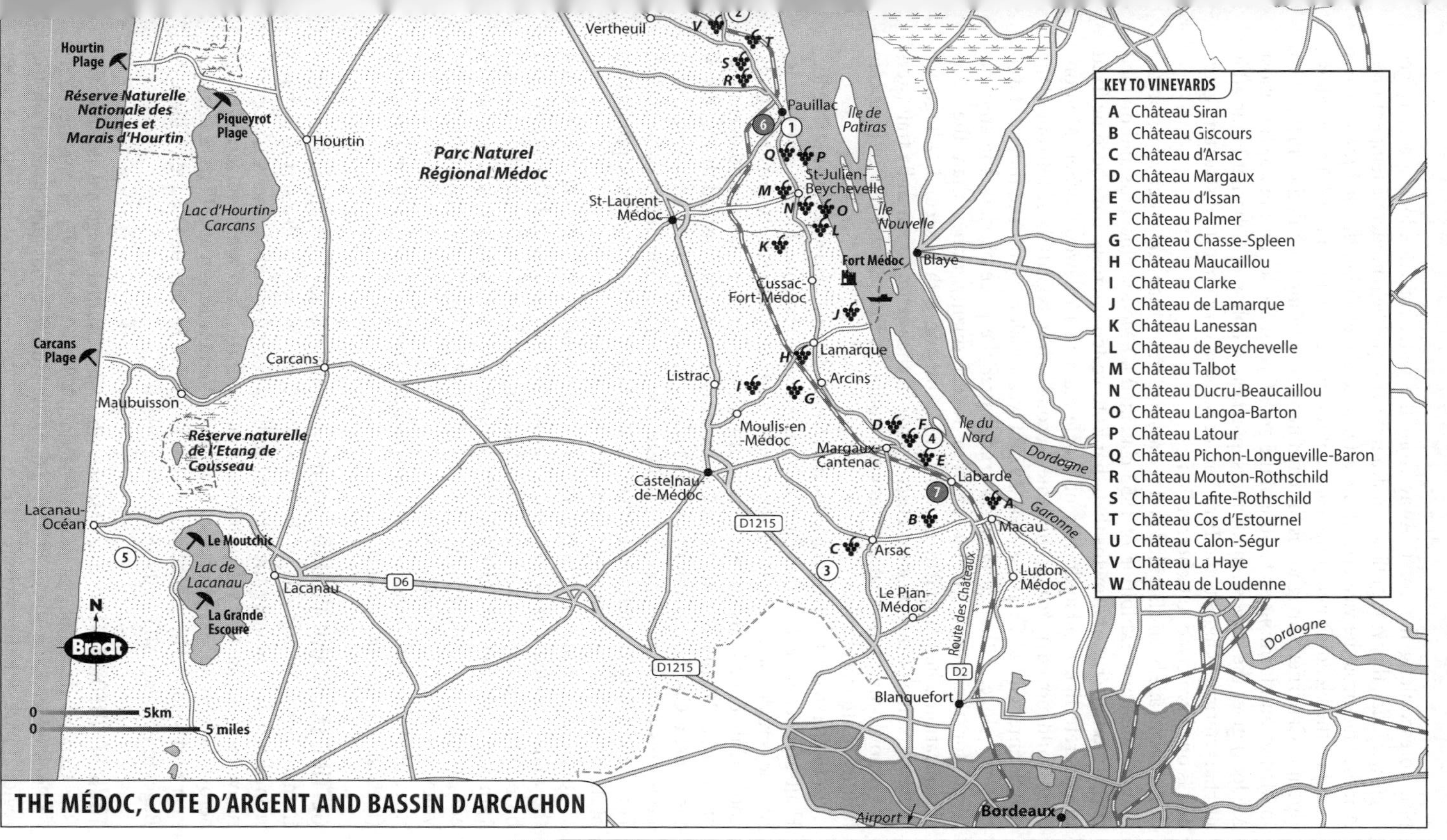

pine forests along the coast. Away from the waterfront, Médoc's gravel ridges overlook *jalles*, the wide gullies that drain the soil and help moderate temperatures. Another factor is the vast size of the estates here – enabling the *maîtres des chais* to adjust the blending and proportions of the grape varieties on each parcel. Slow-ripening Cabernet Sauvignon is the chief here, accounting for half the vines grown in Médoc, and forming up to 80% of the *grands crus*; Merlot (around 35% of most Médocs) gives the wine strength and suppleness; a dollop of Cabernet Franc adds its characteristic bouquet; and Petit Verdot is also a very important structure grape and is often preferred to Cabernet Franc.

Médocs have been classified and reclassified more than any other wines on the planet. The Paris Exhibition of 1855 classified 60 Médoc vineyards and divided them into five *crus* or growths that, thanks to vested interests, have become fixed in concrete like the handprints of movie stars in Hollywood; when Mouton-Rothschild moved up from Deuxième ('second') Grands Cru Classé into one of the five Premier Grand Cru Classés in 1973 it was a major event. And they've stayed that way since. Although *premiers crus* shatter the price barriers, the amounts asked for the other growths tend to reflect quality rather than the 1855 classifications; hence fourth growths may cost more than second. Altogether these are some of the most expensive wines in the world, so naturally fraudsters have moved in; many châteaux now put codes on the seals so you authenticate bottles on their websites.

In 1932, estates in the eight Médoc *appellations* left out of the 1855 rating (Médoc, Haut-Médoc, Saint-Estèphe, Pauillac, Saint-Julien, Margaux, Moulis and Listrac-Médoc) created a syndicate of their own, the Cru Bourgeois (w crus-bourgeois.com). Unlike the Paris ratings, Cru Bourgeois rules have been tweaked over time, and as of 2010, the label no longer designates a château but instead the quality of the wine; a Cru Grand Bourgeois has to be aged in wooden casks; a Cru Grand Bourgeois Exceptionnel has to be château-bottled in a commune of Haut-Médoc. For all the fussiness, there's more than enough to go around: the average production of the whole Médoc area is 112 million bottles a year.

You don't have to go far from Bordeaux to find wine legends: the D2 – nicknamed the *route des châteaux* – into the Haut-Médoc (the southern half) begins just beyond the northern suburbs of Bordeaux. These châteaux date from the 18th and 19th centuries, even though resident proprietors are increasingly rare; corporations and foreign consortiums have bought up some of the most prestigious Médoc vineyards, although foreign ownership is nothing new here – in the 18th century three of the finest châteaux belonged to Irishmen named Kirwan, Dillon and Lynch (the last was once mayor of Bordeaux).

GETTING THERE AND AROUND **TER trains** from Bordeaux to Point-de-Grave stop in many of the Médoc villages, including Pauillac. The area is also served by **buses** from Bordeaux, notably the 705 to Pauillac. For possibilities, see w transports.nouvelle-aquitaine.fr. If you're driving from the north, there are useful **ferries** (*bacs*) across the Gironde (w gironde.fr/bacs) at Le Verdon-Royan and Blaye-Lamarque near Fort Médoc. Hire a **bike** or e-bike at Fun Bike (Passage de Desquet, Village de Bages in Pauillac; 05 56 09 76 62; w funbike.fr).

TOURIST INFORMATION The **Maison du Parc Naturel Régional Médoc** (21 Rue Général de Gaulle, St-Laurent-Médoc; 05 57 75 18 92; w pnr-medoc.fr; f PnrMedoc; 08.30–13.20 & 14.00–17.30 Mon–Fri) has information on the regional park; another website (w medoc-tourisme.com/en), in English, has more information on trails and other activities in the area. Stop at the **Maison du Tourisme et du Vin du Médoc** (La Verrerie, Pauillac; 05 56 59 03 08; w medocvignoble.com; 09.30–19.00 Mon–Sat, 10.00–13.00 & 14.00–18.30 Sun) to find out which châteaux are open for visits, tasting courses and to shop for more than 300 wines from all the Médoc *appellations*, at château prices.

WHERE TO STAY *Map, page 80*

Château de Cordeillan-Bages (28 rooms) Rte des Châteaux, Pauillac; 05 56 59 24 24; w cordeillanbages.com. Set in a sea of vineyards, this lovely place in a 17th-century villa has a heated pool, library & a superb restaurant (€€€€€), where the best local ingredients are enhanced without muss or fuss. Even for a restaurant that tends to be patronised by wine merchants, the choice from among 1,800 bottles in the cellar is astounding. **€€€€€**

La Maison Estournel (14 rooms) Rte de Poumeys, St-Estèphe; 05 56 59 30 25; w egustat-estournel.com. In the 18th-century residence of Louis-Gaspard d'Estournel of Cos d'Estournel (page 87), cushy designer rooms with solid oak floors & a very smart restaurant with a gorgeous terrace (€€€€€) right on the estuary. B/fast inc. **€€€€€**

Relais de Margaux (100 rooms) Chemin de l'Ile Vincent, Margaux; 05 57 88 38 30; w relais-margaux.fr. Where Médoc buyers go to swan around & deduct it all as a business expense. Set in a 55ha park with spa, & an indoor pool, lush gardens, 18-hole golf course, lakeside brasserie & restaurant (€€€); the bedrooms are flowery in a sweet retro way. **€€€€€**

La Maison du Douanier (4 rooms) 2 Rte de By, St-Christoly-Médoc; 05 56 41 35 25; w lamaisondudouanier.com. Situated in a quiet village northeast of Blaignan, this is a big house surrounded by buddleia & other flowering shrubs, where swifts fly in & out of the eaves. From Jun to Sep they run the wooden **La Cabane** (€€€) restaurant, with seafood & vegan choices. B/fast inc. **€€€€**

Hôtel de France et d'Angleterre (45 rooms) 3 Quai Albert de Pichon, Pauillac; 05 56 59 01 20; w hoteldefrance-angleterre.com. Pleasant riverside rooms in a pretty building, near stands selling *bichettes*, little shrimps lightly flavoured with aniseed. The excellent restaurant (€€€) specialises in game dishes. **€€€**

Le Pont Bernet (18 rooms) 1160 Rte de Soulac, Le Pian-Médoc; 05 56 70 20 19; w pont-bernet.fr. Simple, quiet rooms in an inn dating from 1896 in 6ha of grounds, with tennis & a pool. The restaurant (€€) in a garden setting is excellent, & has an award-winning sommelier, & set lunches from €11. **€€**

WHERE TO EAT AND DRINK

In the old days, one of the spin-offs of winemaking in the Médoc was suckling lamb, when vineyards used sheep to keep the weeds down. Lambs, because they bounced around too much and damaged the vines, were confined to the sheepfold and fed only their mother's milk until they were slaughtered two months later. Their pearly meat was a delicacy that died out when chemical herbicides stole the sheep's job. Since 1985, however, *agneau de Pauillac* has made something of a comeback in local butchers' shops and on restaurant menus. From November to March the prize catch is the endangered elver, or *pibale*, the baby eels, only 5cm long, a delicacy that can demand as much as €400 per kilo; although fishing for the 'white gold' is strictly regulated in France, such enormous sums increasingly attract poachers.

Au Marquis de Terme 3 Rte de Rauzan, Margaux; 05 57 08 25 33; w au-marquis-de-terme.com; closed eves Tue, Wed, Sun. At the elegant Château Marquis de Terme, Chef Grégory Coutanceau's menu reads simply 'Foie Gras', 'Trout' & 'Beef', but what he does with them is pretty wonderful. *W/day lunch menu €25, other menus €39–€70.* **€€€€€**

Café Lavinal [map, page 80] Passage du Desquet, Pauillac; 05 57 75 00 09; w jmcazes.com/en/café-lavinal; closed lunch Mon. Retro-style brasserie next to the Château Lynch-Bages, serving French classics, but within range of most pockets. *W/day lunch €19; other menus from €29; much more à la carte.* €€€€€

Nomade 3 Rte des Châteaux, Labarde; 05 56 35 92 38; w restaurant-nomade.fr; closed Sun–Mon. Wonderful innovative cuisine from a young, well-travelled couple of locals, trained by legendary Michelin-starred chef Thierry Marx. *Lunch €35, dinner dégustation €70 – book at least 24hrs in advance as there are only 8 settings.* €€€€€

Le Savoie 1 Place Trémoille, Margaux; 05 57 88 31 76; w lesavoie.net; closed Sun–Mon. Welcoming & informal young team, serving French classics, big salads, seasonal dishes & gorgeous desserts. There's also a wine bar if you just want to taste the local elixir. *Lunch menu du marché €28.* €€€€€

Le Lion d'Or Place de la République, Arcins; 05 56 58 96 79; w leliondor-arcins.fr; closed Sun–Mon. Between Margaux & Pauillac, this is a gourmand landmark: look for nothing but Big Authentic Food & plenty of it. *Lunch menu €25.* €€€€

Le St-Julien 11 Rue St-Julien, St-Julien-Beychevelle; 05 56 59 63 87; w restaurant-le-saint-julien.com; closed Tue–Wed. Another culinary stop among the wine villages, Claude & Rosy Broussard's elegant restaurant in a historic building, with a garden terrace (& their own veg patch), offers an enticing selection of seafood, ravioli filled with truffles & the local lamb. *5 courses €55, 2 for €35.* €€€€

Le Bontemps 5 Place des Commerces, Cussac-Fort-Médoc; 09 83 02 14 16; f; lunch Mon–Fri, also dinner Fri. Creative organic dishes prepared in an open kitchen, run by a French–Japanese couple. *Lunch menu €22.* €€€

BORDEAUX TO MARGAUX All that wine has to go into barrels, many of which are supplied by one of the villages nearest Bordeaux. **Tonnellerie Nadalié** (99 Rue Lafont, Ludon-Médoc; 05 57 10 02 02; w nadalie.fr; for tours by appt mornings Mon–Fri; 90min tour with tasting €12.50) is a traditional family cooperage going back to 1902; the tour takes you through the barrel-making process (more complex than you might think) and explains how the oak influences the wine.

The first village of vinous renown is **Macau**, which also produces artichokes and has a little port, where the Bordelais come at weekends to gobble down *bichettes* (little shrimps). At **Labarde**, next north, the **Château Siran** (Av du Comté Lynch; 05 57 88 34 04; w chateausiran.com; tours & tastings from €12, under 16 free) and its ample *chais* contain some of Margaux's finest Cru Bourgeois Exceptionnels – the very best is stocked in a nuclear fallout shelter (head there if the sirens start to wail); the château, once owned by kin of Toulouse-Lautrec, also has an intriguing collection of wine things, from ancient bottles to Toby jugs. Siran's park is famous for its cyclamens that burst into bloom from late August to early October

Another highly rated vineyard in Labarde, the charming 19th-century neo-Renaissance **Château Giscours** (05 57 97 09 09; w chateau-giscours.com; Apr–Oct 09.30–17.30 daily, Nov–Mar 09.30–17.30 Mon–Fri; 2hr tours in English with tastings from €50, visits to park €6) has revived the *éco-pastoralisme* of old. You can order a picnic to enjoy in the pretty park planted in 1881 and visit the rare breeds of sheep, cows and goats on the organic farm.

Next along the road, in **Arsac**, the blue **Château d'Arsac** (Allée du Comte Arsac-en-Médoc; 05 56 58 83 90; w chateau-arsac.com; book a visit 10.00–14.30 Mon–Sat; grounds 09.00–17.00 Mon–Fri; from €10) is architecturally one of the most striking, beautifully landscaped with a lake. It was once owned by Montaigne's brother, when it was visited by La Boétie, who wrote 'You are at the end of the world, and I love you all the more for it.' The tour includes the colourful contemporary sculpture garden.

MARGAUX-CANTENAC Margaux is noted for the magnificent finesse and delicate perfume of its wines. The **Maison du Vin de Margaux** (Place La Trémoille; 05 57 88

70 82; w vins-de-margaux.fr; ⌚ 10.00–12.30 & 14.00–18.30 Mon–Fri, until 17.00 Sat) dispenses information and sells bottles at château prices. Its renowned Premier Grand Cru, produced by some of the Médoc's oldest vines, hails from the **Château Margaux** (☎05 57 88 83 83; w chateau-margaux.com; ⌚ book 1hr tour & tasting of their Pavillon Rouge 10.00–noon & 14.00–16.00 Mon–Fri; closed Aug & during the harvest; free), just outside the village. The neo-Palladian château, designed in 1802 by Louis Combes, a student of Victor Louis, is set in a pretty English garden.

While in the area, have a look at the early 17th-century **Château d'Issan** (☎05 57 88 35 91; w chateau-issan.com; ⌚ visits & tastings by appt Mon–Fri) set amid the moats of its medieval predecessor. 'For the tables of kings and the altars of the gods', reads the inscription on the gate; they claim their wines were served at the wedding of Eleanor of Aquitaine and Henri Plantagenet in 1152. The neighbouring **Château Palmer** (w chateau-palmer.com) came to Charles Parker, one of Wellington's generals, through marriage and was later purchased by the Pereire brothers (page 93) who built its neo-Renaissance château. Today Palmer is a leader in promoting biodiversity in Médoc, and its wine is often rated just under Château Margaux's.

MOULIS-EN-MÉDOC This charming village northwest of Margaux has an impressive 12th-century fortified Romanesque church, **St-Saturnin**, built reusing Gallo-Roman walls. It boasts an exceptional apse (carved modillions outside and capitals inside, one showing Tobias carrying a fish); the lofty holy water stoup built into the façade was made for the Black Prince to use when he rode into the church! The top wine here comes from the **Château Chasse-Spleen** [map, page 80] (32 Chemin de la Razé; ☎05 56 58 02 37; w chasse-spleen.com; ⌚ mid-Apr–Oct 10.00–13.00 & 14.00–18.00, other times by appt; €10, or €35 with lunch at their excellent wine bar), which earned its name after Byron commented that a glass of it chases away ill humours – although others say it owes its name to Odilon Redon, who often visited his parents next door, and who illustrated Baudelaire's *Fleurs du Mal*, where spleen has a starring role. The castle also offers three beautiful rooms (**€€€€€**) to stay in.

Just opposite the Moulis station, **Château Maucaillou** is dedicated not only to wine but to pulling out all the stops to initiate you into the cult of the 'blood of the vine' at their **Musée des Arts et Métiers de la Vigne et du Vin** (☎05 56 58 01 23; w chateau-maucaillou.com; museum ⌚ May–Sep 10.00–17.00 daily, Oct–Apr at 10.00, 11.00, 14.00, 15.00 & 16.00; €5, plus guided tours of the *chais* etc from €7).

LISTRAC Both Moulis and Listrac are distinguished by their powerful wines, although the fact that they don't 'see the water' prevented them from being classified in 1855; **Château Clarke**, named after the Irish family that built it in 1771 is one of the rising stars of Listrac, after it was entirely recreated from scratch in 1973 by Edmond de Rothschild. From Listrac, take the D5 down towards the Gironde to see the **Château de Lamarque**, this one a rare *château fort*, or castle, built in the 11th century by the cousin of Crusader Gaubert de Fumel – whose descendants still own it today – to defend Bordeaux from Vikings.

FORT MÉDOC (Cussac-Fort-Médoc; ☎05 56 58 98 40; w cussac-fort-medoc.fr; ⌚ May–Sep 10.00–19.00 daily, Apr & Oct 10.00–18.00, Feb–Mar & Nov 13.00–17.00 Sat–Sun; €5, ages 13–17 €3, ages 5–12 €1) Beginning in 1686, the defending job was taken over by this fort along with the Citadel at Blaye and the island Fort Pâté, the three making up the 'Verrou Vauban', the 'lock bolt' of the estuary (page 138). Fort Médoc was begun in 1689 and completed only in 1721, owing to the difficulty of building on marshland. Besides the heavily sculpted Porte Royale, complete with Louis's sun symbol, you can visit the chapel and museum dedicated to local customs, and take in the view across the estuary to the fort's sister citadels.

North of Fort Médoc, signposted off the D2, the eclectic neo-Tudor-Spanish **Château Lanessan** (1870) is the seat of a 350ha estate that has been in the same family since 1790. It has a lovely 7ha English park, garden and greenhouse, and in the stables a **Musée du Cheval** displaying an elegant collection of horse-drawn vehicles from yesteryear, saddles and other antique horsey gear (**** 05 56 58 94 80; **w** lanessan.com; ⌚ 10.00–18.00 daily for guided wine tours; museum €8, guided tours €8, €15 for both).

ST-JULIEN-BEYCHEVELLE St-Julien's wines are distinguished for their fruitiness, delicate bouquet and original character. The Duc d'Épernon, governor of Guyenne and admiral of France (page 119), inherited by marriage the next estate on the grand Médoc tour, which became known as the **Château de Beychevelle** (*becha vela* in Gascon; **** 05 56 73 38 01; **w** beychevelle.com; ⌚ 09.00–12.30 & 14.00–18.00 Mon–Fri; from €18; book ahead for tours & tastings) because every ship that passed in the estuary paid its respects by lowering its sails.

Nearby, the 110ha ivy-covered **Château Talbot** once belonged to John Talbot, Earl of Shrewsbury (page 134; **** 05 56 73 21 50; **w** chateau-talbot.com; tours by appt, from €15). The most distinctive châteaux here are the 18th-century **Château Ducru-Beaucaillou**, and the 18th-century **Château Langoa-Barton**, which unusually for Médoc has its *chais* directly under the château.

PAUILLAC Before settling into the comfortable position of 'capital of Médoc wines', with more Premiers Grands Crus Classés than any other commune, the sprawly town of Pauillac was an important port, and home to one of the oldest sailing clubs in France. Before the 1930s, when the estuary was dredged, steamers would call at the Île de Patiras in the Gironde, where passengers would be transferred to and from Bordeaux by smaller craft. It had to be rebuilt after the RAF and American air force blasted it in the war, killing 45 locals. Nowadays instead of steamers there's a marina, and views over the estuary to the silhouette of the Braud nuclear power plant.

But what people come to ponder at Pauillac is another source of power altogether: some of the most famous wine châteaux in France, where the purest gravelly depths produce full-bodied wines with a distinctive blackcurrant bouquet. For oenophiles, the tour of a Premier Grand Cru Classé must be the equivalent of obtaining a private audience with the pope, but is probably easier to arrange – just book a guided tour weeks in advance.

Approaching from the south, there's **Château Latour** (**w** chateau-latour.com; no visits), a Premier Grand Cru Classé that originally formed part of the same estate as Lafite (see opposite). Purchased for just over €110 million in 1993 by billionaire François Pinault, it has rarely failed to live up to its status. Next north, have a look at the most romantic château of them all, the witch-hat-towered 19th-century Deuxième Grand Cru Classé **Château Pichon-Longueville-Baron** (**w** pichonbaron.com), reflected in its mirror of water.

Just north of Pauillac, the neo-Tudor **Château Mouton-Rothschild** (**** 05 56 73 21 29; **w** chateau-mouton-rothschild.com; ⌚ 09.00–12.30 & 14.00–18.00 Mon–Fri; tours from €65) was bought by Baron Nathaniel de Rothschild in 1853 at an auction. Although he never visited it, he was devastated when it was not selected as a Premier Grand Cru Classé in 1855 – an omission corrected in 1973 (the only one, ever) thanks to the enthusiasm of his great grandson Baron Philippe de Rothschild, who took over the property in 1922 and made it his life's work until he died in 1988;

today it is run by his daughter Baroness Philippine and her three children. The tour takes in the new vat room (2012), the 'theatre of wine', the 100m hall of the Grand Chai, with 1,000 immaculate blond wood barrels lined up with military precision, and the château's collection of wine labels by famous artists (Dalí, Picasso and Warhol), a tradition begun by Baron Philippe in 1945. Perhaps because it belongs to the Rothschilds, the bank-vault atmosphere is unavoidable. The tour continues to a rich museum of art devoted to wine, **Le Vin dans l'Art** – in which the oldest pieces are from ancient Mesopotamia.

Cousins own the big Mouton's eternal rival, the 120ha Premier Grand Cru Classé **Château Lafite-Rothschild** (e visites@lafite.com; w lafite.com; ⌚ by appt, for a maximum of 15 people; ⌚ Nov–Jul 14.00 & 15.30 Mon–Fri; free), which broods over the Pauillac–Lesparre road. Only a tower survives of the medieval castle of the Lafite lords, while the present château dates from the 18th century when this was the most famous wine in France – thanks to the 'Wine Prince', the Marquis Nicolas Alexandre de Ségur, whose bottles were prized by Louis XV, London's élite and Thomas Jefferson, who visited the château when he was Ambassador to France, and became a customer for the rest of his life (one of his bottles from 1787 sold at auction for US$155,500 in 1986). After legendary vintages in the middle of the 19th century (it was declared the top wine at the 1853 Universal Exposition in Paris), it was purchased in 1868 by James de Rothschild, cousin of Nathaniel – who died three months later without ever seeing it, leaving his sons to take charge. Lafite fell on hard times in the first half of the 20th century (the Nazis confiscated both Rothschild estates and raided the cellars) but today it can still make claims to being the most expensive wine in the world (in 2010 three bottles of Lafite 1869 sold for US$232,692 each in an auction in Hong Kong). Visits include Catalan architect Ricardo Bofill's beautiful round *chais* (1987), big enough to hold 2,200 barrels, and the cellars have bottles going back to 1797.

ST-ESTÈPHE This charming village is the last communal appellation of Haut-Médoc, and one that produces wines that need extra-long periods of bottle-ageing, owing to their large quantity of Merlot, which can reach as much as 40% at **Château Cos d'Estournel** (just north of Lafite along the D2; ☎ 05 56 73 15 50; w estournel.com; ⌚ 09.00–17.30 Mon–Fri; from €60, book visits online). By far the most exotic château in the Médoc, it was built in 1791 as a replica of the palace of the Sultan of Zanzibar by its founder Louis Gaspard d'Estournel, nicknamed the 'Maharajah of Saint-Estèphe'.

Here too is **Château Calon-Ségur** (☎ 05 56 59 30 08; tours & tastings by appt), dating from the 12th century and given its heart-shaped device in the 18th century by the aforementioned Marquis de Ségur because he loved it so much. **Château La Haye** (1 Rue St-Affrique; ☎ 05 56 59 32 18; w chateaulahaye.com; ⌚ Apr–Sep; book in advance) was built in 1557 and served as a hunting retreat for Henri II and his official mistress, Diane de Poitiers; their intertwined initials are engraved in the stones. The **Maison du Vin de Saint-Estèphe** (Place des Anciens Combattants; ☎ 05 56 59 30 59; w saint-estephe.fr; ⌚ 10.00–18.00 Mon–Fri, 14.00–18.00 Sat) can tell you more and sells bottles at château prices.

VERTHEUIL Haut-Médoc ends at St-Estèphe; beyond in Médoc (or sometimes 'Bas-Médoc') there are still vineyards, but more marshlands and tiny fishing ports dotted with *carrelets* – wooden fishing huts on stilts. And there's Romanesque art in the 11th-century church of the **Abbaye de Vertheuil** (☎ 05 56 73 30 10; w abbayedevertheuil.com; church ⌚ daily; abbey ⌚ Jul–Aug 14.30–18.30 Tue–Sun, or by appt) endowed with not one but two bell towers and a portal carved with the *Elders of the Apocalypse* and peasants pruning the vines. The interior was redesigned in the 15th century with a striking and unusual barrel-vaulted ambulatory, rib-vaulted choir and choir stalls carved with scenes from monastic life and some unusual sculptures: don't miss the smiling bear grabbing a man by his bottom. The abbey houses the charming **Petit Musée d'Automates**, full of old-fashioned automata inspired by the fables of La Fontaine (05 56 73 30 10; Jul–Aug 11.30–18.30 Tue–Sun, other times by appt; €4/€2).

North in **St-Yzans-de-Médoc** is one last wine stop: the waterfront 18th-century rose-tinted **Château de Loudenne** (05 56 73 17 80; w chateau-loudenne.com; Apr–Sep 10.00–13.00 & 14.00–16.00 Tue–Sat, otherwise book online; free), an organic vineyard in a stunning setting with English gardens, a wine museum and guided tours and tastings.

LESPARRE-MÉDOC The medieval *seigneurs* of lower Médoc were the most loyal to England – fatally so. In 1452 the then baron secretly went to England, promising the king that the Gironde would rise up for him again, encouraging him to send the Earl of Shrewsbury to Bordeaux and Castillon. After the disastrous defeat at the latter, the Baron of Lesparre was banished and beheaded and his castle crumbled away, leaving only the impressive **Tour de l'Honneur** (17 Rue Pierre Curie; m 06 25 77 60 14; w tour-de-lhonneur.jimdofree.com; Jul–Aug 10.00–13.00 & 14.00–16.00 Tue–Sat, Mar–Jun & Sep–Nov 14.00–18.00 Tue–Sat; €5, ages 8–15 €2, under 8 free); today it holds a charming local history museum. Ruins of the long lost Biturige city of Noviomagus (foundations of a 1st-century AD theatre and temple) were uncovered at the **Site Archeologique de Brion** (east of St-Germain d'Esteuil; always), although they weren't the first ones here: a collective passage tomb from c2000BC, the **Allée d'Aquitaine de Barbehère**, used into the Copper Age, is just off the D4 towards Ordonnac.

As you continue north of Lesparre, the vines give way to coastal plains at Queyrac. In **Vensac** you can visit a rare windmill, the **Moulin de Vensac** (05 56 09 45 00; w moulindevensac.fr; Jul–Aug 10.00–12.30 & 14.30–18.30 daily, Jun & Sep 10.00–12.30 & 14.30–18.30 Sat–Sun, Apr–May & Oct 14.30–18.30 Sun; €4.50/€3.50), built in 1858 and still grinding wheat on its millstone. You can also visit the **Phare de Richard** (D2, Jau-Dignac-et-Loirac; 05 56 09 52 39; w phare-richard.com; Jul–Aug 11.00–19.00 daily, Mar–Jun & Sep–Oct 14.00–18.00 Wed–Mon; €2.50, under 10 free). Built in 1843, this 18m lighthouse hasn't guided ships since 1870, but it does offer lovely views and displays on local fishing, oysters, the local fauna, and history of the lighthouses here; in summer you can visit the *carrelet* at its side and have lunch in the snack bar.

THE CÔTE D'ARGENT

In 1905, a Bordeaux newspaperman named this nearly straight 228km beach, wedged between the surf of the Bay of Biscay and the pines, the 'Silver coast'. There is so much sand here that it can be a nuisance. Although we only go as far down as the Bassin d'Arcachon, one of France's oldest resort towns, it's enough to get a taste of the broad sweeping vistas of empty space rare in Europe. If that weren't enough, just on the other side of the dunes are lakes for calmer watersports and superb birdwatching along one of the Continent's major flyways.

Markets here are held at St-Vivien on Wednesdays and daily at Montalivet-les-Bains. Soulac has a daily covered market (closed Mondays in winter).

GETTING THERE AND AROUND Frequent **trains** in the summer and less frequent ones in the winter link Bordeaux to Soulac-sur-Mer and Le Verdon-sur-Mer. In summer, the little open-air **PGVS train** runs along the ocean for 7km from the Phare de Grave in Verdon-sur-Mer to Soulac-sur-Mer (Jul–Aug daily, Apr–Jun & Sep Sat–Sun; see the tourist offices for schedules). **Buses** (w transports.nouvelle-aquitaine.fr) serve all the resorts. For ferries, see page 82.

These flatlands are a great place to get around on a bike, especially along the many designated paths. A very popular 70km *voie verte* runs through the pines from Bordeaux to Lacanau; another, a section of the 1,200km EV1 Atlantic Cycling Route, the Vélodyssée (w cycling-lavelodyssee.com), runs from the ferry landing at Verdon-sur-Mer to the peninsula of Cap-Ferret. Hire bikes at **Cyclo'Star** (9 Rue Fernand-Lafargue, Soulac-sur-Mer; 05 56 09 71 38; w cyclo-star.com), **Fun Bike** (Carcans; 05 56 82 96 74; w funbike.fr) or **Bicy'cool L'Atelier Lacanau** (15 Av Poincaré Lacanau; 05 47 43 02 10; w location-velo-lacanau.com).

TOURIST INFORMATION All the offices listed here share the same website: w medoc-atlantique.com.

Lacanau-Océan Place de l'Europe; 05 56 03 21 01; Jul–Aug 09.00–19.00 daily, other times 09.30–12.30 & 14.00–17.00 Mon–Sat

Le Verdon-sur-Mer Port Médoc; 05 56 09 86 61; Jul–Aug 10.00–13.00 & 15.00–18.00 Mon–Sat, Sep until 17.00

Soulac-sur-Mer 68 Rue de la Plage; 05 56 09 86 61; Jul–Aug 09.00–19.00 daily, other times 09.30–12.30 & 14.00–17.00 Mon–Sat

Vendays-Montalivet 62 Av de l'Océan; 05 56 09 30 12; 09.00–18.00 daily, other times 09.30–12.30 & 14.00–17.00 Mon–Fri, plus Sat in May, Jun & Sep

WHERE TO STAY

Vital Park [map, page 80] (58 rooms) Rte de Baganais, Lacanau Océan; 05 56 03 91 00; w vitalparc.com. Family-style resort hotel with a great staff, spa & pool, close to the action. **€€€€€–€€€€**

Hôtel des Pins (29 rooms) 92 Bd de l'Amélie, Soulac-sur-Mer; 05 56 73 27 27; w hotel-des-pins.com. Founded in 1890, this 3-star hotel has 5 different kinds of room, with views over the pines & sea, & a beach 100m away. The restaurant (lunch menus from €18.50; €€€€) serves plenty of seafood, Chateaubriand, big Charolaise steaks & traditional southwest ingredients given a Thai treatment. **€€€€–€€**

Michelet (19 rooms) 1 Rue Bernard Baguenard, Soulac-sur-Mer; 05 56 09 84 18; w hotelmichelet.fr. In a 19th-century villa, 50m from the central beach, a very pleasant hotel offering a warm welcome. Good b/fast & parking available. **€€**

La Dame de Cœur (11 rooms) Place de l'Église, Soulac-sur-Mer; 05 56 09 80 80; w hotel-ladamedecoeur.com. The Queen of Hearts offers pleasant immaculate rooms & a tapas bar just opposite the basilica. **€**

Villa Zenith Hostel & Surf House (4 rooms & hostel dorms) 16 Av de l'Adjudant Guittard, Lacanau Océan; 05 56 26 36 49; w lacanau-zenith.com. A 5min walk to the beach, this turn-of-the-20th-century villa is laid-back & friendly, with a shared kitchen & yoga classes; a great place to meet fellow surfers. **€**

WHERE TO EAT AND DRINK

Seafood stars, including the freshest oysters, prawns and *gambas* and other shellfish raised around the mouth of the estuary.

La Pêcherie 2 Allée Louis de Foix, Le Verdon-sur-Mer; 05 56 09 60 32; ; closed eves Mon–Thu. Fresh seafood, grilled or *à la plancha* or served on a seafood platter. They also have a limited meat menu for fish haters. **€€€**

Le Bistrot des Cochons 1 Rue du Dr Darrigan, Lacanau; 05 56 03 15 61;

ebistrotdescochonslacanau; 10.00–23.00 daily in season. Tapas, wines & a varied menu that includes the likes of cod ravioli with Thai spices under the wisteria. €€€

Villa Costes 11 Av Sylvain Marian, Lacanau; 05 56 60 80 25; villacostes.fr; eves only. A good place to watch the sunset over cocktails & tapas, before tucking into a gourmet €29 menu. €€€

L'Instant M 8 Rue Fernand Lafargue, Soulac-sur-Mer; 05 57 75 47 81; mika2801; noon–midnight, closed Mon. Fun atmosphere, tasty couscous & dishes *à la plancha*. €€

Le Payotte 7 Bd de la Plage, Lacanau Océan; m 06 99 25 08 51; w la-payotte-lacanau.eatbu.com; summer 11.00–23.00 daily. Burgers, barbecue ribs, tapas, pecan pie & good choice of draught beers. €€

Côté Gam'guette 15 Rte de Soulac, Le Verdon-sur-Mer; 05 56 09 67 55; w jmbertet-aquaculture.fr; mid-Jul–mid-Sep 19.30–midnight. In a picturesque shack, enjoy an evening feast on oysters, *gambas* & frites. Bookings essential; bring cash. €

Judici 15 Rue de la Plage, Soulac-sur-Mer; 05 56 09 81 48; glacesjudici; 09.00–01.00 daily. Nearly a century old now, this is where generations have come for homemade ice cream.

BARS AND NIGHTLIFE In Lacanau summer nights are buzzing ocean side, but quiet towards the lake.

Au Goût'Epic 3 Av Jules Ferry, Lacanau; m 06 88 02 02 97; ; noon–02.00. Exquisite tapas & platters to share & a warm atmosphere. Lots of locals, too.

Le Comptor du Vin 5 Rue Holagray, Soulac-sur-Mer; 05 56 59 73 34; LeComptoirduVin; winter 18.00–midnight Thu–Sun, summer 18.00–midnight daily. Wine bar with tapas & music on some nights.

Le Mulligan 6 Bd de la Plage, Lacanau; m 06 77 85 01 63; lemulliganlacanau; 16.00–02.00 daily. Irish pub/sports bar that draws in the crowds with its fun atmosphere, frequent concerts & good tapas.

Le Kontiki 16 Allée Pierre Ortal, Lacanau; m 06 32 09 01 49; kontiki.lacanau; May–Sep noon–02.00 daily. Bar & disco with a thumping beat & a touch of fun kitsch.

SPORTS AND ACTIVITIES There's no lack of exciting things to do on the Côte d'Argent. The tourist offices can tell you where to parachute, land yacht (*char à voile*), surf, kayak surf, body-board, SUP, canoe, gallop along the sands, or play golf, paintball or tennis. There are 14 places in Lacanau-Océan that rent out surfboards and will teach you how to use them, some of which remain open out of season. Verdon-sur-Mer is renowned for surfcasting, or you can go on an ocean fishing outing with the Vedettes La Bohème (w vedette-laboheme.com).

LE VERDON-SUR-MER Ordered to keep the Gironde ports from being used by the Allies, the Germans held out at Verdon until April 1945, then destroyed all the port installations on their way out. Up towards the **Pointe de Grave**, the northernmost tip of the Gironde, you can climb the pretty **Phare de Grave** (Av du Semaphore; 05 56 09 00 25; w asso-cordouan.fr; Jul–Aug 11.00–19.00 Sun–Fri, May, Jun, Sep & Oct 14.00–18.00 Fri–Mon; €2), built in 1852; it holds a museum dedicated to the history of the Phare de Cordouan and other lighthouses.

Inland, in the Esplanade de la Victoire, is a **monument to Operation Frankton**, erected to commemorate one of the bravest secret missions by British marine commandos in World War II: on 8 December 1942, ten Royal Marines were dropped off here by submarine and rowed 113km up the heavily guarded tidal waters of the Gironde in five two-man 'cockleshell' canoes (kayaks, really) in freezing weather, travelling only by night, carrying limpet mines to sabotage German cargo ships, with the aim of forcing the Nazis to invest a lot more manpower in the area. Two managed to make it to Bordeaux on the night of 11/12 December and completed their mission.

The plan was to escape then to England, but only two marines survived to tell the tale. Lord Mountbatten, Commander of Combined Operations, later wrote: 'Of the many brave and dashing raids carried out by the men of Combined Operations Command none was more courageous or imaginative than Operation Frankton.'

An ancient forest of holm oak survived the war to become a popular picnic spot; dunes divide the ocean from the **Marais du Logit**, a shallow wooded lake, now a nature reserve that encompasses the coastal **Dune des Graves** that starts at the Point de Grave. Along this coast towards Soulac are remnants of the Atlantic Wall: blockhouses, pillboxes, graffiti-covered coastal batteries – the **Batterie Côtière des Arros** is one of the better preserved – and concrete jetties. And there are wild beaches, including naturist **Plage St-Nicolas**.

Phare de Cordouan (05 56 09 62 93; w phare-de-cordouan.fr; Apr–Oct timetable depends on the tide; €15/€11 in Jul–Aug, other times €7/€6 for all; visits last around 4hrs) You can sail over on your own boat (bring cash for the ticket) or take the Vedettes La Bohème from Le Verdon-sur-Mer (05 56 09 62 93; m 06 09 73 30 84; w vedette-laboheme.com; combined ticket €59/€52 (ages 3–15) in Jul–Aug, otherwise €47/€45; book online or phone) – you might well get wet and the rocks can be slippery, so dress appropriately. Designated a World Heritage Site in July 2021, France's last inhabited lighthouse sits on a limestone bump between the Gironde's two main shipping lanes, a notorious graveyard for ships. In the 11th century, a tower was built as a first-line defence; and in the 14th century the Black Prince made it into a lighthouse, manned by a hermit whose job was to feed the fire on the top platform. By 1582 this was falling over, and Louis de Foix was given the task of erecting a new lighthouse. When good King Henri IV came to power, Louis de Foix decided to give the lighthouse a second role, as a monument to the glory of the monarchy, as grand as the ancient lighthouse of Alexandria, laden with sculptures and mini towers.

The result, 67.5m high on a 7m pedestal, was an extraordinary Renaissance confection completed only in 1611 under Henri's son, Louis XIII. In 1788 this frou-frou 'Versailles of the sea' was shorn of many of its frills on the orders of the French navy to make way for a 20m white cone for improved visibility; in 1823 it became the first lighthouse to have a Fresnel lens, invented here by Augustin Fresnel. Two lighthouse keepers hold down the fort and run the guided tours. The first of seven floors houses the king's apartments, and the second a chapel, with a pretty cupola and 17th-century windows. From here you can climb up another 250 steps to the lookout and lantern for a bird's-eye view of the estuary.

SOULAC-SUR-MER Legend has it that Soulac-sur-Mer – 'the Pearl of the Côte d'Argent' – with its pine woods and pretty summer villas is the descendant of the port of ancient Noviomagus, which one cataclysmic day in the 6th century AD sank into the sea. Archaeologists have shown that the legends were true, but this comes as no particular surprise to anyone here; today's Soulac replaces an older Soulac that was methodically swallowed up by sand in the 18th century. As a result of these drifting dunes, little remains of the medieval port where British and Irish pilgrims to Compostela once landed, except for the 11th-century **Basilique Notre-Dame de la Fin des Terres** (Place Aliénor d'Aquitaine; 05 56 09 86 61; 09.00–18.00 daily) and even this was buried twice in the 13th and 18th centuries; in 1859 it was exhumed again, just before the top of the bell tower vanished forever.

This church, now a World Heritage Site, was founded, they say, by St Veronica, an early disciple of Jesus who after the Crucifixion sailed here with her husband Zaccheus and St Martial and built a little oratory, filling it with reliquaries (the Virgin's hair, shoes and milk (*sanctum lac*) which may have given the town its earlier name, Solum Lac). Veronica was buried here in AD70, although her relics were later brought to the safer confines of St-Seurin in Bordeaux (page 72). Rebuilt as a Benedictine abbey in the 11th century, Notre-Dame became a popular pilgrimage site – Louis XI made the journey three times. It has a remarkable apse from the 13th century; inside, the polychrome wooden statue of the Virgin worshipped by the pilgrims is still in place.

Soulac has a small **Musée d'Art et d'Archéologie** (Av El Burgo de Osma; 📞09 75 59 53 81; 🕘 15.00–18.00 Fri–Sun, daily in Jul–Aug; €2.70, under 15 free), housing prehistoric and Gallo-Roman artefacts, including a unique bronze Gaulish boar with an ornate ridgeback that washed up on the beach in 1989. Looking out towards America is a small bronze copy of the **Statue of Liberty** erected in 1980 at the end of Avenue Le Cordouan to commemorate Lafayette's departure for America. Further south is the small resort suburb and beach of **L'Amélie** named after a ship that was wrecked here decades ago: the big dune here is part of the coastal natural park.

VENDAYS-MONTALIVET AND MONTALIVET-LES-BAINS Most of the Germans who come down to the Médoc coast these days couldn't be more harmless; most of them don't even have any clothes on, but leave them at the gate here, at one of Europe's largest naturist resorts, set up in 1950; unlike with the posey beautiful bodies of St-Tropez, the emphasis at Montalivet is good clean bare-naked fun among sand, sea and pines. If you're not quite ready to let it all hang out, there are designated (non-naturist) beaches for textiles at Montalivet and to the north at **Le Gurp**. South of Montalivet, the beautiful white **Plage du Pin Sec** is nearly 4km long and accessible only by one road through the pines; it has a popular surf school, bars, restaurants, free parking and a few ruined blockhouses slowly returning to nature.

LAC D'HOURTIN-CARCANS Stretching 16km from north to south, this is the longest lake in France, home to an insect-eating plant called the *droséra* and otters. The dunes and salt marshes between the west shore and the Atlantic is the **Réserve Naturelle Nationale des Dunes et Marais d'Hourtin**, just south of where the coastal road ends at Hourtin Plage. The beaches along the lake are popular with families. **Piqueyrot Plage** in the northwest by an old fishing village is a lovely spot, and the village of Hourtin to the northeast has the **Île aux Enfants**, a play area with a fort, climbing area, picnic site, etc surrounded by a water-lily-filled moat. **Carcans** and **Maubuisson**, the sports-oriented resorts at the southern end of the lake, also have safe sandy beaches. The **Musée des Arts et Traditions Populaires** (MATP; 129 Av de Maubuisson, Carcans; 📞05 56 03 41 96; **w** musee.matp.carcans.free.fr; 🕘 Jul–Aug 15.30–19.30 Mon–Fri; €2.50, under 17 free) evokes life in the 'other' Médoc, its moors and beaches from the 18th to the 20th century, including the Compostela routes.

South of the big lake, dunes and trees encompass the **Réserve Naturelle de l'Etang de Cousseau** (car park at Marmande on the D6E1; for information: 📞05 56 03 21 01), a nature reserve with a 7.5km path for cyclists and walkers. It hosts migratory waterfowl, such as ospreys and water rails, along with boar, deer, aquatic tortoises, genets, European mink and otters, and 39 kinds of dragonfly. Douse yourself in mosquito repellent in summer.

LACANAU-OCÉAN Since the early 1900s, this has been a popular weekend retreat for the Bordelais, never guessing that the huge rollers that smacked the beach would in the 1960s begin to attract a new breed of tourist – the cream of Europe's surfing fools, who converge here for ten days for stage two of the world surfing championships, Lacanau Pro. For something calmer, there are family-oriented beaches with lifeguards at **Le Moutchic** at the north end of **Lac de Lacanau** and **La Grande Escoure** on the central west shore.

ARCACHON AND ITS BASSIN

Known for its oysters for centuries, Arcachon on Gascony's 250km^2 inland sea only became something more than a village in the mid 19th century thanks to a pair of canny developers, and since then things have grown like Topsy: the gargantuan Dune du Pilat, just south of Arcachon, alone attracts a million visitors a year. Yet many corners have been left untouched by mass tourism: the little villages in the back Bassin could be part of a 17th-century Dutch landscape painting, with their ports sheltering the Bassin's small, shallow-keeled sailing boats called *pinasses* (or *pinassayres*, in Gascon).

Today the whole area is part of several natural parks: there's the Parc Naturel Marin du Bassin d'Arcachon, and the Réserve Naturelle du Banc d'Arcachon (which protects the sandy islets off the Dune du Pilat), while the back Bassin and Teich Delta belong to the Parc Naturel des Landes de Gascogne (page 101).

Arcachon's covered **market** in Place de Gracia is open every morning, and from 17.00 to 19.00 every day in summer. Le Moulleau has an organic market with about 30 producers every July and August on Tuesday mornings.

HISTORY Despite its location near Bordeaux, the Bassin managed to stay out of history, until Louis XVI thought to make the Bassin into a military port and sent down an engineer of the Ponts et Chaussées, Brémontier, to fix the shifting sands. Brémontier built palisades 70m in from the high tide, halting the wind-borne sand to create barrier dunes, which he anchored with a long-rooted grass called *oyat*. To stop the dunes from wandering inland, he spread a mix of seeds of gorse, broom and maritime pines under a network of branches. The gorse sprouted quickly, and held down the soil as the pines established themselves. The Revolution intervened before the military port project ever got under way.

Arcachon itself was a small fishing village until 1841, when its life was turned upside down by the building of a railway line from Bordeaux to nearby La Teste de Buch. This new link neatly coincided with the new fashion for sea-bathing launched by the Duchesse de Berry. Private villas went up here and there, but the resort really took off after 1852, when brothers Emile and Isaac Pereire took over the railway line and extended it to Arcachon. The brothers were descendants of Spanish Jews who found a safe haven in Bordeaux during the Inquisition; their grandfather, Jacob, was famous for inventing the first sign-language alphabet for the deaf in the 1700s.

Emile and Isaac proved just as inventive, but as property speculators, and they laid out their new resort with cute winding lanes according to the Anglophile tastes of Napoleon III. They divided the residential areas into four subdivisions, each named after one of the four seasons. The Ville d'Hiver, sheltered from the ocean winds and always 3°C warmer than the rest of Arcachon, attained full fashion status by the 1860s – Gounod, Debussy, Alexandre Dumas, Napoleon III, Marie Christine of Austria and her future husband Alfonso XII of Spain (who came incognito) were all habitués – and it's never looked back.

GETTING THERE AND AROUND

By train TER trains (**w** transports.nouvelle-aquitaine.fr) run nearly every hour from Bordeaux to Arcachon.

By bus and taxi Five bus routes circle around the Bassin. Download the app My Bus Bassin d'Arcachon for information and tickets (day and weekend passes are available). For a taxi, try Arcachon Aquitaine Taxis (☎ 05 56 83 88 88) or Grégory Taxi Arcachon (m 06 50 56 53 62).

By car Park and ride (*parking relais*) operates in the summer at the entrance to Arcachon (1 Av du Dr Lorentz Monod) with a free bus service into town. There are two underground car parks (on Bd du Général Leclerc/Esp Georges Pompidou and at 14 Rue Jehenne) and several other small payable car parks.

By boat The UBA (Union des Bateliers Arcachonnais; ☎ 05 57 72 28 28; w bateliers-arcachon.com) departing from the Thiers or d'Eyrac jetties make half-hour **ferry shuttles** year-round between Arcachon and Cap-Ferret, with many more services round the Bassin in summer. They also run a Bus de Mer in season between Port de Pêche, Petit Port, Jetée d'Eyrac, Jetée Thiers and Le Moulleau.

There are several **taxi boats**: Bateau Taxi Le Passeur (m 07 63 64 74 74; w taxi-bateau-bassindarcachon.com), which operates year-round, and Allo à l'Eau (m 06 33 33 21 21; w bateau-taxi-arcachon.com) running from April to October.

By bike The Bassin has an extensive network of cycle-tracks. You can hire bikes in all the villages; in Arcachon at Locabeach (☎ 05 56 83 39 64, w locabeach.com) and Dingo Vélos (☎ 05 56 83 44 09; w dingovelos.bike).

TOURIST INFORMATION Arcachon opened a fancy new tourist office, MA.AT, near the train station with a multimedia centre and toy library.

i Andernos-les-Bains Esplanade du Broustic; ☎ 05 56 82 02 95; w andernoslesbains.fr; ⏲ Jul–Aug 09.30–13.00 & 14.30–19.00 Mon–Sat, 10.00–13.00 & 15.00–19.00 Sun, Sep–Jun 09.30–12.30 & 15.00–18.00 Mon–Sat

i Arcachon: MA.AT Place Franklin Roosevelt; ☎ 05 57 52 98 88; w ville-arcachon.fr; ⏲ Jul–Aug 09.30–19.00 daily, Apr–Jun & Sep 09.00–13.00 & 14.00–18.00 Mon–Sat, 10.00–13.00 & 14.00–17.00 Sun, Oct–Mar 09.00–13.00 & 14.00–18.00 Mon–Fri, until 17.00 Sat

i Arès Place À Weiss; ☎ 05 56 60 18 07; w arestourisme.com; ⏲ Jul–Aug 09.00–19.00 daily, Jun & Sep 09.30–12.30 & 14.00–18.00 Mon–Sat, 09.30–12.30 Sun, Oct & Feb–May 09.30–12.30 & 14.00–18.00 Mon–Sat, Nov–Jan 09.30–12.30 & 13.30–17.30 Mon–Fri

i Gujan-Mestras 41 Av de Lattre de Tassigny; ☎ 05 56 66 12 65; w gujanmestras.com; ⏲ 09.30–12.30 & 14.00–17.30 Mon–Sat

i La Teste-de-Buch Rue Victor Hugo; ☎ 05 56 54 63 14; w tourisme-latestedebuch.com; ⏲ 09.00–12.30 & 14.00–17.30 Mon–Fri

i Le Teich Place Pierre Dubernet; ☎ 05 56 22 80 46; w leteich-ecotourisme.fr; ⏲ Jul–Aug 09.30–13.00 &14.00–18.00 daily, Jun & Sep 10.00–12.30 & 14.00–18.00 Mon–Sat, Oct–May 10.00–12.30 & 14.00–17.30 Mon–Fri

i Lège-Cap-Ferret 1 Av Gén. De Gaulle; ☎ 05 56 03 94 49; w lege-capferret.com; ⏲ 09.00–12.30 & 14.00–18.00 Mon–Sat

WHERE TO STAY Cap-Ferret is the trendiest spot on the Bassin these days, but hotels everywhere are on the pricey side; many have rooms in several price categories and can be a good deal outside of July and August, although on the whole if you're staying more than a night or two, you'll do better with a holiday apartment (page 33). This is a prime camping area, where most sites offer cabins, etc, as well as pitches for tents and caravans (see w camping-gironde.fr).

In Arcachon

Hotel les Bains d'Arguin (124 rooms) 9 Av du Parc; 05 57 72 06 72; w thalazur.fr. Set in among the pines & walking distance from the beach, this luxury hotel & spa with thalassotherapy, seawater pools, sauna & hammam will answer your every need. Suites have private jacuzzi on their terraces. **€€€€€–€€€€**

Arc-Hôtel sur Mer (30 rooms) 89 Bd de la Plage; 05 56 83 06 85; w arc-hotel-sur-mer.com. A stylish hotel where the rooms, all with balconies, overlook either water or garden; a 'Californian' jacuzzi is among the other amenities. **€€€€€–€€€**

Le Point France (34 rooms) 1 Rue Grenier; 05 56 83 46 74; w hotelpointfrance.com. A modern hotel in the centre, right across from the beach with easy access to everything in Arcachon. **€€€€€–€€€**

Hotel Altica Port d'Arcachon (46 rooms) 75 Av du Général Leclerc; 05 57 52 06 50; w altica.fr. On the edge of La Teste-de-Buch & the entrance to Arcachon, not far from the port, pine forests & bike paths. **€€€€–€€**

Around the Bassin d'Arcachon

Côté Sable (15 rooms) 37 Bd de la Plage, Cap-Ferret; 05 57 17 07 27; w hotel-cotesable.com. Luxury hotel & spa, with b/fast overlooking the bay & a hotel boat to take you to the Île aux Oiseaux, the oyster huts on stilts & the peaceful waters of the bay. **€€€€€**

Haaïtza (38 rooms) 1 Av Louis Gaume, Pyla-sur-Mer; 05 56 22 06 06; w haaitza.com. A Philippe Starck design project & among the nicest in Pyla, set in the pine woods, a stone's throw from the beach, plus the double Michelin-starred Le Skiff Club restaurant (€€€€€) in an old yacht club atmosphere, & a spa. **€€€€€**

Hotel des Dunes (14 rooms) 119 Av de Bordeaux, Cap-Ferret; 05 56 60 61 81; w hoteldesdunes.com. Woodsy boutique hotel in walking distance of the Cap-Ferret lighthouse & with views over the big dune. **€€€€€**

La Co(o)rniche (11 rooms, 18 cabins) 46 Av Louis Gaume, La Teste-de-Buch; 05 56 22 72 11; w lacoorniche-pyla.com. A legendary hotel by the beach & mighty dune, a neo-Basque wood-&-brick hotel built in 1932 with a stairway down to the beach. In recent years it has gone massively upmarket à la Philippe Starck. The restaurant (€€€€€) has superb seafood. **€€€€€**

La Guitoune (24 rooms) 95 Bd de l'Océan, Pyla-sur-Mer; 05 56 83 00 00; w laguitoune-pyla.com. For years, vintage favourite w/end retreat of the Bordelais; & an excellent restaurant (€€€€€) famous for lobster. **€€€€€–€€€€**

L'Anderenis Boutique Hotel (15 rooms) 9 Bd de la Plage, Andernos-les-Bains; 05 24 18 00 49; w landerenis.com. Light, airy rooms with garden or sea views. Cocktail bar & b/fast with emphasis on organic & local products. **€€€€€–€€€**

La Frégate (29 rooms, 1 apt) 34 Av de l'Océan, Cap-Ferret; 05 56 60 41 62; w hotel-la-fregate.net. Modern hotel complete with a pool. **€€€€–€€€**

Hotel des Pins (13 rooms, plus Gypsy caravan) 23 Rue des Fauvettes, Cap-Ferret; 05 56 60 60 11; w hoteldespins.eu. Delightful 1930s vintage hotel with a good restaurant (€€€€) set in a garden. **€€€**

WHERE TO EAT AND DRINK Although Arcachon has a huge number of restaurants in the high season you need to book several days ahead to have a chance at a table.

In Arcachon

Chez Pierre 1 Bd Prom Veyrier Montagnères; 05 56 22 52 94; w cafedelaplage.com; 08.00–23.00 daily. A local institution with a Michelin Plate, on the beach in the centre of town. Excellent fish & seafood. €€€€€

Club Plage Pereire 12 Bd de la Mer; 05 57 16 59 13; w clubplagepereire.com; 10.00–midnight daily. Enjoying perhaps the most idyllic setting of all, right on the sands towards Le Moulleau. €€€€

Du Soleil Av des Goélands, Plage Pereire; 05 56 83 90 74; w arcachon-bar-soleil.fr; 09.30–02.00 daily. On the beach near Abatilles, a wonderful spot for an evening drink or to watch the sunset. There is a meat menu, as well as the usual fish & oysters. €€€€

Le Bikini 18 Allée des Arbousiers; 05 56 83 91 36; w lebikiniarcachon.com; 09.00–02.00 daily. Where the cool kids go, for a drink or snack by the sea. €€€

Pizzéria Jehenne 19 Rue Jehenne; 05 56 83 20 46; w pizzeria-jehenne.com; daily. Dany Segura has been running this popular pizzeria for more than 40 years. Pizzas, calzone, salads & pasta. In season, book ahead. €€

La Cabane de l'Aiguillon 54 Bd Pierre Loti; 05 56 54 88 20; w lacabanedelaiguillon.com; 11.00–16.00 Tue–Sun. One of many oyster shacks around the bay, & a popular option for a lower-price meal, here you can get a lunch plate of a dozen *huitres* with bread & paté, enough for 2 people, for €20. €

Around the Bassin d'Arcachon

Chez Hortense Av du Sémaphore, Cap-Ferret; 05 56 60 62 56; w chez-hortense.fr; closed Mon–Thu. A local legend, offering a wide variety of succulent seafood, prepared in a wide variety of styles. €€€€€

ONA 3 bis Rue Sophie et Paul Wallerstein, Arès; 05 56 82 04 06; w claire-vallee.com; eves Thu–Sat, lunch Sat–Sun. The first Michelin-starred vegan restaurant, although start planning now – the waiting list for a table is reputed to be 1 year. *Lunch menu €39, dinner & w/end menu €116.* €€€€€

L'Ostalada Lanton; 05 56 60 97 21; w lostalada-lanton.eatbn.com; closed Wed, lunch Sat, dinner Sun. A typical French bistro menu with good choice of meat & fish for those days when you can't face another oyster. *2-course lunch menu €15, 3 courses €17.* €€€€

Chez Pierrette 6 Allée des Cupressus, Piraillon (north of Cap-Ferret); m 06 67 92 60 11; 19.00–01.00 daily. In a traditional Basque house, mojitos & tapas in a relaxed environment. €€€

Le Pinasse Café 2 bis Av de l'Océan, Cap-Ferret; 05 56 03 77 87; w pinasse-café.com; daily. Restaurant plus cabane & sushi bar. €€€

Les Viviers Gujan-Mestras; 05 56 66 01 04; w restaurant-lesviviers.com; daily. The light-filled dining room & terrace restaurant offers a wide selection of shellfish & other denizens of the deep, as well as a tasty beef brochette with cèpes. *3-course lunch menu €15.* €€€

L'Esquirey 9 Av Commandant-Allègre, Andernos-les-Bains; 05 56 82 22 15; w lesquirey-andernos.fr; Jul–Aug daily, Sep–Jun closed Mon–Tue. A haven for oyster-lovers – the freshest of bivalves served in a real cabanon at friendly prices, along with the freshest, tastiest fish the Bassin has to offer. From cheap-&-cheerful oysters to moderate sharing plates (€16–€32). €€€–€€

Station de Gus Cabane 21 at the port in Andernos-les-Bains; 05 57 70 29 12; w stationdegus.fr; 11.30–22.00 daily. Oysters, of course, at a very reasonable price. Cheap & cheerful. €

ENTERTAINMENT AND NIGHTLIFE After dark, much of Arcachon's life gravitates around the **Casino** (163 Bd de la Plage; 05 56 83 41 44; w casino-arcachon.partouche.com) and its bars and restaurant; the roulette and blackjack tables open after 21.00. Younger people tend to head towards Le Moulleau, which is livelier and open later. The local discos put on a number of special nights in the summer: in Arcachon, try the **Metropolitan Club** (4–6 Bd Mestrezat; 09 83 38 03 48; f metropolitainarcachon; 01.00–06.00 Thu–Sun).

SPORTS AND ACTIVITIES The UBA (page 94) offer day and night excursions on the Bassin, including to the **Île aux Oiseaux** given over to seabirds and oyster farms. In the old days, herdsmen in boats would have their horses swim over to the sweet islet pastures; today its landmarks are its picturesque *cabanes tchanquées*, or huts on stilts. Other excursions head to the sandy **Banc d'Arguin**, a wildfowl refuge under the Dune du Pilat; in June sandwich terns nest here in their thousands. They also offer oyster tasting tours, river trips up the Leyre and coastal cruises in the evening.

Sailing is popular and a challenge, with strong currents, sandbanks, channels and occasional high winds, and there are a number of races, including the 18 Heures d'Arcachon sail race in early July; the **Cercle de la Voile d'Arcachon** (Centre Nautique Pierre Mallet, Quai Goslar; 05 56 83 05 92; w voile-arcachon.fr) can help you get on board and offer access for visitors with disabilities. The tourist office can direct you to every other watersport, including rowing, kayaking, kitesurfing and jet ski tours of the Bassin.

Paragliding (*parapente*) off the Dune du Pilat is a year-round thrill: **Waggas** (m 06 32 04 32 07; w waggaschool.com); **Paragliding Arcachon** (m 06 84 77 30 40; w parapente-arcachon.com) and **Pyla Paragliding** (m 06 59 72 55 88; w pyla-parapente.com) all offer the chance to float over the sands. You can take a helicopter ride over the Bassin with **Jet Systems Hélicoptères** (m 06 16 28 27 34; w jet-systems.fr) or go up in a microlight with **Cap Océan Ulm** (m 06 13 80 47 53; w cap-ocean-ulm.com).

You can hit a little white ball around at the beautiful **Golf International d'Arcachon** (35 Bd d'Arcachon, La Teste-de-Buch; 05 56 54 44 00; w golfarcachon.org), or go riding with the **Centre Équestre d'Arcachon** (25 Av Pierre Frondaie; m 06 63 88 74 17; w cearcachon.free.fr). The **Maison de la Nature du Bassin d'Arcachon** (Rue du Port, Le Teich; 05 24 73 37 33; w mnba-leteich.fr) has bikes and canoes to hire for exploring the Réserve Ornithologique du Teich.

Then there are roadside attractions just waiting to keep mum and dad in the poor house. At the **Parc Animalier La Coccinelle** (133 Rte des Lacs, Gujan-Mestras; 05 56 66 30 41; w la-coccinelle.fr; Jun–mid-Sep 10.00–19.30 daily, other times 10.30–18.30 Sat–Sun & school hols; €15.50, ages 2–11 €14), children can feed the lambs and baby goats and ride the rides; **Aqualand** (05 56 66 39 39; w aqualand.fr/bassin-d-arcachon; Jun–mid-Sep 10.00–19.00; €29, ages 4–10 €22, under 4 free) is a big waterpark with rivers, wave pools, and water slides. For the under tens, there's the **Kid Parc Île d'Aventures** (131 Rte des Lacs, Gujan-Mestras; 05 56 66 06 90; w kidparc.com; Jul–Aug 10.00–19.00 daily, Sep–Oct 10.30–18.30 Sat–Sun; €13.90, under 85cm free).

WHAT TO SEE AND DO Facing the Bassin and cooler in the summer, the **Ville d'Été** ('Summerville') has the lion's share of Arcachon's tourist facilities, seaside promenades, sheltered sandy beaches and the casino in the more Disneylandish than outlandish **Château Deganne** (163 Boulevard de la Plage), with the **Palatium** congress centre to keep it company. Just behind it, the **Musée-Aquarium** (Rue Professeur-Jolyet; 05 56 83 33 32; w musee-aquarium-arcachon.fr; undergoing renovations at the time of writing) has a pretty collection of tropical fish, tortoises, seashells, stuffed weasels and shark skeletons. For a rainy day, the MA.AT (page 94) houses **Bunker 502** (09.00–12.15 & 14.00–17.15 Mon–Sat, 10.00–12.15 & 14.00–16.15 Sun; €2, under 10 free) where you can immerse yourself in an authentic underground German telecommunications office with period equipment, dating back to 1943 and only rediscovered in 2015.

The Ville d'Été's most notorious resident was Toulouse-Lautrec, who had a house by the water and liked to swim in the nude, offending the sensibilities of his neighbours. To pacify them, he erected a fence between his house and the beach – then mischievously covered it with obscene drawings. The furious neighbours eventually bought the house and gleefully burned the fence. Their descendants have never really forgiven them.

Inland, the balmy residential quarter, the **Ville d'Hiver** has for a centrepiece the **Parc Mauresque**, named after its fabulously outlandish pseudo-Moorish casino (1864), inspired by the Alhambra and the Great Mosque of Cordoba – but tragically destroyed by a fire in 1977. Inspired by its fantasy, the usually staid 19th-century Bordelais who built villas in the Ville d'Hiver let their hair down, indulging in neo-Gothic, Tyrolean, Tudor, pseudo-medieval and other fond fancies; some 200 of these lacy gingerbread villas survive. Don't miss the fine overall view of the Bassin from the Parc Mauresque gardens and its **Passerelle Saint-Paul** (over adjacent Allée Pasteur), built by Eiffel in 1862, and the observatory, reached by a 19th-century lift.

Since 1950, a new crop of villas has gone up in **Parc Pereire**, overlooking Arcachon's finest beach, **Plage Pereire**. As incredible as it seems, in 1922 someone had the chutzpah to drill for oil right in the middle of the park, only instead of black gold they discovered, at 472m down, a natural spring of mineral water, **Les Abatilles** (157 Bd de la Côte d'Argent; ☎ 05 56 22 38 50; w sourcedesabatilles.com; ⊕ 10.00–11.30 Tue & Thu; €7, under 12 free), which you can visit.

DUNE DU PILAT As the afternoon draws to a close in Arcachon, the thing to do is drive or cycle 8km south, through the laid-back resort areas of **Le Moulleau** and **Pyla-sur-Mer** to the awesome, terrible, extraordinary sight of the Moby Dick of sand piles, at 106m the highest in Europe, at 2.7km the longest. Amid the pine trees there's a payable car park (free for 30mins, €6 for 4hrs, €10 for the day), where you can leave your vehicle.

Excavations in this little chunk of the Sahara have found that Pilat began to form 8,000 years ago, and more or less reached its present dimensions in the 17th century. Like all dunes, it's in a constant state of flux, and every year it creeps about 5m, consuming the pines and forcing the campsites and cafés at its rim to move. A wooden stair with 190 steps helps you get to the top for an unforgettable view – especially at sunset. If you can't resist the urge to roll and slide and scamper down the ocean-side slope, be prepared to face the torturous return trip back up the slippery sands. Often included in the sundown view are schools of bottlenose dolphins and porpoises, who like to frolic just offshore. South of the sand-monster there's **Le Petit Nice** beach, and beyond that a naturist beach, both with lifeguards and snack bars.

AROUND THE BASSIN Ten communes, picturesque little ports with wooden oyster shacks, beaches, a river delta and a bird sanctuary, wait to be savoured around the rim of the Bassin. Try at least once to go out on the water in a traditional *pinasse* – promenades are often offered from the ports of Arcachon, Arès, Andernos and Cap-Ferret.

La Teste-de-Buch East of Arcachon, this village's name recalls the Captals de Buch who lorded it over the Bassin in the Middle Ages, although in those days pine resin rather than oysters was the cash crop. La Teste has some handsome houses dating back to the 18th century, and a covered market on Thursday and Sunday (but daily in summer) and includes in its municipal boundaries the northern half of the **Lac de Cazaux**, the second-largest lake in France, with a calm sandy beach at Cazaux.

Gujan-Mestras The Bassin's oyster capital, Gujan-Mestras, has seven little ports crowded with oyster huts. The critter on Gujan's coat-of-arms, however, is the ladybird beetle, the *barbot* in Gascon, a name that goes back to the early days of the phylloxera epidemic, when the locals noticed that their infected vines invariably swarmed with ladybirds. They accused those helpful insects of spreading the plague, while in fact they were gobbling down the real culprits as fast as they could; the priest at Gujan even held *barbot* exorcisms in the vineyards. When the real, much tinier lice-like pests were discovered, the villagers of Gujan became the butt of jokes from their neighbours, who called them the *barbots*. By the 1920s, Gujan had learned to laugh at itself, and adopted the ladybird as its own, even naming its rugby team the Barbots.

THE OYSTER'S THEIR WORLD

Oysters from the Bassin were popular among rich Romans of Burdigala (Bordeaux), who would set up relays to have them brought to their tables in a few hours. By the Middle Ages, when the old Roman roads were full of mud and potholes, tastes turned to dried oysters put up in barrels, eaten in a sauce or fried. The Bassin's industry remained small and local, however, until 1850, when once again speedy transport, in the form of the railway, allowed the bivalves to chug post-haste to Bordeaux, and then on to Paris in 1857 – at a time when restaurant diners thought nothing of beginning a meal with 10 or 15 dozen.

To prepare the little rascals *à la mode d'Arcachon*: count on a dozen (or more) oysters per person, four (or more) *crépinettes* (small flat sausages cooked in white wine, embedded with truffles if you're lucky), plenty of thinly sliced rye bread and butter and glasses of dry white Entre-Deux-Mers, properly chilled at 6–8°C. Open the oysters and keep cool, and fry or barbecue the sausages just before serving. Then slurp down the oyster, perhaps with a squirt of lemon or a dollop of vinegar and minced shallots, take a bite of hot sausage and buttered bread, then wash it down with a swallow of wine. And repeat and repeat and repeat.

Le Teich Here the Leyre (or L'Eyre), one of the most important rivers of the Landes, drains into the Bassin d'Arcachon, forming the kind of marshy delta beloved of migratory waterfowl flying between Africa and Scandinavia. In 1972, Le Teich's rare environment of saltwater and freshwater bayous was set aside as the **Réserve Ornithologique** (05 24 73 37 33; w reserve-ornithologique-du-teich.com; 10.00–18.00 daily, winter until 17.00, Jul–Aug until 20.00; €9.60, ages 5–12 €7.40; you can rent binoculars on the site). One of the highlights of the Parc Naturel des Landes de Gascogne (page 101), the delta is the nesting ground for several species, especially grey herons, black cormorants, white storks, black and white oystercatchers, egrets, kingfishers, dabbling garganeys and spoon-billed shovelers. Altogether some 280 different species have been sighted. One of the success stories has been the return of the mute swan, which vanished from France at the time of the Revolution; tens of thousands of cranes winter here.

The reserve is divided into four sections, and by taking the 3.5km path from the Maison de la Nature you can visit them all. The **Parc de Causseyre** has several hides and observation posts where you can watch a score of different year-round residents; the **Parc de la Moulette** is where the geese, swans and ducks are concentrated; the small **Parc des Artigues** has a collection of ducks from around the world, at liberty and in large aviaries; and the inaccessible **Parc Claude Quancard** is for wading birds (though there are two observation posts).

The back Bassin At **Biganos**, north of the Leyre delta, many of the old picturesque oystermen's *cabanons* have been converted into holiday homes, while the poor old oystermen, one presumes, now work in the paper mill. The next place, **Audenge**, is a sleepy fishing village where the day's catch is trapped in reservoirs left by the retreating tide – a method of fishing that inspired someone to dig similar tide-fed reservoirs for humans; if the tide is out you can join the locals for a refreshing dip in the public seawater pools. The 18th-century salt pans, the **Domaine de Certes et de Graveyron** (47 Av de Certes; 05 56 82 71 79; w gironde.fr; Jun–Sep 10.00–19.00

daily, Apr–May & Oct 10.00–13.00 & 14.00–18.00 daily, Nov–Mar 10.00–13.00 & 14.00–17.00 daily; free), now form a hauntingly beautiful salt marsh, frequented by eels, white spoonbills and common shelducks, crossed by two paths (6km & 9km, the latter also a bike path). Next to the north is **Lanton**, which has a long beach and a 12th-century church, the oldest on the Bassin. **Andernos-les-Bains**, a lively summer resort with splendid views across the water, and **Arès** both have beaches safe for children.

Lège-Cap-Ferret The northwest curve of the Bassin is sprinkled with little oyster-port resorts set between the calm waters and rough Atlantic. All belong to the peninsula of charming Cap-Ferret. The prettiest of these ports is **L'Herbe**, an intimate hamlet of wooden houses on tiny lanes founded in the 17th century. The commune's 34km of ocean beaches culminate in the sandy tail of the **Pointe du Cap Ferret**, which has long been doing its damnedest to close off the mouth of the Bassin; in the past 200 years the cape has grown 3km and gobbled up several fashionable villas in its wake.

A path leads around to the tip of the cape, with splendid views of the Dune du Pilat, most breathlessly from the top of the 255 steps of the **lighthouse**. The cute little 2km **Tramway du Cap-Ferret** links the Jetée Bélisaire on the Bassin side to the Plage de l'Horizon on the ocean, where surfers ride the big rollers expedited by the Bay of Biscay.

5

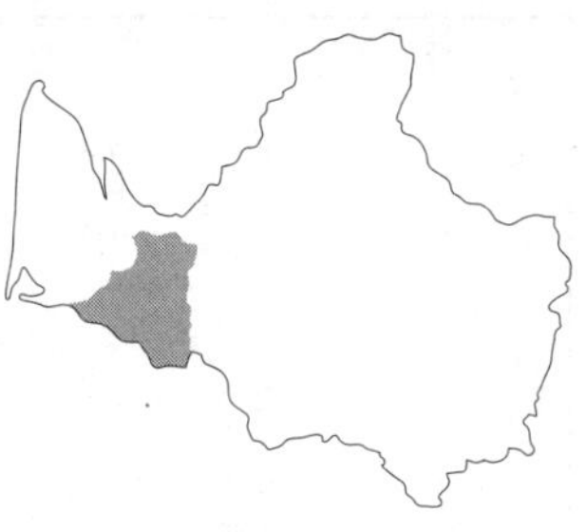

Landes, Graves and Entre-Deux-Mers

This chapter covers three distinct areas which lie to the south and east of Bordeaux. The sparsely populated ferny and piney Landes (the 'moors') that make up the northern section of the Parc Naturel des Landes de Gascogne, and two major Bordeaux wine regions, Graves and Entre-Deux-Mers. Graves is not exactly the name a PR firm would choose, but it isn't so sombre when you remember that here it is to do with gravel ('*les Grabas de Burdeus*' in Gascon) rather than boneyards. The gravel forms a wedge between the Garonne river and the Landes and is endowed with several special microclimates that make it perfect for wine – most famously Sauternes and for the beefy cattle of Bazas. Sleepy rural Entre-Deux-Mers, between the rivers Dordogne and Garonne, is practically synonymous with white wine, but otherwise these gently rolling green hills are terra incognita for most visitors.

PARC NATUREL DES LANDES DE GASCOGNE

The Parc Naturel des Landes de Gascogne was created in 1970, covering 290,000ha from the Bassin d'Arcachon to Brocas in the Landes to safeguard and promote an underpopulated region with a distinct environment and traditions. Managed by landowners, local business people and regional politicians, one goal is to suck in visitors into the pinewoods, passing by villages and medieval churches from the days when most visitors were pilgrims en route to Compostela.

The Gironde section of the park encompasses the upper part of the Leyre (also spelled l'Eyre: there are two intransigent orthographic camps). Nicknamed 'the Little Amazon' you won't find a better river for paddling gently down the stream. Lined with white sandy cliffs, little beaches and lush foliage (willow, oak, ferns, alder), the water is perfectly clear, albeit with a slight orange tint from iron oxide in its sandy bed. And life can seem but a dream where glimpses of civilisation are limited to the rare village or small nautical bases. The season runs from May to September. By starting 100km south in the Landes you can make the voyage last a week (see below and page 103).

GETTING THERE AND AROUND Bus 505 from Bordeaux from the Hôpital Pellegrin tram stop goes to Belin-Béliet by way of Salles and Lugos. For timetables and more information, visit **w** transports.nouvelle-aquitaine.fr.

Canoe hire

Alokanoe 89 Rte de Bayonne, Belin-Béliet; **m** 06 49 21 85 87; **w** alokanoe.fr. Canoes & kayaks, with a base in Salles.

Canoeyre 32 Route de l'Eyre, Pont de Mesplet, Belin-Béliet; **m** 06 25 80 66 33; **w** canoeyre.com/leyre. Kayaks & canoes.

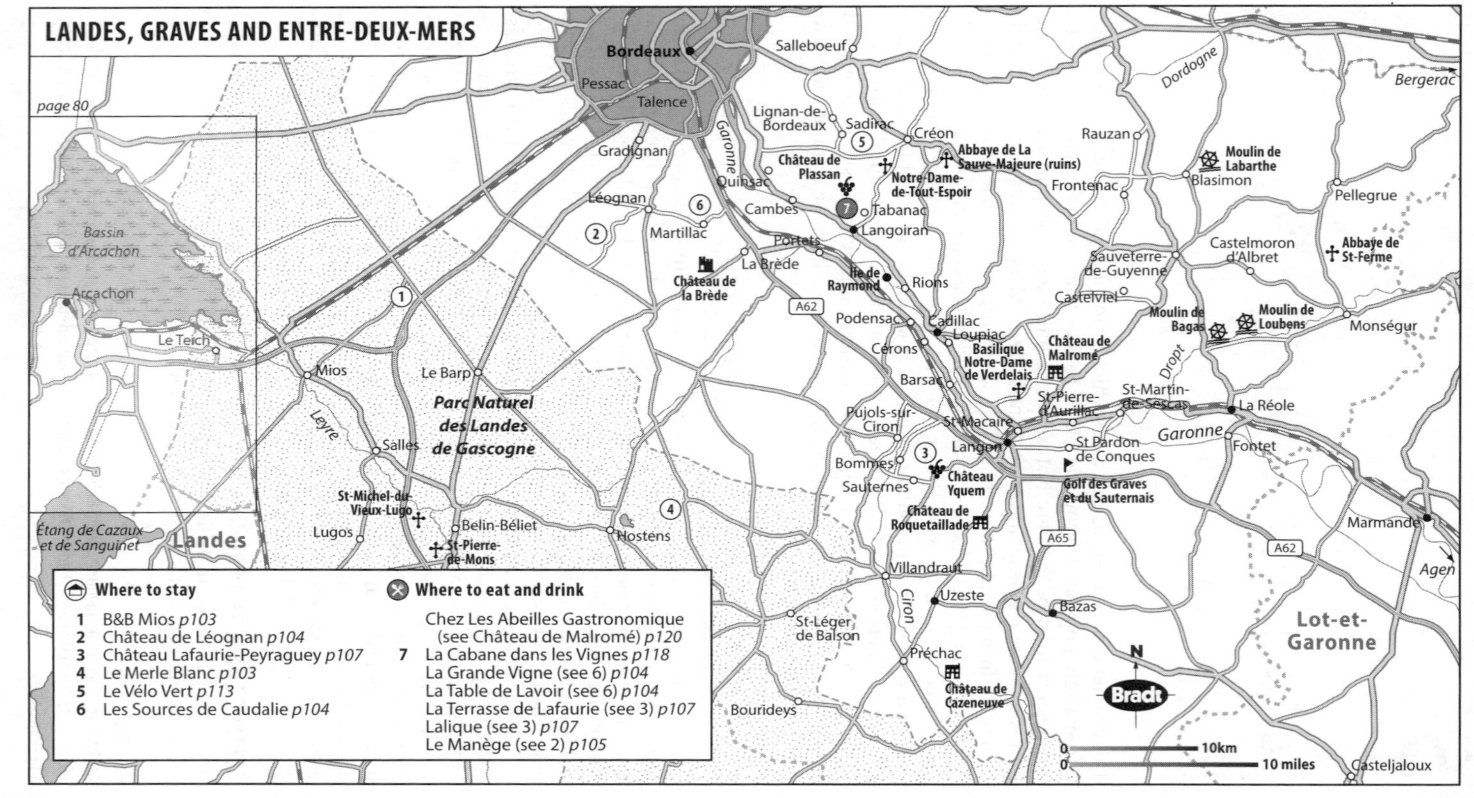
LANDES, GRAVES AND ENTRE-DEUX-MERS
Bordeaux
Pessac
Talence
Salleboeuf
Lignan-de-Bordeaux
Sadirac
Créon
Abbaye de La Sauve-Majeure (ruins)
Notre-Dame-de-Tout-Espoir
Château de Plassan
Gradignan
Garonne
Quinsac
Cambes
Tabanac
Langoiran
Léognan
Martillac
Portets
La Brède
Château de la Brède
Île de Raymond
Rions
A62
Podensac
Cadillac
Loupiac
Basilique Notre-Dame de Verdelais
Château de Malromé
Cérons
Barsac
Pujols-sur-Ciron
St-Macaire
Langon
St-Pierre-d'Aurillac
St-Martin-de-Sescas
La Réole
St Pardon de Conques
Fontet
Bommes
Sauternes
Château Yquem
Château de Roquetaillade
Golf des Graves et du Sauternais
A65
Villandraut
Ciron
Uzeste
St-Léger de Balson
Préchac
Château de Cazeneuve
Bourideys
Bazas
Rauzan
Frontenac
Dordogne
Moulin de Labarthe
Blasimon
Pellegrue
Bergerac
Sauveterre-de-Guyenne
Castelmoron d'Albret
Abbaye de St-Ferme
Castelviel
Moulin de Bagas
Moulin de Loubens
Monségur
Dropt
Marmande
A62
Agen
Lot-et-Garonne
Casteljaloux
page 80
Bassin d'Arcachon
Arcachon
Le Teich
Mios
Leyre
Le Barp
Parc Naturel des Landes de Gascogne
Salles
St-Michel-du-Vieux-Lugo
Lugos
Belin-Béliet
St-Pierre-de-Mons
Hostens
Étang de Cazaux et de Sanguinet
Landes
Where to stay
1 B&B Mios p103
2 Château de Léognan p104
3 Château Lafaurie-Peyraguey p107
4 Le Merle Blanc p103
5 Le Vélo Vert p113
6 Les Sources de Caudalie p104
Where to eat and drink
Chez Les Abeilles Gastronomique (see Château de Malromé) p120
7 La Cabane dans les Vignes p118
La Grande Vigne (see 6) p104
La Table de Lavoir (see 6) p104
La Terrasse de Lafaurie (see 3) p107
Lalique (see 3) p107
Le Manège (see 2) p105
N
Bradt
0 10km
0 10 miles

Lou Canoë 89 Rte de Bayonne, Belin-Béliet; m 06 21 88 42 25; e contact@loucanoe.fr. Canoe & kayak rentals, with optional guides.

T-sur-Leyre Allée de la Plage, Mios; m 06 33 08 20 86; w canoe-t-sur-leyre.fr. Canoes & kayak by the half or whole day.

TOURIST INFORMATION

Parc Naturel des Landes de Gascogne Rte de Bayonne, Belin-Béliet; 05 57 71 99 99; w parc-landes-de-gascogne.fr; 09.00–12.30 & 13.30–17.00 Mon–Fri

Salles 4 Allée du Champ de Foire; 05 56 88 30 11; w rtourisme.com; Jul–Aug 09.00–12.30 & 13.30–18.00 Mon–Sat, 09.00–12.30 Sun, Sep–Jun 09.00–12.30 & 13.30–18.00 Mon–Wed, Fri, 09.00–12.30 Thu. Covers the whole Leyre valley in the Gironde.

WHERE TO STAY AND EAT

La Cabane (21 rooms) 42 Rte de Bordeaux, Belin-Béliet; 09 70 35 77 58; w hotel-lacabane.com. In a woodsy setting, peaceful no-frills rooms & a restaurant (€€) featuring French cuisine with a Western touch (Cowboy roast Camembert). **€€€–€€**

Le Merle Blanc [map, opposite] (7 rooms) Louchats (20km west of Belin-Béliet); 05 56 31 44 30; w lemerleblanc-louchats.fr. Clean, modern & bright, & lovely owners; the restaurant (€€€) is one of the best in the park – really good mussels dishes if they're on the menu. **€€**

Le Résinier (16 rooms) 68 Av des Pyrénées, Le Barp; 05 56 88 60 07; w leresinier.com. Modern rooms spread out between 3 buildings – the stone house, the *bergerie* & annex, all sharing a garden with a heated pool & a restaurant (€€€) – with plenty of Gascon berets, oysters, local veg & meats, & homemade bread. **€€**

B&B Mios [map, opposite] (71 rooms) 6 Rue de Galeben, Mios; 08 92 70 20 70; w hotel-bb.com. Convenient budget hotel off the A63–A660, between Bordeaux, the Bassin d'Arcachon & the Parc Naturel. It doesn't have a pool but it's a couple of minutes' drive from a lake & AquaPark 33 waterpark at Le Barp. **€**

L'Atelier de Chocho 24 Rue du Stade, Belin-Béliet; 05 56 21 95 91; atelier.choch; closed Sun, Mon & eves Tue–Thu. Excellent food here & a young team, with daily changing specials & beautiful desserts. The owner's wife is American. **€€€**

L'Auberge de Lugos 1 Rue Champs de Seuze, Lugos; 05 57 71 95 28; auberge.bistro.gourmand; closed Mon, Tue & eves Sun. Reliable restaurant with 5 tidy rooms (b/fast inc; €), with a big shady terrace under the plane trees. *Good lunch menu €15.50, dinner €25.50.* **€€€–€€**

BELIN-BÉLIET Located both on the River Leyre and the N10 from Bordeaux, Belin-Béliet is a modest place, best known today as the seat of the Parc Naturel. Until the 11th century, however, Belin was the capital of the Kings of Aquitaine and a rival of Bordeaux; it was the birthplace of Eleanor of Aquitaine in 1122. The castle where the most remarkable woman of the Middle Ages first saw the light of day is now little more than a mound located just west of the village centre. The local **Musée d'Histoire** closed, but the friends of the museum are keeping its exhibits at 66 Rue du Stade (05 56 88 17 22; 09.00–noon Sat; free): Iron Age vases, local costumes, items related to traditional Landais industries, and grimoires – old books of magic.

The 11th-century church of **St-Pierre-de-Mons** (2002 Rte de Mons; almost never) south of Belin was built during Eleanor's reign, although its bell tower was only fortified a century later, during the Hundred Years' War – that time bomb left behind by her marriage to Henry II. Inside are four archaic capitals, carved with scenes of mysterious import; Rolands's paladins are said to lie under an ancient pilgrim's cross on an obelisk in the cemetery; pretty paths and a miraculous spring for curing eye diseases are in the surrounding woods.

From Belin-Béliet, take the D110 west and turn right just before the A63 for **Vieux Lugo**. In 1869 Lugos (with an 's') moved to higher, healthier ground 5km west, leaving behind the 11th-century Romanesque church of **St-Michel-du-Vieux-Lugo** (05 57 71 93 05; w vieux-lugo.com; ring ahead) now isolated in a clearing, with very curious murals dated c1500 of the *Seven Deadly Sins* being led off to Hell on the right wall, and *Works of Mercy* on the left.

NORTHERN GRAVES

A 55km gravelly ribbon between Bordeaux and Langon, varying from 15 to 20km in width, is the fief of the Graves appellation. The oldest of all Bordeaux vineyards, it is extremely disparate but basically known for its soft, full-flavoured wines. The cheap quality and sulphur stink of the whites produced here for many years gave Graves a mediocre reputation; nor did anyone protest too loudly when Bordeaux's developers built over vineyard after vineyard. Improvements were recognised with the new Graves classification in 1953, when 13 red wines were given their credentials as a *cru*, joined in 1959 by eight white Graves wines.

As all of the most prestigious *crus* are concentrated near Bordeaux, in Léognan, Pessac and Talence, a vinous civil war of prestige erupted that resulted in 1987 with a secession of the 16 *crus* from the Graves into an appellation of their own called Pessac-Léognan (w pessac-leognan.com); the reds are famous for their nearly infinite capacity for ageing. Then there's Cérons – the demi-sweet intermediary between the dry whites and sweet Sauternes. One winegrower here, however, is far more famous than his wine: a writer known to history as Montesquieu.

GETTING THERE Bordeaux's Tram B ends in Talence; from there take bus 502 for La Brède and Léognan.

TOURIST INFORMATION The tourist office in **Martillac** (3 Place Marcel-Vayssière; 05 56 78 47 72; w tourisme-montesquieu.com; 10.00–13.00 & 14.00–18.00 Mon–Sat) can provide up-to-date details about visits to the wine château and bike hire. The **Maison des Vins de Graves** (61 Cours du Maréchal Foch, Podensac; 05 56 27 41 16; w vinothequedesgraves.com; 10.00–13.00 & 14.00–18.30 Mon–Sat) has tastings, sales and reams of advice.

WHERE TO STAY

Château Pape-Clément [map, page 48] (5 suites) 216 Av Dr N Pénard, Pessac; 05 57 26 58 65; w chateau-pape-clement.fr. This 60ha vineyard was planted in 1300 by Bordeaux archbishop Bertrand de Got before he became pope. The suites in the château (parts of which go back to the 16th century) are gorgeous & romantic; tasting of 3 wines & b/fast inc. **€€€€€**

Domaine de Raba [map, page 48] (11 rooms) 35 Rue Rémi Belleau, Talence; 05 57 26 58 28; w domainederaba-talence.com. A half-hour walk from Haut-Brion, a guesthouse built by Victor Louis & 4 lodges out in the woodland with a big park, indoor pool, spa, 3 restaurants, cocktail & Tiki bars, plus a private 30-seat cinema. **€€€€€**

Les Sources de Caudalie [map, page 102] (43 rooms) Chemin du Bourran, Martillac; 05 57 83 83 83; w sources-caudalie.com. The ultimate word in rustic chic luxury was created by the owners of the nearby Chateau Smith-Haut-Lafitte. Cushy bedrooms are spread out in 6 buildings around a lake, with a spectacular indoor pool. There's a very elegant 2-Michelin-starred restaurant, **La Grande Vigne** (€€€€€), & a simpler bistro, **La Table de Lavoir** (€€€€), set in an old washhouse. But the real story here is wine – you can even bathe in it at the original *vinothérapie* spa. Wine tours, cooking classes & tasting courses are also available. **€€€€€**

Château de Léognan [map, page 102] (5 rooms) 88 Chemin du Barp, Léognan; 05 56 64 14 96; w chateauleognan.fr. In a historic park, a 17th–19th-century château beautifully restored by a couple of Parisians in love with wine & horses;

1 room is a family suite. The old stables now hold a chic restaurant, **Le Manège** (€€€€€), concentrating on local ingredients in classic French dishes. B/fast & classic tour inc. **€€€€**

La Chartreuse des Eyres (5 rooms) 7 Cours Xavier Moreau, Podensac; m 06 20 69 60 65; w lachartreusedeseyres.com. Once home to the Lillet family, now a gorgeous B&B with romantic suites & rooms. Delicious b/fast inc. **€€€€**

Novalis (20 rooms) 9 Av de l'Hippodrome, Gradignan; 05 57 35 37 80; w hotelnovalisbordeaux.com. Convenient for motorists, a smart little hotel with easy free parking. Special w/end family deals inc b/fast for 4. **€€€**

Le Chalet Lyrique (44 rooms) 169 Cours Général de Gaulle, Gradignan; 05 56 89 11 59; w chalet-lyrique.fr. Comfortable ivy-covered hotel & a brasserie (€€) **€€**.

WHERE TO EAT AND DRINK

Le Cohé [map, page 48] 8 Av Roger Cohé, Pessac; 05 56 45 73 72; w le-cohe.fr; closed Mon. Specialising in chic gourmet French cuisine (*supreme de cannette*, lobster medallions in champagne) with all the frills; 3-course weekday lunch €25. €€€€€

Château de Cérons 1 Latour, Cérons; 05 56 27 01 13; w chateaudecerons.fr; summer. On a summer's day few things can match a picnic *à la française* in this 18th-century château's lovely park. Book 24hrs in advance, choose your wine (Graves rouge or blanc or Cérons) & they supply the perfect picnic to go with your bottle, & include a tour & tasting in the price. Adults €49, children under 12 €12. €€€

Le Pistou 8 Av du Général de Gaulle, Martillac; 05 56 72 00 00; w restaurantlepistou.eatbu.com; closed Sun. Big, friendly & popular spot by the village church, featuring traditional dishes with an exotic touch (roasted melon flavoured with tonka beans & peach sorbet…). €€€

L'Esprit des Vins 80 Av Charles de Gaulle, La Brède; 05 56 68 72 60; w lespritdesvins.com; closed Mon, eves Sun. Informal, fun wine bar with a large choice of beers & spirits, with tapas.

La Cave de Léognan 2 Cours du Maréchal Leclerc, Léognan; 05 56 64 19 98; f lacavedeleognan; closed Mon. Charming wine bar run by a fun young couple, Mila & Julien, with more than 500 wines in stock & tasty snacks.

PESSAC (Bus 4 or 24) A victim of Bordeaux's sprawling tentacles, Pessac is the site of a landmark experiment: the **Cité Frugès**. The name commemorates the Bordeaux industrialist who wanted to transform a tract of land near the railway into healthy, affordable housing for 300 families and gave the young Swiss architect Le Corbusier a crack at practising his theories of urban housing. In 1926 he built 51 houses for Henri Frugès: geometric modules with rough concrete skins, brightly painted, with hanging gardens on terraces. The houses had many comforts the old *échoppes* of Bordeaux lacked (central heating, running water and adequate sewerage) but the sight of them drove the Bordelais bananas.

Frugès and his architect were dismissed as lunatics, and, when people reluctantly moved in, the first thing they did was try to make Le Corbusier's modules fit their idea of what a house should look like. Dismayed, Frugès abandoned the project, although up in heaven he must be gratified to see that his *cité* has been slowly stripped of later additions and was designated a UNESCO World Heritage Site since 2016. Visit the **Cité Frugès-Le Corbusier Museum** [map, page 48] (4 Rue Le Corbusier; 05 56 36 56 46; w pessac.fr; Oct–Mar 10.00–noon & 14.00–18.00 Wed–Sat, 14.00–18.00 Sun, Apr–Sep until 19.00; book a tour via 05 57 93 65 40; e kiosque@mairie-pessac.fr).

Château Haut-Brion (135 Av Jean Jaurès, Pessac; 05 56 00 29 30; w haut-brion.com; by appt only 2–3 weeks in advance; free) Founded in 1550, Haut-Brion's elegant reds were rewarded in 1885, when the property became the only non-Médoc wine to be granted Premier Grand Cru status. But Haut-Brion was famous even before then: it was the first wine sold under the name of the estate; 17th-century Londoners called it 'Ho-Bryan' and made it such a success that the owners opened one of London's first luxury restaurants, the 'New Eating House', with a wine cellar on the premises. Later owned by Talleyrand, the estate was purchased in 1935 by American banker Clarence Dillon, whose great-grandson Prince Robert of Luxembourg has been in charge since 2008. In 1983 the family purchased the equally celebrated **Château La Mission-Haut-Brion**. Today the two vineyards are green islands in post-war sprawl, which may be ugly but creates an urban heat island that protects the vines from spring frosts and accelerates the harvest, a plus in years of heavy autumn rains.

CHÂTEAU DE LA BRÈDE (Av du Château, La Brède; 05 57 95 96 25; w chateaulabrede.com; 10.00–18.00 Wed–Sun, see website for schedules of guided tours; €9.50 for castle; €4 the park; €14 for both; ages 16–25 €7.50/€4/€10; ages 7–15 €5.40/€4/€7, under 7 free) Charles-Louis Secondat, Baron de La Brède et de Montesquieu, described his home as 'one of the most pleasant places in France, where Nature puts on her dressing gown as she rises from bed'. He wore a number of hats in his life, not only as a successful winegrower but also as a magistrate in the Parlement de Guyenne and, most memorably of all, as a clear-thinking philosopher of the Enlightenment and author of the best-selling *Lettres persanes*, a satire of French society, and *De l'esprit des lois* (1748), a work proposing the separation of power that became the basis for the Constitution of the United States. Until the line died out in 2004, his descendants lived in the handsome Gothic castle he was born in, defended by wide watery moats. The tour includes Montesquieu's magnificent vaulted library with more than 7,000 of his books and his bedroom, left as it was when he died; he sat writing by the fireplace for so long that one of the firedogs is worn down from his foot resting on it. He created the château's recently restored gardens, and the park, his pride and glory, shaded by cedars planted at the time of the American Revolution which his writings inspired.

PORTETS (10km east of La Brède) This village on the Garonne is the site of the charming **Château de Mongenan** (16 Rue de Mongenan; 05 56 67 18 11; w chateaudemongenan.com; guided tours 14.00–18.00 Sat–Sun, Jul–Aug daily; €10, under 12 free, €15 with Château Lagueloup). It was built in 1736 for Antoine de Gascq, Président of the Parlement de Guyenne and good friend of Montesquieu; together they founded Bordeaux's Académie des Sciences, Belles Lettres et Arts. De Gascq also loved botany and music, thanks to his teacher – Jean-Jacques Rousseau. His natural son and heir, Antoine de Valdec de Lessart (1741–92), served as interior and finance minister under Louis XVI before meeting a sticky end, one of 44 *ancien régime* figures massacred at Versailles en route to the revolutionary tribunal. The rooms, unchanged since 1792, are a museum of 18th-century life with porcelain, textiles, costumes, dolls and so on – including a Masonic Temple.

Nearby the same family's **Château Lagueloup** (2–4 Rue de la Liberté, same contact details) is one of the Gironde's oldest wine estates (it even has the foundations of an early Christian baptistry) with a *chai* filled with all the 19th-century tools and machinery of the first 'mechanical wine cellar' invented by a former owner Jean Descacq. Descacq was so disappointed when a seamstress he loved refused to marry him because he was too poor that he went to work and became a millionaire inventor; the tour includes a wine tasting at the end.

PODENSAC (8km southeast of Portets) This is the home of the famous Bordeaux apéritif Lillet, invented in 1872. At the distillery, **Maison Lillet** (8 Cours du Mal Foch; 05 56 27 41 41; w lillet.com; 10.00–12.30 & 14.00–18.00 Tue–Sat; free), you can see displays of their famous posters and labels from 1900 to 1930, and have a tasting of Lillet, which is currently undergoing something of a revival.

SOUTHERN GRAVES AND THE BAZADAIS

At Barsac, the cold Ciron meets the warmer Garonne and we pass into the magic kingdom of noble rot (see box, page 109), of immaculately kept vineyards and remarkable châteaux from every period; some of the oldest belonging to the Gots, the family of Pope Clement V. Here too is Bazas, a name synonymous with beef and a mighty fine cathedral, or at least a mighty fine façade of one.

Markets are held in Langnon on Fridays, and in Bazas on Saturdays.

GETTING THERE AND AROUND RER trains between Agen and Bordeaux stop in Langon, where you can pick up a bus to Bazas (511 or 512). Hire a bike at the Sauternes tourist office, or at Les Cycles du Bazadais (5 Allée St-Sauveur, Bazas; m 06 69 20 69 66; w les-cycles-du-bazadais.fr) or e-bikes at Mobilêtre (44 Cours du Mal de Lattre de Tassigny, Langon; 09 75 56 54 98; w mobiletre.fr).

TOURIST INFORMATION These share the website: w tourisme-sud-gironde.com.

Bazas 1 Place de la Cathédrale; 05 56 25 25 84; 09.00–12.30 & 14.00–18.00 Mon–Sat, also mid-Jun–mid-Sep 14.30–18.00 Sun

Langon 11 Allée Jean Jaurès; 05 56 63 68 00; 10.00–13.00 & 14.30–18.00 Tue–Fri, also Mon in Jul–Aug

Sauternes 7 Rue Principale; 05 56 76 69 13; May–mid Oct 10.00–13.00 & 14.00–18.00 Tue–Sat

WHERE TO STAY

Château Lafaurie-Peyraguey [map, page 102] (13 rooms) Peyraguey, Bommes; 05 24 22 80 11; w lafauriepeyragueylalique.com. Sleep in a Sauternes Premier Grand Cru Classé château from the 13th century that sold its wine to Thomas Jefferson, with public rooms decorated with Lalique glass. The Michelin-starred restaurant **Lalique** (€€€€€) under young chef Jérôme Schilling is gorgeous; between late May & Oct you can enjoy a more affordable lunch Thu–Mon at **La Terrasse de Lafaurie** with a set menu (€42). You can also book a château visit to see the Lalique-designed chapel, with 3 wines to taste (€20), & a shop selling wines & Lalique glass. B/fast inc. **€€€€€**

Ecolodges Graves & Sauternais (9 lodges) Lac de Seguin, St Pardon de Conques; 05 56 62 25 43; w golf-des-graves.com. Something different: pretty wooden *carrelets* (fishers' cottages on stilts) sleeping 2–4 on the lake by the golf course with kitchenettes, hammocks & spa bath on the terrace. **€€€€€**

Château de Valmont (21 rooms) 22 Rue de la Gare, Barsac; 05 56 27 02 69; w domaine-valmont.com. A pretty 17th-century wine château in the midst of the Sauternes vineyards, with rooms of varying degrees of sumptuousness; plus a pool & good restaurant (€€€€€). **€€€€**

Claude Darroze (16 rooms) 95 Cours du Gral Leclerc, Langon; 05 56 63 00 48; w darroze.com. Hotel in a formal 18th-century building, with comfortable renovated rooms, although Claude Darroze is best known for its Michelin-starred **restaurant** (€€€€€) & terrace under the plane trees, where some of the best traditional Girondin dishes appear on the monthly menu – oysters, foie gras, & game dishes prepared with a light modern touch, along with the famous *soufflé léger au*

Grand Marnier accompanied by a perfect wine list. *3 courses €79, 4 courses €99.* **€€€€–€€€**

Domaine de Fompeyre (35 rooms) Rte de Mont Marsan, Bazas; 05 56 25 98 00; w domaine-de-fompeyre.com. Overlooking Bazas, a bright, modern hotel set in a delightful park, with a tropical garden, pools, lit tennis court & billiard room; the lovely restaurant (€€€) serves delicious seafood & *bœuf bazardais. Menus from €21.* **€€€€–€€€**

Le 23 (8 rooms) 23 Rue Principale, Sauternes; 05 56 27 20 04; w hotelsauternesle23.fr. Comfy rooms, including 2 family rooms in a prettily restored 19th-century stone house, with bikes for guests to pedal through the vines. **€€€–€€**

Hôtel Alienor (20 rooms) Chemin du Pioc, Langon; 05 56 62 15 15; w logishotels.com. A newer hotel in a park, with comfortable rooms. **€€**

Hôtel de Got (11 rooms) Place Gambetta, Villandraut; m 06 68 71 19 76; w hotel-de-got.fr. Typical provincial hotel, near the papal Château de Got, with a simple restaurant (€) & tidy rooms. **€€**

Château Trillon (3 rooms) 13 Cap Lanne, Sauternes; 05 56 27 33 89; w chateau-trillon.fr. Choose between the barrel, cork or bottle room looking across the vines. They also have a *gîte* sleeping up to 8, & an excellent, traditional restaurant, **La Table du Trillon** (€€€), serving seasonal dishes, especially game in season. **€€–€**

Horus (29 rooms) 2 Rue des Bruyères, Langon; 05 56 62 36 37; w hotel-restaurant-horus-langon.com. The falcon-headed Egyptian god's simple family-style hotel & restaurant (€€) serving southwest favourites. **€€–€**

WHERE TO EAT AND DRINK

La Chapelle Château Guiraud, Sauternes; 05 40 24 85 45; w lachapelledeguiraud.com; closed Wed, dinner Mon–Tue. What was a Protestant chapel is now a gourmet restaurant, featuring beef from Bazas but vegetarians will do well too. *W/day lunch menu €25.* €€€€

Auberge de la Haute Lande 5 le Bourg Nord, Bourideys; 05 56 25 74 84; w auberge-de-la-haute-lande.fr; closed Mon, & lunch Sun & Tue. Wonderful food & a warm welcome. Shady terrace for lazy summer dining. *Lunch menus from €12.50.* €€€

Auberge Les Vignes 23 Rue Principale, Sauternes; 05 56 76 60 06; w aubergelesvignes.fr; closed Mon, eves Sun. A charming country inn for lamb & magret grilled in the fireplace. *W/day lunch menu €16.* €€€

Hugo Délices Place de la Cathédrale, Bazas; 05 56 25 54 34; f; lunch Tue–Sun, dinner Fri–Sat. Creative cuisine, with plenty of beef but also vegetarian dishes & fish. *Menus from €19.50.* €€€

Le Boeuf Pop 30 Pl de la Cathédrale, Bazas; 05 56 65 77 56; f Leboeufpop; closed Sun, Mon & eves Tue–Thu. A jolly meat-&-potatoes place but also vegetarian dishes & draft beer. €€€

Le Saprien 14 Rue Principale, Sauternes; 05 56 76 60 87; w restaurant-le-saprien.fr; closed Tue–Wed. Well-prepared fish & market cuisine, with a good wine list & tapas at w/ends. *Lunch menus from €14.* €€€

La Petite Guinguette 2 Chemin de Pasquette, Sauternes; f lapetiteguinguette33; Apr–Sep 18.30–23.00 Thu–Tue. Marie & Guillaume's convivial summer garden party bar with wine, tapas, oysters, music & a play area for the kids is the place to be.

SPORTS AND ACTIVITIES In Villandraut hire a canoe or kayak for a leisurely paddle under the big leafy trees that line the River Ciron from the **Base Nautique Villandraut** (24 Rue Dupuy Jean; 05 56 25 38 65; w basevillandraut.e-monsite.com; May–Sep). In July and August you can book a combination canoe trip down the Ciron with a Sauternes tasting at the Domaine de Carbonnieu departing from Bommes (05 56 63 68 00). The 18-hole **Golf des Graves et du Sauternais** (w golf-des-graves.com) is at St-Pardon-des-Conques east of Lagnon. A bike path links Bazas, Villanraut and Uzeste with the five lakes and lagoons among the pines at the Domaine d'Hostens in the Parc Naturel Régional des Landes de Gascogne.

BARSAC At the village's church of **St-Vincent** (call keyholder Claude Joannet: m 06 30 98 97 60) with its sumptuous Baroque interior you can pay your respects to the

SAUTERNES-BARSAC: THE NOBLEST OF ROTS

Celebrated, simply, as the world's finest dessert wine, golden Sauternes and its twin appellation Barsac owe their inimitable quality to the excellence of their *pourriture noble*, or noble rot (*Botrytis cinerea*), nurtured by the autumnal morning mists formed when the River Ciron meets the warmer waters of the Garonne. *Botrytis* is a fungus that feeds on overripe grapes, dehydrates them, enhances their sugar content, and puffs them up until they look like brown turds. Unfortunately, this metamorphosis doesn't happen uniformly. The most traditional châteaux (like Yquem) harvest the berries literally one by one, selecting each by its degree of noble rot; in some years the pickers will go around the vines as many as 11 times. Add to the high cost of labour the risk: because the grapes are picked late in the year, a good rainstorm could make the overripe grapes pop and replace all the carefully cultivated noble rot with grey rot.

Another factor in the high price: a good Médoc yields 40 hectolitres per hectare; a Sauternes is allowed 25 maximum. Château d'Yquem averages a mere seven and should be aged a minimum of ten years.

The four communes of the Sauternes appellation – Bommes, Fargues, Preignac and Sauternes – lie on the left bank of the Ciron, while Barsac is all by itself on the right bank, where the soil has more limestone and clay, enough to create a subtle difference. Like Médocs, Sauternes-Barsacs were classified in the Paris Exhibition of 1855, and have remained unchanged. Many welcome visitors (w bordeaux-graves-sauternes.com has frequently updated listings). The **Maison des Vin de Barsac et Sauternes** (Place de l'Église, Barsac; m 06 38 47 68 78; w maisondesvinsbarsac.fr; ⌚ closed Mon) sells bottles at château prices and operates as a wine bar with oysters and tapas and more.

patron saint of winegrowers. The story goes that up in heaven St Vincent became so thirsty for fine French wine that God gave him permission to return to earth for one last wine tour if he agreed to come back to paradise at a certain time. Vincent's time ran out, but there was no sign of him. The angels found him in the cellars of Château La Mission-Haut-Brion, and in no state to go anywhere at all, much less to heaven, so they turned him into stone. Vincent wasn't the only one to get soaked around here: note the flood marker of the Garonne high water on 7 April 1770 on the side of the church.

Just north is the handsome Neoclassical **Château Nairac** (Deuxième Cru Classé), built in 1776 by a Huguenot wine merchant, who added the lovely gardens to show off the façade. Another, the **Château Climens** (e visite@chateau-climens.fr; w chateau-climens.fr; ⌚ by appt), was the first biodynamic Premier Cru Classé in Bordeaux. Many consider Climens second only to Yquem. Before crossing the Ciron into the Sauternes, you might look at two non-wine châteaux in **Pujols-sur-Ciron** just southwest of Barsac: the handsome 16th-century **Château de Lassalle**, set in a large walled park; and, 4km south, the **Château de Budos** (196 Av du Jardin), built in 1308 by a nephew of Pope Clement V in a style similar to Villandraut (page 110), and now a striking white ruin enjoying a lovely view of the verdant Ciron valley.

SAUTERNES This village of luscious Grands Crus Classés often seems to snooze away without a care in the world. Among the estates open for visits is the appellation's first organic vineyard, **Château Guiraud** (5 Rue Château Guiraud; 05 56 76 61 01; w chateauguiraud.com; 10.00–18.00 daily; tours with tastings from €22), a Premier Grand Cru Classé with an important conservatory of historic white grape varieties. Just south is the 19th-century Italianate **Château Filhot** (05 56 76 61 09; w filhot.com; 09.00–noon & 14.00–17.00 Mon–Fri; free), a Grand Cru Classé. The lovely park, laid out in 1840, has a *pigeonnier* from the 1600s.

The magnificent 15th–17th-century **Château d'Yquem** (w yquem.fr; tours at 10.00, 11.00, 15.00 & 16.00 Mon–Sat, 10.30 & 14.00 Sun; €84–€300, depending on the wines you want to taste – book online) is just north of Sauternes on the D125. In the same family for more than four centuries, it made international headlines when they sold it to the luxury multinational LVMH. Its pale golden nectar has been the ne plus ultra of Sauternes since the 18th century, a position confirmed since the 1855 classification that put it in a class all of its own as the only Premier Cru Supérieur de Bordeaux. Yquem also produces a rich, dry and more affordable white wine, simply called Y (*'ee-grec'*).

LANGON The largest town of the southern Graves, Langon is also the highest on the Garonne to feel the tide; note the flood markers posted on the corner of Rue Laffargue. Its 13th-century Gothic church of **St-Gervais** (09.00–noon & 14.00–17.00 Tue–Fri, 09.00–noon Sat) with a mighty bell tower inspired by Chartres, contains a surprise: a recently restored and unusual Zurbarán of 1661 (the *Immaculate Conception*, showing the Virgin as a young girl floating in russet clouds on the heads of two cherubs, her dark mantle flowing all around like a bat-winged storm cloud); the local *curé* discovered it by accident in 1966. All the capitals were sold off in 1926 and are now in the Cloisters Museum in New York, but there's a colourful Cavaillé Coll organ from 1857, frequently used in concerts.

VILLANDRAUT South of Langon, there is a definite woodsy Landais air about the birthplace of Bertrand de Got, who was elected Pope Clement V in 1305 at a time when Rome was in the throes of all-out gang warfare and not a very safe place even for the boss. Clement was crowned in Lyon and moved the papal court to Poitiers for a few years before settling in Avignon – the papal spoils after the Albigensian crusade. In the meantime he spent a fortune building up his family's prestige by ordering the construction of a mighty six-towered, moat-girdled **Château de Villandraut** (05 56 25 87 57; w chateaudevillandraut.fr; guided tours: May–Jun 10.00–13.00 & 15.00–18.30 daily, Jul–Sep until 19.00 or by appt year-round; €5/€3). It was finished in seven years (1307–14), a record pace in those days. Set on a plain and without a castle keep, in a style made popular in Wales under Edward I, it became a model for several other fruity-sounding 'clementine' castles in the area. It was quite posh, too – it even had 19 latrines (16 more than Versailles!), but was soundly battered in the Wars of Religion.

West of Villandraut on the D3, the bijou 12th–15th-century church of **St-Léger-de-Balson** has a handsome porch, and some unusual medieval frescoes of labourers, with comic-strip-like captions over their heads – but closed for restoration at the time of writing; while further south **Bourideys** awaits as a perfect and utterly tranquil example of a Landes village.

UZESTE (5km southeast of Villandraut) The Clement V tour continues to this little village founded by the pope's Got (or Goth) ancestors in the 13th century. In 1312, Clement began to pour money into Uzeste for the construction of a small but dignified Gothic **Collégiale Notre-Dame** (w collegiale-uzeste.fr; m 06 09 92

20 23; ⌚ usually; ring to book a guided tour; €5), and the next year declared his intention of being buried there. His request was granted a lot sooner than he had hoped: in 1314, when the Grand Master of the Templars, Jacques de Molay, was burned alive at the stake in Paris, he cried out that both the king and pope who had masterminded the Templars' destruction would follow him to the grave that same year. And so they did – Clement after eating a plate of ground emeralds, prescribed by his doctor for a stomach ache.

Clement's monument to himself in Uzeste suffered when the Protestants whacked his church and tomb (1315–59): his white marble effigy no longer has a face, although the embroidery of the vestments and dragon at his feet show a great attention to detail and hint of what was lost. The church's 14th-century statue of Virgin and Child was once the object of a local pilgrimage against the plague; the stained glass is some of the best from the 19th century.

CHÂTEAU DE CAZENEUVE (Préchac south of Villandraut; ☎ 05 56 25 48 16; w chateaudecazeneuve.com; ⌚ guided tours: Jun–Sep 14.00–17.15 daily, mid-Apr–May & Oct 14.00–17.15 Sat–Sun & hols, check website for extra days; €11.50, students €10.50, ages 5–12 €7) This irregular polygonal château started life as a medieval castle, built in the 11th century by the d'Albrets; Henri IV spent time here with his queen, Margot. Later owners made the castle into a pleasure palace. It has *salles troglodytes* cut into the central court, royal apartments and sculpted chimneypieces, as well as a mill, lake and lovely 40ha 19th-century English-style park along the Gorges du Ciron – now a Natura 2000 site with its towering bamboo forest and Grotte de la Reine Margot, where she is said to have met her lovers via a subterranean passageway.

CHÂTEAU DE ROQUETAILLADE (Mazères, 12km northeast of Villandraut; ☎ 05 56 76 14 16; w roquetaillade.eu; ⌚ Jul–Aug 10.30–18.00 daily (last visit 17.00), Apr–Jun & Sep–Oct & school hols 15.00 & 16.00 daily; €9.50, students & over 6 €6.50, under 6 free; no credit cards) The last of the Graves vineyards are here, along with this remarkable castle high on a spur that has worn some kind of fort since prehistoric times. There are actually two castles, one partly ruined from the 12th century, and the other built in the 14th century by a nephew of Pope Clement in the 'clementine' style, and still inhabited by the same family. In the 19th century, the owners gave Viollet-le-Duc, the restorer of Carcassonne and Paris's Notre Dame, *carte blanche* to give it the full medieval treatment, and he seems to have had a grand old time. Not one to let an idea go to waste, the spectacular stairway he built is the one he had designed in the competition for the Paris Opéra.

BAZAS For the past 2,500 years, Bazas has been the natural capital of a little region of fertile hills south of the Garonne. Up until the Revolution the town even had its own bishop, thanks in part to a unique relic – the blood spilled at the beheading of St John the Baptist, supposedly wiped up with a cloth by a pious woman of Bazas, who just happened to be on the scene and brought the cloth and the new religion home with her.

To shelter the precious relic, a triple church was built on the town's most prominent spot. When this threatened to fall over in 1233, the present **Cathédral St-Jean Baptiste** (⌚ 09.00–18.00 daily) was begun by the seneschal of the King of England. The builders began with the triple portal (echoing the original triple church) and ended with the choir, and this last bit was only completed thanks to subsidies sent over from Avignon by Clement V. In c1500, a Flamboyant rose window (the petals of which contain the 64 names of the bishops of Bazas), pinnacles, buttresses and a gallery were added to set off the three great Gothic doorways. In 1537, some misguided soul decided to gild the lily and stuck another storey on top. When the rampaging Huguenots turned up to wreck Bazas's pride and joy in 1578, the bishop, Arnaud de Pontac, saved the façade by buying it from the Huguenots for 10,000 *écus* (around €350,000 in today's money).

It was worth it: you certainly don't get this kind of theatre in many other places in the Gironde. The central portal is devoted to the Last Judgement, while stacks of virtues, prophets, angels, martyrs and confessors rocket vertiginously up the five arches. Along the lintel are scenes from the life of Bazas's patron saint, John the Baptist. The north portal is dedicated to the Mission of the Apostles, especially that of St Peter; here too are Adam and Eve, Cain and Abel and the Wise and Foolish Virgins. The south portal belongs to the Virgin, showing her Coronation, Dormition and Assumption. The finely detailed arches here are sculpted with signs of the zodiac, scenes of the Virgin's life and the tree of Jesse. Be sure to walk around to see the superb gargoyles, which look ready to launch themselves into space.

The Huguenots did destroy the **interior**, and just as Bishop Pontac, his nephew and great-nephew restored it to its original beauty it was completely wrecked again in the Revolution. To fill the space, furnishings were brought in from deconsecrated churches in the area. South of the cathedral you can visit the pretty **chapterhouse garden**, with a collection of archaeological finds.

Part of the cathedral's charm is its magnificent setting, atop the vast, gently sloping Place de la Cathédrale. This is bordered by arcades and some fine 16th- and 17th-century houses, most strikingly No. 3, the **Maison de l'Astronome** (1530), with ogival arcades and carvings of stars, planets, a blazing comet and a wizard astronomer in a pointy hat. Things get very hot here every 23 June, when bonfires are lit in honour of St John, and the Bazadais leap over the flames. A bull is symbolically offered to the mayor, for Bazas means beef as much as Sauternes means wine; the town is home of its own race of cattle, the *bazadaise*.

Besides entrecôtes, Bazas also offers visitors a **Musée de l'Apothicairerie**, a pharmacy from the time of Louis XV (Rue St-Antoine; book at visit via ☎ 05 56 25 25 84) and a **Musée Municipal** (1 Place de la Cathédrale; ☎ 05 56 25 25 84; ⌚ 15.00–18.00 Tue & Thu, 10.00–noon & 15.00–18.00 Sat; free), with a film on the cathedral, models and artefacts from Roman times to 1945. In the Allées Clemenceau you can pick up the pretty **Promenade de la Brèche** along the ramparts. The artificial **Lac de La Prade**, just east on the D9, has become a nature reserve for herons and other waterfowl, with thousands of orchids; check at the tourist office to see if the 9km path is accessible.

ENTRE-DEUX-MERS

The name comes from *inter duo maria*, 'between the two seas' (the Dordogne and the Garonne) and by the Girondin standards we're talking highlands – an undulating plateau of soft limestone occasionally reaching over 98m in altitude. Its fine blond stone went to build Bordeaux, leaving behind tunnels converted into mushroom farms. On the whole, Entre-Deux-Mers is a tranquil Ruritania, where any village over 2,000 souls seems downright urban; one is proud to be the smallest commune in France.

In the Middle Ages much of this land belonged to the Benedictines, headquartered at the great abbey of La Sauve-Majeure, and they sprinkled the countryside with good Romanesque churches. A century or two later, this peaceful region found itself on the front lines in the Hundred Years' War, which caused such devastation that in the 15th century the French kings repopulated it with northerners (the '*gavaches*' as the Gascons called them) speaking the *langue d'oïl* rather than the local twangy *langue d'oc*.

Entre-Deux-Mers is Bordeaux's largest producer of dry white wines, to the tune of 10 million bottles a year. The diversity of altitudes, soils and influences from its two rivers make this French Mesopotamia a patchwork quilt of microclimates, but for many years Entre-Deux-Mers was the *blanc* that became 'plonk' in English. All has greatly improved since the late 1970s. As usual, Sauvignon is the dominant grape, blended with one or more of the following: Sémillon, Colombard, Ugni Blanc, Merlot Blanc and Muscadelle. Along with white wine, a number of estates produce reds under the appellation Bordeaux or Bordeaux Supérieur. Check it out at the **Maison de l'Entre-Deux-Mers** (16 Rue de l'Abbaye, La Sauve; ☎ 05 57 34 32 12; w vinsentredeuxmers.com; ⌚ 09.00–12.30 & 14.00–17.30 Mon–Fri) by the abbey of La Sauve-Majeure.

EAST OF BORDEAUX Créon holds a very lively **market** on Wednesday mornings, Sauveterre-de-Guyenne on Tuesdays, Rauzan on Saturdays and Monsegur on Fridays.

Getting there and around Nearly all the villages here are served by buses (w transports.nouvelle-aquitaine.fr) from Bordeaux or Libourne.

A beautiful bike path, the 55km **Piste Cyclable Roger-Lapébie** (named after the winner of the 1937 Tour de France), links Bordeaux to Sauveterre-de-Guyenne as part of the V80 Atlantic to Mediterranean route (w en.canaldes2mersavelo.com). Hire bikes from O2 Cycles (m 06 50 02 41 64; w o2cycles.com), who will deliver trekking, racing and e-bikes to Bordeaux station or around the Entre-Deux-Mers.

Tourist information All share the website w entredeuxmers.com.

Créon 62 Bd Victor-Hugo; ☎ 05 56 23 23 00; ⌚ May–Sep 10.00–13.00 & 14.00–17.30

Monségur Pl Robert Darniche; ☎ 05 56 61 39 44; ⌚ Jun–Sep 09.00–13.00 & 14.00–17.00 Tue–Sat

Rauzan 12 Rue de la Chapelle; ☎ 05 57 84 03 88; ⌚ 10.00–noon & 15.30–17.30 daily

Sauveterre-de-Guyenne 20 Place de la République; ☎ 05 56 71 53 45; ⌚ 10.00–13.00 & 14.00–17.30 Tue–Sat

Where to stay

Château Camiac (14 rooms) 1 Rue de la Forêt, Créon; ☎ 05 56 23 20 85, w chateaucamiac.com. A delightful turreted château vintage 1834 with large rooms in an 8ha park, with pool & tennis court. Meals are served out on a magnificent terrace in fair weather. **€€€€€–€€€€**

L'Ilot Vignes (5 rooms & 1 gîte) 2 Lieu-dit Caboz, Rauzan; m 07 70 07 86 93; w ilot-vignes.com. Handsome rooms with Italian showers in a big park with a pool & delicious table d'hôte meals (€29) from Pierre-Yves, owner & former restaurant chef. B/fast inc. **€€€**

Les Secrets Château Pey la Tour (30 rooms) 32 Av de la Tour, Salleboeuf; ☎ 05 56 68 34 41; w secrets-chateaupeylatour.com. A good base for visiting both Entre-Deux-Mers & St-Émilion, this peaceful Logis hotel is 11km north of Sadirac. Its Bistrot Gastronomique (**€€€**) offers contemporary dining in old stone walls or under the cedars. **€€€–€€**

Le Vélo Vert [map, page 102] (5 rooms) 30 Chemin Darrigaut, Sadirac; ☎ 05 56 30 63 26; w chambres-hotes-velovert.com. Charming & rural, with a pool. **€€–€**

Hôtel de Guyenne (12 rooms) Rte de Libourne, Sauveterre-de-Guyenne; ☎ 05 56 71 54 92; w hotel-restaurant-sauveterre.fr. Friendly family-run inn, with a restaurant (**€**) serving €12 menus & pizzas. **€**

L'Archange (4 rooms) 4 Place du 19 Mars 1962, Frontenac; 05 56 30 83 35; w bar-restaurant-larchange.fr. Simple rooms & restaurant (€€) along the Roger-Lapébie bike route. €

Le Monseg (5 rooms) 10 Place Darniche, Monségur; 05 56 61 63 85; f. A lively bar with spacious rooms upstairs; b/fast inc. €

Where to eat and drink

La Pièce de Boeuf 26 Place Darniche, Monségur; 05 56 61 60 28; f lapiecedeboeufmonsegur; closed Mon–Tue. As the name suggests, its speciality is steak; but there are *gambas* & other things, too. *Menu €25*. €€€–€€

Iroko Le Casse, Sadirac; 05 54 49 45 92; f brasseriellroko; closed Sun & eves Mon–Wed. A brasserie with a warm welcome & occasional theme nights. €€

La Maison 2 L'Aiguilley, Rauzan; 05 57 51 76 60; 07.00–22.00 Fri–Wed. Friendly service, pleasant terrace & home cooking make this a popular spot. €€

Lignan-de-Bordeaux Heading east of Bordeaux along the D10/D10E a handful of places discreetly bid a detour. The hamlet of Lignan was once owned by the Knights of St John, who left behind an intriguing Romanesque church of **Ste-Eulalie** with sculpted capitals and fresco fragments. The village's **Musée Archéologique** (43 Rte Entre-Deux-Mers; 05 57 24 11 68; 10.00–noon & 16.00–19.00 Mon–Tue & Thu–Fri; free) founded by a local prehistorian has finds from Palaeolithic to Roman times, and ceramics from Sadirac.

Sadirac Just southeast, Sadirac, with its rich vein of blue clay, has been a pottery-wheeling village since antiquity. In the 18th century, 150 families of potters worked here producing everyday items; today seven of more artistic bent still fire up their kilns: the **Maison de la Poterie** (Pl Fouragnan; 05 56 30 60 03; w maisonpoteriesadirac.fr; 14.00–18.00 Tue–Sat; free) displays historic pieces and contemporary works, with frequent special exhibitions.

Créon East of Sadirac, Créon is one of the larger villages in the pretty emerald corner of hills and valleys nicknamed the 'Little Switzerland' of Entre-Deux-Mers. A bastide of 1316, it was founded by and named after the English seneschal Amaury de Craon, who hoped to dilute the power of the Benedictines at the nearby Sauve-Majeure. Créon retains three sides of arcades in its large central square (now a car park) and a church of **Notre-Dame** rebuilt in the 16th century, as described in the ornate Gothic inscriptions on the wall of its pentagonal apse. Inside, look for the unusually disproportionate 13th-century statue of the Virgin, which long stood in the niche of the 17th-century *clocher-mur*.

Just south of Créon, the fascinating Romanesque church of **Notre-Dame-de-Tout-Espoir** at **St Genès-de-Lombaud** (usually) is built over a Roman villa (two ancient sarcophagi are by the wall). There's good sculpture on the portal and capitals outside and in (one shows a pagan dance), and recently restored murals of the *Pietà* and of *Pope Urban II*, who may have passed through here in 1096 while preaching the First Crusade. An ancient Gallo-Roman altar supports a statue of the same pope. Down in the crypt is a 12th-century black statue of the Virgin, once object of a local pilgrimage.

Abbaye de La Sauve-Majeure (3km east of Créon; 05 56 23 01 55; w abbaye-la-sauve-majeure.fr; mid-Jun–late Sep 10.00–13.00 & 14.00–18.00 daily, Oct–May 10.30–13.00 & 14.00–17.30 Tue–Sun; €6, under 18 & EU citizens under 25 free) This once powerful Benedictine abbey was founded in 1079 by St Gérard de Corbie, who was granted the power of sanctuary and justice by Duke Guillaume IX of Aquitaine. He took its name from *silva major*, 'great forest', which once surrounded it. Its huge Romanesque church dates from the days when it was an important stop on the Compostela pilgrimage, but after damage in the Hundred Years' War, Wars of Religion and the Revolution, it was picked apart by scavengers, leaving only its skeleton.

Few skeletons, however, command such towering presence: three of the 12 massive pillars that supported the triple nave still stand, culminating in a row of five 'bread oven' apses, while the lofty hexagonal bell tower with ogival windows still rises with panache from the fourth bay, now fitted with a viewing platform on top. Two sculpted capitals (the *Sacrifice of Abraham* and *Beheading of St John the Baptist*) are in the second bay, but the most spectacular ones are in the choir and apses, where the eyes and hair of the figures are lovingly detailed: there are scenes of drinking griffons, fighting centaurs, a battle between an asp and basilisk, and scenes from Genesis, Daniel in the lions' den and Samson. To see the rest, you'll have to go to the Cloisters Museum in New York. La Sauve has a good **museum** of its own, in the former monastery, containing a fine statue of St Gérard in a style reminiscent of Chartres, medallions, 13th-century carved keystones, and documents relating to other religious foundations in Entre-Deux-Mers.

The 11th- or 12th-century statue of St James on the flat chevet of La Sauve's parish church of **St-Pierre,** 500m to the west, is one of the oldest that depicts James in pilgrim's garb, with cockleshells, staff and broad-brimmed hat; next to him stand SS Peter and Michael, and the Virgin and Child. There are wonderful expressive modillions all around, and a 13th-century statue of St Peter standing over the main portal; the font is made from a Romanesque capital of Daniel in the lions' den that was salvaged from the abbey. Inside are cartoony 16th-century frescoes, repainted in the 19th century by someone who loved red paint. In 2020 the church was given a 19th-century organ that once belonged to composer Charles Gounod.

Sauveterre-de-Guyenne and around A bastide founded by Edward I in 1283, **Sauveterre** changed hands ten times during the Hundred Years' War, but still managed to hold on to its arcaded square and its four fortified gates. At **Castelviel** (7km southwest on the D230), the elegant south portal of the 12th-century church is a gem, carved with Virtues and Vices, the Labours of the Months and more; Deadly Sins and saints appear on the capitals.

Blasimon (7km north of Sauveterre) was the castrum Blavini Mons and rebuilt as a bastide in 1322, on the orders of Edward II. Outside the centre, the gracefully ruined 8th–12th-century **Abbaye St-Nicolas de Blasimon** is isolated in the little valley of the Gamage (🕘 by appt with Sauveterre's tourist office; page 113). Part Romanesque, part Gothic, the church itself has survived in good nick, complete with a charming façade that takes on a golden patina at sunset. The portal (1170) is exceptionally finely chiselled with scenes of Vices and Virtues, animals and scenes from the hunt; the cloister has a handful of good Romanesque capitals. Just to the north (on the D17) don't miss the 14th-century fortified **Moulin de Labarthe**, built by the abbots of Blasimon and one of the most picturesque watermills in southwest France.

North of Sauveterre in **Frontenac**, the romantic ruins of a 12th-century church and an outpost of the Knights of St John, the **Commanderie de Sallebruneau** (224 Sallebruneau-nord; 📞05 56 80 33 37; **w** assrag.org; 🕘 usually; free), is slowly being restored by volunteers, who have planted a charming medieval garden on the site – replicating the sort of herb garden the Hospitaller Knights themselves would have planted to nurse weary and ill pilgrims en route to Compostela.

Rauzan Further north, this village is huddled under the **Château de Rauzan** (12 Rue de la Chapelle; 05 57 84 03 88; w chateau-fort-rauzan.fr; Jul–Aug 09.30–12.30 & 14.00–18.00, Apr–Jun & Sep–Oct 10.00–12.30 & 14.00–18.00 Tue–Fri, 10.00–noon & 15.30–18.30 Sat–Sun; €4, ages 6–14 €3, under 6 free), a castle built by order of England's King John in the early 14th century. Hotly contested during the various wars, it passed to the Duras clan through marriage in 1478 and was rebuilt and expanded several times. It has a pretty church from the 1200s and, as a centrepiece, an impressive 33m cylinder of a keep pierced with narrow slits for archers.

Rauzan boasts the only subterranean river in the Gironde, which flows through the **Grotte Célestine** (8 Rue Lansade; 05 57 84 08 69; w grotte-celestine.fr; all year but book a day in advance; €8/€5 – children must be 1.20m tall). Discovered in 1845 but only recently reopened, the 45-minute tours (in boots, helmets and headlamps, all of which are supplied) means fun wading in the river under the stalactites.

East of Sauveterre-de-Guyenne to Monségur Charming medieval **Castelmoron d'Albret**, just east of Sauveterre-de-Guyenne, is the smallest commune in France (3.54ha, population 53), squeezed behind its walls on a promontory overlooking a little valley – a pretty place to stop, even though there's nothing in particular to see. To the east stands the fortified 11th-century **Abbaye de St-Ferme** (a corruption of St Fermin – he of the bull-running in Pamplona; 05 56 61 69 92; w abbayesaintferme.jimdofree.com; daily). Although the façade has taken a beating, the interior has an excellent, lively set of capitals illustrating the Old and New testaments; you may have to ask the sacristan to turn on the lights. The *mairie* of St-Ferme is installed in the handsome abbey buildings of 1585, a complex that forms the heart of this peaceful village. North of St-Ferme, **Pellegrue** is yet another bastide from the 13th-century, founded on a rocky spur, with three châteaux decorating the surrounding hills.

Monségur This is the capital of La Petite Gavacherie, the main area in Entre-Deux-Mers resettled by northerners in the 15th century, who to this day are called *gavaches* or *gabots*. Originally the word meant uncouth hillbillies, although these days, realising that everyone is always someone else's hillbilly, this little enclave of northern French descendants take their nickname as a badge of honour. A walled bastide, Monségur was founded in 1265 by Eléonore de Provence, wife of Henri III – one of the few if not the only one founded by a woman (the charter she sent, called the Esclapot, is preserved in the *mairie*). It has kept its arcaded central square, not with the usual medieval *halles*, but a striking 19th-century covered market in iron reminiscent of the old Halles in Paris, alone with lanes of half-timbered houses and a simple Gothic church. Monségur overlooks the River Dropt, and like the Lot-et-Garonne just east, busies itself with plums, prunes and prune *eau-de-vie*.

ALONG THE GARONNE The most dramatic scenery in Entre-Deux-Mers overlooks the Garonne, where instead of white wine vineyards produce mostly fruity red Premières Côtes de Bordeaux from Cabernet Sauvignon and Merlot. Cadillac, Loupiac and Ste-Croix-du-Mont are luscious dessert wines grown on pebbly clay soil on steep hillsides, all rated just a notch below Sauternes-Barsac just over the

Garonne. In Cadillac, learn more at the **Maison du Vin** (D10, Rte de Langon; 05 57 98 19 20; w maisondesvinsdecadillac.com; May–Aug 10.30–13.00 & 14.00–18.00 daily, Sep–Apr 09.00–noon & 14.00–17.00 Mon–Fri) housed in the 18th-century La Closière.

La Réole has a huge Saturday **market** along the Garonne; Cadillac also has a market, on Saturday mornings.

Getting there and away TER **trains** between Bordeaux and Agen call at Cérons (2km from Cadillac), St-Macaire and La Réole.

Tourist information

Cadillac 2 Rue du Cros; 05 56 62 12 92; w destination-garonne.com; 09.30–12.30 & 14.00–17.30 Tue–Sun

La Réole 52 Rue André Bénac; 05 56 61 13 55; w entredeuxmers.com; 09.30–13.00 & 14.00–17.00 Tue–Wed, Fri–Sat

St-Macaire 8 Rue du Canton; 05 56 53 68 00; w tourisme-sud-gironde.com; Sep–Jun 10.00–13.00 & 14.30–18.00 Tue–Sat, Jul–Aug same hours daily

Where to stay

Château de la Tour (32 rooms) D10, Cadillac; 05 56 76 92 00; w hotel-restaurant-chateaudelatour.com. Overlooking the Château de Cadillac, this is an inviting, plush place to stay, with a pool & fitness track in the 3ha grounds, & a *bistronomique* restaurant, **Le Predeille** (€€€€), serving plenty of seafood choices on its idyllic terrace. **€€€**

Le Clos d'Any (5 rooms) 1 Lardon, Fontet; 05 56 61 26 90; w leclosdany.com. Bedrooms (2 for families) with exotic theme in a 12th-century mill, set in a peaceful wooded garden with a heated pool & hammocks. B/fast inc. *Excellent table d'hôte €27*. **€€€–€**

Apparthotel Les Tilleuls (11 studios) 15 Allée des Tilleuls, St-Macaire; 05 56 62 28 38; w tilleul-medieval.com. On the edge of the medieval centre, studios sleeping 2–6. The restaurant, **Le Medieval** (€€€), specialises in seafood under the catalpas. **€€–€**

Le Voyageur (10 rooms) 22 Av du Pont, Cadillac; 05 56 62 65 38; w levoyageur-cadillac.fr. Typical little inn with a restaurant (€€) with a reliable €13.90 lunch menu (& no lack of duck), all *fait maison*. **€**

Where to eat and drink

Aux Fontaines 8 Rue de Verdun, La Réole; 05 56 61 15 25; w restaurant-aux-fontaines.com; closed Mon, & eves Sun & Wed. Elegant 19th-century house with a beautiful summer terrace, & the best food in town & great organic wine choice. *Weekly changing lunch menu €18, dinner menu €37*. €€€€

L'Abricotier 2 Rue Bergoeing, St-Macaire; 05 56 76 83 63; w restaurant-labricotier.com. A charming place to dine with tables in the beautiful garden. Innovative menus & regional specialities, with plenty of fish but also delicious guinea fowl with ceps. Also 3 rooms (**€**) & a pool. *Lunch menus from €25*. €€€€

Auberge Réolaise 5 Rue Gabriel Chaigne, La Réole; 05 56 61 01 33; lunch only, also dinner Thu & Sat. Reliable choice, good for seafood (mussels in chorizo sauce), etc. €€€

Les Perles à Pimpin 31 Rue André Bénac, La Réole; 05 56 71 29 73; f; closed Tue, lunch Wed. Fine views over town & chic décor, & a chalkboard menu. Creative cuisine, vegetarian choices, lavish desserts & homemade ice cream. €€€

Auberge Girondine Le Peyrat, Ste-Croix-du-Mont (along the D10); m 06 34 57 22 49; w auberge-girondine.eatbu.com; lunch Tue–Sun & dinner Sat. Traditional hearty cooking, & succulent *côte de boeuf* waits at this friendly local *cantine. Menus from €24*. €€€–€€

La Petite Naples 7 Rue Porte-de-la-Mer, Cadillac; 05 56 27 47 63; w lepetitnaplescadillac.fr; ⌚ closed Sun–Mon. Excellent trattoria-pizzeria, Neapolitan style, with homemade pasta. Book or risk disappointment. €€€–€€

Auberge L'André 1 Place du Grand Port, Cambes; 05 56 89 85 88; w aubergeandre.fr; ⌚ closed Mon, Tue & eves Sun. On a summer's day, you can spend a lazy lunch or dinner on the banks of the Garonne, dining on lovingly prepared dishes & never want to leave. Often full so be sure to book. *Excellent €17.90 menu.* €€

Le Pampaillet 6 Rue Carnot, St-Macaire; 05 56 62 33 75; w restaurant-saint-macaire.fr; ⌚ 15.00–21.30 daily. Inviting & recently re-opened, with a menu of simple classics (burger etc) & crêpes. €€

C' du Vin 90 Rue Armand Caduc, La Réole; m 06 76 21 68 67; w cduvin.wixsite.com; ⌚ closed Sun–Tue. Great wine bar in the centre focusing on new & unusual wines & beers from the microbrewery next door – all run by women.

La Cabane dans les Vignes [map, page 102] La Côte, Tabanac; m 07 66 67 32 45; w lacabanedanslesvignes.com; ⌚ May–Oct 19.00–22.30 Tue–Sat. Designer organic wine bar with nibbles in a beautiful setting overlooking the vines & the Garonne; booking essential.

Bordeaux to Langoiran From Bordeaux, take the D10 towards **Quinsac**, where Rosa Bonheur (1822–99) spent much of her tomboy childhood at the Château Grimont; one of France's finest animal painters, an outspoken cigar-chomping, trouser-wearing feminist, she was the first woman to be awarded the Grand Cross of the Légion d'Honneur. **Cambes**, a small pleasure port to the southeast, has a good Romanesque church with curious modillions (man-cat, man-owl, cat-snake, fork-tailed mermaid, woman with fangs). On the D240 towards **Tabanac**, you can have a look at the elegant 18th-century **Château de Plassan** (280 Rte des Coteaux) attributed to Victor Louis and architecturally one of the finest wine châteaux in the Bordelais, built with its *chai* as a harmonious Palladian ensemble.

Langoiran This river town 15km upstream from Bordeaux was the first to build docks and boatyards, reaching a heyday in the 17th century. It was defended by the 13th-century **Château de Langoiran** (off the D10 south of town; 05 56 67 12 00; w chateaudelangoiran.com; ⌚ Jul–Aug 10.00–noon & 14.00–19.00 daily, Sep–Jun 14.00–18.00 Sat–Sun, daily in school hols; €4, under 6 free; they also have 2 chambres d'hôtes, b/fast inc; €€), with one of the mightiest donjons in France. After being put to the sack in the Hundred Years' War, it came into the hands of the d'Albrets; damaged again in the Fronde uprisings in 1650, it was abandoned. Volunteers are working on its restoration, while others have revived the Langoiran's historic boatyards, the **Chantiers Navals Tramasset** (Le Torne port; 05 56 67 61 69; w chantierstramasset.fr; ⌚ Jul–Aug 16.30 Wed–Sun; guided tours in French & English €5, combined with the château €8, boat tours €12 with wine tasting, otherwise €3 with a booklet), where they build and restore *gabarres* and other rivercraft the old-fashioned way. There are some handsome medieval houses by the port area and a bridge of 1881 inspired by Eiffel. Overlooking the river in the upper village, the Romanesque church of **St-Pierre-ès-Liens** (Rte de Capian – the D240) has a beautiful 12th-century apse with good sculpture outside and in (the Magi, the man who walks with lions, the fat man with giraffes…).

Rions This picturesque village found itself perched precariously on the frontier between the French and English in the Middle Ages, hence the heavy fortifications that have given it the nickname 'the Carcassonne of the Gironde' – the ruins of the citadel and a watchtower survive, along with the **Porte du Lhyan** (1304), defended by a 24m tower. Downriver towards Paillet is an important wetland reserve, **Île de Raymond**, formed when the Garonne shifted its course.

Cadillac This riverside bastide of 1280 is best known for lending its name to America's luxury dream cars but only by an extremely devious route, thanks to Antoine de Lamothe-Cadillac (page 351). In 1902 a Detroit carmaker took the name Cadillac; it was merged with General Motors in the 1920s, and the rest is history. A full-size Caddy would look like Moby Dick in the main square of Cadillac, and trying to squeeze it under the pretty, lantern-topped 18th-century **Porte de l'Horloge**, the main river gate, would be asking for trouble.

But Cadillac does have something even bigger than its eponymous car: the **Château de Cadillac** (05 56 62 69 58; mid-Jun–late Sep 10.00–13.00 & 14.00–18.00 daily, Oct–May 10.00–12.30 & 14.00–17.30 Tue–Sun; €6, under 18 & EU citizens under 25 free), built in 1598–1620 by Henri III's favourite *mignon* ('cutie-pie', roughly), the fabulously wealthy Nogaret de La Valette, Duc d'Épernon. The story goes that when Henri IV inherited this proud, dangerous and ruthlessly ambitious noble from his predecessor, he made him governor of Guyenne and went out of his way to encourage him to spend as much of his time and money as possible building himself this palace. The result is architecturally a meld of the styles of Henri IV and Louis XIII, but after damage in the Revolution and a century of duty as a women's prison (until 1928) it has lost some of its original sparkle.

Purchased by the state in 1952, the château has great vaulted guard rooms below and painted ceilings above in the main rooms, tapestries from the 13th and 17th centuries (the latter, showing scenes from the life of Henri III, were made here) and, best of all, eight monumental chimneypieces, beautifully sculpted in part by Jean Langlois and decorated with rare marbles, cascades of flowers and fruits, cupids and armour. Also on display are fragments of the grand mausoleum of the Ducs d'Épernon which was located in a rich marble chapel in the nearby church of St-Blaise, until it was bashed in the Revolution.

Loupiac Another village that gave its name to its sweet perfumed wine, Loupiac also prospered in antiquity, judging by its **Villa Gallo-Romain** (St-Romain; m 06 07 01 64 88; w villadeloupiac.wixsite.com; Jul–Aug 14.00–18.00 daily, Sep–Jun 14.00–18.00 Sun for guided tours including a glass of Loupiac wine; €5, ages 12–18 €3, under 12 free). Inhabited from the 1st to 7th centuries AD, the baths and plumbing are well preserved, and the whole is covered with colourful mosaic floors, including one in a pretty heart pattern.

Ste-Croix-du-Mont Up river the third vinous vortex of sweet white wine, St-Croix, sits on an enormous fossilised oyster reef. One of its two châteaux belonged to Pierre de Lancre, a psychotic witch-hunter who terrorised the Basque lands in the 1600s on behalf of the Parlement de Bordeaux. The square in front of the rebuilt Romanesque church enjoys a wide-ranging view of the Garonne valley over towards rivals Barsac and Sauternes.

St-Macaire and around Perched on its rock over the Garonne, **St-Macaire** is one of the Gironde's medieval gems. Originally called Ligena, it assumed the name of its 4th-century hermit Macaire (Makarios) then got a big boost when the kings of England designated it a coin-minting *Ville royale d'Angleterre*. It was on the river and bustling, and what could go wrong? But in the 18th century the Macariens woke up one morning to find their quays left high and dry when the Garonne altered its course, and taking away any impulse to modernise its narrow lanes and medieval houses. Three fortified gates still defend the village, including the **Porte de l'Horloge**, equipped with a watchtower, bell and a clock. Best of all is the irresistible, irregular **Place du Mercadiou**, lined with Gothic arcades and houses in a variety of styles from the 13th to the 16th centuries.

Sitting atop the village ramparts, **St-Sauveur** (Place de l'Église; 05 57 36 24 64; usually) was part of a 12th-century Benedictine priory built on the site of St-Macaire's hermitage. It has a sculpted portal and tympanum, damaged in the Revolution; inside the painting on the capitals was restored making them look as odd as painted Greek statues – but in both cases that's what their sculptors intended. The murals in the vaults from the 1400s on the *Apocalypse* and *Golden Legend* look as if the restorer in 1825 went a bit mad there too, but recent studies say he only altered a few of the colours. There are some very unusual scenes here, of the angel cracking open the book of seven seals, while the Son of Man is shown with a double-edged sword over his mouth (page 125). St-Sauveur's cloister and priory buildings, with their wide-ranging views over the countryside, are a favourite setting for summer fêtes.

The beloved summer home of Nobel-prize-winning novelist François Mauriac (1885–1970), the **Domaine de Malagar** (05 57 98 17 17; w malagar.fr; 45min guided tours: 10.30, 11.30, 14.30, 15.30, 16.30 & 17.30; €8, ages 12–25 €6, under 12 free), is 3km northwest. It belonged first to his great-grandfather, and since 1985 to the Conseil Régional d'Aquitaine. A treat for French literature fans, Malagar is preserved as it was during the lifetime of the author of *Thérèse Desqueyroux*; there are exhibits on his life and times, and visitors can ramble in its lovely park.

The 14th-century **Château de Malromé** (6km northeast of St-Macaire in St-André-du-Bois; 05 56 76 25 42; w malrome.com; Jul–Sep 11.00, 14.30 & 16.00 Wed–Sun, Oct–Jun 11.00 & 15.00 Wed–Sun (closed Jan); check website for specialised visits during the year; €12, EU citizens aged 18–26 €8, under 18 free) was completed in the 18th and 19th centuries by the Counts of Toulouse-Lautrec. Young Henri often spent his summers here with his mother, and died here in 1901, aged only 37, burned out from alcoholism and syphilis. The tour takes in nine rooms from his time and his summer atelier, and has contemporary art exhibits, a restaurant, **Chez Les Abeilles Gastronomique** [map, page 102] (May–Oct, Wed–Sun; lunch menu €19, dinner €58; **€€€€**) and 43ha of vineyards. 'I'll drink milk when the cows start eating grapes,' Toulouse-Lautrec would thunder at his doctors, and the château's red Bordeaux Supérieur made of 70% Merlot was one of his favourites.

Henri de Toulouse-Lautrec is buried, rather uncomfortably one imagines for a hard-living, keen-eyed observer of Parisian low life, next to his mother in the cemetery of the prim and proper 17th-century **Basilique Notre-Dame de Verdelais** (1 Place des Allées, Verdelais; 05 57 98 34 90; w sanctuairedeverdelais.fr; 09.30–noon & 14.30–18.00 daily), with its skyscraper belltower, located just to the southwest. This is the most famous pilgrimage church in the Gironde, with its miracle-working statue of the Virgin (from the 12th or 14th century). The church's little **museum** (Jul–Sep 14.00–18.30 Tue–Sun; free) has an impressive collection of ex-votos from sailors and landlubbers attesting to her powers of intervention.

Further up the Garonne, **St-Pierre-d'Aurillac** has a pleasant beach and a Merovingian sarcophagus in front of its church, but the most tempting stop between St-Macaire and La Réole is **St-Martin-de-Sescas**, to see the magnificent portal of its 12th-century church of **St-Martin** with its six rainbow arches filled with intricate, lace-like carvings of birds, rabbits, trees, leaves and male and female figures representing the Seven Deadly Sins, along with other capitals, warning of other (mainly sexual) sins. Other capitals inside, especially those supporting the triumphal arch, are strange and mysterious.

La Réole and around In AD977, the Benedictines received a charter from the Duke of Gascony to refound a Carolingian-era priory at Squirs on the Garonne, which had been left in ruins ever since the Vikings hooliganned their way through in AD848. The Benedictines renamed the priory after their Rule (Regulam), hence La Réole, and Richard the Lionheart gave it a set of walls to match its strategic position over the river and to defend its river trade, especially in wine. Until the English created a rival port, Libourne on the Dordogne, La Réole could proudly claim to be the second town in Guyenne. In 1856, the completion of the Canal Latéral à la Garonne (or Canal de Garonne; which carries on downriver to Langon) put the nail in the coffin of its river trade.

Le Réole is full of fascinating corners. It presents a stately façade, especially with the mass of the 18th-century **Prieuré des Bénédictins** on its terrace overlooking the railway and river. Many of the old priory buildings are now used by the city – the panelled and stuccoed Louis XV **Salle d'honneur** is now the mayor's office; the impressive vaulted cellars house the library. Among the medieval boutiques and houses is the oldest **Hôtel de Ville** in France, built in the early 1200s by order of Richard the Lionheart, pierced with irregularly placed mullioned windows; it was later converted into a prison, with a market *halle* below.

Rue Peysseguin is a charming street, site of La Réole's synagogue; Bordeaux's Parlement met between 1653 and 1678 in a handsome 15th-century mansion on Côte St-Michel. In 1230, an English architect under Henry III designed La Réole's **Château des Quat'Sos** ('of the four sisters'), its name referring to the massive round towers at each angle, although only one 'sister' still stands; this castle suffered 12 different sieges, the last in 1629. It remained the property of the kings of England until the end of the Hundred Years' War and was always heavily garrisoned; the Black Prince spent a good deal of time here.

Just over the bridge from La Réole, **Fontet** has a surprise: a group of farm buildings containing the **Musée d'Artisanat et Monuments d'Allumettes** (matchstick models) (Couture; 05 56 71 21 17; w museeallumettes.com; guided tours Mar–Sep 14.00–18.00 daily; €5/€2.50), including nothing less than the Largest Matchstick Buildings in the World (Rheims Cathedral and the Château de Versailles) made by Gérard Gergeres, along with old farm tools and some rather dodgy paintings.

Just north, on the River Dropt, you can look at a pair of attractive watermills: the fortified **Moulin de Bagas** (Rte du Dropt, Bagas) built in 1316 by the Benedictines of La Réole, and, 2.5km further up, the even more impressive 11th-century **Moulin de Loubens**; in the 18th century, they added a bridge-dam of arcades leapfrogging over the stream, giving the mill its nickname, the 'Petit Chenonceau'. The Romans liked this area as well: the ruins of Gallo-Roman villas have been discovered about every 2km along the valley.

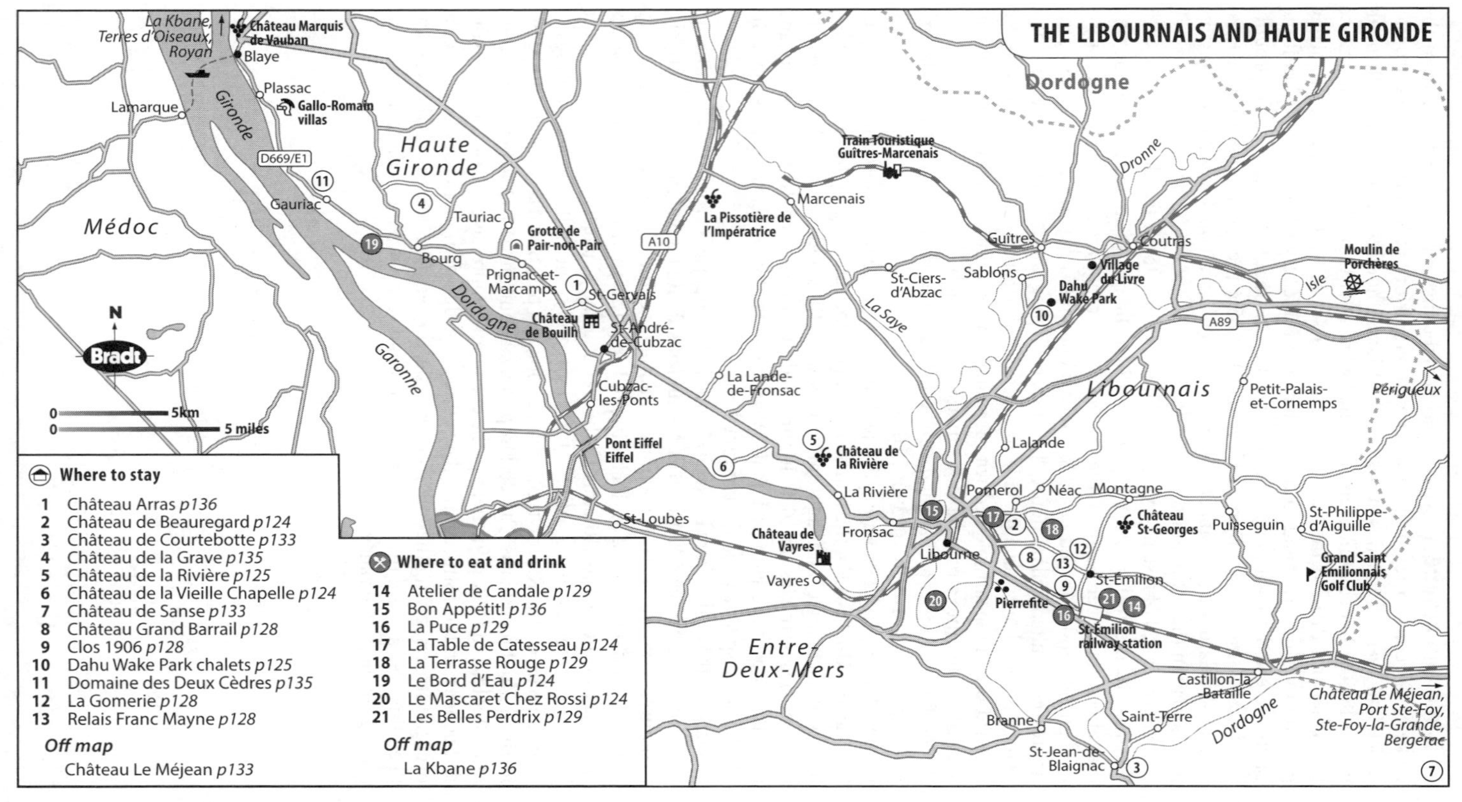
THE LIBOURNAIS AND HAUTE GIRONDE
La Kbane, Terres d'Oiseaux, Royan
Château Marquis de Vauban
Blaye
Plassac
Gallo-Romain villas
Lamarque
Gironde
D669/E1
Haute Gironde
Gauriac
Médoc
Tauriac
Grotte de Pair-non-Pair
Bourg
Prignac-et-Marcamps
St-Gervais
Château de Bouilh
St-André-de-Cubzac
Dordogne
Garonne
Cubzac-les-Ponts
Pont Eiffel Eiffel
N
Bradt
0 5km
0 5 miles
A10
La Pissotière de l'Impératrice
Marcenais
Train Touristique Guîtres-Marcenais
Dordogne
Dronne
Guîtres
Coutras
Village du Livre
Dahu Wake Park
Sablons
St-Ciers-d'Abzac
La Saye
La Lande-de-Fronsac
Moulin de Porchères
Isle
A89
Libournais
Petit-Palais-et-Cornemps
Périgueux
Château de la Rivière
La Rivière
Fronsac
Château de Vayres
Vayres
St-Loubès
Lalande
Pomerol
Néac
Montagne
Château St-Georges
Puisseguin
St-Philippe-d'Aiguille
Grand Saint Emilionnais Golf Club
Libourne
Pierrefite
St-Émilion
St-Emilion railway station
Entre-Deux-Mers
Castillon-la-Bataille
Branne
Saint-Terre
St-Jean-de-Blaignac
Dordogne
Château Le Méjean, Port Ste-Foy, Ste-Foy-la-Grande, Bergerac
Where to stay
1 Château Arras p136
2 Château de Beauregard p124
3 Château de Courtebotte p133
4 Château de la Grave p135
5 Château de la Rivière p125
6 Château de la Vieille Chapelle p124
7 Château de Sanse p133
8 Château Grand Barrail p128
9 Clos 1906 p128
10 Dahu Wake Park chalets p125
11 Domaine des Deux Cèdres p135
12 La Gomerie p128
13 Relais Franc Mayne p128
Off map
Château Le Méjean p133
Where to eat and drink
14 Atelier de Candale p129
15 Bon Appétit! p136
16 La Puce p129
17 La Table de Catesseau p124
18 La Terrasse Rouge p129
19 Le Bord d'Eau p124
20 Le Mascaret Chez Rossi p124
21 Les Belles Perdrix p129
Off map
La Kbane p136

6

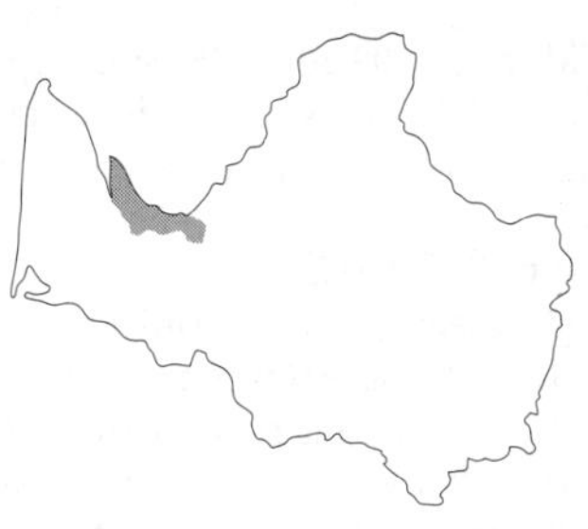

The Libournais and Haute Gironde

When Bordeaux talks about 'right bank' wines, it refers to the prestigious vineyards surrounding the Gironde's second city of Libourne – including the renowned wines of St-Émilion and Pomerol but many other (and more affordable!) good ones. St-Émilion is also the most beautiful town in the department, in the most beautiful setting, and gets the most tourists, but there are other treasures here too, including a historic train to ride. There are more wines and castles to discover in the Haute Gironde along the estuary, but it gets a tenth as many tourists; it also offers some superb birdwatching.

LIBOURNE AND AROUND

In 1269, Sir Richard de Leyburn, of Leybourne, Kent, Lieutenant of Henry III, was ordered to found a port bastide to double the export capacities of Bordeaux, and located the perfect site on the deep tidal waters of the River Isle just before its confluence with the Dordogne, 100km from the Atlantic. Renamed Leyburnia, then Frenchified to Libourne, it soon grew into the Gironde's second port, shipping wine to England and carrying sea salt into the interior. It has a surprising secret: in December it's the address of Père Noël. All the letters sent by French children end up in his special office here, where 60 elves help him sort the post. In September, surfers and kayakers gather at the Port du St-Pardon to ride the *mascaret* (tidal bore) on the Dordogne – it's only about a metre high but it's long and fun.

Libourne has held **markets** on Tuesday, Friday and Sunday mornings in Place Abel-Surchamp for the past 600 years.

GETTING THERE AND AROUND

By train Libourne's station (Av de Gallieni) is on the main Paris–Bordeaux LGV line, with eight stops a day; it also has TER connections to Coutras, Périgueux and Bergerac.

By bus and taxi Calibus (**w** calibus.fr) serves the surrounding area (including Pomerol, Guîtres and Vayres) from the *gare routière* next to the station. Other buses (**w** transports.nouvelle-aquitaine.fr) go on to St-Émilion.

For taxis, try Taxi Libournais (**m** 06 02 11 79 04; **w** taxi-libourne.fr).

By bike Hire an e-bike by Libourne's port from **Lovelec33** (Espl de la République; **m** 06 82 72 15 64; **w** location-velo-electrique-libourne.fr; from €26 for a half-day to €168/week).

TOURIST INFORMATION Libourne's go-getter **tourist office** (42 Place Abel-Surchamp; ☎ 05 57 51 15 04; **w** tourisme-libournais.com; ⏱ Jul–Aug 09.30–19.00

Mon–Sat, 09.30–13.00 Sun, Sep–Jun 09.30–12.30 & 14.00 Mon–Sat) offers tickets for **river cruises** to the Château de Vayres (€18, ages 6–18 €15, family of 4 €49) and lists a full range of activities on nearby lakes and rivers.

WHERE TO STAY

Château de Beauregard [map, page 122] (5 rooms) 73 Rue de Catusseau, Pomerol; 05 57 51 13 36; w chateau-beauregard.com. Sleep in a famous Pomerol estate's 18th-century *chartreuse* (the model for the Guggenheims' Mille-Fleurs mansion on Long Island) overlooking a beautiful park. **€€€€€**

Château de la Vieille Chapelle [map, page 122] (4 rooms) Lugon et L'Ile-du-Carney, 14 km west of Libourne; 05 57 84 48 65; w chateau-de-la-vieille-chapelle.com. Lovely tranquil rooms near the river on a wine estate that once formed part of a 12th-century church. Evening meals available for around €20. **€€€**

La Tour du Vieux Port (15 rooms) 23 Quai Suchet, Libourne; 05 57 25 75 56; w latourduvieuxport.com. Next to Libourne's landmark tower on the River Isle, a Logis hotel with a wide choice of décors. **€€**

Mercure Libourne Saint Émilion (81 rooms) 3 Quai Suchet, Libourne; 05 57 25 64 18; w all.accor.com. Big modern chain hotel, with good views. **€€**

WHERE TO EAT AND DRINK

La Table de Catusseau [map, page 122] 86 Rte de Catusseau, Pomerol; 05 57 84 40 40; w latabledecatusseau.fr; closed Sun–Mon. Elegant, contemporary & fresh & something different – the chef hales from New Caledonia. Charming service. *Excellent w/day menu du marché €25, dinner from €38.* **€€€€**

Cosy Tourny 12 Cours Tourny, Libourne; 05 57 51 68 91; w cosytourny.business.site; closed Mon & eves Sun. Pretty patio & chimney within that matches its name. Always a good soup, salads, duck & vegetarian choices. Very popular, so book well in advance. *Menu €35.* **€€€**

Le Bord d'Eau [map, page 122] 4 Rue Poinsonnet, Fronsac (just west of Libourne); 05 57 51 99 91; closed Mon–Tue. A pretty spot for lunch or dinner, on the river itself. Fish & meat dishes, with homemade bread. **€€€**

Le Mascaret Chez Rossi [map, page 122] Av du Port du Roy, Libourne (south of the centre by the Dordogne); 05 57 84 79 10; f; closed Mon–Thu. Bucolic setting, charming service & delicious €30 menu. **€€€**

Chez Rémi 6 Rue Fonneuve, Libourne; 05 57 51 27 71; closed Mon & eves Sun. A local favourite for its traditional, old-fashioned dishes & big portions. *Lunch formule €14.* **€€**

WHAT TO SEE AND DO After the French sacked Libourne in 1294, the English surrounded the town with high walls and towers; the large cylindrical **Tour Richard**, named after the son of Edward III, still overlooks the Isle at the Grand Port. Here and there you can see old wine warehouses and merchants' houses, mostly from the 18th century, especially in Rue Victor Hugo and Rue Fonneuve. Both lead into the central square, **Place Abel Surchamp**, with its arcades, covered market, 16th-century houses and the **Hôtel de Ville**, built in 1429 and restored when the 19th-century infatuation for neo-Gothic was at its peak. Upstairs, the **Musée des Beaux-Arts** (05 57 55 33 44; 14.00–18.00 Tue, 09.30–13.00 & 14.00–19.00 Wed–Sat; free) features the lively horse paintings of Libourne native René Princeteau (1844–1914), who was the friend and first teacher of Toulouse-Lautrec, and a sprinkling of minor works by Le Brun, Bartolomeo Manfredi, Jacopo Bassano, Picabia, Foujita and Dufy. Don't miss the quirky statue on the landing of the monumental stair: *La France* embracing a bust of the worst Bourbon wastrel, Louis XV.

DOWNRIVER FROM LIBOURNE Across the Dordogne, the 16th–17th-century **Château de Vayres** (63 Av de Libourne, Vayres; 05 57 84 96 58; w chateaudevayres.com;

🕘 Jul–mid-Sep 14.00–18.30 daily, Apr–Jun & mid-Sep–Nov guided tours 15.00, 16.00 & 17.00 Sun & hols; €12.50/€10, park only €8 from age 5 up) was once owned by Henri IV, and is endowed with a magnificent stairway sweeping down to the water via a formal riverside park. The refined, decorative east gallery is attributed to Louis de Foix, architect of the lighthouse of Cordouan; the furnishings are Louis XIII and Louis XIV, although it's best known for its 17th- and 18th-century tapestries.

Further downriver, the little bastide town of **St-Loubès** gave the world one of its first silent film comedians and one of Charlie Chaplin's inspirations, Max Linder (1883–1925, born Gabriel Leuvielle). He shot three of his films in St-Loubès before shooting himself, and is buried in the village cemetery.

FRONSAC Just west of Libourne, this town is synonymous with red wines that had a better reputation and were pricier than those of St-Émilion in the 18th and early 19th century before almost disappearing. Now revived, Merlot again is a dominant grape, with high proportions of Cabernet Sauvignon and Cabernet Franc. Visitors are welcome at the loveliest estate, the grand 14th-century **Château de la Rivière** [map, page 122] (Rue Goffre, La Rivière; 05 57 55 56 56; 🕘 book a guided tour at 10.30, 14.30 & 16.30 Mon–Sat; from €9), and to spend the night in one of their five rooms (b/fast inc; **€€€€€**).

The church at the village of **La Rivière** houses a tall 14th-century alabaster statue of the Virgin and Child, while **La Lande-de-Fronsac** to the northwest has a remarkable 11th-century church of **St-Pierre** with a tympanum intricately carved with a scene from the first vision of the Apocalypse: 'He had in His right hand seven stars, out of His mouth went a sharp two-edged sword….' Lively scenes of hunters, musicians, etc fill the surrounding arches. The elongated apse has curious modillons as well. No-one has any idea who sculpted it, or when.

NORTH OF LIBOURNE Up the Isle from Libourne, **Guîtres** is a popular stop for its **Abbatiale** (05 57 69 10 34; w abbatialedeguitres.fr; 🕘 late Jun–early Sep 14.00–18.00 daily; during Aug–mid-Sep concerts at 17.00 Sun are free), a church the size of a cathedral begun by the Benedictines in 1080 and finished in the 1400s. Despite fortifications added during the Wars of Religion, it was damaged on several occasions and restored in 1839. Inside it has a pretty colonnaded apse, and you can usually go up to admire the remarkable carpentry holding up the roof.

The **Train Touristique Guîtres-Marcenais** (13 Av de la Gare; 05 57 69 10 69; w trainguitres.fr; 🕘 runs Jun–Sep 15.30 Sun; Jul–Aug €14, ages 5–11 €8, Jun & Sep €12/€7.50) pulled by a steam or diesel engine chugs 13.5km through pretty countryside from Guîtres to Marcenais and back in 3 hours on the Blaye-to-Coutras line which closed in 1938. The station at Guîtres has a small **train museum** to get you into the mood, and if you've ever watched those old Westerns where baddies make a getaway on a handrail car, the **Vélorail du Pays Gabay** (🕘 May–Oct 09.30–14.30 daily; €30 for 5 places) offers a chance to do it on a 16km track through the forest.

Three kilometres south of **Guîtres**, learn how to wakeboard at the **Dahu Wake Park** [map, page 122] (10ter Champ de Gougeon, Sablons; m 07 56 94 70 81; w dahuwakefamily.com) featuring the world's longest cable ski (580m). They also have five floating chalets (**€€€€€**).

West of Guîtres, **St-Ciers-d'Abzac**'s 12th-century church of **St-Martin-du-Bois** used to attract pilgrims with stunted children. It has curious modillions and a curiouser apse, sheltering a venerated block of sandstone called La Feyra that once formed part of a Neolithic monument; it is rumoured to turn three times at the ringing of the Angelus.

Just east of Guîtres, the **Village du Livre** (Laubardemont, Sablons; ☎05 57 41 14 11; **w** levillagedulivre.com; ⏰ 10.00–18.00 Tue–Sat; €8, under 14 free) occupies a former flour mill, where the Dronne flows into the Isle. It's now a kind of second-hand bookshop plus, with some 2 million volumes in a series of rooms dedicated to toy models, historic postcards, an old schoolroom, musical instruments, religion, gastronomy, etc.

Coutras, located near the confluence of the Dronne and Isle, witnessed a major battle in the Wars of Religion in 1587. This was won by the Protestants for Henri of Navarre over the 27-year-old Duc de Joyeuse, whose entrails were solemnly buried in the floor of the church of **St-Jean Baptiste**, which was mostly rebuilt in the 1800s. In 1981, Merovingian sarcophagi from the 5th–7th centuries were discovered here with rich jewels now in Bordeaux's Musée d'Aquitaine.

Further east up the Isle, the flour-milling **Moulin de Porchères** (1679 Rte de l'Entre-Deux-Mers, Porchères; ☎05 57 40 86 60; **w** moulindeporcheres.jimdofree.com; ⏰ mid-May–early Nov 10.00–18.00 Tue–Sun; €7/€5) offers tours of the mill, last modernised in the 1930s, and hires out water bikes for pedalling on the river; there's also a *guinguette* for lunch.

POMEROL Although the growing area is a mere 3 by 4km, Pomerol produces some of the most distinctive wines in France, noted for their power and bouquet. As in neighbouring St-Émilion, the soil is very complex; here the best vintages take years to come into their own. Merlot is the predominant grape, making up 95% of the most celebrated of all Pomerols, Château Pétrus, considered by many to be the best Merlot in the world. Wines from nearby Néac and Lalande come under the appellation Lalande-de-Pomerol (and are certainly more reasonably priced). Pomerol's **Maison des Vins** (8 Rue Tropchaud; ☎05 57 25 05 88; **w** vins-pomerol.fr; ⏰ 09.30–noon & 14.30–17.30 Mon–Fri) sells bottles at château prices. You can also take a 90-minute tour of a Pomerol vineyard in an electric tuk-tuk (book via the Cordeliers, page 130; €35/€30).

ST-ÉMILION AND AROUND

In 1999, UNESCO designated St-Émilion as a World Heritage Site for being 'an outstanding example of a historic vineyard landscape that has survived intact and in activity to the present day'. Set in a natural amphitheatre, mellowed to the colour of old piano keys, the town has been restored to its former beauty. But leave your high heels at home: lanes called *tertres,* unevenly paved with granite blocks from Cornwall (the ballast of England's wine ships), are so steep that handrails have been installed down their centres. For all that, St-Émilion keeps its greatest secrets underground – not only the ruby nectar in its cellars, beloved by medieval popes and English kings, but Europe's largest subterranean church. Ideally arrive early to avoid the crowds of day trippers, or stay overnight.

HISTORY The town's destiny was set in motion in the 8th century AD with the arrival of a Benedictine hermit from Brittany named Émilion. His piety attracted others, who enlarged the natural shelters in the hillside. When the founder died, this primitive monastery took his name: Sent-Melyon in Occitan. The walled town that grew up here controlled this section of the Dordogne and received its first charter

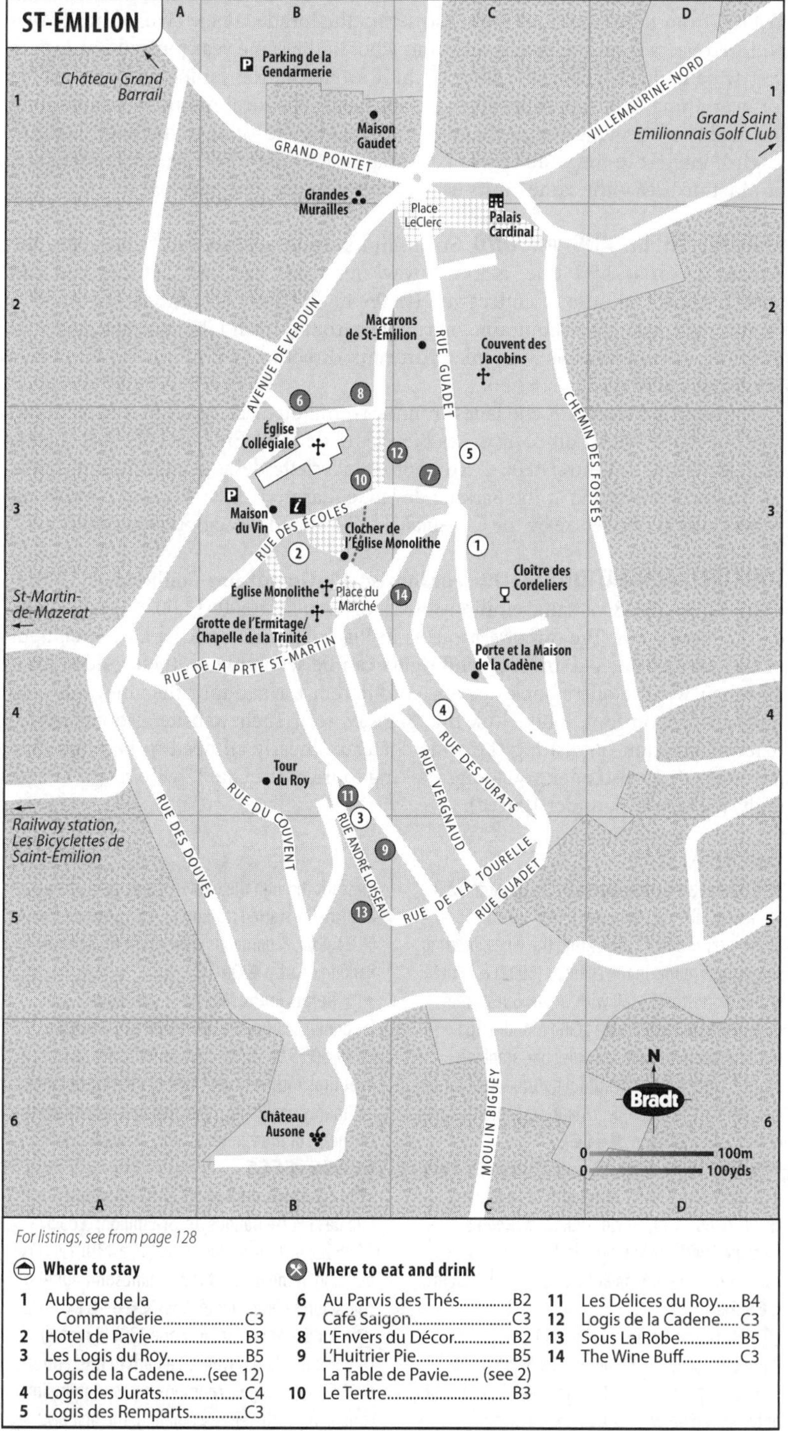

For listings, see from page 128

Where to stay

1 Auberge de la Commanderie C3
2 Hotel de Pavie B3
3 Les Logis du Roy B5
Logis de la Cadene ......(see 12)
4 Logis des Jurats C4
5 Logis des Remparts C3

Where to eat and drink

6 Au Parvis des Thés B2
7 Café Saigon C3
8 L'Envers du Décor B2
9 L'Huitrier Pie B5
La Table de Pavie ...... (see 2)
10 Le Tertre B3
11 Les Délices du Roy B4
12 Logis de la Cadene C3
13 Sous La Robe B5
14 The Wine Buff C3

in 1199 from John Lackland, who also set up the Jurade, a new civil authority of a hundred peers from the bourgeoisie and who, in the same year formed Bordeaux's first wine guild. Up until the time of the Revolution, the Jurade was responsible for everything from tax collecting and organising the local militia to maintaining the quality of the wine – wine that was imported by the tonne to the English court. English interest in the wine was so keen that in 1289 Edward I set the limits of the production area – the same limits used to this day (see box, page 132).

GETTING THERE AND AROUND St-Émilion's **train station** [127 A4], on the Bordeaux–Sarlat TER line, is 2km away, but from April to October you can book a tuk-tuk shuttle to collect you (m 06 40 83 62 60; €4). **Buses** 314 and 315 (w transports.nouvelle-aquitaine.fr) run year-round from Libourne station to St-Émilion; in summer bus 302 links Bordeaux direct to St-Émilion via Libourne. For **taxis**, call m 06 40 83 62 60.

The beautiful vineyards and lanes around St-Émilion make for a fun spin on a **bike**; hire one at the tourist office or at Les Bicyclettes de Saint-Émilion [127 A4] (Planté Blé, 1km from the centre; m 06 98 16 10 86; w bicyclettesdesaintemilion.simplybook.it). There's free **parking** at the Parking de la Gendarmerie [127 B1] and payable car parks closer to the centre by the Collégiale [127 B3] and Place Bouqueyre.

TOURIST INFORMATION The **Office de Tourisme du Grand Saint-Émilionnais** [127 B3] (05 57 55 28 28; w saint-emilion-tourisme.com; 10.00–13.00 & 14.00–18.00 daily, closed Mon–Tue out of season) is in Place des Créneaux Le Doyenné. Four of the town's principal **underground sights** can be seen only on their guided tour; and their website offers bookings for ten different ways to tour the vineyards – by tourist train, on foot, e-bike, tuk-tuk, Segway, etc). Their website also has up-to-date information on visiting the wine châteaux (nearly all need to be booked in advance). They also offer hour-long walking tours of the Cité UNESCO (in French daily at 15.00; €13, under 10 free).

WHERE TO STAY

Château Grand Barrail [map, page 122] (46 rooms) Rte de Libourne (D43); 05 57 55 37 00; w grand-barrail.com. Amid the vines, offering sumptuous rooms in the château (1902) & in the modern guesthouse, all with views. Guests may never want to leave: there's Cinq Mondes Spa, outdoor pool, Turkish bath, cosy bar, smoking room & cigar bar & a beautiful gourmet restaurant (€€€€) in the glassed-in Mauresque dining room or in the Grand Salon. €€€€€

Clos 1906 [map, page 122] (4 rooms, 1 apt) 4 La Gaffelière-Ouest, 2km south of St-Émilion; m 06 76 69 15 11; w clos1906.com. Rooms furnished with antiques on an 18th-century estate with a pool & an antique gallery. B/fast inc. €€€€€

Hotel de Pavie [127 B3] (17 rooms) 5 Place du Clocher, St-Émilion; 05 57 55 07 55; w hoteldepavie.com. A luxurious Relais & Château hotel spread between 2 buildings, reached by a glass lift through the garden. There is an elegant 2-Michelin-starred restaurant, **La Table de Pavie** (€€€€€), & gorgeous views from the terrace. Parking nearby. €€€€€

Relais Franc Mayne [map, page 122] (5 rooms) La Gomerie, 2km west of St-Émilion; m 07 50 55 06 99; w chateaufrancmayne.com. A beautiful 16th-century château offering gorgeous bedrooms (including 1 perched in a cedar tree) in the heart of the vineyards. Wine tours & b/fast inc. €€€€€–€€€€

Les Logis du Roy [127 B5] (5 rooms) 7 Rue de la Porte Bouqueyre, St-Émilion; 05 57 74 15 26; w leslogisduroy.com. In a 13th-century building in the heart of town, handsome suites of character, sleeping up to 4. €€€€€–€€€

La Gomerie [map, page 122] (5 rooms) 5 La Gomerie, 20min walk on a path to the centre; 05 57 24 68 85; w chambreshotessaintemilion.com. In an 18th-century building, the first B&B

in town & it's still one of the best. Excellent b/fast inc. €€€€

Logis des Remparts [127 C3] (9 rooms) 18 Rue Gaudet, St-Émilion; 05 57 24 70 43; w logisdesremparts.com. Sweet & pretty with a little inner courtyard, pool & walled garden; also a rare private car park. €€€€

Auberge de la Commanderie [127 C3] (17 rooms) 2 Rue de la Porte Brunet, St-Émilion; 05 57 24 70 19; w aubergedelacommanderie.com. A former Templar possession, where the 8 Girondins hid during the Terror (page 130). Now a tidy contemporary hotel, with dbls & family rooms. Parking €15/night. €€€

Logis des Jurats [127 C4] (3 rooms) 6 Rue des Jurats, St-Émilion; m 06 74 76 20 38; w logisdesjurats.com. In the centre, with a wood-&-stone décor, including 2 family rooms. Friendly host, parking & garden; b/fast inc. €€€–€€

WHERE TO EAT AND DRINK

La Terrasse Rouge [map, page 122] 1 Château La Dominique, 5km northwest; 05 57 24 47 05; w laterrasserouge.com; closed Tue. Chic terrace & chic cuisine overlooking the garnet-coloured roof of the chai designed by Jean Nouvel with views across to the famous Premier Grand Cru Cheval Blanc vines. *€45 lunch menu*. €€€€€

Les Belles Perdrix [map, page 122] Château Troplong-Mondot, 5km east of St-Émilion; 05 57 55 38 28; w troplong-mondot.com; closed Sun–Mon & lunch Tue. Idyllic setting with a panoramic terrace, where Michelin-starred chef David Charrier whips up gorgeous seasonal *haute cuisine. W/day lunch €48, total blowout menu €145*. €€€€€

Logis de la Cadene [127 C3] 3 Place du Marché au Bois; 05 57 24 71 40; w logisdelacadene.fr; closed Sun–Mon. One of the oldest restaurants in town, founded in 1848, has a fresh new look, & very arty Michelin-starred cooking by young chef Alexandre Baumard, as well as 5 designer rooms (€€€€€). *W/day lunch menus from €44*. €€€€€

Atelier de Candale [map, page 122] 1 Grandes Plantes, St-Laurent-des-Combes, 3km southeast of St-Émilion; 05 57 24 15 45; w atelierdecandale.com; May–Sep closed eves Mon–Sun, Oct–Apr closed Mon–Sun. Gorgeous views over the vines & contemporary cuisine. *Lunch menu €28*. €€€€

L'Envers du Décor [127 B2] 11 Rue du Clocher; 05 57 74 48 31; w envers-dudecor.com; daily. Opened in 1987 & still going strong; an excellent wine bar-bistro famous for its lamb shoulder & *soufflé au Grand Marnier. Lunch menus from €32*. €€€€

L'Huitrier Pie [127 B5] 11 Rue de la Porte Bouqueyre; 05 57 24 69 71; w lhuitrier-pie.com; closed Tue–Wed. 'The Oystercatcher' in a 16th-century building is one of the best new spots in town, fresh & creative, using nearly all organic produce; gorgeous plates & a pretty patio. *Menus from €36*. €€€€

La Réserve du Presbytère 22 Grand Rue, Montagne, 5km north of St-Émilion; 05 57 79 03 43; w lareservedupresbytere.fr; closed Mon & eves Sun. Delicious *bistronomique* cuisine by a young enthusiastic team with their own vegetable & herb garden in this pretty wine village. Special dinner & cinema eves 1st Fri of each month. *3-course lunch menu from €27, dinner €46, Sun lunch €35*. €€€€

Le Tertre [127 B3] 5 Rue Tertre de la Tente; 05 57 74 46 33; w restaurantletertre.com; closed Wed–Thu. Since 2020 the young owners of this beautiful restaurant in the heart of St-Émilion have seduced the town with their fresh modern cuisine on a menu that changes every 2 months. Superb wine list, too. €€€€

Café Saigon [127 C3] 21 Rue Guadet; 09 53 00 00 19; w cafe-saigon-saint-emilion.business.site; daily. Exceptional Vietnamese cuisine, all freshly made & served with a smile. €€€

Caffé Cuisine 9 Place du Marché, Branne, 8km south; 05 57 24 19 67; f; closed Mon & eves Sun. Pretty terrace overlooking the Dordogne & a fresh market menu that literally changes every day; tapas & pizzas too. €€€

Les Délices du Roy [127 B4] 1 Rue de la Porte Bouqueyre; 05 57 51 95 68; w lesdelicesduroy.fr; closed Mon & eves Sun. Everything is homemade here, including good vegetarian & pescatarian choices, terrines, salads & their special duck burger with foie gras. Sautéed potatoes but no frites, *jamais!* €€€

La Puce [map, page 122] 323 Grand Bigaroux, Saint-Sulpice-de-Faleyrens (2km south);

☎05 57 24 71 18; ⏲ lunch only Mon–Fri.The 'Flea' (a term of endearment in French) serves 1 menu (€14), & it's all solid *grandmère*-style cuisine. Filled with locals. €

Au Parvis des Thés [127 B2] 1 Place Pioceau; ☎05 57 50 58 87; w macarons-saint-emilion.fr. Delightful tearoom & gorgeous pastries.

Sous La Robe [127 B5] 21 Rue André Loiseau; ☎05 57 24 56 80; f souslarobesaintemilion; ⏲ Thu–Mon 17.00–midnight. Cool wine bar with excellent little plates & frequent live music at w/ends.

The Wine Buff [127 C3] 2 Rue du Marché; m 06 28 80 21 52; w thewinebuff.com/st-emilion; ⏲ 10.00–18.00 daily (in winter ring ahead). To go to St-Émilion without stopping for a glass & tapas with the entertaining & knowledgeable Paddy & Pilar would be to miss one of the town's great experiences. Fabulous range of wines to take home, too.

SHOPPING Macarons made according to a recipe invented by local nuns in 1620 are sold from the town's oldest shop, **Macarons de Saint-Émilion** [127 C2] (9 Rue Guadet; ☎05 57 24 72 33; w macarons-saint-emilion.fr). **Maison du Vin** [127 B3] (Place Pierre Meyrat; ☎05 57 55 50 55; w maisonduvinsaintemilion.com; ⏲ Jul–Aug 09.30–19.00 daily, other times 09.30–12.30 & 14.00–18.30) sells wine at château prices, and also does tastings (€28) and wine classes.

SPORTS AND ACTIVITIES **Hot-air balloon flights** are offered by Bordeaux Montgolfière (m 06 19 58 52 61; w bordeaux-montgolfiere.fr; €248 pp) over St-Émilion or Entre-Deux-Mers and La Ferme du Ciel (☎05 57 33 52 60; w lafermeduciel.eu; from €219 pp) over the vines and the Gironde.

You'll find one of the top golf courses in France, designed by Tom Doak, at **Grand Saint Emilionnais Golf Club** [map, page 122] (172 Goffre, Gardegan-et-Tourtirac; ☎05 57 40 88 64; w segolfclub.com).

WHAT TO SEE AND DO

A walk around St-Émilion

Entering the town from the south on the D122, you'll pass a **public park** built around the **Maison Gaudet** [127 B1], home of the Girondin deputy Marguerite-Élie Guadet, who managed to flee Robespierre's executions in Paris with seven other Girondins. They hid out for nine months in St-Émilion, but all but one were eventually captured by Robespierre's henchmen and guillotined – ironically, only a few days before 9 Thermidor, when Robespierre himself got the chop. Across the road, rising abruptly out of a vineyard, the **Grandes Murailles**[127 B1], a 20m wall with ogival arches, is all that remains of a Dominican monastery built in 1287; as it was outside the walls, it was easy prey for a marauding French army in 1337.

Just beyond is the main entrance to St-Émilion, the **Place Leclerc** [127 C2]. Take the first left to see the substantial remains of the once-sumptuous **Palais Cardinal** [127 C1], built in 1316 by the Cardinal de Ste-Luce, nephew of Pope Clement V. Continue up Rue Gaudet, where just beyond Place du Chapitre the Dominicans rebuilt their **Couvent des Jacobins** [127 C2], after a donation in 1378 by the English Lieutenant of Aquitaine, Jean de Neville. Until the Revolution, this church held the town's main pilgrimage attraction: a statue of St Valéry, patron of St-Émilion's vintners (now in the Collégiale). Brides would gently wipe the statue with their handkerchiefs while wishing to become pregnant; Valéry's exact role in the matter was the cause of many pleasantries.

Further up, where the street forks, take Rue des Cordeliers for the **Commanderie** [127 C3], an old Templar outpost (now a hotel) and the **Cloître des Cordeliers** [127 C3] (2 bis Rue de la Porte-Brunet; ☎05 57 24 42 13; w lescordeliers.com; ⏲ Apr–Oct 11.00–19.00 daily), built in 1383. The pretty twin-columned 14th-century Franciscan cloister is a peaceful place – and this being St-Émilion, it's now used as a wine bar, while the former church is a huge wine and gift shop. Some 20m below is an astonishing termitary of 3km of tunnels, where since 1892 they have aged bubbly and slightly sweet Crémant de Bordeaux, invented by a Monsieur Meynot, when there was a slump in wine sales. Book tours and tastings via the Les Cordeliers website (€11, students & ages 10–17 €9.90, under 10 free), or take an electric tuk-tuk tour (€25, ages 3–18 €20, under 3 free), which includes an above-ground tour of St-Émilion.

Backtrack to Rue Gaudet and Rue de la Cadène, which soon passes under the 16th-century arch of the **Porte et la Maison de la Cadène** [127 C4], 'of the chain', by which a street could be quickly closed off in case of emergency. Note the half-timbered house on the left, decorated with a pair of grotesque heads and dolphins. Further up, Rue Gaudet runs into **Place du Marché** [127 B3], a magnificent urbane stage set built over the town's first cemetery, its cafés shaded by a Liberty Tree planted during the 1848 Revolution.

St-Émilion Souterrain (45min guided tours from the Place d'Église Monolithe; ⌚ 10.30–17.30 daily; book at the tourist office or online: €12, students & ages 10–17 €9, under 10 free but need a ticket) The largest underground church in Europe at 11m high, 38m long and 20m wide, St-Émilion's **Église Monolithe** [127 B3] and its sister church in Aubeterre (page 157) were begun under the shadowy 12th-century lord they both shared, the Viscount Pierre Castillon, who perhaps hoped to draw in some of that lucrative Compostela pilgrim trade with a pair of truly exceptional shrines. The Église Monolithe is a primitive and uncanny place, supported by ten rough, ill-aligned pillars – although it seems less uncanny now, with lighting and metal supports around the pillars. The bas-reliefs – the unusual four-winged angels, a figure playing a rebec, a dragon and a dragon-slayer – hint of a mystic initiation in the womb of the earth. The Gothic portal, with its eroded tympanum showing a Last Judgement, the windows and the bell tower are all later additions.

The first to dig here, however, was the saintly hermit, who excavated the **Grotte de l'Ermitage** [127 B4], where he retreated and died in AD767. His one amenity was running water from a natural spring, which he could also use to baptise converts. Carved in the stone is the saint's 'chair of meditation', now known as the *siège de la fertilité* where women would come to sit and fall pregnant within the year (there are still requests for its services, and the tourist office keeps a dossier of 'St-Émilion's babies'). The adjacent 8th-century **catacombs** originally had no door, so bodies were deposited through the funnel-like cupola: around the vault are engraved figures of three corpses with upraised arms, weird zombies symbolic of the Resurrection.

The tour also includes the 13th-century **Chapelle de la Trinité** [127 B4], decorated with very odd murals in the choir: a beardless Jesus in a diamond, with the four symbols of the Evangelists with a curious sun face above and a dragon with a bishop's head below.

Clocher de l'Église Monolithe [127 B3] (Place de Cloché; ⌚ same hours as tourist office; €2) The town's landmark 11th–15th-century bell tower and spire rises 68m, the second highest in the Gironde after St-Michel of Bordeaux. If you have the puff, you can climb the 198 steps for a superb 360-degree view over the rooftops.

Église Collégiale [127 B3] (Place Meyrat; ⌚ same hours as tourist office in the former refectory) This hotchpotch of a church was begun in 1110 – the period of its west portal, Byzantine cupolas, and frescoes of a devil, St Catherine and the Virgin on the right wall of the nave. The north portal has a tympanum adorned with a Last Judgement from 1306; in the choir are 15th-century stalls and the treasure, where the relics of St-Émilion are currently installed.

ST-ÉMILION IN THE BOTTLE

On the steep slope just west of St-Émilion stood an imperial Roman villa believed to have belonged to the poet and governor Ausonius (page 73), who lent his name to one of the greatest and smallest of the St-Émilion vineyards, **Château Ausone**. St-Émilion's reputation soared in the Middle Ages; it was the *vin honorifique* for the French, the 'king of wines' for the English. No-one can really explain why it's so good except for the intangible qualities of the *terroir*: the soil has no prominent characteristic besides its complexity, with clay and chalk present in most places – hence the predominance of Merlot, which does well in clay and ripens well in its cooler temperatures, mixed with Cabernet Franc (or Bouchet, as it's called here), producing softer, less tannic wines than its Médoc. It has also been subject to some of the strictest quality controls in France. Estates were small to begin with, compared with others in the Bordelais, and in 1921 it was decided to limit the growing area to that decreed by Edward I in the 13th century.

In 1948 the medieval Jurade was reincarnated. Clad in swish scarlet caps and robes trimmed in ermine, members announce the Ban des Vendanges, or beginning of the harvest (third Sunday in September), with a procession to the top of the Tour du Roy. The jurats also gather in May to taste each new wine to judge whether or not it will evolve to merit the name St-Émilion, announcing the crucial *jugement du vin nouveau* the third Sunday in June.

Unlike the Médoc, St-Émilion frequently updates its classifications based on quality. The last revision in 2012 divides the châteaux into Premiers Grands Crus Classés A (of which there are four: Ausone, Angélus, Cheval Blanc and Pavie), followed by 14 others distinguished by Classé B, followed by 85 Grands Crus Classés. All have to undergo a second tasting two years after the harvest to merit their labels. Below these come St-Émilion Grands Crus, and plain St-Émilions and the satellites: Lussac–St-Émilion, Montagne–St-Émilion, Puisseguin–St-Émilion and St-Georges–St-Émilion.

Tour du Roy [127 B4] (Rue des Jurats; ⌚ see tourist office; €2, under 6 free) This 32m donjon is all that remains of the Norman castle built by French king Louis VIII in c1224 or English king Henry III in c1237, with 118 steps (a bit complicated if a lot of people are going up and down at the same time), but you'll be rewarded at the top with more grand views.

AROUND ST-ÉMILION Nearly every little village around St-Émilion has a Romanesque church worth a look. One of the best, **St-Martin-de-Mazerat** (1137), is less than a kilometre west; it has a richly carved south portal, but an amputated bell tower, chopped off on the order of the Jurats to prevent the Huguenots from using it to lob cannonballs on St-Émilion. Due west of St-Émilion, overlooking the Dordogne on the D19, is the largest menhir in the Gironde, the 4.8m **Pierrefite**. This gets a big summer solstice party – no druids, but old jazz, bonfires, floating candles in the Dordogne, food and wine.

North of St-Émilion, **Montagne** has three Romanesque churches, with 12th-century **St-Martin** in the centre and less than a kilometre away, the 11th-century **St-Georges-de-Montagne** built over a Roman structure; it sports a curious bell tower, curious sculptures around the door, and curious modillions (moustache man, the anal exhibitionist, two men embracing, puking man…). Others adorn the triumphal arch and blind arcades around the apse; the naked men with belts around their middles are thought to be warnings against homosexuality in the clergy, who would have been the only ones to see them.

The 18th-century **Château St-Georges** (Rte de St-Émilion, Montagne; 05 57 74 62 11; w chateau-st-georges.com; Easter–early Nov by appt; from €9) is the most beautiful estate in the area, incorporating several towers from the original castle and a magnificent garden stair. They offer, among other visits, an *étape vigneronne* – a tour among the vines, tasting and a picnic with wine for a minimum of four people (book online; €45, ages 5–12 €26).

EAST OF ST-ÉMILION

Following the River Dordogne up to the department that takes its name, you'll find the site of a famous battle at Castillon-la-Bataille (today scene of a massive summer re-enactment) and the unofficial capital of the river's most curious fish – the lamprey.

Castillon's **market** is on Monday morning; Ste-Foy's on Saturday morning is huge and in 2021 was chosen as the most beautiful in the Gironde.

TOURIST INFORMATION

Castillon-la-Bataille 5 Allées de la République; 05 57 40 27 58; w castillonlabataille.fr; 10.00–noon & 14.00–18.00 Tue–Sat

Ste-Foy-la-Grande 102 Rue de la République; 05 57 46 03 00; w tourisme-dordogne-paysfoyen.com; 09.30–12.30 & 14.00–18.00 Mon–Sat. The office has a museum of the town's history.

WHERE TO STAY

Château de Courtebotte [map, page 122] (6 rooms, 2 cottages, 1 tree house) St-Jean-de-Blaignac; 05 57 84 61 61; w chateaudecourtebotte.com Gorgeous rooms designed with a mix of antique & contemporary in a 17th-century château overlooking the Dordogne. **€€€€–€€€**

Château de Sanse [map, page 122] (16 rooms) Sanse, Ste-Radegonde; 05 57 56 41 10; w chateaudesanse.com. A beautifully restored 18th-century castle where most spacious bedrooms have a terrace or balcony, & a heated pool. The pretty restaurant (€€€€) has its own veg garden & views; they also have a painting studio & offer courses. **€€€–€€**

Château Le Méjean [map, page 122] (5 rooms) Labarthe, Pessac-sur-Dordogne; 05 57 49 57 94; w chateau-lemejean.com. Geneviève & the grandly moustachioed Pierre-Marie are lovely hosts at their 19th-century home, with a garden. Pierre-Marie is a master frame gilder & can demonstrate his art. B/fast inc. **€€€–€€**

Grand Hotel (17 rooms) 117 Rue de la République, Ste-Foy-la-Grande; 05 57 46 00 08; w grandhotel-sainte-foy.com. Not really very grand but okay white rooms in a century-old building, with a bar & patio. **€€–€**

WHERE TO EAT AND DRINK

Auberge St-Jean 8 Rue du Pont, St-Jean-de-Blaignac; 05 57 74 95 50; w aubergesaintjean.com; closed Wed, & eves Tue & Sun. On the banks of the Dordogne, mouth-watering Michelin-starred cuisine on a short menu. *Set menus from €62.* €€€€€

Au Fil de l'Eau 3 Rue de la Rouquette, Ste-Foy-la-Grande; m 06 19 65 21 80; w aufildeleau-33.fr; daily. Part retro piano bar, with fine cocktails & restaurant, & lovingly prepared dishes made from local & organic ingredients. *3-course menu €33.* €€€

Le Cabestan Ferme du Pêcheur 2 Rte du Port de Peytor, Saint-Terre; m 06 20 89 41 84; w lamproie.fr; Jun–Sep. Where else can you dine with the lamprey fishers? Besides lamprey in several ways, there's eel, or Wels catfish & chips, & non-fishy things. As they say: 'Lamprey is the Proust madeleine of the Bordelais!' *Lunch menu €14.90.* €€

SPORTS AND ACTIVITIES Paddle a 9m native American-style canoe down the Dordogne with a nature guide through **Balade au fil de l'eau en Canoë Rabaska** (62 Rue des Sables, L'Ilot, Port Ste-Foy; m 06 81 38 44 21; w canoe-rabaska.com) or try **Galo Canoë Kayak** (Allée Paul Ducou, Port Ste Foy; 05 53 24 86 12; w canoe-kayak-port-ste-foy.com) for kayaking and stand-up paddleboarding. They also offer two-day journeys, plus there's a beach nearby.

SAINT-TERRE 'Holy Land' is the home of something that exists only in France: the Confraternity of the Lamprey, who meet in February with big silver lamprey medals around their necks to cook up pots of *lamproie à la bordelaise*, the favourite dish of Rabelais, and one they claim still graces the table of the British royal family.

The **Jardin de Lamproie** (20 Rue Charles de Gaulle; 05 57 55 28 28; 08.00–18.30 daily) will teach you all about this 340-million-year-old remarkably un-cuddly, ugly, blood-sucking parasite that missed the evolutionary boat, probably because it doesn't seem to have any eyes. The recipe requires slicing off the tail of a live lamprey, collecting the blood and removing the poisonous dorsal cartilage (ingesting some by mistake is said to have killed Henri I), then stewing it in its blood with leeks, onion, shallots, *jambon de Bayonne* and a bottle of St-Émilion.

CASTILLON-LA-BATAILLE This wine town saw the last battle of the Hundred Years' War on 17 July 1453. John Talbot, the Earl of Shrewsbury and 'English Achilles', was at Mass when a spy told him that the French, camped near the Dordogne, were retreating. Talbot at once gathered his forces, hopped on a horse and charged, only to lead his men straight into a wall of artillery. Because he was so conspicuous in his Sunday finest (once, when he was held hostage, he had vowed to the French king to never wear armour against the French), Talbot was one of the first of 4,000 to die, when his horse, hit by a cannonball, fell on him, making it easy to finish him off with an axe. The French paid tribute to him by erecting the monument in the field where he died in medieval chivalry's last great battle (it still stands 2km east of town, on the Route du Monument Talbot). In summer, the **Re-enactment of the Battle of Castillon** (Château Castegens, in Belvès-de-Castillon; 05 57 40 14 53; w bataillede castillon.com; mid-Jul–mid-Aug, with events in the medieval village starting at 18.30, battle starts at 22.30; €29, ages 5–12 €14.50, under 5 free; book via the website) is one of the great summer events of the Gironde, featuring 600 volunteers, 40 knights, sound and light and pyrotechnic excitement. In town, the **Maison du Vin** (6 Allées de la République; 05 57 40 00 88; w castillon-cotesdebordeaux.com; 08.00–noon & 14.00–17.30 Mon–Fri, May–Sep also Sat; free) eagerly waits to introduce you to the pleasure of Castillon Côtes de Bordeaux.

There are fine viewpoints north of Castillon: from **St-Philippe-d'Aiguille** and the mill at Candelaïre with an orientation table, although the main reason for heading this way (if you like a good Romanesque church) is to see the ornate façade of the 13th-century **St-Pierre** at **Petit-Palais-et-Cornemps**. On either side of the main door are figures inspired by antique sculpture, especially the relief of the man pulling an arrow or spine from his foot.

STE-FOY-LA-GRANDE At the crossroads of the Gironde, Dordogne and Lot-et-Garonne, this bustling market town was founded as a bastide by Alphonse de

Poitiers in 1255. Like Bergerac just east it was a Huguenot stronghold, and to this day it has a sizable Protestant population. Although none of the architecture is particularly out of the ordinary, there are some fine half-timbered houses from the 15th–17th centuries, a 13th-century Gothic church with a 60m tower, and the arcaded **Place Gambetta**. And you can find out more about the local Sainte-Foy Côtes de Bordeaux at the **Maison des Vins** (21 Rue Pasteur; 09 61 22 31 91; w saintefoy-cotesdebordeaux.com; 14.30–17.30 Tue, Thu–Fri, 09.30–12.30 Sat).

THE HAUTE GIRONDE

The Dordogne grows wider and wider and browner and browner as its sweet waters mix with the Garonne and the salt of the estuary. In its last stretch, Bordeaux's left bank is lined with limestone cliffs, yet more vineyards, and a charming corniche road. Two important towns wait on the big estuary, Bourg and Blaye with its famous citadel guarding the entrance to Bordeaux, both of which produce wine; the estuary acts like a giant hot-water bottle that keeps the vines a little warmer and drier than those on the Médoc side. Like many minor appellations, Côtes-de-Bourg wines mature earlier than Bordeaux's big boys; the **Boutique Côtes-de-Bourg** (Place de l'Eperon, Bourg; 05 57 94 80 20; w cotes-de-bourg.com; 10.00–12.30 & 14.00–18.00, closed mornings Mon) has a list of producers and bottles at château prices. Premières Côtes-de-Blaye is its much larger northern extension. For a map and more information, stop at the **Maison du Vin** (12 Cours Vauban, in Blaye; 05 57 42 94 20; w boutique.vin-blaye.com; 09.00–12.30 & 14.00–19.00 Mon–Sat).

GETTING THERE AND AROUND Buses 201 and 202 (w transports.nouvelle-aquitaine.fr) from the Cité du Vin tram stop in Bordeaux go to Bourg and Blaye via the train station at St-André-de-Cubzac, which also has TER train connections with Bordeaux. All take about 90 minutes from Bordeaux to Blaye.

There's also a **ferry** from Lamarque to Blaye (05 57 42 04 49; w gironde.fr/bacs) which runs from 07.15 to 18.00 Monday to Friday and until 20.30 between mid-July and mid-September, and also from 09.00 to 18.30 on Saturday and Sunday.

TOURIST INFORMATION The tourist offices of Blaye and Bourg share the same website: w bbte.fr.

Blaye 1 Place de La Citadella; 05 57 42 12 09; 10.00–13.00 & 14.00–18.30 daily, till 17.00 Oct–Mar. They offer a full menu of guided tours of the citadel and its bowels, by foot or little train, which goes as far as the Roman villas at Plassac.

Bourg Place de la Libération; 05 57 68 31 76; 09.30–12.30 & 14.00–18.00 Tue–Sun, Oct–May closed Sun. They hire out e-bikes.

WHERE TO STAY

Château de la Grave [map, page 122] (4 rooms) La Grave, Bourg; 05 57 68 41 49; w chateaudelagrave.com. Sleep like a royal in a genuine castle, restored in Louis XVIII style & amid vineyards, with lovely views from the heated pool. **€€€€**

Auberge du Porche (8 rooms) 5 Rue Ernest Régnier, Blaye; 05 57 42 22 69; w auberge-du-porche.com. A picturesque old stone inn with luminous rooms, some overlooking the estuary & a bar. Free bikes for guests. **€€€**

Clos Réaud de la Citadelle (5 rooms) 8 Rue des Maçons, Blaye; m 06 99 44 43 34; w closreaud-citadelle.com. Rooms with big Italian showers in an 18th-century building, in a park, with a pool, spa & sauna. B/fast inc. **€€€**

Domaine des Deux Cèdres [map, page 122] (4 rooms) 26 Rte des Astéries, Gauriac, between Bourg & Blaye; 05 57 64 88 65; w domainedesdeuxcedres.com. Eric & Sophie run this charming B&B in a garden setting with a pool & spa. Delicious table d'hôtes available (€28); b/fast inc. €€€

Château Arras [map, page 122] (3 rooms) 1 Les Arrats, St-Gervais, near the Grotte de Pair-non-Pair; 05 57 43 00 35; w chateaudesarras.fr. 2 sisters run the vineyard by this 18th-century château. B/fast inc. €€–€

WHERE TO EAT AND DRINK In local bakeries look for the toasted almonds *pralines de Blaye*, invented by the chef of the Maréchal de Plessis-Praslin, governor of the citadel in 1649.

Le Gavroche 12 Rue Neuve, Blaye; 05 57 58 21 03; restaurantlegavroche; closed Mon & eves Sun & Thu. Contemporary cuisine from new owners in a handsome stone-walled room. *Tasty menus from €17.20.* €€€

Les 4 Baigneurs 7 Cours du Port, Bourg; 05 57 32 30 54; w les4baigneurs.fr; closed Mon & eves Wed, Thu & Sun. Bistro with an open kitchen, serving inventive takes on familiar dishes. *W/day lunch €26.* €€€

La Kbane [map, page 122] 4 bis Quai d'Orio, Saint-Ciers-sur-Gironde; 09 72 84 54 62; w lakbane.com; Apr–Oct daily, Sep–Oct lunch daily & eves Fri–Sat. By the Port des Callonges & Terre d'Oiseaux, laid-back place with a wooden deck & playground. *Lunch formules from €14.90, popular Sun lunch land or sea menus from €19.* €€

Tropidella 9 Rue du Couvent des Minimes, Blaye; m 06 33 31 00 67; w tropidella.com; closed Mon–Tue & eves Sun. A surprise in the old citadel – fast food, South American style, with great juices & ales to go with chilli con carne & *grand cru* hot chocolate. €€–€

Bon Appétit! [map, page 122] Pain de Sucre, St-Seurin-de-Bourg; m 06 18 43 39 53; ; closed Mon–Wed, but check. Informal riverside *guinguette* with a wooden deck & succulent rotisserie chicken, magret & flaky *tourtière aux pommes*. €

Café Bourg'joie 61 Rue Valentin-Bernard, Bourg; 09 83 77 49 56; w cafe-bourg-joie.fr; daily. Laid-back bar with frequent concerts.

Cave de l'Estuaire 18 Course Vauban, Blaye; 05 57 33 04 18; w cavedelestuaire.com; closed Sun–Mon. Wine & spirit shop plus a wine bar with tapas; oysters & prawns on Fri–Sat.

SPORTS AND ACTIVITIES The Haute Gironde is popular cycling territory, featuring 100km of the 800km V80 Atlantic to Mediterranean route, but there are other *voies vertes* and *boucles* (circular routes) on sleepy back roads. Rent an e-bike from the tourist office at Bourg.

ST-ANDRÉ-DE-CUBZAC AND AROUND This important crossroads town, with the last bridges over the Dordogne, was the birthplace of Jacques Cousteau in 1910, and who is buried in the village cemetery. In his honour, St-André erected a statue in a roundabout of a dolphin holding Cousteau's famous red *bonnet* in its mouth.

Just north of town, the vast 16th-century **Château de Bouilh** (for sale at the time of writing) was derelict until the day when the governor of Guyenne, Jean-Frédéric de La Tour du Pin Gouvernet invited Louis XVI to visit, only to have the king reply: 'But there is no château in Guyenne to receive me!' Du Pin decided to remedy the situation, commissioning Victor Louis to make Bouilh worthy of a royal visit, with a pavilion embraced by a massive hemicycle. Begun in 1787, tools were downed when Du Pin was guillotined – and the interiors have remained untouched ever since. On Rue Robillard, on the edge of St-André, another, much smaller spread from the 16th century, the **Château Robillard**, has one of the oldest plane trees in France, over 300 years old, growing at the entrance.

South of St-André, the iron bridge along the RN10 at **Cubzac-les-Ponts** was designed by Eiffel in 1882 and 1889. It is considered his most important bridge, supported by majestic cathedral-like arches, and was later restored by his engineer grandson after the Nazis bombed it, hence its nickname, Pont Eiffel Eiffel. Superstitious locals whistle before crossing it. A wine château in **Marsas** (north of St-André) has the most memorable name in Bordeaux: **La Pissotière de l'Impératrice** (w lapissotieredelimperatrice.com), the 'Empress's Chamberpot', so-named after Josephine, who, on her way to meet Napoleon, felt nature's call in this patch of vines.

For centuries, the pale limestone from the quarries at **Prignac-et-Marcamps** – which were photogenic enough to be used as a set in Robert Hossein's 1982 film of *Les Misérables* – was the most sought-after building stone of Bordeaux. In **Tauriac** just north of Marcamps the 12th-century church of **St-Étienne** has rare Merovingian capitals and two carved tympanums.

GROTTE DE PAIR-NON-PAIR (Prignac-et-Marchamps; 05 57 68 33 40; w pair-non-pair.fr; guided tours in French: 15 Jun–15 Sep, roughly every hour 10.00–18.30 Tue–Sun, until 17.30 other times; €8, EU citizens ages 18–25 €6.50, under 18 free; ring to book as numbers are limited) Discovered in 1881, the cave yielded a rich store of finds from the Mousterian (80,000BC) to the Périgordien Supérieur (18,000BC) – tools of flint and bone, and piles of animal bones left over from thousands of prehistoric feasts. Unusually for a dwelling area, it was also decorated with etchings, as well as rare paintings, tragically washed away in 1899 by an imbecile who wanted to clean them using a hose from a vineyard pump. The etchings, in places scratched one over the other, include mammoths, deer and bison, and most notably a Megaloceros (giant elk) and a horse in flight, head turned dramatically back towards an unseen pursuer. The cave's funny name, 'Even-Odd', is derived from a village that once stood nearby, lost by its *seigneur* in a game of heads-or-tails.

BOURG This charming medieval and 18th-century town is still on the Dordogne, just before it joins the Gironde. Pleasure boats bob in the port, linked by hundreds of steps to the upper town spread over a natural terrace. This was first fortified by the English, and after numerous attacks the castle was reconstructed in the 18th century as a folly, and torched in 1944 by the retreating Germans out of spite. A small replacement (private) stands in the Parc de la Citadelle, with its gardens of magnolias.

The **Musée de la Citadelle** (Place d'Armes; 05 57 68 23 57; Jun–Sep guided visits at 10.00, 11.30, 14.00, 15.30 & 17.00 daily, Mar–May & Oct Sat–Sun only; €5, ages 10–15 €1.50, under 10 free) offers a fine collection of landaus, omnibuses, cabriolets, phaetons, gigs and coupés, including one that belonged to Tzar Nicolas. The tour includes the quarries below the citadel, where seven enormous tanks were used to store fuel during World War II – a project begun by the French before the war, then finished by the Germans. You can still see the *Frisco*, an Italian tanker ship sunk by the Germans in 1944, sticking out of the water off Bourg's port.

Bourg has a remarkable covered **Lavoir** or washhouse of 1828 in Place du Chenal, nicknamed the '*chambre des députées*' by the town's men (who were forbidden to enter). An old sea gate bears the town's last vestige of English heraldry.

The narrow D669/E1, or 'flowery corniche road', passes tiny villages and semi-tropical gardens, estuary islands and *carrelets* – the picturesque wooden huts on stilts used for fishing in big nets. In **Gauriac**, the houses are cut straight into the limestone. At **Plassac** you can visit the excavations of three Gallo-Roman villas from the 1st–6th centuries AD, next to the **Musée Gallo-Romain** (05 57 42 84 80;

w villagalloromaine-plassac.fr; ⌚ Mar–Oct 10.00–12.30 & 14.00–17.30 daily, summer until 18.30; €5, ages 8–16 €3). This contains a virtual 3D model of the 2nd-century villa, and recreations of its wall paintings; there are the colourful mosaics, bronzes, coins, ceramics, a strange statuette of a three-horned bull and an explanation on the villa's underfloor heating system.

BLAYE Occupying a limestone spur over the Gironde, Blaye has been inhabited since 5000BC and entered the history books as Blavia, a camp of Roman legionnaires; Ausonius called it 'The Star and Key of Aquitaine', as its Latin motto proudly proclaims. When Louis XIV's engineer Sébastien Vauban was charged with improving the citadel at Blaye to defend Bordeaux from the English and Dutch, he concluded what was really needed was a new series of fortifications at the narrowest, most defensible part of the Gironde, at the medieval castle at Blaye and on the little Île Pâté and over the water at Fort Médoc so any enemy ship that dared to approach would be within the range of a French cannon.

To build the massive 44.5m walls of citadel in 1686–89, 250 houses had to be razed along with the Abbaye de St-Romain, the 8th-century AD burial site of Roland, Lord of Blaye, nephew of Charlemagne and hero of the great medieval epic, the *Chanson de Roland*. Some 300 years after Roland, its prince was the troubadour Jaufre Rudel. Although his castle was mostly destroyed by Vauban, two towers remain north of the Place d'Armes to give at least some physical credence to his strange and mystical story: in 1147, a pilgrim told him of the beauty of Melisande, Countess of Tripoli, and Jaufre fell passionately in love with her sight unseen. He composed songs for her (six have survived) and went on the next Crusade to find her. But he became feverishly ill and the Crusaders left him to die in a fisherman's hut, when Melisande appeared saying, 'You were right to seek me, Jaufre, even if it has cost you your life… Rest assured that you will find me as you dreamed.' He smiled and died, and she entered a convent the next day. The story inspired writers from Petrarch to Rostand (*La Princesse lointaine*) to Heine, who has the lovers reunited as ghosts in a poem from his *Romanzero*.

At the end of World War I, the army abandoned the 'Verrou Vauban' ('Vauban's Bolt'), and in 2008 the Citadelle, Fort Paté and Fort Médoc were made UNESCO World Heritage Sites, and the English, Dutch and everyone else are welcome to invade its confines. You can go on a guided tour of its **Souterrains** (underground passages; ☎ 05 57 42 12 09; ⌚ 14.30 year-round, Mar–Oct also at 16.00, mid-Jun–mid-Sep also at 11.00; €7.50, ages 5–12 €5.50, under 5 free), departing from the Place d'Armes.

The prison (later converted into a bakery) houses a small **Musée d'Archéologie** (Rue de la Manutention; m 06 82 34 72 66; ⌚ mid-Mar–Sep 11.00–12.30 & 13.30–19.00 daily, Oct–mid-Mar 13.30–17.30 daily; €5, ages 5–12 €4, under 5 free, €7/€4.70 combined admission with the Conservatoire de l'Estuaire), covering 7,000 years of Blaye's history, including finds from the long-lost abbey and displays on the history of bread-making. Upstairs, the **Conservatoire de l'Estuaire** (☎ 05 57 42 80 96; ⌚ Apr–Oct 14.00–18.00 daily; €3/€1.50) offers changing exhibits on the natural and manmade history of the estuary. The citadel even has its own micro-organic vineyard, the **Clos de l'Echauguette** (☎ 05 57 42 94 20; w vin-blaye.com; 90min tours & tastings €5), which like many organic vineyards in the area uses horses instead of tractors.

Of the many other wine châteaux that welcome visitors, the **Château Marquis de Vauban** (Rte des Cônes; ☎ 05 57 42 80 37; w vignobles-le-cone-de-vauban.fr; ⌚ Apr–Oct; from €12 for a carriage tour, €33 for a visit with lunch) is only a 15-minute walk north of Blaye and offers horse-drawn carriage and little train tours, tastings and lunch.

Further up the estuary, beyond the nuke plant, there's a nature reserve along one of France's main migration routes, the **Terres d'Oiseaux** (Les Nouvelles Possessions, Braud-et-St-Louis; ☎ 05 57 32 88 80; **w** terresdoiseaux.fr; ⏲ 10.00–18.00 daily, mid-Jun–mid-Sep until 20.00, Nov–Feb 10.00–18.00 Mon–Fri; €6, ages 5–12 €4, under 5 free). There are six observation posts and four walks in the park. Bring your binoculars.

7

Northern Périgord

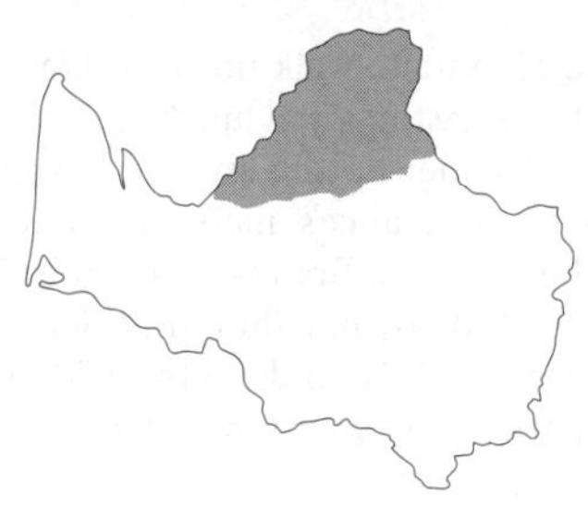

Petra sis ingratis, cor amicis, hostibus ensis
Haec tria si fueris Petra-cor-ensis eris

(A stone to the unpleasant, a heart to the friendly, and iron to the enemy
If you're all three, then you're a Périgourdin)

This northernmost half of the département of the Dordogne, home to its capital, Périgueux, is known as 'White and Green Périgord' (white after the colour of the stones, green after the lush river valleys and forests). It was the cradle of troubadours, a land of truffles, foie gras and caviar, 'the nearest thing to Paradise this side of Greece', as Henry Miller wrote.

If Périgord could make a wise guy from Brooklyn go soppy, there must be something to it. It fulfils a communal dream for a comfortable place, a simpler, rural idyll of beauty and pleasure. Ironically, this Paradise is the result of long centuries of war and poverty and neglect. So is much of the architecture that charms us today – the medieval castles, churches and villages are only that way because no-one ever had the wherewithal to improve them.

PÉRIGUEUX

Set in a privileged, fertile valley on the River Isle, the capital of the Dordogne département is a cheerful city of 31,600 people who print all the postage stamps in France. The old streets around its famous five-domed cathedral have been intelligently restored to give the city a lively and lovely heart. Another plus are two excellent museums, old and new, offering a chance to get to know what life was like here in the time of Asterix.

HISTORY Like Périgord, Périgueux's name comes from the Gaulish nation known as the Petrocorii ('the four tribes'), who according to Caesar sent 6,000 troops to aid Vercingetorix in his final defeat against Rome. Originally living in an oppidum on the heights of the left bank of the Isle, they settled down to enjoy the *pax Romana* on the fertile plains of the Isle's right bank and build a new town they called Vesunna after their sacred spring. By the 3rd century AD, it had 20,000 Gallo-Roman citizens, who were renowned for their iron-working skills.

Vesunna was still in its first bloom when the barbarian Alemanni came and crushed it under their heels in AD275. Raped and pillaged into a state of shock, the locals destroyed their own temples and basilicas for stone to build a wall, contracting themselves into the space of a village. As the years (and more unpleasant barbarians) passed by, this bristling remnant of Vesunna even lost its proud name: it became known as Civitas Petrocoriorum, the town of the Petrocorii, or just the Cité, as it's known to this day. Clovis, the first king of the Franks, captured the Cité and his successors fought over it; in the Dark Ages, the 24 towers of the wall were converted into donjons by rival factions of gangster-nobles.

The Rise of Puy-St-Front As the Cité declined, a new bourg of artisans and merchants grew up around the nearby hill (*puy*) around the tomb of St Front, a 4th-century AD follower of St Martial, the Apostle of Gaul. Over the years his legend evolved to make Front into no less than a personal acquaintance of Jesus who lived in a state of perpetual virginity. Baptised by the hand of St Peter, he chased the devils and dragons out of the pagan temple of Vesunna by blasting open an enormous breach in the walls. Thanks to the pilgrims who stopped at this superhero's tomb, mercantile Puy grew larger than its rival, the noble Cité. In 1182 Puy began its own wall. It also was a firm ally of France against the English.

The English weren't half as much trouble as the counts of Périgord. One of the worst, Roger Bernard (who liked to catapult messengers he didn't like into the river), pillaged and partly destroyed Puy in 1246 just to show who was boss. After this outrage, the future saint Louis IX, with more than human patience, brokered an agreement that united Puy-St-Front and the Cité into one town and freed it of homage to the counts, with a new motto: *Fortitudo mea civium fides* ('My strength lies in the trust of my fellow citizens').

One can almost hear the counts scoff. In 1357, while the French were distracted by the capture of John the Good, Count Archambault V and his brother, Cardinal Hélie de Talleyrand, pounced and grabbed Périgueux with English aid. Although Du Guesclin chased the English out in 1369, Count Archambault managed to stay put by promising loyalty to the crown of France; instead, he took money from England to stir up as much trouble as possible until the exasperated French came back to give him the boot. His castle, built over the Roman amphitheatre, was demolished, his goods confiscated and given to the canons of St-Front.

Périgord's Bastion of Catholicism In the 15th century, the battered survivors slowly rebuilt, putting the city back on its feet just in time for more trouble in the Wars of Religion. Périgueux was as firmly Catholic as Bergerac was Protestant, but the Huguenots were quicker off the mark: in 1575 they killed the Bishop of Périgueux, then, disguising themselves as peasants, entered and captured the city. Salt was rubbed into Périgueux's wounds when the Treaty of Beaulieu (1576) made the city a safe haven for Protestants; so miserable were the Catholic majority that the triumphal arch they erected for the visit of Henri, King of Navarre, read '*Urbis Deforme Cadaver*'. In pity the Sénéchal André de Bourdeilles offered to buy the town back for the Catholics and, failing that, he captured Périgueux in 1581 by using the same peasant-disguise ruse as the Huguenots.

More trouble In spite of it all, the burghers of Périgueux had maintained the privileges bestowed by St Louis. They were exempt from royal taxes and military service; they had their own constitution and elected officials. In 1635, when Louis XIII imposed a tavern tax, the result was a riot. The mayor had to bolt, the tax clerk was tossed down a well; the Croquants (page 10) took to the forests and fought the king's men until 1641. Louis XIV cast a cold eye on these goings-on, and by the end of his reign, he had rubbed out all traces of Périgueux's privileges and independence.

In 1790, when the Revolution divided France into départements, the worthies of the Dordogne could not choose a capital: as Périgueux, Bergerac and Sarlat all had valid claims, it was decided that they would alternate. Périgueux drew the longest straw and got to be capital first, and inertia has done the rest to make sure it never went anywhere else.

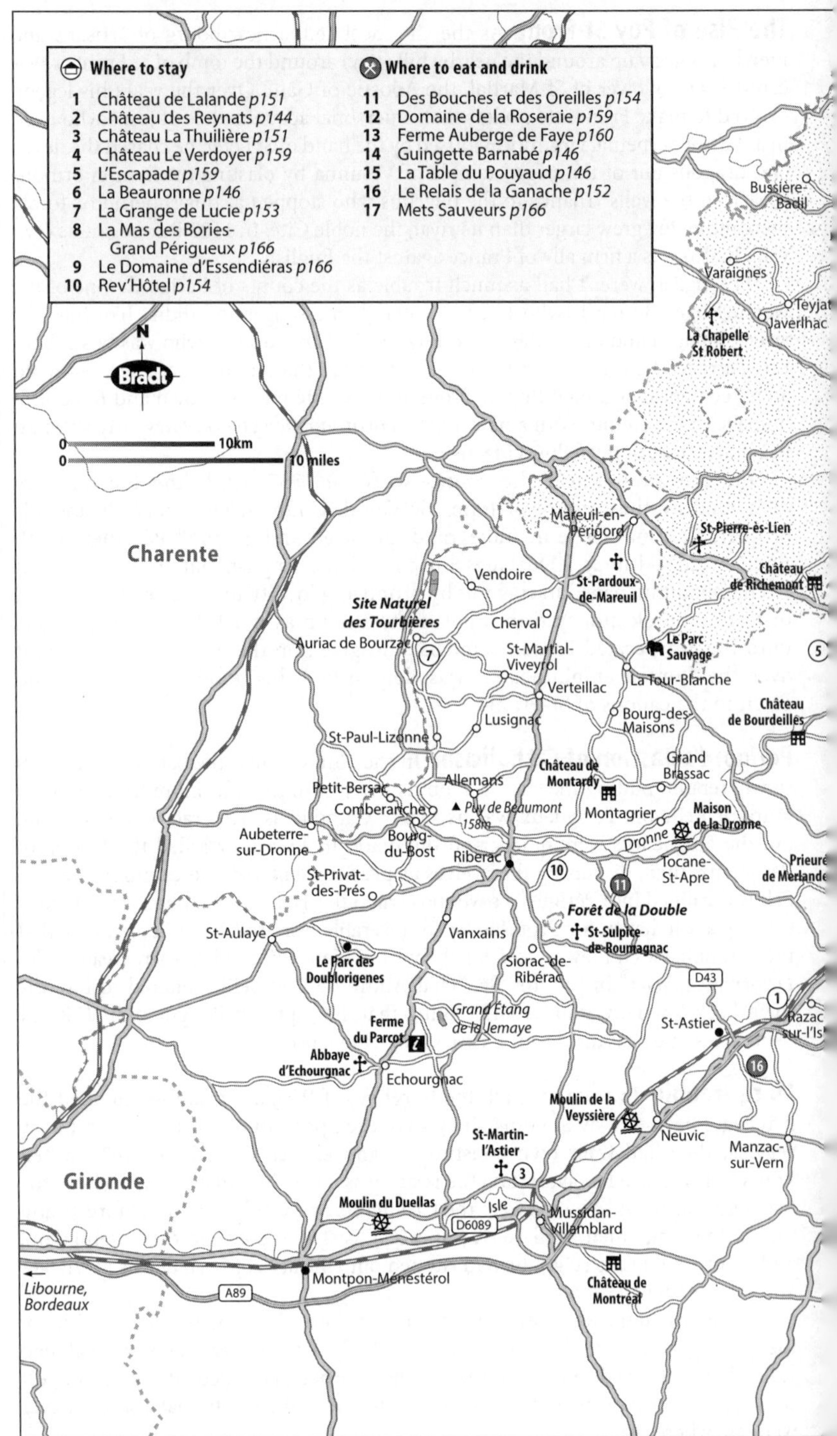

Where to stay
1 Château de Lalande p151
2 Château des Reynats p144
3 Château La Thuilière p151
4 Château Le Verdoyer p159
5 L'Escapade p159
6 La Beauronne p146
7 La Grange de Lucie p153
8 La Mas des Bories-Grand Périgueux p166
9 Le Domaine d'Essendiéras p166
10 Rev'Hôtel p154
Where to eat and drink
11 Des Bouches et des Oreilles p154
12 Domaine de la Roseraie p159
13 Ferme Auberge de Faye p160
14 Guingette Barnabé p146
15 La Table du Pouyaud p146
16 Le Relais de la Ganache p152
17 Mets Sauveurs p166
N
Bradt
0 10km
0 10 miles
Charente
Gironde
Bussière-Badil
Varaignes
Teyjat
Javerlhac
La Chapelle St Robert
Mareuil-en-Périgord
St-Pierre-ès-Lien
Château de Richemont
Vendoire
St-Pardoux-de-Mareuil
Site Naturel des Tourbières
Cherval
Auriac de Bourzac
St-Martial-Viveyrol
Le Parc Sauvage
La Tour-Blanche
Verteillac
Bourg-des-Maisons
Château de Bourdeilles
Lusignac
St-Paul-Lizonne
Grand Brassac
Château de Montardy
Petit-Bersac
Allemans
Comberanche
Puy de Beaumont 158m
Montagrier
Maison de la Dronne
Aubeterre-sur-Dronne
Bourg-du-Bost
Dronne
Riberac
Tocane-St-Apre
Prieuré de Merlande
St-Privat-des-Prés
Forêt de la Double
St-Aulaye
Vanxains
St-Sulpice-de-Roumagnac
Le Parc des Doublorigenes
Siorac-de-Ribérac
D43
Grand Étang de la Jemaye
St-Astier
Razac sur-l'Is
Ferme du Parcot
Abbaye d'Echourgnac
Echourgnac
Moulin de la Veyssière
Neuvic
St-Martin-l'Astier
Manzac-sur-Vern
Moulin du Duellas
Isle
D6089
Mussidan-Villamblard
Libourne, Bordeaux
Montpon-Ménestérol
A89
Château de Montréal

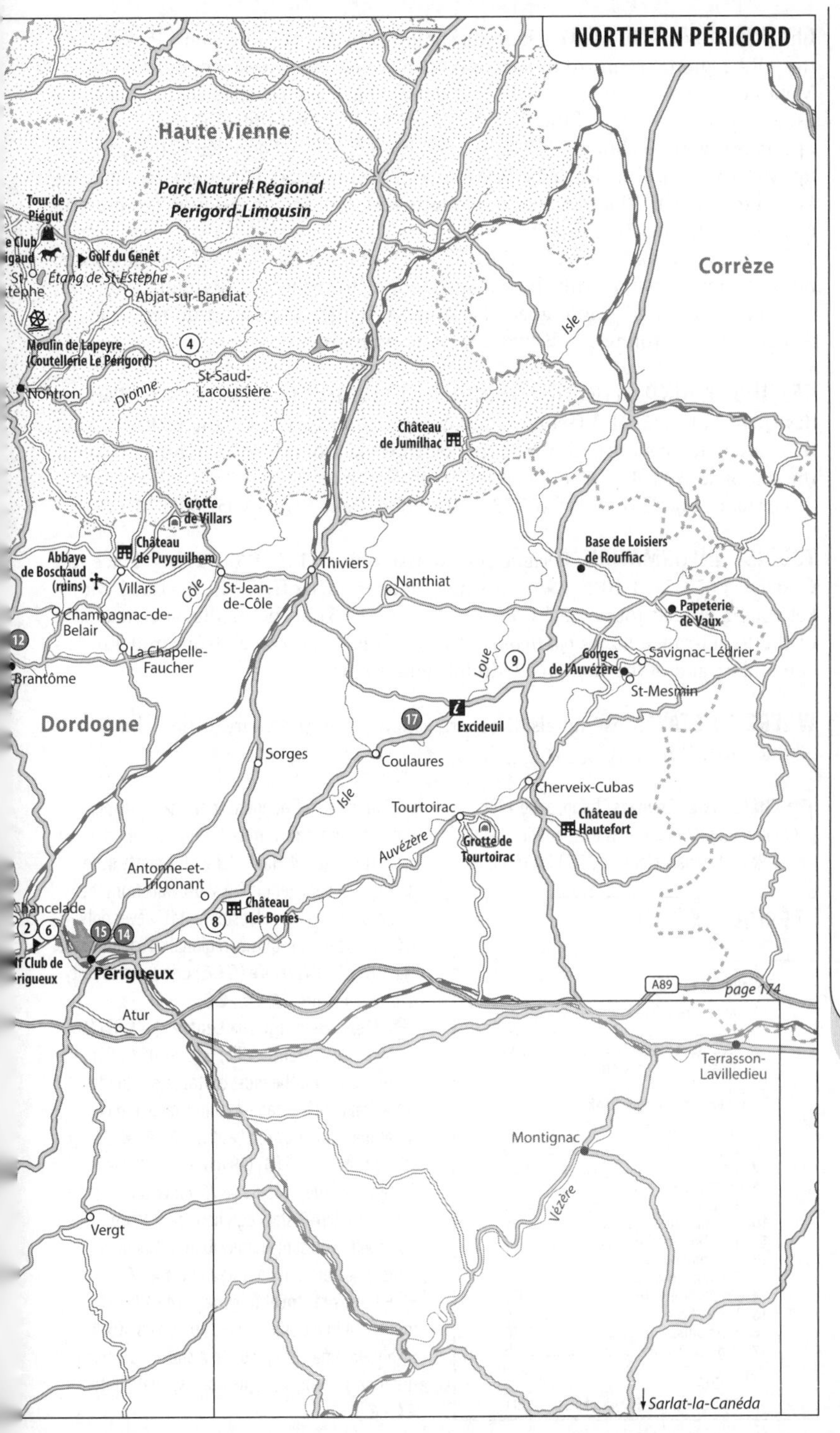
NORTHERN PÉRIGORD
Haute Vienne
Parc Naturel Régional
Perigord-Limousin
Tour de Piégut
Golf du Genêt
Étang de St-Estèphe
Abjat-sur-Bandiat
Moulin de Lapeyre (Coutellerie Le Périgord)
St-Saud-Lacoussière
Nontron
Dronne
Isle
Corrèze
Château de Jumilhac
Grotte de Villars
Château de Puyguilhem
Abbaye de Boschaud (ruins)
Villars
Côle
St-Jean-de-Côle
Thiviers
Nanthiat
Base de Loisiers de Rouffiac
Papeterie de Vaux
Champagnac-de-Belair
La Chapelle-Faucher
Brantôme
Loue
Gorges de l'Auvézère
Savignac-Lédrier
St-Mesmin
Excideuil
Dordogne
Sorges
Coulaures
Cherveix-Cubas
Tourtoirac
Château de Hautefort
Grotte de Tourtoirac
Auvézère
Antonne-et-Trigonant
Château des Bories
Chancelade
Périgueux
A89
page 174
Atur
Terrasson-Lavilledieu
Montignac
Vézère
Vergt
Sarlat-la-Canéda

GETTING THERE AND AWAY The **train** station [145 A1] (11 Rue Denis Papin) is on the TER regional train from Bordeaux to Limoges, via Mussidan and Montpon-Ménestérol and Libourne. It's 4½–5 hours from Paris (change in Limoges), or usually quicker by way of the LGV to Libourne and then the TER train. Another option is the 01 bus linking Périgueux (via Brantôme) to Angoulême, there to link up with the Paris–Bordeaux LGV. Another TER line links Périgueux to Agen via Les Eyzes, Sarlat, Villefranche-de-Périgord and Monsempron-Libos (where you can pick up the bus to Cahors).

Périgueux station is also the centre of the Dordogne's **bus** network (w transports.nouvelle-aquitaine.fr) with buses year-round to Riberac, Mareuil, Nontron, Excideuil, Salagnac, Montignac, Sarlat and Bergerac, plus summer lines to Aubeterre-sur-Dronne, Les Eyzies, Domme and more.

GETTING AROUND Périgueux is small enough to visit on foot. The city's free **Parking des Quais** [145 D6] (Bd Georges Saumande) is convenient for the cathedral, but there are many paying and free car parks scattered around. You can **hire a car** near the station at Ada [145 A1] (4 bis Rue Henri Barbusse; 05 53 05 40 28; w ada.fr).

For **taxis**, call Allô Taxis (05 53 09 09 09) or Taxis Verts (05 53 04 14 14).

TOURIST INFORMATION Périgueux's **tourist office** [145 B6] (9 bis Place du Coderc; 05 53 53 10 63; w tourisme-grandperigueux.fr; 09.30–18.00 Mon–Sat) offers guided tours (each tour €6, ages 6–11 €3) of the medieval centre, and of the Renaissance *hôtels particuliers* two or three days a week from mid-June to September, and of the Roman city in July and August.

WHERE TO STAY Most hotels here are chains, but there are other choices in Chancelade, 6km west.

Château des Reynats [map, page 142] (13 rooms, plus 37 rooms in the Orangerie) 15 Av des Reynats, Chancelade; 05 53 03 53 59; w chateau-hotel-perigord.com. The classy place to stay – a handsome turreted, 19th-century château converted into a 4-star hotel,with a pretty little park with a pool, tennis & a short walk from the golf course. The formal restaurant (eves only; €€€€€) serves exquisite regional specialities; the glass-terraced **Verrière** (€€€) bistro serves tasty €28–€32 menus. **€€€€–€€**

Mercure Périgueux Centre [145 B2] (66 rooms) 7 Place Francheville; 05 53 06 65 00; w all.accor.com. The most central, close to the cathedral with a garage & comfortable rooms decorated with art from Lascaux. **€€€–€€**

Bristol [145 B1] (29 rooms) 37–9 Rue Antoine Gadaud; 05 53 08 75 90; w bristolfrance.com. A modern 3-star Logis hotel near Place Roosevelt, with some family rooms. Parking & b/fast available, but no restaurant. **€€–€**

Comfort Hotel Régina [145 A1] (41 rooms) 14 Rue Denis Papin; 05 53 08 40 44; w hotelregina-perigueux.fr. A short walk from the train station, a simple no-fuss chain hotel. **€€–€**

PÉRIGUEUX
For listings, see above

Where to stay

1	Mercure Périgueux Centre	B2
2	Bristol	B1
3	Comfort Hotel Régina	A1
4	Ibis Périgueux Centre	C7

Where to eat and drink

5	66 Degrés	C1
6	Chez Wouam	C6
7	Epicurien	C5
8	Hercule Poireau	C6
9	L'Essential	C6
10	La Peniche	D3
11	Le Chai Bordin	B6
12	Le Cosy Bar	B6
13	Le Seizième	B7
14	The Silver Owl	C5
15	Veloc Café	C6
16	Vinobilis	B6
17	Watson's Pub	C6

Off map

Le Rocher de l'Arsault ... D1

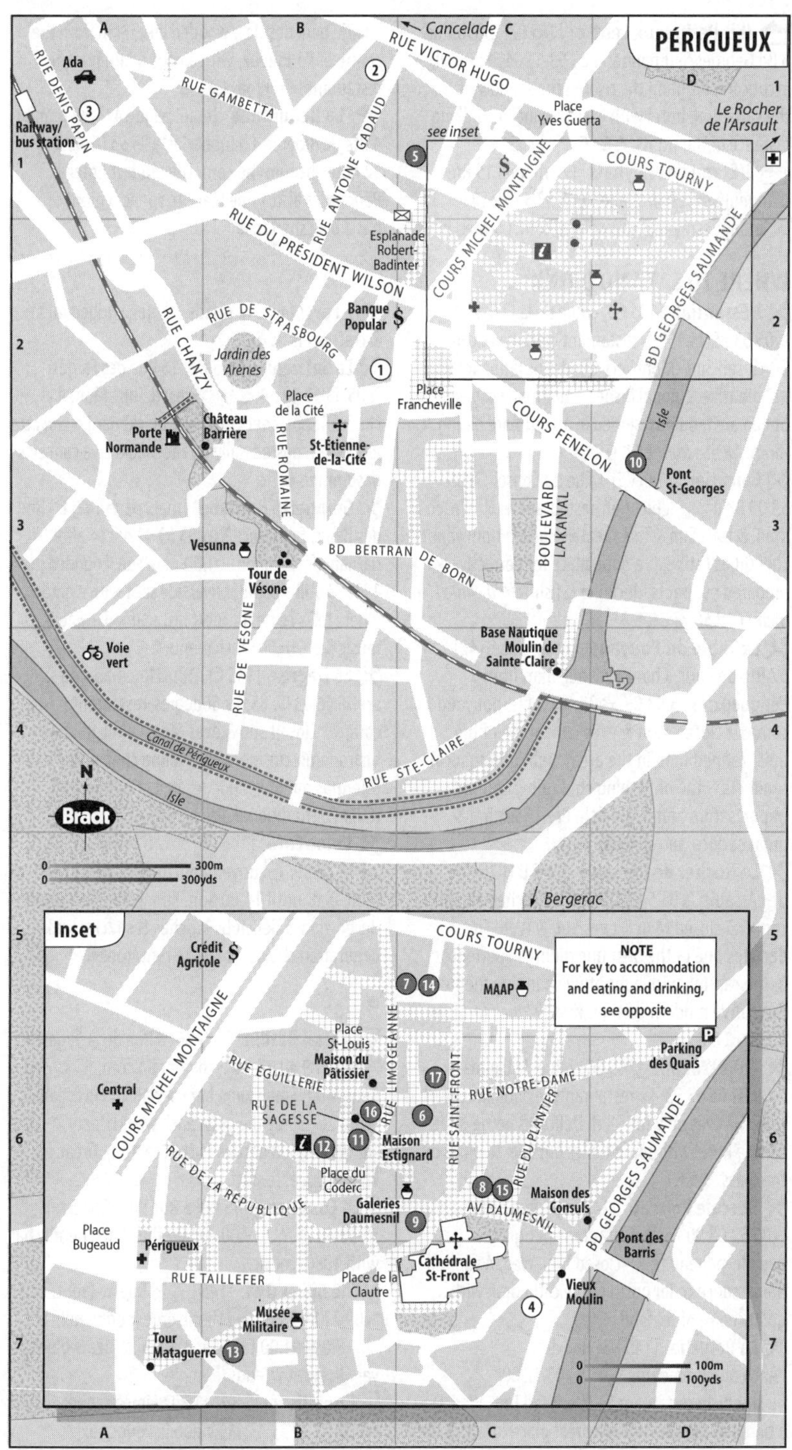
PÉRIGUEUX
Cancelade
Rue Victor Hugo
Rue Gambetta
Rue Denis Papin
Ada
Railway/ bus station
Place Yves Guerta
Le Rocher de l'Arsault
see inset
Cours Tourny
Rue Antoine Gadaud
Cours Michel Montaigne
Rue du Président Wilson
Esplanade Robert-Badinter
Bd Georges Saumande
Banque Popular
Rue de Strasbourg
Rue Chanzy
Jardin des Arènes
Place de la Cité
Place Francheville
Cours Fenelon
Isle
Château Barrière
Porte Normande
Rue Romaine
St-Étienne-de-la-Cité
Pont St-Georges
Boulevard Lakanal
Vesunna
Tour de Vésone
Bd Bertran de Born
Base Nautique Moulin de Sainte-Claire
Voie vert
Rue de Vésone
Canal de Périgueux
Rue Ste-Claire
Isle
Bradt
300m
300yds
Bergerac
Inset
Crédit Agricole
Cours Tourny
NOTE
For key to accommodation and eating and drinking, see opposite
MAAP
Place St-Louis
Maison du Pâtissier
Rue Limogeanne
Parking des Quais
Rue Éguillerie
Central
Rue Notre-Dame
Rue de la Sagesse
Rue Saint-Front
Maison Estignard
Rue du Plantier
Place du Coderc
Rue de la République
Galeries Daumesnil
Maison des Consuls
Av Daumesnil
Bd Georges Saumande
Place Bugeaud
Périgueux
Pont des Barris
Cathédrale St-Front
Rue Taillefer
Place de la Claütre
Vieux Moulin
Musée Militaire
Tour Mataguerre
100m
100yds

Ibis Périgueux Centre [145 C7] (88 rooms) 8 Bd Georges Saumande; 05 53 53 64 58; w all.accor.com. Right on the river in the shadow of the cathedral, hotel with easy parking, in walking distance of the sights. €€–€

L'Étang des Reynats (21 rooms) 15 Rte d'Angoulême, Chancelade; 05 53 54 79 58; w letangdesreynats.site-solocal.com. Located in a large park beside a wooded lake, 3km from the centre of Périgueux, with a pool & family-style restaurant (€€) too. €€–€

La Beauronne [map, page 142] (22 rooms) 4 Rte de Riberac, Chancelade; 05 53 08 42 91; w hotel-beauronne.com. The reddest hotel in Périgord is also a fine place to spend a night or 2, & has a bike shelter. €

WHERE TO EAT AND DRINK

L'Essential [145 C6] 8 Rue de la Clarté; 05 53 35 15 15; w restaurant-perigueux.com; closed Sun–Mon. Very good reputation for its imaginative regional dishes – not many choices, but all are fabulous, served in an intimate dining room. *Menus from €52.* €€€€€

Epicurien [145 C5] 1 Rue du Conseil; 05 53 09 88 04; w lepicurien-restaurant.fr; closed Wed, & eves Sun & Tue. Creative cuisine from young chef Gilles Labbé, & a good place for perfectly prepared escargots, duckling & fish. *W/day lunch menu €19.50.* €€€€

La Table du Pouyaud [map, page 142] 57 Rte de Paris, Champcevinel, 3km from Périgueux; 05 53 09 53 32; w table-pouyaud.com; closed Mon & eves Sun. Some of the most refined food in the area, highlighting local products – the only thing chef Gilles Gourvat imports from afar is the fish. Pretty setting & great service, too. €€€€

Le Rocher de l'Arsault [145 D1] 15 Rue de l'Arsault; 05 53 53 54 06; w rocher-arsault.com; closed Mon & eves Sun & Wed. For decades one of the best fine dining experiences in the capital, with a monthly changing menu & creative modern cuisine. *W/day lunch formule €23.* €€€€

Chez Wouam [145 C6] 2 Rue de Lanmary; 09 81 05 53 93; w restaurantchezwouam.eatbu.com; eves only Tue–Sat. Delicious home-style cuisine here, with some tables outside, & wines by the glass. €€€

Hercule Poireau [145 C6] 2 Rue de la Nation; 05 53 08 90 76; w restaurant-perigueux-hercule-poireau.fr; closed Tue–Wed. A vaulted Renaissance cellar north of the cathedral, with a good choice of seafood. €€€

La Peniche [145 D3] Rue de l'Ancienne Préfecture; 05 53 03 12 00; w lapenicherestaurant.fr; closed Tue–Wed. On a barge in the Isle, this is a great place to watch the sunset over tapas or salads, burgers, grilled meats & craft beers. €€€

Le Seizième [145 B7] 16 Rue des Farges; 05 53 53 12 54; f; closed Sun–Mon. A cheerful spot; check out their blackboard *menu du jour* (€16), posted daily on Facebook. Live concerts in summer. €€€

Guingette Barnabé [map, page 142] 80 Rue des Bains, Boulazac; 05 53 53 41 45; w alfred-barnabe.fr; noon–01.00 Tue–Sun. Founded in 1935, & still a popular riverside spot with a garden, where folks come for cocktails, seafood, oysters, music & a €16.50 lunch menu. €€

66 Degrés [145 C1] 18bis Rue Gambetta; m 06 46 03 08 85; w 66degres-restaurant.com; closed Sun & eves Mon. Colourful funky bistronomic cuisine with a young chef whose day's offerings might include Asian, Latin American, Italian or traditional dishes. €€–€

Veloc Café [145 C6] 7 Av Daumesnil; m 06 33 48 22 89; f unvelopourtous; 07.30–20.30 Mon–Sat, until 14.00 Sun. Fun, colourful vintage decoration & delicious lunches & snacks, with vegetarian choices; bikes to rent, too. €

Bars

Le Chai Bordin [145 B6] 8 Rue de la Sagesse; 09 81 89 40 95; w lechaibordin.com; closed Sun–Mon. Small wine bar specialising in organics (with 20–30 by the glass each week), tasty snacks & 1,500 bottles to choose from. Great knowledgeable staff.

Le Cosy Bar [145 B6] 3 Rue de la Sagesse; 05 53 53 60 78; 19.00–02.00 Thu–Sat. Friendly bar with 1980s music.

The Silver Owl [145 C5] 25 Rue St-Front; 09 72 89 13 21; f thesilverowlperigueux; 18.00–01.00 Tue–Sat. Cocktails, jazz & blues; very lively at w/ends.

Vinobilis [145 B6] 11 Rue Limogeanne; m 07 75 22 75 43; f VinobilisPerigueux;

⌚ 11.00–19.00 Tue–Thu, 11.00–21.00 Fri–Sat, 11.00–15.00 Sun. Wine bar with both French & foreign bottles, & platters to nibble out on the terrace; good for a light lunch.

Watson's Pub [145 C6] 17 Rue St-Front; ☎ 05 53 45 95 24; w watsons-pub.fr; ⌚ 08.00–02.00 daily. Draught beers & rum cocktails, plus a tapas & pub menu in a cosy atmosphere near the cathedral.

SHOPPING There's a daily morning market in the *halles* in Place du Coderc [145 B6] and a big market on Wednesdays and Saturdays in Place de la Clautre [145 B7] in front of the cathedral. From mid-November to March the *marché au gras* (duck, foie gras and truffles) takes place in Place St Louis [145 B5] on Wednesday and Saturday mornings. A clothes and accessories market is held all day Wednesday in Esplanade Robert-Badinter and Place Bugeaud.

SPORTS AND ACTIVITIES The **Voie Verte des Berges de l'Isle** [145 A4] (V90; w af3v.org/les-voies-vertes) is a beautiful cycling/walking path through the city and along the Isle, part of the 104km route to the Gironde. Because of the many train stations, it's easy to return to your starting point. You can hire a bike at **Veloc Café** (see opposite).

Golf Club de Périgueux Bd de Saltgourde, Marsac-sur-l'Isle; ☎ 05 53 53 02 35; w golfdeperigueux.com. Beautiful 18-hole course.

Le Périgord en Montgolfière m 06 87 84 43 55; w leperigordenmontgolfiere.fr. Hot-air balloon ascents from €190.

Périgueux Canoë-Kayak [145 C4] Base Nautique Moulin de Sainte-Claire; ☎ 05 53 04 24 08; w perigueuxcanoe.org. Not only rentals, but fascinating guided day & night tours in long canoes.

OTHER PRACTICALITIES

$ **Banque Popular** [145 B2] 23 Place Francheville

$ **Crédit Agricole** [145 B5] 17 Bd Montagne

Centre Hospitalier de Périgueux [145 D1] 80 Av Georges Pompidou; ☎ 05 53 45 25 25; w ch-perigueux.fr

Pharmacie Central [145 A6] 3 Bd Michel Montaigne

Pharmacie Périgueux [145 A7] 12 Place Bugeaud

Post office [145 C2] 1 Rue de 4 Septembre

WHAT TO SEE AND DO

Cathédrale St-Front

Cathédrale St-Front [145 C7] (Place de la Clautre; ☎ 05 53 53 10 63; ⌚ 09.00–18.00 daily; free; the tourist office offers 1hr guided tours of the roof (in French) over age 8 only; book at m 06 16 79 03 97; €6, ages 8–10 €3.50) This is the fourth church built here, on the summit of the *puy* over the Isle. A 6th-century AD chapel holding the relics of St Front was replaced in 1074 with a much larger church, to draw in pilgrims on the way to Compostela. In 1120, when this new church burned down, it was decided to build something extraordinary with five domes on a Greek cross, similar to St Mark's in Venice. By the 19th century this marvel was a rickety disaster waiting to happen. After the Huguenots had damaged it in 1575 and destroyed the tomb of St Front, a streak of thoughtless restorations exacerbated the typical problems of old age.

Viollet-le-Duc, who restored Notre-Dame in Paris and Carcassonne, wanted to have a crack at it, but his rival Paul Abadie was given the nod in 1852. Abadie loved Romanesque churches so much that he devoured them whole; he started by demolishing the north dome which caused all the others to collapse, so he demolished much of the rest and spent the next 50 years rebuilding it. There's nothing medieval about the peculiar scaly domes and their knobby lanterns you see today; they're pure Abadie.

But for all its sheer awfulness, St-Front was much praised in its day, and Abadie became a favourite at the famously philistine court of Napoleon III; he would later copy his Périgueux domes for the new church of Sacré-Coeur on Montmartre in Paris. The people of Périgueux, who had no say in the state-run restoration, initially hated it. But the result is breathtakingly exotic from a distance, especially at night when St-Front is illuminated and reflected in the waters of the Isle.

From **Place de la Clautre** [145 B7] you can see what survives from the church of 1074: the austere façade fitted with the odd Roman fragment, lateral walls that now form an open courtyard, the bottom two-thirds of the squarish 57m **bell tower**, built in a style unique for the Middle Ages that may have inspired Abadie's eccentricity. There are two **confessions** (tomb-shrines of saintly confessors) – one under the bell tower and the other under the west dome – and the little **cloister** with a 'pine cone' at its centre, a copy of a common Roman motif (the Vatican has a famous one in a courtyard), that originally topped the bell tower.

The cavernous, breathtakingly ugly interior, with its fake painted masonry joints, is mostly Abadie's work too. The most lingering impression is one of vastness (no wonder – it's one and a half times the length of a football pitch). Between Abadie and the Protestants, little of interest survived. Highlights include the huge chandeliers, which Abadie had designed for Paris's Notre Dame for Napoleon III's wedding, and a bombastic Baroque walnut retable from a Jesuit seminary.

Medieval streets around St-Front The north door of the cathedral opens on to **Avenue Daumesnil** [145 C6], the centre of a fascinating web of 15th- and 16th-century pedestrian lanes. Much of the stone of their urbane houses was quarried from ancient Vesunna, and residents often leave their gates open to let passers-by admire their curved inner stairs. The **Vieux Moulin** [145 C7], perched on a river wall on Boulevard Georges Saumande, is a relic of the grain monopoly once held by the canons of St-Front. Just down the street, the 15th-century **Maison des Consuls** [145 C6], the old seat of city government, reflects Périgueux's late medieval-Renaissance heyday; there are beautiful views of the ensemble over the willowy banks of the Isle from the **Pont des Barris** [145 D7].

Back up in Place Daumesnil, enter the picturesque **Galeries Daumesnil** [145 C6] by way of Rue de la Clarté: these are a set of old courtyards opened up to the public, and named after Pierre Daumesnil (see opposite) who was born at 7 Rue de la Clarté in 1776. Long narrow pedestrian **Rue Limogeanne** [145 B6] has been Périgueux's busiest shopping street since the Middle Ages and is lined with Renaissance-era houses; no. 5, the **Maison Estignard** [145 B6], is especially lovely with its dormers, mullioned windows and carvings of salamanders – a way of flattering François Ier, whose emblem they were. In pretty **Place St-Louis** surrounded by restaurants and cafés, the **Maison du Pâtissier** (1518) [145 B6] has a sculpted porch and an inscription warning that anyone who speaks badly behind people's backs is not welcome inside, for 'The greatest glory is to displease the wicked.'

Musée d'Art et d'Archéologie du Périgord (MAAP) [145 C5] (22 Cours Tourny; ☎ 05 53 06 40 70; w perigueux-maap.fr; ⌚ Apr–Sep 10.30–17.30 Mon, Wed–Fri, 13.00–18.00 Sat–Sun, Oct–Mar 10.00–17.00 Mon, Wed–Fri, 13.00–18.00 Sat–Sun; €6, ages 18–26 €4, under 18 free) This museum has something for every taste. The important prehistoric section has one of the oldest complete skeletons ever found, the 70,000BC Neanderthal *homme de Régourdou* (page 180). There are Upper Palaeolithic carvings and engravings on bone and stone, among them the strange, disembodied *Parade of Bison* from Chancelade and a disc carved with does. From later millennia there's Gallo-Roman jewellery, domestic items and mosaics, an Alemanni sword, Visigothic and Frankish blades, a 6th-century Visigothic sarcophagus, a lacy fragment of a Carolingian chancel, and strange faces and slatternly mermaids that once adorned St-Front, a jewellery box that belonged to Fénelon's family, and ceramics and enamels from Limoges.

The paintings aren't overwhelming, but there is the *Diptyque de Rabastens* (1286), a rare work painted on leather from Toulouse, a Canaletto and Dutch works, and 20th-century works by Périgourdins, including sculptures by Jane Poupelet (page 155).

Much of the ethnographic collection (from New Caledonia, the Cook Islands, Papua New Guinea and Africa) was brought back by Admiral Bougainville, who sailed around the world in 1768 for King Louis XV and introduced Europe to the flowers that bear his name, along with masks, idols and other art, including a 5m seashell necklace used as money. He also (unwittingly) took along Jeanne Baret, the first woman to circumnavigate the globe (page 156).

Musée Militaire de Périgord [145 B7] (32 Rue des Farges; 05 53 53 47 36; w museemilitaire-perigord.fr; 14.00–18.00 Mon–Sat; €5, under 12 free) Founded and staffed by the Veterans of Périgord, this museum has a wide-ranging collection of arms and armour, battle flags and wild Zouave uniforms and everything else military, dating from the Middle Ages up to the war in Algeria. The Germans are of course well represented, notably by a whole cabinet of *Pickelhauben* – those old spiky Prussian helmets.

There are mementos of Périgord's heroes, notably the feisty General Pierre Daumesnil who fought with Napoleon in Egypt, lost a leg at Wagram near Vienna and was given what seemed to be the equivalent of a desk job as commander of the Château of Vincennes – in charge of the biggest arsenal in France. When the Allies took Paris in 1815, they (and Daumesnil's own superiors) demanded that he surrender Vincennes. He refused. They offered him a million-franc bribe, and when the Prussian negotiator arrived, Daumesnil waved a lighted paper in front of the mountain of powder he was guarding and frightened the daylights out of him. '*Je rendrai Vincennes quand on me rendra ma jambe!*' ('I shall surrender Vincennes when they give me back my leg!') he told them. They didn't, and Vincennes remained the only part of France never to surrender. Finally the new king, Louis XVIII, came in person to accept the keys. In a humiliated France, Daumesnil's defiance made him a hero. Later the old rascal confided: 'That refusal was my heritage to my grandchildren.'

He died of cholera in 1832, and in Cours Michel Montaigne, there's a statue of him from that year, pointing with pride at his peg leg.

Place Francheville [145 C2] Once the no-man's land between the Cité and Le Puy St-Front and then a car park, Place Francheville is now a rather lovely garden square. The tourist office's medieval-Renaissance guided tour will get you inside the last remnant of Puy's walls here, the **Tour Mataguerre** [145 A7]. Decorated with fleurs-de-lys, it was repaired in 1477 with the forced labour of men inflicted with the scourge of 15th-century Périgueux – leprosy.

Vesunna: Musée Gallo-Roman [145 B3] (Parc de Vésone; 05 53 53 00 92; w perigueux-vesunna.fr; Jul–Aug 10.00–19.00 daily, Apr–Jun & Sep 09.30–17.30 Tue–Fri, 10.00–12.30 & 14.30–18.00 Sat–Sun, Oct–Mar 09.30–12.30 & 13.30–17.00 Tue–Fri, 10.00–12.30 & 14.30–18.00 Sat–Sun, Jan 6–30 closed; €6, students €4, under 18 free; combined tickets with MAAP €9/€6) Périgueux's oldest bits are the stars of its newest attraction designed by Jean Nouvel. Delicate, almost immaterial glass walls hang from a parasol roof, which protects the impressive remains of a 1st–3rd century AD domus, a fancy patrician villa with paintings, mosaics and heated baths discovered in 1959, which you inspect up close from the walkways just above. The numerous finds excavated over the years are displayed on the two balconies.

Tour de Vésone [145 B3] According to ancient writers, this fantastical ruin once stood in the exact centre of Vesunna, in the middle of a peristyle square. It was the temple of the city's tutelary deity, some murky Celtic goddess who didn't like to be named. Today it stands alone in a park, an enigmatic stone and brick cylinder 20m high, with its breach attributed to St Front. Imagine this great cylinder as it must have appeared in the Middle Ages, still surrounded by some of its columns. Note the row of sockets about 6m from the top; beams projected from here to hold up the cornice and roof, which would have been domed or conical – recalled in the unique, odd circular lantern on the top of St-Front's bell tower. It's the very image of the Tour de Vésone; this iconic, almost magical building must still have held Périgueux in its spell, and the Romanesque builders were able finally to capture it and Christianise it.

St-Étienne-de-la-Cité [145 B3] (Rue Romaine) The centre of the old Cité is marked by Périgueux's oldest church, founded over a Temple of Mars in the 6th century. In the 12th century it was rebuilt in a style that became the prototype of the Périgourdin domed Romanesque church, with wide Byzantine cupolas not only over the crossing but cupping the length of the nave. Originally St-Étienne had four of these, culminating in a huge bell-tower porch; those busy Huguenots unkindly, and none too neatly, tore off the front half.

The two surviving bays are not only an important lesson in the origins of Périgourdin Romanesque, but are steeped in shadowy medieval solemnity, an atmosphere so lacking in St-Front. The first dome, from the early 1100s, is solid and primitive, lit only by tiny windows; the second, from around 1160, is elongated, lighter, and supported by twinned columns. Inside, the arch from the tomb of Bishop Jean d'Asside (d1169) frames the Romanesque baptismal font, and there's a medieval curiosity: a carved 12th-century Easter calendar. Back in the age of slow communications, each diocese had to puzzle out the right Sunday for Easter by observing the moon and calculating from a chart like this one.

Elsewhere in the Cité Just north of St-Étienne, the **Jardin des Arènes** [145 B2] traces the lines of the ancient amphitheatre, where up to 30,000 spectators cheered gladiators to death. Now it's practically toothless; after serving as the base for the castle of the bloody-minded counts of Périgord, it was enthusiastically razed in 1391. Just southwest stands the **Château Barrière** [145 B3], a *maison forte*, or strong house, built into the walls of the Cité for a loyal retainer of the counts. Next to the château is a rare 13th-century Romanesque house; across the street the Gallo-Roman **Porte Normande** [145 A3] is a sole survivor of the wall thrown together by the citizens of Vesunna after the invasion of the Alemanni; originally it stood about 10m high, a jigsaw of columns and temple fragments.

ABBAYE DE CHANCELADE (Rte des Carrières, 6km west of Périgueux; **m** 06 46 78 94 37; **w** abbaye-chancelade.com; ⌚ 14.30–17.30 Mon–Fri, guided tours in French 15.00 Tue–Fri & Sun; donations) Chancelade is an enchanting spot with a spring and an Augustinian abbey founded in 1133. In 1370 the English gave the monks the bum's rush and converted the abbey into a fort that only fell when the great Bertrand du Guesclin stormed up the ladder and split open the head of the English captain. The main church, with its arcaded, three-tiered bell tower, was restored in the 1600s, although the 13th-century frescoes of Catholicism's two tallest saints, Christopher and Thomas à Becket, have survived.

In the 12th century, monks from Chancelade founded the **Prieuré de Merlande** (📞05 53 03 52 80; 🕘 09.00–noon & 16.30–17.30 Mon–Thu, 09.00–noon Fri–Sat) in a forest clearing 6km north off the D2. One of the original two domes was smashed by the English; the rest was fortified in the 16th century and wrecked again in the Revolution. Somehow the capitals on the blind arcading of the choir have survived, with interwoven designs of animals and monsters.

South of Périgueux on the D2, the hamlet of **Atur** has a 12th-century Romanesque church with a newly discovered mural of *The Kiss of Judas* and a Lanterne des Morts (page 201); 21km south on the D8, **Vergt** stands as a rare monument to the very seldom seen positive side of the counts of Périgord, in this case Archambault III, who in 1285 founded this pleasant bastide best known for its strawberry festival in May, when local bakers produce a tart so big it fills the entire *halle* in the centre.

SOUTHWEST OF PÉRIGUEUX: DOWN THE RIVER ISLE

Once past Périgueux, the busy A89 to Libourne and Bordeaux skirts the valley, leaving the quieter D6089 to meander along the south bank of the pretty River Isle, in no hurry to meet the Dordogne. Its clear waters were once popular with some pretty big fish–sturgeon; after a somewhat disastrous start to the local caviar industry, it's now going strong.

St-Astier holds a big **market** on Thursdays, Mussidan-Villamblard on Saturdays and Montpon-Ménestérol on Wednesdays.

TOURIST INFORMATION All the tourist offices listed here share the same website (**w** tourisme-isleperigord.com).

ℹ Montpon-Ménestérol Place Clemenceau; 📞05 53 82 23 77; 🕘 09.00–noon & 14.00–17.30 Mon–Fri, mornings only Sat

ℹ Mussidan-Villamblard Place de la République; 📞05 53 81 73 87; 🕘 09.00–12.30 & 14.00–17.00 Tue–Thu, mornings only Sat

ℹ Neuvic Place de la Mairie; 📞05 53 81 52 11; 🕘 Jul–Aug 09.30–12.30 Mon, Sat, 09.30–17.30 Tue, Wed, Fri, afternoon only Thu, Sep–Jun 09.30–noon & 14.00–17.00 Tue, Wed, Fri, mornings only Sat

ℹ St-Astier 1 Rue de la Fontaine; 📞05 53 54 13 85; 🕘 09.30–noon & 14.00–18.00 Mon–Fri, Jul–Aug 09.30–noon & 14.00–18.00 daily

WHERE TO STAY

Château de Lalande [map, page 142] (17 rooms) 57 Rte de S-Astier, Annesse-et-Beaulieu; 📞05 53 54 52 30; **w** chateau-lalande-perigord.com. Beautiful rooms of character in an ivy-covered château & historic park, with great hosts, an elegant gourmet restaurant (€€€€€) & an outdoor pool. **€€€€**

Château La Thuilière [map, page 142] (5 rooms) 38 Rte de St-Martin, St-Front-de-Pradoux; **m** 06 45 35 36 82; **w** chateaulathuiliere.com. Charming 19th-century Tudor-style mansion with a park & a pool. There are king-size beds in all the rooms, & cosy public rooms with a fireplace. The hosts serve a superb table d'hôte, with a vegetarian option by request. **€€€€**

Le Lion d'Or (8 rooms) Place de l'Église, Manzac-sur-Vern; 📞05 53 54 28 09; **w** lion-dor-manzac.com. 3-star Logis hotel in a former coaching inn, with a restaurant (€€€) featuring the local sturgeon & beef. **€€**

Le Sorbier (12 rooms) 6 Rte de Bordeaux, Razac-sur-l'Isle; 05 53 03 55 65; w lesorbier.eu. Tidy roadside inn with a good, recently remodelled, restaurant (€€€) & pool. **€€**

WHERE TO EAT AND DRINK

Le Relais de la Ganache [map, page 142] La Bassonie Nord, St-Astier; 05 53 09 67 33; w laganache.fr; eves only & Sun lunch, closed Mon. Gourmet dining in a renovated stone barn, plus stable boxes for your horse & 3 comfy rooms (**€€**) if you want to stay. There's just 1 menu (see the website; €32), but it's top-notch. €€€

Ô petit Gavroche 10 Rue Marl Foch, Montpon-Ménestérol; 05 53 80 04 01; w opetitgavroche.fr; closed Tue–Wed. Classic & creative cuisine with a touch of Italy & Spain in many dishes. *Menus €23–€29*. €€€

Auberge du Musée 6 Rue Raoul Grassin, Mussidan; 05 53 80 56 45; w aubergedumusee.com; closed eves Mon, Wed, Sun. Hearty local fare & big salads & a €13.50 lunch menu, with more elaborate fare in the evenings. €€

Le Kayola 18 Rte de St-Astier, Neuvic; 05 53 81 26 08; w le-kayola-neuvic.fr; closed eves Sun–Tue. Classic French dishes, all *fait maison* with an excellent-value €13.50 4-course lunch. €

ST-ASTIER This pleasant town on the Isle, 15km southwest of Périgueux, is named after the 7th-century AD hermit St Asterius, who in turn gave his name to the massive 11th-century fortified **church of St-Astier** (2 Rue du 20 Août), with sculpted figures on the façade that recall its days as a pilgrimage church. There's a pretty park on the riverbank and a pretty bridge over the Isle, but St-Astier is best known for its **lime quarries** (28 bis Rte de Montanceix, La Jarthe; 05 53 54 13 85; visits: Jul–Aug 09.30 Wed; €4, you must book), producing fine plaster often used in the renovation of historic buildings.

NEUVIC Downriver from St-Astier, you can visit the ivy-covered **Moulin de la Veyssière** (05 53 82 03 07; w moulindelaveyssiere.fr; 09.00–noon & 14.00–18.00 Mon–Sat; free), which produces flour and walnut, hazelnut and almond oils; they also have a small museum. The big and beautiful Renaissance **Château de Neuvic** (m 06 36 83 85 52; w fondation-isle.e-monsite.com; tours: Jul–Aug 10.30, 14.30 & 16.30 Tue–Sat, other times 1st w/end of each month; €6, ages 8–16 €3, under 8 free, inc access to the botanic park) is now a foundation for children in need but is open for tours. Its 6ha park is now a **botanic park** (Apr–Oct 10.00–noon & 14.00–18.00 Mon–Fri; €4, ages 8–16 €2) with a romantic Diana's Bath in an 18th-century grotto, and can be visited independently of the château.

These days Neuvic is best known for caviar. The Isle once hosted huge numbers of sturgeon, which migrated up the Gironde to spawn. In the early 20th century, the legend goes, an exiled Russian princess was appalled to see the fishermen feed the eggs to their poultry…and it wasn't long before the caviar industry took off, so much so that the sturgeon were fished to near extinction. Today its sturgeon are farmed and produce 24 tonnes of caviar a year; learn all about it at **Caviar de Neuvic** (05 53 80 89 57; w visites.caviar-de-neuvic.com; book 2hr tours in English online, from €19).

MUSSIDAN This large village on the Isle was twice in its history singled out for tragedy. During the Wars of Religion, all the Protestants in the vicinity took refuge there and fought bravely against the Catholics. They surrendered when their lives were guaranteed, but the Catholics were only joking; most were hanged, and Mussidan was razed. Henri IV, in honour of the town's sufferings, had it rebuilt. In 1944, the Resistance was very active in the surrounding forests, and were in town on 11 June 1944 when an armoured German train pulled up at the station with a machine gun, and a battle began. In reprisals, 52 people were rounded up and executed, the town was pillaged and about to be razed again when the Gestapo chief decided Mussidan had suffered enough.

You can get a good feel for Périgord's past at the **Musée André Voulgre** (4 Rue Raoul Grassin; 05 53 81 23 55; w museevoulgre.fr; Sep–May 09.00–noon & 14.00–17.00 Mon–Fri, Jun–mid-Jul 09.00–noon & 14.00–17.00 Tue–Sat, mid-Jul–Aug 09.00–noon & 14.00–18.00 daily; €5, ages 6–18 €2.50), with 5,000 items from Périgourdin daily life going back 200 years, including a tractor from 1920, built of parts salvaged from a World War I tank.

Just north of Mussidan, the 12th-century church at **St-Martin-l'Astier** has a very unusual octagonal choir. The partly medieval, partly 16th-century **Château de Montréal** (private), 7km east of Mussidan, belonged to Claude de Pontbriand, who accompanied Cartier to Canada and named the new French town on the St Lawrence after his home in Périgord – or so goes one possible explanation for Montreal's name.

MONTPON-MÉNESTÉROL The last town on the Isle in the Dordogne, only half an hour from St-Émilion on the A89, is nicknamed the 'Organ capital of the Aquitaine' (musical organs, that is) with ten beautiful instruments, including one of the oldest in France, built in 1660. These are at five different locations around town, gathered together by local enthusiast and organist Francis Chapelet. On Thursday afternoons in July and August the tourist office (page 151) takes visitors on tours to hear them all played. There's a beach on the river, and kayaks to hire at the **Moulin du Duellas** (m 06 15 19 11 18).

WEST OF PÉRIGUEUX

It was Jules Verne who dubbed the northern Périgord 'Green', where deep forests, shady rivers and the hills remain lusciously verdant even in midsummer. Between the Dronne and the Isle is the 50,580ha Forêt de la Double, interspersed with lakes and moody wetlands (some created by medieval monks to farm fish for Lent). It was long a refuge for bandits and anyone on the run.

The great oaks were all cut down in the 17th and 18th centuries – by barrel-makers, charcoal-burners, glass-blowers and tile-bakers – leaving an impoverished, malarial swamp. Napoleon III initiated a scheme to recolonise the forest, draining swamps and replanting the trees, which led to a brief population surge in the late 19th century. The Maquis were active here, until the Germans burned the forest. Most of the trees have since regrown but it's as empty as ever – a lonesome, poetic place of old farms (the Ferme du Parcot, page 157, is a rare survivor) and yet on these quiet roads there's a remarkable amount of things to see and do.

There are **markets** on Friday in Riberac and Monday in Tocane-St-Apre.

TOURIST INFORMATION **Riberac**'s tourist office (05 53 90 03 10; w en.perigordriberacois.fr; 09.30–12.30 & 14.00–18.00 Mon–Fri, 10.00–13.00 Sat) is at Place du Général de Gaulle.

WHERE TO STAY

La Grange de Lucie [map, page 142] (5 rooms) La Côte, Auriac de Bourzac; 05 53 90 28 53; w lagrangedelucie.com. Tranquil B&B with pleasant rooms that can sleep up to 4. There are a pool & hammocks in the orchard, & a lounge with books & games; table d'hôte 3 nights a week. B/fast inc. **€€**

Restospa Gassyhotel (6 rooms) St-Paul-Lizonne; 05 53 91 51 25; gassyhotel. In spite of its name, gas-free red-&-white rooms with a pool & a bar. €

Rev'Hôtel [map, page 142] (29 rooms) Rte de Périgueux, Riberac; 05 53 91 62 62; w rev-hotel.fr. Just outside the centre, a pleasant no-fuss 2-star hotel. €

WHERE TO EAT AND DRINK

Aux Délices de la Treille 18 Porte de Méribel, Montagrier; 05 53 91 12 63; w aubergeauxdelicesdelatreille.fr; mid-Jun–mid-Sep daily, mid-Sep–mid-Jun closed Wed & eves Tue. Combination village bar, tabac, grocer & restaurant under a trellis of vines, serving tasty renditions of the classics, with plenty of salads & seafood. *Lunch menu €15.90*. €€€

Le Chabrot 8 Rue Gambetta, Riberac; 05 53 91 28 59; lechabrotriberac; closed Wed & eves Mon–Thu, Sat. Regional dishes cooked with pizzazz. Named after the southwest custom of adding a splash of wine to the dregs of soup & sipping it right out of the bowl. *Menus from €16*. €€€

Rouge Le Bistrot Place des Tilleuls, Tocane-St-Apre; 05 53 90 26 37; w rougelebistrot.com; 08.00–14.00 & 19.00–midnight Mon, 11.00–14.00 Tue–Fri. Excellent dishes on an ever-changing blackboard menu, with a terrace overlooking all the action in the main square. €€€–€€

Des Bouches et des Oreilles [map, page 142] 2 Place Roger Nadal, Douchapt; 05 53 90 08 08; dbetdo.fr; closed Sun–Mon & lunch Sat. West of Tocane-St-Apre, informal & friendly, often featuring live music. *Menu from €12.50*. €€

L'Escapade Gourmande 2 Av de Verdun, Riberac; 05 24 14 11 62; lescapaderiberac; closed lunch Sun. Italian & French dishes, & excellent pizzas. €€

Le Citronnier 3 Place Nationale, Riberac; 05 53 90 22 72; ; 11.00–21.00 Tue–Sat. Handsome terrace out front & good €16 *plat du jour*. They often do special G&T nights with platters of nibbles. €€

Le Bar du Midi 35 Place Nationale, Riberac; 05 53 90 02 96; 07.00–20.00 Mon–Sat. Always packed in summer. Great coffee, great atmosphere & light lunches. €

SPORTS AND ACTIVITIES **Camping du Pré Sec** (Tocane-St-Apre; 05 53 90 40 60; w campingdupresec.com) rents out kayaks and SUPs from a few hours to up to two days. You can also hire canoes and kayaks from **Canoë Riberac** (Camping municipal, Riberac; m 06 77 30 89 63; w daviddessaigne.wixsite.com/canoeriberac). If rowing boats are more your thing, rent one at **Maison de la Dronne** (134 Moulin du Pont, Tocane-St-Apre; 05 53 91 35 11; maisondeladronne24; Jun–Sep Wed–Mon) for drifting down the Dronne, or take one of their tours, with oars or motors (night tours Wed).

TOCANE-ST-APRE The D710 from Périgueux meets the lovely Dronne river in this pretty village. It has a rare collection of 19th-century dresses and coifs gathered by Ginette Valprémy, a seamstress who was a major figure in preserving Périgord's traditional songs and dances: the **Musée du Costume** (m 06 81 29 55 28; w musee-tocane.fr; Jun–Sep 14.30–18.30 Tue–Sat, other times by appt; €4, under 15 €2) is in the central 17th-century Hôtel Paradol.

There's a good dolmen nearby and Gallo-Roman excavations that suggest folks have long forded the river here. You should too, following signs for **Montagrier**. The rewards are superb panoramas into the Dronne valley, the 12th-century **Moulin de la Dronne** (converted to an electric plant in 1906; 05 53 91 35 11; May–Sep 10.00–17.00 Wed–Mon) and a 12th-century domed church, **Ste-Madeleine**, with a three-lobed apse and carved capitals.

Grand Brassac north of Montagrier has the even more extraordinary 12th-century **SS Pierre et Paul** – a genuine church-castle with crenelated towers and walls. Not surprisingly it was never taken by an enemy. Then there's an unusual double-decker sculpted tympanum over the north portal that has retained some of its original paint. Inside three domes hover on pendentives, and there's an elaborate 17th-century wooden tabernacle. The beautiful 14th–19th-century **Château de Montardy** (to visit call 05 47 94 00 07; free), just west on the D93, has belonged to the same family since 1427.

RIBERAC With 3,800 souls, Riberac on the Dronne offers a dollop of urbanity in the Forêt de la Double. After the Vikings rowed past in AD848 on their way to pillage Brantôme, it was fortified with a castle that stood for a thousand years. In the mid 12th century it gave birth to quixotic troubadour Arnaut Daniel, whose verse is so complex that it is well-nigh impossible to translate without losing its charm. Dante met his shade in Purgatory, where Arnaut speaks the only line in Provençal in the *Divine Comedy* – a language Dante himself considered using for his masterpiece before opting for Italian.

Riberac has a charming town hall with turrets, and a pair of striking churches. **Notre-Dame de la Paix** (637 Rue de la Nouvelle Église) has domes with fish-scale tiles and a bell tower that looks like it was inspired by a Lanterne des Morts, while the 12th-century Romanesque **Collégiale de Riberac** (40 Rue Notre Dame; mid-Mar–Oct 14.00–18.00 Tue–Sat, otherwise by appt with the tourist office) was restored in the 1980s with a façade that would look nice on a school gymnasium; it has a pretty apse decorated with 17th-century paintings.

AROUND RIBERAC: THE ROMANESQUE CIRCUIT This corner of Périgord is peppered with Romanesque churches. The signed circuit begins at **Allemans** (up the D709), then passes another church at **St-Paul-Lizonne**, where in the 1680s the priest commissioned a local deaf artist named Arnaud Paradol to paint the ceiling with a charming vision of the *Rapture of St Paul*, with plenty of cherubs and bubbling clouds all around the edges of the starry sky. Paradol wasn't the only artist to come from the village: one of France's first female sculptors, Jane Poupelet (1874–1932), was born and is buried here. Poupelet spent time in the Paris circle of Auguste Rodin and Antoine Bourdelle, then worked with American sculptor Anna Coleman Ladd, making masks for soldiers who had their faces blown apart during World War I; both were awarded the Légion d'Honneur for their work.

Next on the circuit is **Lusignac**, a film set of a medieval village. Here the fortified church of **St-Eutrope** resembles the Mother of God's attic, filled with clutter, discontinued models of saints, vases of dusty artificial flowers and holy pictures that look as if they were clipped from magazines. The next stop, **St-Martial-Viveyrol**, has remnants of frescoes, while **Cherval** to the northeast has the 11th-century **St-Martin**, which doesn't look like much but inside is one of the most beautiful of them all, with a cluster of five domes.

La Tour-Blanche gets its name from the ruined *Turris Alba* 'White Tower' built in the 10th century over a Gaulish fort, said to be the oldest still standing in France; Henri IV lodged here for several weeks, although a few years later he would have been more comfortable in the handsome **Manoir de Roumailhac** (1617) in the centre. There are 30 excellent Romanesque carved capitals to see in the 12th-century priory of **St-Cybard-de-Cercles** and a trio of mini museums (05 53 91 11 98; w la-tour-blanche-cercles.fr; Jul–Aug 15.00–18.00 Tue–Sun; €1.50 for all 3): the **Musée de la Ferblanterie** dedicated to tin with more than 1,000 items; the **Musée des Minéraux** with a local's geological collection; and the **Musée de Records** with choice items in the order of a giant replica of a French postage stamp. It also has a rare 14th-century **windmill** and, in the same area, **Le Parc Sauvage** (Le Claud; m 07 66 79 42 84;

w leparcsauvage.com; ⌚ Apr–Jun & Sep–Oct 10.00–18.00 Wed–Sun, Jul–Aug & school hols 10.00–18.00 daily; €8, ages 3–12 €5), part rescue centre for wounded wild animals, part educational farm, part deer and wallaby woodland and part falconry show (11.15 & 16.30) run by an enthusiastic young team.

Bourg-des-Maisons has a big church, **Ste-Marie**, with rare 14th–16th-century frescoes inside, among them a *Last Supper* and a figure with an enormous sword; **Vendoire** further northwest has yet another, from the 17th century, with a façade decorated with columns in the style of the nearby Charente. In the meantime, learn all about peat bogs at the **Site Naturel des Tourbières** (05 53 90 79 56; f tourbieresvendoire24; ⌚ year-round; museum ⌚ May–Sep 10.00–17.00 Tue–Sun, with special activities on Fri; €5), with a nature trail.

VANXAINS Once upon a time this quiet village was the seat of the Vicomte de la Double. It has an elegant Romanesque church with fine carved capitals, and a line of menhirs at **Sauteranne** which is impossible to find unless you get someone to direct you. In 1747, it was the birthplace of Suzette Labrouse, 'the Prophetess of the Revolution', who went to Paris, where she met Marat, Dr Guillotin, Desmoulins and, most disastrously, Robespierre, who persuaded her to go to Rome to tell the pope to give up his temporal power. The pope disagreed and locked her up in Castel Sant'Angelo.

West of Vanxains, **Le Parc des Doublorigenes** (Le Petit Moucaud, St-Vincent-Jalmoutiers; m 06 33 81 26 15; w doublorigenes.com; ⌚ May–Jun 10.30–19.00 Sat–Sun, Jul–Aug 10.30–19.00 Tue–Sun; €6, children €5) offers a lazy day out in loungers and quirky wooden sculptures, cultural and 'nonchalant activities' and all kinds of games.

ST-AULAYE Some of the prettiest Dronne valley scenery is around St-Aulaye, at the edge of the Double forest. It has a rare 11th-century bridge by a picturesque mill and will teach about the neighbouring Charente's famous brandy at the **Musée du Cognac et du Vin** (1 Rue du Dr Rousseau; 05 53 90 81 33; ⌚ Jul–Aug 15.00–18.30 Sat–Sun; €2.30, under 15 €0.75). Recently the village has declared itself the 'Terre de Pastel' – not the Toulouse version of pastel (page 361) but the artistic one, with a **Musée du Pastel** (39 Rue du Dr H Lacroix; 05 53 90 81 33; ⌚ ring for hours) displaying a rotating collection of art.

St-Aulaye was the last home of Jeanne Baret (1740–1807), the first known woman to travel around the world. Disguised as a man, she enlisted as the assistant to her lover, naturalist Philibert Commerçon, who was in ill health, and sailed with Louis Antoine de Bougainville's expedition; in Rio de Janeiro she helped gather the specimens of the flower that took Bougainville's name. She left the ship in Mauritius (Bougainville was relieved, as it was illegal at the time to have a woman in a crew), where she ran a successful tavern. There she met and married Jean Dubernat, a native of St-Aulaye where they settled after she completed her circumnavigation of the globe. For more, seek out Danielle Clode's book, *In Search of the Woman Who Sailed the World* (page 398).

IN THE FORÊT DE DOUBLE To the east along the D43, **Siorac-de-Riberac** has yet another fortified Romanesque church, while the church of **St-Sulpice-de-Roumagnac** 3km further boasts a beautiful 17th-century wooden retable. The D43 continues east towards St-Astier on the Isle (page 152), with grand views most of the way. Alternatively, south of Siorac the bucolic **Grand Étang de la Jemaye** offers the chance to swim in pure nature.

In the very heart of the forest, the monks at the **Abbaye d'Échourgnac** (☎ 05 53 80 82 50; **w** abbaye-echourgnac.org; no visits, but retreats possible), who arrived in 1868, were one of the first positive things to happen to the local economy. Now replaced by cloistered nuns, they are famous for their cheeses, especially La Trappe, which you can purchase at the convent shop along with other goodies produced in local convents and monasteries. Just east of Échourgnac, one of the last examples of traditional rural architecture in the region, the **Ferme du Parcot** (☎ 05 53 81 99 28; **w** parcot.org; ⏱ Jul–Aug 10.30–12.30 & 14.30–18.30 daily, May–Jun & Sep 14.30–18.30 Sat–Sun), is open for tours, and doubles as a Double information centre.

WEST TO AUBETERRE-SUR-DRONNE West of Riberac and north of the river, you can get a bird's-eye view of the area from the top of **Puy de Beaumont** on a little road off the D709. The little bridge at **Comberanche** will take you back over the Dronne to **Bourg-du-Bost**, with another 12th-century church, **Notre-Dame de l'Assomption** (⏱ usually) with a tall defensive tower over the dome and colourful murals, including a St Christopher. Next here is **Petit-Bersac**, where archaeologists have uncovered a Gallo-Roman settlement and have collected the finds in a small **Musée Gallo-Romain** (⏱ Jul–Aug 14.30–18.00 daily; other times ring Mme Duprat on ☎ 05 53 90 17 45).

Another little road leads due south of Petit-Bersac to **St-Privat-des-Prés** where the 11th-century church sports a porch and belt of nine blind arches across the façade and good modillions. In the village centre, St-Privat's **Musée du Patrimoine en Miniature** (☎ 05 53 91 22 87; ⏱ Jul–Aug 15.00–18.00 Tue–Sun; ask at the *mairie* if it's closed) is the lifelong project of Dr Jean Nicolas, who in his retirement built scale 1:100 models of some of the world's greatest cathedrals and castles. The **Musée de la Vie de la Village** (same details) is chock-full of tools and curiosities recreating a 19th-century village street.

AUBETERRE-SUR-DRONNE The real attraction in this neck of the woods is 2km over in the Charente. A beautiful hill town of ivory stone, Aubeterre has more history and mystery than it has room for. Much of it is concentrated in the **subterranean church of St-Jean** (☎ 05 45 98 65 06; ⏱ Jul–Aug 09.30–19.00 daily, Sep–Jun 09.30–12,30 & 14.00–18.00 daily; €8, students & ages 13+ €4, ages 8–12 €3, under 8 free). First excavations in the cliff over the Dronne began on a small scale in Merovingian times, when the rare total-immersion baptismal font was cut into the floor. This early cave church soon became a favourite place to await the trump of doom; behind the font a necropolis is jammed with a hundred hollows chiselled in the stone.

In the 12th century, just when Aubeterre found itself on a major route to Compostela, Pierre de Castillon, the Crusader Viscount of Aubeterre, brought back an important relic from the Holy Land (if anyone knows what it was or is, they aren't telling) and ordered the cave to be enlarged to hold a magnificent 6m stone **reliquary** in the form of the Holy Sepulchre. If St-Émilion's Église Monolithe (page 131) – another project of Pierre de Castillon – is the largest in Europe, Aubeterre's is the tallest in the world, nearly 20m high and supported by two blackened columns as thick as sequoias.

Whatever was in the reliquary must have been powerful, judging by the many subsequent tombs facing it instead of Jerusalem. But what could have been an even older holy place was discovered by accident in 1963 when a passing truck caused the pavement outside the church to collapse, revealing what looks like an ancient *mithraeum* – a subterranean chamber lined with benches on either side, where adherents of Mithras (the favourite god of the Roman legions) would be baptised in the hot blood of a bull sacrificed on ground level.

Compostela pilgrims had another important stop in Aubeterre, just up the hill: the 11th-century church of **St-Jacques**. Although the Protestants smashed it up, they spared the magnificent three-arched Romano-Hispano-Moorish façade. Bolted on to the upper left of the façade are the black fragments of an equestrian statue, believed to have been either Charlemagne or Santiago (St James in his Spanish role as a Moor-slaying crusader).

Although the right arch has been eroded, the central and especially the left arch are richly decorated with patterns and six panels of the zodiac – although, unlike most zodiacs, each scene features a fellow (a chef?) sitting by a cooking fire. The monsters on the capitals are a treat: winking cats with two bodies, biting birds and quadrupeds with silly bearded heads (with extra pairs of heads like grinning balloons strapped to their backs). On the far left side of the left arch, note the centaur with a bow, and on the right a horse with an arrow piercing its neck. Inside is the only other bit salvaged from Huguenot fury: an 11th-century statue of the Virgin holding Jesus in her right arm instead of the usual left, a deviation believed to be mystically significant, although nobody knows exactly how.

BRANTÔME AND THE PARC NATUREL RÉGIONAL PÉRIGORD-LIMOUSIN

The gentle Dronne meanders through delightful Renaissance Brantôme, one of the gateways into the lush wooded Parc Naturel Régional Périgord-Limousin (**w** pnr-perigord-limousin.fr), created to develop opportunities in rural communities while preserving the area's natural heritage and culture, villages and some of the most beautiful châteaux you'll ever see. Do it from a bike saddle on the Flow Vélo (**w** laflowvelo.com), a bucolic 290km *voie vert* replacing the old rail link from Thiviers to the sea via Nontron and Javerlhac.

Brantôme has its **market** on Fridays, Thiviers and Nontron on Saturday mornings.

GETTING THERE AND AROUND Public transport is pretty sparse here; besides the buses from Périgueux (page 144), there are links to Nontron (bus 20) & Piégut (bus 21) from Angoulême. See **w** transports.nouvelle-aquitaine.fr.

TOURIST INFORMATION

Brantôme 2 Rue Puyjoli de Meyjounissas; 05 53 05 80 63; **w** perigord-dronne-belle.fr; Jun–Sep 10.00–18.00 daily, Oct–Dec & mid-Feb–May 10.00–noon & 14.00–17.00 Wed–Mon

Jumilhac le Grand Place du Château; 05 53 52 55 43; same website & hours as Thiviers, but closed Nov–early Apr

Mareuil 12 Rue Pierre Degail; 05 53 05 62 41; **w** perigord-dronne-belle.fr; 09.00–noon & 14.00–16.00 Mon–Thu, closed Wed mornings

Nontron 1 Av du Général Leclerc; 05 53 56 25 50; **w** tourisme-nontron.fr; 09.30–12.30 & 13.30–17.00 Mon–Fri, 09.30–12.30 Sat

St-Jean-de-Côle Rue du Château; 05 53 62 14 15; same website & hours as Thiviers

Thiviers 8 Place Foch; 05 53 55 12 50; **w** office-de-tourisme-perigord-limousin.jimdosite.com; 09.30–12.30 & 14.00–17.30 Mon–Sat, 09.30–12.30 Sun, Sep–Jun closed Sun, & afternoons Mon & Sat.

Varaignes 1292 Rte de Terres Rouges; 05 53 56 35 76; **w** tourisme-nontron.fr; 14.00–17.00 Mon, Fri–Sat, 09.00–noon Thu.

WHERE TO STAY

Le Moulin de l'Abbaye (20 rooms) 1 Route de Bourdeilles, Brantôme; 05 53 05 80 22; **w** moulinabbaye.com. On the Dronne, this romantic, ivy-covered Relais & Châteaux is spread among a converted watermill, a carpenter's house & a Cure's residence, set in a garden. The Michelin-starred restaurant (€€€€€) serves exquisite dishes on the riverside terrace. **€€€€€**

Moulin du Roc (15 rooms) Av Eugène Le Roy, Champagnac-de-Belair; 05 53 02 86 00; w moulinduroc.com. Dreamy spot in a charming old mill on the Dronne northeast of Brantôme, with beautiful rooms, pool, tennis, bar & gastronomic restaurant (€€€€€) with 900 wines to choose from. **€€€€€**

Moulin de Vigonac (10 rooms) Vigonac, Brantôme; 05 53 05 87 59; w moulindevigonac.com. The ruins of a 16th-century mill belonging to the abbey, later used as a slipper factory, have been stunningly restored as a 4-star hotel, with big luminous rooms, a heated pool in the lovely garden, & excellent restaurant (€€€€€, eves only). **€€€€–€€€**

Charbonnel (18 rooms) 57 Rue Gambetta, Brantôme; 05 53 05 70 15; w hotelrestaurantcharbonnel.com. A local institution on the Dronne; many of the elegant rooms have river views, while the excellent restaurant (€€€€) has a flowery terrace right on the water. Free parking 5mins away. **€€€**

Hostellerie les Griffons (10 rooms) Grand Rue, Bourdeilles; 05 53 45 45 35; reserve via w booking.com. Charming antique-furnished 17th-century inn by the château, with a garden & pool. **€€€**

L'Escapade [map, page 142] (4 rooms) Clos Bois, 5km northwest of Brantôme; m 06 22 18 47 35; w chambredhotelescapade.business.site. Isabelle runs a peaceful retreat in a gorgeous garden setting, with a pool. Delicious b/fast inc. **€€€**

Hostellerie St-Jacques (13 rooms) 10 Rue du Grand Étang, St-Saud-Lacoussière (west of Nontron); 05 53 56 97 21; w hostellerie-saint-jacques.com. A charming hotel with comfy rooms, a heated pool in the garden & an exceptionally good restaurant (€€€€) with plush red seats & enchanting terrace. **€€€–€€**

Hôtel de France et de Russie (11 rooms) 51 Rue du Général Lamy, Thiviers; 05 53 55 17 80; w thiviers-hotel.com. Rooms in various sizes & styles in this old stone inn of 1776. Its name comes from the many Russians who frequented Thiviers in the late 19th century, including the supplier of the foie gras to the Tsar. It's also a bike hotel. **€€€–€**

Grand Hôtel Pélisson (15 rooms) 3 Place Agard, Nontron; 05 53 56 11 22; w hotel-pelisson-nontron.com. A traditional hotel in what was an 18th-century convent, then a posthouse, with an inner courtyard & pool & bike garage. The restaurant (€€€) serves the classics; note the certificate from Napoleon III dated 1867, proclaiming the inn was the official provider of foie gras to the imperial table. **€€**

Hostellerie du Périgord Vert (23 rooms) 6 Av de Thiviers, Brantôme; 05 53 05 70 58; w hotel-hpv.fr. This ivy-swathed building is a delightful Logis de France hotel with modern rooms, spa & pool, & good restaurant (€€€€) featuring succulent meats. **€€–€**

Château Le Verdoyer [map, page 142] (5 rooms) Champs Romain near St Saud-Lacoussière; 05 53 56 94 64; w verdoyer.fr. A large family-oriented complex, offering rooms in the castle & a campsite with tents etc to rent. Facilities include indoor & outdoor pools, tennis, mini-golf, bike rentals, elegant restaurant (€€€€) & snack bar. **€**

Les Conches (3 rooms) 38 Av de Verdun, Thiviers; m 06 86 20 61 92; w chambre-hote-dordogne.com. Lovely old farmhouse & hosts, with a pool & garden; eve meals available. B/fast inc. **€**

WHERE TO EAT AND DRINK

L'Escapade des Sens 51 Rue du Général Lamy, Thiviers; 05 53 62 19 23; w lescapade-des-sens.com; closed Mon & eves Sun, Thu. Young chef Nicolas Cousinou trained in Monaco with Alain Ducasse so knows a few things about fine cuisine. *W/day lunch, 2 courses €16, evening menus from €30.* €€€€

Moulin du Grand Étang St-Estèphe; 05 53 60 41 69; w moulindugrandetang.com; closed Mon–Tue. Bucolic, gourmet dining by the lake. *W/day lunch menus from €19.* €€€€

Domaine de la Roseraie [map, page 142] (Récré gourmande) Les Courrières, just north of Brantôme; 05 53 45 77 04; w domainedelaroseraiebrantome.com; closed Mon & eves Sun. In a 17th-century chartreuse in the middle of a rose garden, with a beefy menu, & burgers, too. €€€€–€€€

La Table d'Emilie 28 Rue Victor Hugo, Brantôme; 09 52 83 53 35; w latabledemilie.restaurant; closed Mon & eves Sun, Wed. Popular, friendly bar & brasserie, with vegetarian choices & an excellent tournedos Rossini if you feel like a splurge. €€€

Le St-Jean St-Jean-de-Côle; 09 70 35 57 20; w le-stjean.fr; closed Sun–Mon. Oldest restaurant in the village; informal place with a terrace serving duck classics. *Menus from €19.50.* €€€

Les Promenades de Bourdeilles Rue de l'Église, Bourdeilles; 05 53 03 43 70; w restaurantlespromenades.com; closed Wed, Thu & eves Sun. The place to stop for lunch or dinner while visiting the château, with a convivial terrace & chef does lovely things with mushrooms & seafood. Chalkboard menu: *3 courses for €31.* €€€

Ferme Auberge de Faye [map, page 142] Faye, 3km south of Brantôme; 05 53 05 85 84; w ferme-auberge-de-faye.fr; closed Sun–Mon. Exceptional home-cooking & jolly host. Book long in advance. *Set menus with wine from €29.* €€

SPORTS AND ACTIVITIES The mayor of Nontron (1 Place Alfred Agard; 05 54 60 84 00; w nontron.fr) rents out city and mountain **e-bikes** by the day, weekend or week (€10/€15/€40). In Brantôme hire a **canoe** at Allo Canoës (Les Prés; m 06 01 78 29 58; w allocanoes24.com) for up to 3 hours or at Brantôme Canoë (14 Av André Maurois; 05 53 05 77 24; w brantomecanoe.com) who also do SUPs. **Boat rides** are available through Croisières de Brantôme (m 06 29 77 98 97; w brantomecroisieres.com; Apr–Oct; €9, ages 2–12 €6, for a 50min cruise on the Dronne). There's a 9-hole course at **Golf du Genêt** (St-Barthélémy de Bussière; m 06 01 71 07 42) and opportunities to go riding north of Nontron with the **Horse Club Mérigaud** (Mérigaud, St-Estèphe; m 06 10 08 08 71; f Merigaud-Horseclub).

BRANTÔME Brantôme makes a neat bookend to Sarlat (page 193). Both are essentially aristocratic preserves – Sarlat is where the elite built their townhouses, and Brantôme is where they parked their younger sons in a five-star abbey. The setting is perfect; beneath the cliffs and forested hills, the centre is on an island in the Dronne, with the water lazily flowing on all sides, enough to call it 'the Venice of Périgord'. A charming 16th-century dogleg bridge, the **Pont Coudé** with a Renaissance pavilion, built by a dreamy abbot to watch the reflections in the river water, crosses from the island town to the white pile of the abbey.

The **Abbaye de Brantôme** (05 53 05 80 63; mid-Feb–Dec 10.00–17.00; tickets from the tourist office: tours of the church, cloister & bell tower €8/€6, under 12 free; visits to the caves & Musée Fernand Desmoulin €6.50/€4.30; combined tickets €10/€6.50), so they say, was founded by Charlemagne in AD769 to house the relics of St Sicaire, a slave of Herod who converted to Christianity after participating in the Massacre of the Innocents. Sacked by the Vikings in the 11th century, it was rebuilt beside the river against a steep bank. During the Hundred Years' War, it was defended by the Barons of Bourdeilles, and it survived the Wars of Religion thanks to one of their descendants, Pierre de Bourdeilles (see box, opposite).

The 11th-century **church**, after suffering a string of bad luck and reconstructions, was given the *coup de grâce* when it was handed over to the ham-fisted 19th-century architect-restorer Paul Abadie. The church had already lost its dome back in the 13th century; after the Abadie treatment, only a bas-relief of the *Massacre of the Innocents* under the porch and a carved capital, now used as a font, survived. Of the cloister, rebuilt in the 16th century, only one gallery remains.

The best bits of the abbey (the bits you buy tickets for) are behind its Renaissance façade, in the caves in the cliff where the first monks lived, around the **fountain of St Sicaire**. Built on a spur of the cliffs is another wonder, the slightly tipsy **bell tower** (the oldest in France), with its Merovingian base, pyramid roof and complex tiers of windows and arches from the 11th century which attest to the abbey's former grandeur. It's 130 steps up for the big views.

THE FRISKY ABBÉ DE BRANTÔME

Pierre de Bourdeilles (1540–1614), from the very noble family just down the river, was one of those younger sons who ended up here. He became abbot at the age of 22 and used the abbey's revenues to finance his escapades as a soldier of fortune and lover of court ladies: he accompanied Mary Stuart to Scotland, visited Morocco, Portugal and Venice, and planned an expedition to Peru, only to be frustrated by the Wars of Religion. He rendered a genuine service to his abbey by keeping the Huguenots at bay, diplomatically appealing to the Protestant leader – an old companion-in-arms.

But when Henri III vetoed a promotion, he was so furious he decided to go to Spain and fight against France, only to be gravely injured falling off his horse. Using his abbey as his pen name, Brantôme spent the rest of his life convalescing while writing gossipy accounts of his time (the *Vies des hommes illustres et des grands capitaines* and the scandalous *Vies des dames galantes*). Brantôme was a one-man tabloid, offering an insider's account of what was really going on behind the arrases. It was such spicy stuff that he left instructions for his heirs to wait 50 years before publishing his books, to make sure all his subjects were dead. He is still celebrated for his wit and worldly cynicism, but mostly survives these days in French books of quotations, imparting such louche epigrams as *'D'un veille poule on fait le meilleur bouillon'* ('An old chicken makes the best soup') and *'Toute belle femme s'estant une fois essayée au jeu d'amour ne le désapprend jamais'* or, as we might say, 'Once you learn to ride a bike you never forget.' His bust, overlooking the pool of the Fontaine Médicis, still casts a worldly eye over Brantôme.

All this is a prelude to something so ancient and strange you half expect Indiana Jones to leap out with a flaming torch: a huge temple carved out of the cliff focused on a colossal relief, known as the **Grotte du Jugement Dernier**. No-one knows its exact age or what the complex composition really represents. The huge shadowy figure that dominates the scene is said to be Christ, but looks more like some emanation from the prophetic works of William Blake. The rows of heads recall the Celts, like the carved heads on the modillions of Romanesque churches. Saints or angels look up to the deity, their faces too eroded for identification. The *Crucifixion* on the next wall is said to date from the 17th century.

After all this, the tour ends with the slightly eerie **Musée Fernand Desmoulin**, filled with the paintings of the Nontron-born Desmoulin (1853–1914), a friend of Zola and follower of spiritualist Allan Kardec. In this world Desmoulin was known for his portraits of great men; in the beyond he is known for the drawings he made between 1900 and 1902 in complete darkness with the aid of a medium.

Château de Bourdeilles (7km southwest of Brantôme; 05 53 03 73 36; w chateau-bourdeilles.fr; Jul–Aug 10.00–19.30 daily, May–Jun, Sep–Oct 10.00–13.00 & 14.00–18.00 daily, Nov–Apr 10.00–13.00 & 14.00–17.30 Tue–Sun, closed Jan; €9.50/€6.30, under 5 free) Seat of the oldest of Périgord's four baronies, Bourdeilles is so old that the first barons lived in fairy-tale times, when they slew griffins and transported themselves to Jerusalem and back by means of an ointment extracted from a dragon's ear. As time went on, their castle found itself on the frontier between English Guyenne and France, in a commanding position over the river. In 1259, St Louis ceded Bourdeilles to the English. However, not all members of the family agreed to the switch in allegiance, and they built the magnificent 35m octagonal keep, which failed to keep the English out until 1376, when that flower of French chivalry Du Guesclin took the castle back for France. Brantôme was born here in 1540 (see box, page 161).

The adjacent Renaissance château is a rare one designed by a woman – Brantôme's wealthy, widowed sister-in-law, Jacquette de Montbron, a favourite of Catherine de' Medici who was left a substantial sum in the queen's will in 1589. Jacquette worked especially hard on her sumptuous Salon Doré, its ceiling beautifully painted by Ambroise Le Noble, a member of the Mannerist Fontainebleau school.

Bourdeilles later fell into the clutches of the anachronistic bad boys, the Comtes de Périgord, who used it as a robbers' hideout. The King confiscated it as soon as he could, and for a while in the 18th century Jacquette's proud palace was reduced to a silkworm farm, then a saltpetre works. It was in a sad state until a wealthy descendant of the family bought it in the 1960s, fixed it up, filled it with antiques and donated it to the department.

The tour includes both the **keep** with its 2.5m-thick walls, and views that make the slog up worthwhile, as well as the château. Its armoury is full of decorative weapons and rooms richly decorated with 16th- and 17th-century furniture from Spain and Burgundy, including a 16th-century German *Dormition of the Virgin*, the Burgundian tomb of Jean de Chabannes, a tapestry showing François Ier, with his falconers, and a gilt Spanish bed fit for a king – in fact the bed of François's arch-rival, the megalomanic emperor Charles V.

Château de Richemont (St-Crépin de Richemont, 9km northwest of Brantôme; ☎05 53 05 72 81; ⌚ mid-Jul–Aug 10.00–18.00 daily; €5/€3) In 1564–68, Brantôme built this château where he wrote most of his works, and declared in his will that no matter what, his family must never ever sell it off, but keep it in his memory. And so they have, and have recently opened it for visits. You can see the great man's bedroom and the chapel, where he lies buried under the epitaph he composed.

MAREUIL-EN-PÉRIGORD This slightly bedraggled corner of Périgord was the fief of the barons of Mareuil, who had their seat at the slightly bedraggled 15th-century **Château de Mareuil**, rebuilt after the former model was destroyed in the Hundred Years' War (☎05 53 60 74 13; ⌚ Jun–Sep 10.00–13.00 & 14.00–17.00 Mon–Sat, 14.00–17.00 Sun; €7.50). Once property of the famous Baron Talleyrand, it has a Flamboyant Gothic chapel, dungeons, Louis XV furniture, and a museum of memorabilia on Maréchal Jean Lannes, an ancestor of the current owners, who served in the Grande Armée all across Europe and in 1809 famously complained: 'This Napoleon is going to get us all killed!' He died months later, his legs crushed by a cannonball.

Mareuil was the birthplace of troubadour Arnaud de Mareuil, son of a poor castle workman. Dante sent him to Purgatory, although his only sin was to be admired. His poetry, so celebrated in his day, is nearly impossible to translate, 'the result of a technique honed down to the point where all signs of effort vanish…resulting in a poetry of extraordinarily gentle and delicate beauty' (Anthony Bonner).

Just south of Mareuil, the 12th-century church of **St-Pardoux-de-Mareuil** is a sombre model with an impressive bell tower, while to the east the fortified church of **St-Pierre-ès-Liens** at **Vieux-Mareuil** has three domes crowning the length of its nave. The pretty little River Belle flows through the centre; it's a protected area, home to otters and 18 kinds of bat.

CHÂTEAU DE PUYGUILHEM (14km northeast of Brântome, near Villars; 05 53 54 82 18; w chateau-puyguilhem.fr; Jul–Aug 10.00–12.30 & 14.00–18.30 daily, Apr & Sep 10.00–12.30 & 14.00–17.00 Tue–Sun, May–Jun 10.00–12.30 & 14.00–18.30 Tue–Sun, Oct–Mar 10.30–12.30 & 14.00–17.30 Wed–Sun; €6, under 18 & EU citizens under 26 free, €10 combined with Brantôme Abbey's caves) Périgord claims to have 1,001 châteaux; of that number, the most splendid is arguably this Renaissance jewel. Built in 1524 by the first president of the Parlement of Bordeaux, Mondot de la Marthonie, its roof-line forest of richly carved dormers and chimneys is just as impressive when viewed from within – it looks like the hull of a ship. Saved from collapse in the 1930s, Puyguilhem has been refurnished with period pieces and Renaissance tapestries; the star is the chimney, sculpted with the *Labours of Hercules*.

GROTTE DE VILLARS (Le Cluzeau, Villars; 05 53 54 82 36; w grotte-villars.com; Jul–Aug 10.00–19.00 daily, Apr–Jun & Sep 10.00–noon & 14.00–19.00 daily, Oct 14.00–18.00 daily; €10.50, students €8.50, ages 5–11 €7) Périgord's largest underground network, this cave extends some 13km and combines natural art – brilliant white translucent stalactites and draperies (now stage for a new *son et lumière* production) – with drawings in magnesium oxide, dating back to 17,000BC. The authenticity of the blue outline of a galloping horse and 'sorcerer' was confirmed by the dense layer of concretions formed over the pictures. Outside, a 'Prehistoric Garden' evokes Magdalenian times.

Some 2km from Villars, out in a meadow, stand the impressive ruins of the chapterhouse and cloister with curiously asymmetrical arches of the **Abbaye de Boschaud** (1154–59), one of four Cistercian foundations in Périgord.

NONTRON AND AROUND High on its promontory, Nontron (in Celtic, 'the valley of ash trees') began as an oppidum over the River Bandiat. It won't take too long to exhaust its charms: there are a few picturesque medieval streets to explore in the lower town, and in the upper town an 18th-century château in Place Fort. Since the 15th century, Nontron has been famous for its knives with boxwood handles – the smallest of which can be folded into a hazelnut shell. Watch them being made at the **Coutellerie Nontronnaise** (Place Paul Bert; 05 53 56 01 55; 09.00–noon & 12.30–17.30 Mon–Fri; free) and buy them at the shop (33 Rue Carnot; 05 53 60 33 76; 09.30–noon & 14.00–19.00 Tue–Sat).

A newer company, **Coutellerie Le Périgord,** has a workshop in the **Moulin de Lapeyre** (St-Estèphe, 7km north Nontron; 05 53 05 35 82; w couteau-leperigord.com; mid-Jul–Aug 14.00–19.00 Mon–Sat; €7/€3) where they also mill walnut oil and flour, and have on display 3,000 historic tools. Just north, **Étang de St-Estèphe** is a beautiful wooded lake with a sandy beach. Just west of the lake, a signposted path leads to a stream tumbling through granite boulders called the 'Devil's Chaplet', where the large boulder, the **Roc Branlant**, rocks when touched.

East of Nontron, tiny **Abjat-sur Bandiat** would like you to stroll through its Jardin des Légendes, with artworks evoking local tales. Signposted from the centre, with a little car park, is the steep path up to the **Saut du Chalard**, a lovely waterfall of the Dronne. Another pretty spot, where the Dronne cascades among the boulders, is the **Trou de Philippou**, signposted from the church in **St-Saud-Lacoussière**. St-Saud too has a lake with a beach; so many cèpes grow in these woods in autumn that the village holds a special mushroom market when the baskets overflow (ring the *mairie*: 05 53 56 97 03).

Further north, the striking, cylindrical 23m **Tour de Piégut** stands isolated on a spur, once visited and wrecked (as usual) by Richard the Lionheart in 1199.

A bit further north, where the tip of Périgord is wedged between the Charente and Limousin, detour to medieval **Bussière-Badil**, site of famous May ceramics fair, to see its beautiful, fortified 12th-century church of **Notre-Dame-de-la-Nativité** (⌚ 09.00–18.00 daily), a hotchpotch of Romanesque styles: Limousin in the octagonal bell tower and the flat pendentives under the dome; Charente in the animals and foliage sculpted on the arches of the porch and in the strange, if sadly eroded, figures on the tympanum on the west façade; and Périgourdin in the capitals and cupola. The whitewashed interior, with its 15th-century rose window and listed Renaissance gilded statue of the Virgin, is as impressive as a basilica, although the nave is curiously misaligned with the apse, and the walls and columns aren't exactly straight – hence the buttresses added later. Look for the capital with a hairy green man and woman.

VARAIGNES West of Nontron, on the Limousin frontier, Varaignes won an award for its restorations, especially for its 13th–16th-century **château** (sadly minus its magnificent Flamboyant portal, sold in the 1920s to an American). This now houses the **Atelier-Musée des Tisserands et de la Charentaise** (☎05 53 56 23 66; ⌚ mid-Jul–Aug 10.00–noon & 14.00–18.00 daily, school hols 14.30 Thu with demonstrations (best to ring); €3.80/€2.30), where you can learn all about the local textile industries, and in particular how to make the thick and comfy wool-lined *charentaise*, the ne plus ultra of slippers.

In nearby **Teyjat**, the **Grotte de la Mairie** has 40 beautiful engravings of animals from the late Magdalenian period (11,000BC), discovered in 1889, although it's now closed to the public; finds are in the **Espace Pierre Bourrinet** (☎05 53 56 23 66; ⌚ Jul–Aug 14.30–18.30 Wed–Mon; €3.80/€2.30, under 10 free). South of Varaignes, the 11th-century church at **La Chapelle-St-Robert** is, like Bussière's, a mix of styles, with a big octagonal bell tower. Inside is a 13th-century Spanish *Crucifixion* brought back from the Battle of Lepanto, and a curious medieval mural of the Baptism of Christ. In its sister village of **Javerlhac**, there is a 13th-century abbey church, a château from the 1400s with a tubby tower, and the Versailles of pigeonniers, with niches for 1,500 birds.

UP THE CÔLE TO ST-JEAN-DE-CÔLE To the east of Brantôme, the D78 follows the little River Côle through peaceful landscapes of happy cows. One of the first villages, **La Chapelle-Faucher**, sleeps peacefully on its hill belying the horrible events that happened here in 1569, when the powerful Huguenot Admiral Gaspard de Coligny massacred 300 Catholics – an act avenged three years later by the Catholics who first tried to assassinate him in Paris, and then, fearing his vengeance, slaughtered every Protestant they could find in the St Bartholomew's Day massacre in Paris, making sure Coligny was dead by stabbing him, throwing him out the window and then cutting off his head.

St-Jean-de-Côle is as pretty a village as you could ask for, gathered on the banks of the Côle (spanned here by a Gothic humpback bridge), each house crowned by a steep tile roof that won the village a prize for the best roofs in France. It was a busy place in the Middle Ages; the Templars were here, and in the 12th century the inhabitants built themselves a domed church dedicated to **St-Jean-Baptiste**. No-one knows how the secrets of dome building were passed on, but in St-Jean they bungled it so often that they settled in the end for a less precarious wooden roof. The bell tower and modillions sport some delightful carvings, especially one of God modelling Adam out of clay. St-Jean's handsome 15th–17th-century **Château de la Marthonie** was remodelled by the same Mondot de la Marthonie responsible for Puyguilhem, and might be open for visits in July and August.

THIVIERS Further up the Côle, this town surrounded by ducks is the foie gras capital of Green Périgord, and pays tribute to the goose that lays its golden egg, or rather contributes its gorged liver, at the **Maison du Foie Gras** (in the same building as the tourist office; ⌚ same hours; free; tastings €3.50). Its 12th-century church of **Notre-Dame de l'Assomption** (16 Rue Jean Jaurès) originally had two domes, which collapsed, and a curious bell tower with homey domestic dormer windows in its roof.

Place Jean Paul Sartre commemorates the philosopher of existentialism who spent his miserable childhood and summer holidays in the house (with the white shutters) with a grandfather who for 40 years refused to speak to his wife because she had no dowry – perhaps the inspiration for Sartre's remark that 'Hell is other people.' If Sartre hated Thiviers (he wasn't very kind in *Les Mots*), Thiviers returned the favour, but now all is forgiven.

CHÂTEAU DE JUMILHAC (Jumilhac-le-Grand; m 06 82 09 65 83; w chateaudejumilhac.com; guided tours: ⌚ Jun–Sep 10.00–19.00 daily, plus Jul–Aug night visits with dinner Tue, Apr–May & Oct–mid-Nov 14.00–18.00 daily, Jan–Mar & mid-Nov–Dec 14.00–18.00 Sat–Sun; €9.50, students €7.50, under 12 €5.50, gardens only €4/€3/€2) North and east of Thiviers, the ferny forested frontier of the Limousin is the least populated area in Périgord, an ideal location for Sleeping Beauty's forgotten castle. Destroyed on several occasions during the Hundred Years' War, Jumilhac was rebuilt by Antoine Chapelle, an alchemist and a master of forges who made such fine cannons for Henri IV and loaned him so much money that the king made him a count.

Chapelle converted his spread into a fantasia of towers, turrets and chimneys coiffed with blue slate pepper-pots ('the most romantic roofs in France', according to Gustave Doré, who borrowed them for some of his fairy-tale engravings) topped with an equally fantastic array of forged-iron decorations. The Chambre de la Fileuse, built into the thickness of the wall, has naïve murals imitating tapestries, painted for the lady whose portrait is over the door and who had nothing to do but spin when her jealous husband confined her here, smuggling out love letters to her shepherd sweetheart amid her bobbins. Although the poor woman never spun straw into gold à la Rumpelstiltskin, there is a **Galerie de l'Or** in the *chai* (Place du Château; 05 53 52 55 43; ⌚ same as the tourist office (page 158); €3, under 11 free), which includes pieces of gold in their raw state discovered in the Gallo-Roman mines at Fouilloux; nuggets are still occasionally found in the Isle and Auvézère (page 167).

East of Thiviers, there's some fine countryside along the upper reaches of the Isle, especially around the D67. **Nanthiat** has a château with a pair of pepper-pots of its own, and a handsome Romanesque church, with a rare altar cross in front.

EAST OF PÉRIGUEUX

Once past Jumilhac, the Isle loops down to pick up the waters of the Auvézère just before Périgueux. In the 1500s this was full of iron forges, one of which remains in the wooded gorges of the Auvézère. This is the country of the battling troubadour Bertran de Born, and of fungi worth their weight in gold: truffles.

Excideuil's **market** is on Thursdays, and Hautefort's on Wednesday mornings.

TOURIST INFORMATION

Excideuil 1 Place du Château; 05 53 52 29 79; w naturellementperigord.fr; ⌚ Jul–Aug 10.00–1300 & 14.00–18.00 Mon–Sat, 09.30–13.00 Sun, Jun & Sep closed Sun, Oct–May closed Sun–Wed

Hautefort In the Hôtel-Dieu, Place Marquis Jacques-François de Hautefort; 05 53 50 40 27; w vezere-perigord.fr; 10.30–12.30 & 15.00–18.30 daily

WHERE TO STAY

Le Domaine d'Essendiéras [map, page 142] (12 rooms) St-Médard d'Excideuil; 05 53 55 34 34; w essendieras.fr. On a 360ha estate atop one of the Dordogne's highest hills, suites in a 16th-century château & rooms in a 19th-century château, plus gîtes, a campsite, 9-hole golf course, restaurant (€€€), lakes, pools, & more. **€€€€–€**

La Mas des Bories-Grand Périgueux [map, page 142] (11 rooms) 51 Rte de Limoges, Antonne-et-Trigonant; 05 53 02 23 52; w masdesbories-dordogne.fr. Lovingly renovated old stone farmhouse with rooms & apts for families. There's an infinity pool & tennis courts, plus a bar & restaurant (€€€), where Madame Ugolini cooks up delicious meals. **€€€–€€**

Hostellerie La Charmille (9 rooms) Antonne-et-Trigonant; 05 53 06 00 45; w lacharmille.fr. A large ivy-covered house of character, offering renovated, bright rooms, bar & a good restaurant (€€€) serving southwest favourites on the summer terrace. **€€**

Vue du Château d'Excideuil (6 rooms, 2 apts) 26 Av Andre Audy, Excideuil; m 07 66 68 10 06; w vueduchateau.fr. Charming Paula & Brian run this attractive B&B in a big white *maison de maître*, with a garden & saltwater pool, in walking distance of town. Table d'hôte (€32.50) available. Excellent b/fast inc. **€€**

Auberge de la Truffe (20 rooms) Place du Village, Sorges; 05 53 05 02 05; w auberge-de-la-truffe.com. A local institution, with traditional rooms overlooking the garden & an indoor pool. The restaurant (€€€€) specialises in truffles, as well as rather less pricey delights, with (truffle-less) lunch menus from €15. They also do cookery courses. **€€–€**

Au Périgord Noir (27 rooms) La Genèbre (D704), Hautefort; 05 53 42 77 50; w hotel-perigord-noir.fr. Modern hotel on a hill with superb views across to the château, plus a pool & restaurant with a magnificent terrace. **€**

Hostellerie du Fin Chapon (11 rooms) 3 Place du Château, Excideuil; 05 53 62 42 38; w lefinchapon.com. Old-fashioned rooms in the posthouse of 1751. **€**

WHERE TO EAT AND DRINK

Auberge du Parc Place René Lavaud, Hautefort; 05 53 50 88 98; w aubergeduparc-hautefort.fr; 09.00–23.00 Thu–Sat, daytime Sun. Classic village restaurant & bar, with tasty takes on the local duck & pork, walnuts, etc (& mushrooms, in season). Also has 5 rooms (€) upstairs. *Lunch formules from €17.90*. €€€

L'Aventure Place de l'Église, Hautefort; 09 66 90 07 71; w aventurehautefort.com; closed Tue & eves Mon. Best-selling photo-journalist author Christophe Géral has settled back in his home town to take up the reins of his family restaurant with his son. Pleasant terrace under the horse chestnut trees & slow-cooked meat dishes. *2-course menu €22*. €€€

Le Troubadour 1 Place Eugène le Roy, Hautefort; 05 53 51 61 49; w letroubadour-hautefort.fr; closed Mon & eves Sun. A short but elegant carte, gourmet burgers with foie gras. *2-course lunch menu from €16 exc Jul–Aug*. €€€

Mets Sauveurs [map, page 142] Brasserie Le Mayne, St Martial d'Albarède (just west of Excideuil); 05 53 62 02 40; w metssaveurs.fr; closed Sun–Mon & eves exc Fri–Sat. Contemporary, well-prepared local ingredients, with a daily 3-course €18.50 *formule* with a glass of wine, but fine choices on the other menus too, from €26. €€€

Favard (Chez Franca Nathalie) Place Goumandie, Cherveix-Cubas; 05 53 51 35 69; closed Mon & eves Thu. Popular old-fashioned restaurant serving *cuisine de terroir* – delicious *touran, pâté de foie gras truffé*, homemade desserts, etc. *Excellent €22 formule*. €€

SPORTS AND ACTIVITIES Enjoy the beautiful wooded *plan d'eau* with a beach, adventure playground, wakeboarding, canoes, paths, and more at the **Base de Loisiers de Rouffiac** (Lanouaille; 05 53 52 68 79; w rouffiac-loisirs.fr). They also have bungalows (€) for overnight stays. At **Le Chercheur d'Or** (05 55 00 83 59;

w lechercheurdor.org; ⌚ Jul–Aug Wed, Thu, Sat; €20/€16; book at the Excideuil tourist office) professional gold miner Philippe Roubinet will show you how to pan for nuggets. **Vert'Auvézère** (Le Bourg Cubas, Cherveix-Cubas; **m** 06 15 45 55 19; **w** vert-auvezere.fr) can arrange white-water kayaking on the Auvézère, plus canoeing, rock climbing and speleology.

EXCIDEUIL The busiest market town in the region, charming Excideuil once belonged to the vicomtes of Limoges, who built its vertiginous landmark, the **Château d'Excideuil** with a double square donjon and handsome Renaissance gate on a butte of Jurassic limestone. Richard the Lionheart attacked it three times in 1182 without success, but in 1420 the English did finally succeed and wrecked the town and its church of **St-Thomas**, which explains its curious mix of Romanesque and Gothic styles, though not its crazy steeple made of reinforced concrete in 1936 with a crown on its head. Excideuil prospered from its nearby iron mines and forges, especially after Louis XI exempted it from paying taxes in 1482.

Place Bugeaud in front of St-Thomas has a pretty swan fountain donated by yet another Périgourdin military hero, Thomas Robert Bugeaud (1784–1849). After serving as major in the Napoleonic wars, he returned to his family estate in nearby Lanouaille and his other passion – agriculture – and served as Excideuil's mayor. He rejoined the army as a general under Louis Philippe in 1831 and in 1836 he was sent to crush the revolt of Abd el Kader in Algeria, and eventually was made governor general, never losing a battle with his tactics of 'flying columns' (the Razzia) and ruthlessness.

Bugeaud's interest in road building and agriculture saw the French colonial occupation of Algeria jump from 17,000 to 100,000. His statue in Allée André Maurois was repatriated (just in time!) from Algiers to France in 1962, and in 1999 was erected here.

COULAURES Excideuil's River Loue flows into the Isle just west at Coulaures, where the 15th–18th-century **Château de la Cousse** stands over the two rivers with pretty views from its park, garden, chapel and tower (☎ 05 53 05 01 12; ⌚ Jul–late Sep 13.00–19.00 daily; free). Between Coulaures, Savignac-les-Églises, Mayac and Saint-Jory-las-Bloux, the wooded **Causse de l'Isle** is the northernmost of the limestone plateaux that stretches across southwest France to the Mediterranean; now a protected natural area, it's dotted with *bories* (drystone huts), and crossed with paths, picnic areas and a playground (the car park, off the D74, is signposted 'Causse de Savignac').

UP THE GORGES DE L'AUVÉZÈRE East of Excideuil, the Auvézère, the main tributary of Vézère (page 172), hurtles down from the Massif Central. Although it's fairly calm as it passes **Cherveix-Cubas** – with a Lanterne des Morts in its cemetery, a slender cross-topped version of the one in Sarlat (page 201) – upstream it hurtles through a narrow cleft in the limestone, a pristine playground with cliffs to climb and caves to explore. Head to the sweet little village of **St-Mesmin**, where there's a bucolic walk along the river (wear good shoes; not suitable for young children); other paths are more *sportif*.

Further upstream are two evocative relics of rural industry. The riverside **forge** (Rte des Forges; ☎ 05 53 52 29 79; **w** ecomuseesdelauvezere.fr; ⌚ Jul–Aug 10.00–18.00 daily, Jun & Sep closed Mon–Tue; €6, under 8 free) at **Savignac-Lédrier** dates back to the 15th century, although the remains are mostly early 19th century; the forge was in use (it was the only French furnace using charcoal) until 1975. Further upstream, at Payzac, they made paper for butchers from 1861 to 1968 at the **Papeterie de Vaux** (✆ 05 53 62 50 06; **w** ecomuseesdelauvezere.fr; ⏲ Jun 10.00–12.30 & 14.00–18.30 Tue–Fri, 14.00–18.30 Sat–Sun, Jul–Aug 10.00–12.30 & 14.00–18.30 Tue–Sat, 14.00–18.30 Sun; €7/€3, under 7 free; ring ahead for guided tours in English). It's the last paper mill in Europe from the period in near mint condition.

HAUTEFORT

Château de Hautefort (✆ 05 53 50 51 23; **w** chateau-hautefort.com; ⏲ Jun–Aug 09.30–19.00 daily, Sep 10.00–18.00 daily, Oct 14.00–18.00 daily, Mar & early Nov 14.00–18.00 Sat–Sun, Apr–May 10.00–12.30 & 14.00–18.30 daily; €10/€5.50, under 7 free; see website for special events & summer night visits) This famous citadel high over the Auvézère was the fief of the Lastours, whose baron Gouffier de Lastours fought in the First Crusade alongside Godefroy de Bouillon. The medieval castle passed in the 12th century to the family of famous troubadour Bertran de Born (see box, below).

In the early 1600s the castle was rebuilt as a palace in the Loire style by François de Hautefort, first Marquess of Hautefort in 1614. His grandson was the famous miser, Jacques-François de Hautefort. According to the gossip of the day, Jacques-François was the model for Harpagon in Molière's *L'Avare* (though Molière lowered

BERTRAN DE BORN, TROUBADOUR AND WARRIOR

The career of Bertran de Born (c1140–1214) makes mincemeat of the romantic Hollywood stereotype of troubadours as long-haired, love-lorn wimps. Although capable of writing delightfully about love, he liked nothing better than stirring the pot, which he did through his battle songs and the topical, satirical songs called *sirventes*: 'I want great barons always/ to be angry with one another.' And elsewhere: 'Peace does not comfort me/ I am in accord with war/ Nor do I hold or believe/ Any other religion.' The minor nobility of Aquitaine listened, and agreed; feudal anarchy between the overlords offered their only chance for independence and profit.

In his day, Bertran was feared by all for his biting satire, so much so that he was blamed for the death of the Young King, Henry Court-Mantel, Henry II's heir and older brother of Richard the Lionheart. The chroniclers tell the story: Bertran through 'ruse and felony' had kicked out Hautefort's co-owner, his brother Constantine. Constantine appealed to Richard, the Governor of Aquitaine, for justice. Bertran resolved to seek aid in other quarters, and wrote a series of *sirventes* taunting his friend Henry Court-Mantel, whom Bertran knew was sick with jealousy of Richard; the Lionheart already ruled Aquitaine and attracted great renown and money for his exploits, while his older brother chafed with little to do (and a small allowance) while waiting to inherit the throne of England.

Bertran's satires had their doleful effect in the spring of 1183, when a general uprising against Richard's tyranny broke out across Aquitaine. The Young King joined the rebels, at first reluctantly, and then wholeheartedly when Henry II came down in person to aid Richard. The Young King was now fighting not only his brother but his father too, and he raised money for his mercenaries by plundering; after a raid on the treasure at Rocamadour, he sickened along the road, and died at Martel.

Grief-stricken, old King Henry blamed Bertran for his son's death, and sent Richard and Alfonso II of Aragon to besiege Hautefort. Bertran scorched the earth

his miser to bourgeois status); when Jacques-François fell ill his doctor prescribed 'English pills', which brought about his death – they cost so much he couldn't bear to swallow them.

His beautiful sister, Marie, was nicknamed Aurore by the French court. Yet even rarer than her beauty was her even-handedness – Marie was both the lover of the melancholic Louis XIII and best friend of the wife he abhorred, Anne of Austria. Marie's devotion to the queen made her the enemy of Cardinal Richelieu, who went to the extreme of presenting a rival for the king's affections, a young man named Cinq-Mars; when that ploy only resulted in the king having two loves instead of one, Richelieu threatened to leave the king's service himself if he didn't dump Marie. She was only reinstated in court after Louis's death in 1643.

Although it survived the Revolution (as a prison), Hautefort was derelict in 1929, when the Baron and Baronne de Bastard undertook its restoration, finally finishing it in 1968. In the autumn of that same year Hautefort went up in a blaze that could be seen across half of Périgord. But after the shock of losing 39 years of work in one night, the now widowed baroness amazed everyone by simply starting all over again, completing the work by the time she died in 1999. Besides the château, the visit includes the panoramic terraces and the immaculate French gardens, the park, and vegetable garden of heritage vegetables; seeds are for sale in the shop.

before them so they would have nothing to eat. But when Alfonso asked him as an old friend for sustenance, Bertran offered his army ten days' food for the promise that they would not attack the weakened south wall of Hautefort. Of course, that was precisely where the Aragonese began their attack, and Bertran surrendered at once to spare further damage to his beloved castle.

Bertran was carted off before King Henry, who received him in a towering rage, and determined to have him put to the sword. Then he said: 'Bertran, Bertran, once you said that you never needed more than half your wits. Surely now you need them all!' 'My lord, what I said is true,' Bertran replied in tears. 'Although since the day of the death of your son, the beautiful and valiant Young King, I have lost all my wits, judgement, and mind.'

His grief so moved the king that he fainted, and when he recovered he wept and said: 'Ah Bertran, unhappy Bertran, it was only right that you have lost your wits in losing my son, for he loved you more than any other man in the world. And I, for love of him, return to you your liberty, goods, and castle. And I will add 500 marks to rebuild the south wall of your castle. Thanks to this letter from my son Richard, I know of your worthy conduct in the siege of Hautefort. It is as much for your noble acts as a soldier as for your celebrated talents as a troubadour that you have earned today my clemency.'

If Bertran had used his grief to get out of a jam, it was nonetheless sincere – his famous *planh* (lament) for the Young King is one of the masterpieces of Occitan literature.

Yet for all his love of war, Bertran died in a monastery, but Dante still sent him straight to Hell to wander about as a headless trunk, holding his head aloft as a lantern. The head explains: 'Know that I am Bertran de Born, who gave evil counsel to the Young King and made father and son rebel against one another… Because I parted those who were joined, I carry my brain parted from its roots in this trunk.'

Hôtel Dieu de Hautefort (Musée de la Médecine) (Place Marquis J F de Hautefort; 05 53 50 40 27; w musee-hautefort.fr; May 10.00–noon & 14.00–18.00, Jun–Sep 10.00–19.00 daily; €7/€5, under 13 free) This hospital, unique in France, was founded by the perhaps not so miserly Jacques-François in 1669, in the form of a Greek cross with a dome. Each wing was designed to take in precisely 11 old men, 11 boys and 11 young women and was known as the hospital of 33 years, recalling the age of Christ when he died. After the Revolution, it also took in abandoned children and operated until 1995; since then it has been a museum of medicine, with an old apothecary, uniforms, liturgical items, medicines, dentists and gynaecologist offices and a room dedicated to Louis Pasteur.

TOURTOIRAC (8km west of Hautefort) This typical village on the Auvézère is far more famous than you might guess. It made speleology headlines in 1995, with the discovery of the **Grotte de Tourtoirac** (w grotte-de-tourtoirac.fr; Jul–Aug 09.30–19.30, May–Jun & Sep 10.00–noon & 14.00–18.00 daily, Apr & Oct 14.00–18.00 daily, Mar & Nov 14.00–18.00 Sat–Sun, last admission 1hr before closing; €9.90/€7.10 inc audio guide in English, under 6 free), with a whole panoply of rare formations along a subterranean river; in 2010, with the construction of a lift, it was opened to the public. Dress warmly and avoid high heels. Because of the walkway, it's accessible to wheelchair users.

Tourtoirac's 11th-century abbey church of **St-Pierre-ès-Liens** (Jul–Aug 10.30–12.30 & 15.00–18.00 daily) still has its cupola behind a lofty *clocher-mur*, along with some delightful carvings on the capitals of its ruined chapterhouse. Part of the abbey contains the **Musée du Royaume d'Araucanie et de Patagonie** (now run by the *mairie*, but closed at the time of writing). The kingdom's founder, Orélie Antoine de Tounens (1825–78), was a charismatic character, the eighth of nine children but the one with great ambitions. With his family's support he sailed to Chile in 1858 and learned Spanish. When he found out that the native Mapuche tribe, who lived in southern Chile on land unclaimed by Spain (and who had signed a treaty with Spain in 1641, marking the River Biobio as the frontier), were fighting for their independence, de Tounens bought a poncho and joined them, learned their language and convinced them to elect him King Antoine I, under a progressive constitution of a parliamentary monarchy based on the *coyag*, the traditional Mapuche assembly.

The Chileans were not amused and captured him in 1862, only sparing him execution because they thought he was mad. But he never gave up his claim and, impoverished, spent his last years with his nephew, Tourtoirac's butcher; a plaque on a small shop notes the spot. By 1883 the Chilean army had seized all the Mapuche lands. But to this day they are fighting to regain their sovereignty.

King Antoine left no heir, so willed the crown to a friend, and since then the title of pretender has been carried on by voting. The current pretender, Frédéric Luz, elected in 2018, works for Mapuche rights; you can learn all about the Araucania at w araucanie.com and visit the **royal tombs**. Antoine I's is marked with a stele and crown, copied by the stonecutter from the king of hearts on a playing card.

SORGES Sorges is the centre of the Dordogne truffle-dom and home of the **Écomusée de la Truffe** (2 Rte des Truffières; 05 53 05 90 11; w ecomuseedelatruffe.com; mid-Jun–mid-Sep 10.00–12.30 & 14.00–18.00 daily, mid-Sep–mid-Jun 10.00–12.30 & 14.00–17.30 Mon–Sat, Dec–Jan 10.00–12.30 also Sun; €5/€2.50). There's a 3km truffle path to walk where you can learn all you've ever wanted to know about the 'black diamonds'. Sorges and the Causses de Thiviers and Lalbenque (page 283) are among the richest sources in southwest France.

FOR THE LOVE OF TRUFFLES

In 1974, a Parisian banker came home to find that his cook had served his last truffle to her friends. He shot her. The judge refused to try him because it was a crime of passion 'completely understandable and completely forgivable'.

The *tuber melanosporum* or Périgord black truffle, the most muskily orgasmic food on earth, can easily incite folly, if not bankruptcy. There are more than 70 kinds of truffle, but only the white ones can hold a candle to the ineffable melanosporum. In the late 19th century, France produced some 1,000 tonnes per year. Today the whole country manages around 40 tonnes.

For once climate change is not the culprit. The 19th-century bounty was a by-product of the phylloxera epidemic that decimated French vineyards in the 1870s. Farmers, desperately seeking new crops, planted sapling oaks in known limestone-rich truffle zones, hoping the spores would, in their secretive symbiotic way, spread to their roots. The result exceeded their wildest dreams. A delicacy once reserved for royalty became so common that country folk ate them whole. Even British recipes at the time would recommend adding a handful to a dish.

That golden truffle age ended with another catastrophe – the First World War that bled France white. The subsequent lack of rural manpower, and the Great Depression coincided with the end of the 30-year productive life of the *champs truffiers*. When gourmets were ready to indulge again, truffles had become scarce.

Cultivating truffles began in earnest in the 1970s, when INRA, the French agricultural research institute, patented a technique of inoculating roots, giving the tree a 20–30% chance in ten years of producing truffles. Today some 80–90% of French truffles are cultivated, but the *cavage* (finding them) remains labour-intensive: any truffle that has survived droughts, heatwaves, winter freezes and wild boar (who get most of them) must be snuffed out by specially trained dogs or pigs. The pigs are almost invariably female; the sexy pheromone in truffles, androstenol, is nearly identical to one produced by male pigs – and human male armpits. Visit a winter truffle market (the weekly one in Lalbenque claims to be the world's biggest; page 39) and the aroma will hit you in waves, a shocking wall of wild, pungent perfume, the Chanel No. 5 of the earth.

Sorges also has a 12th-century church, **St-Germain d'Auxerre**, hiding behind a Renaissance portal, although you may find the 15th-century **Château des Bories** more rewarding (13km south at **Antonne-et-Trigonant**; ☎ 05 53 06 00 01; **w** site-des-bories.business.site; 🕘 13.00–19.00 Mon–Sat; €5.50/€4). The last castle on the Isle before Périgueux, it is considered the archetype of all Périgourdin châteaux, with symmetrical round towers, a Gothic kitchen, huge chimney and monumental stair.

8

The Vézère Valley

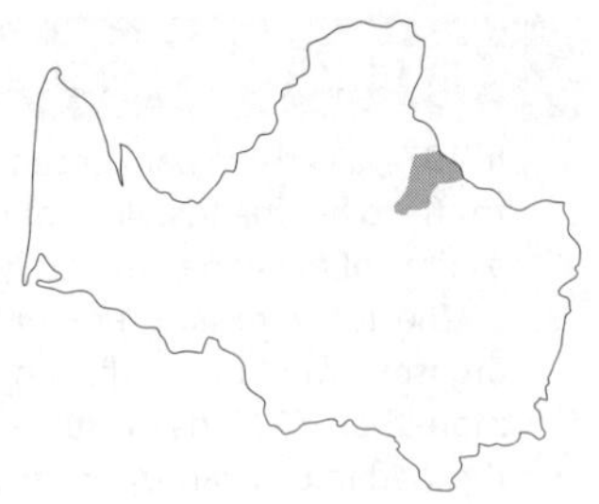

One of the most striking things about a visit to the Vézère Valley is the contrast between the lush, civilised Périgord Noir countryside of golden stone farmhouses, villages, châteaux and medieval churches, surrounded by meadows, bucolic woodlands and laughing streams – and the outlandish history that lies beneath the surface, back when cavemen and cavewomen were jumping all over it. The river itself was more dramatic, too, when the first humans arrived some 400,000 years ago, flowing 30m higher than it does today. But it was more than gorgeous landscapes that attracted these Palaeolithic pioneers – the Vézère's bulging cliffs were pocked with caves and shelters, there was fresh water, river pebbles and flint for manufacturing tools, and, most importantly, there were thundering herds of bison and reindeer that funnelled down the valley before the glaciers of the last ice age. Over the millennia, the hunters left us an extraordinary record of their passing in the valley's most secret caves, so secret that new ones are still being discovered

ART BEGINS HERE

Art is art. Everything else is everything else.

Ad Reinhardt

Two-thirds of the prehistoric decorated caves known in the world are in southwest France. Created by a people so ancient that they are almost impossible to imagine, it is difficult to look at the caves as works of art and not as brief, mysterious encounters with another world. The fact that there may well have been a ritualistic or supernatural motivation behind the paintings takes nothing away from their aesthetic value; art has always willingly served religion. *Homo sapiens sapiens* were considered to be our intellectual equals, with a keen eye for observations, a capacity for abstract or symbolic expression, and imaginative innovation. 'This is the infancy of art, not an art of infancy', as the saying goes.

Prehistory itself is a recent field. Until the 19th century, Stone Age artefacts (tools, decorated throwing sticks, carvings in bone or stone, staffs, 'Venuses') were considered to be 'thunderstones', somehow created by lightning. In 1859, the discovery of tools in the same strata as the bones of extinct animals led to an increased interest in the field – further fuelled by the publication of Darwin's *On the Origin of Species* the same year. The idea that a stone-tool culture was also capable of the 'noble' art of painting was much more difficult to comprehend. When the stunning cave paintings of Altamira in northern Spain were discovered in 1879, all but a tiny handful of scholars believed they were a hoax.

The Doubting Thomases began to change their minds in 1895, with the discovery of paintings and wall incisions – and a prehistoric lamp – in the

(page 214). As the earth heated up, the big game retreated northwards, and a curtain falls on Act I of the history of art.

To date, 25 decorated caves and 147 shelters have been discovered in the Vézère Valley, a UNESCO World Heritage Site since 1979. Its mystique has drawn holy men from afar – one of Europe's most important Tibetan monasteries is near Le Moustier. Visiting is easy – sights are well signposted and spread at intervals along the main roads – and there are more than enough to endanger your fiscal well-being.

HISTORY

For centuries the Vézère Valley was best known for the psychopathic Counts of Périgord and their reign of terror on their own people (page 176). It yielded the first clue of a much older history in 1862, when a deposit of carved flints and bones was uncovered at La Madeleine, including the image of a mammoth engraved on a mammoth tusk. It caused a sensation; no-one had imagined that mammoths and humanity coexisted at the period – henceforth known as the Magdalenian (c15,000–10,000BC). The quest for 'antediluvian man' was on. One of the most important discoveries occurred in 1888, during the excavations for a rail line between Périgueux and Agen, when workers at a hamlet called Cro-Magnon, discovered five Magdalenian-era skeletons with big brain cavities, among them a woman, a foetus and a man over 6ft tall, the *Homo sapiens sapiens*, or Cro-Magnons.

Seven years later, the first Magdalenian paintings in France were discovered at Les Eyzies' Grotte de la Mouthe. In 1908, the finding of 70,000-year-old Neanderthal bones and their effects at Le Moustier made Mousterian synonymous with Middle

Vézère Valley's Grotte de La Mouthe. A 23-year-old priest named Henri Breuil was invited to trace the drawings, beginning the career of 'the father of prehistory'. Once Breuil and his fellow pioneer Denis Peyrony knew what to look for, important discoveries followed quickly; in 1901, the men discovered the reliefs and paintings in Les Combarelles and Font-de-Gaume, both near Les Eyzies. Local boys began to explore the countryside around their villages. In 1922 they discovered Pech Merle in the Lot, in 1940 Lascaux, with art so magnificent that there's the temptation to stand Breuil's description of the cave as 'the Sistine Chapel of prehistoric art' on its head, and say that the Sistine Chapel is the Lascaux of the Renaissance.

Intriguingly, these first artists achieved many of the aims of contemporary art. They suggest far more than they actually show and invite the viewer to participate actively in their meaning; they make admirable use of their environment and the nature's palette (bulges in the stone wall give animals a three-dimensional feel, the shadows suggest water, a protrusion becomes the muzzle of a horse); they are not bound as compositions into the artificial rigours of a canvas, much less to any sensation of up and down or north or south. Most of all, they combine their formal perfection with a function and meaning that, even if the exact nature of it may never be discovered, leaves a powerful and poignant impression even after thousands of years. Nothing means as much or will ever be as immediate as the animal world was to these first artists, at a time in nature before such things as 'they' and 'us'. The only 20th-century composition that comes close to the impact of Lascaux is Picasso's *Guernica*, a work about technological advances in death.

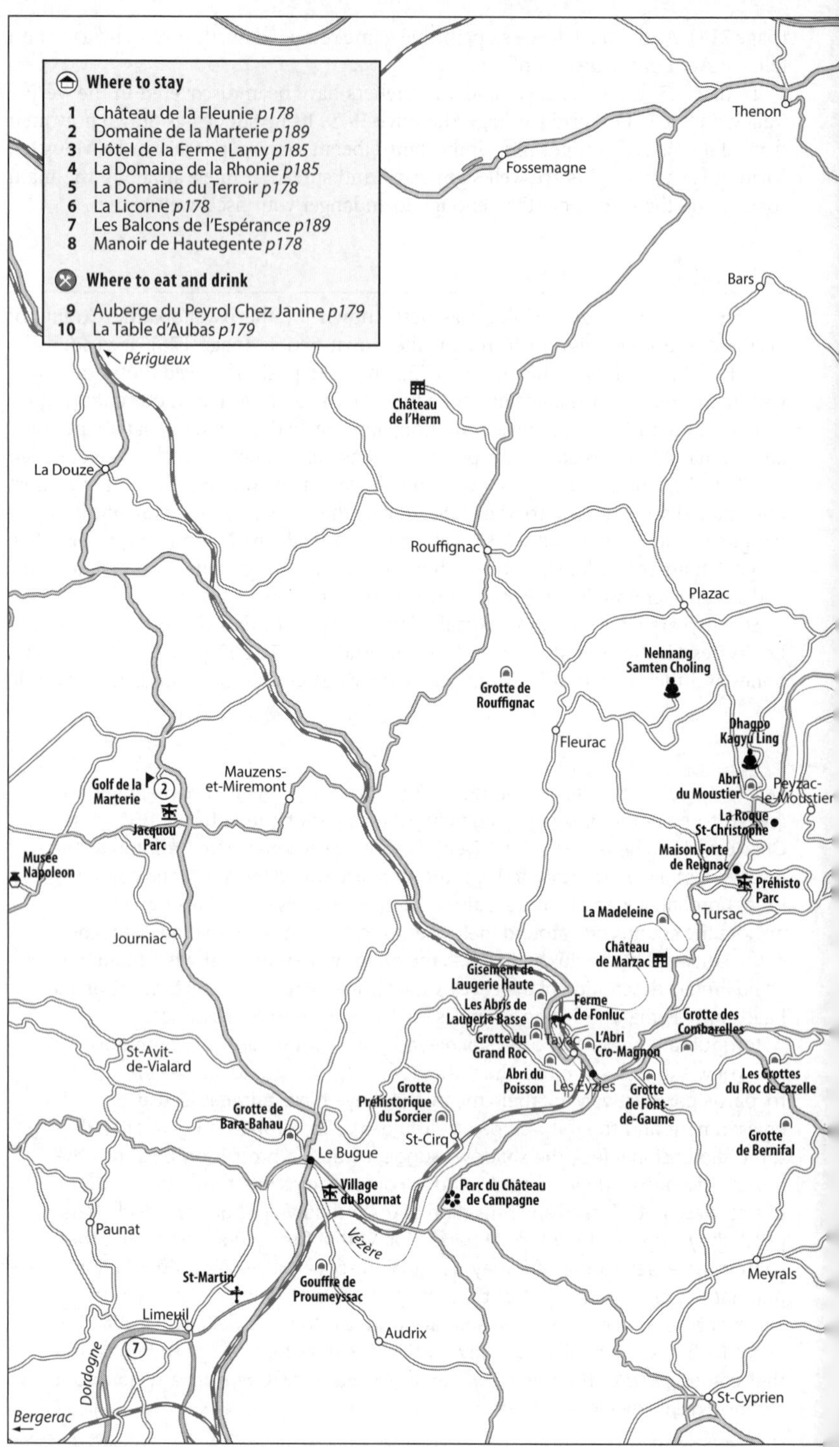
Where to stay
1 Château de la Fleunie p178
2 Domaine de la Marterie p189
3 Hôtel de la Ferme Lamy p185
4 La Domaine de la Rhonie p185
5 La Domaine du Terroir p178
6 La Licorne p178
7 Les Balcons de l'Espérance p189
8 Manoir de Hautegente p178
Where to eat and drink
9 Auberge du Peyrol Chez Janine p179
10 La Table d'Aubas p179
Thenon
Fossemagne
Bars
Périgueux
Château de l'Herm
La Douze
Rouffignac
Plazac
Nehnang Samten Choling
Grotte de Rouffignac
Fleurac
Dhagpo Kagyu Ling
Abri du Moustier
Peyzac-le-Moustier
Golf de la Marterie
Mauzens-et-Miremont
Jacquou Parc
La Roque St-Christophe
Musée Napoleon
Maison Forte de Reignac
Préhisto Parc
La Madeleine
Tursac
Journiac
Château de Marzac
Gisement de Laugerie Haute
Les Abris de Laugerie Basse
Ferme de Fonluc
Grotte des Combarelles
Grotte du Grand Roc
Tayac
L'Abri Cro-Magnon
St-Avit-de-Vialard
Abri du Poisson
Les Eyzies
Grotte de Font-de-Gaume
Les Grottes du Roc de Cazelle
Grotte Préhistorique du Sorcier
Grotte de Bara-Bahau
St-Cirq
Grotte de Bernifal
Le Bugue
Village du Bournat
Parc du Château de Campagne
Paunat
Vézère
Meyrals
St-Martin
Gouffre de Proumeyssac
Limeuil
Audrix
Dordogne
St-Cyprien
Bergerac

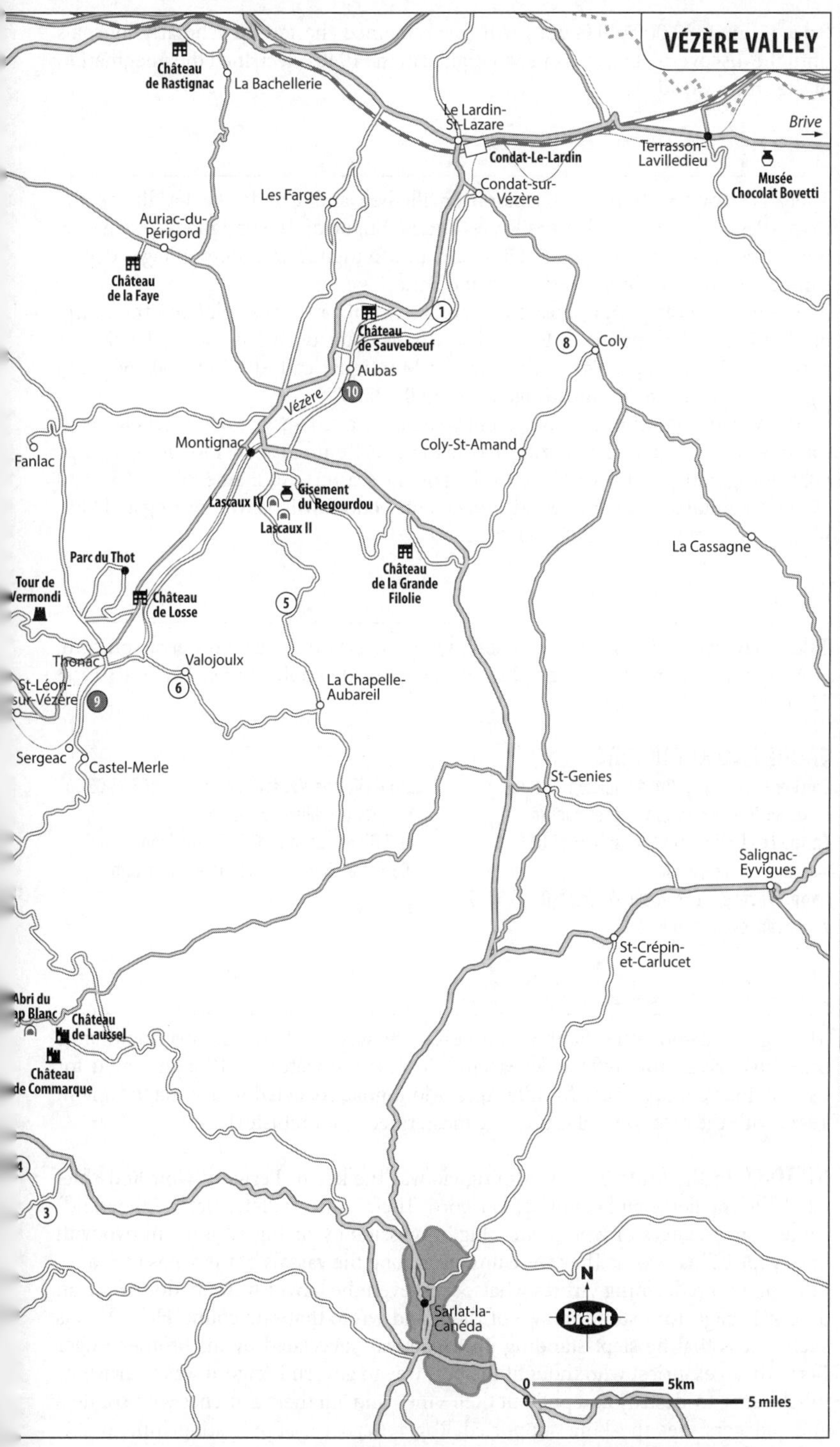

VÉZÈRE VALLEY
Château de Rastignac
La Bachellerie
Le Lardin-St-Lazare
Condat-Le-Lardin
Terrasson-Lavilledieu
Brive
Musée Chocolat Bovetti
Condat-sur-Vézère
Les Farges
Auriac-du-Périgord
Château de la Faye
Château de Sauvebœuf
Coly
Aubas
Vézère
Montignac
Coly-St-Amand
Fanlac
Lascaux IV
Gisement du Regourdou
Lascaux II
Parc du Thot
Château de la Grande Filolie
La Cassagne
Tour de Vermondi
Château de Losse
Thonac
Valojoulx
St-Léon-sur-Vézère
La Chapelle-Aubareil
Sergeac
Castel-Merle
St-Genies
Salignac-Eyvigues
St-Crépin-et-Carlucet
Abri du Cap Blanc
Château de Laussel
Château de Commarque
Sarlat-la-Canéda
N
Bradt
0 5km
0 5 miles

Palaeolithic (c80,000–40,000BC). All this remained the fare of scholarly journals until the discovery of Lascaux in Montignac in the 1940s electrified the imagination of the entire world.

GETTING THERE AND AROUND

There are **train** stations at Terrasson-Lavilledieu and Condat-Le Lardin on the Brive–Périgueux line, and at Les Eyzies and Le Bugue on the Périgueux–Agen line. **Buses** (w transports.nouvelle-aquitaine.fr) to Montignac and other villages depart from the stations at Brive, Périgueux and Sarlat.

The massive **car** park opposite Lascaux IV is only a short stroll from the centre of Montignac. Parking in Les Eyzies in season is notoriously frustrating; try the car park at 19 Avenue de la Forge. For a **taxi** in Montignac call 05 53 51 80 46; in Les Eyzies 05 53 29 28 74; in La Bugue 05 53 07 22 97.

The Vézère communities have recently launched a self-service **e-bike** scheme with stations at Montignac, Les Eyzies, La Bugue and Rouffignac (w mobility-parc.net; €0.01 to sign up, plus €2–€3/hr depending on the season). Aquitaine Bike (05 53 30 35 17; w aquitainebike.com; see ad, 2nd colour section) will deliver touring and kids' bikes to your hotel, from €90 for 4 days.

SPORTS AND ACTIVITIES

Take a **riverboat** ride from Terrasson's Quai du Lavoir (w gabare-terrasson.com; May–Sep). There are **riding stables** at the Ferme de Fonluc in Les Eyzies (05 53 35 30 06; w fonluc.com).

CANOE AND KAYAK HIRE

Canoës Courrèges Rte du Buisson, Le Bugue; m 06 86 26 72 88; w canoe-courreges.fr
Canoë Les Eyzies Les Eyzies; 05 53 06 91 89; w canoes-3drapeaux.fr
Canoë Vézère St Léon-sur-Vézère; 05 53 50 67 71; w canoevezere.com
Canoës Vallée Vézère Les Eyzies; 05 53 05 10 11; w canoesvalleevezere.com
Les 7 Rives Chemin de St-Pierre, Montignac; 05 53 50 19 26; w canoe-montignac.com

MONTIGNAC, LASCAUX AND AROUND

Montignac sits on either bank of the Vézère, its wooden balconies overlooking its once busy river port reflected peacefully across the waters. Although feared for its ferocious counts in the Middle Ages, Montignac rocketed to a sweeter fame in 1940, with the discovery of one of the masterpieces of prehistoric art.

HISTORY In the Middle Ages, Montignac was the key to Périgord Noir and chief citadel of the fierce bad counts of Périgord. Their name Taillefer (later Talleyrand) came from an ancestor who made a big impression by slicing a Viking in two with one swipe of his sword. They were unique among the vassals of the kings of France in having no redeeming virtues whatsoever; even the hawkish troubadour Bertran de Born (page 168) stood in awe of them and wrote that one count, Hélie V, was such a cuss that he slept standing up. Hélie was succeeded by his brother Roger Bernard, an ex-priest who thought the best way to govern Périgord was to crush its inhabitants, to 'destroy and pull out their vines' and 'fill their churches with soldiers and pillagers'. Yet the king supported Roger Bernard, appreciating him for his skill at stomping on lesser barons – to the king's mind the fewer nobles the better, especially in this den of cut-throats.

But Roger Bernard's even nastier son, Archambault V, changed sides and swore allegiance to England, and took advantage of a truce to surround Périgord with castles. He captured Domme by surprise, burned the church with all the people inside, then hunted down all the women who escaped, forcing them to cut off their dresses at the waist for easier raping. Archambault attacked the monasteries and royal officers, declaring himself the absolute sovereign of Périgord, and, to show he meant business, destroyed half of Périgueux. The good folk of Périgord begged Charles VI for relief and in 1394 the king sent down an army to punish Archambault, destroying his fortresses and besieging Montignac for a month. Archambault sued for a truce and offered to pay a huge fine; but as soon as the royal army turned its back, Archambault tortured and hanged the king's commander.

Archambault died before the king could punish him again, leaving an heir – Archambault VI – who proved to be even worse, terrorising Périgord with murder and mayhem, laughing at royal orders to behave. He didn't laugh so hard in 1397, when once again Montignac was besieged and Archambault was forced to surrender. The king gave Montignac to his brother, Louis d'Orléans (who had to sell it for ransom money when he was captured at Agincourt), while Archambault hightailed it to London, where he connived and made everyone around him miserable until his death in 1430. By the 18th century, Talleyrand blood had cooled enough to produce a diplomat, the famous sallow-faced Charles (1754–1838), who quit Napoleon's foreign ministry in protest against his wars, and then after Waterloo negotiated the peace that allowed France to keep its old borders.

The discovery of Lascaux One morning in September 1940, two local teenagers and two young refugees from Paris equipped themselves with lanterns and set off up the hill, determined to find a legendary secret treasure. A recent storm had uprooted a tree growing over the vault of the cave, causing part of it to collapse. The boys enlarged the opening and fumbled their way into a treasure beyond anyone's dreams, one that had been virtually vacuum-sealed when the entrance was blocked by an ancient landslide.

Within a week the world's authority on decorated caves, the 73-year-old Abbé Breuil, had made his way to Montignac and was ravished by what he called the 'Sistine Chapel of Prehistoric Art'. He made Lascaux's young discoverers responsible for guarding the cave – which they did vigilantly, with shotguns. But by the early 1960s it had become clear that Lascaux's worst enemy wasn't something to shoot at, but the 'white disease' caused by carbonic acid from the breath of a million visitors; within 15 years of its discovery, the masterpiece that had endured for millennia was beginning to fade under a film of white calcite deposits. On 20 April 1963 Lascaux was closed to the public by André Malraux. Disappointment was so universal that the département financed a replica, Lascaux II, which opened in 1983. Lascaux III is a unique set of five ultralight exact replica shells that went on an international tour. And as of 2016, we are on to Lascaux IV, created after concerns that millions of visitors were damaging the hill around the original cave.

TOURIST INFORMATION

Montignac 1 Place Bertran de Born; 05 53 51 82 60; w lascaux-dordogne.com; Jul–Aug 09.30–18.30 daily, Sep–Jun 09.30–13.00 & 14.00–18.00 daily. Pick up their useful town plan.

Rouffignac Place Simone Veil; 05 53 05 46 46; w rouffignac-perigordnoir.fr; in season only 09.30–13.00 & 14.00–17.00 Mon, Wed, Sat–Sun

Terrasson-Lavilledieu Rue Jean Rouby; 05 53 50 37 56; 10.00–noon & 14.00–18.00 Mon–Sat

WHERE TO STAY

Montignac

Hôtel de Bouilhac (10 rooms) Rue du Dr Mazel 05 53 51 21 46; w hoteldebouilhac-montignaclascaux.fr. In a listed 17th-century *hôtel particulier*, elegant dbls & family suites, with a gastronomic restaurant (€€€€€) in the vaulted cellar. **€€€€€–€€€€**

Château de Puy Robert (20 rooms & gîtes) 865 Rte de Valojoulx; 05 53 51 92 13; w puyrobert.fr. This 4-star hotel, in a romantic 10ha park a short walk from Lascaux IV, occupies a bijou 19th-century château & its *gentilhommière*, each room stylishly decorated with modern fabrics, English furniture & antiques. There's also a pool & spa. **€€€€€–€€€**

Hostellerie La Roseraie (10 rooms) Place d'Armes; 05 53 50 53 92; w laroseraie-hotel.com. In a large 19th-century house, a charming place where you can forget about the world outside. The elegant restaurant (€€€€) is one of the best in town, & the attractive gardens have a rose tunnel & pool. **€€€€€–€€**

Le Lascaux (10 rooms) 109 Av Jean Jaurès; 05 53 51 82 81; w hotel-lascaux24.fr. A good-value, slightly old-fashioned Logis hotel. **€€**

Le P'tit Monde (15 rooms) 54 Rue du 4 Septembre; 05 53 51 32 76; w hotel-montignac.fr. Cheap & cheerful 2-star hotel in the centre, with a walled garden, pool, sauna, jacuzzi & ping pong out back. **€**

Around Montignac

Manoir de Hautegente [map, page 174] (17 rooms) 3km north on the D62 in Coly-St-Amand; 05 53 51 68 03; w manoir-hautegente.com; Apr–Oct. A magnificent, ivy-covered 18th-century manor with antique-furnished rooms. Its idyllic 14ha park is crossed by a clear, ambling trout stream, & there's a large pool & massages on the riverbank; plus a playground, horses, chickens & rabbits, & bikes & e-bikes to rent. Superb b/fast (€18) & creative gourmet restaurant (€€€€), one of the best in the valley. **€€€€**

Archambeau (21 rooms) Place de l'Église, Thonac; 05 53 50 73 78; w hotel-restau-archambeau.com. Just south of the Château de Losse, a Logis hotel with shipshape contemporary rooms in a traditional stone house, plus a good restaurant (€€€) with a lovely summer terrace, & a heated pool & spa for relaxing after seeing the sights. **€€€**

Château de la Fleunie [map, page 174] (33 rooms) Rue du Aubas, Condat-sur-Vézère, 10km northeast of Montignac; 05 53 51 32 74; w lafleunie.com. Unpretentious rooms in a 12th–15th-century château, set in a 106ha estate with tennis courts, pool & a sauna. There are 2 restaurants, the Gastronomique (€€€€) in a very elegant stone-walled setting or the informal Grill Piscine (€€) for lunch in summer. **€€€**

La Licorne [map, page 174] (5 rooms) Valojoulx, 6km south of Montignac; 05 53 50 77 77; w licorne-lascaux.com. The Unicorn offers rooms sleeping up to 4 in 13th- & 17th-century buildings with a pool. Peace reigns. Meals available to guests. B/fast inc. **€€€**

La Domaine du Terroir [map, page 174] (20 rooms) Fougeras, La Chapelle-Aubareil; 05 53 51 04 17; w ledomaineduterroir.fr. Off the beaten track some 7km south of Montignac but worth the effort: the family-friendly farm-hotel-restaurant (€€€) offers panoramic views from its 25ha park & heated hilltop pool. There's a play area for the kids, too. **€€€–€€**

Auberge de Castel-Merle (9 rooms) Sergeac; 05 53 50 70 08; w hotelcastelmerle.com; Apr–Oct. This pretty hotel in a former farmhouse is peaceful & charming, & near a river beach. B/fast inc. **€€**

Hôtel de l'Abbaye (10 rooms) Coly-St-Amand; 05 53 51 68 50; w hoteldelabbaye-lascaux.com. Little old-fashioned place in a little old-fashioned village, with a restaurant (€€€) serving the classics. **€€–€**

WHERE TO EAT AND DRINK A lot of folks head to nearby St-Léon for lunch or dinner.

Montignac

Aux Berges de la Vézère Place Tourny; 05 53 50 56 31; w restaurant-montignac.fr; closed Mon, eves Wed & Sun. Finding contemporary cuisine with riverfront views in a tourist town isn't a given, but chef Lionel Lascaud does it with panache. They also do excellent pizzas. €€€

Le 4 Lacoste, south of the centre; 05 53 51 86 92; w le-4.eatbu.com; closed Wed & eves Sun. Wendy & Christopher offer big salads & set menus with interesting choices such as cod with chorizo crumble & quinoa. *Menu €28.* €€€

La Chaumiére 53 Rue du Quatre Septembre; 05 53 50 14 24; closed Tue, Wed & lunch Sat. A great little place to recharge after Lascaux, serving up hearty dishes with a cheesy northern French influence, but of course there's duck too – after all, this is the Dordogne! €€

Around Montignac

Le Petit Léon St-Léon-sur-Vézère; 05 53 51 18 04; w restaurantlepetitleon.fr; May–Oct, closed Mon–Wed. Pretty garden restaurant in the centre, where young New Zealand chef Nick Honeyman (who worked in Paris at L'Astrance & L'Arpège) serves one exquisite, changing set menu. Choose between 4 courses (€50) or 7 (€65). €€€€€

Auberge du Peyrol Chez Janine [map, page 174] Les Soles, Sergeac; 05 53 50 72 91; w hotel-loupeyrol-dordogne.com; Mar–Jun & Sep–Dec lunch Tue–Thu, lunch & dinner Fri–Sun, Jul–Aug lunch & dinner Tue–Sun. A family inn (which also has 5 rooms; €) offering a lovely picture-window overview of the Vézère landscape to go with the likes of foie gras in Monbazillac, truffle omelettes & magret with herbs. €€€

La Poste St-Léon-sur-Vézère; 05 53 50 73 08; closed eves Mon. Pleasant beamed dining room & terrace, with something for everyone – everything from escargots & confits (their speciality since 1948!), to burgers, vegetarian dishes & good homemade frites. *Menu €26.* €€€

La Table de Jean Coly-St-Amand; m 06 42 48 19 49; w latabledejean.com; closed Mon & eves Tue. Excellent bistronomic cuisine. *Lunch menu €26.* €€€

Les Agapes Impasse de la Halle, Terrasson-Lavilledieu; 05 53 50 14 75; LesAgapes24; Aug daily. In the heart of the old town, with 3 outdoor terraces & solid unfussy food. *Menus from €18.* €€€

La Table d'Aubas [map, page 174] Aubas, by the Château de Sauvebœuf; 05 53 50 48 57; ; closed Sun & eves Mon. A big terrace at this restaurant-bar, & kindly priced food in a friendly atmosphere, good for families, & only a few minutes' drive from Lascaux. *Lunch menu €15.* €

Smoovie Grignothéque St-Léon-sur-Vézère; m 06 07 24 20 01; Grignotheque; closed Wed, Sat & eves Tue, Sun. A godsend for vegans & vegetarians in the former boulangerie. €

MONTIGNAC The tourist office occupies one of the most striking buildings in town, the 14th-century **Hôpital de St-Jean**, with its chapel, the **Prieuré St-George** at its side. The bust of a man with the show-stopping beard is of Eugène Le Roy, who worked as Montignac's tax collector before he hit the big time with his novel *Jacquou Le Croquant* (page 21). In medieval **Rue de la Pégerie** (named after the tolls charged on a long-gone bridge) is a house Henri IV gave to his mistress, Gabrielle d'Estrées (no. 1), and at no. 16 the home of fiery revolutionary Élie Lacoste (1745–1806), first head of the new Dordogne department, and who (much to the relief of France) brought down Robespierre and Saint-Just during the Terror.

The medieval bridge was washed away in a flood and it took 200 years before there was another, the **Pont de Pierre** of 1777 (which proved its mettle, withstanding the floods of 1924 and 1960). Cross it for Place de la Libération, from where you can walk up to the **Château de Montignac** (no entrance, but take Rue des Jardins to Rue de la Tour allowing a closer look), seat of the wicked Counts. Later the d'Albrets added the fat round tower and mighty wall, pierced with artillery openings during the Wars of Religion; inherited by Henri IV, he sold it to the Hauteforts to pay off his debts. Quarried for its stone after the

Revolution, it was later owned in the early 1900s by a mayor who cleared much of what survived away to build his villa and *orangerie*.

Below, **Place Joubert** honours the town's famous author of the *Pensées*, Joseph Joubert (1754–1824), who penned aphorisms and notes, many worthy of Montaigne but published only after his death. Nearby is the church **St-Pierre-ès-Liens**, 13th century, rebuilt in the 20th, where the treasure is the *Death of St Bruno* by Baroque painter Juan Sánchez Cotan, who is otherwise famous for his still-life tableaux.

GROTTES DE LASCAUX

Centre International de l'Art Parietal (Lascaux IV) (Av de Lascaux; ☎ 05 53 50 99 10; w lascaux.fr; ⏲ 10 Jul–Aug 08.00–22.00 daily, May–Jun 09.00–19.00 daily, Oct–7 Nov 09.30–19.00 daily, 8 Nov–2 Jan 10.00–18.00 daily; tickets bookable online: €21, ages 5–12 €13.50, under 5 free, 2hr cave visits with torches €30 for all. See website for packages with Parc du Thot, page 182; Laugerie Basse, page 187; and Grotte du Grand Roc, page 187) Set in a bunker at the base of the hill, full of high-tech gimcrackery, the star attraction is a perfect replica of the entire Grotte de Lascaux, with its 600 paintings and more than 1,500 engravings. But no-one can explain how an artist limited to a lamp of animal fat and juniper twigs could get the proportions of a 4.8m bull so perfectly. For Cro-Magnon artists not only drew with the unerring line of a Matisse, but mastered techniques forgotten until the Renaissance – note the three-quarter, twisted turn in the animals' heads, the Impressionistic use of perspective in the legs of running horses.

Scattered among the animals is a vocabulary of mysterious symbols reminiscent of Joan Miró. And what of the Dr Seuss-ish beast dubbed the 'unicorn', the only known 'imaginary' creature discovered in prehistoric art? Was all the painting done for a single religious rite and sealed off, never to be revisited? The original entrance to Lascaux I has never been found. Allow 3 hours to see it all, including Lascaux III and a 3D theatre. There's a bar/restaurant on the site, and special evenings that combine tours with dinner.

Lascaux II (200m below the original cave; ☎ 05 53 51 95 03; w lascaux-ii.fr; ⏲ mid-Apr–Jun 09.30–12.30 & 14.00—18.00 daily, Jul–late Aug 09.00–19.00 daily; late-Aug–Sep 10.00–12.30 & 14.00–17.30 daily; tickets bookable online €15, ages 5–12 €10) This incredibly painstaking reproduction of the two most beautiful chambers, the Hall of the Bulls and the long narrow Diverticule Axiale, was painted over 15 years by Monique Peytral with the same colours and techniques used 17,000 years ago. Tours here allow more time and a more intimate experience than in Lascaux IV, the guides illuminating the art with imitation Cro-Magnon torchlight. The tour includes a visit to the modern entrance of Lascaux I.

Gisement du Regourdou (800m up from Lascaux II; ☎ 05 53 51 81 23; w regourdou.fr; ⏲ Apr–Jun & Sep 11.00–18.00, Jul–Aug 10.00–19.00, Nov, Feb–Mar 13.00–18.00, all daily; €7, ages 6–12 €4) Farmer Roger Constant was fascinated by Lascaux, and in 1954, hoping to find the original entrance to the cave, began digging, uncovering a collapsed karst cavity. Instead he found a Neanderthal mandible. He contacted the authorities who sent in a team who uncovered a nearly complete, well-preserved skeleton (minus the skull) of a Neanderthal man named Regourdou 1 – and a brown bear. Covered with an enormous slab weighing 850kg, it may be the oldest tomb in the world, from the Mousterian era (c90,000BC); nearby other bones were found in small stone boxes in what looked like a bear cult cemetery. It inspired Constant to buy three bears to live on the site (now there are six), create a museum in his house to contain the bones, fossils and flint tools and open it up to visitors.

Regourdou was explored again in 2013–14, and current thought is that the bear 'cemetery' was natural even though there are signs of cutting on the bones. Opinion may change again – since the discovery of the cave of Bruniquel (page 341), people are willing to admit that Neanderthals were far more sophisticated than anyone imagined.

COLY-ST-AMAND This tiny village, 6km east of Montignac, is named after a remarkable fortified abbey **church** (05 53 51 98 92; 09.30–12.30 & 14.00–18.00 daily) that looms like a skyscraper over its valley. Built in the 1120s, it was so strong that the Huguenots who took shelter here in 1575 withstood six days of close cannon fire. It is stirring, wholesome Romanesque, unusually built on a slope (the walls of the nave converge slightly, to create a curious perspective). The dome hovers 30m over the nave: stand under it and sing, and like all true Romanesque churches it rings like a bell. Some 5km southwest is one of the Dordogne's dreamiest châteaux, the 14th–15th-century **Château de la Grande Filolie** (private), so perfect that, as Périgord novelist Marc Blancpain put it, 'one could believe it grew here, as mushrooms grow in the humid sweetness of an autumn night'.

UP THE VÉZÈRE FROM MONTIGNAC

Auriac-du-Périgord Here the 14th–16th-century **Château de la Faye** was wrapped around a medieval keep. The château's chapel of St Rémy was famous throughout Périgord; nicknamed St Remèdi, he was so reputed for his healing juju that all the features of his statue were rubbed off by people vigorously rubbing the afflicted parts of their bodies against him.

Château de Sauvebœuf (Aubas; m 06 74 65 89 54; w lechateaudesauveboeuf.com; Apr–mid-Oct 14.00–18.00 Mon–Fri, Jul–Aug 14.00–19.00 Mon–Fri; €8.50, ages 6–18 €5, guided visit of museum €8.50/€5, combined €12/€10; in late October they do a pretty good haunted Halloween castle) The Vézère glides under this classic, severe 17th-century château. Its predecessor, built in the 14th century to defend Montignac, was flattened on the orders of Richelieu, to punish the owner for killing a man in a duel. Louis XIII's mistress, Marie de Hautefort (page 169), was so upset over this scarring of her beloved Périgord that she had it rebuilt. It passed to Victor Riquetti in 1743, the father of the Count of Mirabeau of the French Revolution; today its advertising executive owner Claude Douce has filled it with period furnishings, a Cabinet of Curiosities, and a **Musée de Préhistoire** with nearly half a million artefacts. One of the fountains that once adorned the gardens is in Clairac (page 316).

Above Aubas you can walk up along the signposted trail to a spectacular belvedere over the valley from **L'Escaleyrou** cliff, nicknamed the 'end of the world'.

Le Lardin-St-Lazare Here is the 15th-century **Château de Peyraux** (privately owned, but gardens open in summer; ask at the Terrasson tourist office, page 178), while a 7km detour west will take you to a place called **La Bachellerie** – its name derived, like the English 'bachelor', from *bas-chevalier*, the lowest, youngest order of knights. It is the address of the singular **Château de Rastignac** (1811–17) built for the Marquis Chapt de Rastignac by a Périgourdin architect named Mathurin Blanchard (although some say it was Charles-Louis Clérisseau, a friend of Thomas Jefferson, when he served as ambassador to France, which might explain why it looks like the prototype for the rear façade of the White House in Washington). The resemblance was enough to infuriate the retreating Nazis in 1944, who got symbolic revenge on Roosevelt by burning the original (along with 33 paintings by Cézanne, Manet, Renoir, Matisse and Van Gogh that had been hidden here by the Bernheim-Jeune gallery when the war broke out).What you see today is a careful restoration. It cannot be visited.

Terrasson-Lavilledieu The Vézère enters the Dordogne at Terrasson, a rare industrial town in a daydreamy region. But the centre remains a place of considerable charm, with its gurgling fountains, boutiques and spectacular gardens, where swans glide under the 12th-century 140m **Pont Vieux**, the first stone bridge over the river.

Terrasson grew up around the **Abbaye Saint Sour**, founded in AD560 by a very suspect holy man named St Sorus, who washed up here from the Mediterranean and let his two pet doves decide where to settle. When they finally stopped flying around, the cry went up: '*Terra sunt*!' ('They've landed!') – hence Terrasson. St Sour's church, last repaired in 1889, has, in spite of its name, some sweet medieval and 19th-century stained glass that recounts his legend.

Above it are the delightful **Jardins de l'Imaginaire** (Place de Genouillac; ☎05 53 50 86 82; w jardins-imaginaire.com; ⊕ Apr–early Oct 10.00–17.30 Wed–Mon; €8, ages 10–18 €5, under 10 free), evoking gardens through the centuries and across cultures. There's a grand cascade and fountain centrepiece – an idea borrowed from Renaissance Italy – and a *roseraie* where new varieties are developed. A new walkway up the **Falaise du Malpas** – the 300m long sandstone cliff that dominates the town – allows you to get a majestic view over the roofs and valley.

Top it off with a visit to a chocolate factory. Just east of the centre, the shiny **Musée Chocolat Bovetti** (☎05 53 51 81 53; w bovetti.com; ⊕ Aug 10.00–17.00 daily, other times 10.00–12.30 & 14.00–18.00 daily, visits in English Jul–Aug 11.00 daily; €3.90, ages 3–12 €3.40) offers tours with tastings and a boutique.

MONTIGNAC TO LES EYZIES

Parc du Thot (Along the D706, Thonac; ☎05 53 50 70 44; w parc-thot.fr; ⊕ 10.00–17.00 daily, Jul–Aug 10.00–19.30 daily; €10.50, ages 5–12 €6.80, with Lascaux IV €24.60/€15.90, with Lasaux IV & Laugerie Basse €31.40/€20.50) Thot is dedicated to the environment of the Lascaux artists, with a 3D film on the climate change that brought the Cro-Magnons here, and a park with animals portrayed in the cave – the deer and bulls and the animals that found a last refuge in Poland: European bison and Przewalski's horses, plus a pack of wolves, just because. You can have a go at cave painting or hurtling a spear.

Château de Losse (Rte des Eyzies, Thonac; ☎05 53 50 80 08; w chateaudelosse.com; ⊕ May–Jun & Sep noon–18.00, Jul–Aug 11.00–18.00, all daily; €9.50, students €8, ages 5–11 €6, under 5 free) In 1576, this castle, the base of one of Périgord's noblest families, was converted into an elegant Renaissance palace with a massive terrace by Jean II de Losse, former page of François Ier, who served all the sons of Catherine de Medici, and tutored Henri IV. Completely furnished with tapestries, porcelains and other 16th- and 17th-century pieces, it has immaculate Renaissance gardens and a picnic area; you can arrive by canoe, and there's a garden restaurant and tearoom.

Thonac and Plazac An immense bell tower is **Thonac**'s landmark, but the main attraction is a leaning tower 2km away on the Plazac road, called the **Tour de Vermondi**, next to a manor. The story goes that a girl was imprisoned here to keep her away from her lover. When he came and sang at its foot, the tower was so moved that it bent over to allow the two to kiss and never quite straightened up again. There are lovely views from here, and towards **Plazac**, with a bijou square, a 14th-century church, episcopal palace and a medieval garden. Since 1974, it's also hosted a Tibetan Buddhist centre, **Nehnang Samten Choling** (w nehnangsamtencholing.wixsite.com), and a new temple, the **Dhagpo Kagyu Ling** (Landrevie; 05 53 50 70 75; w dhagpo.org).

Due north of Thonac, **Fanlac** is so perfectly preserved in the aspic of time that it was chosen as the location for the French TV film based on *Jacquou Le Croquant*.

Rouffignac-St-Cernin-de-Reilhac Many Dordogne villages have been twinned with one in Germany. In the case of Rouffignac, it marks a special act of forgiveness – in 1944, in reprisal for Resistance activity, the retreating Nazis burned it to the ground and murdered six inhabitants, events recalled in the Espace Mémoire next to the tourist office. Only the church of **St-Germain** remained, or at least most of it – the Romanesque apse is rebuilt, but an admirable Renaissance doorway of 1530 survives, carved with mermaids. If it's open, don't miss the Flamboyant Gothic interior.

Rouffignac has even greater claims to fame: the **Grotte de Rouffignac**, 'the Cave of a Hundred Mammoths' (5km south, off the D32; 05 53 05 41 71; w grottederouffignac.fr; Apr–Jun & Sep–Oct 10.00–11.30 & 14.00–17.00 daily (no reservations; arrive early to make sure of a timed ticket), Jul–Aug 09.00–11.30 & 14.00–18.00 daily (tickets sold throughout the day until sold out); €8, ages 6–12 €5.30; dress warmly, picnic area by the entrance). Here an electric train waits to trundle you 4km down into the bowels of the earth as the guide illuminates the vivid etchings, drawings of mammoths and woolly rhinoceroses, and niches in the clay floor formed by generations of hibernating bears, restlessly spinning. The ceiling of the innermost chamber is an excellent pastiche of horses, mammoths, bison, and an ibex.

Rouffignac is a good example of the way people only see what they expect to see. Unlike many caves, its entrance has always been open, and for centuries locals would come down and take scary walks or even Sunday afternoon promenades, leaving their names and dates behind on the walls and ceilings. Only in 1956 did someone notice that their graffiti covered vigorous prehistoric masterpieces.

The savage, ruined towers of the sinister **Château de l'Herm** (6km northwest of Rouffignac; 05 53 05 46 61; under restoration until 2027), loom in a remnant of the Fôret de Barade, once Périgord's darkest wood. Few castles in France are so bloodstained: legend tells of the 13th-century Baron de l'Herm, whose daughter Jeanne fell in love with a page. By a freak accident, the young man accidentally cut off Jeanne's hand when they first embraced; a wax one was made in its place, and in remorse the young husband swore to obey her blindly whenever she raised it. Unfortunately he became a violent drunkard, and came home one day to find her listening to a troubadour. In a jealous rage he would have slain the singer, but Jeanne raised her wax hand, and the troubadour made good his escape – only to hear Jeanne's screams as her husband cut the rest of her to bits.

Windows and openings were cut into the round feudal towers when a third tower was added by l'Herm's later owner, an ambassador of François Ier named Jean III de Calvimont. Calvimont had spent long periods in Italy, and graced his residence with a Flamboyant Gothic portal guarded by men-at-arms, a superb stone spiral staircase and carved fireplaces, now surreally suspended over the floorless void. Calvimont died a mysterious violent death and left l'Herm to his five-year-old daughter, Marguerite. His widow immediately married a neighbour, Foucauld d'Aubusson, and married Marguerite to his diabolical son, François, to make sure the property stayed in the family. But François was already in love with Marie de Hautefort (aunt of the mistress of Louis XIII), and as Marguerite grew older and François's debts grew larger, he had her strangled, beginning a new 80-year-long streak of murders at and around l'Herm involving the Calvimonts, d'Aubussons and anyone connected with them. By 1652, when all the claimants had self-destructed, the château was put up for auction but no-one wanted it. It was eventually converted into a farm and abandoned in 1862.

Sergeac This village also has a pretty Romanesque church and a sculpted 15th-century roadside 'Hosanna' cross at the entrance to the village. In prehistoric times, Sergeac was the most densely populated spot in the valley outside Les Eyzies. At **Castel-Merle** (D65; 05 53 50 79 70; w castel-merle.com; Jul–Aug 10.00–18.00 Sun–Fri, May & Sep 14.00–18.00 Sun–Fri; €7.50, ages 6–10 €4.50) 11 shelters were inhabited from 85,000BC by the Neanderthals, who were replaced in 35,000BC by the first Cro-Magnons. In one were found very early Magdalenian-era sculptures, and blocks of stone carved with mysterious symbols dated to 32,000BC. While visiting you can get in the Stone Age groove and learn all about carving flint, starting a fire in prehistoric times and how to hurl a throwing stick.

St-Léon-sur-Vézère Charming St-Léon was once a stopping point for pilgrims to Compostela: today its many restaurants offer an ideal stopping point for lunch. Overlooking the willows weeping into the river and a pedestrian bridge, its stunning Romanesque **church**, with its *lauze* roofs, broad square tower and three pointy-topped apses, looks more Burgundian than Périgourdin. Inside a learned priest left a beautifully made display explaining the sacred geometry of the church's proportions.

LES EYZIES-DE-TAYAC AND AROUND

The rivers Vézère and Beune meet at Les Eyzies, the 'World Capital of Prehistory' where the first known bones of our immediate ancestors were discovered just above the train station. As the valley's chief crossroads, with remarkable decorated caves, prehistoric shelters (abris) and deposits (gisements) in every direction, and an important prehistory museum, Les Eyzies is swamped with summer visitors, all watched over by a lumpish creature representing Cro-Magnon man, sculpted in 1930 by Paul Dardé and a grave insult to the painters of Lascaux.

TOURIST INFORMATION Les Eyzies' office is at 19 Avenue de la Préhistoire (05 53 51 82 60; w lascaux-dordogne.com; Jul–Aug 09.30–18.30 daily, Sep–Jun 09.30–13.00 & 14.00–18.00 Mon–Sat).

WHERE TO STAY

Les Glycines (25 rooms) 4 Av de Laugerie, Les Eyzies; 05 53 06 97 07; w les-glycines-dordogne.com. Smart 4-star hotel in a posthouse of 1862 where Prince Charles & Yves Montand stayed, in a 3ha garden setting (with plenty of wisteria (*glycine*) in June), with an outdoor pool & a counter-current indoor pool & spa. There's an excellent gourmet restaurant, Le 1862 (€€€€€) for dinner & a bistro (€€€) for lunch, both supplied by the hotel's organic garden & beehives. **€€€€**

Le Centenaire (19 rooms) 2 Av du Cingle, Les Eyzies; 05 53 06 68 68; w hotelducentenaire.fr. Founded in 1964, 100 years after the first Palaeolithic discoveries in the area, this hotel is central yet seems far from the summer brouhaha in its walled garden with a heated pool, sauna &

gym & exquisite, creative cuisine in the restaurant (€€€€€). **€€€€–€€€**

Ferme de Tayac (5 rooms) Tayac, Les Eyzies; m 06 37 85 29 09; w fermedetayac.com. Next to the fortified church of Tayac, this is a very charming place to stay in a 900-year-old monastery, converted into a farm with lovely warm rooms dedicated to musicians, pool, gardens & everything else you could want. Great hosts, too. B/fast inc. **€€€**

Hôtel de la Ferme Lamy [map, page 174] (5 rooms) 305 Rue Lamy-Boyer, Meyrals; 05 53 29 62 46; w sarlat-dordogne-lamy.com. Halfway to Sarlat, a B&B with rooms of character, with bare beams, a garden & a vast pool. *Meals €32/€16 adults/children*. **€€€**

Hôtel des Roches (41 rooms) 15 Av de la Forge, Les Eyzies; 05 53 06 96 59; w roches-les-eyzies.com. At the foot of the cliffs by the river, a modern hotel with a large lawn, pool & comfortable rooms, & parking. **€€€**

Hostellerie du Passeur (19 rooms) Place de la Mairie, Les Eyzies; 05 53 06 97 13; w hostellerie-du-passeur.com. Super central with comfortable rooms & a warm dining room, & a new heated pool in the gardens. Southwest menus in the pleasant restaurant (€€€€) with its seductive riverside terrace. **€€€–€€**

Moulin de la Beune (20 rooms) 2 Rue du Moulin Bas, Les Eyzies; 05 53 06 94 33; w moulindelabeune.com. A friendly hotel in a pretty ivy-covered mill immersed in greenery filled with birdsong & the sounds of a gurgling stream. Another fine restaurant (€€€), whose weekly menu is posted on their website. **€€**

La Domaine de la Rhonie [map, page 174] (12 rooms & a gîte) Boyer, Meyrals; 05 53 29 29 07; w sarlathotelperigord.com. Stay on a goose farm, with comfortable bedrooms, covered heated pool, as well as a host of indoor & outdoor games. The excellent restaurant (€€€) specialises in you know what, but there are other things as well. **€**

WHERE TO EAT AND DRINK It's very touristy here, so easy to get a so-so meal. Do try the hotel restaurants.

Auberge de Layotte 10km from Les Eyzies at Layotte, Tursac; 05 53 06 95 91; w aubergelayotte.com; Mar–Nov, best to book a week in advance. The jovial family that runs this auberge serves up more than the usual southwest farm offerings. Be sure to come hungry – there's only 1 menu (€37, under 10 €12), but it's guaranteed to be a treat, & includes 3 starters, 2 main courses, cheese, dessert, wine, aperitif, digestive & coffee. €€€

Mentalo 1 Av de la Forge; 05 53 06 92 01; f; Thu–Tue. Friendly atmosphere, tasty pizzas & a €15 *menu du jour* – what's not to like? €

WHAT TO SEE AND DO

Musée National de Préhistoire (1 Rue du Musée; 05 53 06 45 65; w musee-prehistoire-eyzies.fr; Jul–Aug 09.30–18.30 daily, Jun & Sep 09.30–18.30 Wed–Mon, Oct–May 09.30–12.30 & 14.00–17.30 Wed–Mon; €6, under 18 free) Tucked under the cliffs that dominate Les Eyzies, and sharing the terrace with the hapless caveman statue, the village's 16th-century castle was slowly being cannibalised for its stone when it found a new role in 1918 as a museum. This is now dwarfed by the expansion of 2004 – altogether the perfect prehistory aperitif.

If, technologically, humankind got off to a slow, painstaking start (see the flint blades), the opposite is true in art: some rooms form a kind of Louvre of prehistory, with the largest collection anywhere of reliefs and sculpture in stone, bone and ivory. There are bas-reliefs of shapely Magdalenian women, mammoths butting heads etched on a staff, the famous *Bison Licking Its Flank* from La Madeleine and the *Aurochs du Fourneau-du-Diable*; there are rough carved vulvas and delicate ornate phalluses that make you wonder which sex carved which.

Abri Pataud (20 Rue du Moyen Age; 05 53 06 92 46; w mnhn.fr; Jul–Aug 10.00–13.00 & 14.00–18.00 daily, May–Jun & Sep 10.00–noon & 14.00–18.00

Sun–Thu, Apr–mid-Oct 10.00–noon & 14.00–18.00 Mon–Fri; €5, EU citizens under 25 free) Under a rocky overhang in the centre of Les Eyzies, Upper Palaeolithic hunters came to live on 40 separate occasions over a span of nearly 15,000 years, leaving more than a million artefacts. A museum contains key finds, including one of the oldest known bas-reliefs, of an ibex dated to 18,000BC.

Centre d'Accueil du Pôle International de la Préhistoire (30 Rue du Moulin; 05 53 06 06 97; w pole-prehistoire.com; Sep–Jun 09.30–17.30 Mon–Fri, 10.30–17.30 Sun, Jul–Aug 09.30–18.30 daily; free) Opened in 2010, this welcome centre aims to tie all the strands of prehistory together, putting the Vézère Valley in perspective with up-to-date findings from around the world. They have set up a 15km (or 8km) trail, **La Boucle de la Micoque** along the river for a trek through the history and geology of the valley.

L'Abri Cro-Magnon (2 Chemin de Cro-Magnon; 05 53 13 58 54; w abri-cromagnon.com; Jul–Aug 10.00–19.30, Apr–Jun & Sep check website; €7.50, students €7, ages 5–16 €4) In 1868, the first bones of *Homo sapiens sapiens* were discovered near the station here; there are exhibits on the archaeology of the period, interactive displays (in English) on the evolution of man and a story of a Cro-Magnon family in holograms.

St-Martin-de-Tayac (6 Rue de l'Église, north of the train station) One of the most fortified of fortified Romanesque churches, St-Martin has a watchtower instead of bell tower, and a majestic *lauze* roof and antique columns on the porch. Inside it's austere, dark, mysterious.

Grotte de Font-de-Gaume (1 Av des Grottes; 05 53 06 86 00; w sites-les-eyzies.fr; guided tours (some in English) mid-Sep–mid-May 09.30–12.30 & 14.00–17.30 Sun–Fri, mid-May–mid-Sep 09.30–17.30 Sun–Fri; €11.50, under 18 & EU citizens under 25 free; Nov–Mar free 1st Sun of the month; book online well in advance) Thirteen visitors at a time are allowed into Font-de-Gaume, a 10-minute walk east along the D47. It has nothing less than the finest polychrome prehistoric paintings open to the public in France, although as in Rouffignac (page 183) the cave was visited centuries before the the artwork was actually 'discovered' in 1901.

It's a bit of a steep walk up to the entrance. Inside, beyond a narrow passage called 'the Rubicon', the walls are adorned with beautiful paintings and engravings in remarkable flowing lines dating from c12,000BC, created with the same drawing and colour-blowing techniques used at Lascaux: magnificent friezes of red and black bison on a light background, reindeer, horses with legs and heads partially formed by natural features in the cave walls.

The guide will adjust the lighting to bring out the extraordinary fullness and depth of the art. The partially painted, partially engraved black stag and kneeling red doe are unique in the canon of Upper Palaeolithic art, and only become visible after the guide carefully traces out the lines with a light. The stag is leaning over delicately to lick the doe's brow, an image of tenderness as sublime as it is startling, and one that questions a lot of commonly held assumptions about life 14,000 years ago.

Grotte des Combarelles (1km up the D47 from Font-de-Gaume; see Font-de-Gaume) Discovered the same year as Font-de-Gaume, here some 800 different engravings dated 12,000–10,000BC have been distinguished in the cave's last 122m, including 140 horses and 48 rare human representations – hands, masks, women and a seated person. Originally these were painted as well, but because the entrance was open to the elements the humidity has made nearly all the colour disappear. Many are incomplete, most are superimposed in wild abandon, and others only appear when lit from various angles. Some of the art is exceptional – the horse, the lioness, and the reindeer leaning forward to drink from a black cavity suggesting water.

Abri du Poisson (D47; ⌚ book in advance at Font-de-Gaume) This shelter has a rare relief of a fish – a beautiful salmon over a metre long. It is nearly detached from the ceiling; a devious local mayor had sold it secretly to a museum in Berlin, but the French found out just in time and classified the site, preserving the fish in situ. There are a number of other shelters here in the Gorge d'Enfer, but all are closed.

Grotte du Grand Roc (D47 towards Périgueux; ☎ 05 53 06 92 70; w grotte-grand-roc.fr; ⌚ early Jul–Aug 10.00–19.30 daily, early Apr–early Jul, Oct–early Nov 10.00–13.00 & 14.00–18.00 daily, Feb–early Apr & Nov–Dec 10.00–12.30 & 14.00–17.00 daily; €8.60, ages 5–12 €5.90, for combined tickets see website) With an entrance halfway up a cliff, this is a fairy work by Mother Nature, boasting a rare 'forest' of minerals and crystals and extremely rare triangular formations; others resemble coral, some thumb their nose at the law of gravity.

Les Abris de Laugerie Basse (Next to the Grand Roc; ☎ 05 53 06 92 70; w abris-laugerie-basse.fr; ⌚ same as Grand Roc; €9, ages 5–12 €6.40, for combined tickets see website) Located under a cliff, amid troglodyte houses, these were among the first (1863) and most important shelters ever excavated. Inhabited from 15,000 to 10,000BC, some 600 pieces of *art immobilier* were found here. A 3D film at the entrance, reconstructions and a digital tablet loaned to visitors explain what's what.

Gisement de Laugerie Haute (D47; ⌚ book in advance at Font-de-Gaume – you can combine it with Abri du Poisson) If you're especially keen, you can survey 42 levels of human habitation excavated over the last 120 years, at the bottom of the cliff. When the massive top terrace of the cliff collapsed in c14,000BC, it had already been home to people for 11 millennia. There are Solutrean (20,000BC) engravings and a carved gutter, an early attempt to solve a problem that would ever after plague humanity – leaking roofs.

NORTH OF LES EYZIES-DE-TAYAC

La Roque St-Christophe (Peyzac-le-Moustier; ☎ 05 53 50 70 45; w roque-st-christophe.com; ⌚ Nov–Jan 10.00–17.00 daily, Feb–Mar & Oct 10.00–18.00, Jul–Aug 09.30–19.30; €10, students under 25 €7, ages 5–13 €5) This sheer cliff boasts the longest natural terrace in Europe, over 300m long, sliced into five shelves, like the curved prow of a cruise ship. Inhabited from Mousterian times by Neanderthals until the Wars of Religion, the Roque housed about 1,000 people. After the AD900s, it was fortified against the Vikings sailing up the Vézère. There is a reconstruction of a medieval building site and information panels describe the ecosystem of the cliff, and a new virtual-reality film on the site that took six years to make.

Elsewhere in Peyzac-le-Moustier, the **Abri du Moustier** (off limits) is another hoary site in the annals of prehistory. Excavations begun in 1908 have produced such a wealth of material that the last half of the Middle Palaeolithic era is known as the Mousterian culture (roughly 100,000–35,000BC).

Château de Marzac (Tursac; m 06 06 42 58 59; w chateaudemarzac.com; ⌚ Jul–Aug 09.45–19.00 daily; book a session online for a team of 4–12 people: €16, ages 6–12 €13) This beautiful 14th-century château hosts an escape game in which you have 90 minutes to get in and out (there are two to choose from, in English as well as French). The former owners, the de Fleurieu family, hosted the Franco-Japanese painter Foujita during World War I.

Maison Forte de Reignac (Tursac; w maison-forte-reignac.com; ⌚ 10.00–18.00 daily, summer until 19.00; €9, ages 14–18 €6.50, ages 5–13 €4.50) This picturesque medieval fortress-manor built beneath and into the rock is the only residence of its kind to survive in France. It has loopholes and bartizans, furnished rooms, underground vaults, a museum of prehistoric finds from the site and 60 authentic frisson-giving torture instruments.

La Madeleine (Le Petit Marzac, Tursac; ☎ 05 53 46 36 88; w la-madeleine-perigord.com; ⌚ Sep–Jun 10.00–18.00 daily, Jul–Aug 09.30–20.00 daily; €7.90, students €5, ages 5–12 €4, with audio-guide (bring your phone & earphones), €2 extra to visit the traditional farm, or €4 on its own) Over the Lespinasse bridge from Tursac, the excavations begun here in 1863 have yielded some 600 pieces of *art immobilier*, giving the name Magdalenian to the greatest age of Palaeolithic art. Although the finds are now in Les Eyzies' museum, the path from the car park leads to the ruins of a troglodyte village similar to the Roque St-Christophe: a 10th-century fort carved into the living rock, a 15th-century chapel, and, on the promontory, a ruined château.

Préhisto Parc (La Faure Reignac; ☎ 05 53 50 73 19; w prehistoparc.fr; ⌚ Jul–Aug 10.00–19.30 daily, other times check website; €8.50, students €7.50, ages 5–13 €4.80) If after all this, you still can't imagine daily life at the dawn of time, Tursac offers life-size outdoor dioramas featuring hunters killing mammoths, woolly rhinos and bears, shamans, wall painters, families, etc.

EAST OF LES EYZIES-DE-TAYAC

Les Grottes du Roc de Cazelle (D47, Rte de Sarlat; ☎ 05 53 59 46 09; w rocdecazelle.com; ⌚ Jul–Aug 10.00–20.00 daily, May–Jun & Sep 10.00–19.00 daily, mid-Nov–Christmas hols 11.00–17.00 daily; €8.50, students €7.50, ages 5–13 €4.80) Inhabited from prehistoric times to 1966, these cave dwellings in, under and around the natural cliff terrace evoke the millennia, starting with Palaeolithic mannequins doing Palaeolithic things, medieval tunnels, and troglodyte structures including a restored farm entirely cut out of the rock, along with real farm animals.

Grotte de Bernifal (Meyrals, 6km from Les Eyzies on the D47, then 500m walk from the road; m 06 74 96 30 43; ⌚ by appt; €8, under 18 free) A privately owned cave on the left bank of the Petite Beune, this has some 125 Magdalenian-era figures, which a family member will illuminate with a flashlight in the pitch darkness…for a completely different experience. There are more than 20 mammoths, and a wild ass, and rarest of all, a human face, staring out of the night of time.

Abri du Cap Blanc (Marquay, 6.5km from Les Eyzies on the D48; ☎ 05 53 59 60 30; w sites-les-eyzies.fr; ⌚ guided tours mid-May–mid-Sep 10.00–18.00 Sun–Fri, mid-Sep–mid-May 10.00–12.30 & 14.00–17.30; €8, under 18 & EU citizens under 25 free; reserve online) Here 30 people at a time are allowed in to see the shelter's remarkable, vigorous, 13m frieze of nearly life-size horses and bison in high relief, following the natural contours of the limestone cliff.

Château de Commarque (05 53 59 00 25; w commarque.com; May–Jun & mid-Sep 11.00–19.00 daily, Jul–Aug 10.30–19.30 daily, mid-Sep–Oct 13.00–18.00 daily; €8.80, students €7, ages 13–17 €5, ages 6–12 €4, inc audioguide in English or guided tour) Just beyond Cap Blanc up the Grand Beune valley rise the majestic, romantic ruins of the 12th–13th-century castle betrayed to and ruined by the English in the Hundred Years' War; the elegant keep was added in the 16th century. After 400 years of abandonment a descendant of the original builders purchased the castle and opened it to visits. It's a 500m walk from the car park through the woods. Every year it hosts new activities.

On the cliff opposite, **Château de Laussel** (private) sits over the Gisement de Laussel (100,000–17,000BC), which produced the famous relief of the Vénus de Laussel, holding her bison horn (now in Bordeaux).

LE BUGUE-SUR-VÉZÈRE TO LIMEUIL

There are even more caves around Le Bugue, the market town at the southern crossroads of the Vézère, and plenty to entertain the family with a unique aquarium, a theme park, a water park, and a golf course. Limeuil, where the river joins the Dordogne, is as cute as a button.

Market days in Le Bugue are Tuesday and Saturday.

TOURIST INFORMATION

Le Bugue Place de l'Hôtel-de-Ville; 05 53 51 82 60; w lascaux-dordogne.com; 09.30–13.00 & 14.00–18.00 Mon–Sat

Limeuil Jardin de la Mairie, D31; 05 53 63 38 90; w lascaux-dordogne.com; 10.00–13.00 & 14.00–18.00 Mon–Thu (in season)

WHERE TO STAY

Domaine de la Marterie [map, page 174] (5 lodges) 210 Allée du Golf de la Marterie, Saint-Félix-de-Reilhac, 11km north of La Bugue; 05 53 05 61 00; w leslodgesdugolfdelamarterie.com. Peaceful, luxurious wooden lodges opened in 2020 next to the golf course, with heated pool, & spa, & good bistro (€€). €€€€€

Les Balcons de l'Espérance [map, page 174] (19 rooms) Gorceval, Limeuil; m 06 88 82 54 30; w balconsdelesperance.fr. Set in a lofty position just west of Limeuil, minimalist rooms, a pool, spa & bar/restaurant with a vegetarian menu (€) & stunning views over the valley. €€

Le Royal Vézère (53 rooms) Place de l'Hôtel-de-Ville, Le Bugue; 05 53 07 20 01; w hotel-royal-vezere.com. This big white hotel beside the river has the only rooftop pool & terrace in the valley. The restaurant (€€) serves traditional Périgourdin cuisine. €€–€

Le Cygne (12 rooms) 2 Rue du Cingle, Le Bugue; 05 53 06 01 16; w lecygne-perigord.com. The friendly 'Swan' is in a busy spot but it's not too noisy at night & has a shaded garden. The popular restaurant (€€€) serves regional favourites. €

Paris (17 rooms) 14 Rue de Paris, Le Bugue; 05 53 07 28 16; w hotel-bugue-perigord.com. Located in the town centre, this has simple rooms, bar & shady terrace. €

WHERE TO EAT AND DRINK

Le Moulin du Porteil Campagne; 05 53 54 48 73; w moulin-du-porteil.com; daily. Lovely restaurant (also 4 rooms; €€) in a former mill with a gorgeous garden terrace & food to match; limited choices, but all delicious. *2 courses €29, 3 for €33.* €€€

À l'Ancre de Salut Rue du Port, Limeuil; 05 53 63 39 29; 08.00–midnight daily. In the former boatmen's union; bar & brasserie out on a lovely riverside terrace, perfect on a lazy summer's day. €€

Da Francesco 78 Rue de Paris, Le Bugue; 05 53 08 41 57; w da-francesco-perigord.fr; closed Jan & Nov. Tasty *cucina italiana*, with bruschetta, pasta, pizza, seafood & panna cotta. €€

Le Menhir 68 Rue de Paris, Le Bugue; 05 53 07 58 00; w le-menhir.eatbu.com; 08.00–23.00 Tue–Sun. Reliable restaurant-bar with a terrace & smile to go with the *steak frites*, burgers, salads & pizzas. €€

Au Bon Accueil Near the top of Limeuil; 05 53 63 30 97; w au-bon-accueil-limeuil.com; Apr–Oct. A sweet place with tables under a century-old wisteria – the scent is hypnotic when in full bloom – & southwest treats. They also have 4 rooms (**€€**) 50m away. €

Crêperie l'Abreuvoir 31 Grand Rue, Le Bugue; 09 82 25 35 45; daily. Cheap & cheerful, with a lot of savoury & sweet choices. €

WHAT TO SEE AND DO

Aquarium du Périgord Noir (99 Allée Paul Jean Souriau; 05 53 07 10 74; w aquariumperigordnoir.com; Jul–Aug 10.00–19.00 daily, Feb–Jul & Sep–11 Nov 11.00–18.00 daily; €15.90, ages 4–12 €12.90) Although freshwater fish lack the glamour of their salty kin, this, the largest freshwater aquarium in Europe, brings out the charms of pike, sturgeon, eels and turtles in imaginative indoor and outdoor settings. But along with fish there are reptiles – lizards (including iguanas), and alligators in the bayou – and a big touching pool. And there's more kid fun in the same complex: a mini Jungle Golf and the Prehistoric mirror maze, and burgers and crêpes, too.

Parc le Bournat (191 Allée Paul-Jean Souriau; 05 53 08 41 99; w parclebournat.fr; Apr–Sep 10.00–18.00 daily; €16, Jul–Aug €18, ages 4–12 €10/€11, family discounts available) As roadside attractions go, this is an ambitious one: The 'hive' is a reconstructed village set up by Paul-Jean Souriau to take visitors back to 1900, complete with costumed villagers performing tasks of old, including carving *sabots*, or wooden clogs – you can understand how one of these tossed into a machine would be 'sabotage'. There are farm animals, fairground rides, including a vintage rollercoaster, musicians, a restaurant, and occasional night visits with special performances.

Grotte de Bara-Bahau (2km to the northwest; 05 53 07 44 58; w bara-bahau.fr; Feb–Oct 10.00–noon & 14.00–17.30 Tue–Sun; €7.50, ages 6–15 €5.30) This 100m cave, a steep walk up from the car park, belonged to the bears for millennia before graffiti artists moved in some 17,000 years ago. Its walls, 'as soft as white cheese' as one prehistorian put it, are covered with bear-claw marks and flint-blade carvings from the Middle Magdalenian culture, discovered in 1951 by France's Jacques Cousteau of caves, Norbert Casteret, and his daughter Maud; among them are an aurochs, horses, hand or claw marks, a phallus, and other mysterious signs – and a very rare silhouette of a bear.

Gouffre de Proumeyssac (3km south of Le Bugue on the D31E; 05 53 07 27 47; w gouffre-proumeyssac.com; Jul–Aug 09.00–19.00 daily, Apr–Jun & 1–15 Sep 09.30–18.30 daily, Mar & 16 Sep–Oct 09.30–noon & 14.00–17.30 daily, Feb & Nov–Dec 14.00–17.00 daily; €11.60, students €9.90, ages 4–15 €8.30; tour with descent in basket €19.80, under 16 €13.30) For centuries Proumeyssac was protected by demonic legends that claimed the abyss was a volcanic crater full of flames, where unfortunate travellers had perished (or were pushed). It was sealed up in 1778 until 1907 when the enclosure collapsed. Before it could be covered again, a local daredevil installed a windlass and lowered himself on a rope – the ancestor of the 'basket' cage that for years was the only way into the gouffre. It's nicknamed the 'Crystal Cathedral', from its extraordinary domed chamber of yellow and white stalactites and draperies, complete with new sound and lighting effects. Geologists suspect there may be an even larger abyss just underneath.

AROUND LE BUGUE

Parc du Château de Campagne (Rte de Les Eyzies, Campagne; ⌚ Apr–Oct 10.00–18.00, Mar & Nov 10.00–16.00; free) This handsome 15th-century château was given a William Morris neo-Gothic facelift in the 19th century. There was no tinkering, however, with its magnificent trees planted in the mid 19th century (sequoias, cypresses, plane trees) in the Romantic English-style park with a 139-step forest stair, the Chemin des Dames. The surrounding 337ha forest, a Réserve Biologique, is free to explore year-round.

Grotte Préhistorique du Sorcier (Rte de St-Cirq, 5km east of Le Bugue, ☎ 05 53 07 14 37; ⌚ book ahead; €8, students €6, ages 5–13 €3.50) In a very lush setting this little cave has, along with drawings of animals, a rare human figure from c17,000BC. He doesn't really look like a sorcerer to us, but he is extremely well endowed, which has made him a prehistoric celebrity. The guide is good (one speaks English), there's a small museum, the setting is beautiful and you can climb higher up for a lovely view over the Vézère.

Jacquou Parc (D710, 10km north of Le Bugue at Mortemart; ☎ 05 53 64 15 57; w jacquouparc.fr; ⌚ Jun–Aug 10.00–18.30 daily, Apr–May 10.30–17.30 Sat–Sun & hols; €18, €13 after 16.00, children under 85cm €16.50/€13, over 65 & students €14.50/€13) Combined water park and mini theme park, with a toothsome cartoony Jacquou Le Croquant as a mascot.

Musée Napoleon (Cendrieux, 14km northwest of Le Bugue; ☎ 05 53 03 24 03; w musee-napoleon.fr; ⌚ guided tours Apr–Sep, check website for hours; €8, under 12 free) Founded in the 18th-century Château La Pommerie, this museum displays some 500 objects that once belonged to France's emperor and his family, along with

LA DOUCE LIMEUIL

In the 16th century, Isabelle de Limeuil, daughter of the *seigneur* of Lanquais (page 225), put the little town's name on the tip of every tongue in Paris. Rhapsodised by Brantôme as 'La Douce Limeuil', she was the loveliest of Catherine de' Medici's bevy of ladies-in-waiting, jokingly known as the 'flying squadron'. As queen mother, Catherine employed astrologers and sorcerers to get her way, and, like the wicked witch in Snow White, once sent a poisoned apple to an enemy; nor was she above using the virtue of her flying squadron to seduce great Protestant nobles of France, in the hope that a conquest in the bedroom would translate somehow into a conquest for the Church. Catherine sent Isabelle to charm one of the most powerful – the Prince de Condé, the great grandson of St Louis. When a growing waistline betrayed the fact that she'd succeeded only too well, Catherine sent her home in disgrace. After the baby's birth, Catherine had a change of heart, and gave Isabelle in marriage to a social-climbing Italian banker to whom she owed money.

dioramas with lead figures evoking the age of Napoleon. Monsieur De Witt, your affable guide, is a descendant of Napoleon's youngest brother Jérôme, and cousin to the current pretender to the throne.

LIMEUIL The lords of lofty Limeuil, where the Vézère meets the Dordogne, defended their patch with walls and three mighty gates. The snug village inside, with cobbled streets and stone cottages laced with ivy and roses, is almost too cute to be real. At the top, the former park of the château is now **Les Jardins Panoramiques** (Places des Fosses; 05 53 63 32 06; w jardins-panoramiques-limeuil.com; Apr & Oct 10.00–18.00 Sun–Fri, May–Jun & Sep 10.00–18.00 daily, Jul–Aug 10.00–20.00 daily; €9, students €7.20, ages 6–18 €6, under 6 free), consisting of six gardens – sun, medieval, magic, colours, water and insects – with beautiful views.

There's a Renaissance statue of the Virgin in Limeuil's church and, outside the village on the road to Le Bugue, the Romanesque church of **St-Martin** (09.00–18.00 daily) built in 1194 by King Richard the Lionheart as an expiatory chapel for the murder of Thomas à Becket by his dad (see the Latin dedication carved in the stone). The building is one of Richard's few good deeds in his native Aquitaine; the choir still has a few paintings. Down by its once important port there's a popular **beach**, campsite and canoes and kayaks to rent.

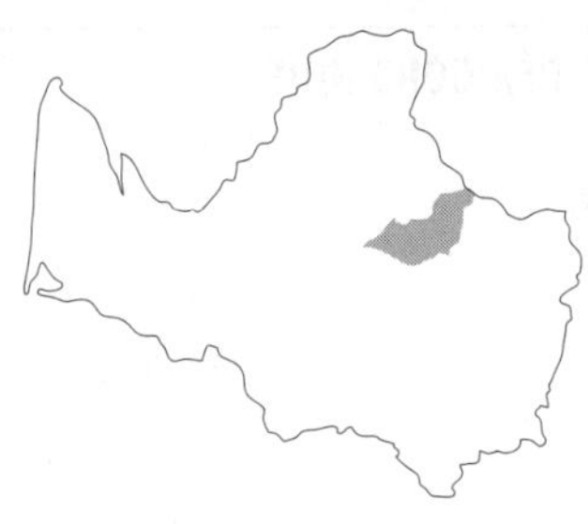

Sarlat and Périgord Noir

When the French dream of Périgord and its charms, it's usually Périgord Noir, the black Périgord, of truffles, or dark walnut groves, or the big river that often turns into a black mirror as the sun goes down, or maybe the dark caves with their secrets from the night of time. Besides its natural beauty and easy living, Périgord Noir also claims an unfairly large share of the region's attractions, including the prehistoric charms of the Vézère Valley (but we've put that in its own chapter, page 172). Here, instead we start with the regional capital Sarlat, one of the most beautiful and distinctive towns in France and the choicest stretch of the Dordogne as it flows out of Quercy past stunning villages such as Domme and La Roque-Gageac, and a mini-Rhineland with a castle around each bend.

SARLAT-LA-CANÉDA

'Mon Dieu, there's nothing here but foie gras!' muttered an old farmer, brought by his relatives to Sarlat for a Sunday afternoon promenade. Of course he's right: nearly every boutique glitters with stacks of shiny tins and jars. But such rich stuff fits Sarlat perfectly well, for, cocooned inside its clinking ring of sprawl, this golden Renaissance town is architecturally the foie gras of southwest France.

HISTORY It was Clovis, they say, who founded a church at what is now Sarlat, and Charlemagne who stopped here after Roncesvalles to drop off a fragment

THE DORDOGNE, RIVER OF HOPE

Its name simply means the Dore water, '*Dore d'eau*' gushing from the volcanic Mont Dore in the Auvergne, before shooting through the steep gorges of the Corrèze to the mellower countryside at Beaulieu; by the time it appears in Quercy, under the watchful eye of the mighty feudal castle of Castelnau (page 237), the river's queenly character has been completely formed.

From here on it meanders down to the Garonne in elegant hairpin turns, or *cingles*. At Bergerac, the Dordogne becomes a wine river, providing the perfect climatic conditions for the likes of Monbazillac and St-Émilion. To defend such a prize, enough châteaux were built along its banks during the Hundred Years' War to make it the Loire Valley of the Middle Ages. Even a hard-boiled Brooklynite like Henry Miller couldn't resist its charms: 'France may one day exist no more, but the Dordogne will live on just as dreams live on and nourish the souls of men.' Today it's the only river in France classed as a World Biosphere Reserve by UNESCO, proving its French nickname, 'La Rivière Espérance' – Hope River.

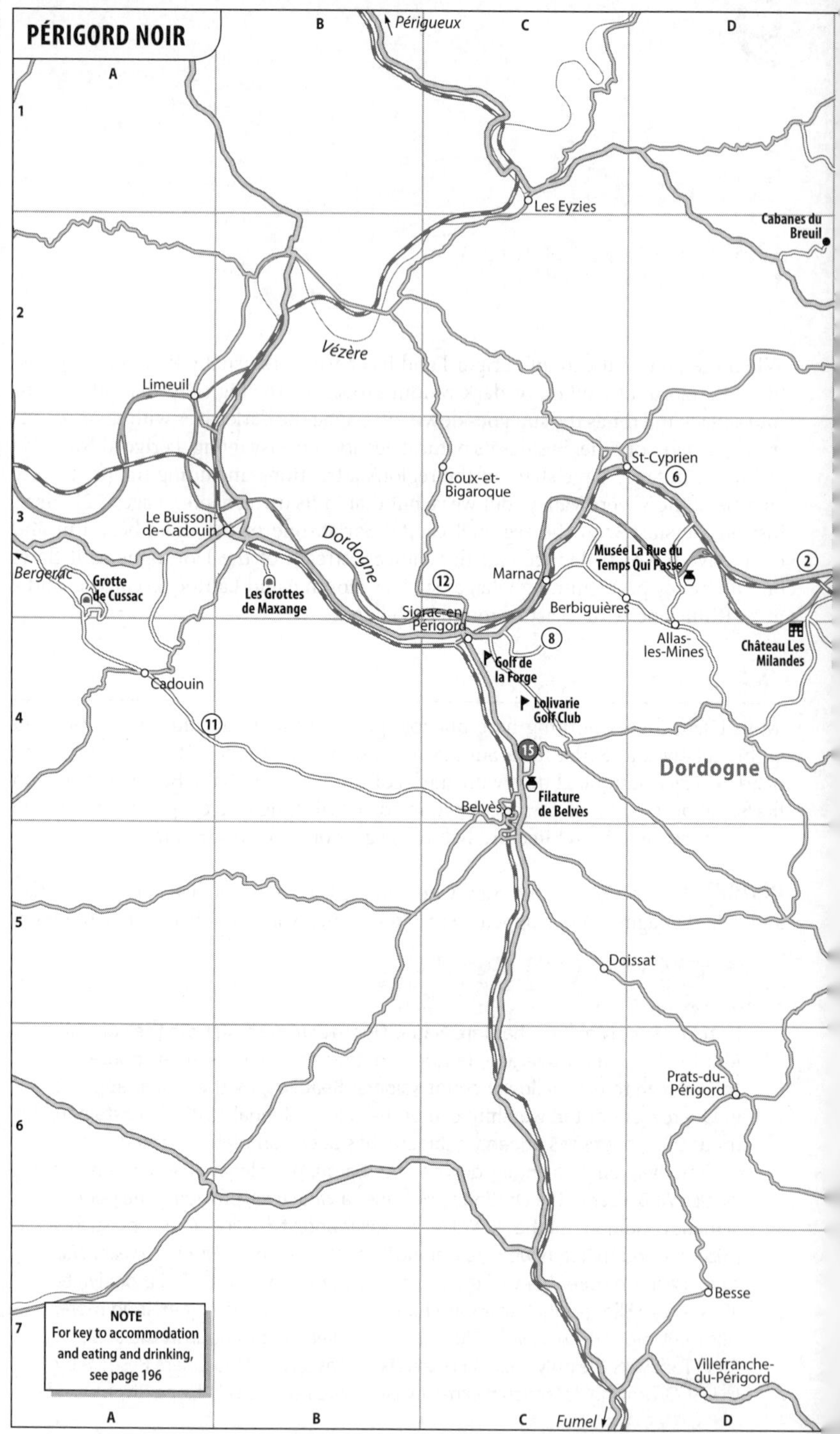

PÉRIGORD NOIR
Périgueux
Les Eyzies
Cabanes du Breuil
Vézère
Limeuil
St-Cyprien
Coux-et-Bigaroque
Le Buisson-de-Cadouin
Dordogne
Bergerac
Grotte de Cussac
Les Grottes de Maxange
Musée La Rue du Temps Qui Passe
Marnac
Berbiguières
Siorac-en-Périgord
Allas-les-Mines
Château Les Milandes
Golf de la Forge
Cadouin
Lolivarie Golf Club
Dordogne
Filature de Belvès
Belvès
Doissat
Prats-du-Périgord
Besse
Villefranche-du-Périgord
Fumel
NOTE
For key to accommodation and eating and drinking, see page 196

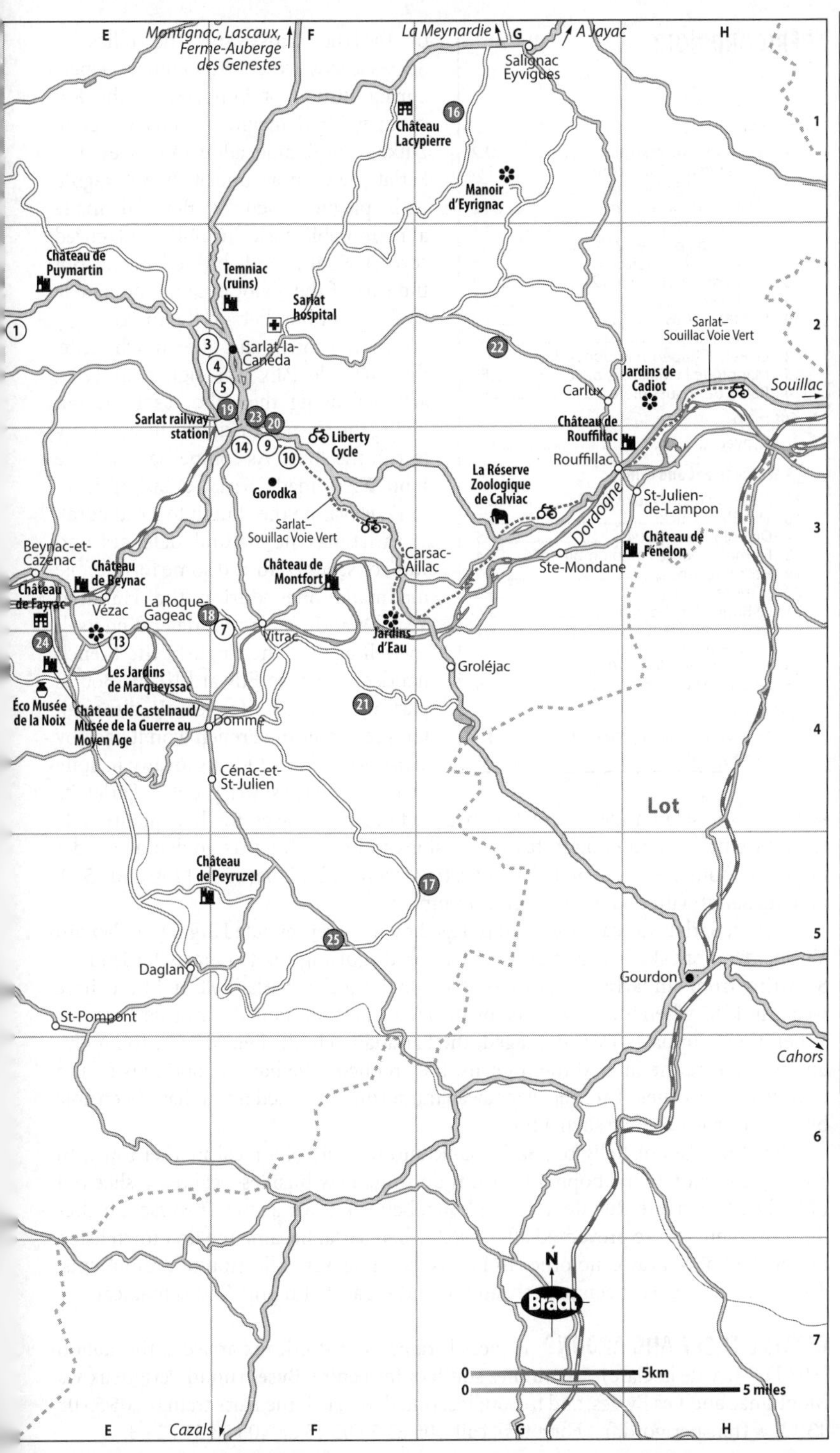

Montignac, Lascaux, Ferme-Auberge des Genestes
La Meynardie
A Jayac
Salignac Eyvigues
Château Lacypierre
Manoir d'Eyrignac
Château de Puymartin
Temniac (ruins)
Sarlat hospital
Sarlat-la-Canéda
Sarlat railway station
Liberty Cycle
Gorodka
Sarlat–Souillac Voie Vert
La Réserve Zoologique de Calviac
Carlux
Jardins de Cadiot
Souillac
Château de Rouffillac
Rouffillac
St-Julien-de-Lampon
Dordogne
Château de Fénelon
Ste-Mondane
Carsac-Aillac
Château de Montfort
Jardins d'Eau
Beynac-et-Cazenac
Château de Beynac
Château de Fayrac
Vézac
La Roque-Gageac
Vitrac
Groléjac
Les Jardins de Marqueyssac
Éco Musée de la Noix
Château de Castelnaud/Musée de la Guerre au Moyen Age
Domme
Cénac-et-St-Julien
Lot
Château de Peyruzel
Daglan
St-Pompont
Gourdon
Cahors
Cazals
Bradt
N
0 5km
0 5 miles

PÉRIGORD NOIR
For listings, see opposite unless otherwise stated

Where to stay

1	Aux Bories de Marquay	E2
2	Domaine de Monrecour *p206*	D3
3	Hostellerie de Meysset	E2
4	Hostellerie La Verperie	F2
5	Hôtel de Compostelle	F2
6	L'Atelier d'Epicure *p212*	D3
7	La Ferme Fleurie *p206*	F4
8	La Grande Marque *p212*	C4
9	La Hoirie	F3
10	La Mas de Castel	F3
11	La Salvetat *p212*	A4
12	Le Petit Chaperon Rouge *p213*	C3
13	Manoir de la Malartrie *p206*	E4
14	Relais de Moussidière	F3
Off map		
	A Jayac	G1

Where to eat and drink

15	Auberge de la Nauze *p213*	C4
16	The Black Duck	G1
17	Diabolo Fraise *p204*	G5
18	Ferme Auberge Le Colombier *p207*	E4
19	Hel's Kitchen	F2
20	L'Orient Express	F2
21	La Borie Blanche *p207*	F4
22	La Garrigue Haute *p204*	G2
23	Le Grand Bleu	F2
24	Le Près Gaillardou *p207*	E4
25	Le Saint Martial *p207*	F5
Off map		
	Ferme-Auberge des Genestes	F1
	La Meynardie	G1

of theTrue Cross and the relics of St Sacerdos, the 6th-century leper-curing Bishop of Limoges. In the 8th century, Charlemagne's grandson, Pépin, Duke of Aquitaine, added an abbey, and Sarlat grew up around it. It was raging with plague when St Bernard made a memorable visit in 1147 and cured several victims with blessed bread. But the rule of the abbot became intolerable to the good burghers of the increasingly mercantile town, and after much strife, the Livre de Paix was signed in 1299, acknowledging the abbot as boss, but giving the town councillors the authority to run the show. As compensation, Pope John XXII made Sarlat a bishopric in 1317, elevating the church to a cathedral.

Sarlat has no natural defences and was constrained to add some formidable manmade ones during the Hundred Years' War. In return for defending itself so well against the English, the French handed it over to Edward III in 1360 as part of the ransom for Jean II, although ten years later the French won it back by arms. As a reward for its loyalty in spite of it all, Charles VII granted Sarlat its symbol – the salamander (a creature believed to have an asbestos-like quality, able to endure fire) – and enough tax concessions to bring about its golden age and a building boom; nearly all of its *hôtels particuliers* were built between 1450 and 1500, gracing Sarlat with a rare architectural unity.

In 1574, Sarlat was captured and pillaged by the irrepressible Huguenot Captain Vivans, who sneaked in during Carnival by disguising his troops as harlequins. Smarting from embarrassment more than anything else, Sarlat held tight for three weeks in 1587 when it was besieged by the fanatical Protestant Vicomte de Turenne. When their ramparts were damaged, the Sarladais rebuilt them during the night, and when Turenne offered them terms, they replied: 'We have a good master and don't want any other.' Turenne went away muttering, ashamed not to have been able by force or ruse 'to take such a town'.

After the Wars of Religion, Sarlat sank into the role of a local market town. In 1827, the town fathers, hoping to drum up some new business, carved a slice out of its heart to create Rue de la République, better known as the Traverse. Further 'improvements' were prevented after 1962, when Sarlat became the first town listed under the Loi Malraux; no other in France has a denser collection of monuments. The entire centre has been pedestrianised and is gaslit at night. And is magical.

GETTING THERE AND AROUND Regional **trains** from Bordeaux arrive at the station [198 D7] (Av de la Gare), 15 minutes south of the centre. **Buses** run to Périgueux via Montignac and Les Eyzies, and to Souillac, timed to match the Paris trains (05 53 08 43 13; w transperigord.fr). For a **taxi**, call 05 53 59 02 43 or 05 53 31 62 43.

The most convenient **car parks** are off the north end of the Traverse [198 C4], and Place de la Grande Rigaudie [198 C5]; there's also free parking in Place des Cordeliers [198 B1]. **Hire a bike** or e-bike at Liberty Cycle [198 D7] (Av du Périgord; 07 81 24 78 79; **w** liberty-cycle.com; Apr–Nov 10.00–18.00 daily).

TOURIST INFORMATION Sarlat's **tourist office** [198 C4] (05 53 31 45 45; **w** sarlat-tourisme.com; Jul–Aug 09.00–19.00 Mon–Sat, 10.00–13.00 & 14.00–18.00 Sun) is at 3 Rue Tourny. They offer 90-minute guided tours in summer (May–Jun & Sep 14.00 Thu, Jul–Aug 11.00 Thu; €7.50, ages 12–18 €4.50, under 12 free).

WHERE TO STAY You'll find nearly as many places to choose from around Sarlat, as in the centre, with the added bonus of a little peace and quiet, although almost all are closed from November to March.

In and near Sarlat centre

Les Suites Sardalais [198 C3] (5 suites) 5 Rue d'Albusse; 05 53 30 50 38; **w** les-suites-sarladaises.fr. Gorgeous antique furnished self-catering suites & apts in the 17th-century Hôtel de Leydis; 3 nights minimum stay. **€€€€**

Plaza Madeleine & Spa [198 B1] (41 rooms) 1 Place de la Petite Rigaudie; 05 53 59 10 41; **w** plaza-madeleine.com. Near the medieval centre, converted from a 19th-century town house, with a cocktail & wine bar, heated pool, spa & a rare private garage. It was where the Hollywood stars stayed in 2020 during the filming of *The Last Duel* in Beynac. **€€€€**

Montaigne [198 C6] (28 rooms) 2 Place Pasteur; 05 53 31 93 88; **w** hotelmontaigne.fr. Attractive older hotel, 200m from the historic centre, renovated in 2019; bright rooms with queen- or king-size beds. **€€€**

Hostellerie de Meysset [195 E2] (30 rooms) 62 Rte d'Argentouleau; 05 53 59 08 29; **w** hotel-meysset.com. A hilltop hotel with modern rooms 2km northwest of Sarlat with wonderful views, park & pool; it's equally pleasant sitting on the restaurant terrace (€€€€), dawdling over locally sourced, contemporary dishes almost too pretty to eat. **€€€–€€**

La Couleuvrine [198 D2] (26 rooms) 1 Place de la Bouquerie; 05 53 59 27 80; **w** la-couleuvrine.com. Bedrooms, each with its own character in Sarlat's 14th–18th-century ramparts, including 5 big ones for families. The excellent restaurant (€€€) features market-fresh produce & the world's best walnut ice cream. Parking 400m away €10/day. **€€€–€€**

Le Renoir [198 C7] (36 rooms) 2 Rue de l'Abbé Surguier; 05 53 59 35 98; **w** hotel-renoir.sarlat.com. In a quiet lane in the centre; a former distillery, now a Best Western hotel with an old cinema-inspired décor, plus a bar, garden & pool. Free parking nearby. **€€€–€€**

Hostellerie La Verperie [195 F2] (24 rooms) 15 Allée des Acacias; 05 53 59 00 20; **w** laverperie.com. A short walk from the centre, peaceful, cosy & suitable for families, with a pool & games. Good restaurant (€€) in a glass atrium. **€€**

Hôtel de Compostelle [195 F2] (23 rooms) 66 Av de Selves; 05 53 59 08 53; **w** hotelcompostelle-sarlat.com. Modern rooms near the centre, with a lap pool & sauna. **€€**

Saint-Albert [198 C6] (25 rooms) 22 Av Général Leclerc; 05 53 31 55 55; **w** hotelsaintalbert.com. Basic rooms & wine bar in a *hôtel particulier* at the north entrance of the old town. **€€**

Hôtel des Récollets [198 A2] (16 rooms) 4 Rue J-J Rousseau; 05 53 31 36 00; **w** hotel-recollets-sarlat.com. Small rooms around a 17th-century cloister in a quiet corner west of the Traverse. Private parking, free bike garage & a shuttle for hikers are a bonus. **€€–€**

La Maison du Notaire Royal [198 C2] (4 rooms, 1 gîte) 4 Rue Magnanat; 05 53 31 26 60; **w** sarlat-chambres-hotes.com. Climb the steps to the big oak doors of this B&B, once home of a captain in the Hundred Years' War. The large-ceilinged rooms & eclectic antiques are perfect for a total immersion in Sarlat's atmosphere. Friendly owners. Free motorcycle & bike garage. B/fast inc. **€**

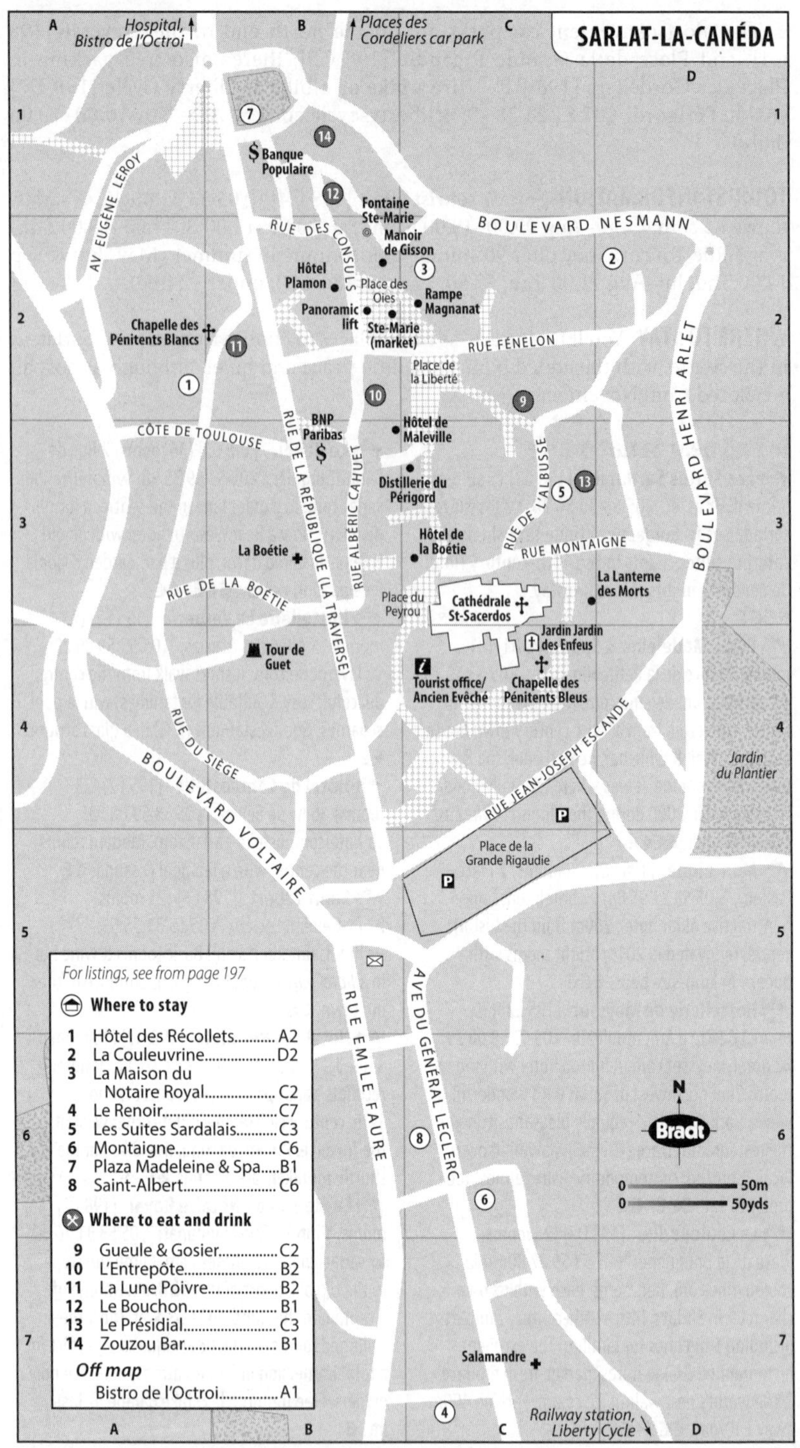

SARLAT-LA-CANÉDA
Hospital, Bistro de l'Octroi
Places des Cordeliers car park
Banque Populaire
Fontaine Ste-Marie
Manoir de Gisson
Hôtel Plamon
Place des Oies
Rampe Magnanat
Panoramic lift
Ste-Marie (market)
Chapelle des Pénitents Blancs
Place de la Liberté
BNP Paribas
Hôtel de Maleville
Distillerie du Périgord
Hôtel de la Boétie
La Boétie
La Lanterne des Morts
Place du Peyrou
Cathédrale St-Sacerdos
Jardin Jardin des Enfeus
Tour de Guet
Tourist office/ Ancien Evêché
Chapelle des Pénitents Bleus
Jardin du Plantier
Place de la Grande Rigaudie
Salamandre
Railway station, Liberty Cycle
BOULEVARD NESMANN
AV EUGÈNE LEROY
RUE DES CONSULS
RUE FÉNELON
CÔTE DE TOULOUSE
RUE DE LA RÉPUBLIQUE (LA TRAVERSE)
RUE ALBÉRIC CAHUET
RUE DE L'ALBUSSE
RUE MONTAIGNE
BOULEVARD HENRI ARLET
RUE DE LA BOÉTIE
RUE DU SIÈGE
BOULEVARD VOLTAIRE
RUE JEAN-JOSEPH ESCANDE
RUE EMILE FAURE
AVE DU GÉNÉRAL LECLERC
Bradt
N
0 50m
0 50yds
For listings, see from page 197
Where to stay
1 Hôtel des Récollets A2
2 La Couleuvrine D2
3 La Maison du Notaire Royal C2
4 Le Renoir C7
5 Les Suites Sardalais C3
6 Montaigne C6
7 Plaza Madeleine & Spa B1
8 Saint-Albert C6
Where to eat and drink
9 Gueule & Gosier C2
10 L'Entrepôte B2
11 La Lune Poivre B2
12 Le Bouchon B1
13 Le Présidial C3
14 Zouzou Bar B1
Off map
Bistro de l'Octroi A1

Around Sarlat

Aux Bories de Marquay [195 E2] (5 rooms & a gîte) 254 Rte de la Bouyerie, Marquay, 8km northwest of Sarlat; 05 53 29 67 02; w auxboriesmarquay.fr; see ad, page 215. Charming B&B in a golden stone country house in a delicious rural setting with a pool, spa & superb table d'hôte. Excellent b/fast inc. €€€€€

Relais de Moussidière [195 F3] (35 rooms) Rte des Moussidière, 3km south of the centre; 05 53 28 28 74; w hotel-moussidiere.com. Built as a charterhouse in a 7ha park with century-old trees with a pool & lake, with simple modern rooms; bar but no restaurant. €€€€

La Hoirie [195 F3] (44 rooms) Rue Marcel Cerdan, La Giragne, 2.5km south of Sarlat; 05 53 59 05 62; w lahoirie.com; Apr–15 Nov. A former hunting lodge, with modern rooms, friendly staff, a pool in the park, & an excellent restaurant (€€€) with a fireplace & veranda. €€€€–€€€

La Mas de Castel [195 F3] (19 rooms) Rte de Sudalissant, 2.5km towards Souillac; 05 53 59 02 59; w hotel-lemasdecastel.com. Peaceful, bright pastel rooms near the pool in the midst of a beautiful garden, plus a bar. €€€–€€

A Jayac [195 G1] (12 rooms) Laval de Jayac, 24km northeast of Sarlat; 09 75 78 86 46; w hotelajayac.com. Little Logis hotel in a stone farmhouse, with simple rooms, a seasonal restaurant (€€) & a pool. €€–€

Ferme-Auberge des Genestes [195 F1] (9 rooms) St-Geniès, 12km north of Sarlat, just off the D704; 05 53 28 97 71; w lesgenestes.pagesperso-orange.fr; Easter–Oct. A good reason to stay here is that you can fill up at their superb farm restaurant & go straight to bed for a post-prandial nap (€). €

WHERE TO EAT AND DRINK

In and around Sarlat centre

Le Présidial [198 C3] 6 Rue Landry; 05 53 28 92 47; w lepresidial.com; closed Sun, lunch Mon–Tue & mid-Oct–mid-Apr. Beautiful *lauze*-roofed 17th-century royal courthouse, with an elegant dining room & garden. One of the best places to savour some of the Dordogne's more extravagant regional dishes; great wine list too. *Excellent w/day lunch menu €26.* €€€€€

Le Grand Bleu [195 F2] 43 Av de la Gare; 05 53 31 08 48; w legrandbleu.eu; closed Mon, eves Sun & lunch Tue–Wed. Superbly crafted fresh seafood dishes star front & centre here. *W/day lunch €26.* €€€€

Gueule & Gosier [198 C2] 1 Rue Salamandre; 05 79 87 21 03; w gueule-et-gosier.fr; closed Tue. Housed in the 15th-century Hôtel de Grézel, creative take on traditional Périgourdin cuisine. *Menu €28.* €€€

L'Entrepôte [198 B2] 5 Rue Albéric Cahuet; 05 53 29 05 30; Restaurant-LEntrepôte; closed Sun & lunch Mon. Pretty stone walls & a young, enthusiastic staff. Good-value menu on the chalkboard: *€26.* €€€

Bistro de l'Octroi [198 A1] 111 Av de Selves; 05 53 30 83 40; w lebistrodeloctroi.fr; Mon–Fri. The former customs & tax office at the north entrance to Sarlat is now a pleasant bistro with freshly prepared dishes & a glassed-in terrace. *Lunch menu with wine & coffee from €15.* €€

L'Orient Express [195 F2] 45 Av de la Gare; m 07 86 23 08 09; 08.30–19.15 daily. Fatima makes the best couscous in the Dordogne. €

La Lune Poivre [198 B2] 5 Rue Jean-Jacques Rousseau; m 06 81 58 88 30; 18.00–02.00 daily. Frank is your very simpatico host in this cosy bar, with great music, too.

Le Bouchon [198 B1] 1 Rue de la Paix; 05 53 59 09 84; noon–14.00 & 18.30–01.00 Tue–Sat. Medieval charm & lively atmosphere, with tapas, cheese & charcuterie platters, wine & craft beers.

Zouzou Bar [198 B1] 9 Place de la Petite Rigaudie; m 06 63 22 88 98; 19.00–midnight Tue–Fri, 19.00–02.00 Sat. Inviting wine bar, with great cocktails & nibbles, as well as wines by the glass.

Hel's Kitchen [195 F2] 13 bis Av Aristide Briand; m 06 31 58 73 30; Hels-Kitchen-Sarlat; 10.00–01.00 Tue–Sat. Popular live music bar (rock, blues, soul, electronic & more).

Around Sarlat

La Meynardie [195 G1] Meynardie, Salignac-Eyvigues; 05 53 28 85 98; w domainedelameynardie.com; closed Tue, eves Mon, lunch Sat. Young Michelin-starred chef Adrien Soro has made this former *ferme-auberge* in a 14ha park into a gastronomic mecca. The veg come from just down the road, the superb country bread is baked every day & the meats & seafood are carefully sourced. *Exquisite w/day lunch menu €39.* €€€€€

The Black Duck [195 G1] Le Sol, St-Crépin-et-Carlucet, just outside Salignac; 05 53 28 80 51; w theblackduck.fr; Tue–Sat. Irish pub grub & southwest French cuisine get along very nicely here. Try the *mousse au chocolat à la Guinness.* €€

SHOPPING Sarlat hosts a huge market on Wednesday mornings and all day Saturdays in Place de la Liberté, with an added *marché au gras* and truffle market from December to February. There's also the covered market in the church of Ste Marie (Tue–Sun). Since 1861, Place de la Liberté has been the site of the **Distillerie du Périgord** [198 C3], where you can try the original Pastis Lapouge, Périgord's own rendition of the famous Marseille apéritif, and an array of fruity *eaux-de-vie*.

OTHER PRACTICALITIES

$ Banque Populaire [198 B1] 1 Rue de la République
$ BNP Paribas [198 B3] 21 Rue de la République
Hospital [195 F2] Le Pouget, Rue Jean Leclaire; 05 53 31 75 75; w ch-sarlat.fr
+ La Boétie [198 B3] 30 Rue de la République
+ Salamandre [198 C7] 17 Av Thiers
Post office [198 B5] 8 Place du 14 Juillet

WHAT TO SEE AND DO

Place de la Liberté All of the medieval lanes in Sarlat lead to this urbane, elongated vortex of a square. The 17th-century **Hôtel de Ville** is here, next to the **Hôtel de Maleville** [198 B3], a 16th-century combination of three older houses, with two Renaissance façades – one French, one Italian. It belonged to Jean de Vienne, a local boy who owed his rise to high office to Henri IV (see the portrait medallions of the king and a woman – either Henri's wife Marie de' Medici, or his mistress Gabrielle d'Estrées). It was later owned by the family that produced Jacques de Maleville, a key author of Napoleon's Code Civil.

The north end of the square is framed by the carcass of the church of **Ste-Marie** [198 B2] and a massive bell tower, completed in 1507. After being used to store saltpetre during the Revolution, it was sold for a pittance to a speculator, who lopped off its chancel and converted its chapels into shops; now it houses a covered market – with 15m-high doors designed by Jean Nouvel and a secret **panoramic lift** [198 B2] (05 53 31 45 45; €5, ages 6–12 €1, under 6 free) waiting to take you 45m up for views over Sarlat's roofs.

The picturesque **Rampe Magnanat** [198 C2] to the right of the market has been used by a score of French film directors for their climactic duel scenes, swords clashing in front of the 13th–15th-century **Manoir de Gisson** [198 B2] (05 53 28 70 55; w manoirdegisson.com; Apr–Jun & Sep 10.00–18.30 daily, Jul–Aug 10.00–19.00 daily, Oct–Nov 10.00–18.00 daily; €8.50, students €7.50, ages 10–17 €4.80, under 10 free) and its hexagonal tower; most of the furnishings are from the 17th-century and there's even a typical cabinet of curiosities. To its left, the mansion overlooks the old goose market, **Place des Oies** [198 B2], with its statue of the three geese that laid Sarlat's golden egg, or rather gave up their livers for its foie gras.

Rue des Consuls Among the magnificent *hôtels particuliers* here, the **Hôtel Plamon** [198 B2] (nos. 8–10) stands out; it was owned by a prosperous family of drapers, who added a new floor every century or so – early Gothic on the ground floor, Flamboyant Gothic on the first and Renaissance on the second. Opposite is a curious cave-like **Fontaine Ste-Marie** [198 B2] from the 15th century; the River Cuze passed openly under the Hôtel de Plamon as a pestilent sewer until it was covered over in the 19th century.

Cathédrale St-Sacerdos

Cathédrale St-Sacerdos (Place du Peyrou; m 07 70 54 03 28; ⌚ usually) This church with impressive flying buttresses and garlic bulb steeple replaces the old abbey church founded by Clovis – of which only the much-restored 12th-century **Chapelle des Pénitents Bleus** in Cour des Fontaines survives. The cathedral had to be reconsecrated in 1273, after a disgruntled monk with a crossbow shot the abbot while he was saying Mass. In 1504, Bishop Armand de Gontaut-Biron demolished this version (except for its Romanesque *clocher-porche*) in order to construct something grander. Unfortunately, it took until the dull 17th century to complete and holds nothing as fine as the bishop's own tomb at Biron (page 227).

Adjacent to the cathedral, the former bishopric or **Ancien Évêché** (now the tourist office), has a handsome top-floor gallery in brick that looks as if it escaped from Italy – not surprising, as it was built by a cousin of Catherine de' Medici, Cardinal Niccolò Gaddi, who added Bishop of Sarlat to his titles in 1533.

Hôtel de la Boétie

Hôtel de la Boétie [198 C3] Opposite the cathedral in Place du Peyrou stands the most lavishly ornate town house in Sarlat (1525). The modern entrance is through the wide round arch of a former shop; richly ornamented mullioned windows dominate the upper three floors, squeezed between a vertiginously steep gable. The decoration reaches a curlicue frenzy in the dormer window, in frilly contrast with the sombre black *lauzes* of the roof.

The *hôtel particulier* was built by the father of the precocious humanist poet Étienne de la Boétie, who was born here in 1530. A student of the classics, Étienne was only 18 when he wrote his *Discours de la servitude volontaire*, asking why people willingly give up their liberty to support tyrants, when tyrants could never exist without people willing to give up their freedom, the most precious thing of all. Instead he suggested 'voluntary servitude' – obey the State or Church, pretend to believe what they say to believe from prudence (or, in those days, survival). Your mind, said La Boétie, belongs to you.

These were radical ideas then, and, even when his dear friend Michael de Montaigne published La Boétie's papers after his premature death at the age of 32, he discreetly omitted the *Discours*, although it greatly influenced his own thinking (it would only appear in 1576 in a collection of 'libellous' Protestant writings). After his death, La Boétie was the subject of Montaigne's beautiful *Essay on Friendship* – and the inspiration for all of his subsequent essays.

La Lanterne des Morts

La Lanterne des Morts [198 C3] Behind the cathedral, the Benedictine cemetery, the **Jardin des Enfeus** [198 C4], consists of 12th–15th-century tombstones excavated and arranged on terraces. Above looms a giant stone bullet of a tower, the largest of several 'Lanterns of the Dead' in these parts – they can be found all over France, but most thickly in Aquitaine and all date from the 1100s.

A *lanterne* is round and sometimes square, with at least three small windows near the top. In the old days, it's said a light would be hoisted up on a pulley to shine through the slits. Most, like this one, are found in cemeteries, although they are sometimes built into churches; the strange cupola on Périgueux's St-Front may be one. Beyond hints from folklore, we have no idea what purpose they served, but we can guess that it's something genuinely old and strange, perhaps a survival of the old Celtic religion – the tower with small windows at the top is a form reminiscent of the *cella* in a Gallo-Roman temple. Were they lighthouses, guiding the souls of the dead? A fascinating thing about Sarlat's Lanterne des Morts is its upper chamber. It's sealed off, completely, mysteriously inaccessible, and no-one alive knows what's inside.

Présidial [198 C3] North of the cathedral, Rue de l'Albusse leads to the handsome Présidial, the seat of a royal court set up by Henri II in 1552, in defiance of local wishes, to administer local justice; it has the very unusual polygonal lantern on the loggia. It's now a fine restaurant (page 199).

Across the Traverse The Traverse divides wealthy Sarlat from the steeper, more piquant neighbourhood to the west, where some alleys are scarcely wide enough to walk arm in arm. In its intimate scale, the **Chapelle des Pénitents Blancs** [198 B2] in Rue Jean-Jacques Rousseau seems like a walrus. Further south are Rue du Siège and a stretch of Sarlat's walls that survived demolition; in Rue Rousset there's a second tower, the 15th-century crenellated **Tour de Guet** [198 B4].

Outside the centre South of the centre in Sarlat's lesser-known half, **Gorodka** [195 F3] (La Canéda; m 06 83 36 77 96; w gorodka.com; ⌚ Jul–Aug 18.00–23.00 daily, or by appt; €10, under 12 free) invites you to hang up your *idées fixes* at the door. Beyond wait 2ha of art in galleries and in the woods, presided over by a giant neon dragonfly. Parisian artist Pierre Shadmoukine has been at it since the 1970s and there are works by other artists; some may be in residence – musicians, dancers, or performance artists – so you never know what to expect. At night the follies are illuminated, and there's a chambre d'hôte (**€**).

In the 8th century AD Duke Pépin built the first citadel on the natural belvedere at **Temniac** [195 F2] (Rte de Temniac, 2km north of Sarlat), north of the centre. In the 1200s the bishops of Sarlat used the site for a palace; it was rebuilt in the 15th century, and today stands in ruins, around the bishops' tower and the pure Périgourdin Romanesque **Chapelle de Notre-Dame** (closed).

THE PLATEAU OF PÉRIGORD NOIR Sarlat's lofty wooded hinterland is a peaceful place these days, but its striking castles show it wasn't always the case. Right in the middle of the 'golden triangle' of Sarlat, Lascaux and Les Eyzies is the **Château de Puymartin** [195 E2] (off the D47, 8km northwest of Sarlat; ☎ 05 53 59 29 97; w chateau-puymartin.com; ⌚ Apr–Jun & Sep 10.00–18.00 daily, Jul–Aug 10.00–17.00 daily (mystery of the Dame Blanche 17.00–19.00 Wed–Sun, 10.00–18.30 Mon–Tue, *soirées* 19.30–midnight Tue), Oct–Nov 10.00–17.30 daily; €10, ages 13–18 €7, ages 6–12 €5). This twin-turreted 15th–16th-century storybook castle, set in a handsome park, was the Viscount of Turenne's headquarters when he besieged Sarlat, but afterwards managed to stay out of history, although it has a well-documented 16th-century ghost. Thérèse de Saint-Clar, the 'Dame Blanche', was caught by her husband in the arms of her lover and imprisoned in the north tower for years. Rooms are fitted with 17th–19th-century furnishings, painted beams, wall paintings and Aubusson tapestries.

Just north on winding little roads, the **Cabanes du Breuil** [194 D2] (St-André-d'Allas; m 06 80 72 38 59; w cabanes-du-breuil.com; ⌚ Apr–Sep 10.00–20.00 daily, Oct 10.00–noon & 14.00–19.00 daily, 1–11 Nov 14.00–18.00 daily; €5.50, ages 13–17 €4.50, ages 2–12 €3) is a hamlet of tiny, drystone huts with breast-shaped stone roofs, the kind of place where Astérix or Obélix would feel perfectly at home. Similar *cabanes* (or *bories* or *gariottes)* exist in Provence and in Ireland, where they're called *clochans*, but whole villages of them are rare, and these are a historical monument. No-one knows who built them, or how long ago; the most likely answer is shepherds, who kept them in repair over the centuries.

In St-Crépin-et-Carlucet to the northeast, the **Château Lacypierre** [195 F1] (Le Bourg; m 06 48 71 30 16; w chateau-lacypierre-perigord.fr; guided tours in English: Jul–Aug 15.00 & 17.00 Mon–Thu, 15.00 Fri, 17.00 Sun, Apr–Jun & Sep–Oct 15.00 daily; €7.50, ages 7–12 €4) is a bijou 15th-century model, built by the Benié de Lacypierre family of magistrates and soldiers who served the kings of France. In the 19th century it became a farmhouse. The guides, Florence and Isabelle, grew up here and their mother wrote a history of its owners, which adds to its special charm.

Up the road, **Salignac-Eyvigues** is clustered under the impressive 11th–17th-century towers of the **Château de Salignac** (m 06 51 03 01 16; w billetweb.fr/visite-du-chateau-de-salignac; Jul–Aug 10.00–18.00 daily, May–Jun & Sep closed Tue; €6, under 18 free) built by François Fénelon's feudal ancestors, and hotly disputed in all the region's wars. After decades of abandon, it was purchased in 2006 by a family of gung-ho restorers, and you can visit their work in progress and buy a drink or ice cream in the cellar bar.

A hilltop on the edge of the village has something exceptional: the 17th-century **Manoir d'Eyrignac** [195 G1] (05 53 28 99 71; w eyrignac.com; Nov–Mar 10.30–12.30 & 14.30–nightfall daily, Apr & Oct 10.00–18.00 daily, May–Sep 09.30–19.00 daily; €13.50, ages 11–17 €8.90, ages 5–10 €6.90, family of 2 adults & up to 3 children €42; discounts if you book online). The first thing to know about Eyrignac is that it has been in the same family for over 500 years. And while exploring these 10ha of classic *jardin à la français*, you might conclude that current owner Patrick Sermadiras and the 21 generations that preceded him were put on earth for no other purpose than to make this lovely thing possible.

Like many great French gardens, it's not about flowers. The emphasis is on grand axes and patterns of sculpted bushes and hedges. There are seven different gardens, but everyone's favourite is the White Garden, with its abundance of pure white roses and frog fountain to complement the magnificent views over the countryside and surrounding woodland.

CARLUX TO DOMME: PAYS DU FÉNELON

This lush, far eastern corner of Périgord Noir takes up the River Dordogne as it winds out of Quercy (page 232). A good way to see it from Sarlat is take the D47/D478 to Carlux, then circle back west, or pedal the *voie verte* on the former Sarlat–Souillac railway line. Both banks of the river are lined with peaceful campsites and beaches, a far cry from the Hundred Years' War, when it divided the French to the north and the English to the south.

TOURIST INFORMATION The office at Gare Robert Doisneau in **Rouffillac-Carlux** (05 53 59 10 70; w fenelon-tourisme.com; May–Jun 10.30–12.30 & 13.00–17.00 daily, Jul–Aug 10.00–18.00 daily, Sep 10.00–18.00 Mon–Fri, 10.30–12.30 & 14.00–18.00 Sat–Sun, Oct–Apr 11.00–13.00 & 14.00–17.00 Tue–Sat) covers this whole area.

WHERE TO STAY AND EAT

La Villa Romaine (17 rooms) 12 Rue Marius Rossillon, Carsac-Aillac; 05 53 28 52 07; w lavillaromaine.com. The Romans were here, & now you can be too in the stone walls of this comfy 4-star hotel with a gourmet restaurant (**€€€€€**) & pool & park. **€€€€**

Le Relais du Touron (17 rooms) 3881 Rte de Gourdon, Carsac-Aillac; 05 53 28 16 70; w lerelaisdutouron.com. Very pleasant, peaceful hotel surrounded with direct access to gardens & pool from most rooms. The restaurant (eves only; €€€) puts on a good spread. €€

Delpeyrat (10 rooms) La Tavernerie, Carsac-Aillac; 05 53 28 10 43; w hotel-delpeyrat.fr. A charming family-run option by a park, with an excellent restaurant (€€) in the wood-beamed barn & pretty terrace under the trellis. €

Ô Moulin Place Martin Dolt, Carsac; 05 53 30 13 55; w latabledumoulin.com; closed Wed, lunch Tue, dinner Sun. Carsac has no fewer than 5 watermills, but only one offers superb market cuisine with a creative touch. It's tiny, excellent, with tables out on the lawn & you won't get in unless you book. *Menus from €35.* €€€€

L'Escapade Le Bourg, Carlux; 05 47 96 92 45; w lescapade-perigord.fr; closed Sun & eves Wed. Also 3 rooms (€) at this bar-restaurant, serving good, simple food. *4-course menus €13.50.* €€

La Garrigue Haute [195 G2] Prats-de-Carlux; 05 53 29 80 08; w lagarriguehaute.fr; Easter–Oct, eves only. Now run by the 7th generation, this is one of the few *ferme-auberges* specialising in goose as well as duck; booking essential. Also 7 peaceful rooms (€). *Superb menus from €21–€33.* €€

Diabolo Fraise [195 G5] Bourg, Nabirat (just south of Groléjac); 05 53 59 36 83; f Café-Restaurant-Le-Diabolo-Fraise; lunch only Mon–Fri. Rural France at its best; charming village, charming owner, & superb garden-fresh dishes. Only 1 menu – best to book & warn madame if there's something you can't eat. €

SPORTS AND ACTIVITIES Hire a bike in Sarlat (page 197) or at **Périgord Vélo** (Carsac-Aillac; m 07 88 09 71 45; w perigordvelo.com; May–Sep daily). **Canoë Dordogne Explorando** (Groléjac; m 06 74 24 40 81; canoedordogne.com) and **Canoë Carsac** (Les Bories Basses, Carsac; m 06 12 28 45 49; w canoe-carsac.com) rent out canoes and kayaks for a few hours or up to ten days.

CARLUX AND AROUND A big village north of the river, **Carlux** has a pair of romantic castles to admire: the mighty ruins of the 12th-century **Château de Carlux** in the centre and the 16th-century **Château de Rouffillac** [195 H3] (w chateauderouffillac.com) on a remarkable site in a holly-oak forest overlooking the Dordogne, now beautifully restored by its English/American owners and available to rent. In between, the delightful family-run **Jardins de Cadiot** [195 G3] (05 53 29 81 05; w lesjardinsdecadiot.com; May–Oct 10.00–19.00 daily; €7.50, students €6, under 15 free) were created 30 years ago, offering ten themed gardens with more than 2,000 plants, dotted with sculptures. Recently the old train station at Carlux has been converted into the **Gare Robert Doisneau** (home to the tourist office, page 203), with a permanent exposition of the 'slice of life' photos the famous photographer took during his holidays in this area before World War II, and which just go to show some things never change.

The bridge over the Dordogne here leads to **St-Julien-de-Lampon**, named after one of the few Gothic churches in the area; if it's open, pop in to see the 16th-century courtly paintings in the apse. Just to the west is **Ste-Mondane**. Mothers are often saints, but few are ever canonised, what with the Church's fantasies about virginity. One who made it into the ranks was Mondane, the mum of Sarlat's patron, St Sacerdos, who spent her later years in a cave here.

Although the cave is no longer a pilgrimage site, visitors still come to see the majestic **Château de Fénelon** [195 H3], piled on a set of terraces, defended by a triple ring of walls and gate towers (05 53 29 81 45; w chateau-fenelon.fr; Jul–Aug 10.30–18.30 Sun–Fri, Apr–Jun & Sep 10.30–12.30 & 14.30–18.00 Wed–Fri & Sun, Oct 14.00–17.00 Wed–Fri & Sun; €10, ages 12–17 €6.50, ages 5–11 €5.50). The Fénelons, here since the 11th century, converted to Catharism and held out against the Albigensian Crusaders, then rebuilt their castle in 1300 and swore allegiance to Edward III. When it was captured by the French in the early 15th century, it passed to the ancient Salignac family who added 'de la Mothe-Fénelon' to their name. One member, Bertrand de Salignac de la Mothe Fénelon, who served as ambassador to Scotland and England (1548–75), had the sticky task of keeping Elizabeth I on France's side after the St Bartholomew's Day massacre in 1572. Rebuilt in the 1600s as a lordly residence, it's one of the last châteaux crowned by a *lauze*-covered roof. The magnificent cedar of Lebanon by the gate was planted to celebrate the birth of François in 1651, a 13th child but one whose brain soon attracted attention (see box, page 241). The visit includes the medieval kitchens, the great Renaissance hall, a collection of 15th–18th-century arms and a display on wolf hunting, a cabinet of curiosities, and more.

CARSAC-AILLAC AND AROUND West, where the little River Enéa flows into the Dordogne, **Carsac-Aillac** has 16th–17th-century *lauze*-roofed houses, with the ruins of its castle on the hill. It has a charming 11th-century Romanesque church, **St-Caprais** (1 Place Martin Dolt; ☎05 53 59 03 16; ⌚ 08.30–19.30 daily). Damaged by the English, the nave and chapels were rebuilt in the 1500s, creating a striking interior of ogival vaults and capitals carved with surprising classical scenes, including a baby Hercules strangling the serpents that crept into his cradle. When the church was restored in 1940, new works, the stained glass and the Stations of the Cross were commissioned from Russian artist Léon Zack.

Just across the Dordogne, **Groléjac's** web of medieval streets conceals a little 18th-century château and a Romanesque church. Back over the bridge, you can visit the rare birds, animals and reptiles in the **Réserve Zoologique de Calviac** [195 G3] (Sous le Roc, Calviac-en-Périgord; ☎05 53 28 84 08; **w** reserve-calviac.org; ⌚ Feb–Mar & Oct–11 Nov 13.30–18.00, Apr–Jun & Sep 10.00–19.00 daily, Jul–Aug 09.30–19.00 daily; €14, students & ages 13–18 €12, ages 3–12 €9.50), a non-profit organisation linked to the Durrell Wildlife Conservation Trust, dedicated to the protection of endangered species from Madagascar, the Americas and Oceania.

Just outside Carsac, the bucolic **Jardins d'Eau** [195 F3] (St-Rome; ☎05 53 28 91 96; **w** jardinsdeau.com; ⌚ May–Aug 10.00–19.00 daily, Sep 11.00–18.00 daily; €8.50, students €7, ages 6–11 €5) has 3ha of pretty water gardens, with 55 kinds of water lily and 30 varieties of lotus, plus Europe's only water labyrinth. It's a paradise for dragonflies, and the kids can feed the koi.

The corniche road, the D703 between Carsac and **Vitrac**, passes the spectacular **Château de Montfort** [195 F3], hanging dramatically over one of the Dordogne's tightest loops. Mentioned in the 9th century as *monti forti*, it was owned by the late Francophile Saudi millionaire Gaith Pharaon, earning himself the local nickname the 'Pharaoh of the Valley of Kings'.

DOMME TO CASTELNAUD

The bastide of Domme, one of the great belvederes over the Dordogne, surveys the river as it winds west towards famous beauty spots such as La Roque-Gageac and Jardins de Marqueyssac and castles, castles, castles. From the mighty Château de Beynac, you can count six, including the menacing hulk of the Château de Castelnaud and the Renaissance Les Milandes, now a museum dedicated to its late great owner, Josephine Baker. This stunning region, a favourite for hot-air balloon flights and kayaking (in August there are even river traffic jams!), has always been a crossroads, these days for tourists but in the old days for merchants and armies – these castles weren't built for decoration.

Villefranche-du-Périgord's market is on Saturday, but it runs daily in autumn when the mushrooms are in season. In July and August, the tiny hilltop village of Loubéjac south of Villefranche is famous for miles around for its excellent Thursday-night market.

TOURIST INFORMATION

Beynac La Balme; 05 53 31 45 45; w sarlat-tourisme.com; Apr–Sep 10.00–13.00 & 14.00–17.00 daily, Oct 14.00–17.00 Fri, 10.00–noon & 14.00–17.00 Sat

Domme Place de la Halle; 05 53 31 71 00; w tourisme-domme.com; 10.00–12.30 & 13.30–18.00 daily, Dec–Feb school hols only

Villefranche-du-Périgord Rue Notre Dame; 05 53 29 98 37; w perigordnoir-valleedordogne.com; Jul–Aug 10.00–12.30 & 14.00–18.00 daily, other times closed Sun–Mon

WHERE TO STAY

Manoir de la Malartrie [195 E4] (5 rooms, 2 apts) Vézac; 05 53 29 03 51; w chambresdhotes-lamalartrie.com. Stunning place to stay in evocative, romantic rooms overlooking the Dordogne, with an elegant salon, heated pool & sheltered Mediterranean gardens in the cliffs. **€€€€€–€€€€**

Château de Maraval (4 rooms) Cénac-et-St-Julien; 05 53 31 82 77; w chateaudemaraval.fr. Just below Domme, in a 4ha park, pretty château with a heated pool & spa, & contemporary bedrooms. B/fast inc. **€€€€**

Domaine de Monrecour [195 D3] (31 rooms, 8 apts) Monrecour, St-Vincent de Cosse, 2km from Beynac; 05 53 28 33 59; w monrecour.com. In the 16th century, the barons of Beynac built this *maison de maitre* amid their vines, now a smart hotel. Two heated pools, pétanque court & playground wait in the 12ha park. A restaurant (€€€€) opened in 2020, with a bistro & gastronomic menus, & 500 tempting wines to choose from, visible behind glass. **€€€€–€€**

L'Esplanade (15 rooms) 2 Rue Pont Carral, Domme; 05 53 28 31 41; w esplanade-perigord.com. Family run & tranquil, with cosy rooms, some overlooking the Dordogne. The restaurant (€€€) serves some of the richest food in all of Périgord; lovely asparagus dishes when in season. **€€€**

Plaisance (40 rooms) Le Port, Vitrac; 05 53 31 39 39; w hotelplaisance.com. Made of stone, with a long garden terrace overlooking the river; there's a pretty restaurant (€€€€), heated pool & tennis. **€€€–€€**

Hôtel du Château (12 rooms) 2 Rue de la Balme, Beynac; 05 53 29 19 20; w hotelduchateau.fr. A tranquil hotel on the road up to the castle; its traditional restaurant (€€€) with a riverfront terrace makes good use of quality ingredients. **€€**

La Bastide (8 rooms) Rte de Cahors, Villefranche-du-Périgord; 05 53 30 22 67; w hotellabastide.fr. Little hotel with contemporary rooms & a gastronomic restaurant (€€€€), specialising in seafood, as well as lamb & beef dishes (€52 menu). There's a pretty pool & garden out back. **€€**

La Belle Etoile (13 rooms) La Roque-Gageac; 05 53 29 51 44; w logishotels.com. A modest but welcoming family hotel with a terrace & pretty views of the river & village. The excellent restaurant (€€€) attracts locals from far & wide. **€€**

Le Clos Roussillon (30 rooms) Vitrac; 05 53 28 13 00; w closroussillon-perigord.com. Pleasant, peaceful hotel with a pool, garden & 3 kinds of room to choose from. **€€**

Hostellerie Maleville-Pontet (13 rooms) Beynac, on the riverbank; 05 53 29 50 06; w hostellerie-maleville.com. Family-run since 1871, this pleasant Logis de France has a terrace right on the beach. **€**

La Ferme Fleurie [195 F4] (8 rooms) Le Colombier, La Roque-Gageac; 05 53 28 33 39; w fermefleurieperigord.com; Apr–Oct. Stay with the 6th generation of delightful owners on this farm with a garden & table d'hôte (€) located just outside the village. **€**

La Treille (7 rooms) Vitrac-Port; 05 53 28 33 19; w latreille-perigord.com. Right by the river, comfy rooms in an old inn, plus an excellent restaurant (€€€) serving French classic & exotic dishes as well. **€**

WHERE TO EAT AND DRINK

Le Saint Martial [195 F5] Le Bourg, St-Martial-de-Nabirat (9km southeast of Domme); 05 53 29 18 34; w lesaintmartial.com; Wed lunch–Sun. Colourful contemporary cuisine. *Menus from €45.* €€€€€

O' Plaisir des Sens D703, La Roque-Gageac; 05 53 29 58 53; w restaurant-o-plaisirdessens.com; closed Sun–Mon. Come here for Bruno Marien's beautifully presented dishes served in the handsome courtyard. *Exceptional w/day lunch menu €36.* €€€€€

Cabanoix Chataigne & Cie 3 Rue Geoffroy de Vivans, Domme; 05 53 31 07 11; w restaurantcabanoix.com; closed Tue–Wed. If you love foie gras, come here. Also succulent beef, pork & duck *tatin de Canard Forestier*. Vegans & vegetarians can ring ahead & order a meal just for them. *Menus from €26.* €€€

Le Fat Pig La Roque-Gageac; 05 53 30 13 38; w fat-pig.fr; closed Thu. Same owners as Sarlat's Gueule & Gosier & just as good – all fresh, delicious & *fait maison. 2-course menu €24, 3 courses €28.* €€€

Le Petit Paris Daglan; 05 53 28 41 10; w le-petit-paris.fr; closed Mon. Tiny Daglan boasts the best restaurant south of Domme, in a big stone house that once served as the local bar-tabac, with a table outside in the square. *Menus from €29.* €€€

Les Près Gaillardou [195 E4] D703 Gaillardou, La Roque-Gageac; 05 53 59 67 89; w lespresgaillardou.com; closed Wed & eves Sun & Tue. Limited menu but highly recommended for its quality, served in a charming stone building or on the summer terrace. €€€

Le Tournepique Castelnaud-la-Chapelle; 05 53 29 51 07; w restaurantletournepique.fr. Right on the river, Basque cuisine on a flowery terrace with seafood, omelettes & summer salads & *la potence de boeuf* (steak flambéed on an iron hook). €€€

Auberge de la Rode Place de la Rode, Domme; 05 53 28 36 97; f Auberge-De-La-Rode-Domme; closed eves Tue. A reliable old favourite, with duck but also seafood & mushroom risotto. Save room for one of their luscious desserts. €€€–€€

Ferme Auberge Le Colombier [195 E3] D703, La Roque-Gageac; 05 53 28 33 97; closed Mon & eves Sun. Feast on homegrown Périgourdin goodies with a twist (*crumble de confit, magret à la plancha*) in this former tobacco barn. *Menus €20–€35.* €€

La Borie Blanche [195 F4] 6km east of Domme, off the D50; m 06 50 32 18 05; daily. Something different at this friendly *ferme-auberge*, with their own succulent grilled beef on the menu instead of duck. *Menus from €19.* €€

La Forge St-Pompont; 05 53 28 89 09; f Restaurant-La-Forge; lunch only exc Fri, closed Sat–Sun. New restaurant in the old blacksmith's shop, offering big smiles & good cooking. Try the cheesecake for dessert. €€

Ô Faim Goût'R Mets Rue Notre Dame, Villefranche-du-Périgord; 05 53 30 16 45; w ofaimgoutrmets.wixsite.com/ofgm; 09.30–15.00 & 17.30–midnight Tue–Sat. Young chef prepares some surprises in this brasserie, with a good choice of craft beers. €€

Le Chalet Le Bras, Domme; 05 53 29 32 73; 09.00–22.00 daily. Riverside brasserie by the beach, with steak frites, salads, etc with views of the cliffs & passing kayaks. €€–€

Pizzeria des Templiers Place Porte des Tours, Domme; m 06 02 29 04 30; f; closed lunch Wed & Sat. Pizzas, pasta & salads, on a pretty outdoor terrace. €

SPORTS AND ACTIVITIES

Hot-air balloon trips

Montgolfière Châteaux Les Louardes, Beynac-et-Cazenac; m 06 71 14 34 96; w montgolfiere-chateaux.fr. Hot-air balloon rides from €190 pp.

Montgolfière du Périgord Clos Saint Donat, La Roque-Gageac; 05 53 28 18 58; w montgolfiere-du-perigord.com. Balloon tours from €215 pp; also special flights for families with kids ages 7–11 for €110 pp.

Périgord Dordogne Montgolfières Castelnaud; m 06 83 26 47 66; w perigord-dordogne-montgolfieres.com. Balloon tours from €205 pp (ages 6–12 €115 pp).

Other activities

Beynac Gabarres Beynac; 05 53 28 51 15; w gabarre-beynac.com; May–Sep 10.00–18.00, Apr & Oct 11.00–17.00 daily; €9, ages 4–12 €5, children go free on morning departures. Riverboat cruises.

Canoë Dordogne La-Roque-Gageac; m 06 08 54 86 89; w canoesdordogne.fr. Kayaks for 1–4 people.
Couleurs Périgord Chemin de la Dordogne, Vézac; m 06 81 68 43 11; w ladordogneencanoe.com. Multi-day kayaking, rock climbing, caving, etc.

Norbert Gabarres La Roque-Gageac; 05 53 29 40 44; w gabarres.com; late May–Sep 09.30–18.00 daily, Oct afternoon only; €10.90, under 13 €8.50. 1hr tours of the cliffs & châteaux on this stretch of the Dordogne.

DOMME Honey-hued Domme is a bastide, but one whose classic grid plan was transplanted on to a 250m bluff over the Dordogne, earning it the nickname the 'Acropolis of Périgord'. Philippe III founded it in 1281, and, although he granted it many favours, he had to resort to threats to get the locals to build and settle his baby – including only paying his workers in leather coins 'minted', or rather cut out, at the mint in Place de la Rode, Domme's oldest building.

Despite its natural defences, Domme was captured several times: by the English, the counts of Périgord and, in 1588 during the Wars of Religion, by Henri of Navarre's captain, Geoffroy de Vivans – although only on the fourth try, after he established a secret arms depot halfway up the cliff and laid coats on the bare rock to muffle the noise of their approach.

These days it's much easier to drive up through the 13th-century **Porte des Tours** (Apr–Sep 14.15–17.00 Fri–Sun; €4, students €3, under 12 €2), framed by two fat guard towers built by Philip the Fair. These were converted into prisons in 1307 when the king ordered the arrest of the Knights Templars; some of them lingered here until 1318, engraving crucifixes and other mysterious graffiti on the walls. Domme's other gates are also intact: the arched **Porte de la Combe** to the south and the **Porte del Bos**, still grooved for its portcullis.

As with any bastide, the focal point of Domme is its market square, **Place de la Halle**, although no other bastide square is quite like this: the church gives on to the **Belvédère de la Barre**, with views stretching from Montfort to Beynac. When Vivans made it over the cliff he took care to destroy the **church**, which is why the current one isn't much. However, Place de la Halle boasts other fine buildings: the turreted Governor's House from the 1500s, now the tourist office, and **Oustal de Périgord** (05 53 31 71 00; May–Jun & Sep 10.30–12.30 & 14.30–18.00 daily, Jul–Aug 10.30–19.00 daily; €5, students €4, under 12 €3), with rooms fitted out 19th-century style.

The charming 17th-century *halle* offers more than the usual turnips and carrots – the entrance into Domme's very bowels, through the **Grotte de Domme** (05 53 31 71 00; w sites-domme.com; tours: Jul–Aug 10.30–19.00 daily, Apr–Jun & Sep 10.30–12.30 & 14.30–18.00 daily, Feb–Mar & Oct 11.00 & 14.00–16.00 daily; €9, students €7.50, under 12 €6.50). Although the lower part of the cave was used as a refuge during the Hundred Years' War, the upper part, where fossilised bison and deer bones have been found, was discovered only in 1954; beyond is a stalactite phantasmagoria that ends with a ride in a glass lift up the cliff, depositing you near the Jardin Publique, with the option of walking back to the Belvédère along the cliff walk.

Just below Domme in **Cénac-et-St-Julien**, some exceptionally lively Romanesque sculpture is concentrated in **Notre-Dame-de-la-Nativité** (1090s). Vivans smashed this church as well, but fortunately gave up before reaching the apse. Nearby, on the grounds of the **Château du Thouron**, is a massive plane tree planted in 1750, called **Thermidor** after the name for the summer month on the Revolutionary calendar.

A DETOUR SOUTH OF DOMME TO VILLEFRANCHE-DU-PÉRIGORD All is rural tranquillity south of Domme, especially along the D60, fringed by chestnut forests and meadows. The Brigadoon stillness that reigns here (except during the autumn,

PÉRIGORD'S MAYPOLES

A common sight in these parts is a tall pole, usually from a poplar, decorated with hoops and *tricouleurs* and a sign reading *'Honneur à Notre Maire'*, or *'Honneur au Patron'* or *'à Notre Élu'*, or *'aux mariés'* with the names of a newly married couple. They are called *arbres de Mai*, or maypoles, and are erected at boozy confabs known as Plantations de l'Arbre de Mai. Once up, they are meant to gradually rot away rather than ever be taken down. The Périgourdins have been planting maypoles ever since Gallo-Roman times, when a newly elected official would be honoured with a similar pole crowned with a garland.

when the hunters are out) makes the few 'sights' somehow more magical for being unexpected. The elongated village of **Daglan** with its curious, fortified, cross-shaped **Château de Peyruzel** [195 E5] (private) from the 1600s, has drystone cabanes and walls that testify to its past as a vine-growing area before phylloxera. The **Maison de la Pierre Seche et du Causse** (05 53 29 88 84; w maisonpierreseche.org; Apr–Oct 10.30–12.30 & 14.30–17.00 Tue–Fri; free) tells their story. Medieval **St-Pompont**, just west, has a pair of châteaux and a mini-maze of medieval houses huddled beneath the fortified church and gate. Further south lies remote **Prats-du-Périgord**, with an even mightier 12th-century church of **St-Maurice** with a 20m *clocher-mur* and 16th-century château.

From Prats (Occitan for 'meadows'), follow the signs for **Besse**, an even tinier hamlet, with yet another château and an overbearing fortified 11th-century church of **St-Martin**. This one is special: not only has it held on to its *lauze* roof, but also a vigorous sculpted porch. There's God sternly appearing in the Garden of Eden, a rarely depicted scene of an angel placing a hot coal on the lips of Isaiah (Isaiah 6: 6–8), another upside-down angel rescuing St Peter from prison, St Eustache the hunter pursuing a stag and St Michael killing the dragon.

To guard Périgord's southernmost marches, Alphonse de Poitiers founded the bastide of **Villefranche-du-Périgord** 7km further south in 1261. Although the grid plan and a fountain survive from Alphonse's day, Villefranche's central square has taken a lot of licks, leaving only one row of arcades facing the stone-pillared *halle*. The church sharing the square is a more maladroit than usual 19th-century rebuilding of the original; adjacent to the tourist office, the **Maison de la Châtaigne** is devoted to the town's famous chestnuts and ceps (and has the same hours; page 206).

LA ROQUE-GAGEAC The car park along the Dordogne is five times as large as the entire village of La Roque-Gageac, heightening the effect of a two-dimensional stage set. In truth, there isn't room for much depth when you build into the face of an overhanging cliff; the warm stone houses and their brown roofs are piled against it so harmoniously they almost look as if they have grown there naturally. An **exotic garden** of cacti and palms thrives by the little 16th-century **church**. Reality does intrude occasionally, when bits of the cliff break off and fall like meteors through the roofs.

For a 180-degree view over the Dordogne, climb up the stair in the cliff to the **Fort de la Roque-Gageac** (05 53 31 04 08; w fortdelaroquegageac.com; Apr–mid-Nov 09.30–19.30; €6.50, students €5.50, ages 5–13 €3.50), where big metal columns now hold up the roof after it part collapsed in 2010. A film shows what it was like when the fort was the last refuge for locals in case of attack. At the eastern end of La Roque stands the manor house once owned by Jean Tarde, a humanist scholar and friend of Galileo who left a moving chronicle of the devastation wrought by the Wars of Religion in the area.

LES JARDINS SUSPENDUS DE MARQUEYSSAC [195 E4] (05 53 31 36 36; w marqueyssac.com; Apr–Jun & Sep 10.00–19.00 daily, Jul–Aug 09.00–20.00 daily, Feb–Mar, Oct–14 Nov 10.00–18.00 daily, 15 Nov–Jan 14.00–17.00 daily; book tickets online €9.90, ages 10–17 €5, under 10 free, combined with Castelnaud (see below) €19/€9.50, candlelit eves (Jul–Aug dusk–midnight Thu) €20/€10) One of the beauty spots of France, these gardens laid out in the 16th century are gloriously romantic, with waterfalls, rockeries and 150,000 ancient box hedges (which managed to survive the recent nasty infestation of box-hedge-eating caterpillars) trimmed in extravagant forms and laid out on terraces with enchanting views over the river. A pleasant tearoom waits by the exit.

CHÂTEAU DE BEYNAC [195 E3] (Beynac-et-Cazenac; 05 53 29 50 40; w chateau-beynac.com; 10.00–19.00 daily; €9.50, ages 12–16 €7; park at the top or it's a good 20min walk up) You've probably spotted this mighty castle of 1,115m looming high over the Dordogne. Barons of Périgord, the Beynacs were every bit as daunting and fierce as their castle. When Richard the Lionheart made it known that he meant to confiscate their land and give it to his devoted Captain Mercadier, the Beynacs joined forces with Fortanier of Gourdon, whose father and brothers had been killed by Richard, and who had vowed to seek revenge. In March 1199, when Richard and Mercadier came down to besiege Châlus (a castle just over the border in the Limousin), Fortanier shot an arrow that caught the king in a gap in his armour. Richard died a few days later, and not long after that the Beynacs liquidated Mercadier. Problem solved.

In 1214 Simon de Montfort attacked Beynac and its baron, who was nicknamed the 'Arca satana' (Satan's Bow), for being a devoted friend of the Cathar-friendly Count Raymond VI of Toulouse. Although de Montfort spared Satan's Bow when King Philippe Auguste personally intervened, he destroyed the château's most imposing towers. During the Hundred Years' War, French Beynac fought a constant war against English Castelnaud across the river, although all the quarrelling had a happy ending when a Beynac daughter married the Marquis of Castelnaud in 1761.

The interior of the castle has been through numerous transformations: there's a monumental 17th-century stairway, a Grand Siècle salon with a sculpted wooden chimney carved with mythologies, a *Sacrifice of Isaac* done with provincial panache, and late 15th-century frescoes in the Oratory (which, stylistically, are only about 400 years behind Tuscany) of the *Last Supper*, the *Pietà* and the *Man of Sorrows*. In the *Last Supper*, note the rare portrayal of the occasion's *maître d'* – St Martial, the apostle of Aquitaine.

CHÂTEAU DE CASTELNAUD AND MUSÉE DE LA GUERRE AU MOYEN AGE [195 E4] (Castelnaud-la-Chapelle; 05 53 31 30 00; w castelnaud.com; same as Marqueyssac, see above; €11.90, ages 10–17 €6, combined with Marqueyssac €19/€9.50) Opposite Beynac, the powerful hulk of its eternal nemesis, Castelnaud stands undaunted on the limestone cliffs. First mentioned in 1214, when its Cathar lord was chased out by Simon de Montfort, Castelnaud's rulers, the Caumonts, stuck with the English during the Hundred Years' War and let them use it as a base from which to terrorise the surrounding countryside. Then they let Henri IV's Huguenot Captain Geoffroy de Vivans use Castelnaud for similar exploits, although by that time the family had moved out of the stark, dark little rooms of this feudal fort into Les Milandes (see opposite). Abandoned after the Revolution, the castle is rather appropriately once again full of catapults, swords and crossbows. There are films on medieval warfare, and in summer they shoot off the trebuchets.

Below the castle, the **Éco Musée de la Noix** [195 E4] (Domaine de Vielcroze; 05 53 59 69 63; w ecomuseedelanoix.fr; Apr–11 Nov 10.00–19.00 daily; €5, ages 10–17 €4, under 5 free) occupies an 18th-century farm amid 7ha of walnut groves, where you learn about the nutty side of Périgord Noir, and dine on walnut dishes in the little restaurant.

CHÂTEAU LES MILANDES [194 D4] (05 53 59 31 21; w milandes.com; Feb–Mar 14.00–18.00, Apr–Jun 09.30–19.00, Jul–Aug 09.00–20.00, Oct–Nov 09.30–18.00; €12.50, ages 5–16 €8 (mid-May–11 Nov bird of prey show inc, see website for times), best to book online) A wooded road from Castelnaud follows the river past the 14th–17th-century Château de Fayrac [195 E3] (private) to this Renaissance beauty built by François de Caumont for his bride, Claude de Cardaillac, which he filled with frescoes and sculptures. Their grandson, raised as a priest, took his conversion to Protestantism so seriously that he smashed all these worldly things to bits. After passing through other hands and falling into ruin, it was purchased in 1900 and restored by a local industrialist.

In the 1930s, while Josephine Baker was on holiday in the Dordogne, Les Milandes cast a spell on her almost as powerful as the spell she had cast over Paris with her joyful, exuberant versions of the Charleston and Black Bottom. Of all the black Americans who came to France to escape racism at home, Josephine Baker was the most successful, becoming the highest-paid performer in Europe, enabling her to rent in 1940, then in 1946 purchase Les Milandes and the surrounding 243ha. Her goal was to create a 'Global Village' with her husband, bandleader Jo Bouillon. They adopted 12 children of every race and creed, her 'Rainbow Tribe', and ran an amusement park and a restaurant, put on shows and hosted anti-racism conferences. But she was terrible with money and she fell so deeply into debt that in 1964 Les Milandes went into administration – Brigitte Bardot, a huge fan, launched an appeal but by 1968 Baker's dream château went to the highest bidder. Another fan, Princess Grace, found her a home in Monaco, and she had just started a comeback tour in 1975, trying to make money to pay back her debts, when she died. In 2021, she became one of the only women, and the first person of colour, to be interred in the Pantheon in Paris, alongside Rousseau and Voltaire.

Today Les Milandes is a wonderful shrine to Josephine Baker's memory, filled with her glamorous costumes and her famous skirt of upturned bananas; there are hundreds of photos, posters, recordings of her songs and films of her extraordinary dance moves. But there are also displays on her work in the Resistance that won her the Légion d'Honneur in 1961, and her work in the American civil rights movement, when she was the only woman to speak at Martin Luther King's March on Washington in 1963. Admission includes the beautiful gardens, and in season a demonstration of falconry, complete with a mechanical rabbit and ferret. The lovely Flamboyant Gothic chapel, where Josephine and Jo were married, is currently undergoing restoration. There's a bar/brasserie on the property, and just down the lane from the château, a house has on its corner a statue of the Virgin Mary carved with Josephine's features.

ST-CYPRIEN TO LIMEUIL

The next west bridge over the Dordogne is at St-Cyprien, a village overlooking the fertile alluvial plain that has long been the source of its fat, contented air. South of the river the splendid Gothic cloister at Cadouin recalls its pilgrimage heyday, while further south is the hill town of Belvès with its secret underground world and

Villefranche-du-Périgord, set among mushroom-, chestnut- and wild-boar-filled woodlands. Then the Vézère kicks in at Limeuil (page 192).

Markets are held at St-Cyprien on Sundays, Belvès on Saturdays, Le Buisson on Fridays and Siorac on Wednesdays.

GETTING THERE The Sarlat–Bordeaux RER line runs through here five or six times a day, with stations at Siorac and Le Buisson de Cadouin; the latter is also on the Périgueux–Agen line, along with Villefranche-du-Périgord, Belvès and Siorac.

TOURIST INFORMATION All share the same website: w perigordnoir-valleedordogne.com.

Belvès 1 Rue de Filhols; 05 53 29 10 20; Apr–Sep 10.00–12.30 & 14.00–17.30 daily, May & Oct closed Mon

St-Cyprien Place Charles de Gaulle; 05 53 30 36 09; 10.00–12.30 & 14.00–18.00 Mon–Sat

WHERE TO STAY

Le Clément V (10 rooms) 15 Rue Jacques Manchotte, Belvès; 05 53 28 68 80; w clement5.com. A former *épicerie* converted into a charming hotel with a wide choice of rooms & suites, furnished with antiques. **€€€€€–€€€**

Hôtel des Augustins (12 rooms) 49 Rue Gambetta, St-Cyprien; 05 53 28 73 08; w hoteldesaugustins.com. This historic inn of 1880 has been given a new lease of life, with contemporary rooms, a gourmet restaurant (€€€), bar & big wine cellar. **€€€**

L'Atelier d'Épicure [194 D3] (9 apts) Argentonesse, Castels, near St-Cyprien; 05 53 30 40 95; w latelierdepicure.com. New arty apts on an 18th-century farm complex, with a pool & spa. The excellent restaurant (€€€) is worthy of the hotel's name. **€€€**

Relais du Périgord Noir (41 rooms) Place de la Poste, Siorac-en-Périgord; 05 53 31 60 02; w relais-perigord-noir.fr. Well-equipped 3-star hotel with a bar, wine bar/restaurant (€€€), fitness room, pool & tranquil garden; massages available. **€€€–€€**

Villa Marguerite (5 rooms) 2 place Géraud de Salles, Cadouin; m 06 16 10 34 99; w villa-marguerite-cadouin.com. Big bourgeoise house with a garden & rooms of character; tasty table d'hôte available. B/fast inc. **€€€–€€**

Auberge de la Petite Reine (55 rooms) Siorac-en-Périgord; 05 53 31 60 42; w hotelperigordnoir.com; Jun–Nov. Near the Lolivarie Golf Course, a club-like family-oriented hotel with a good restaurant (€€), covered pool & other sports in a large park. **€€**

La Salvetat [194 A4] (6 rooms, 3 gîtes) La Salvetat, Rte de Belvés, Le Buisson-de-Cadouin; m 06 38 21 16 95; w lesalvetat.com. Rooms in a 12th-century *presbytère* in a pretty garden setting, surrounded by 14ha of meadows, with a pool & e-bike hire service. Delicious table d'hôte meals €25. B/fast inc. **€€**

Le Home (10 rooms) Place de la Croix-des-Frères, Belvès; 09 70 35 03 65; w restaurant-hotel-lehome.com. Recently renovated rooms, & a popular restaurant (€€€) with plenty of seafood choices. **€€**

Auberge le Trèfle à Quatre Feuilles (5 rooms, 1 gîte) 174 Rue de la Gare, Siorac-en-Périgord; 05 53 31 60 26; w letrefle4feuilles.com. Simple hotel near the castle, with rooms in a country style. Intimate restaurant (€€€) featuring creative dishes with locally sourced ingredients, served on a pretty summer terrace. **€**

La Grande Marque [194 C4] (5 rooms, 4 flats) Marnac, east of Siorac; 05 53 31 61 63; w lagrandemarque.fr. Very friendly English owners run this lovely chambre d'hôte set in its own park with breathtaking views. Delicious dinners (€€) prepared each evening from local farm ingredients. **€**

Le Chambellan (13 rooms) Place de l'Église, Coux et Bigaroque; 05 53 29 90 11; w hotel-chambellan.fr. Simple, peaceful rooms sleeping up to 7; 800m from the beach with a good restaurant (€€) & playground. **€**

Le Petit Chaperon Rouge [194 C3] (6 rooms) La Faval, Coux-et-Bigaroque; 05 53 29 37 79; w chaperonrouge.fr. Hidden among trees, Little Red Riding Hood's rooms offer old-fashioned comfort, while the restaurant (€€) with its plants & fairy lights overlooking the valley, is enchanting. €

WHERE TO EAT AND DRINK

Auberge l'Espérance Av des Sycomores 3, Le Buisson-de-Cadouin; 05 53 74 23 66; w lesperance.eatbu.com; closed Tue–Wed. A local favourite, with good reason: it has a bucolic garden terrace, superb creative dishes – & very pretty pet chickens. *W/day lunch menu from €29.* €€€€

Auberge de la Nauze [194 C4] Fongauffier, Sagelat (north of Belvès); 05 53 28 44 81; w aubergedelanauze.com; Jul–Aug closed Mon–Tue, other times closed Mon, eves Tue & lunch Sat. Contemporary cuisine served on a pretty terrace, & a good mix of seafood & meat choices. Also 6 rooms (**€€–€**). *4-course menu €38.* €€€

Les Terrasses de la Côte Rouge 6 Rue de la Côte Rouge 2, Cadouin; m 06 38 99 73 02; w lesterrassesdelacoterouge.fr; closed Wed. Charming owners, charming terrace looking over the abbey bell tower, & charming organic cuisine with an Italian touch; vegan dishes offered too. Bookings essential. €€€–€€

Le Médiéval 34 Rue Jacques Manchotte, Belvès; 05 53 30 29 83; f LeMedievalBistrot.fr; daily. Popular bistro with a Breton touch & succulent steaks. €€

Restaurant de l'Abbaye 1 Place de l'Abbaye, Le Buisson-de-Cadouin; 05 53 63 40 93; closed Mon & Thu & eves Sun. Very popular spot (be sure to try the garlic soup). *Lunch menus from €17.50.* €€

Planche et Plonk 34 Rue Jacques Manchotte, Belvès; 05 53 28 21 70; w planchesetplonk.com; closed Mon–Tue. Huge wine list, superb *fromage et charcuterie* platters & cosy atmosphere run by Damon & Graham, who also operate a wine shop by the covered market. Above the bar, *2 chambres d'hôte* (**€€**). Ask about their Oct–Mar gourmet w/ends.

SPORTS AND ACTIVITIES **Canoë River** (Le Buisson de Cadouin; 05 53 22 95 88, 05 53 08 28 57 (Oct–Apr); w canoe-river.com) rents canoes and kayaks by the hour or day. There's enough flat land here for golf courses: the 9-hole **Golf de la Forge** [194 C4] (Siorac-en-Périgord; 05 53 31 99 76; w golfdelaforge.fr) and the 18-hole **Lolivarie Golf Club** [194 C4] (St-Germain-de-Belvès; 05 53 30 22 69; w lolivariegolfclub.com).

ST-CYPRIEN In the Middle Ages the Romanesque church with its bulky 12th-century bell tower had an important relic for pilgrims – the Sainte-Épine, or holy thorn, which monks rubbed against the clothes of sick people. Today it's best known for its recently restored organ and summer concerts.

MUSÉE LA RUE DU TEMPS QUI PASSE [194 D3] (Sandou, Allas-les-Mines, just east of Berbiguières; 05 53 28 27 82; w musee-laruedutempsquipasse.fr; Apr–Jun & Sep 10.00–noon & 14.00–18.00 Fri–Tue, Jul–Aug 10.00–18.00 daily, Oct–11 Nov 14.00–18.00 Fri–Tue; €7.50, ages 6–12 €6) A father–daughter team have recreated a nostalgic street of *la douce France* of yesteryear (1840–1960 to be precise) with authentic antiques, signs and more, and where you can even taste the drinks popular a century ago in the bistro.

BELVÈS There's another bridge at Siorac, once the port for the ancient hill town of Belvès, 5km south. Known as the city of seven bell towers, it has been inhabited for donkey's years – its name comes from a local Celtic tribe, the Bellovaques. It went from a fortified Roman *castrum* to an English town in the Middle Ages; a ring boulevard now replaces the walls that surrounded it. Within the ring, however, the old plan remains intact, as a kind of proto-bastide, the straight narrow lanes lined with Gothic and Renaissance buildings.

In the central Place d'Armes stands a last relic of Belvès's defences, the **Tour des Fillols**, and a 15th- and 16th-century ***halle***, supported by 23 pillars, one still bearing the chains from pre-Revolutionary days when it doubled as a pillory. In the 12th century those folks who couldn't afford to build a house, dug one 6m underground: known as **Les Troglos de Belvès**, some were inhabited into the 18th century (fascinating guided tour (English by request) Mon–Sat via the tourist office, ring to book; €7, students €5.50, children €4.50). One of the bell towers belongs to the Gothic church **Notre Dame de l'Assomption** (05 53 29 10 20; daily); when it was restored, its colourful, homespun 16th–19th-century murals of virtues, saints and prophets were revealed.

For a real taste of homespun, however, head down just south to the 15th-century watermill housing the **Filature de Belvès** [194 C4] (Fongauffier, Monplaisant; 05 53 31 83 05; w filaturedebelves.com; Jun & Sep 14.00–18.00 Sun–Fri, Jul–Aug 10.00–19.00 daily, Oct–May 14.00–18.00 Mon–Fri; €8.50, ages 6–18 €6, under 6 free) dedicated to the wool industry. Ten historic machines transform raw wool into yarn, notably for the Aubusson tapestry works; there are demonstrations, hands-on activities and games, and a boutique.

BACK ON THE DORDOGNE

Le Buisson-de-Cadouin This village, once known only for its beaches and train station, now has its share of attractions. Start with the exotic **Jardin de Planbuisson** (18 Rue Montaigne; 05 53 57 68 02; w planbuisson.com; Apr–Jun & Sep–Oct 10.00–noon & 14.00–18.00 Wed–Sun, Jul–Aug 10.00–19.00 daily; €7, ages 12–18 €3), the obsession of the late Michel Bonfils, who in the 1990s became so fascinated by bamboo that he planted 240 varieties, in one of the most important collections in Europe – along with rare grasses and trees from around the world.

Then, in 2000, Angel Cabellero discovered the **Grottes de Maxange** [194 B3], 'the cave of stars' (Mestréguiral; 05 53 23 42 80; w lesgrottesdemaxange.com; guided tours Apr–Jun & Sep 10.00–noon & 14.00–18.00 daily, Jul–Aug 09.30–19.00 daily, Oct 10.00–noon & 14.00–17.00; €8.90, ages 4–12 €5.90). Formed 60 million years ago, Maxange is famous for the exquisite quality and beauty of its crystallised formations created by the special porous qualities of the limestone.

The same year, another speleologist, Marc Delluc, discovered something even rarer: the **Grotte de Cussac** [194 A3], with such startlingly beautiful pictures of animals traced in the clay 30,000 years ago that it was soon dubbed 'the Lascaux of engravings'. It was also the first decorated Palaeolithic cave that also contained skeletons laid out in a ritual manner. Because it has dangerous levels of carbon dioxide, it may never be opened to the public – although the *Atelier des facsimilés du Périgord* is creating a digital replica: stay tuned.

Cadouin In 1115, a holy man named Géraud de Salles and a group of canons from Périgueux's St-Front founded a monastery at the end of a wooded valley. Four years later they built a vast Romanesque church and cloister in the Norman style; at the end of the 15th century the cloister collapsed and was lavishly rebuilt by masons from Languedoc and the Rouergue. Why such an ambitious enterprise in the middle of the forest? Because in 1117 the abbey bagged a relic that put it square on the pilgrims' path – the Saint Suaire, the cloth used to wrap the head of Christ at his burial. Pilgrims en route to Compostela poured in, as well as Eleanor of Aquitaine, Richard the Lionheart and St Louis.

The centre of the village has a sturdy Flamboyant ***halle*** supported on stone pillars, facing the **Abbey Church** consecrated in 1154. All the austere decoration of the asymmetrical façade is in triplicate: three flat buttresses, three doorways, three windows and nine blind arches, while the interior, with its three naves and domes, has been stripped bare by Cadouin's 19th-century restorers to reveal the vigorous architecture in all its purity. The reliquary holding the Saint Suaire hung behind the altar; only the dangling chains remain.

The star of the show is the lovely, Flamboyant Gothic **Cloister** (05 53 63 36 28; w cloitre-cadouin.fr; Jan–Jun & Sep–Oct 10.00–13.00 & 1400–18.00 daily, Jul–Aug 10.00–19.30 daily, Nov–Dec 10.00–13.00 & 14.00–17.00 daily; €7.20, ages 5–12 €4.40, under 5 free, combined ticket with Château de Biron (page 227) €12.50/€8). This took so long to build that even a remote spot like Cadouin fell under the spell of the Renaissance before it was completed; while the older galleries have Gothic pinnacles carved with curly kale and thistles, the west gallery, built in the 1500s, is entirely Renaissance. The reliefs offer a hearty mix of sacred and profane, and include an anti-feminist trilogy: Samson and Delilah, a scene from the Lays of Virgil, and a courtesan straddling Aristotle (her name is Phyllis; this is from a medieval legend warning against the vanity of scholars).

In 1934, a scientific examination of the Saint Suaire showed it to be a fine Egyptian weaving from the 11th century. An even greater embarrassment was the discovery that what for centuries had been considered a decorative border was in fact an Arabic inscription in praise of Allah. Today it discreetly lies in a copper gilt reliquary in a little museum in the Salle Capitulaire.

10

Bergerac and the Bergeracais

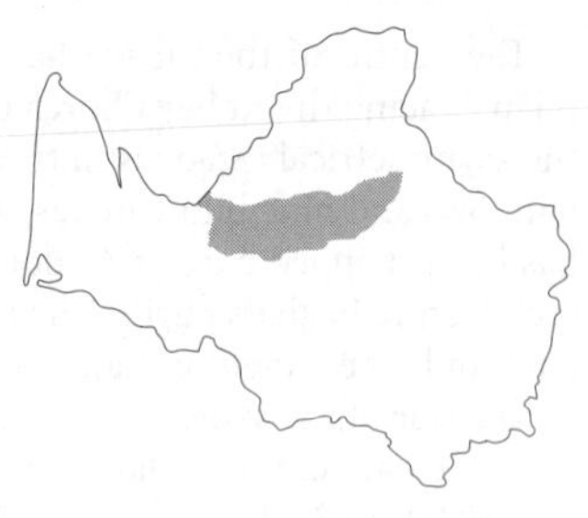

After White, Green and Black Périgord, this westerly region of département 24 has been christened 'Purple Périgord' for its fine wines – including tannin-rich Pécharmant and two sweet golden wines, Monbazillac and Saussignac. Before straightening out, the big river has a last madly scenic curly fling just up from the city around Trémolat. The *pays* of Bergerac, often on the frontlines of the wars that rocked southwest France, also boasts the beautiful film-set village of Issigeac, two exceptionally pretty bastides, Monpazier and Eymet, and the enormous castle at Biron, home to one of the four barons of Périgord.

BERGERAC

Bergerac, known far and wide as the name of a poetic cavalier with a big nose who never set foot there, is a lively little city where a cluster of medieval, half-timbered houses bask by the old river port. Perhaps, back in the days when Bogart could seduce Bacall by blowing smoke in her face, it would have been dubbed Nicotine-Brown Périgord: tobacco, first popularised in France by Catherine de' Medici (who used it to cure her migraines), was once a major crop.

HISTORY Bergerac's name is derived from *Braca* ('breeches') which suggests its first industry was producing Gaulish trousers. It grew up around a feudal castle, but really took off as a town in the 12th century with the construction of a bridge – at that time the only one on the river; from there it naturally evolved into a commercial centre and port. The bridge also brought trouble: in 1345, Henry of Grosmont brought his army here and routed the French in the Battle of Bergerac, and demolished much of the town.

Like most of France's self-reliant mercantile communities, the Bergeracois converted to Protestantism with gusto; during the Wars of Religion it was known as the 'French Geneva'. In 1553, all the churches were dismantled for stone to build ramparts; in 1567, they destroyed the bridge to keep any Catholics from crossing over. Although a peace treaty was signed in 1577, the strong religious convictions of its merchants spelt the slow death of Bergerac as a commercial city. First the walls of the city were destroyed by Richelieu in 1620; in 1681 dragoons arrived to force the Huguenots to convert to Catholicism; then in 1685 Louis XIV revoked the Edict of Nantes, denying them the right to worship. By the end of the 17th century, an estimated 40,000 inhabitants had emigrated to England and Holland. The city revived only at the end of the 19th century thanks to tobacco and wine.

GETTING THERE AND AWAY Bergerac's **airport** at Roumanières (3km south on Rte d'Agen; 05 53 22 25 25; **w** bergerac.aeroport.fr) is the busiest in the Dordogne.

Buses (☎ 09 70 87 08 70; w transports.nouvelle-aquitaine.fr) link it to Périgueux, to Eymet and Marmande, and to Issigeac and Villeneuve-sur-Lot for only €2 – on the condition you book before 17.00 the day before; all of these go by way of Bergerac's **train station** [221 C1], on the Bordeaux–Sarlat line. There are several car hire firms at the airport; Avis and Europcar also have offices near the station.

GETTING AROUND Bergerac is easily do-able on foot, with several payable **car parks** by the centre at Place Forail [221 C5], Place des Carmes [221 C3] and Place Gambetta [221 A3].

If you need a **taxi**, call ☎ 05 53 23 32 32.

TOURIST INFORMATION Bergerac's **tourist office** [221 A5] (☎ 05 53 57 03 11; w pays-bergerac-tourisme.com; ⌚ May–Sep 10.00–19.00 daily, Oct–Apr 09.30–13.00 & 14.00–18.30 Mon–Sat) shares the new Quai Cyrano with the Espace Vin at 1 Rue des Récollets. They also rent out bikes.

WHERE TO STAY

Bergerac centre

France [221 A3] (20 rooms) 18 Place Gambetta; ☎ 05 53 57 11 61; w hoteldefrance-bergerac.com. Central & stylish, with good soundproofing, a heated pool & garage. **€€€–€€**

Le Bordeaux [221 A2] (40 rooms) 38 Place Gambetta; ☎ 05 53 57 12 83; w hotel-bordeaux-bergerac.com. Modern hotel in the centre by the Saturday morning market, with a garden, pool & secure parking. **€€**

Ludik for rêveurs [map, page 218] (46 rooms) 9 Rte d'Agen; ☎ 05 53 24 89 76; w ludikresort.com. In a peaceful spot towards the airport, a concept hotel based on games, with a pool, bars (one has 700 board games), billiards & restaurant (€) for guests only. **€€**

Brithotel du Commerce [221 A3] (35 rooms) 36 Place Gambetta; ☎ 05 53 27 30 50; w brithotel.fr. Comfortable, well-equipped rooms, but you're best off asking for one facing away from the square. Bike shelter & bar. **€€–€**

L'Atypic [221 B4] (8 rooms) 3 Rue du Dragon; ☎ 05 53 74 19 79; w hotel-restaurant-atypic.com. Recently renovated rooms near the market, & a surprise – Peruvian/Columbian restaurant (€€) with *cevice*, empanadas & other South American treats. **€€–€**

Around Bergerac

La Chartreuse de Bignac (12 rooms) St-Nexans, 12km southwest of Bergerac; ☎ 05 53 22 12 80; w abignac.com. Peaceful & comfy rooms with wooden floors & beams in an old charterhouse, in a park with a pool & 360-degree views over the hills, plus a home cinema down in the vaulted cellar. The hotel garden supplies the gourmet restaurant (€€€€) with an open kitchen & wine bar. **€€€€€–€€€**

Relais de la Ribeyrie (8 rooms) 74 Rte de Périgueux, Lembras, 4km northeast of Bergerac; ☎ 05 53 27 01 92; w logishotels.com. An old posthouse, with basic rooms. The restaurant (€€) serves classic southwest offerings. **€**

WHERE TO EAT AND DRINK

Bergerac centre

L'Imparfait [221 A5] 8 Rue des Fontaines; ☎ 05 53 57 47 92; w imparfait.com; ⌚ daily. Fresh & sunny gourmet cuisine based on top-notch ingredients, served on a pretty summer terrace. *Menus from €32*. **€€€€€**

La Table du Marché [221 B4] 21 Place Louis de la Bardonnie; ☎ 05 53 22 49 46; w table-du-marche.com; ⌚ closed Sun–Mon. Fresh & inventive cuisine by master chef, with a short menu including a daily vegan dish, with lots of flowers. *W/day lunch €29.50*. **€€€€€**

La Kour [221 A7] 4 Rue Fonsivade; m 06 62 96 87 66; f restolakour; ⌚ 15.00–late Mon–Sat, Sun brunch by reservation. Where the cool kids go on the left bank, with its *brocante* atmosphere & tapas, exotic dishes, great music & live events. **€€€€**

Le Vin'Quatre [221 B5] 14 Rue St Clar; ☎ 05 53 22 37 26; w levinquatre.fr; ⌚ closed Wed

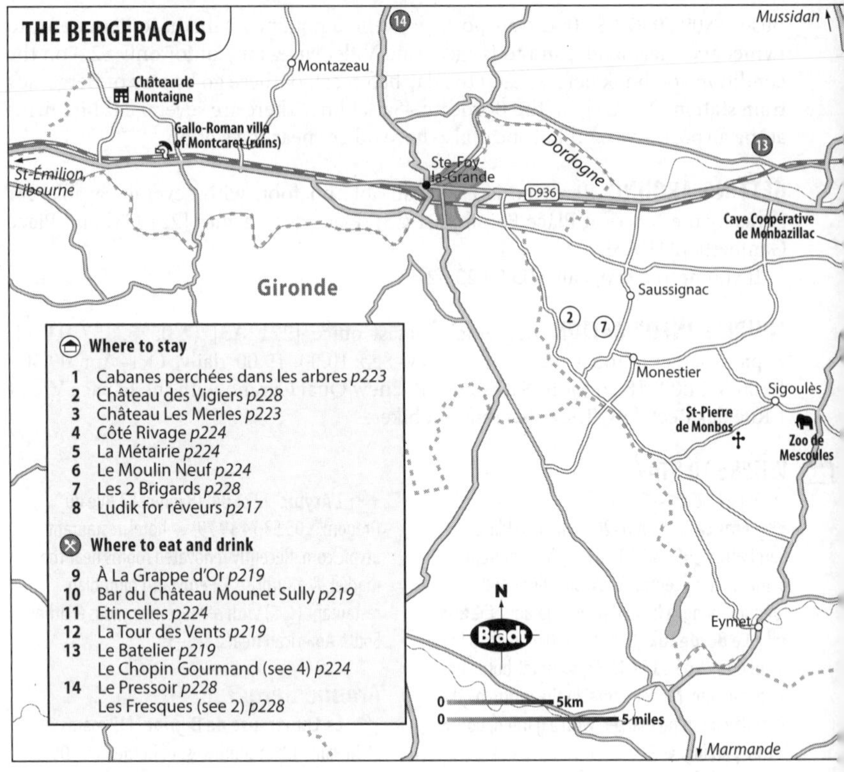

& lunch Mon–Tue & Thu. English chef Charlie Ray's imaginative delicious cuisine has made this charming spot with a few tables out in the lane a favourite; vegetarian & vegan options too. *3 courses €36.* €€€€

Aux Tabliers Noirs [221 C5] 24 Rue du Guesclin; 09 81 34 62 08; w auxtabliersnoirs.fr; closed Sun–Mon & lunch Tue–Wed. Fred & Mathilde are the lovely young couple behind this relaxed bistro; the place in the Dordogne for bouillabaisse. Good veggie dishes too. *3-course menu €34.* €€€

D'un Terroir à l'Autre [221 B2] 51 Rue Ste Catherine; 05 24 10 56 14; w dunterroiralautre.com; closed Mon–Tue & eves Sun. Unusual dishes from organic ingredients, including spicy hot & vegetarian choices, prepared by a young couple who met in Zanzibar. €€€

Le Bistro d'en Face [221 A7] 1 Rue Fénelon; 05 53 61 34 06; f lebistrodenface24; 09.00–18.00 Mon–Thu, 09.00–22.00 Fri–Sat. Arty colourful contemporary cuisine & views from the riverside terrace. €€€

Le Confluence [221 B4] 16 Rue du Col. De Chadois; 05 53 24 30 63; w restaurant-le-confluence.com; closed Sun. Limited menu but everything is refined & delicious, prepared by a chef who worked in the top restaurants in Lyon. *3 courses €33.* €€€

Le Bistro du Coin [221 B4] 6 Rue du Colonel de Chadois; 05 53 57 77 56; f Le-Bistro-Du-Coin-Bergerac; closed Sat–Sun. Bistronomic cuisine, with delicious couscous & daube often on the menu. *Lunch menu from €16.* €€

Chez Albert [221 C4] 93 Rue Neuve d'Argenson; 05 53 27 88 16; 09.30–20.00 Mon–Sat. Cheap & cheerful café for a quick lunch by Les Carmes car park, famous for their croque-monsieur. €

Fleur d'Oranger [221 B3] 30 Rue de la Résistance; 05 53 63 40 36; closed Sun–Mon. Tearoom with homemade pastries, ice cream, milkshakes & more, plus soups & salads for a vegetarian lunch.

L'Art et L'Envie [221 A4] 12 Grand Rue; 05 53 63 94 47; w artetvin-bergerac.fr; closed

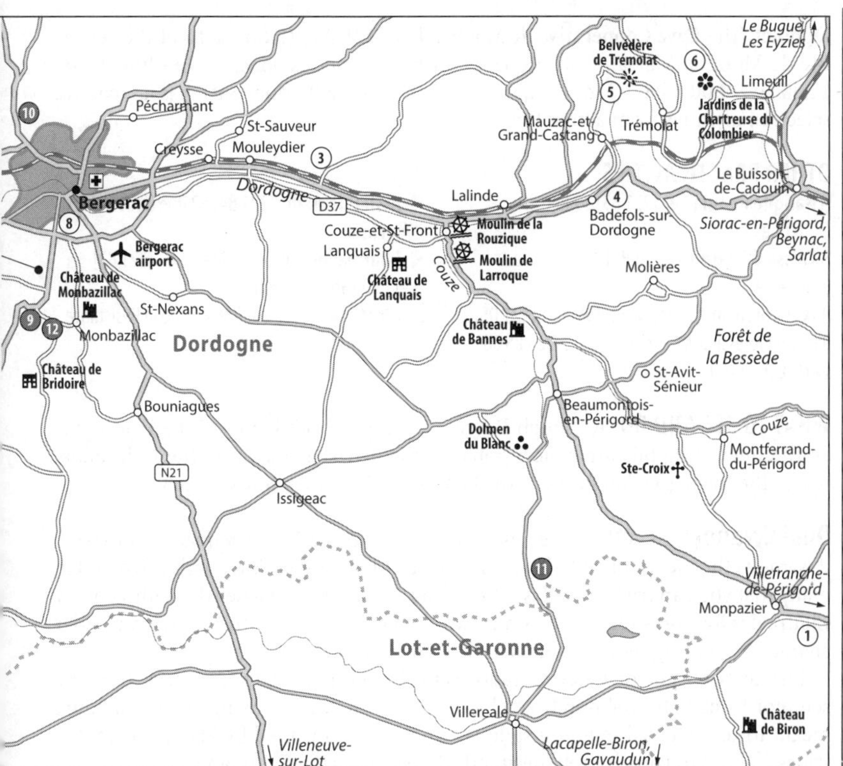

Sun–Mon. Stylish wine & tapas bar naturally starring Bergerac, but also others & spirits.

Around Bergerac *Map, above*

La Tour des Vents Moulin de Malfourat, Monbazillac; 05 53 58 30 10; w tourdesvents.com; closed Mon–Tue. Contemporary Michelin-starred cuisine in a beautiful setting renowned for its famous 360-degree view over the vines. Also a more affordable bistro (€€€). *Menus from €54.* €€€€€

À La Grappe d'Or Le Peyrat, Monbazillac; 05 53 61 17 58; w alagrappedor.fr; closed Mon. An old favourite, featuring simple but well-prepared duck, beef, fish – & duck heart brochette. *3 course menu €28.50.* €€€

Le Batelier 18 Rue de la Résistance, Prigonrieux, 6km west of Bergerac; 05 53 57 76 32; w le-batelier.business.site; closed eves Sun–Wed. It might not look like much, but there's a lovely terrace under the mulberry tree, warm welcome & dishes with a tropical island touch. €

Bar du Château Mounet Sully 2km northwest of Bergerac on the Rte de Mussidan; m 06 85 47 95 20; f; 18.00–02.00 Sat. Charming setting for a wine bar with platters at the striking 16th–19th-century château that once belonged to the Comédie Française actor Jean Mounet-Sully, born in Bergerac in 1841 (during the day you can also book a guided tour to the rest of the château: min 6 people for €10 pp).

La Maison Vari Le Bourg, Monbazillac; 05 53 73 52 96; w chateau-vari.com; 11.00–17.00 daily. Wine bar on an organic wine estate, with vegetarian & meaty light meals & a shop.

SHOPPING There's a covered **market** [221 A4] (Mon–Sat) in Place Louis de la Bardonnie, and outside stalls on Saturdays and Wednesdays around Notre-Dame church. Bergerac hosts a flea market the first Sunday morning of each month in Place Gambetta and there's an organic market on Tuesday mornings in Place

Doublet. The **Cave Coopérative de Monbazillac** [221 A7] (5km south of the centre, Rte de Mont de Marsan; 05 53 63 65 06; cavemonbazillac; Sep–Jun 10.00–12.30 & 14.00–18.00 Mon–Sat, Jul–Aug 09.00–19.00 Mon–Sat) has a massive selection of wines from across the region.

OTHER PRACTICALITIES

$ Banque Populaire [221 B3] 19 Rue Ste-Catherine
$ Caisse d'Epargne [221 B3] 22 Rue de la Résistance
Centre Hospitalier Samuel Pozzi [221 D5] 9 Bd du Professeur A Calmette; 05 53 63 88 88; w ch-bergerac.fr
Assier Gemelli [221 B4] 52 Rue Neuve d'Argenson
PharmaConfiance Du Marché [221 B3] 9–11 Rue Ste-Catherine
Post office [221 B3] 36 Rue de la Résistance

WHAT TO SEE AND DO Although Bergerac occupies both banks of the Dordogne, all the interesting bits are concentrated in the pedestrian area on the right bank, where the town grew up in the 14th–17th centuries – Bergerac's heyday.

Quai Cyrano [221 A5] (1 Rue des Récollets; 05 53 63 57 55; w quai-cyrano.com; same as the tourist office) This is the centre of Bergerac's wines, with 160 on offer, many that you can try by the glass after 17.00. It also encompasses the 16th-century **Cloître des Récollets** [221 A5] with its wooden gallery, home to a Franciscan order charged with bringing Protestants back to the Catholic fold.

Just to the right of Quay Cyrano waits *Désillusion totale* [221 A6], by Paris sculptor Daniel Hourdé purchased by the mayor in 2017 – a winged human figure meant to recall a bird in an oil spill wearing a mask inspired by Pacific northwest tribes – about to launch itself, hesitantly, into or over the Dordogne.

Musée de Tabac [221 A5] (Place du Feu; 05 53 63 04 13; w bergerac.fr; 10.00–12.30 & 14.00–18.00 Tue–Fri, 14.00–18.00 Sat–Sun; €4.50, under 18 free; no smoking!) Some of the finest buildings are in the Place du Feu, a pretty square shaded by an enormous tree tucked in the lanes behind *Total Disillusionment*. Housed in the handsome Maison Peyrarède (1604), this museum recalls the days when the Bergeracais grew a thousand varieties of Nicotiana (named after the 16th-century French diplomat Jean Nicot, who introduced tobacco to France). It traces the history of tobacco through some pretty spectacular tobacco art, including a bowl from Cameroon that seems to be an intricately carved biography of the smoker, paintings by Teniers and Meissonnier showing happy snuff-takers and puffers, and an 1850 Viennese meerschaum cigar holder carved with a Sicilian wedding.

Behind the tobacco museum in Place du Dr Cayla is Bergerac's strange and chilly 19th-century **Protestant Temple** [221 A5], where occasional services are held for the last die hard Calvinists.

BERGERAC

For listings, see from page 217

Where to stay

1 Brithotel du Commerce ... A3
2 France ... A3
3 L'Atypic ... B4
4 Le Bordeaux ... A2

Where to eat and drink

5 Aux Tabliers Noirs ... C5
6 Chez Albert ... C4
7 D'un Terroir à l'Autre ... B2
8 Fleur d'Oranger ... B3
9 L'Art et L'Envie ... A4
10 L'Imparfait ... A5
11 La Kour ... A7
12 La Table du Marché ... B4
13 Le Bistro d'en Face ... A7
14 Le Bistro du Coin ... B4
15 Le Confluence ... B4
16 Le Vin'Quatre ... B5

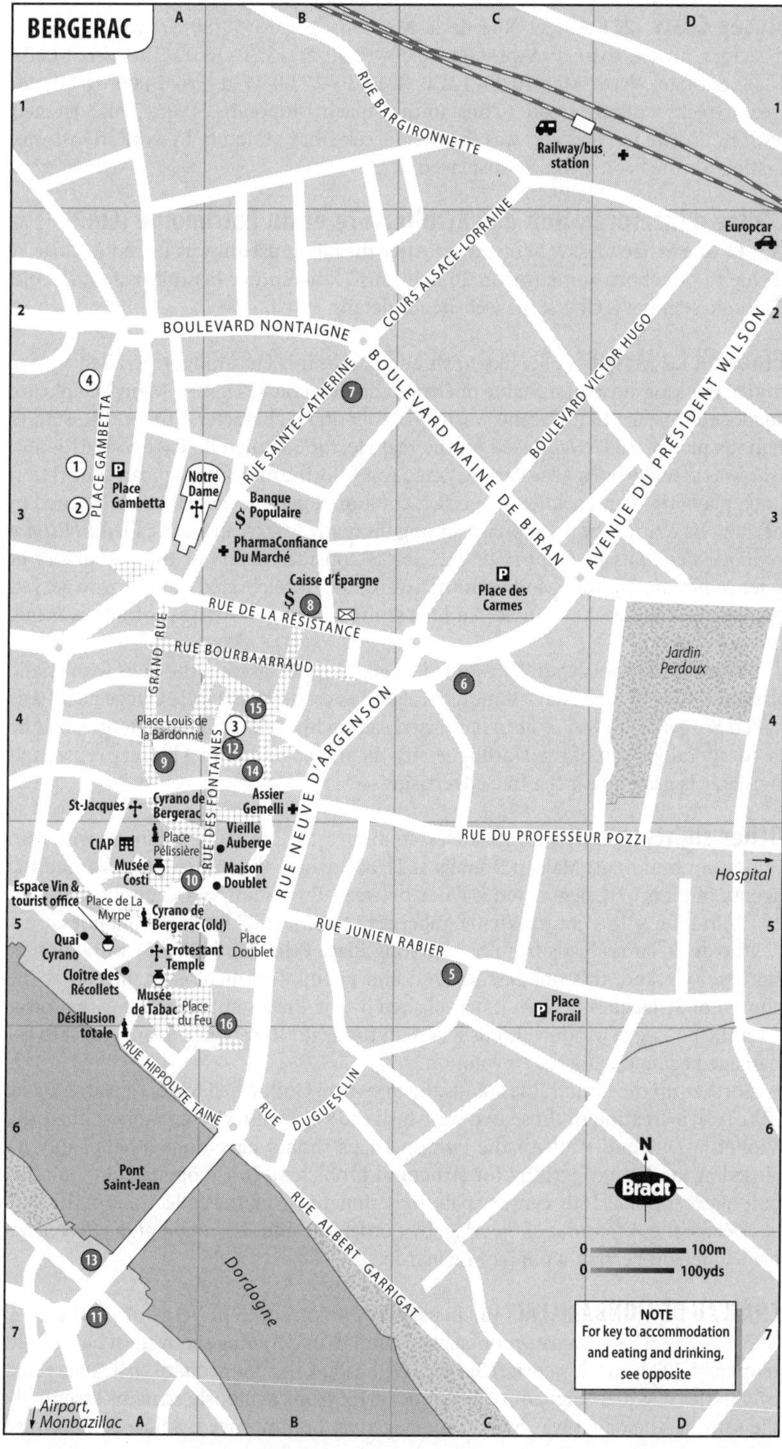
BERGERAC
Rue Bargironnette
Railway/bus station
Europcar
Cours Alsace-Lorraine
Boulevard Nontaigne
Place Gambetta
Rue Sainte-Catherine
Boulevard Maine de Biran
Boulevard Victor Hugo
Avenue du Président Wilson
Notre Dame
Banque Populaire
PharmaConfiance Du Marché
Caisse d'Épargne
Place des Carmes
Rue de la Résistance
Rue Bourbaarraud
Grand Rue
Jardin Perdoux
Place Louis de la Bardonnie
Rue des Fontaines
Rue Neuve d'Argenson
St-Jacques
Cyrano de Bergerac
Assier Gemelli
CIAP
Place Pélissière
Vieille Auberge
Rue du Professeur Pozzi
Musée Costi
Maison Doublet
Hospital
Espace Vin & tourist office
Place de La Myrpe
Cyrano de Bergerac (old)
Place Doublet
Rue Junien Rabier
Quai Cyrano
Protestant Temple
Cloître des Récollets
Musée de Tabac
Place du Feu
Place Forail
Désillusion totale
Rue Hippolyte Taine
Rue Duguesclin
Pont Saint-Jean
Rue Albert Garrigat
Dordogne
Bradt
100m
100yds
NOTE
For key to accommodation and eating and drinking, see opposite
Airport, Monbazillac

Musée Costi [221 A5] (1 Rue de la Mission; ☎ 05 53 58 80 87; w bergerac.fr/directory/musee-costi; ⊕ Apr–Oct 10.00–12.30 & 13.30–18.00 Tue–Fri, 14.00–18.00 Sat–Sun, Nov–Mar 10.00–12.30 & 13.30–17.00 Wed–Fri, 14.00–18.00 Sat; free) Greek sculptor Costi (Constantin Papachristopoulos, 1906–2004) trained with Bourdelle in Paris and was the first Greek since antiquity to work in lost wax casting for the bronze figures displayed here.

Centre d'Interprétation de l'Architecture et du Patrimoine (CIAP) [221 A5] (1 Rue St-Jacques; w bergerac.fr) After the city museum was forced to close, it is due to be reborn sometime in 2022 in this 17th-century Petite Mission, the old Catholic seminary. Check the website for details.

Place de La Myrpe Folks like to sit and gab in this charming, tree-filled square under the long nose of a **Statue of Cyrano de Bergerac** [221 A5]. Many people are surprised to learn that Cyrano wasn't just a fictional character. Edmond Rostand's famous play of 1897 was based on the real Hector Savinien de Cyrano (1619–55), who was actually born near Paris. Cyrano was fully the man for his picaresque times: poet, playwright and soldier – a perfect combination, especially if one happened to be gay. His writings were popular; among his many works, an essay called *L'Histoire comique des États et Empires de la Lune* is considered one of the precursors of science fiction. He was good with the sword, too, a celebrated duellist who served his king in a number of battles. And his schnoz, in his surviving portraits, was big, but not *that* big.

When Cyrano was young, he joined a company of Gascons, the boys with all the flash and style in those days. Among his family's estates was a little village near Paris called Bergerac, and so to fit in he started calling himself Cyrano de Bergerac. If he is not literally a son of the Dordogne, he will always be one in a literary sense, and Bergerac is grateful for the free advertising.

Other sights Rue des Conférences continues to Rue des Fontaines, with two important buildings: **Maison Doublet** [221 B5], where the future Henri IV and the agents of Henri III negotiated a truce between Protestant and Catholic forces in 1577, and the 14th-century **Vieille Auberge** [221 B5], at 27 Rue des Fontaines.

Rue de St-James leads from here to long **Place Pélissière** [221 A5] with another statue of Cyrano, this one less stylised and in full Technicolor, gazing up at the church of **St-Jacques** [221 A4], demolished by the Protestants except for the tower with the bulls-eye window; Louis XIV sent funds for its rebuilding only for it to get damaged again during the Revolution.

Further up the Grand Rue stands the lofty neo-Gothic bell tower of **Notre-Dame** [221 A3], a creation of those two busy beaver 19th-century re-creators of the past, Viollet-le-Duc and Paul Abadie (who perhaps should have done a better job; it's closed at the time of writing for structural problems). If it reopens, don't miss its pair of exceptional 16th-century paintings, donated from the collections of the Duc d'Orléans: the *Adoration of the Magi* by Pordenone and *Adoration of the Shepherds* by Gaudenzio Ferrari, a pupil of Leonardo.

CHÂTEAU DE MONBAZILLAC [map, page 218] (6km south of Bergerac on the D13; ☎ 05 53 61 52 52; w chateau-monbazillac.com; ⊕ undergoing renovation but should reopen in 2022; check website) Set on a high ridge, this four square château erected by Charles d'Aydie, Seigneur of Bergerac in 1550, miraculously remains essentially the same as the day it was built, undamaged and unimproved: a nice compromise between the necessities of defence and beauty. The owners were Protestants after 1607, made vicomtes by Henri IV, and they used the castle as a venue for theological discussions and as a refuge for persecuted pastors, until the viscountess neatly recanted the day she heard of the Revocation of the Edict of Nantes. Now owned by the Monbazillac wine co-opérative, displays will concentrate on wine when it opens, along with changing exhibits. The grounds are planted with vines (in autumn you can examine the rather ugly noble rot on the grapes).

EAST OF BERGERAC

Swollen with the waters of the Vézère at Limeuil (page 192), the Dordogne whiplashes two more times on either side of Trémolat before settling down by Bergerac and the first of the vineyards that the river wears like a green sleeve down to the sea. Since the opening of Bergerac airport to international flights in 2002, this has been a popular spot for second homes, although the gorgeous scenery and wine might have something to do with it, too!

Lalinde holds a **market** on Thursdays and Saturdays, and a fair on the second Thursday of each month. Tuesdays and Saturdays are market days in Beaumontois, and Thursday in Monpazier.

GETTING THERE The Sarlat–Bordeaux RER line runs through here five or six times a day, with stations at Trémolat, Lalinde and Creysse.

TOURIST INFORMATION All the offices listed here share the same website: w pays-bergerac-tourisme.com.

Beaumontois-en-Périgord 16 Place Jean Moulin; 05 53 22 39 12; 09.00–12.30 & 15.00–18.00 Mon–Sat, Sep–Jun closed Sat
Lalinde Jardin Publique; 05 53 61 08 55; 09.30–12.30 & 14.00–17.30 Mon–Fri
Monpazier Place des Cornières; 05 53 22 68 59; 09.00–12.30 & 14.00–17.30 Mon–Fri, Jul–Aug daily
Trémolat In the centre; 05 53 22 89 33; May–Sep 09.30–12.30 & 14.00–17.30 Mon–Thu

WHERE TO STAY

Cabanes perchées dans les arbres [map, page 218] (6 rooms) Roussille, Capdrot, 3km from Monpazier; m 06 87 05 48 75; w cabanes-perchees-dans-les-arbres.com. A 12ha park with big oaks, a lake & rustic chic treehouses, 4 with spa baths, 1 for families plus an Institut de Beauté & e-bikes to rent. B/fast inc. **€€€€€**

Edward I (17 rooms) 5 Rue St-Pierre, Monpazier; 05 53 22 44 00; w hoteledward1er.com; Mar–Dec. Boutique hotel in a 19th-century mini-château on the edge of the bastide, with an attractive swimming pool where the moat might have been. There's a small but excellent restaurant (€€€€), bike rental, electric vehicle & Tesla charging stations. **€€€€€**

Le Vieux Logis (23 rooms) Rue des Écoles, Trémolat; 05 53 22 80 06; w vieux-logis.com. An enchanting sybaritic sort of place that people put on bucket lists. This ivy-covered 17th-century manor has been a Relais & Châteaux hotel since the 1950s, with a dreamy French garden & pool. The Michelin-starred restaurant in a former tobacco barn has long been one of the very best in the region (€€€€€), but there's also a bistro with a €19 lunch menu. **€€€€€**

Château Les Merles [map, page 218] (14 rooms, 3 villas) 3 Chemin des Merles, Mouleydier; 05 53 63 13 42; w lesmerles.com. Beautiful 17th-century château 14km west of Bergerac, with a pool, tennis court, 9-hole golf course, & gourmet restaurant (€€€€) with wonderful menus to choose from, including a 3-course vegetarian (€27.50) & wines available by the glass. Culinary packages available. **€€€€**

Le Prieuré du Château de Biron (5 rooms, 1 apt) Biron; m 06 84 31 38 38; w leprieurebiron.com; Easter–Oct. Very atmospheric & peaceful with beamed ceilings & thick stone walls of the 12th-century priory next to the castle, plus a pretty garden. B/fast inc. **€€€€**

La Métairie [map, page 218] (10 rooms) Millac, Mauzac-et-Grand-Castang; 05 53 22 50 47; w la-metairie.com. On the idyllic Cingle de Trémolat, plush tranquil rooms in a lovely century park of shaded lawns, with an infinity pool & very warm welcome. Elegant seasonal restaurant (**€€€€**) with a light, modern touch & superb seafood. **€€€€–€€€**

Côté Rivage [map, page 218] (7 rooms) Badefols-sur-Dordogne, Lalinde; 05 53 23 65 00; w cote-dordogne.com. Right on the river, sweet place with a pool & restaurant, **Le Chopin Gourmand** (**€€€**), often filled with locals. **€€**

Le Moulin Neuf [map, page 218] (6 rooms) Paunat, Ste-Alvère; 05 53 63 30 18; w the-moulin-neuf.com. Northeast of Trémolat, enchanting English-owned B&B with pretty rooms in the old mill surrounded by gardens. B/fast (inc) served under the arbour. **€€**

WHERE TO EAT AND DRINK

Etincelles [map, page 218] Le Bourg, Ste-Sabine-Born, south of Beaumontois; 05 53 74 08 79; w gentilhommiere-etincelles.com; closed Tue–Wed & lunch every day exc Sun. Let young chef Vincent Lucas wow you with his spontaneous dishes in a bucolic setting for €75. Book at least a day ahead. Also 4 rooms (**€€€**) & a pool. **€€€€€**

La Bastide 52 Rue St-Jacques, Monpazier; 05 53 22 60 59; w restaurant-labastide.fr; closed Mon–Wed & eves Sun. An old favourite that has upped its game in recent years; the ingredients are still mostly local, but the result on your plate is fresh, modern & exceptionally good. *Menu €35*. **€€€€**

Auberge des Marronniers Le Bourg, Lanquais; 05 53 24 93 78; closed Tue–Wed. Traditional down to the checked tablecloths; dine by the fireplace, or on the summer terrace. *Lunch menu from €14.50*. **€€€**

La Table de Léo Le Bourg, St-Avit-Sénieur; 05 53 57 89 15; w latabledeleo.fr; closed Mon–Wed & eves Sun. A smart little restaurant with a terrace by the abbey, with a short but delicious €35 menu. **€€€**

Le Coulobre 36 Place de la République, Lalinde; 05 53 61 04 04; w lecoulobre.com; daily. Brasserie, offering a wide choice of classic fare, plus burgers (including fancy ones with foie gras & onion jam), pasta & pizza. One of the few in the region serving andouillette if you're a tripe sausage fan. *3-course lunch €14.50*. **€€€**

Le Croquant 28 Rue St-Jacques, Monpazier; 05 53 22 62 63; closed Mon & eves Sun. Jolly place, where you can nibble *tapas de terroir* & other local goodies; it's small so best to book. **€€**

Le Poquelin Place de la Bastide, Molières; 05 53 63 48 77; f; closed Mon–Tue. Nice village atmosphere at this bar/bistro, with burgers & *plats du jour*, & very popular theme nights. **€€**

Le Relais Saint-Sauveur 2 Rue de Gaffan, St-Sauveur, 10km northwest of Lanquais; 05 53 22 16 50; f lerelaissaintsauveur24; closed Mon & eves Tue–Thu & Sun. Great place where fine ingredients are given a colourful Reunionais touch. There are 2 terraces, & a red piano if you feel like bursting into song. *W/day lunch menus from €14.50, dinner €31*. **€€**

Chez Claudette Rue Foussal, Beaumontois-en-Périgord; 05 53 23 95 23; lunch Mon–Sat, eves Thu–Fri. Cheap, cheerful & reliable, offering family-style cuisine. Best to book. **€**

Bière de la Bastide 10 Rue St André, Monpazier; 05 53 27 72 49; w bierebastide.com; 11.00–19.00 Wed–Thu, Sun, 11.00–22.00 Tue, Fri–Sat. Award-winning ales, plus light meals & cheese & charcuterie platters. Ring ahead to book a brewery tour & tasting.

Le Bistoufly 6 Rue de la Premiere Armée, Lalinde; 05 24 10 35 81; f; 19.00–02.00 Fri–Mon, also Sun brunch. Cocktail bar that often does special evenings; always good to book.

COUZE-ET-ST-FRONT (East of Bergerac) The Dordogne is so clear here that from the 15th to the 19th century this village became the area's chief paper maker, producing a high-quality product sold throughout Europe. Two mills are still at it: the **Moulin de Larroque** (05 53 61 01 75; w moulindelarroque.com; boutique ⌚ 09.00–noon & 14.00–18.00 Mon–Fri) makes art paper in the traditional way; the **Moulin de la Rouzique** (Rte de Varennes; 05 53 24 36 16; w moulin-rouzique.com; ⌚ Apr–Jun & Sep–Oct 14.00–18.00 Sun–Fri, Jul–Aug 10.00–19.00 daily – see website for times of guided tours; €8.50, students €7.30, ages 6–18 €6, under 6 free) was restored in 1991 as an *écomusée* of paper. It has a rare collection of watermarks, and offers demonstrations of paper-making from rags during the guided tours; there's also a boutique so you can take some home.

The D37 continues to the 'Unfinished Louvre of Périgord', the **Château de Lanquais** (m 07 57 09 99 99; w chateaudelanquais.fr; ⌚ often, but ring first; €6). Here are two stout 15th-century towers with a Renaissance pavilion that closely resembles the Lescot wing of the Louvre. Some say it was financed in part by Catherine de' Medici as a thank you after the sister of the lord, Isabelle de Limueil (page 191), served in her 'Flying Squadron'. Work was interrupted when Henri de La Tour d'Auvergne, a Protestant cousin and associate of Henri IV, lobbed 200 cannonballs at it; he later became the master of the château, duke and peer of France, and filled it with furniture and fireplaces carved by itinerant Italian craftsmen, completing it in 1604.

LALINDE Further east, this busy market town was one of the first English bastides in Aquitaine, founded by Henry III in 1267. Lalinde still has its market square and one of its six original gates, the **Porte de Bergerac**, restored after the Wars of Religion; today the town extends between the Dordogne and the 19th-century **canal** built between Mauzac and Tulières, to avoid the Saut de la Gratusse rapids.

Before the canal, boatmen from Lalinde made a good living navigating all the *gabarres* through the rapids, helping their business by warning of a great serpent that gobbled up anyone who foundered. A waterside **Chapelle de St-Front** was built by the most dangerous stretch, opposite Lalinde's river terrace.

TRÉMOLAT The boundaries of this charming village match the outlines of a 6th-century AD estate owned by the parents of Trémolat's patron, St Cybard. Signs of a Carolingian chapel, built to mark Cybard's miracles, can still be traced in the nave of the 12th-century church of **St-Nicolas**. If attacked, the population retreated into the mighty bell tower-keep; it even has cute dormer windows so they'd feel at home. There's a beach by the Base Nautique on the river if you need a dip and spectacular views from the **Belvédère de Trémolat**, just to the west.

Just east, the **Jardins de la Chartreuse du Colombier** (D31 Rte de Limeuil; m 06 84 60 74 75; w chartreuseducolombier.com; ⌚ Apr–mid-Oct 10.00–19.30 Wed–Sun; €7, under 12 free) opened in 2014. Belonging to a 17th-century charterhouse villa, these Florentine-inspired gardens invite a wander through Baroque pavilions, ancient roses, box hedges and fountains.

SOUTH OF THE DORDOGNE You might consider a little micro-tourism circuit through the woods here. Due south of Trémolat and southeast of Lalinde is the tiny, unfinished bastide of **Molières**, founded in 1284 by Jean de Grailly, seneschal of Edward I, complete with a large Gothic church built by a Plantagenet architect. It once had an impressive castle (notable for the quantity and quality of its latrines!) and a ghost: in 1361, the young Blanche de Bourbon is said to have died here, poisoned by order of her husband Pedro the Cruel and thrown into a well, but still has a habit of wandering the streets.

Continue south through the valley of the Couze, dotted with prehistoric cave shelters, one of which for 40 years was the abode of St Avitus (AD480–570), a Visigoth soldier who became a holy hermit and performed miracles. So many pilgrims came that in the 11th century the Augustinian fathers founded an abbey on a promontory, around an immense fortified church, **St-Avit-Sénieur**. Despite the terrifying aspect of its towers, the abbey was sacked three times. The Salle Capitulaire has a small museum (☎ 05 53 22 39 12; ⏰ Jun–Sep daily; free) with bits discovered during archaeological digs in 1960. On summer nights its walls are turned into a canvas of images, *Les Murmures de St Avit*.

From St-Avit, the D26 winds southeast through the **Forêt de la Bessède**, the largest forest in the département, to **Montferrand-du-Périgord**, a hilltop village dominated by the ruins of a medieval castle. It has a pretty 16th-century *halle* and a Romanesque church by the cemetery, although even better is the Romanesque church at **Ste-Croix** (take the D26E), with a stern *clocher-mur* and good carved capitals inside.

Northwest of Ste-Croix, another English bastide, **Beaumontois-du-Périgord**, was founded in 1275 by a lieutenant of Edward I, Lucas de Thaney, who honoured Edward's father, Henry III, by laying out the streets in the form of an H. One mighty gate remains of the ramparts, the **Porte de Luzier**, as well as the striking 13th-century English Gothic church, **St-Laurent-et-St-Front**, with its fortified bell towers, which could probably lick even St-Avit's church in a pitched battle. Yet it's not all tough stuff: the west front has a carved porch and frieze depicting the four Evangelists, a hunt, a king and a mermaid.

The landmark here is the perfectly preserved 14th-century **Château de Bannes** (private) set high on a crag over the Couze valley and last rebuilt by the bishop of Sarlat. The Neolithic Périgourdins were here, too, leaving an impressive megalithic gallery, the **Dolmen du Blanc**, just over 3km to the south along the D676, on the left side of the road.

MONPAZIER During the Hundred Years' War, Monflanquin, Villeréal and Castillonnès (now in the Lot-et-Garonne) held the front lines against the English at Beaumontois and at Monpazier, 'the most perfect bastide'. Founded by Edward I in 1284, Monpazier might have been perfect but it had a perfectly rotten 14th century, kicked like a football from side to side in the Hundred Years' War – *routiers* pillaged it, and a streak of bad harvests was followed by a typhoid epidemic. The local lepers were blamed, and a few were burned alive. Then in 1350 came the Black Death.

Amid the terrors of the next round of wars, over religion this time, the Duke of Sully recorded a story about Monpazier worthy of Monty Python: by sheer coincidence Monpazier decided to raid Villefranche-du-Périgord to the east, on the very same night that Villefranche decided to do the same to Monpazier. By chance each militia took a different path; each was delighted to find no defenders, and carried their booty back – to ransacked homes. An agreement was struck, and both sides gave back everything they stole.

In spite of it all, Monpazier has held itself together remarkably well, from its fortified church (still bearing its Revolutionary slogan, that 'The People of France believe in a Supreme Being and the Immortality of the Soul') to its 16th-century *halle*, complete with its original grain measures. The *cornières* around the square are picturesquely irregular, and narrow spaces were left between the houses – not to give the residents air or light so much as a place to throw their rubbish. In 1637 crowds gathered in the square to watch Buffarot, the leader of the Croquants, broken on the wheel. Today they gather for the Thursday market.

An interpretation centre, **Bastideum** (8 Rue Galmot; ☎ 05 53 57 12 12; **w** bastideum.fr; ⏰ Apr–Jun & Sep 10.00–13.00 & 14.30–18.00 Tue–Sun, Jul–Aug

10.00–19.00 daily, Oct 14.00–18.00 Tue–Sun; €4.80, ages 18–25 €3.50, ages 6–17 €2.80) in the former convent of the Récollets is dedicated to Monpazier's history and building, and has medieval games to try.

CHÂTEAU DE BIRON (45km southeast of Bergerac; 05 53 63 13 39; w chateau-biron.fr; Jul–Aug 10.00–19.30 daily, Sep–Jun 10.00–13.00 & 14.00–18.00 (Nov–Dec until 17.00); €9, ages 5–12 €6, combined with Cadouin cloister, page 214, €12.70/€8) You can see this mighty bruiser of a castle long before you get anywhere near it. The steep isolated hill was a natural stronghold, and saw its first fort in the 11th century to command the northern approaches to the Agenais. In 1189 Gaston de Gontaut, chief of the four barons of Périgord (and an ancestor of Lord Byron), got his hands on it, and they were like glue – the Gontauts held on to it for 24 generations, until the early 1900s.

Over the centuries they added and added to the pile, creating one of the most eclectic castles in France. The first Gaston built the square 12th-century keep, or Tour Anglaise, while Romanesque walls and the Tour du Concierge (with Renaissance dormers) date after the siege in 1212 by Simon de Montfort.

The next important building spree was initiated by Pons de Gontaut-Biron, who accompanied Charles VIII on his invasion of Italy in 1497. Pons returned to Biron determined to add some quattrocento glamour with the delicate Pavillon de la Recette and a two-storey chapel – the ground floor was a parish church for the village, and the upstairs reserved for the nabobs. This held two 14th-century masterpieces, a *Pietà* and *Mise au Tombeau*, which to the chagrin of many were sold by the Gontaut-Birons in the early 1900s to the Metropolitan Museum in New York, leaving only the tombs of Pons de Gontaut-Biron, carved with the *Resurrection of Lazarus* and *Christ Appearing to His Disciples*, and his brother, Armand, bishop of Sarlat (d-1531), with three Virtues.

A third round of building was begun by Baron Armand de Gontaut, a Maréchal de France (1524–92), who died fighting the Catholic League at the side of Henri IV. His hot-headed son Charles continued the fight, receiving 32 wounds in battle. Henri rewarded him by raising Biron to a duchy, and making Charles ambassador to England; but Charles found peace boring, and in 1602 he was un-duked and beheaded at the Bastille for conspiracy against the king (hence Biron's story of a headless ghost). Work was taken up again in the 18th century, but left incomplete at the time of the Revolution; since then, each year new bits have been restored and reopened, from the dungeons and enormous kitchen to the tower. Every year there's a new contemporary art exhibit: past ones have been dedicated to Miró and Calder.

BATTLE OF THE BARONS

Why were there four barons (Bordeilles, Mareuil, Beynac and Biron) of Périgord? Because four were needed to carry the throne of a newly elected bishop in Périgueux on their shoulders into the Cathedral of St-Front, which was a great honour. But each baron was prouder than the next, and every time there was a new bishop to carry, arguments broke out over who would stand in front. The issue became so heated between the barons of Biron and Bordeilles that in 1532, when there was a new bishop, each showed up with thousands of partisans armed to the teeth. In the end, peace was made when the consuls of Périgueux agreed that the canons of the cathedral would carry the bishop from then on.

SOUTH AND WEST OF BERGERAC

Rolling hills, woodlands and bastides dot the land in between the vineyards south and west of Bergerac. Before the Dordogne flows into the Gironde (page 135), it passes the château of one of the most original thinkers of the Renaissance: Michel de Montaigne.

The Sunday morning **market** in Issigeac takes over the whole town in summer and draws people from miles and miles around.

TOURIST INFORMATION Both share the website **w** pays-bergerac-tourisme.com.

Eymet 45 Place Gambetta; 05 53 23 74 95; 10.00–12.30 & 14.00–18.00 Mon–Sat, Sep–Apr closed Mon

Issigeac Place du Château; 05 53 58 79 62; 10.00–12.30 & 14.00–18.00 Mon–Sat, 10.00–12.30 Sun, Sep–Apr closed Mon

WHERE TO STAY

Château des Vigiers [map, page 218] (70 rooms) Monestier, 4.5km west of Saussignac; 05 53 61 50 00; **w** vigiers.com. A member of the Small Luxury Hotels of the World, this 16th-century wine château & contemporary relais, built in the style of the local tobacco barn, overlooks a lake & 27-hole golf course. Other goodies include a deluxe spa, heated pools & a Michelin-starred restaurant **Les Fresques** (€€€€€), under Chef Didier Casaguanas, plus a **bistrot** (€€€) & a menu of experiences to match your interests. **€€€€€–€€€€**

Château de Bouniagues (1 room, 3 apts) Place de l'Église, Bouniagues; 05 53 23 08 65; **w** chateaudebouniagues.com. Beautiful apts in a 15th-century castle. **€€€**

Les 2 Brigards [map, page 218] (5 rooms) Cablanc, Monestier; **m** 06 31 64 99 37; **w** les2brigards.com. Brigards Patrick & Jean Paul will instantly make you feel at home in their ivy-covered shabby chic 17th-century *maison de maître*, with comfy rooms & large pool in a 2ha park. Table d'hôte available 3 nights a week, & they'll pack a picnic for your outings. B/fast inc. **€€€**

Villa Corisande (4 rooms) 27 Bd National, Eymet; **m** 06 08 18 89 71; **w** villacorisande.com. Charming rooms in a 1920s house with a pool & garden. **€€**

WHERE TO EAT AND DRINK

L'Atelier 66 Tour de Ville, Issigeac; 05 53 23 49 78; **w** latelierissigeac.com; closed Tue–Wed. Superb contemporary cuisine on a terrace in the pretty medieval village, in winter around a cosy fireplace. **€€€€**

La Brucelière Place de la Capelle, Issigeac; 05 53 73 89 61; **w** labruceliere.com; closed Tue–Wed. An old postal stage has been restored as a lovely restaurant where David Douet is renowned for his seasonal dishes & seafood. Also 5 rooms (b/fast inc; **€**). *W/day lunch menu €25.* **€€€€**

Andine Place Gambetta, Eymet; 09 81 18 33 41; **w** andine.eu; closed Sun–Mon. 2 Peruvian chefs have charmed this old bastide with their *pisco sours, causa, ceviche*, & much more; vegetarian choices, too. **€€€**

Bucket's Auberge Inn Le Bourg, Montazeau; 09 83 43 14 41; **w** buckets.fr; closed Tue–Wed. Seasonal bistronomic cuisine with an exotic touch, plus a shady terrace & lovely summer salads. *Menus from €28.* **€€€**

Le Pressoir [map, page 218] 20 Rue de Montpon, St-Meard-de-Gurcon; 05 53 80 56 78; **w** opressoir.com; closed Wed. A lovely stop between Bergerac & St-Émilion, where everything is prepared fresh; try the local sturgeon. *W/day lunch menu €16, dinner from €32.* **€€€**

Walnut 41 Bd National, Eymet; 05 53 24 03 68; **w** walnutbistro.com; closed Mon–Tue. Young, enthusiastic owners run this cool bistro, serving up exciting contemporary cuisine; also great choice of wines & cheese, charcuterie or veggie platters. **€€€**

Aroy Jung Le Bourg, Bouniagues; **m** 07 80 97 56 47; **w** aroyjungbylefromageamalices.business.site; closed eves Sun. Something different – spicy Thai dishes & Thai beer or cheesy raclette & fondues. **€**

Shabby Chic Corner 3 Rue Ernest Esclargon, Issigeac; 05 53 63 96 24; Shabby-Chic-Corner-salon-de-thé; 10.30–17.30 Thu–Tue. A chance for a proper cuppa (also good coffee) with homemade goodies & sandwiches in a 15th-century house.

Café Tortoni Av de Ste-Foy, Eymet; 05 24 10 62 32; LeTortoniEymet; daily. Lively spot for a drink or superb bar food, Italian dishes & excellent burgers, & perfect homemade chips.

ISSIGEAC (18km southeast of Bergerac) This medieval picture-postcard village, enclosed in a circular wall, is filled with artisans and boutiques (Coloratura on the Grand Rue does stunning nature prints). Among its charms are a late Gothic church with a good porch, a massive palace of the bishops of Sarlat (1660, now the tourist office), and the half-timbered Maison de Têtes, decorated with leering faces.

CHÂTEAU DE BRIDOIRE (Ribagnac, 12km south of Bergerac; m 06 30 39 38 22; w chateaudebridoire.com; Apr–Jun & Sep–Oct 14.00–18.00 Sat–Sun & hols, Jul–Aug 10.00–19.00 daily; labyrinth Jul–Aug; €9.50, students €8.50, ages 4–12 €6.50, labyrinth €8.50/€5.50/€7.50, château & labyrinth €16/€10/€14) A beautiful château, rebuilt after it was destroyed in the Wars of Religion, Bridoire was purchased in 1987 by the infamous Emperor Bokassa of the Central African Republic, then left in a lamentable state of dereliction. Now restored, visitors can play medieval games, following clues through a natural labyrinth. They also do haunted house evenings – check the website.

ST-PIERRE DE MONBOS (18km southwest of Bergerac, Thénac, signposted just beyond Sigoulès; always) This isolated Romanesque church has four remarkable 11th-century (or even older) capitals in the presbytery that have somehow survived all the wars and tumult; with reliefs of a hunt, animals real and imaginary, disembodied heads and couples having sex. Tradition has it you should stick your finger in the hole by the hunter sounding his horn for good luck. A curious little oculus illuminates the presbytery (there are also lights by the door).

ZOO DE MESCOULES (La Pleyssade, Mescoules, 17km southwest of Bergerac; m 06 99 74 57 77; w zoo-de-mescoules.com; Apr–Jun & Sep 14.00–18.30 Tue–Sun, Jul–Aug 10.00–19.00 daily, Oct–Mar 14.00–18.30 Wed, Sat–Sun & school hols; €10, ages 3–12 €8) This small private zoo boasts the biggest reticulated python in Europe, plus Nile crocodiles, giant tortoises, wallabies, racoons and bouncy castles.

EYMET A pretty bastide, founded in 1270 by Count Alphonse de Poitiers of Toulouse, Eymet's market square still has its evocative *cornières,* and more unusually a donjon – it was one of the few bastides to have a castle. In the past few decades it has become best known as the most English spot in all Dordogne-shire, with one in six inhabitants from the UK, and an English grocer.

THE GALLO-ROMAN VILLA OF MONTCARET (38km west of Bergerac, just north of the D936; 05 53 58 50 18; w villa-montcaret.fr; late May–late Sep 09.30–12.45 & 14.00–18.00 Tue–Sun, other times 10.00–12.30 & 14.00–17.30 Tue–Sun; €4, under 18 & EU residents under 25 free) In 1887, workmen digging next to Montcaret's church struck their shovels on the rock-hard mosaic floors of the luxurious baths of a 2nd–4th-century AD Gallo-Roman villa. The villa was known to the builders of the church, who incorporated a funerary stele into the apse (along with a primitive Carolingian relief of Adam and Eve) and reused some Roman capitals

MICHEL DE MONTAIGNE

Few have had the advantage of the wise and gentle upbringing of Michel de Montaigne, the eldest of eight children raised 'without whip or tears' by a humanist Catholic father and Jewish mother converted to Protestantism. His father sent him to spend his first three years with a peasant family so he would understand the life of the people. Latin was his first language (his father only hired Latin-speaking servants); he learned Greek as a child's game and was always accompanied by a musician to alleviate any signs of boredom. After his studies, he entered the legal and public career destined for him; as a member of the Parlement in Bordeaux, he met his dear friend, La Boétie (page 201).

He served Charles IX so well the king awarded him the collar of the Order of Saint Michael, the highest award a French noble could hope for. In 1565 he married Françoise de la Cassaigne, who provided him with such a large dowry that in 1571 Montaigne could afford to retreat to his château. He was 38 at the time, and vowed to spend his life doing nothing; instead, he invented the essay (*essai* in French, or 'try' or 'experiment'), a collection of which he first published in 1580.

The freest French thinker of the 16th century, Montaigne was also the most sceptical, the product of his heartfelt sorrow at the dogmas, cruelty, hypocrisy, legal double dealings, and fanaticism of his day; he once said that if he were accused of stealing the towers of Notre Dame in Paris, he would flee France rather than risk standing trial.

In his writings he reasoned that if human beliefs through the ages have fluctuated so violently, if one age's reason and common sense would seem ridiculous to the next, then the only sane response to the world was not to believe in its external things and accept constant mutability and chaos with a smile. '*Que sais-je?*' ('What do I know?') was his motto, and he had it inscribed over the château door. He also recognised that we lead double inner lives and that all conclusions are…inconclusive. 'Nothing is so firmly believed as that which a man knows least,' he wrote. It's almost certain that Shakespeare read him, and that Hamlet (or Jacques in *As You Like It*) could never have existed without Montaigne.

The truth is he didn't retreat to his ivory tower at all, and in his lifetime was better known for his statesmanship. He composed many of his essays while travelling. In 1580 he was in Italy where he learned to his surprise he had been elected Mayor of Bordeaux. He reluctantly returned and served two terms and was admired as a moderating influence; he was the first to attempt to classify Bordeaux's wines and he did try to reconcile Catholics and Protestants (which earned him, thanks to fanatic Catholics, a brief spell in the Bastille!), and he was also able to keep Bordeaux loyal to Henri IV.

for its columns. It had a lavish triclinium, or dining room now part of the museum flanking the excavations.

CHÂTEAU DE MONTAIGNE (St-Michel-de-Montaigne, north of Moncaret; 05 53 58 63 93; **w** chateau-montaigne.com; book guided tours online Wed–Sun; château & tower €14, or €7 each) This château was purchased by wealthy herring merchant Raymond Eyquem, in 1477. In 1533, it saw the birth of his great-grandson Michel

Eyquem de Montaigne, but in 1885, it went up in flames (the current château was rebuilt in the Viollet-le-Duc neo-medieval/Renaissance style).

Luckily the fire spared Montaigne's home within a home, the round tower where he wrote his famous *Essays* while sipping his beloved wine. There's a tiny chapel on the ground floor, its altar painted with a scene of St Michael and the dragon, of which Montaigne said: 'I like to light a candle to St Michael, and to his serpent, too.' Stairs wind up to the bedroom, equipped with a handy toilet, and to his famous inner sanctum, where he could sit at his desk surrounded by bookshelves and windows, with a stone armchair niche in the wall for quiet readings. His books are gone, but the beams still bear 57 Greek and Latin maxims that Montaigne inscribed on them to ponder; you can see a few he scratched out when he tired of them. He died here in 1592, and his heart is buried in the village church.

11

The Dordogne Quercynoise

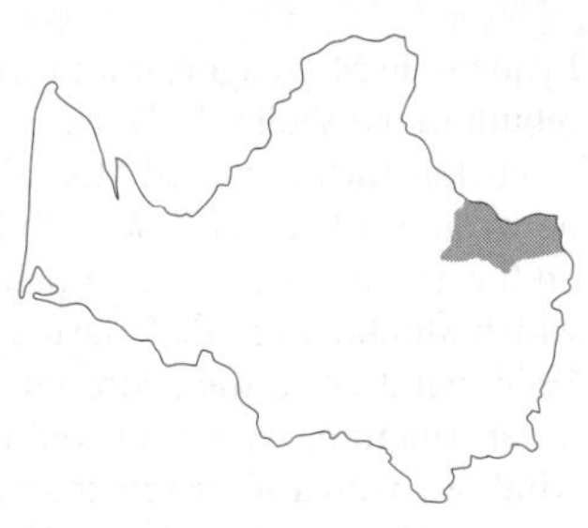

Before gracing the département that bears its name, the Dordogne winds through the Lot, or Quercy. This means *causses* – rugged limestone plateaux, shot with green velvet valleys and pocked by cliffs, caves and chasms, the spectacular maw at Padirac and vertiginous cliff-hugging Rocamadour, which draws in nearly as many visitors as Disneyland, Paris. Yet the rest, the gorgeous villages and châteaux are so unspoiled and low key that if they were any more relaxed, no-one would ever get out of bed.

GETTING THERE AND AWAY

BY AIR Brive-Souillac Airport (☎ 05 55 22 40 00; **w** aeroport-brive-vallee-dordogne.com) is the closest, with regular flights from Paris Orly and others in season.

BY TRAIN The Paris Austerlitz–Toulouse line stops a couple of times a day at Souillac, but for other places, get off at the busier station at Brive; ditto if you're coming from Bordeaux on the Tulle line. Transfer to the Brive–Figeac line (**w** ter.sncf.com/occitanie) for St-Denis-lès-Martel, Padirac-Rocamadour and Gramat. For Biars-sur-Céré, Bétaille (4km from Carennac) and Vayrac, transfer to the Brive–Aurillac line.

BY BUS LiO bus 887 links Biars-sur-Céré to St-Céré, St-Jean-Lespinasse and Bretenoux. In July and August and at weekends in June and September, the same 877 bus runs between Biars-sur-Céré and Souillac, stopping at Lacave, Rocamadour, Padirac and Bretenoux. Souillac is also linked to Sarlat by bus (☎ 05 53 08 43 13; **w** transperigord.fr).

ST-CÉRÉ AND AROUND

The largest town in these parts, St-Céré is romantically set on the banks of the Bave, or 'babbler', which tumbles down the causse to join the Dordogne. St-Céré reached its peak in the 15th century and has never had any compelling reason to change much since then, now hosting a small art colony inspired by Jean Lurçat who made his home here; it also hosts a renowned summer opera festival.

St-Céré is also the main market town in the area, with **markets** on Saturday in the *halles* and Place Jean Jaurèes and on Sunday morning in Place de la République. Bretenoux holds markets on Tuesday and Saturday mornings.

TOURIST INFORMATION St-Céré's **tourist office** (☎ 05 65 33 22 00; **w** vallee-dordogne.com; ⌚ 10.00–12.30 & 14.00–18.00 Mon–Sat, plus Jul–Aug 10.00–13.00 Sun) is at 13 Av François de Maynard.

WHERE TO STAY

Villa Ric [map, page 234] (5 rooms) Rte de Leyme, 2km south of St-Céré; 05 65 38 04 08; w villaric.com. Big luminous rooms in a lush garden with a beautiful pool & views over St-Céré. It operates on HB terms – & the food is delicious. **€€€€€**

Trois Soleils de Montal (29 rooms) St-Jean Lespinasse, St-Céré; 05 65 10 16 16; w 3soleils.fr. This large, ivy-covered villa occupies an extensive park by the Château de Montal; most rooms have balconies, some have AC. For dinner choose between the exquisite Michelin-starred **Les Prés de Montal** (€€€€€), or its annex **L'Informel** (€€€) which is really good, too. **€€€**

Auberge de la Fontaine (9 rooms) Autoire; 05 65 10 85 40; w auberge-de-la-fontaine.com. Logis hotel in an old stone inn & the best restaurant (€€) in the village. **€€€–€€**

Relais de Castelnau [map, page 234] (40 rooms) Rte de Padirac, Loubressac; 05 65 10 80 90; w relaisdecastelnau.com. Modern rooms & spectacular views over the valley towards Castelnau; heated pool & tennis. The restaurant (€€€) serves local specialities. **€€€–€€**

Domaine de Borie (6 rooms) Rue du Quartier de Borie, Bretenoux; 05 65 38 41 74; w domaine-de-borie.com. A chambre d'hôte with a panoramic terrace in a 14th-century farm, where writer Pierre Loti spent his childhood summers in the 1860s. B/fast inc. **€€**

Victor Hugo (16 rooms) 7 Av des Maquis, St-Céré; 05 65 38 16 15; w hotelsaintcere.com. A 16th-century inn in the centre, with an excellent market-based restaurant (€€). **€€–€**

Auberge du Vieux Port [map, page 234] (8 rooms) Port de Gagnac, Gagnac-sur-Cère; 05 65 38 50 05; w auberge-vieuxport-lot.com. East of Bretenoux, beside the river, in a calm location, charming place now run by the 3rd generation. With bright renovated rooms & excellent restaurant (€€€) with a secret Norwegian omelette recipe. **€**

Hôtel Le Touring (28 rooms) Place de la République, St-Céré; 05 65 38 30 08; w hoteldutouring.fr.hoteldutouring.eu. Central hotel, with recently renovated rooms & a sunny roof terrace. **€**

WHERE TO EAT AND DRINK

Au Déjeuner de Sousceyrac Rue Pierre Benoit, Sousceyrac; 05 65 33 00 56; closed Mon & eves Sun. Named after a 1931 novel by Pierre Benoit, & Michelin-starred since 2008, Patrick Lagnès's lovely little restaurant lures gourmets into the Ségala, featuring local ingredients; there are also 10 rooms (**€€**). *Menus €30–€100*. **€€€€**

Bistrot de Bacchus 2 Rue des Roubinets, St-Céré; 05 81 71 60 45; f; closed Sun & eves Mon. Just off the main square, with a terrace for perfect people-watching & perfectly crafted dishes, served with a smile. Often full, so do book. **€€€**

Bistrot Puymule 1 Place de l'Église, St-Céré; 05 65 34 27 40; f lebistrotpuymule; closed Sun–Mon. Very pretty contemporary cuisine & good vegetarian dishes, great atmosphere; & yummy desserts. *Lunch menus from €17*. **€€€**

L'Entre-Pots 5 Rue Centrale, St-Céré; 05 65 33 71 93; closed Sun, eves Tue–Thu & lunch Sat. Excellent versions of traditional duck dishes, generous portions (the frites are famous) & great atmosphere. **€€**

Le Vieux Pigeonnier [map, page 234] Py, Loubressac; 05 65 38 52 09; w levieuxpigeonnier.fr; May–Sep daily. Simple place to sit by the pool & nibble meat from the grill, salads, crêpes & ice cream, & look out over Castelnau. **€€**

Il Etait Une Fois 13 Rue Pasteur, St-Céré; 05 65 40 51 16; closed Sun–Mon. Tearoom with the most heavenly cakes in town.

DORDOGNE QUERCYNOISE

Where to stay

1 Auberge du Vieux Port *see above*
2 Château de la Treyne *p239*
3 La Noyeraie Rocamadour *p246*
4 La Terrasse *p239*
5 Le Petit Relais *p246*
6 Le Pont de l'Ouysse *p239*
7 Le Troubadour *p246*
8 Les Vieilles Tours *p246*
9 Relais de Castelnau *see above*
10 Villa Ric *see above*

Where to eat and drink

11 Auberge Le Roc du Berger *p246*
12 Ferme Auberge du Gouffre du Blagour *p251*
13 La Bonne Famille *p240*
14 La Ferme de la Truffe *p240*
15 La Table du Moulin *p240*
16 Le Vieux Pigeonnier *see left*
17 Les Saveurs d'Uxellodunum *p240*
18 Les Tilleuls *p251*

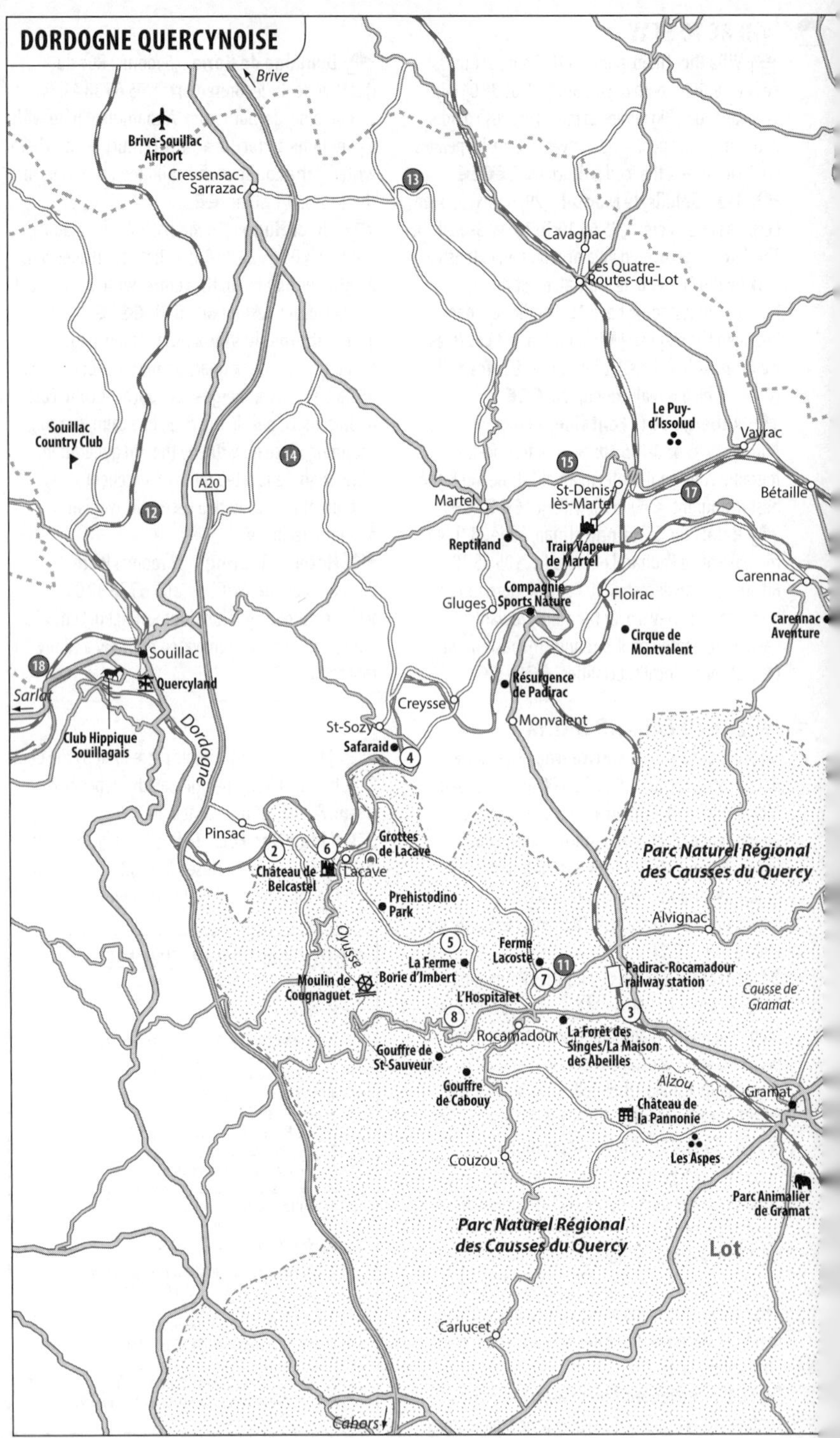
DORDOGNE QUERCYNOISE
Brive
Brive-Souillac Airport
Cressensac-Sarrazac
13
Cavagnac
Les Quatre-Routes-du-Lot
Le Puy-d'Issolud
Vayrac
Souillac Country Club
14
A20
15
St-Denis-lès-Martel
17
Bétaille
Martel
12
Reptiland
Train Vapeur de Martel
Carennac
Compagnie Sports Nature
Gluges
Floirac
Carennac Aventure
Cirque de Montvalent
Souillac
18
Quercyland
Sarlat
Résurgence de Padirac
Creysse
Club Hippique Souillagais
Dordogne
Monvalent
St-Sozy
Safaraid
4
Pinsac
2
6
Grottes de Lacave
Parc Naturel Régional des Causses du Quercy
Château de Belcastel
Lacave
Prehistodino Park
Alvignac
Oyusse
5
Ferme Lacoste
11
La Ferme Borie d'Imbert
Padirac-Rocamadour railway station
Moulin de Cougnaguet
7
Causse de Gramat
L'Hospitalet
8
3
Rocamadour
La Forêt des Singes/La Maison des Abeilles
Gouffre de St-Sauveur
Alzou
Gouffre de Cabouy
Gramat
Château de la Pannonie
Les Aspes
Couzou
Parc Animalier de Gramat
Parc Naturel Régional des Causses du Quercy
Lot
Carlucet
Cahors

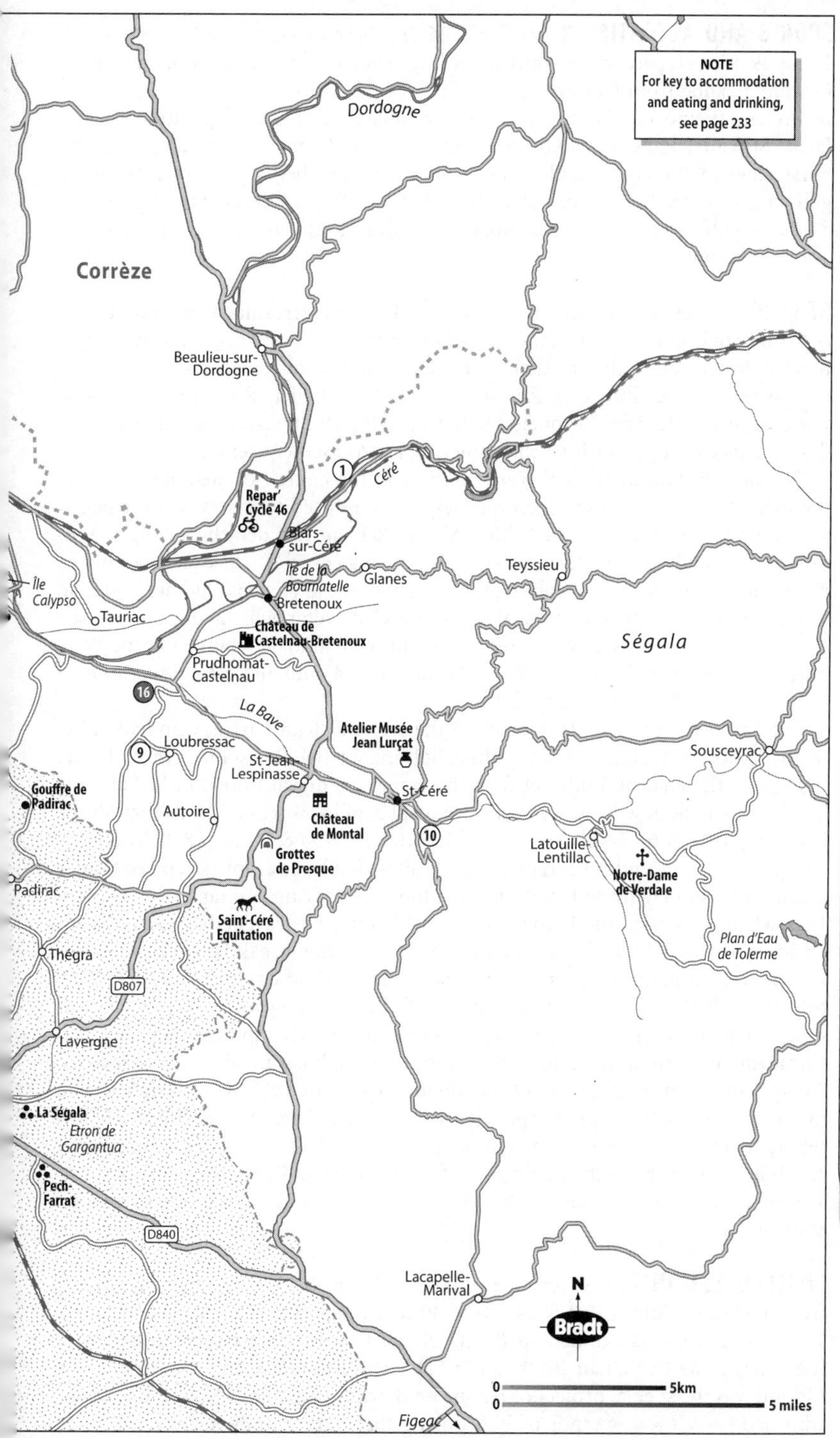

NOTE
For key to accommodation and eating and drinking, see page 233
Dordogne
Corrèze
Beaulieu-sur-Dordogne
Cère
1
Repar' Cycle 46
Biars-sur-Cère
Île de la Bournatelle
Glanes
Teyssieu
Île Calypso
Tauriac
Bretenoux
Château de Castelnau-Bretenoux
Ségala
Prudhomat-Castelnau
16
La Bave
Atelier Musée Jean Lurçat
9
Loubressac
St-Jean-Lespinasse
Sousceyrac
Gouffre de Padirac
St-Céré
Autoire
Château de Montal
10
Latouille-Lentillac
Grottes de Presque
Notre-Dame de Verdale
Padirac
Saint-Céré Equitation
Plan d'Eau de Tolerme
Thégra
D807
Lavergne
La Ségala
Etron de Gargantua
Pech-Farrat
D840
Lacapelle-Marival
N
Bradt
0
5km
0
5 miles
Figeac

SPORTS AND ACTIVITIES Repar'Cycle 46 (La Serre Conte Haut, Girac; m 06 71 68 49 17; w reparcycle46.com) has a huge choice of all kinds of **bikes** to hire. Or hire a **canoe** from Copeyre Canoë (05 65 32 72 61; w copeyre.com) – start in Bretenoux and paddle down as far as Souillac. Saint-Céré Équitation (Donat Haut, St-Jean Lagineste; m 06 66 25 33 33; w saint-cere-equitation.com) offers **horse rides** in the countryside from 1 hour up; and there's an attractive 9-hole **golf** course under the château at Golf de Montal (St Jean Lespinasse; 05 65 10 83 09; w golf-montal.fr). For **boating** and **ziplining**, and more, on Lac Tolerme, see w letolerme.fr.

ST-CÉRÉ The town's beautiful market square, **Place du Mercadial**, is surrounded by half-timbered buildings; the stone benches on the Rue Pasteur corner were once used by fishermen to display their catch. Other medieval-Renaissance houses are everywhere, especially along Rue du Mazel, Rue d'Ollier, Rue St-Cyr, Impasse Lagarouste and Quai des Récollets. On the latter, look for the 18th-century **Chapelle des Récollets**, decorated with a charmingly painted casement ceiling.

The first visitors to St-Céré were pilgrims at the church of **Ste-Spérie**. Spérie, the daughter of the lord of St-Laurent-les-Tours, refused to marry a noble pagan and literally lost her head over him. She picked up her detached noggin and, being a tidy soul, gave it a last wash before expiring (AD794). The exact spot of her martyrdom is marked with a black grid in front of the altar steps, and her bones lie in the Carolingian crypt, along with a curious Celtic altar, which you can only see on 12 October, her feast day. The rest of the church had to be rebuilt after the Wars of Religion, but there's an impressive altarpiece (1714) and interesting *Adoration of the Magi* (1860) by Henriette Haillot.

The first artist to establish himself in the area was Jean Lurçat, who had fallen in love with it during the war, while fighting in the Resistance. In 1945, he purchased the château built between the craggy medieval towers of St-Laurent-les-Tours, which now hosts a permanent display of his works at the **Atelier Musée Jean Lurçat** (05 65 38 28 21; Apr–Sep 10.30–12.30 & 14.30–18.30 Tue–Sun, €4, ages 12–16 €2, under 12 free). Lurçat (1892–1966) was a close friend of Ranier Maria Rilke and Heinrich Heine and first took up weaving and tapestry design in 1917 when he became too ill to fight in World War I. He travelled in Spain, North Africa and the Middle East, and was marked by the streak of fantasy, colour and interest in natural forms in the local art. In 1937, after being thunderstruck by the sublime 14th-century tapestries of the Apocalypse in Angers, Lurçat went on to become a one-man renaissance of French tapestry. He designed extraordinary brilliantly coloured cartoons for Aubusson; his masterpiece, in Angers, the 80m long *Le Chant du Monde*, begun in 1957, was designed as a modern response to the great Apocalypse. He is buried next to his wife and fellow resistant Simone (d-2009) in the little cemetery at St-Laurent, under a sun symbol reading 'C'est l'Aube' – the beginning of a phrase he had engraved on his sword as a member of the Académie: 'It's the dawn of a new age, when men will stop behaving like wolves...'

CHÂTEAU DE MONTAL (St-Jean-Lespinasse; 05 65 38 13 72; w chateau-montal.fr; Jul–Aug 10.00–12.30 & 14.30–16.30 daily, Sep–Jun 10.00–12.30 & 14.00–17.30 Wed–Mon; €8, under 18 & EU citizens under 26 free, combined with the Château de Castelnau-Bretenoux €12) Just outside St-Céré, the Château de Montal was the special project of Jeanne de Balzac, daughter of Robert de Balzac, who had served as governor of Pisa during the Wars of Italy. Jeanne, who had accompanied him, had fallen in love with the Italian Renaissance, and decided to replant some of it in *la France profonde* as a surprise gift for her own son, Robert, while he was fighting in Italy; much to Jeanne's despair, he was killed before ever setting eyes on it.

After surviving intact until the late 19th century, Montal was bought by a greedy speculator who spent 22 years stripping it. In 1908, when only the frame of the staircase remained, oil tycoon Maurice Fénaille stepped in, bought Jeanne's château, repurchased as many of its original works as he could, and had copies made of the rest. During World War II Montal had a very famous guest – the *Mona Lisa* was one of the masterpieces from the Louvre hidden here from the Nazis.

Step inside the rough walls and a magical courtyard opens up, decorated with lovely façades, ornate dormers and a sculpted frieze more than 30m long, attributed to the same sculptors who worked in Biron (page 227); note the intertwined initials of Jeanne and her sons Robert and Dordé. Seven Renaissance portrait busts of Jeanne and her family, among the finest in France, occupy the niches between the windows. The decoration around one of the windows, where legend has it Jeanne often sat, watching for Robert's return, sums up her sorrow – a knight holds a scroll reading *Plus d'espoir* ('no more hope'). Death accompanies a decapitated youth gripping his skull.

The interior is just as beautiful as the courtyard: the meticulous grand stair in the Italian style, carved in golden cream stone, the grand chimney supporting a heraldic stag with golden antlers, the guard room vaulted with 'basket handle' arches, the walnut table carved from a single tree, the rooms filled with Renaissance furniture, ceramics, paintings, tapestries (including a fascinating series on croquet) and 17th-century German stained glass. Even the graffiti on the walls is quality – left by Léon Gambetta of Cahors, the hero of 1870.

The village's 12th-century church of **St-Jean-Baptiste** (🕘 by request from the *mairie*: 05 65 38 02 64) has interesting murals from two periods in the 15th century.

NORTH OF ST-CÉRÉ

Château de Castelnau-Bretenoux (05 65 10 98 00; w castelnau-bretenoux.fr; 🕘 Jul–Aug 10.00–19.00 daily, Sep–Apr 10.00–12.30 & 14.00–17.30 Wed–Mon, May–Jun 10.00–12.30 & 14.00–18.30 Wed–Mon; €8, under 18 & EU citizens under 26 free, combined with the Château de Montal €12) The River Dordogne bristles with castles, but burnished red Castelnau is the oldest and most redoubtable of all, rising on a conical, 229m outcropping over its confluence with the Cère. Although a fort stood here since the 8th century, the current castle was begun in 1100, evolving over the centuries. It is considered the second military castle in France after Pierrefonds in the Oise. Which is only fair, as the lords of Castelnau claimed to be 'the second barons of Christendom'.

In 1184, when their liege lord the Count of Toulouse put them under the suzerainty of the Viscounts of Turenne, they were so insulted that only after the King of France intervened did they agree to pay the most begrudging tribute to Turenne: one egg, ceremoniously transported by a yoke of four oxen. In 1851 most of the château was damaged by arson, but Jean Mouliéret, tenor at the Opéra Comique, came to the rescue, rebuilding and sumptuously refurnishing one wing. Inside you can see the Grande Salle, where the États du Quercy once met, the chapel, vaulted cellars and the deep, long-forgotten oubliettes, where seven skeletons were discovered. Mouiéret's *objets d'art*, photographs of himself in various roles, late medieval triptychs, furniture, paintings, medieval sculptures and other fascinating bits – most unlabelled – give the Lot's most-visited castle the air of an upscale *brocante*.

Clustered at the foot of the behemoth, the hamlet of **Prudhomat-Castelnau** is worth a stop for its 15th-century **Collégiale de St-Louis**, with Renaissance windows in the choir and fine sculpted choir stalls.

Bretenoux The main urban venture of the barons of Castelnau was the bastide of Bretenoux, which they founded on the left bank of the Cère in 1277. Its grid plan survives, as do medieval arcades and houses in Place des Consuls. It also has a pleasant picnic spot over the bridge on the **Île de la Bournatelle**. It's all very jammy, especially just north at **Biars-sur-Cère**, home to Andros, maker of France's most famous confiture, Bonne Maman.

Glanes Just east of Bretenoux, this is the epicentre of red and rosé **Coteaux de Glanes**, one of France's least-known wines, with a production area limited to 30ha. Visit the Co-operative, **Les Vignerons du Haut-Quercy** (84 Route de Pontouillac, Glanes; ☎05 65 39 73 42; w coteauxdeglanes.fr; ⌚ 10.00–noon & 15.00–19.00 Mon–Sat).

Beaulieu-sur-Dordogne It would make the angels weep to go this far east and not hop over into the Corrèze to see the tympanum of the *Last Judgement* on the abbey church **St-Pierre**, one of the masterpieces of French Romanesque. Stylistically similar to Carennac (page 241) here Christ has his arms outstretched in triumph while a carnival of apocalyptic monsters roll below across the lintel, supported by a strange figure Freda White described as 'flowing upward like a flame of prayer'. It would inspire Abbot Suger, inventor of Gothic architecture, in his choice of a tympanum for St-Denis in Paris.

EAST OF ST-CÉRÉ: THE SÉGALA This sparsely populated region is the 'rye land' where wheat refuses to grow, where limestone gives way to grey granite on the frontier of the Cantal, legendary as the cold spot of France. There are a few things to see in this far, obscure corner of Quercy, although the deep chestnut forests, heather and pure air have something to be said for them. Aim for the striking 15th-century pilgrimage church of **Notre-Dame de Verdale**, near **Latouille-Lentillac**, clinging precariously to the rock face high over the Tolerme gorge – you can take the narrow road off the D30 to the top. There's a **Sentier Art Nature** path bordered by 20 works by local artists.

Further east, old grey **Sousceyrac** is the largest town in the Ségala, once fortified (see the Porte Notre-Dame, topped with a chapel). The Viscounts of Turenne are responsible for the 15th-century **Château de Grugnac**, 1km north, still bearing its *lauze* roof; the department's more recent bosses have endowed Sousceyrac with the **Plan d'Eau de Tolerme** (8km south), the largest body of water in the Lot and one of the most beautiful.

WEST OF ST-CÉRÉ From St-Céré the D673 ascends past the village of **St-Jean-Lespinasse** and to the **Grottes de Presque** (St-Médard-de-Presque; ☎05 65 40 32 10; w grottes-de-presque.com; ⌚ guided tours in English Jul–Aug 09.30–18.30 daily, closed Jan–late Mar, for other months see website; €8.50, ages 5–11 €5). Famous for their enormous columns, Presque offers chambers full of draperies, stone waterfalls and other geological wonders, most strikingly the 'candles' in the 'Hall of Wonders', brilliant white and 8.5m tall.

Another 4km down the D673, a right turn will take you to the little village of **Autoire**. Often picked out as an example of a true Quercynois village, its steep brown-tiled roofs form an exquisite ensemble around the church; it earned its nickname

'Le Petit Versailles' in the 1700s when nobles chose Autoire to build their country manors. It sits under the majestic **Cirque d'Autoire**, which you can explore (wear non-slip shoes) on the 5.6km Circuit ENS ('Sensitive Natural Space') trail. This leads up in 1.2km to the 35m waterfalls of the River Autoire which is most impressive after the spring or autumn rains. The path then climbs to a tremendous bird's-eye view stretching to the Dordogne valley from the 150–200m limestone walls of the cirque, near the picturesque ruins of a château des Anglais, built into the cliff. If the weather is hot, go in the afternoon when you'll be in the shade.

From here the D135 leads to another exceptionally lovely village, **Loubressac** – an eagle's nest with 'one of the finest views in the realm' according to 17th-century writer Savinien d'Alquié – overlooking the confluence of the Bave, the Cère and the Dordogne. American poet and novelist W S Merwin lived here for decades, and beautifully evoked life here in *The Lost Upland: Stories of Southwestern France.*

DOWN THE DORDOGNE: CARENNAC TO LACAVE

This stretch of the river flows around islets and high cliffs as it curls past châteaux, a fascinating Romanesque abbey connected with the sweet-tempered archbishop Fénelon, the handsome medieval town of Martel and the stalactite phantasmagoria at Lacave.

Martel's **market** takes place in its 18th-century *halle* on Wednesday and Saturday mornings.

TOURIST INFORMATION

Carennac Cour du Prieuré; 05 65 33 22 00; w vallee-dordogne.com; 10.00–12.30 & 14.00–18.00 Mon–Sat, plus Jul–Aug 10.00–13.00 Sun

Martel Place des Consuls; 05 65 33 22 00; w vallee-dordogne.com; Apr–Oct 10.00–12.30 & 14.00–18.00 Mon–Sat, plus Jul–Aug 10.00–13.00 Sun

WHERE TO STAY

Château de la Treyne [map, page 234] (16 rooms) La Treyne, Lacave; 05 65 27 60 60; w chateaudelatreyne.com. This 14th-century château set high above the river & its splendid formal gardens is the luxury showpiece of the region: stately gardens, antique furnishings, tapestries, magnificent rooms with river views, along with a large pool & stone terrace, not to mention a highly rated restaurant (€€€€€) in the candlelit dining room. €€€€€

Le Pont de l'Ouysse [map, page 234] (14 rooms) Lacave; 05 65 37 87 04; w lepontdelouysse.fr. In a magical garden setting under the Château de Belcastle along the banks of the 'emerald' Ouysse, this hotel founded in 1884 has been in the same family for 5 generations. French country-style rooms have waxed parquet floors & there's a heated pool & formidable Michelin-starred restaurant (€€€€€) & wine cellar. €€€€€

La Terrasse [map, page 234] (15 rooms) Le Bourg, Meyronne; 09 74 56 65 30; w hotel-la-terrasse.com. The old riverside château of the bishops of Tulle is now a delightful hotel run by the charming Françoise. It's still very medieval, with spiral stone steps, big wooden doors & atmospheric rooms. There's also a pool & a fine restaurant (€€€€) either on the terrace or stone vaulted banquet hall. €€€–€€

Auberge de l'Ile (18 rooms) Creysse; 05 65 32 22 01; w auberge-de-lile.com. On the banks of a laughing stream, historic inn with modernised rooms, attentive service & informal restaurant (€€) offering good-value lunches, big salads & omelettes. €€

Auberge des Sept Tours (7 rooms) Av de Turenne, Martel; 05 65 37 30 16; w auberge7tours.com. Pleasant & peaceful family hotel with flowery bedrooms that sleep up to 4, a playground & shady terrace & good restaurant (€€€). €€

Domaine du Bougayrou (4 rooms, 2 gîtes) Lacave; 05 65 32 68 74;

w domainedubougayrou.com. Serene 18th-century *maison de maître* in a large wooded park with a pool. Table d'hôte in the eves. B/fast inc. **€€**

Domaine les Falaises (15 rooms) Gluges, Martel; 05 65 27 18 44; w les-falaises.com. Charming place with a perfect setting under the cliffs, beautiful gardens & an excellent restaurant (€€€) with a €28 menu. **€€**

Hostellerie Fénelon (15 rooms) Carennac; 05 65 10 96 46; w hotel-fenelon.com. At the entrance to the village, authentic provincial rooms, & a pool as well. In the garden dining room (€€€) all the menus are a good bet. **€€**

Grangier (18 rooms) Le Bourg, St-Sozy; 05 65 32 20 14; w hotel-grangier.com. In a stone building of 1880, with recently renovated rooms, garden terrace, pool, delightful owners & good restaurant (€€), with a chalkboard menu. **€€–€**

WHERE TO EAT AND DRINK

Saveurs des Halles Rue Sans-Lys, Martel; 05 65 37 35 66; w restaurant-saveurs-des-halles-martel.fr; closed Wed–Thu. Rich, beautifully prepared gourmet cuisine. *3-course lunch menu €32*. €€€€€

La Ferme de la Truffe [map, page 234] Pouzols, Cuzance (9km west of Martel); m 06 89 97 84 39; w lafermedelatruffe.fr; Apr–mid-Jul closed Mon, Wed & Sun, eves Tue & Thu, mid-Jul–Sep closed Sun–Mon & eves Tue, Oct–Nov & Mar lunch only Fri–Sat. Your best chance for a truffle feast here, along with organic veg from the garden & lamb. Book a day in advance to choose your main course. *Menus €28–€75*. €€€€

La Table du Moulin [map, page 234] Les Landes, 3km east Martel; 05 65 37 40 69; w moulincastagne.com; closed Mon & winter. For generations the Castagné family has run a walnut oil press in 47ha of groves (on Tue & Thu in Jul–Aug you can watch the mill in action), & now run this rustic chic restaurant in a charming 14th-century inn, serving generous menus prepared in an open kitchen (the beef rib cooked in a kamado is mouth-wateringly tender). €€€€

Au Hasard Balthazar Rue Tournemire, Martel; 05 65 37 42 01; w auhasardbalthazar.fr; closed eves Sun, lunch Mon–Tue. Superb renditions of local products, big salads & wines by the glass. *3-course menu €31*. €€€

La Bonne Famille [map, page 234] Le Bourg, Sarrazac, Cressensac-Sarrazac (13km northwest of Martel); 05 65 37 70 38; w labonnefamille.fr. In a tiny village, a legendary restaurant & hotel (formerly known as Aussel; rooms **€**) now in the 4th generation & still well worth the journey. *Menus €30 for 3 courses*. €€€

Les Saveurs d'Uxellodunum [map, page 234] Ferme de Roubegeolles, Vayrac; 05 65 32 40 60; f fermederoubegeolles. Good €22 duck-based menus & lunches from €12. In 2018 an ancient Gaulish oven was found on the farm, the inspiration for their *banquets Gaulois* (Jul–Aug Thu–Fri) prepared by chef Jean-Paul Romac, an expert on cuisine Gauloise, accompanied by tales of the famous battle & sometimes sword fights; games for the kids too. Book. €€€

Le Petit Moulin Rue Droite, Martel; m 06 59 59 27 66; w petitmoulinmartel.com; daily. Delicious *cuisine bistronomique* with light dishes, foie gras but also vegan options. Also 5 contemporary rooms (**€€**) & a rare wine bar in this area. *3-course lunch €23*. €€

Maison Sophie Place des Consuls, Martel; 05 65 27 87 34; daily. Combination boutique & restaurant, offering colourful plates & vegetarian cuisine. €€

Plein Sud Place des Consuls, Martel; 05 65 37 37 77; closed Mon & eves Tue. A good place to find reliable, satisfying pizzas & other inexpensive fare. €€

Le Pourquoi Pas? Le Barry, Floirac on the D43; m 06 87 20 84 78; w lepourquoipas.fr; Jul–Aug Tue–Sun, Sep–Jun eves Wed–Sun. Great atmosphere at this beer bar & garden with 60 local & Belgian beers, crêpes, theme nights, & games. €

SPORTS AND ACTIVITIES **Compagnie Sports Nature** (Gluges; 05 65 32 27 59; w compagnie-sports-nature.com) offers a full range of outdoor activities, from canoeing and SUP to caving, canyoning and rock climbing the cliffs of the Dordogne and Lot. **Carennac Aventure** (La Prade, Carennac; m 06 30 87 66 65;

w carennac-aventure.fr) offers canoes/kayaks from 1½ hours to 6 days, canoraft, mountain bike hire, paintball and more. You can also hire canoes and kayaks from **Safaraid** (Camping Les Borgnes, Saint-Sozy near Lacave; 05 65 37 44 87; w canoe-kayak-dordogne.com).

CARENNAC From the river, Carennac presents an enchanting higgledy-piggledy cluster of roofs, walls and turrets around its honey-coloured **Prieuré St-Pierre** (05 65 33 22 00; 10.00–12.30 & 14.00–17.30 daily; €3). Founded in AD932 by Frotard, Vicomte de Cahors, the priory was given to Cluny in 1040. Fortified in the 16th century, it managed to repulse Protestant attacks, preserving some fine Romanesque art by the school of Toulouse: the 12th-century tympanum, showing Christ blessing in a mandorla, surrounded by the Evangelists and Apostles. In the shadowy interior, capitals carved with primitive birds, animals and monsters add to its atmosphere of archaic mystery.

The **cloister** with its one Romanesque and three Flamboyant Gothic galleries was rescued from its fate as a pigsty in 1928. After the Revolution, when most of

FÉNELON, OR A GOOD MAN IN BAD TIMES

If I could come back as anyone, I'd like to be Fénelon's valet.

Voltaire

Known for his gentle eloquence as the 'Swan of Cambrai', François Salignac de la Mothe-Fénelon, born in the nearby Château Fénelon, was given the special task of bringing Protestant women back to the Catholic fold. Gentle, reasonable, well spoken and extremely tolerant for his bigoted age, Fénelon was so successful that he attracted the attention of Madame de Maintenon, morganatic wife of Louis XIV and herself a convert to Catholicism. In 1689 she had Louis appoint Fénelon as tutor of his 7-year-old grandson and heir, the singularly charmless Duke of Burgundy. He was given the prestigious post of Archbishop of Cambrai.

From that exalted position Fénelon would aim a surprise satirical shot right at his boss: *Les Aventures de Télémaque* (1693) was an assault on the tyranny of Louis and all absolute monarchs, disguised as an adventure novel written for the instruction of his royal pupil. Shortly afterwards the archbishop fell on to the wrong side of the Inquisition for defending his cousin, the mystic Madame Guyon, who believed in the possibility of abandoning the soul to God's love outside the Church. 'It is hard to get a great prelate condemned for trusting overmuch in the love of God,' as Albert Guérard commented – but he was.

Shocked, Louis immediately dismissed Fénelon from his tutorial post (all of his work went down the drain anyway, when the duke died three years before his terrible grandfather). Even worse, *Télémaque* was published in court without its author's permission; Louis read it with such fury that he ordered Fénelon never to leave Cambrai. Without him, his beloved Carennac fell into ruin. As a posthumous apology for Fénelon's treatment, Philippe, regent for Louis XV, had *Télémaque* printed; in the 18th century it went into more than 180 editions. It is 'the true key to the museum of the 18-century imagination', according to historian Jean-Claude Bonnet, and the first great work of the Enlightenment.

the carvings were hammered, the villagers sold off the priory's art, except for their beloved 15th-century *Mise en Tombeau* (in the Salle Capitulaire), a poignant composition of eight intricately detailed figures. The Virgin's arms reach out stiffly in grief; Nicodemus and Joseph of Arimathea, in Renaissance costumes, hold the shroud, while John, Mary Magdalene and the women in biblical draperies mourn. Here too are 17th-century bas-reliefs on the *Life of Christ* and a *Pietà* carved in stone.

At the south end of the cloister, the old kitchen with its monumental fireplace and refectory has been converted into a culture centre. During the work, a 15th-century mural was uncovered, on a common medieval theme: the *Dit des Trois Morts et des Trois Vifs* – three skeletons warning three cavaliers to reflect on earthly vanity. The 16th-century deanery, or Château des Doyens, now houses the **Espace Patrimoine** (05 65 33 81 36; Easter–Sep same hours as the church) with exhibits covering art, history and the natural environment. In the 17th century, the deanery became a personal fief of the Salignac de la Mothe-Fénelon family, who owned châteaux on either bank of the Dordogne; in 1674, it was inherited by François (1651–1715), the Archbishop of Cambrai (see box, page 241), who, at least according to tradition, wrote his famous romance in the 'Tour de Télémaque'. The Île Barrade, facing Carennac, was renamed Île Calypso after the island in the novel.

AROUND CARENNAC Crossing the bridge over the Dordogne from Carennac, a right turn will take you to **Tauriac**, where the Gothic church of **St-Martial** (05 65 38 53 33; 09.00–18.00 daily) has 16th-century frescoes on the figures who prefigured the birth of Christ: Adam and Eve, the 12 sibyls and 16 prophets, along with scenes of the Passion.

A left turn at the bridge will lead you to **Vayrac** and the D119, leading up to **Le Puy-d'Issolud**, a broad plateau that in 2001 archaeologists confirmed was the site of the fabled oppidum with the ululating nursery rhyme of a name, Uxellodunum. After capturing Cahors, Julius Caesar was niggled enough to come in person to sort out this last pocket of resistance to his legions, where the Gauls who escaped from Alesia made their last stand. Ruins have been identified as belonging to Celtic fortifications, camps and temples. Finds are now in the museum in Martel and you can take a guided tour of the site starting from the car park at the Fontaine de Loulié in **St-Denis-lès-Martel** (w uxellodunum.com; Jun–late Sep 10.00 Tue–Sat, max 30 visitors at a time; free – book online).

MARTEL Proud, staunchly medieval Martel, the 'City of Seven Towers', resolves under the microscope to a rustic village of 1,400 souls. Martel means 'hammer', like the three hammers on its coat of arms, and like the hammer wielded by Charles Martel, scourge of the Muslims; legend credits this grandfather of Charlemagne with founding the city in the AD700s. Severely depopulated over the last century, today many of its houses are now summer homes. Still, the population isn't nearly big enough for Martel. However small, this is a real city, and, beautiful as it is, it wears a melancholy air with so few around to share its beauty.

In central Place des Consuls are the covered market and huge **Palais de la Raymondie**, begun by the viscounts in c1300. Now Martel's town hall, it also hosts the **Musée Gallo-Roman d'Uxellodunum** (05 65 37 43 13; w amismuseeraymondie.org; mid-Jun–mid-Sep 15.30–18.30 Wed–Fri; €2.50, ages 12–18 €1, under 12 free), with prehistoric and Gallo-Roman finds from Puy-d'Issolud, old maps and pharmacy jars. Its bell tower is one of the famous seven.

Another is the tower of **St-Maur** (05 65 37 34 53; usually), a fortified but exquisite Gothic church built into the walls with a tympanum from the mid 1100s sculpted with the *Second Coming of Christ*, while the rest, rebuilt in the 14th century, has excellent stained glass from 1511 with scenes of the Passion. A few sculptural decorations can be seen in the odd corners; for a puzzle, see if you can find the three sleeping monks – the two angels under blankets don't count.

For the other five towers, you'll need to tour the rest of Martel. It won't take long: there are scarcely more than a dozen streets. One of the towers is the **Maison Fabri**, behind the market, where Henri Court-Mantel was welcomed by Viscount of Turenne after pillaging Rocamadour in 1183 – then sickened and died (page 244). The **Tour de Tournamire** at the northern gate doubled as a prison.

Martel has more recent attractions, too. The **Train Vapeur de Martel** (05 65 37 35 81; w trainduhautquercy.info; Apr–Sep, check website for departures & book online; steam train: return €11, ages 4–11 €7, diesel train: €8.50/€5.50) offers a thrilling 90-minute journey from Martel to St-Denis-lès-Martel, skirting cliffs over the Dordogne. This was once part of the Bordeaux–Aurillac line of 1889, built to compete with the riverboats. The train used to transport truffles to Bordeaux, hence its name, Le Truffadou. In the station, there's a **museum** (€1) of train things – uniforms, watches and clocks, signals and posters.

Then there's the compelling (and well-heated) **Reptiland** (05 65 37 41 00; w reptiland-le-renouveau.fr; Feb–Jun & Sep–Nov 10.00–18.00 Tue–Sun, Jul–Aug 10.00–18.30 Tue–Sun, closed Dec–Jan; €10.50, ages 4–12 €7) housing 92 species of crocs, snakes, spiders and other cold-blooded beasts, all described in loving detail in French and English.

GLUGES The Dordogne is at its scenic best between Martel and Souillac, meandering through dramatic countryside, and often hemmed in by steep cliffs. Directly south of Martel, the riverside village of Gluges fairly cowers beneath one of these lofty rock walls. The church of **St-Pierre-ès-Liens** is half cut into the rock; the local baron, Gérard de Mirandol, built it after his return from the Crusades in 1095. It has a good set of modillions; Edith Piaf used to spend her holidays here and paid for the windows, and swore the priest to secrecy until after her death in 1963. A cave, converted to a fortress in the Middle Ages, can be reached by a stairway carved into the cliff.

Across the Dordogne along the D43, the **Cirque de Montvalent** was formed by the river ages ago before it chose its present course. Further south, towards Montvalent village is the **Résurgence de Padirac** – where the underground river (page 250) surfaces in a bucolic turquoise pool. From Gluges, the D23 to Creysse follows the river – it's terrifically scenic, if a bit dangerous, climbing up and down the cliffs on a single lane. **Creysse** is worth a stop, too – it's an exquisite village built around a Romanesque church.

LACAVE Further downstream, this well-named village can show you one of France's most spectacular subterranean wonders, open to the public since 1906, the **Grottes de Lacave** (05 65 37 87 03; w vert-marine.com; guided tours: mid Feb–early Nov 10.00–noon & 14.00–17.00 daily, 1st 3 weeks in Aug 09.30–18.00 daily (be sure to arrive 30mins in advance of your tour); €12, ages 14–20 €10, ages 4–13 €7.50). From the entrance, you'll travel 400m down on an electric train into the caverns – 1.5km of them, including the 'Lac des Mirages', where the reflections of stalactites in the water look just like an underwater city. Some of the caverns are illuminated by black light for their strange phosphorescent effects.

Then there's **Prehistodino Park** (Rte de Rocamadour; 05 65 32 28 28; w prehistodino.com; May–Jun & Sep 10.00–19.00 daily, Jul–Aug 10.00–20.00

daily, mid-Nov–Christmas & Feb school hols 11.00–17.00 daily; €8.90, students €7.90, ages 5–13 €4.90) with life-size models of dinosaur favourites, including an electronically animated T-Rex and a suitably roar-filled soundtrack, plus a reconstruction of a Neolithic village.

From Lacave the D43 continues to Souillac (page 251) passing the **Château de Belcastel** in a perfect cliff-top setting over the river to meet one of the most graceful iron bridges you'll ever see, at **Pinsac**; an anonymous engineer of the Ponts et Chaussées, France's national public works office, designed it in the 1930s.

ROCAMADOUR

Rocamadour proudly bills itself as the 'Second Site in France', after Mont St-Michel. The two share extraordinary, fantastical settings, the very kind of naturally sacred places that attract legends like lightning rods. Rocamadour is the medieval French equivalent of a Pueblo village in North America, a vertical cliff-dwellers' town, the beautiful golden stone houses and chapels piled up one on top of another over a deep ravine, while far, far below the little River Alzou continues its work of aeons, cutting even deeper into the gorge. There are several approaches: the most dramatic road is by way of Carlucet, east of the N20 and south of Rocamadour, a narrow winding road that comes out directly under the cliff.

HISTORY The late 11th-century origins of Rocamadour's cult of the Black Virgin are murky enough, and coincide neatly with the founding of the hostel at L'Hospitalet at the top of the cliff and the sudden flood of passing pilgrims. On the other hand, the Benedictines of Tulle, the promoters of Rocamadour, were hardly the only ones suddenly to find saintly relics – the money-generating roadside attractions of the Middle Ages – along the busy Way to Compostela.

The cult's legitimacy was given a big boost in 1166, when a man's body was discovered buried near the altar. This had to be St Zaccheus (dAD70), the diminutive publican who climbed the tree to see Jesus. After the Crucifixion, he, his very tall wife, St Veronica (of the holy handkerchief), and St Martial fled Palestine and arrived in Soulac-sur-Mer (page 91). After Veronica died, Zaccheus came here and built the first sanctuaries in the cliff-face. The locals called him 'the lover' or Amator for his devotion, and hence RocAmadour, the lover of rock. A second attraction was Durandal, the sword of Roland; just before he died at Roncesvalles, the hero confided his blade to St Michael, and the Archangel hurled it like a javelin straight into Rocamadour's cliff, where it remains to this day.

Yet always, the chief attraction was the blackened statue of the Virgin, whose cult grew by leaps and bounds at the time of the Crusades. Rocamadour's first important patron was Henry II of England, who endowed much of its treasure. His wayward eldest son, the Young King, Henry Court-Mantel – companion of Bertran de Born (page 168) – stole it in 1183 to pay his *routiers* in his war against his own father. By the time the plunderers reached Martel, the Black Virgin got her revenge, striking young Henry down with a fever. Full of remorse, he asked his father's forgiveness, had a halter placed on his neck and laid naked in a bed of ashes and died. The Bishop of Limoges refrained from excommunicating the dead man when his grieving father promised to replace Rocamadour's losses.

The story had the same effect as the doings of the royals in today's tabloids, and made Rocamadour even more famous. Saints Louis, Dominic, Bernard, Anthony of Padua, Engelbert and the blessed Raymond Lull came, as did the kings of France and countless others, especially on the days of pardon and plenary indulgence, when the chronicles say 30,000 thronged into the village. Others who came were less willing: thousands of criminals, Cathars and men who broke the Truce of God by fighting during Lent were ordered by ecclesiastical courts to make the pilgrimage to Rocamadour, to climb up the famous steps on their knees, to be bound in chains and led to the Virgin to confess and be purified by the priest. The priest would then strike off the chains, and present the shriven one with a certificate to take home as proof.

Rocamadour suffered a near-fatal setback during the Wars of Religion, when the Huguenot captains Bessonies and Duras came to lay waste and desecrate the shrine, leaving only the Virgin and her bell intact; what treasure was replaced afterwards was taken during the Revolution. After nearly three centuries of neglect, the bishops of Cahors began to (over) restore the shrines in the 1850s – giving the buildings a slight Disneyland-ish air that only increases in the high summer, when the crowds can barely squeeze into the narrow lanes. Arrive early in the morning to avoid the worst; better still, go in the early autumn when Rocamadour is at its most magical.

GETTING THERE AND AROUND For getting there, see page 232. If you're coming by train, Rocamadour is 4km from the station; book a **taxi** (m 06 07 14 72 36) to meet you.

Only the **cars** of visitors with bookings in the village hotels are allowed. In July and August the nearer **car parks** outside the gates fill up fast, but there are always places at the bottom, where a **little train** (05 65 33 65 99; w lepetittrainderocamadour.com; 10.00–19.30 daily; €3, ages 5–9 €2, return €4/2.50) runs every 15 minutes between the car park in the valley and the Cité Médiévale. Or park in the P2 in L'Hospitalet, Rocamadour's upper district, where you can walk down to the medieval Cité Médiévale – the steps aren't steep, but there are 223 of them – or take the two **public lifts** (05 65 33 67 79; w ascenseurincline-rocamadour.com; 09.30–19.00 daily; under 8 free) to the level of the sanctuaries (one way €2.70, return €4.30) or the Cité (€4.20/€6.20).

Rent a **bike** or e-bike at Lot & Bike (Le Château; m 06 14 65 77 62; w location-velo-lot.com) to explore the surroundings.

TOURIST INFORMATION Rocamadour's **tourist office** (05 65 33 22 00; w vallee-dordogne.com; Jul–Aug 09.30–19.00 daily, Sep–Jun 10.00–12.30 & 14.00–18.00 daily) is at the top at L'Hospitalet. Call them for current information on guided tours.

WHERE TO STAY A big advantage of staying in or near Rocamadour is seeing it the first thing in the morning, or in the evening after all the daytrippers have gone.

In Rocamadour

Les Esclargies (16 rooms) Chemin des Esclargies, L'Hospitalet; 05 65 38 73 23; w esclargies.com. On the corniche road, set amid the ancient oaks & in walking distance of Rocamadour this peaceful hotel has a heated pool, garden, bikes to hire & parking. **€€€€**

Beau Site (37 rooms) Rue Roland-le-Preux; 05 65 33 63 08; w beausite-rocamadour.com. In a medieval house, with contemporary rooms, some sleeping 4. The restaurant, **Jehan le Valon** (€€€€) is one of the best in town, with a panoramic dining room & pretty garden. **€€€€–€€**

Hostellerie Bellevue (13 rooms) L'Hospitalet; 05 65 33 62 10; w hotel-bellevue-rocamadour.com. Hotel from 1938 with view across to Rocamadour with decent 2-star rooms & parking, with a good restaurant (€€€) serving big salads & traditional dishes. **€€**

Le Relais Amadourien (23 rooms) Rte de Château, L'Hospitalet; 05 65 34 39 19;

w relais-amadourien.com. Renovated rooms, including some for families, in a park. €€–€

Le Terminus des Pèlerins (12 rooms) Place de la Carretta; 05 65 33 62 14; w terminus-des-pelerins.com. If you want to pay less in the centre, you won't do better than this simple Logis de France; the restaurant (€€€) serves traditional Quercy cuisine & snails. €€–€

Lion d'Or (72 rooms) by the Porte du Figuier, 05 65 33 62 04; w liondor-rocamadour.com. Wide choice of traditional rooms in 2 buildings 50m apart, some with spectacular views. Typical Périgord cuisine in the restaurant (€€) overlooking the Alzou gorge. €€–€

Around Rocamadour *Map, page 234*

Les Vieilles Tours (15 rooms) 3km west at Lafage; 05 65 33 68 01; w vtrocamadour.com. Rooms in a sturdy manor house built & added to between the 13th & 17th centuries; there's a panoramic heated pool, restaurant (€€€) & excellent €12 b/fast. €€€

Le Petit Relais (9 rooms) Calès, 13km northwest; 05 65 37 96 09; w hotel-petitrelais.fr. Country chic atmosphere, a pool & a superb restaurant (€€€€), featuring the best of the southwest. Well worth considering HB terms. €€€–€€

La Noyeraie Rocamadour (3 rooms, 1 studio) En Caminou, 3.9km east of Rocamadour; 05 65 40 43 91; w lanoyeraierocamadour.com. Charming traditional rooms on a farm. Host James makes a tasty table d'hôte; b/fast with homemade pastries inc. €€

Le Troubadour (10 rooms, 3 apts) Belveyre, 1km north of L'Hospitalet; 05 65 33 70 27; w hotel-troubadour.com. Peaceful & well-kept Logis hotel on 4ha of land, with a garden, pool & magnificent views of the *causse*, & a restaurant (menu €34; €€€). €€–€

WHERE TO EAT AND DRINK Locally Rocamadour is synonymous with creamy, flat cylinders of goat's cheese: *AOP cabécou de Rocamadour* (w aop-rocamadour.com). Connoisseurs like them ripe, pungent and coated with a tawny crust – the perfect accompaniment to a well-aged Cahors. If you haven't been previously introduced, you may want to start with a fresh white *cabécou*, or have it grilled – as a starter with salad. A couple of farms are open for tourists, including **La Ferme Borie d'Imbert** [map, page 234] (2km from Rocamadour on the Rte de Sarlat/Souillac; 05 65 33 20 37; w laboriedimbert.com; 10.00–19.00 daily, shorter hours out of season – check their website) and the **Ferme Lacoste** [map, page 234] (Les Alix; 05 65 33 62 66; 09.30–noon & 14.00–18.00 Mon–Sat, but ring first).

Auberge Le Roc du Berger [map, page 234] Bois de Belveyre, Rte de Padirac; 05 65 33 19 99; w rocduberger.fr; last w/end of Mar–Sep daily, Oct Sun & eves Sat. A great place for grilled lamb, trout, or duck, salads & potatoes, but you'll need a car. *Menus €22*. €€

L'Estanquet Place de l'Europe, L'Hospitalet; 05 65 10 98 08; f LaillierCalore; daily. Contemporary dishes & big salads at this bistro with a sunny terrace. *Menus from €20*. €€

Le Quercygnac Place Bernard de Ventadour; m 06 18 36 29 41 f; daily. A young team runs this restaurant near the Porte du Figuier, with a delicious €14.90 lunch menu, *tartines* (French *bruschetta*), salads & great music. €€

La Maison de Famille Porte Salmon; 05 65 50 20 61; f; 10.00–21.00 daily. Shady terrace with views, crêpes & salads. €

Café Théâtre Côté Rocher Rue Roland-le-Preux; 05 65 10 93 39; f CoteRocher; 17.00–00.30 Mon–Tue, Thu–Sat. Snack bar & comedy, a great way to spend a night in the Cité Médiévale, if your French is up to it.

WHAT TO SEE AND DO

Cité Médiévale The pilgrims would enter Rocamadour through the 13th-century **Porte du Figuier**, one of four gates that defended the village's one real street. Once in, past a gauntlet of souvenir shops, you'll find a second gate, **Porte Salmon** (and the lift to the Holy City). Beyond this is the 15th-century Palais de la Couronnerie, now the **Hôtel de Ville,** where a beautiful tapestry of local flora and fauna by Jean Lurçat (page 236) is on display (🕘 Jul–Aug 09.30–18.30 daily, Sep–Jun 10.00–noon & 14.00–17.30 Mon–Sat; €2). The street continues through another gate into the **Quartier du Coustalou**, the prettiest and least restored part of the village, with jumbly little houses and a fortified mill.

The Holy City From Place de la Carretta the great stair, the 216-step **Grand Escalier**, leads up into the holy city; pilgrims still sometimes go up them on their knees. The first 144 steps lead to the **Place des Senhals**, where merchants sold holy medals (*senhals* in Occitan) made of lead and stamped with a picture of the Virgin. Rocamadour's oldest street, **Rue de la Mercerie**, extends from here, with the 14th-century **Maison de la Pomette** at its end. From here, continue up through the gate under the over-restored **Fort**, sometime residence of the bishops of Tulle.

Parvis de St-Amadour At the top of the Grand Escalier, this small square is the centre of the holy city, where the pilgrims could visit seven churches, just as in Rome, but in a very abbreviated space. Today only **Notre-Dame** and **St-Sauveur** are open (🕘 Jul–Aug 08.00–21.00 daily; Sep–Jun 08.30–18.30 daily); for **St-Michel**, **SS Anne and Blaise** and L'Hospitalet and the **Crypt of St-Amadour**, you need to take the tourist office's guided tour.

The 11th-century **Basilique St-Sauveur** makes good use of the cliff for a wall. Over the altar hangs a painted wooden 16th-century Christ crucified on a tree, his right side instead of the customary left pierced by the lance. Steps lead down into another of the seven churches, the simple 12th-century **Crypt St-Amadour**, where the relics of the saintly hermit were venerated. The Parvis also has the **Musée Trésor d'Art Sacré** (closed except for special occasions) dedicated to the composer Francis Poulenc, an atheist who converted to Catholicism after a vision here in 1936 and composed his *Litanies à la Vierge Noire de Rocamadour*. Inside are precious medieval reliquaries from Limoges, stained glass and 17th-century ex-votos.

Parvis Notre-Dame On the other side of St-Sauveur another 25 steps lead up to the church of **Notre-Dame** and the Flamboyant Gothic **Chapelle Notre-Dame**. This dates from 1479, after a rock crashed off the cliff through the original sanctuary. Inside, the miraculous Black Virgin holds court. Carved from walnut in the 11th century, she sits stiffly on her throne, almost a stick figure, the Christ Child balanced on her knee. Ex-votos testify to her heavenly influence: many are from Breton sailors saved from shipwreck after praying to the Virgin of the Rocamadour – including Jacques Cartier, who returned safely from his three voyages to Canada. Miracles were often foretold by the ringing of the 9th-century bell hanging from the roof. Chains from pilgrim petitioners still hang in the back of the chapel. Outside, high in the rock above the door, **Durandal** (page 244) is still embedded in the stone, fastened by a chain to keep it from falling on someone's head.

Sharing this upper square with Notre-Dame is the **Chapelle St-Michel**, with the overhanging cliff for a roof, decorated on the outside with colourful 12th- or 13th-century frescoes representing the *Annunciation* and *Visitation*. The patron of travellers, St Christopher, is painted below; to catch a glimpse of him was good luck, so he was always made extra big. Nearby, tucked in the rock is the newest chapel – to **Notre-Dame de l'Ovalie** (aka rugby!) Further up, a hairpinning path lined with the **Stations of the Cross** (or the much easier lift from the Parvis de St-Amadour) takes you up to the ramparts of the 14th-century **château** (€2 for the vertiginous view) and **L'Hospitalet**, the district named after a hostel-hospital founded in 1050 by Hélène de Castelnau for pilgrims en route to Compostela.

Le Rocher des Aigles (Marcayou, L'Hospitalet; 05 65 33 65 45; w rocherdesaigles.com; Apr–Jun & Sep daily, see website for times, Jul–Aug 10.00–20.00, shows at 11.00, 14.30, 16.00 & 17.30 daily; arrive 10mins before the show; €11, ages 4–13 €7; bring a hat) The eagle's nest atop Rocamadour is a real one, thanks to the breeding programme for endangered birds of prey (including a condor) and parrots from Costa Rica. Watching them soar high over Rocamadour is pretty impressive, and you can visit them all before or after the show. Try to go to the last spectacle, when they bring out the owls.

Parc Durandel (Marcayou, L'Hospitalet; m 06 19 39 18 00; w parcdurandal.com; mid-Jul–late Aug shows at 11.30 & 16.00 Sun–Thu; €12, ages 7–15 €10, under 7 free; arrive 30mins before the show) Good clean medieval fun for the whole family – equestrian displays, jousting, and a lot of joshing about.

Grotte des Merveilles (L'Hospitalet; m 07 88 26 84 78; w grottedesmerveilles.com; Jul–Aug 10.00–18.00 daily, May–Jun & Sep–Oct hours change frequently – see website, closed Nov–Apr; €8, ages 5–11 €5) L'Hospitalet was first inhabited in the Upper Palaeolithic era. This cave in the village centre has, besides stalactites, lakes and fantastical rock formations, some rather deteriorated negative hands and animal drawings dating back to 30,000BC, which suggests that this might have been a sacred place long before any of its stories were written.

La Forêt des Singes (Rte de Gramat, L'Hospitalet; 05 65 33 62 72; w la-foret-des-singes.com; Apr–early Nov daily, see calendar on the website; €9.50, ages 5–14 €5.50) You can meet, perhaps more intimately than you might wish, the 150 friendly Barbary apes at liberty here.

La Maison des Abeilles (Rte de Gramat, L'Hospitalet; 05 65 33 66 98; w abeilles-rocamadour.com; Apr–Oct 10.30–12.30 & 14.00–19.00 daily; free) Walk into a living beehive; there's also a film, a display of historic hives and more on apiculture, plus tasting of the *pain d'épices* (a bit like gingerbread) and a honey boutique.

Near Rocamadour On the blue-green River Ouysse, the **Moulin de Cougnaguet** is an impressive mill built by monks in 1350, fortified against flour thieves and – by the looks of it – against time as well; its four millstones can grind 3 tonnes of grain each day. Herbert the miller will demonstrate (Calès, 9km west on the D673; 05 65 32 63 09; w cougnaguet.com; Apr–Oct 10.30–noon & 14.00–18.00; €5). There are geological attractions just south of Rocamadour – the **Gouffre de St-Sauveur**, a round, deep, blue-green pit, and **Gouffre de Cabouy**, the resurgence in the canyon of the Ouysse.

THE CAUSSE DE GRAMAT AND PADIRAC

The Causse de Gramat is the upper crust of an extraordinary subterranean world of lakes and rivers. The *causse* itself has a peculiar fascination in the spring and early summer, when the scrub oak and juniper, wild flowers, eglantine and

above The monstrous, ever-growing Dune du Pilat, Europe's biggest sand pile (SS/S) page 96

below *Cabanes tchanquées*, built for supervising oyster beds in the Bassin d'Arcachon (SP33/S) page 96

bottom Lacanau-Océan on the Côte d'Argent is popular with surfers (ap/S) page 92

above France's largest fortified mill, the Moulin des Tours in Barbaste, was once owned by Henri IV (v/S) page 306

left The 700-year-old Pont Valentré in Cahors was built, according to legend, with aid from the devil (GB/S) page 262

below left The Tour du Roy is all that remains of St-Émilion's medieval castle (SLC/SET) page 132

below right The Château de Beynac, once home of the powerful baron known as 'Satan's Bow' (tr/S) page 210

above **Romanesque at its best: Moissac Abbey's 11th-century cloister** (ADT82) page 349

right **St-Front's exotic domes rise over Périgueux's skyline** (d/S) page 147

below **A bird's-eye view of Brantôme – the 'Venice of Périgord' – and its famous abbey** (BF/S) page 160

above **Canoeing is a great way to explore the region's many rivers. Pictured here: La Roque-Gageac on the Dordogne** (w/S) pages 21 & 209

left **Climbing the Rocher d'Anglars at St-Antonin-Noble-Val, in the Gorges de l'Aveyron** (ADT82) page 342

below **Cycling along the Canal Latéral à la Garonne between Toulouse and Bordeaux, one of the region's many bike paths** (ADT82) page 21

above **Rocamadour provides a spectacular backdrop to the September Mongolfiades balloon festival** (tr/S) pages 41 & 244

below left **Summer fêtes are non-stop: medieval ones, like this one in Cadouin, are especially popular** (JR/PdB)

below right **The tall ships at Bordeaux's river and wine festivals evoke the wine trade of yore** (JL/S) page 52

above **A rare pig snuffling out Périgord's 'black gold' (most truffle hunters now use dogs)** (P1b/S) page 171

left **Geese and ducks are a mainstay of the local cuisine** (MP) page 36

below **In St-Émilion the grape harvest, or *vendange*, is still done by hand** (SLC/SET) page 132

above *Carrelets* – wooden fishing shacks on stilts – line the Gironde estuary (BZ/S) page 137

right Eating lamprey stewed in wine is the test of a true Bordelais (FdC/SET) page 134

below Farming oysters in the Bassin d'Arcachon (En/S) page 93

above **Place de la Liberté, in the heart of Renaissance Sarlat-la-Canéda** (JC/S) page 200

honeysuckle soften the land; the flocks of the *causse* – a local breed of sheep called the *caussenarde* whose eyes are protected from the sun by natural black spectacles – forage on wild herbs, butterflies flutter by and buzzards and kestrels slowly circle the horizons. Holiday people fill the houses, and the cafés and restaurants are open – often a welcome sight after you've travelled for miles without passing a sign of human life.

Come in the winter, and the *causse* becomes a study in grey desolation, the colour drained out of it, the oaks clinging dismally to their brown leaves in the sodden mists. The villages seem sad and empty, or locked up altogether; the buzzards and kestrels are still there, but now they seem sinister as they circle over silent, overcast ridges.

TOURIST INFORMATION Gramat's office (05 65 33 22 00; w vallee-dordogne.com; 10.00–12.30 & 14.00–18.00 Mon–Sat, plus Jul–Aug 10.00–13.00 Sun) is on the D807.

WHERE TO STAY AND EAT

Hostellerie du Causse (31 rooms) Rte de Cahors, Gramat; 05 65 10 60 60; w hostellerieducausse.com. Modern rooms in a pretty garden setting with a heated pool & an exceptional restaurant (€€€€) with dishes all *fait maison*. **€€€–€€**

Hôtel Le Centre (19 rooms) Place de la République, Gramat; 05 65 38 73 37; w lecentre.fr. A new fun, colourful makeover of a once rather drab hotel & a very good restaurant (€€€). **€€**

Le Relais des Gourmands (16 rooms) 2 Av de la Gare, Gramat; 05 65 38 83 92; w relais-des-gourmands.com; closed Mon & eves Sun. Reopened in late 2021 after a fire, with a pool & garden; superb dining (€€€) on locally sourced lamb, duck; also a superb *tatin de foie gras*. **€€**

Le Grand Couvent (28 rooms) 33 Av Louis Mazet, Gramat; 05 65 38 73 29; w grandcouventgramat.fr. In a 10ha park, a 5min walk from the station, simple rooms, very welcoming to pilgrims & a good restaurant (€€). B/fast inc. **€€–€**

Le Lion d'Or (15 rooms) 8 Place de la République, Gramat; 05 65 10 46 10; book on w booking.com. Old coach inn in a handsome stone building, & good restaurant (€€) in the dappled shade of the trellis. **€€–€**

Hôtel du Château (28 rooms, 1 gîte) Place de la Mairie, Alvignac (midway between Rocamadour & Padirac); 05 65 33 60 14; w hotelduchateaualvignac.fr. Ivy-covered inn with simple rooms & a pool, & an excellent restaurant (€€€); lovely owners. **€**

Les Coeurs Gourmands 1 Rue de la Poste, Gramat; m 06 81 17 13 14; 07.00–22.30 Mon–Sat. Modern, friendly spot right in the heart of the village, with tasty home-cooked set menus & excellent beers. **€€**

GRAMAT Located on the River Alzou, the pleasant if not terribly remarkable capital of the *causse* has only a 15th-century clock tower and a watchtower to recall the days before the Wars of Religion. Gramat's baron, Gontaut d'Auriolle, was a Protestant ally of Henri IV, but, unfortunately for the town's historical preservation, everyone else in the vicinity remained Catholic. These days Gramat acts as Rocamadour's overflow tank, with a surprise: the **Musée Insolite du Coiffeur Barbier** (160 Rue Alexandre Dumas; 05 65 33 76 48; w museeinsoliteducoiffeurbarbier.fr; 10.00–12.30 & 15.00–19.30 Tue–Sun; €4), in a 1920s salon, displaying more than 4,000 objects on the history of hairdressing from 1850 to 1950.

On the edge of Gramat, the excellent **Parc Animalier de Gramat** (05 65 38 81 22; w gramat-parc-animalier.com; Apr–Jun & Sep–Oct 10.00–18.30 daily, Jul–Aug 09.30–19.00 daily, Nov–Apr 13.30–17.30 daily; €14, ages 4–11 €9, under 4 free) is home to 250 different European animals and birds, aurochs, wolves, bears and Barbary apes (and funky punk chickens and curly-haired pigs) in a large wooded park.

AROUND GRAMAT The most important tumulus in the Lot, known as the **Étron de Gargantua** ('Gargantua's turd'), is just east (on the D15) and covered with flowers that don't grow anywhere else (the name Gramat comes from the Celtic *grammat*, or tumulus). Other Neolithic sites in the vicinity include good dolmens at **Pech-Farrat** (east off the N140), **La Ségala** (up the Alzou from Gramat) and **Les Aspes** (to the west on the D39). Northeast of Gramat, **Lavergne** has an impressive *pigeonnier*; the village's Romanesque church of **St-Blaise** has modillions carved with lively human and animal faces. Another 2.5km to the north, **Thégra** has a harmonious 15th-century château.

West off the D39, the **Château de la Pannonie** (Rte de la Pannonie, Couzou; 05 65 33 71 71; w lapannonie.com; guided tours: Jun, Sep–Oct 11.00, 14.30–16.30 Wed–Mon, Jul–Aug 11.00, 14.30–17.30 daily; €6/€4) was built as the pleasure dome of a Rocamadour merchant in the 15th century then expanded in the classical style in the 18th century; a rare grand house in the Lot from that period.

GOUFFRE DE PADIRAC (Padirac; 05 65 33 64 56; w gouffre-de-padirac.com; mid-Jul–late Aug 08.00–20.30 daily, Apr–early Nov shorter hours, closed Fri; boat ride & audio guided visit: €19.50, students €18, ages 4–12 €14.50; special exploring activities: €140/€80 – book timed tickets online to avoid the queues) A *gouffre* is a chasm which is easy to remember if you recall that French trappers named the burrowing critters they found in America *gaufres*, or gophers. Had a gopher dug the pit in Padirac, it would have to have been the size of the Titanic – this chasm plunges down 90m before forming 21km of galleries. But not only is the Gouffre de Padirac spectacularly huge, much of it is spectacularly beautiful. Bring a sweater: down below the temperature is a constant 13°C.

For centuries the opening, 35m diameter, was regarded as the entrance to hell. In 1889, Edouard Martel, one of the founding fathers of speleology, made the first scientific exploration of the *gouffre*; by 1898 it was opened to the public. Remarkably, tools and animal bones from c50,000BC were found 8km from the entrance.

The 90-minute visit starts with a descent by lifts or stairs into the cool depths of the cavity, formed by water dissolving the limestone over millions of years. This chamber was once domed; now the floor is covered by a pyramid of rubble from the roof. You'll wander past a spring and down a long underground canyon. At the end, gondolas wait to row you along the **Rivière Plane**, the 'smooth river', which flows underground into the Dordogne; in 1996 a diver-speleologist discovered the exact point of its resurgence, under the Cirque de Montvalent (page 243). Along this shadowy River Styx the most extraordinary decoration is the **Grande Pendeloque**, or Great Pendant, an enormous stalactite that almost touches the water.

When you disembark on the far bank, you'll walk through the narrow **Pas du Crocodile**, past a 40m stalactite pillar into the **Salle des Grands Gours**. A *gour* is a natural limestone dam, and here the *gours* create a pretty series of basins of clear water, flowing one into the other, with a 6m waterfall and a green lake at the end. Beyond lies another little lake, the **Lac Supérieur**, fed only by rainwater penetrating the limestone.

None of this, however, prepares you for the climactic **Salle du Grand Dôme** – an un-collapsed *gouffre*, a majestic vaulted space which soars up to 93m and in volume could contain two cathedrals of Notre-Dame; as you climb the steps through this fantastical space, with a grandiose view over the lakes, the only way you can take in the immensity is to note how very tiny all the people look at the far end.

SOUILLAC

This town may not look like much from the dusty stretch of the N20 that passes through it, but its abbey church makes it a mandatory stop to see a jewel of Romanesque sculpture, and it has a museum of the first robots. Souillac likes to call itself the 'Gateway to the South', based on the tradition that cicadas, the totem insect of the French Midi, will sing only once you cross over the 45th parallel. Its name, however, actually comes from the Celtic *souilh*, mudflat, the kind that boars like best – hence the bristling swine on its coat of arms.

TOURIST INFORMATION Souillac's office (05 65 33 22 00; w vallee-dordogne.com; 10.00–12.30 & 14.00–18.00 Mon–Sat, plus Jul–Aug 10.00–13.00 Sun) is on Boulevard Louis Jean Malvy.

WHERE TO STAY AND EAT Located midway between Sarlat and Rocamadour, Souillac makes a good stopover.

La Vieille Auberge (9 rooms) 1 Rue Récège; 05 65 32 79 43; w la-vieille-auberge.com. Pool, sauna, hammam & jacuzzi, & well-equipped rooms & a gastronomic restaurant (€€€) filled with light. There are another 25 rooms with balconies around the pool in its annexe, **Le Quercy. €€€–€€**

Les Ambassadeurs (22 rooms) 12 Av du Général de Gaulle; 05 65 32 78 36; w ambassadeurs-hotel.com. Classic Logis hotel with a pool & good traditional cuisine (€€€), popular with the locals. **€€**

Le Grand Hôtel (30 rooms) 1 Allée de Verninac; 05 65 27 76 21; w legrandhotel.net. Vintage 1905, central & comfy enough accommodation with new young owners. The bar/bistronomic restaurant (€€) serves classic dishes. **€**

Le Pavilion Saint Martin (11 rooms) 5 Place St-Martin; 05 65 32 63 45; w hotel-saint-martin-souillac.com. Atmospheric hotel in a medieval building, with some fun touches (some rooms sleep 5). Buffet b/fast (€12) in the vaulted cellars. **€**

Le Beffroi 6 Place St Martin; 05 65 37 80 33; f lebeffroisouillac; closed Sun & eves Mon. A jovial place with tables spread out in the medieval centre & creative but unfussy cuisine make this one of the best in town, plus live music some evenings. **€€€**

Ferme Auberge du Gouffre du Blagour [map, page 234] Lachapelle-Auzac (just north of Soulliac); 05 65 37 83 93; w gouffredublagour.com; Jul–early Sep lunch Wed–Sun. This spring-filled *gouffre* is a trout farm, with a restaurant where you can feast on a €21 menu starring smoked & grilled trout. You can also fish & pay by the kilo, or visit their boutique. **€€**

Les Tilleuls [map, page 234] 143 Rte de Sarlat; 05 65 27 28 53; f restaurantlestilleuls46; closed eves Wed & Sun. Very pretty terrace & a constantly changing menu, all fresh & great value for money. **€**

SHOPPING Souillac's big **market** takes place in Place de l'Abbaye on Fridays. There are smaller **fruit-and-vegetable markets** on Monday and Wednesday mornings in Place Doussot and Place St-Martin, in July and August, and also a **clothes and bric-a-brac** market on the first and third Friday of each month.

SPORTS AND ACTIVITIES **Souillac Country Club** (Le Mas Del Teil, Lachapelle-Auzac; 05 65 27 56 00; w souillaccountryclub.co.uk), a resort with holiday rentals and a restaurant, boasts an 18-hole **golf** course. For **riding** excursions, try the Club Hippique Souillagais (Chemin Corpus Christi; ☎ 05 65 32 64 62; w centre-equestre-souillac.fr).

Quercyland (Rue des Ondines, Souillac; ☎ 05 65 32 72 61; w copeyre.com; ⌚ May–Sep 11.00–20.00 daily; €10) waits to entertain the kids with bouncy castles and a waterpark; they also offer **canoe and kayak** descents down the Dordogne.

WHAT TO SEE AND DO

Abbatiale Ste-Marie (Place Pierre Betz; ⌚ 08.00–19.30 daily; free) The origins of Souillac are typical: an abbey was founded here in the early AD900s and reached its glory days in the 12th century. A village grew up around its walls and the abbey took some hard knocks in the wars before a fire in the 1570s finished it off, leaving only the church and massive 16th-century bell tower of St-Martin. The philistines of Louis XIV's time worked some outrageous butchery on the church, covering its stately domes with a fake gable roof, destroying one of the finest carved portals in France, and plastering over everything inside. All that has since been cleared away and, although it may still be hard to imagine the church of Ste-Marie in its original splendour, the essentials remain.

Its denuded state, in fact, makes it easier to appreciate the authority and perfection of the architecture. Ste-Marie is Romanesque at its most Roman, striving above all for monumental presence. This is best seen outside in the apse; one suspects the architect had had a good long look at the ancient palaces and public baths in Rome (some of which were still in good nick in the 1100s). The interior is even better: a single nave, graceful and strong. Of the three domes, the earliest is oddly squared, showing the Islamic origins of the technique.

The surviving fragments of the **portal** have been reconstructed inside the main door. The wild scene on top, showing a fellow with some serious devil troubles, represents St Theophilus the Penitent. Archdeacon of Adana (in Turkey), this Theophilus was wrongly thrown out of his office and in revenge sold his soul to the devil; of course the devil got it in writing. Theophilus later repented so sincerely that the Virgin Mary went down to hell and snatched the contract from the devil. The three vignettes in the crowded relief show the signing, the devil attempting to carry Theophilus away and, above, the Virgin and an angel pulling him up into heaven. Just why this obscure saint should have such a prominent place on the portal is a good question, but then perhaps he isn't so obscure after all – this story is one of the sources for the legend of Faust. Flanking the relief are the two figures without which no French portal would be complete: St Peter and St Paul.

Outstanding as these reliefs are, the eye is inevitably drawn below to the Prophet Isaiah. As Freda White noted, 'This statue is alive.' It is commonly called the 'dancing' Isaiah. Poised on one foot, with stone draperies flowing, the composition is unlike anything else produced in the Middle Ages. Most striking of all is the extreme stylisation: studied and consistent, a vision of form that is the work of a great artist – one of the greatest between the Greeks and Donatello.

Musée de l'Automate (Esplanade Alain Chastagnol, opposite Ste Marie; ☎ 05 65 37 07 07; w musee-automate.fr; ⌚ Apr–Jun, Sep & Oct 14.00–18.00 Wed–Sun, Jul–Aug 09.00–12.30 & 14.00–18.00 daily, other times ring ahead; €9/€7.50, ages 5–12 €3) A fascinating museum, this claims to be the largest collection in Europe of mechanical dolls and toys, some from as far back as 1870 – and nearly all are in working order. They haunt the premises, eating, drinking, playing banjos, waiting for the metro, dancing with snakes, jumping through hoops and doing every other trick that clockwork and circuitry can accomplish, all to special sound and light effects.

Musée de la Vieille Prune (41–43 Av Jean Jaurès; 05 65 32 78 16; w lavieilleprune.com; 08.30–noon & 14.00–17.30 Mon–Fri; free) The 'Old prune museum' is not a portrait gallery of wrinkly old people but the home of the Distillerie Louis Roque, where plums are apotheosed into a lip-smackingly smooth *eau-de-vie*.

12

The Lot: Quercy

Outsiders often tend to lump the Lot together with neighbouring Dordogne because the northern reaches of the department include that famous river (which we have put in our Dordogne Quercynoise chapter). But the Lot's heartstrings and history have always pulled it in the other direction – to the south. It occupies half of the ancient province of Quercy, the northernmost lands of the medieval Counts of Toulouse and Occitanie. Instead of the green-shire beauty of the Dordogne, the Lot is more cowboy rough-and-tumble, its landscape tossed up in limestone plateaux called *causses* – a huge swathe down the middle is now a Regional Natural Park and UNESCO World Geopark. What soil it has is said to be the worst in France (the truffles and Malbec vines don't mind that at all), but its air is also the cleanest; with so little light pollution, you can see a billion stars.

Sometime in the past, the letters in the Celtic name Olt were jiggled to create 'Lot' for a river with more curls, or *cingles*, in it than Goldilocks' ringlets; if you stretched it out from its source in the Lozère to Aiguillon, where it flows into the Garonne, it would measure 471km – all that to travel a mere 270km as the crow flies. It wanders through three distinct landscapes. Above Vers it is closed in by blond and ochre limestone cliffs, where you'll find the most striking castles, the fabulous cave of Pech Merle and St-Cirq-Lapopie. West of Vers the cliffs have been worn down into *cévennes*, rounded hills covered with scrub oak. West of Cahors, the typical landscape is asymmetrical – *cévennes* on one bank, spacious valley on the other, much of it covered with oak forests, the rest with vines producing *vin de Cahors*.

CAHORS

The immediate surroundings of Cahors are some of the most discouraging landscapes in all France. The anomic clutter of the newer parts of town matches them well, but persevere – in the middle you'll find a medieval city of surprising subtlety and character. Its star attraction is the Pont Valentré, which, as any Frenchman will tell you, is the most beautiful bridge on this planet.

HISTORY 'Quercy' may evoke oaks (as in the Latin *quercus*), the tree that covers much of its territory, but the name is really derived from its never-say-die Cadurcii, the fierce Gaulish tribe who had their capital Divona Cadurcorum in this tight twist of the River Lot. Divona was the name of the sacred spring that still flows under the riverside cliffs, or perhaps of the Celtic goddess who presided over it. In 51BC, after Caesar's defeat of Vercingetorix at Alésia, the feisty Cadurcii still refused to surrender until Caesar diverted the physical manifestation of their goddess Divona – their water supply.

Under Roman rule, Divona Cadurcorum boasted an aqueduct, public baths, an arena and a theatre for 6,500. A civil war among the Franks in the AD570s left it thoroughly trashed, but fortunately, not long after, a strong-willed bishop named

Desiderius, later to be declared St Didier – or St Géry, as the locals like to call him – was also royal treasurer to King Dagobert, and he found enough loose change to resurrect Cahors at a time when little else was being built in Gaul.

Further insults were in store – unwelcome visits by Vikings, Magyars and Arabs – but Cahors survived to find a brilliant career in the Middle Ages. The bishops still ruled, gradually gaining control of most of the Lot valley and becoming a factor that even the French kings and the counts of Toulouse had to take into consideration. Under their stable rule, the town began to learn to make money. The founders of this great foray into modern capitalism seem to have been Italians, 'Lombard' merchants who fled north to the relative safety of the bishops' domains from the terrors of the Albigensian Crusade in the early 1200s.

Throughout the 13th century these families and their colleagues perfected their skill at merchant finance and moneylending. They became familiar figures in all the trade fairs and business centres of Europe, so prominent – and predatory – that Caorsin became a synonym for a usurer. Dante mentions them in the *Inferno* (Canto XI, 50), where he put the Caorsins down with Sodom in the third circle of hell. No doubt they laughed all the way to the bank. The king of France needed them, whenever he was in the mood for a campaign; the noblemen and the Church needed them too, and they got on just fine with the town's bishops.

As their wealth piled up, the merchants translated it into impressive palaces, a new set of fortifications, magnificent bridges and the completion of the cathedral. Even more money flowed in after 1316, when a Cahors merchant's son named Jacques Duèze became Pope John XXII at age 72...who then surprised everyone by living for another 18 years. John reigned from Avignon, and founded a university in his hometown that lasted until 1751, when the jealous scholars of Toulouse succeeded in having it merged into their own. During the religious wars, Cahors with its still-influential bishops remained stoutly Catholic. In 1560, there was a bloody massacre of Protestants; 20 years later, Henri of Navarre stormed the city, and in retaliation the future king allowed his troops to give the place a thorough pillaging.

In June 1949, thanks to an initiative by local teacher Émile Baynac and Robert Sarrazac, a Resistance leader and co-founder (with American Garry Davis) of the World Citizens Movement in 1945, Cahors became the first to declare itself a World City, Cahors Mundi. The event was celebrated the following year on the Pont Valentré with founder of the UN's FAO (Food and Agricultural Organization) and Nobel Peace Prize recipient Lord John Boyd Orr and André Breton (other early supporters were Albert Camus and Albert Einstein – and 239 other communes in the Lot). Another Resistance fighter, Cahors mayor Maurice Faure, who served in the national government, was the last surviving signer of the Treaty of Rome that created the EU when he died in 2014.

LOT: QUERCY

Where to stay

1 Château de Mercuès *p259*.......C4
2 Château de Rouffiac *p285*.......A4
3 Comfort *p271*.......G4
4 Domaine de La Barthe *p259*.......C4
5 Hotel au Charme du Levat *p282*.......D6
6 La Bergerie *p259*.......D4
7 La Combe de Redoles *p274*.......F5
8 La Métairie des Songes *p290*.......C2
9 Le Clos des Dryades *p274*.......D4
10 Le Grézalide *p265*.......F3
11 Le Manoir Enchanté *p271*.......H4
12 Le Vinagrou *p282*.......E6
13 Maison Duler *p282*.......C6
14 Mas de Redoulès *p274*.......F5
15 Mas del Lum *p274*.......G3
16 Mas Des 3 Ânes *p265*.......E4

Where to eat and drink

17 Aux Délices de la Serpt *p290*.......B3
18 Château de Chambert *p285*.......B5
19 Château de Haute-Serre *p282*.......D5
20 Delicatessens *p290*.......D2
21 Ferme Auberge de Larcher *p265*.......E3
22 La Garenne *p259*.......D5
23 La Poule au Pot *p291*.......B4
24 Le Caillou *p285*.......A5
25 Le Gindreau *p290*.......C4
26 Un Canard sous l'Olivier *p290*.......D3

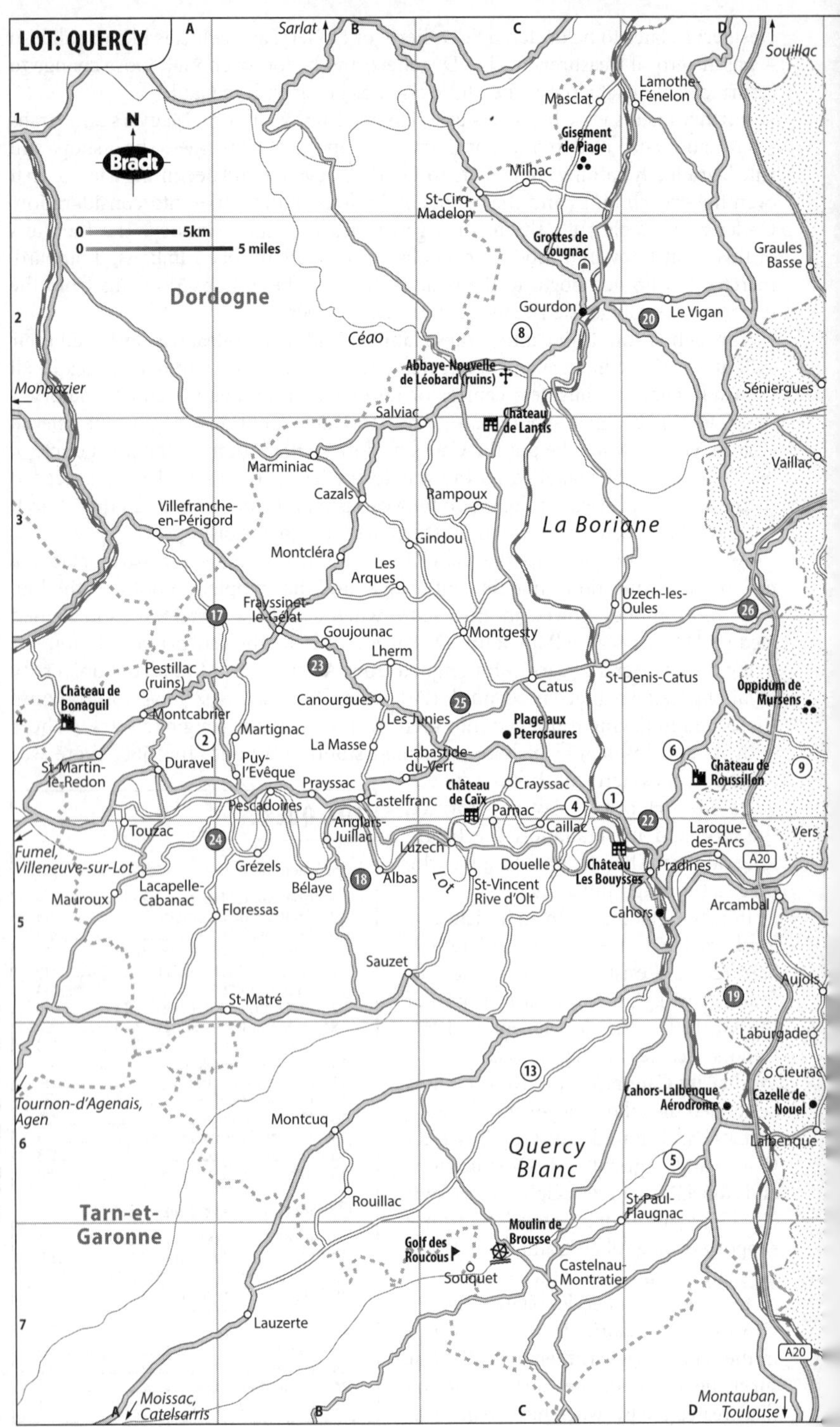
LOT: QUERCY
Bradt
N
0 5km
0 5 miles
Sarlat
Souillac
Masclat
Lamothe-Fénelon
Gisement de Piage
Milhac
St-Cirq-Madelon
Grottes de Cougnac
Graules Basse
Dordogne
Gourdon
Le Vigan
Céao
Abbaye-Nouvelle de Léobard (ruins)
Séniergues
Monpazier
Salviac
Château de Lantis
Marminiac
Vaillac
Cazals
Rampoux
Villefranche-en-Périgord
La Boriane
Gindou
Montcléra
Les Arques
Uzech-les-Oules
Frayssinet-le-Gélat
Goujounac
Montgesty
Lherm
Pestillac (ruins)
St-Denis-Catus
Catus
Oppidum de Mursens
Château de Bonaguil
Canourgues
Les Junies
Plage aux Pterosaures
Montcabrier
Martignac
La Masse
Labastide-du-Vert
Château de Roussillon
St-Martin-le-Redon
Duravel
Puy-l'Evêque
Prayssac
Château de Caïx
Crayssac
Pescadoires
Castelfranc
Parnac
Caillac
Laroque-des-Arcs
Vers
Touzac
Anglars-Juillac
Luzech
Fumel, Villeneuve-sur-Lot
Grézels
Douelle
Château Les Bouysses
Pradines
A20
Lacapelle-Cabanac
Albas
Lot
Bélaye
St-Vincent Rive d'Olt
Mauroux
Arcambal
Floressas
Cahors
Sauzet
Aujols
St-Matré
Laburgade
Cieurac
Cahors-Lalbenque Aérodrome
Cazelle de Nouel
Tournon-d'Agenais, Agen
Montcuq
Lalbenque
Quercy Blanc
Rouillac
St-Paul-Flaugnac
Tarn-et-Garonne
Moulin de Brousse
Golf des Roucous
Souquet
Castelnau-Montratier
Lauzerte
Moissac, Catelsarris
Montauban, Toulouse

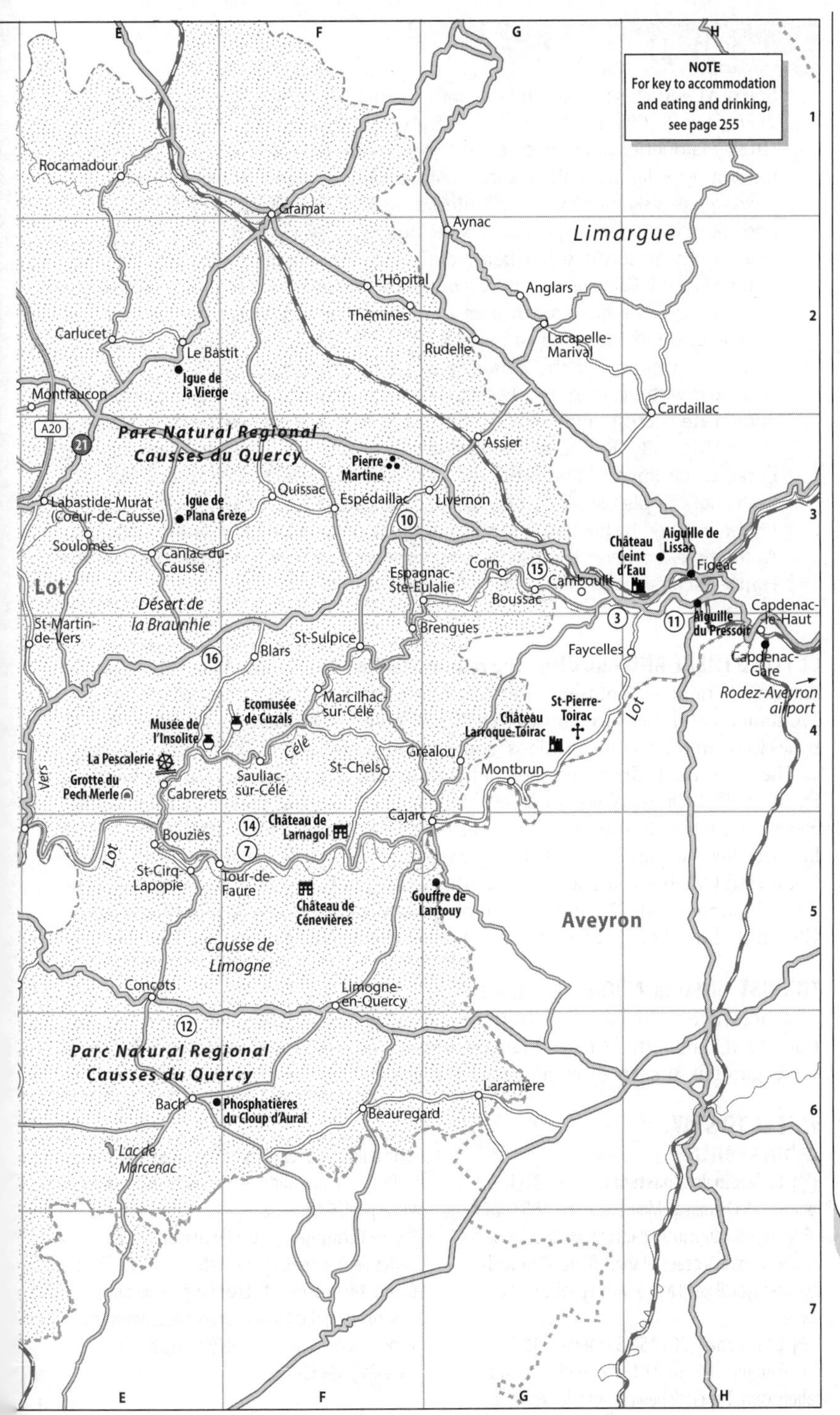
NOTE
For key to accommodation and eating and drinking, see page 255
Rocamadour
Gramat
Aynac
Limargue
L'Hôpital
Anglars
Thémines
Carlucet
Le Bastit
Rudelle
Lacapelle-Marival
Igue de la Vierge
Montfaucon
Cardaillac
A20
21
Parc Natural Regional Causses du Quercy
Assier
Pierre Martine
Quissac
Labastide-Murat (Coeur-de-Causse)
Igue de Plana Grèze
Espédaillac
Livernon
10
Soulomès
Caniac-du-Causse
Château Ceint d'Eau
Aiguille de Lissac
Corn
15
Figeac
Lot
Espagnac-Ste-Eulalie
Camboulit
Boussac
Désert de la Braunhie
Capdenac-le-Haut
St-Martin-de-Vers
Brengues
3
11
Aiguille du Pressoir
St-Sulpice
Faycelles
16
Blars
Capdenac-Gare
Rodez-Aveyron airport
Ecomusée de Cuzals
Marcilhac-sur-Célé
Musée de l'Insolite
Château Larroque-Toirac
St-Pierre-Toirac
Lot
Célé
La Pescalerie
Grealou
Vers
Grotte du Pech Merle
Sauliac-sur-Célé
St-Chels
Montbrun
Cabrerets
Château de Larnagol
14
Cajarc
Bouziès
7
Lot
St-Cirq-Lapopie
Tour-de-Faure
Gouffre de Lantouy
Château de Cénevières
Aveyron
Causse de Limogne
Concots
Limogne-en-Quercy
12
Parc Natural Regional Causses du Quercy
Laramière
Bach
Phosphatières du Cloup d'Aural
Beauregard
Lac de Marcenac
E
F
G
H
1
2
3
4
5
6
7

THE POET OF THE NIPPLE

Son of a Cadurcien mother and the Norman poet Jean Marot, *valet de chambre* of François Ier, Clément Marot (1495–1544), went into the service of the king's sister, Marguerite d'Angoulême, and soon made his mark at court for his elegant verse, if not for his personal charms; contemporaries described him as looking 'like a skinned rat'. Marguerite was known for protecting Protestants, and Marot was often suspected of being one, especially in 1526 when he was chucked into prison for eating bacon during Lent – although his eloquent plea to the king, the *Épître au roi*, got him out of the calaboose overnight.

Marot was the first French poet to write in sonnets. When he got into trouble again in 1534, and was forced into exile in Italy, he regained favour with the invention of the *blason* (a short poem eulogising an attribute of a lady) with his *Blason du beau tétin* ('to the beautiful nipple'). It was an immediate success, and Clément, 'the Prince of Poets', was welcomed back to court in 1536. But he was too honest to take much comfort in fashion; bored by his imitators, he wrote the *Contre-blason du laid tétin* ('anti-blason to the ugly nipple'), setting a new fad for indelicate satires. Then he published *L'Enfer*, inspired by his stay in prison and today considered his greatest work. At the time, however, it caused such an uproar that he was forced to leave France yet again, and died alone in Turin in 1544.

GETTING THERE AND AROUND The **railway station** [260 A5] on Avenue Jean Jaurès has direct trains to Gourdon, Souillac, Brive, Paris and south towards Caussade, Montauban and Toulouse. **Buses** (08 05 36 06 60; w lio.laregion.fr) leave several times a day to Monsempron-Libos (some go only as far as Puy l'Évêque) and Figeac.

The city is easily doable on foot, but parking can be a challenge. The **city bus line**, Évidence (08 06 80 10 60; w bus-evidence.fr), provides free park-and-ride shuttles every 15 minutes to the Chartreuse car park [260 B7] just south of the centre and Ludo-Rollès car park [260 C3] to the east; other car parks are at the north end of Boulevard Gambetta at Place Charles-de-Gaulle [260 C4] and south over the Pont Louis Philippe [260 C7], and in an underground garage called l'Amphithéâtre [260 C6] under the Allées Fénelon because they found the Roman arena at one end.

TOURIST INFORMATION The **tourist office** [260 C6] (05 65 53 20 65; w cahorsvalleedulot.com; 09.00–19.00 Mon–Sat, 10.00–18.00 Sun) is off Boulevard Gambetta at Place François Mitterrand. Ask for the guide to the city's secret gardens, tucked away in unexpected places.

WHERE TO STAY

Cahors centre

Le Jardin du Moustoulac [260 A3] (4 rooms) 175 Chemin du Moustoulac; m 06 98 42 07 36; w lejardindumoustoulac.com. Modern house & comfy rooms in a peaceful spot off the D8 towards Pradines (you'll need a car) with a pool. B/fast inc. **€€€**

Le Divona [260 A5] (38 rooms) 113 Av André Breton; 05 65 21 18 39; w divona-hotel-cahors.com. The city's newest hotel looks like a white bunker, but each room has lovely views over the Pont Valentré, and there's parking & a heated indoor pool. **€€€–€€**

Le Terminus [260 B4] (20 rooms) 5 Av Charles de Freycinet, by the station; 05 65 53 32 00; w terminus-1911.fr. Charming, resolutely retro & ivy-covered, this hotel has recently renovated rooms in various sizes, & a very pretty bistro (€€€€€). **€€€–€€**

Jean XII [260 C4] (9 rooms) 2 Rue Edmond Albe; 05 65 35 07 66; w hotel-jeanxxii.com. Simple rooms (including a quad) by the tower of the 14th-century Palais Duèze, built by the pope's brother. **€€**

La Chartreuse [260 C7] (50 rooms) St-Georges; 05 65 35 17 37; w hotel-la-chartreuse.com. Overlooking the Lot, just south of the centre; modern rooms & a good traditional restaurant (€€€) with a terrace on the water. **€€**

Brit Hotel France [260 B5] (70 rooms) 252 Av Jean Jaurès; 05 65 35 16 76; w ahors-france.brithotel.fr. Chain hotel near the station & Pont Valentré. **€**

La Chantrerie [260 C5] (3 rooms) Rue de la Chantrerie; m 06 84 76 84 23; w lachantrerie.fr. Tucked in the pedestrian lanes behind the cathedral, characterful studios. **€**

Near Cahors

Château de Mercuès [256 C4] (30 rooms) Rte du Château, Mercuès, 5km northwest of Cahors; 05 65 20 00 01; w chateaudemercues.com. Sitting on a spur high above the Lot valley, this Relais et Châteaux hotel occupies the count-bishop's palace (page 265). Rooms (2 are in the towers) are fitted with large marble baths & canopy beds, & outdoors are gardens, spa pool, tennis & tremendous views. Guests can visit the huge wine cellars. Michelin-starred **Le Duèze restaurant** (€€€€€) is the best in town, but there's also an excellent bistro in the courtyard with a €45 lunch formule. **€€€€€**

Domaine de La Barthe [256 C4] (5 rooms, 2 gîtes) 1 Rue des Granges, Espère, 8km west of Cahors; 05 65 30 92 34; w domaine-de-labarthe.com. Set back in a beautiful park with ancient olive trees, this 18th-century *gentilhommière* is filled with antiques, books, art & family heirlooms & gorgeous rooms, all south facing with views. There's a heated saltwater pool, spa, mountain bikes & lovely English-speaking owners. B/fast inc. **€€€€**

Le Mas Azemar (5 rooms) Rue du Mas-de-Vinssou, Mercuès; 05 65 30 96 85, w masazemar.com. At the foot of the mighty castle, this 18th-century farmhouse in a mature park with a heated pool offers large antique-furnished bedrooms; table d'hôte available eves for €39 all included. B/fast inc. **€€€**

La Bergerie [256 D4] (10 rooms) 8km north of Cahors on the N20 in St-Pierre-Lafeuille; 05 65 36 82 82; w labergerie-lot.com. Modern Logis hotel, each room with a private little terrace & view. The restaurant (€€€) offers modernised versions of cuisine quercynoise. **€€**

Le Clos Grand [260 A3] (20 rooms) 12 Rue des Claux Grands, Pradines, 6km northwest of Cahors; 05 65 35 04 39; w leclosgrand.fr. 5 generations have run a restaurant (€€) here since the 1930s & added rooms in the 1970s, with balconies overlooking the park. **€**

WHERE TO EAT AND DRINK

La Garenne [256 D5] 5km north on the D820; 05 65 35 40 67; w la-garenne-cahors.com; closed Wed & eves Mon–Tue. Pretty setting in a 19th-century farm, famous for its superb land-&-sea dishes such as *couronne de St-Jacques à la truffe* & *filet de bœuf Rossini. Menus from €36, w/day lunch €22.* €€€€

Le Marché [260 C5] 27 Place Chapou; 05 65 35 27 27; w le-marche-cahors.fr; closed Sun–Mon. Near the covered market, with fresh market-based dishes on a weekly changing menu, & vegetarian & vegan dishes by request. *3-course w/day lunch €24, dinner €36–€54.* €€€€

L'Ô à la Bouche [260 C6] 56 Allées Fénelon; 05 65 35 65 69; w loalabouche-restaurant.com; closed Sun–Mon. New address for this old favourite, featuring dishes designed, as the name promises, to make your mouth water. *Lunch menus from €22.50.* €€€€–€€€

Côté Sud [260 D5] Place Champollion; 05 65 53 15 16; w cuisine-cotesud.com; closed Sun–Mon. Right behind the cathedral, with a summer terrace; David Blanco prepares colourful contemporary dishes that never fail to hit the spot. *3-course menu €33.* €€€€–€€€

La Petite Auberge [260 D6] 144 Rue St Urcisse; 05 65 35 06 05; f; 11.00–22.00 Thu–Mon. Near the marble clock, part restaurant with a delicious €29 menu, with good vegetarian choices, & part tearoom with organic teas, coffees & homemade pastries. €€€

Bistro de L'Isa [260 C5] 67 Bd Gambetta; 05 65 35 22 35; w bistrodelisa.fr; daily. Bar/brasserie serving French classics along with duck (of course), pizzas & snacks; also Sun brunch.

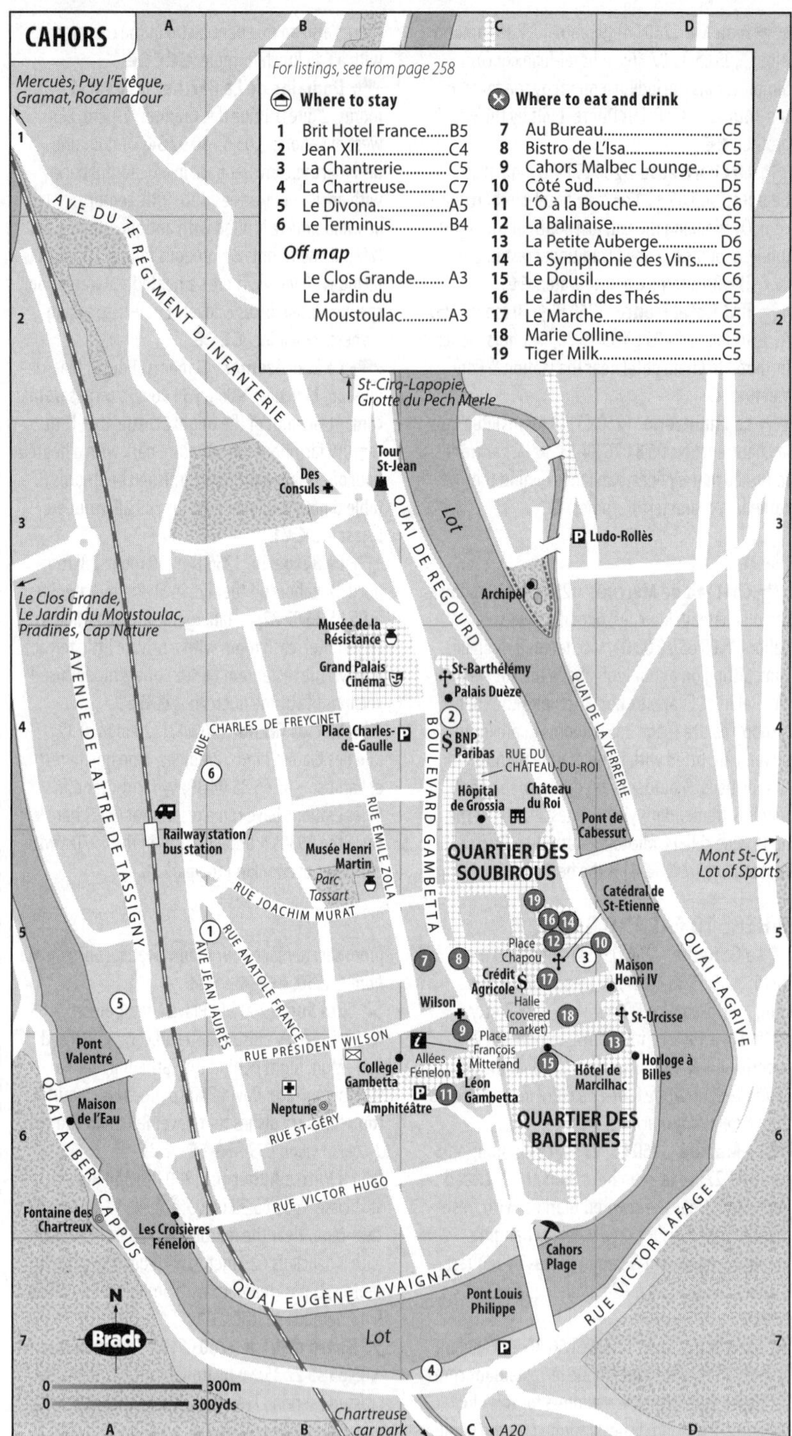
CAHORS
For listings, see from page 258
Where to stay
1 Brit Hotel France......B5
2 Jean XII.........................C4
3 La Chantrerie............C5
4 La Chartreuse...........C7
5 Le Divona...................A5
6 Le Terminus..............B4
Off map
Le Clos Grande........ A3
Le Jardin du Moustoulac............A3
Where to eat and drink
7 Au Bureau.................................C5
8 Bistro de L'Isa..........................C5
9 Cahors Malbec Lounge...... C5
10 Côté Sud...................................D5
11 L'Ô à la Bouche......................C6
12 La Balinaise.............................C5
13 La Petite Auberge................ D6
14 La Symphonie des Vins...... C5
15 Le Dousil...................................C6
16 Le Jardin des Thés................ C5
17 Le Marche.................................C5
18 Marie Colline...........................C5
19 Tiger Milk..................................C5
Mercuès, Puy l'Evêque, Gramat, Rocamadour
St-Cirq-Lapopie, Grotte du Pech Merle
Le Clos Grande, Le Jardin du Moustoulac, Pradines, Cap Nature
Mont St-Cyr, Lot of Sports
Chartreuse car park
A20
AVE DU 7E RÉGIMENT D'INFANTERIE
AVENUE DE LATTRE DE TASSIGNY
QUAI DE REGOURD
QUAI DE LA VERRERIE
QUAI LAGRIVE
QUAI ALBERT CAPPUS
QUAI EUGÈNE CAVAIGNAC
RUE VICTOR LAFAGE
RUE CHARLES DE FREYCINET
BOULEVARD GAMBETTA
RUE ÉMILE ZOLA
RUE JOACHIM MURAT
AVE JEAN JAURÈS
RUE ANATOLE FRANCE
RUE PRÉSIDENT WILSON
RUE ST-GÉRY
RUE VICTOR HUGO
RUE DU CHÂTEAU-DU-ROI
Lot
Des Consuls
Tour St-Jean
Ludo-Rollès
Archipel
Musée de la Résistance
Grand Palais Cinéma
St-Barthélémy
Palais Duèze
BNP Paribas
Place Charles-de-Gaulle
Hôpital de Grossia
Château du Roi
Pont de Cabessut
Railway station / bus station
Musée Henri Martin
Parc Tassart
QUARTIER DES SOUBIROUS
Catédral de St-Etienne
Place Chapou
Maison Henri IV
Crédit Agricole
Halle (covered market)
St-Urcisse
Wilson
Place François Mitterand
Allées Fénelon
Léon Gambetta
Collège Gambetta
Amphithéâtre
Hôtel de Marcilhac
Horloge à Billes
Neptune
QUARTIER DES BADERNES
Pont Valentré
Maison de l'Eau
Fontaine des Chartreux
Les Croisières Fénelon
Cahors Plage
Pont Louis Philippe
Bradt
N
0 300m
0 300yds

Tables on the pavement are great for people-watching. €€€–€€

Au Bureau [260 C5] 73-67 Bd Gambetta; 05 65 30 17 58; 09.00–23.00. Cheap & cheerful bar-brasserie with pub food, burgers, veggie platters, mojitos and more. €€

La Balinaise [260 C5] 219 Rue Maréchal Foch; 09 52 35 07 39; w labalinaise.fr; closed Sun. Authentic dishes from Bali, packed full of flavour. Small, so be sure to book. €€

Le Dousil [260 C6] 124 Rue Nationale; 05 65 53 19 67; w ledousil.free.fr. Restaurant-wine bar near the covered market, with tapas & daily specials. €

Le Jardin des Thés [260 C5] 12 Rue Daurade; m 06 88 04 60 00; Le-Jardin-des-Thés-La-Suite; 10.00–18.30 Tue–Sat. Fine teas of course, but also cakes & tasty vegetarian lunches. €

Marie Colline [260 C5] 173 Rue Clemenceau; 05 65 35 59 96; lunch only Mon–Fri. Excellent vegetarian restaurant, offering a choice of 2 different plats du jour each day plus a choice of starters & magnificent desserts. €

Cahors Malbec Lounge [260 C5] Place François Mitterrand; 05 65 23 82 35; w vindecahors.fr; 15 Jun–Oct 11.00–19.00 Tue–Sat, Oct–mid-Jun 11.00–13.30 & 16.00–19.00 Tue–Sat. By the tourist office, chic wine bar for a full-on Malbec experience.

La Symphonie des Vins [260 C5] 42 Rue Daurade; 05 65 35 47 94; w lasymphoniedesvins.fr; noon–02.00 Tue–Sat. Malbec here but also a long list of other wines & excellent tapas, including mini burgers & desserts.

Tiger Milk [260 C5] 49 Rue Clémont Marot; m 06 11 96 71 82; ; 18.00–02.00 Wed–Sat, 11.30–16.00 Sun. Cool, atmospheric, inventive cocktail & tapas bar.

SHOPPING Cahors's award-winning covered market [260 C5] (daily exc Sun) is at the south end of Place Chapou; on Wednesday and Saturday mornings it fills the square. Every first and third Saturday there is a clothes and flea market spread all along Boulevard Gambetta and the Allées Fénelon.

SPORTS AND ACTIVITIES In summer you can pretend you're on the Riviera at **Cahors Plage** [260 C7] by the Pont Louis-Philippe.

Archipel [260 C3] Quai Ludo Rolles, Île de Cabessut; 05 65 35 05 86; mid-Jun–mid-Sep 10.00–18.00 daily; €4.20, ages 3–12 €3.45. With a huge pool, whirlpool, children's area, beach & more.

Cap Nature [260 A3] Pradines; 05 65 22 25 12; w capnature.eu. Adventure park also offering waterskiing, wakeboarding, kayaking, etc.

Les Croisières Fénelon [260 A6] Quai Valentré, Allées des Soupirs; 05 65 30 16 55; w bateau-cahors.com; 80min cruises Jul–Sep 11.00, 15.00 & 16.30 daily, Jun Sat–Sun only; €11.50, ages 5–13 €5. They also offer special w/end cruises on the Lot.

Lot of Sports [260 D5] m 06 80 45 33 31; w lotofsports.fr. Their centre is on Mont St-Cyr, Cahors's belvedere, offering archery, frisbee golf & mountain bike hire.

OTHER PRACTICALITIES

$ **BNP Paribas** [260 C4] 15 Bd Gambetta

$ **Crédit Agricole** [260 C5] Place Chapou

Hospital [260 C4] 52 Place Antonin Bergon; 05 65 20 50 50; w ch-cahors.fr

+ **Des Consuls** [260 B3] 2 Place des Consuls

+ **Wilson** [260 C5] 36 Bd Gambetta

Post office [260 B6] 257 Rue Président Wilson

WHAT TO SEE AND DO

Boulevard Gambetta [260 C4/5] A canopy of plane trees shades the city's main shopping street, replacing its medieval walls. Near the tourist office in Place François Mitterrand, an appropriately Flamboyant **monument to Léon Gambetta** [260 C6], shows Cahors's Republican hero pointing dramatically, perhaps accusingly, north towards Paris. As a lawyer and politician, Gambetta was a strong opponent of Napoleon III. After France's defeat in 1870, he declared the Third Republic in Paris, and then dramatically escaped from the city in a balloon while the Prussians were besieging it. After that, he raised new armies in the south (though the Prussians whipped them too), and eventually became premier; all France mourned in 1882 when he accidentally killed himself while cleaning a gun.

If you stroll to the end of the Allées Fénelon behind Gambetta, have a look at the handsome **Collège Gambetta** [260 B6] on the right with its octagonal red-brick bell tower, a survivor of the 17th-century Jesuit college that stood here first. The Allées are closed off by a pretty **Neptune fountain** [260 B6]; turn right here for Rue du Président Wilson.

Pont Valentré [260 A6] (At the end of Rue Wilson) If anything is a sign of opulence in a medieval city, it's the bridges. Cahors had three, where one would have sufficed, and the two that have disappeared, demolished in 1868 and 1907, were almost as good as this one.

The Pont Valentré survived because it carried little traffic. Begun in 1308, and financed with the help of Pope John, the bridge nevertheless took 70 years to complete. With the Hundred Years' War in full swing, it isn't surprising that defence became the major consideration. The three towers that look so picturesque are three rings of defences to keep the English out; each had its portcullis, and slits for archers and boiling oil.

You can be sure the Devil had something to do with it. Here after working on the project for decades, the master builder made a deal with Old Nick: if he would do whatever the builder told him to do with his supernatural powers to finish the bridge, he would forfeit his soul. After the bridge was finished, the builder tricked him, of course, by giving him a sieve and ordering him to fetch water, but the Devil got his revenge by sending a demon to steal one of the stones near the top of the central tower, which had to be replaced every day. In the 19th century, restorers added the stone carved with a devil to trick Satan into thinking his orders were still being followed.

Once over the bridge, turn left to visit the old pumping station, the **Maison de l'Eau** [260 A6] (05 65 53 04 99; 10.00–13.00 & 15.00–19.00 daily; free) with its original machinery intact. Some 200m further down, under the cliff, the medieval **Fontaine des Chartreux** [260 A6] is fed by the underground streams of the causse; hundreds of ancient coins discovered in the depths, confirm the popular belief that this was the ancient spring Divona.

Cathédral de St-Étienne [260 C5] (Place Chapou; 05 65 35 27 80; 09.00–19.00 daily; free) Medieval Cahors is clustered east of Boulevard Gambetta under its mighty cathedral. Begun in the 10th century on the site of St Didier's 7th-century church, this was the second of the domed churches of Périgord and Quercy, directly inspired by St-Étienne in Périgueux. Not completed until the 1400s, its western and eastern ends were completely rebuilt, resulting in a not unlovely architectural mongrel, a kind of Romanesque-on-Gothic sandwich.

The severe **façade**, the typical broad *clocher-mur* of a Quercy church writ large, was redone in the 14th century, when the original entrance was moved around to the side – then walled in and forgotten until 1840. This, the **north portal**, is one of the finest in southern France. In the centre, Christ in a mandorla is flanked by angels tumbling down out of the heavens, and scenes of the martyrdom of St Stephen; below are the Virgin Mary and ten apostles (there wasn't room for 12). The borders and modillions are fascinating, with a full complement of monsters, scenes of war and violence, and unusual decorative rose motifs that seem to prefigure the trimmings on Cahors's Renaissance palaces.

The entrance is via the beautiful **tri-lobed portal** tucked in the south. Turn around to see the finely drawn frescoes (c1320) high above the west door, a series of scenes from Genesis. The other surviving original paintings decorate the first of the two mighty domes in the nave. These include the *14 Lapidateurs* with their stones, ready to lapidate poor Stephen and ensure his status as the first Christian martyr. The new windows, with designs by Gérard Collin-Thiébaut imprinted on glass and installed in 2013, aren't to everyone's liking, to put it mildly.

In 1330, the original east end was replaced with a Gothic apse, an odd structure built on the plan of a pentagon which from the outside looks like a separate building. Inside, it contains some fine sculptural work and 17th-century paintings in its side chapels. More of the same can be seen in the Flamboyant **cloister** (1509). Tragically, Henri IV's lads did a thorough job of smashing up the capitals in 1580, but enough remains, or has been restored, to allow you to appreciate one of the finest sculptural ensembles of the southwest. Note in one corner the winsome *Vierge des Litanies*. The carvings around the arches facing the centre have an M C Escher quality, metamorphosing from a leaf of curly kale into an ocean wave into a dog licking its legs.

The cloister's **Chapelle St-Gausbert** has 15th-century frescoes representing a not very dire *Last Judgement*, along with portraits of the 93 bishops of Cahors and what remains of the treasure, notably its relic – the *coiffe* or cap Jesus wore when he was buried, which was pinched from Constantinople during the Fourth Crusade of 1204.

Place Chapou [260 C5] This elongated square in front of the cathedral extends to the covered **market** [260 C5]. Note the old painted shop sign, preserved on the façade of the Crédit Agricole bank: Bazar Genois – Gambetta Jeune et Cie, put up for an Italian immigrant grocer who earned his immortality for being the father of Léon.

Quartier des Badernes South of the cathedral, this was the popular quarter of the city – though it had its share of palaces, mostly along Rue Nationale, the main street in medieval times; at its beginning, the **Hôtel de Marcilhac** (no. 116) [260 C6] has a lovely Baroque carved door. The narrow lanes to the left off Rue Nationale, give an idea of how dense urban life was in Cahors, with numerous half-timbered houses, and medieval palaces along Rue Lastié; many of these have big, pointed arches facing the street for the business façades and elegant twinned windows on the family quarters upstairs. Another feature is the *soleiho*, a sun porch on the top; in Renaissance palaces they are often made of brick arches and called *mirandes*. The neighbourhood's church, **St-Urcisse** [260 D5], stands at the end of Rue Clemenceau with a 13th-century statue of the Virgin on the façade; if it's open, don't miss the set of carved capitals with fond naïve scenes of *Adam and Eve* and the *Life of Christ*. In Place St-Urcisse by the river, the hypnotic **Horloge à Billes** [260 D6] created by Michel Zachariou keeps the time with 54 marbles. Here too is the most impressive medieval palace of them all, the **Maison Henri IV** [260 D5] (271 Quai Champollion) where the future king parked himself while his troops ransacked the city. For a view of Cahors's medieval skyline most people never see, cross over the bridge here, the Pont de Cabessut.

Quartier des Soubirous [260 C5] North of the cathedral extends what was the wealthy merchants' quarter; *soubirous* means superior, for the way it climbs uphill.

Its spine, **Rue du Château-du-Roi** [260 C4], is an elegant street reminiscent of Siena or Perugia. Its most impressive façade is at no. 102, the 13th-century **Hôpital de Grossia** [260 C4]. Across from the Hôpital, the **Château du Roi** [260 C4] was one of Cahors's grandest palaces in the 1300s, built by the pope's brother-in-law but it was thoroughly wrecked in the 19th century when the state converted it into a prison; the tall donjon inside, visible only from the riverfront, once had a tall chimney as a landmark for river boatmen. Plans are to make it into a hotel and cultural centre.

St-Barthélémy [260 C4] (Rue St-Barthélémy, at the top of the Soubirous; 05 65 21 30 91) This austere church with a triple arcaded bell tower was one of the earliest in Cahors, site of an abbey founded by St Didier; in 2019 a 7th-century AD skeleton of a woman was found outside the portal, along with fragments of Merovingian pots. In 1244 Jacques Duèze, a merchant's son born nearby, was baptised at St-Barthélémy, and, when he became Pope John XXII, he rebuilt the church in the Gothic style while his brother rebuilt the **Palais Duèze** [260 C4] nearby. Of the palace only the lofty tower survives, again more reminiscent of Tuscany than France. The best surviving parts of the medieval walls are here: the **Barbacane** and the massive 30m **Tour St-Jean** [260 B3], which did double duty: its other name is the Tour des Pendus, 'Tower of the Hanged Men'.

Musée de la Résistance [260 C4] (Place Général de Gaulle; someday) The old museum was demolished to make way for the new Grand Palais Cinéma, where its collections are due to reopen in a new space nearby.

Musée Henri Martin [260 B5] (792 Rue Emile Zola; 05 65 20 88 66; ring for opening hours) After years of renovations and a new addition, this museum in the 17th-century Bishop's Palace finally reopened in 2022, and features 60 works by the endearing pointilliste Henri Martin, who lived in Labastide-du-Vert (page 288). It also holds the Symbolist paintings by Lotois painter Edmée Larnaudie (d2001), items relating to the World Citizen Movement, and archaeological finds, including a three-fingered Neolithic goddess from Capdenac and an Iron Age relief of what looks like a birth scene. Just behind it, the bishop's garden, planted with sequoias and Japanese magnolias, is now **Parc Tassart** [260 B5], with a playground and a pair of swans.

CASTLES AROUND CAHORS First built by Waiofar, Duke of Aquitaine in the 8th century, the medieval **Château de Roussillon** [256 D4] (**w** chateau-de-roussillon.com) is a romantic sight isolated 8km north of Cahors in St-Pierre-Lafeuille. Although one of the city's chief defences, it never saw much action; in 1355, during the Hundred Years' War, its lord welcomed the English inside until the Consuls of Cahors paid them to go away. Cannibalised for its stone since the 18th century, it was purchased in 1958 by a couple of teachers who restored three of its eight towers; today their son rents it out as a wedding and party venue.

Even more striking is the **Château de Mercuès**, prominent – or rather unavoidable, on its hilltop over the D811 – 5km northwest of Cahors. Its name, first mentioned in the 7th-century AD chronicles of St Didier, comes from the 'Camp of Mercury'. The castle was built as a stronghold, but it soon became the pleasure dome of the count bishops of Cahors. In 1563, the Protestants smoked the then bishop out and caught him climbing out of a window; they made him ride backwards on a donkey dressed in mock papal regalia before he was rescued, and his embarrassment was so acute that he died shortly after. The castle burned in the 17th century; when a plague hit Cahors, the bishop offered refugees shelter at Mercuès – in exchange for rebuilding his spread. Any bishop would be proud of the vast wine cellars; still they gave it all up in 1909 and today it's a hotel (page 259).

THE CAUSSES DU QUERCY

Northeast of Cahors are the lofty lonesome causses, which most people only see on their way to Rocamadour (page 244). These great limestone plateaux, pocked full of karstic chasms (*gouffres*), sinkholes (*igues*) and subterranean rivers, are now part of the Parc Naturel Régional Géoparc Mondial UNESCO Causses du Quercy, nicknamed the 'Black Triangle' for very starry nights. To the east of the park is a nearly-as-empty micro-region of chestnut forests and meadows of wildflowers called the Limargue with some charming villages, and the remains of one of the most blustering castles ever built.

TOURIST INFORMATION The tourist office of **Labastide-Murat** (aka Coeur-de-Causse; 05 65 21 11 39; w tourisme-labastide-murat.fr; Jun–Sep 09.00–13.00 & 14.00–18.00 Mon–Sat, plus Jul–Aug 09.00–13.00 Sun, Oct–May 09.00–13.00 & 14.00–18.00 Mon, Wed–Thu only) is at 9 Place de la Mairie. Also see the **Parc Naturel Régional Causses du Quercy** website, w parc-causses-du-quercy.fr.

WHERE TO STAY

Le Grézalide [257 F3] (20 rooms) Le Bourg, Grèzes (between Espédaillac & Livernon); 05 65 11 20 40; w grezalide.com. Rooms in the contemporary art-filled Château de Grèzes with a room for every mood, a restaurant (guests only; €€€) plus a pool, billiards, bikes, pétanque, massages & a telescope. **€€€€–€€€**

La Garissade (18 rooms) 20 Place de la Mairie, Labastide-Murat; 05 65 21 18 80; w garissade.com. Comfortable old stone Logis inn & a good restaurant (€€€) – bistro for lunch & more ambitious evening dining, all *fait maison*. **€€**

Hostellerie La Terrasse (13 rooms) Place de Larroque, Lacapelle-Marival; 05 65 40 80 07; w hostellerie-la-terrasse.com. The architecture won't win prizes, but the dining room (€€€) has panoramic views of the castle. The food is lovely; menus from €30. **€€–€**

Mas Des 3 Ânes [257 E4] (5 rooms, 1 gîte) 570 Rte du Pech de Gignous, Blars; 09 61 67 68 40; w lemasdes3anes.com. Simple B&B with peaceful rooms, a pool & starry nights. Table d'hôte available by request. B/fast inc. **€**

WHERE TO EAT AND DRINK

L'Assiérois Place de l'Église, Assier; 05 65 40 56 27; w lassierois.com; closed Mon & eves Sun & Wed. Refined contemporary dining in the old village inn, with extra special gourmet takes on the classics. *Menus from €36.* €€€

Osteria Il Grappolo Le Bourg, Montfaucon; 05 65 31 11 80; w osteriailgrappolo.com; lunch Tue–Sun, dinner Fri–Sat. An excellent Italian restaurant with a chef from Piedmont, who prepares exquisite dishes from the region such as *plin* (meaty melt-in-your-mouth ravioli). €€€

Ferme Auberge de Larcher [257 E3] D677 Labastide-Murat; 05 65 31 10 39; w fermedelarcher.com; Jul–Aug daily, Jun & Sep Sat–Sun. Duck, lamb & veal are raised here, now run by the 5th generation, & served in generous portions. Be sure to book. *Menus from €15.90.* €€

Auberge de Beauville Le Bourg, Espédaillac; 05 65 40 55 62; lunch Tue–Sun. A historic stone inn with checked tablecloths & a terrace, & a young chef, serving up a satisfying €15 lunch. €

LABASTIDE-MURAT (Or **Coeur-de-Causse** since 2016, when all the surrounding villages were sucked in to make one commune) This important population centre on the causses was founded in the 13th century by Fortanier, lord of Gourdon, and was named after him until 1852, when the village decided to rename itself to honour native son Joachim Murat (1767–1815). Yet, despite his adventurous career – as Bonaparte's aide-de-camp he distinguished himself with gut-busting courage and bravado, was promoted to marshal, married Napoleon's sister Caroline, and was crowned King of Naples, before trying to return to Naples after Waterloo and getting himself shot on the spot – Murat never forgot the folks back home. He built a château for his brother André – a rare example of the Empire style in this neck of the woods – and sent letters to his mum, now displayed in the **Musée Murat** (in his father's auberge; 05 65 24 97 82; 15 Jul–15 Sep 10.00–noon & 15.00–18.00 Wed–Mon; €3/€1.50); among the period furniture and other memorabilia is a giant family tree showing Murat's relationship with most of the crowned heads of Europe.

Vaillac, now part of Coeur-de-Causse, is the seat of a formidable feudal castle and Romanesque church, where a medieval relief of the Virgin of Rocamadour was discovered. **Soulomès** 3km southeast, was one of several commanderies of the Knights of St John in the region, and their 12th-century Gothic church of **Ste-Marie Madeleine** has unusual 16th-century frescoes on the *Life of Christ* – scenes of Jesus taking a stroll with Mary Magdelene, Doubting Thomas and the resurrected Christ with a knight of St John.

NORTH OF LABASTIDE-MURAT As a foil to French-founded Labastide-Murat, Edward II founded the charming hilltop bastide of **Montfaucon** in 1292; if the church is open, pop in to look at the 17th-century altarpieces. Two kilometres north of Montfaucon, **Séniergues** is a minor gem, a picturesque rural hamlet with a 12th-century Romanesque church and splendid views all around. **Le Bastit**, another important Templar commandery serving passing pilgrims, has one of the causse's most spectacular avens (natural wells) or sinkholes, the **Igue de la Vierge** [257 E3]. The pilgrim's route, in this case between Rocamadour and Compostela, was often marked by wayside crosses: west, in **Carlucet**'s hamlet of **Graules Basse**, there is a unique one with mysterious stone pendants.

DÉSERT DE LA BRAUNHIE To explore this wildest, most desolate part of the causse, take the small roads east of Labastide-Murat. On the west edge of La Braunhie, **Caniac-du-Causse** has, under its modern church, a 12th-century crypt containing the 11th-century reliquary of St Namphaise, a friend of Charlemagne who fought against the Saracens in Quercy and then returned to live as a hermit, wandering about excavating drinking holes for the flocks, earning himself the sincere devotion of Lotois shepherds. The local answer to fertility drugs is to crawl under his reliquary. There are traces of a Roman road nearby.

Some things do grow in La Braunhie – eglantine, juniper, twisted little oaks, gorse, brambles and other prickly things. East of Caniac, you can visit its most dramatic feature, the **Igue de Plana Grèze**, a 271m deep sinkhole descending into an underground river – it's inaccessible but panels explain what's down there. A path carved out of the stone links the pit to a dolmen, as if it were part of the sacred site.

Picturesque, sleepy villages to aim for include **Blars** (south of the D653 to Figeac), with a Romanesque church with carved capitals and reliefs, **Quissac** and **Espédaillac**, the latter seat of another commandery of the Knights of St John, the former with a *pietà* in its church from the 1600s. Just northwest of **Livernon**, you can see the biggest dolmen in the Lot, the **Pierre Martine** [257 F3] (off the D2; walk through the scrubby trees to the end of the field). Its 22-tonne table stone stretches 7m, but, massive as it is, it would wiggle at the touch of a finger until 1948, when it cracked; now concrete blocks support it. Livernon's **church** has a beautiful fortified Romanesque bell tower, and there's a pretty fountain in the centre called the **Boudoulou**.

The N140 traces an important pilgrim route to Rocamadour, remembered in **L'Hôpital**, where the Knights of St John ran a hostel, although just a chapel survives. Further southeast, tiny **Thémines** has a fine *halle* with a *lauze* roof, while, yet further along, **Rudelle** is a rather dilapidated 13th-century bastide, defended by a battlemented **church** built by Bertrand de Cardaillac which looks like an overgrown rook from a chessboard.

For a scenic detour, take the D40 north from Thémines up to **Aynac**, where a striking **château** (private) was built in the 15th century by the sister of Galiot de Genouillac of Assier, its four towers crowned with breast-shaped, slate-coated cupolas; the delicate bas-relief over the door fits in perfectly, although it dates from 1895. Aynac's Romanesque church of **St-Geniès** has an octagonal tower and carved capitals. People here were once famous for their height – a skeleton found near the château was 2.4m tall.

For a pretty drive from Aynac, circle around on the D39 to Leyme, then follow the D48 down to **Lacapelle-Marival**, an attractive village of sun-warmed limestone, old towers and a tiny 14th-century *halle*. The powerful Cardaillac family built one of their principal residences, the **Château de Lacapelle-Marival** (m 07 87 14 71 36; w ap-chateau-lacapelle-marival.fr; ⏲ guided tours Jul & Aug; €5, under 18 free), smack in the middle of the village to use its walls as an outer ring of defences. Inside are a handful of 15th-century frescoes, and 17th-century *grisailles*. It's often used for exhibitions.

ASSIER This tidy commune belonged to the irrepressible cannonballing Galiot (Galahad) de Genouillac (1465–1546). In 1494 he famously saved the life of Charles VII in Naples, then became François Ier's Captain General of Artillery, Master of the Horse and Lieutenant General of Guyenne. In 1515 Galiot helped the king beat the redoubtable Swiss pikemen at the Battle of Marignano by blowing them away, on a massive scale, with his cannons – the first time anyone ever employed them so in battle.

Galiot bought up the largest property in all Quercy and made two rich marriages to finance a building programme that was pharaonic for the Lot in 1526: a Loire Valley-style château in an immense quadrangle, numerous windmills and barns, a vaulted, 55m stable (still standing in the village), a forge, a church, and a *jeu de paume* for court tennis matches. The pile was inherited by the dukes of Uzès, who cared little for it, and by 1786 it had reached such a state of decay that the owners let the locals take the stone for a small fee; wherever you see a carved stone in a local house, you can bet it came from the château. When Prosper Mérimée, inspector of historical monuments, came to Assier in 1841, he was touched by the romantic ruin of Galiot's pride and put it on his register to prevent the rest from going to hell. Only the relatively simple west wing of the quadrangle, the guards' quarters, remains of the once enormous **Château d'Assier** (☎ 05 65 40 40 99; w chateau-assier.fr; ⏲ mid-May–Aug 10.00–12.30 & 14.00–18.30 Wed–Mon, other times by appt; €4, under 18 & EU citizens under 26 free).

The exterior façade of this wing is framed by two of the château's original four towers, one sheathing Galiot's humble medieval birthplace. The once ornate dormers have all been stripped off, except for one on the left; the niche over the entrance once held an equestrian statue of Galiot. The interior façade, however, is still a handsome Renaissance work; large stone-framed windows alternate with walls bearing medallions of Roman emperors, while bands of a frieze show swords and cannons relating to Galiot's deeds or those of Hercules, with whom Galiot fancied a resemblance. The interior, described by Brantôme as 'the best furnished in France with its vast piles of silver, tapestries and silks', now contains only one of its former score of grand stairways, decorated with a handsome pilaster carved with grotesques, Hercules and the Nemean Lion and Galiot's trophies. A pendant in the vault, showing Hercules wrestling with Ateneus, is inscribed with Galiot's motto: *J'aime fort une* (meaning either 'I love fortune' or 'I love one very much' – in Galiot's case, himself). There's an exhibit on his career, and a hologram of his armour sent over by the Metropolitan Museum in New York.

The man's overweening self-esteem is most manifest today in **St-Pierre d'Assier** (1540–49), the church he built as a shrine to himself. The 100m sculpted frieze that encircles the exterior is devoted to cannons, battles and artillery, with nary a Christian symbol in sight – and may have been inspired by Trajan's column, which Galiot would have seen in Italy. On the tympanum, framed in a Doric temple front, we see the Virgin looking quite pleased to accept Galiot's sword and insignia from an angel, while two other angels unfurl banners reading *Vivit d. Jac. Galeotus!* ('Long live Galiot!'). Inside, under the exceptional 'spider's web' star vaulting, is Galiot's tomb, topped with a statue of you-know-who in his battle gear, leaning nonchalantly against a cannon, with a braggart's epitaph and his *J'aime fort une* motto. The old warrior died peacefully in bed aged 81 and, according to the dictates of his will, 500 priests gathered to give him a rousing send-off at his funeral.

On the road to Lacapelle-Marival, you can see Galiot's ***pigeonnier***, the Rockefeller Center of *pigeonniers*, 11.5m high with 2,300 varnished nests, one for each acre of his realm.

CARDAILLAC Cradle of one of the oldest and most powerful families of Quercy, the name Cardaillac once made people tremble in their boots, but today it means a delightful old *village perché* where dogs snooze in the middle of the lane. Only fragments recall its mighty citadel demolished by Cardinal Richelieu to punish Cardaillac for being a Protestant safe haven – Jeanne de Cardaillac, mother of Madame de Maintenon and future mother-in-law of Louis XIV, was an important Reformation figure. Other important members were Guillaume de Cardaillac, bishop of Cahors, who fought with Simon de Montfort in the Albigensian Crusade, and Hugues de Cardaillac, who wrote a code regulating the use of cannons in warfare (1346) – a code that his neighbour Galiot probably broke at Marignano. The village has marked out a walk through the *quartier du fort*, the site of the old citadel on its rocky spur, still dominated by the Cardaillacs' 21m **Tour de Sagnes**.

FIGEAC

Figeac, the metropolis of the Célé valley, has more than one feather in its cap. It gave the world Jean-François Champollion, the linguistic wizard who cracked Egyptian hieroglyphics, and Charles Boyer, the archetypical French lover of the silver screen (and the inspiration for Warner Bros' cartoon skunk, Pepé le Pew). Near the frontiers of the Aveyron, Figeac is the second city of the Lot, with all of 9,000 people; it has more obelisks than Paris, and lays fair claim to flexing the Lot's industrial muscle, thanks to the aeronautics manufacturer Ratier.

But for the casual visitor, it's Figeac's medieval heart of golden sandstone that comes as the most charming surprise of all – it's arguably the most beautiful medieval French city that most people (including the French themselves!) have never heard of. There may be no canals, but there's something vaguely Venetian about Figeac, beginning with its medieval plan, full of curving lanes and irregular, asymmetrical little squares, offering a wealth of visual surprises. The stone houses are so tall and densely built that many are topped with covered rooftop terraces that the Venetians call *altane* and the Lotois call *soleihos*, which not only offered city-dwellers a breath of fresh air but came in handy for drying fabrics, fruit and nuts. As in Venice as well, the ground floors were given over to stocking merchandise, while the merchants lived upstairs on the *piano nobile*, usually lit with the most elaborate windows of the building.

HISTORY The story goes that Pepin the Short, father of Charlemagne, was resting on the banks of the Célé in AD753, thinking of founding an abbey when he saw doves suddenly fly up in the form of a cross. '*Fiat là!*' ('Let it be there!') exclaimed Pepin. He then founded the abbey on the site of St-Sauveur, which, the legend continues, was consecrated two years later by Pope Stephen II himself. The hamlet that grew up around it was called Figiacus. In AD866 Vikings made it all the way up here and killed 60 monks.

As was often the case, the hamlet around the abbey expanded into a town. The Knights Templar set up an important commandery in 1184. Figeac flourished from wool and flax industries along the River Célé and from the pilgrims heading to Rocamadour or Compostela, and chafed at being bossed around by an abbot. In 1302 Philip the Fair replaced monastic rule with that of seven consuls, one for each quarter, with a Viguier in charge of administering royal justice; he even granted it the right to mint money. It was the beginning of Figeac's prosperity; it became a trade and banking centre. Apparently, like their brethren in Cahors, they were known for cutting a close deal.

As in many mercantile towns, Protestantism made many converts in Figeac, although the Calvinists only took control in 1568 when their captain bribed the wife of a consul to steal her husband's keys while he slept and toss them over the gate. In 1598 the Edict of Nantes made Figeac a Protestant safe town; Henri IV's brilliant minister, the Duke de Sully, took refuge here after the king's assassination. Sully had remained Henri IV's right-hand man (and a Protestant) even after the king decided that Paris was worth a Mass; as the powerful superintendent of finances he performed the seemingly impossible task of filling the king's war chest, promoting agriculture and building roads all across France while lowering taxes and balancing the budget.

If the Calvinists damaged much of Figeac's ecclesiastical patrimony, the Nazis struck at the inhabitants themselves. During the war, Ratier was forced to make parts for the Luftwaffe. The Maquis launched a secret attack on the plant on 19 January 1944. The Nazi reprisals came the following May, when the Das Reich division turned up and helped the SS round up 800 men and sent them to Montauban to be interrogated; 540 men and eight women were deported to German labour and concentration camps; 170 never returned.

GETTING THERE AND AROUND The nearest **airport**, Rodez-Aveyron (05 65 42 20 30; w aeroport-rodez.fr) is a 45-minute drive to the east. By **train**, Figeac's station is on the Brive–Toulouse branch line, with direct services to Assier, Gramat, Rocamadour-Padirac, Capdenac, and to Rodez. LiO **buses** (w lio.laregion.fr) link Figeac to Cahors via Cajarc, Tour-de-Faure (near St-Cirq-Lapopie) and Vers; other buses link Figeac to Cardaillac and Lacapelle-Marival. There are several free car parks on the northeast side of town and over the Célé at Jean Jaurès.

TOURIST INFORMATION Figeac's **tourist office** (05 65 34 06 25; w tourisme-figeac.com; 10.00–12.30 & 14.00–18.00 Mon–Fri, Sat until 17.00) is in the Hôtel de La Monnaie in Place Vival.

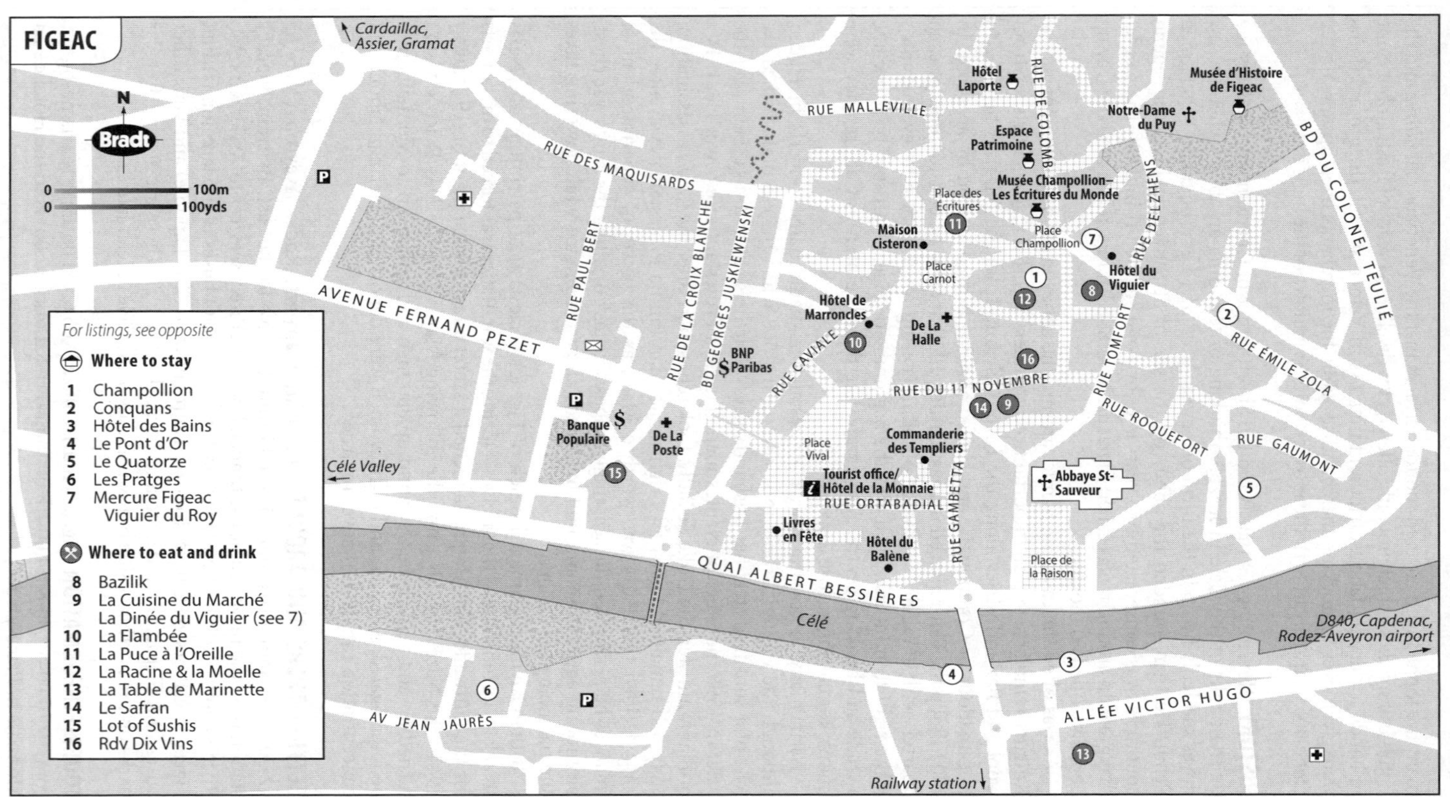
FIGEAC
Cardaillac, Assier, Gramat
N
Bradt
0 100m
0 100yds
For listings, see opposite
Where to stay
1 Champollion
2 Conquans
3 Hôtel des Bains
4 Le Pont d'Or
5 Le Quatorze
6 Les Pratges
7 Mercure Figeac Viguier du Roy
Where to eat and drink
8 Bazilik
9 La Cuisine du Marché
La Dinée du Viguier (see 7)
10 La Flambée
11 La Puce à l'Oreille
12 La Racine & la Moelle
13 La Table de Marinette
14 Le Safran
15 Lot of Sushis
16 Rdv Dix Vins
RUE MALLEVILLE
RUE DES MAQUISARDS
RUE DE COLOMB
BD DU COLONEL TEULIÉ
RUE DELZHENS
RUE ÉMILE ZOLA
RUE TOMFORT
RUE ROQUEFORT
RUE GAUMONT
RUE DU 11 NOVEMBRE
RUE CAVIALE
BD GEORGES JUSKIEWENSKI
RUE DE LA CROIX BLANCHE
RUE PAUL BERT
AVENUE FERNAND PEZET
RUE ORTABADIAL
RUE GAMBETTA
QUAI ALBERT BESSIÈRES
ALLÉE VICTOR HUGO
AV JEAN JAURÈS
Célé
Célé Valley
D840, Capdenac, Rodez-Aveyron airport
Railway station
Hôtel Laporte
Espace Patrimoine
Musée Champollion– Les Écritures du Monde
Musée d'Histoire de Figeac
Notre-Dame du Puy
Place des Écritures
Maison Cisteron
Place Champollion
Place Carnot
Hôtel du Viguier
Hôtel de Marroncles
De La Halle
BNP Paribas
Banque Populaire
De La Poste
Place Vival
Commanderie des Templiers
Tourist office/ Hôtel de la Monnaie
Abbaye St-Sauveur
Livres en Fête
Hôtel du Balène
Place de la Raison

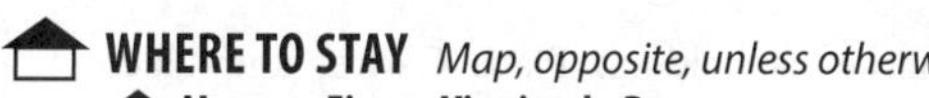

WHERE TO STAY *Map, opposite, unless otherwise stated*

Mercure Figeac Viguier du Roy (21 rooms) 52 Rue Emile Zola; 05 65 50 05 05; w cite-hotels.com. Former home of the royal judge, built in 1302 & added to over the centuries, all impeccably restored & furnished in a contemporary style. **La Dinée du iguier** (€€€€) is Figeac's gastronomic haven. **€€€€**

Comfort Hotel [257 G4] (42 rooms) Rond point du Drauzou, Ceint d'Eau, 5km west of the centre; 05 31 86 00 01; w comforthotelfigeac.com. Modern & comfortable, good for motorists, with a restaurant (€) featuring pizzas, grilled meats & salads; also pool, playground & pétanque. **€€€–€€**

Conquans (4 rooms) 38 Rue Emile Zola; m 06 84 72 98 28; w chambre-dhotes-conquans.com. Big beautiful contemporary rooms in an atmospheric 14th-century house; charming owner. Delicious b/fast inc. **€€€–€€**

Hôtel des Bains (19 rooms) 1 Rue du Griffoul; 05 65 34 10 89; w hoteldesbains.fr. The former public bath house is now a very pleasant 2-star hotel with contemporary rooms directly over the Célé, near the medieval centre. **€€€–€€**

Le Pont d'Or (35 rooms) 2 Av Jean Jaurès; 05 65 50 95 00; w hotelpontdor.com. Comfortable, recently renovated hotel by the river, with a pretty terrace, pool & fitness room, & a restaurant (€€€) featuring regional dishes. **€€€–€€**

Le Quatorze (14 rooms) 14 Place de l'Estang; 05 65 14 08 92; w le-quatorze.fr. Bright, cheerful rooms in the centre, in 3 19th-century houses cobbled together. Garage for cars & bikes, & e-bike rechargers, & nice owners. **€€€–€€**

Les Pratges (5 rooms) 6 Av Jean Jaurès; 05 65 50 01 42; book on w booking.com. Rooms with a pool, great hosts & pretty terrace. B/fast inc. **€€€–€€**

Le Manoir Enchanté [257 H4] (3 rooms) 193 Rte de la Tour Negre, 5km south of Figeac; m 06 29 70 78 37; w lemanoirenchante.com. Traditional B&B-style rooms in a 16th-century manor house. B/fast inc. **€€**

Champollion (10 rooms) 3 Place Champollion, 05 65 34 04 37; w hotelchampollion.fr. Small, with simple, stylish rooms in the centre, with friendly staff & a bright bar full of locals. **€**

WHERE TO EAT AND DRINK *Map, opposite*

La Table de Marinette 51 Allée Victor Hugo; 09 70 35 31 72; w restaurant-table-marinette.fr; closed Thu–Fri. One of the best, with an optional vegetarian menu. *Lunches from €22.* €€€€

Le Safran 17 Rue de Clermont; 05 65 38 45 41; w le-safran.wixsite.com/Figeac; closed Tue. Lots of well-prepared seafood here, flavoured with the local saffron, with mussels in 8 different ways. *Lunch formule €17–€22.* €€€€

La Cuisine du Marché 15 Rue Clermont; 05 65 50 18 55; w lacuisinedumarchefigeac.com; closed Sun & lunch Mon. Eat out under the stone arches of this restored wine cellar behind St-Sauveur specialising in seafood & *foie gras poêlé. Excellent €33 menu.* €€€€–€€€

La Puce à l'Oreille 5–7 Rue St-Thomas; 05 65 34 33 08; f puceaoreille; closed Sun–Mon. In a 15th-century mansion with a pretty patio, just a few short steps away from the Champollion museum. *€28 duck menu, other menus from €35.* €€€

La Racine & la Moelle 6 Rue du Consulat; 09 83 53 81 58; closed Sun–Mon. Opened in 2018, the Root & the Marrow, run by French Julie & Irish Michael, has won over the Figeacois in a big way with their superb modern but unfussy dishes. €€€

La Flambée 26 Rue Caviale; 05 65 34 72 12; w restaurant-flambee-figeac.fr; closed Sun & eves Wed. Traditional Lotois dishes, *salades composés. W/day lunch €13.50.* €€

Lot of Sushis 2 Place Besombes; 05 65 34 13 01; w lot-of-sushis.com; closed Sun–Mon. There's more than sushi here, including soups & yakitori. €€

Bazilik 14 Rue Baduel; m 06 62 00 21 98; lunch only. Vegetarian/vegan restaurant, offering a choice of 2 menus daily. €

Rdv Dix Vins 8 Rue de Clermont; m 06 76 69 75 31; f; 11.00–23.00 Tue–Sat. Warm, friendly atmosphere, great choice of wines & cheese & charcuterie.

SHOPPING The Saturday morning **market** is held on Place Carnot and Place Champollion. The **bookshop**, Livres en Fête (27 Rue Ortabadial; 05 65 34 43 11; w lelivreenfete.fr), has a selection in English.

OTHER PRACTICALITIES

$ **Banque Populaire** Place Léon Bescombes
$ **BNP-Paribas** 26 Bd Juskienwenski
Hospital 33 Rue des Maquisards; 05 65 50 65 50; w ch-figeac.fr
De La Halle 42 Rue Gambetta
De La Poste 9 Bd Juskienwenski
Post office 8 Av Fernand Pezet

WHAT TO SEE AND DO

Hôtel de la Monnaie (Place Vival) The tourist office occupies this elegant 13th-century palace, one of the finest secular buildings of the period in France. Philippe IV granted Figeac the privilege of minting its own coins, a dandy boost to commerce in those days; the ground floor with its pointed arches was used as a bank, while on top is a typical *soleiho*.

Just west of Place Vival runs charming Rue Caviale, where the **Hôtel de Marroncles** at no. 30 hosted Louis XI in 1463. Rue Caviale gives into Place Carnot, Figeac's ancient market square, although since 1988 sadly lacking its 13th-century grain *halle*. Note the well-preserved 13th–17th-century **Maison Cisteron** in the corner, with a turret: this was the residence of Pierre de Cisteron, master armourer of Louis XIV and a Huguenot. Just before revoking the Edict of Nantes, Louis sent down a special safeguard for Cisteron, to keep him from the persecutions he had in store for Protestants not so dear to his heart.

Commanderie des Templiers (41 Rue Gambetta; m 06 22 41 44 86; w commanderie-des-templiers.com; guided tour in French: Jun 10.30–noon & 13.30–18.30 Tue–Sat, Jul–Aug 10.30–18.30 daily, Sep 13.30–18.00 Mon, 14.00–18.00 Sat; €5, ages 8–16 €4, under 8 free) The whole block south of Place Carnot once belonged to the Knights Templars and the whole has been beautifully restored and furnished. There's also a three-room chambre d'hôte (**€€€€–€€€**) – just don't expect any modern conveniences!

Place Champollion For centuries this held Figeac's chestnut market; until the 19th century chestnuts were staple in the local diet, ground into flour for bread. The butchers had their stands under the ogival arches; note, too, the 12th-century Maison du Griffon at no. 4. The square is named after the 14th-century birthplace of Jean François Champollion (1790–1832), who by age 14 could rattle away in Latin, Greek, Hebrew and Arabic. He was always fascinated by Egyptian hieroglyphics, and when he finally saw a copy of the British Museum's Rosetta Stone in 1822, he made his great discovery and confirmed his belief that the 'pictures' were a form of writing. The alphabet-covered **Musée Champollion–Les Écritures du Monde** (05 65 50 31 08; f MuseeChampo; Apr–Jun & Sep–Oct 10.20–12.30 & 14.00–18.00 Tue–Sun, Jul–Aug 10.30–18.30 daily, Nov–Mar 14.00–17.30 Tue–Sun; €5, ages 13–18 €2.50, under 13 free) offers four floors of somewhat didactic displays; there are three mummies and a small but choice collection of ancient Egyptian and Coptic art, as well as a painting of our man in Egypt, dressed in native costume, looking for all the world like a brigand with his bushy black beard and scimitar. In the **Place des Écritures**, Champollion's bicentenary in 1991 was celebrated with the installation of a giant facsimile of the Rosetta Stone in the pavement, designed by American artist Joseph Kosuth.

Espace Patrimoine (8 Rue de Colomb; ☎ 05 65 50 05 40; ⌚ Apr–mid-Jul & mid-Sep–Oct 14.00–18.00 Tue–Sun, mid-Jul–mid-Sep 10.30–noon & 14.00–18.00 daily; free) The *mairie* has a permanent exhibition of the history and heritage of Figeac, with frequent special exhibitions. Rue de Colomb has some of Figeac's most aristocratic houses.

Hôtel Laporte (3 Rue Malleville, just off Rue de Colomb; m 07 68 11 33 02; ⌚ guided tours in English: Jul–Aug 10.00–13.00 & 14.00–18.00 Mon–Fri; €5, under 16 free) This is a private museum that evokes life in 17th-century Figeac, with costumes and antiques.

Notre-Dame du Puy (1 Rue Victor Delbos; ⌚ usually) Figeac's churches haven't withstood the trials of time as successfully as its secular buildings. This much-tampered-with 12th-century church overlooking the town replaces an ancient chapel where the Virgin made a rose bloom on Christmas Day, and retains some 14th-century carvings on its portal and capitals. The ornate 17th-century rooms of the former seminary here house Figeac's attic – the **Musée d'Histoire de Figeac** (Cour de Puy; ☎ 05 65 50 31 08; ⌚ Jul–Aug 14.30–18.30 daily; €3.50, ages 13–18 €2) with a mix of prehistoric relics, paintings, gifts from President Pompidou and other odds and ends.

The most picturesque descent from Notre-Dame is by way of Rue Delzhens, past the seat of the king's judge, the **Hôtel du Viguier** (1300s, now a hotel), to Rue Roquefort, where at no. 12 are the elegant remains of the house built by Galiot de Genouillac (page 267).

Abbaye St-Sauveur (6 Rue du Monastère; ☎ 05 65 10 90 31; ⌚ 09.00–19.00 daily) Encased in a forgettable 19th-century façade and bell tower crowned with a giant bread box, only St-Sauveur's large size hints that this was Figeac's famous medieval church. The chapterhouse (now a chapel off the right aisle) was given its remarkable ogival vaulting in the 15th century; in the 17th century, to cover up some of the damage caused in the Wars of Religion, a local sculptor added the naïve painted reliefs of the Passion – including a *Last Supper* of roast hamster and a bizarre scene of baby Jesus sleeping sweetly on a cross, dreaming of his future torments. In the adjacent riverside **Place de la Raison** stands a small obelisk, a monument to Champollion.

Just before the river, Rue du Balène winds past the **Hôtel du Balène** with its huge ogival door and Flamboyant windows. From here Rue Orthabadial, once the realm of the medieval abbey gardener, returns you to the Hôtel de la Monnaie.

AROUND FIGEAC Mysterious 8m obelisks or Aiguilles 'needles' were erected in the 12th century – the **Aiguille de Lissac** [257 H3] to the west (Rte de Lissac, facing the university) and the **Aiguille du Pressoir** [257 H3] to the south, on the Colline du Cingle – part of a 4.5km hike rewarded with great views. Their original purpose has been forgotten, but they may have been set up by the abbey of St-Sauveur, either to lift the spirits of pilgrims, or to set the limits within which fugitives were guaranteed the abbey's asylum.

THE UPPER LOT AND CÉLÉ VALLEYS

Although the rivers Célé and Lot are less than 7km apart at Figeac, they don't meet up until they reach Bouzies, near St-Cirq-Lapopie. We'll start with the Lot's merriest river, the Célé (from the Latin *celer*, or rapid), born in the Cantal. Once past Figeac this clear shallow stream splashes through gentle valleys and steep gorges protected by cliff forts, the so-called *châteaux des anglais*. Along the way are two fascinating outdoor museums, and one of the best decorated caves still open to the public at Pech Merle.

Next we follow the River Lot west from its debut in the department at Capdenac. Until the 1700s both the river valleys were famous for saffron, grown mostly as a dye back then, and in recent decades the crop has been revived.

GETTING AROUND Several buses a day run between Cahors station and Figeac (page 269). The Célé valley is ideal walking country, along the GR651 (the alternative Compostela route from Figeac to Cahors; download the map at w tourisme-lot.com).

TOURIST INFORMATION

Cajarc La Chapelle; 05 65 40 72 89; w tourisme-figeac.com; May–Sep 09.30–12.30 & 14.00–18.00 Mon–Sat

Capdenac-Gare Place du 14 Juillet; 05 65 64 74 87; w tourisme-figeac.com; May–Sep 10.00–noon & 14.00–17.00 daily, winter Tue & Fri only

St-Cirq-Lapopie Place du Sombral; 05 65 31 31 31; w cahorsvalleedulot.com; 10.00–18.00 daily

WHERE TO STAY Things close up tight here from November to March.

Le Saint Cirq (29 rooms) Tour-de-Faure; 05 65 30 30 30; w hotel-lesaintcirq.com. Opposite St-Cirq-Lapopie, smart hotel with a spa & a pool. **€€€€–€€€**

La Truite Dorée (28 rooms) Rue de la Barre, Vers; 05 65 31 46 13; w latruitedoree.fr. A beloved institution, now in the hands of the 5th generation. Good rooms in an old stone farmhouse & a pool, spa, & a great restaurant (€€€) with 2 lovely terraces – trout in various forms, but also duck, truffles & a sublime cassoulet. *W/day lunch menu €20.* **€€€**

Les Gabarres (28 rooms) Le Roucayral, Tour-de-Faure; 05 65 30 24 57; w hotellesgabarres.com. A modern hotel in a quiet corner, but with nice views of tree-covered cliffs from some rooms; there's a pool & pool bar. **€€€–€€.**

Mas del Lum [257 G3] (4 rooms) Domaine des Villedieu, Boussac (between Figeac & Corn); 05 65 40 06 63; w mas-del-lum.fr. A bucolic, authentic retreat on an organic farm built in the 18th century; pool & gorgeous views. B/fast inc. **€€€–€€**

La Combe de Redoles [257 F5] (5 rooms, 1 gîte) Combe de Redoles, Tour-de-Faure; m 07 84 56 25 63; w lacombederedoles.com. Waken to the morning chorus in the sweet rustic farm, 2km from St-Cirq, with lovely hosts; open all year. B/fast. **€€**

Le Clos des Dryades [256 D4] (5 rooms, 3 gîtes) Le Bois Noire, St-Géry, Vers; 05 65 31 44 50; w leclosdryades.com. Stay like a dryad among the oak trees with Sabrina & Sébastien at this charming B&B with a pool & delicious evening meals (€22) on request. **€€**

Le Relais de la Tour (11 rooms) Place Lucteur, Capdenac-le-Haut; 05 65 11 06 99; w lerelaisdelatour.fr. Rooms in a 15th-century building up in the fortified village near the museum, with home-cooking (€€) in the restaurant. **€€**

Mas de Redoulès [257 F5] (3 rooms) Nougayrac, St-Martin-Labouval, 6km northeast of St-Cirq-Lapopie; m 06 31 79 63 86; w saint-cirq-lapopie-redoules.com; see ad, page 295. French Marie and Irish Antoine run this delightful wisteria-draped 18th-century property in the meadows which once served as an inn for boatmen and a silkworm farm. Guests can use the summer kitchen and barbecue. **€€**

Auberge du Sombral (8 rooms) St-Cirq-Lapopie; 05 65 31 26 08; w aubergelesombral.wordpress.com. In a medieval house in the centre, charming rooms under its steep-pitched roof, plus a traditional restaurant (€€). Very peaceful at night. €€–€

Hôtel des Grottes du Pech Merle (14 rooms) 2432 Rte du Célé, Cabrerets; 05 65 31 27 02; w hoteldesgrottes.com. Pleasant 2-star family-run hotel with views over the cliffs, restaurant (€€) with traditional & vegetarian dishes, & a pool. €€–€

Hôtel de Paris (14 rooms) 12 Av Gambetta, Capdenac-Gare; 05 65 64 75 91; w hoteldeparis-capdenac.fr. Traditional little hotel from 1954, with basic renovated rooms, restaurant (€) & bar. €

La Peyrade (10 rooms) 52 Rue Lapeyrade, Cajarc; 05 65 10 42 03; w hotel-gite-lapeyrade.fr. Modern & welcoming, with family rooms & studios & a restaurant (€€) for guests only. €

La Treille (4 rooms) Montbrun; 05 65 40 77 20; book through Gîtes de France: w gites-de-france.com. Basic rooms on a farm nicely located right on the river. €

WHERE TO EAT AND DRINK

L'Allée des Vignes 32 Bd du Tour de Ville, Cajarc; 05 65 11 61 87; w alleedesvignes.com; closed Mon–Tue, lunch Wed–Thu, eves Sun; out of season usually eves Fri–Sat, lunch Sun. Top Michelin-starred cuisine, making superb use of the local saffron by French-Mexican chef Claude-Emmanuel Robin & his Russian wife, Evgenia. €€€€€

Jeu de Quilles 7 Bd du Tour-de-Ville, Cajarc; 05 65 33 71 40; f jeu-de-quilles; closed Sun–Mon. Casual chic restaurant-wine bar featuring market cuisine on a small menu, with frequent live music. *Lunch menu €20, dinner around €30.* €€€€

Le Gourmet Quercynois Rue de la Peylorie, St-Cirq-Lapopie; 05 65 31 21 20; w restaurant-legourmetquercynois.com. Near the top of the village, this is the restaurant of Le Saint Cirq hotel, specialising in duck. *Excellent €28.50 menu.* €€€

L'Oustal Le Bourg, St-Cirq-Lapopie; 05 65 31 20 17; w loustal46.fr; closed Sat. Head down below the church for an excellent chalkboard €21 lunch menu, often featuring lamb. €€

Le Paradou Cénevières; m 06 72 50 43 79; f LeParadou46; eves only, closed Sun–Mon. Popular laid-back bar-resto in the old schoolhouse with a pretty courtyard serving burgers, magrets & other French-style pub grub. €€

Le Titruc Marcilhac-sur-Célé; m 06 34 36 54 60; eves only, closed Mon, Wed–Thu. A different menu every evening at this sweet little village restaurant, all homemade & always vegetarian choices. €€

Les Deux Vallées Gare de Conduché, Bouziès; 05 65 24 58 92; w les2vallees.fr; 09.00–21.00 Tue–Sun. The old train station, lovingly converted into a bar-restaurant & *gîte d'etape* (€) where you can sit out by the old towpath & cliffs. Tasty cuisine *de terroir*. €€

Les Fadas Place du Sombral, St-Cirq-Lapopie; 05 65 31 91 69; f; 10.00–22.00 Wed–Mon. Opposite the tourist office, combination shop, cocktail bar, tapas & organic restaurant. Homemade ice cream, too. €€

Lou Bolat Place du Balat, St-Cirq-Lapopie; 05 65 30 29 04; w loubolat.fr; daily. Café-restaurant-glacier near the top, with a terrace overlooking the village, serving classics (coq au vin, *omelettes aux truffes de Lalbenque*) & 30 kinds of homemade ice cream. €€

O'louise Cabrerets; 05 65 21 23 64; f Restaurant-Olouise-Cabrerets; lunch only. Informal spot with pizzas & cuisine by a very good-humoured granny. €

SPORTS AND ACTIVITIES In 1990 the Lot was made navigable between St-Cirq-Lapopie and Luzech, thanks to the installation of 14 locks.

Cajarc Nature Evasion 7 Place du Faubourg, Cajarc; m 06 46 86 08 35; w canoe-cajarc.fr. All kinds of watercrafts.

Chill-Lot Cénevières; 05 81 42 95 00; w chill-lot.com. Offers kayaks, SUPs, mountain bikes, fishing boats, pedalos, camping in tepees & yurts.

Kalapca Bouziès; 05 65 24 21 01; w kalapca.com. They offer a host of activities, from rock climbing, Via Ferrata, caving in underground rivers, zipline, kayaks & more.

Lot & Bike 1 Bd du Tour de Ville, Cajarc; m 06 23 11 62 50; w location-velo-lot.com. Hires out all kinds of bikes.

Lot Adventure 4 Place du Faubourg, Cajarc; m 06 23 02 43 66; w lotaventure.jimdo.com. Offers canoes, SUPs, rock climbing in the Lot & Célé valleys & caving expeditions. Also at St-Cirq-Lapopie/Torre de Faure.

Nature et Loisirs Sauliac-sur-Célé; ☎ 05 64 30 25 60; w nature-et-loisirs.com. Paddle your kayak gently down the stream.

Passion Aventure Rte de St Chels, Marcilhac-sur-Célé; m 06 10 73 73 12; w location-canoe-cele.com. Also rents out canoes & kayaks.

Seven Wonders Cruise Bouziès; ☎ 05 65 31 72 25; w croisieres-saint-cirq-lapopie.com; ⌚ Apr–Oct; 70min *gabarre* ride €14, ages 3–12 €9. They also hire out boats, canoes & *gabarres*, for up to 12 people.

DOWN THE CÉLÉ FROM FIGEAC West of Figeac, aim for the picturesque riverside D41; just beyond the Ratier plant, on a hill, is the much restored, fat-towered 15th–16th-century **Château Ceint d'Eau** [257 H3]. Soon to the right, just beyond a ruined Romanesque chapel, is a road leading up to the tiny, charming village of **Camboulit**. The valley narrows past **Boussac**, where overhanging cliffs were used as shelters or fortresses in the Middle Ages. In and around **Corn**, an old farming village, are fortified caves from the Hundred Years' War, as well as a pair of 17th-century châteaux on either side of the river.

Espagnac-Ste-Eulalie The most photographed spot along the Célé, this tiny hamlet huddles in the shadow of a unique church tower. Crowned by an openwork timbered chamber with a bell from the 1500s and a pointy octagonal roof, the whole is almost too quaint to be real. This belongs to a convent fittingly named **Notre-Dame du Val Paradis** (w espagnac-ste-eulalie.fr; ⌚ guided tours: Jun–Sep 10.30–12.30 & 16.00–18.00 Sun–Thu, 10.30–12.30 Fri; €2), founded in the 12th century but greatly expanded in the next by its benefactor, Aymeric d'Hébrard of Cajarc, a bishop of Coimbra in Portugal.

The bell tower isn't the only quaint thing here. A pentagonal apse rears up abruptly, a full storey higher than the rest of the church. There are three tombs: those of Aymeric d'Hébrard, the knight Hugues de Cardaillac-Brengues (d1342), and his elegant wife, Bernarde de Trian, niece of Pope John XXII. The lofty choir is decorated with the arms of the Cardaillacs and little mitred heads. On the high altar, a gilt wooden retable from the 1700s displays a badly restored copy of an altarpiece by Simon Vouet, showing Louis XIV's mum, Anne of Austria, floating up to heaven in the guise of the Virgin of the Assumption.

Brengues The next village is an old Cardaillac fief, built on a bluff over the river that conceals a *château des anglais*. The Hébrards came from the next village down the Célé, **St-Sulpice**, partially built into and growing out of the curve of its cliff; its much-restored 12th-century château is still in the family that produced bishops, soldiers and diplomats who served in important posts across Europe. The Hébrards owned so much of the Célé valley that it was nicknamed the 'Hébrardie'.

Marcilhac-sur-Célé With a population of 240, this is one of the larger villages in the valley. It owes its existence to a powerful **Abbaye St-Pierre de Marcilhac** (☎ 05 65 40 68 44; w abbayedemarcilhac.com; ⌚ 08.00–18.00 daily; free) first mentioned in the will (AD654) of St Didier, who wanted to be buried there. By the 12th century the abbey possessed more than a hundred properties, including Rocamadour. Its abbots, however, singularly failed to foresee Rocamadour's potential – unlike the bishops of Tulle, who took it over and made it a prestigious pilgrimage site. When the pilgrims (and profits) starting piling into Rocamadour, Marcilhac wanted it back, leading to an unseemly conflict that saw each side booting out the other's monks. In the end, Marcilhac surrendered its claim in exchange for cash. The abbey was badly pillaged in the Hundred Years' War. The Hébrards took it under their wing in 1451 and rebuilt the damaged bits in the Gothic style, which was then damaged in turn by the Protestants. A few monks stuck it out until the Revolution.

There are more ducks than people here now, but along the Célé they are still defended by the thick medieval buttresses topped with little carved figures mysteriously called 'conspirators' heads'. The path from Place des Platanes leads past the Romanesque chapterhouse, with capitals carved with scenes of heaven and hell in two distinct styles. The grandiose ruins of the bays and narthex of the Romanesque church form a kind of courtyard around what is now Marcilhac's parish church, rebuilt by the Hébrards in the Gothic style to replace the once-vast Romanesque model. The interior is decorated with Hébrard coats of arms and 15th-century frescoes, 17th-century panelling and a copy of a Van Dyck *Virgin and Child*. Note the angel's head with a teasing smile, on the pew with the heraldic carvings. The original church's south portal has a rare Carolingian tympanum, a triangular composition of bas-reliefs. Christ on top is framed by symbols of the sun and moon, while two angels below grip instruments of the Passion, and at the bottom stand SS Peter and Paul.

Sauliac-sur-Célé This old village is a lovely place for a riverside picnic, overlooking a dilapidated château, and is home to the excellent **Écomusée de Cuzals** [257 F4] (05 65 22 58 63; w musees.lot.fr/ecomusee-de-cuzals; Jun & Sep 14.00–18.00 Wed, Sun, Jul–Aug 10.00–18.00 daily; €5, ages 12–26 €2.50, under 12 free; cash only). This recreates two farms with original buildings, one pre-Revolutionary, the other from the 19th century, along with little museums of crafts, agriculture, water and natural sciences; there are old tractors, many in working order, a dentist's surgery from 1900, an antique carousel, demonstrations of all manner of local crafts (especially on Sundays), and a snack bar.

Cabrerets Heading west on the D41 is another partly outdoor museum: the one and only **Musée de l'Insolite** [257 E4] ('Museum of the Unusual'; Liauzu, Cabrerets; 05 65 30 21 01; w museedelinsolite.com; Apr–Jun & Sep–Oct 09.00–19.00, Jul–Aug 09.00–20.00; €3, ages 4–13 €2). Since 1988, Bertrand Chenu has been busy creating this cliff-side wonderland of surreal craziness and belly laughs at the world. The explanations are as funny as his creations; even if you don't speak French you can usually get the gist.

Down by the road, stop by **La Pescalerie** [257 E4], a resurgent spring with its picturesque abandoned mill. Further along, set back against the cliffs of the Célé, is one of the most dramatic *châteaux des anglais*, begun in AD745 by Waiofar, Duke of Aquitaine, although this one is better known as the **Château du Diable** – devils and Englishmen being frequently synonymous in medieval France. Downstream, on a high bluff is the much-restored 14th-century **Château de Cabrerets**.

Grotte du Pech Merle [257 E4] (4km above Cabrerets; 05 65 31 27 05; w pechmerle.com; Apr–early Jul & Sep–Oct 09.30–noon & 13.30–17.00 daily, early Jul–Aug 09.00–17.00 daily; €14, ages 5–14 €8.50, under 5 €3.50 – book timed tickets online & choose between tours in French or English) Pech Merle rivals Font-de-Gaume (page 186) as the finest polychrome painted cave still open to the public. Your ticket includes the **Musée de Préhistoire Amédée-Lemozi** with a collection of tools and art ranging from the Lower Palaeolithic to the Iron Age, as well as a film; there's also a snack bar and picnic grove.

The original entrance to the cave, blocked up at the end of the last ice age, was only rediscovered in 1922 by 16-year-old André David, son of the owner of Pech Merle, and his friend Henri Dutertre who wormed and scrambled their way through a narrow 122m passage and found exactly what they dreamed of finding – a beautiful cave filled with beautiful art. Some 80 drawings of animals and humans and hundreds of symbols decorate a third of Pech Merle's passageways, spanning three distinct periods (20,000–15,000BC).

Highlights include a great spiral frieze of mammoths, horses and bison, mysterious 'hieroglyphs', footprints left by a woman and child at least 12,000 years ago, 'the wounded man' – a long figure pierced by arrows – extremely rare cave pearls (*pisolites*), and the two beautiful spotted horses, reminiscent of ancient Chinese horses, one with its delicate head drawn on a natural protuberance in the rock. The spots spill out of the outlines while six feminine 'negative hands' seem to be yearning to stroke or hold the horses. Over the horses is a rare picture of a fish – a large pike.

DOWN THE LOT: CAPDENAC TO ST-CIRQ-LAPOPIE

Capdenac-le-Haut This lofty and charming medieval hill town enjoys 'one of the most beautiful settings in France', according to Prosper Mérimée, who saw them all while visiting all the monuments of France. It was one of the keys to Quercy, and was constantly besieged throughout its history, and often resisting, thanks to several springs excavated in the rock, notably the **Fountain des Anglais**, which is really ancient Roman. Capdenac was first inhabited in Neolithic times, yielding the torso of the Lady of Capdenac, from c3000BC. You can see a cast of her, as well as other odds and ends, in the 13th-century 110m-tall donjon's little **Musée de Capdenac-le-Haut** (Place Lucter; 05 65 38 32 26; Apr–Jun & Sep 10.30–11.30 & 14.00–17.00 Mon–Sat, 14.00–17.00 Sun, Jul–Aug 09.30–12.30 & 14.30–18.30 Mon–Sat, 14.30–18.30 Sun; €2.50, ages 12–25 €2, under 12 free). Around it are the terraced gardens of the five senses, a pair of Gothic gates, lanes of sunny limestone houses and views of the Lot and the village's own ugly stepsister, the industrial railway junction of **Capdenac-Gare**.

St-Pierre-Toirac [257 G4] Downriver, the D662 rises to pretty **Faycelles,** with its panoramic views over the valley and medieval cross, before swooping down to this tiny village and its remarkable 12th-century fortified **church**. The interior is exceptional for its beautiful lines and its 50 sculpted capitals in at least two distinct styles – and many are so inexplicably whacky that it's been called the 'apogee of Romanesque surrealism', while others are strikingly primitive, perhaps borrowed from an earlier church. Several Merovingian sarcophaguses lay outside.

The **Château Larroque-Toirac** [257 G4] (m 06 12 37 48 39; w chateau.toirac.free.fr; guided tours (French only): May–Jun 14.00–18.00 Sun, Jul–Sep 10.30–noon & 14.00–18.00 daily; €8, ages 4–12 €4, under 4 free) dates from the same time. It passed to the Cardaillac family, whose fidelity to France in the Hundred Years' War invited numerous sieges before the English succeeded in taking the castle in 1372. Incredibly, the high, pentagonal donjon, now topped with a sloping roof, originally stood 33m higher before the Revolution; a spiral Romanesque stair leads up to some fine chimneypieces, wall and ceiling murals and furnishings. Behind the castle are some curious troglodyte dwellings.

Prettily situated **Montbrun**, the next village, has the ruins of another Cardaillac castle, overlooking the grand belvedere on the south bank, known as Saut de la Mounine (Monkey's Leap). The lord of Montbrun, furious at his daughter's choice of lovers, had ordered her to be thrown off the cliff; a kindly hermit dressed a monkey in the girl's clothing and hurled it in her place. The sight made her father deplore his cruelty, and when he found out he had been duped he forgave his daughter. What she thought about him isn't recorded.

Cajarc Next downriver, spread across a loop of the Lot, is saffron-growing Cajarc, a riverside resort with a beach, an extremely popular *plan d'eau*, and host to a very lively festival dedicated to African culture in summer. Novelist Françoise Sagan (1935–2004) was born here and in 1954 at age 18 rocked the French literary world with her bestseller *Bonjour Tristesse* (her grave is in Cajarc's Cimetière de Seuzac). French President Georges Pompidou had a holiday home here, which is now dedicated to changing exhibits of contemporary art in the **Maison des Arts Georges Pompidou** (134 Av Germain Canet; 05 65 40 78 19; w magcp.fr; whenever there's an exhibition; free). There are many fine medieval houses in the teardrop-shaped boulevard (especially the 13th-century **Maison de Hébrardie**) and, on the edge of town, the ruined 12th-century chapel of an asylum for lepers. Less than a kilometre north, there's a pretty waterfall, the **Cascade de la Cogne** (although it dries up in the summer).

This area, between the rivers Célé and Lot, is rich in dolmens: there's a pair of good ones along the D82, west of **Gréalou**, and another two on the D17 just north of **St-Chels**. Four kilometres south of Cajarc, a path off the D146 towards St-Clair leads to the **Gouffre de Lantouy**, filled with emerald-green water, and, according to the locals, a monster.

Château de Larnagol [257 F5] (Rue du Château, Larnagol; 05 65 23 39 79; mid-Apr–Jun & mid-Sep–Oct 14.30–18.00 Wed, Fri, Sun, Jun–mid-Jul 14.30–19.00 Tue–Wed, Fri, Sun, mid-Jul–mid-Sep 11.00–12.30 & 14.30–19.00 Fri–Sun, Wed; €8, under 12 free) A 12th-century Cardaillac castle, Larnagol was transformed into an elegant residence in the 1600s with elegant Italian gardens; until 2011 it was the long-time home of master ironworker Raymond Subes. Today it's undergoing a painstaking restoration; one room is set aside as a chambre d'hôte (w chateaudelarnagol.business.site; b/fast inc; **€€€€€**).

Château de Cénevières [257 F5] (D8; 05 65 31 27 33; w chateau-cenevieres.com; mid-Apr–Nov 10.00–noon & 14.00–17.00 Sun–Fri; €8, guided tours €9, ages 7–15 €4; book tickets online) Perched on a lofty cliff over the river, this castle marks a strategic point that has been fortified since the cows came home. In the 1500s its owner, Flottard de Gourdon, was a master of the royal artillery who served François Ier with his buddy Galiot de Genouillac, and married Marguerite de Cardaillac. The château was enlarged in the Renaissance style; Flottard's son Antoine converted to Protestantism, and in 1580 the future Henri IV stopped here, to plot his attack on Cahors. During the Revolution, local *sans-culottes* arrived ready to burn this symbol of feudalism to the ground. The custodian invited them in – to the wine cellar. They were soon drunk as skunks. Afterwards they half-heartedly vandalised a bit, then staggered home.

Near the entrance stands the little Protestant temple added by Antoine Gourdon. Of the medieval castle only the donjon remains, although it's hardly recognisable behind the ornate dormers and windows that stylistically meld it to the Renaissance sections added by Flottard and son. Ten rooms are richly appointed with period furnishings and ancient tapestries; there's an ornate chimney, a complex stair, charmingly painted coffered ceilings, a vast kitchen and an unusual Cabinet d'Alchimie decorated with 16th-century frescoes; never fully explained, the paintings seem to express some alchemical allegory.

St-Cirq-Lapopie The setting is spectacular; St-Cirq hovers 100m above the Lot, overlooking the kind of dramatic, sheer cliffs beloved of Romantic poets. Its architecture is pure, harmoniously medieval. It was elected the favourite village of the French a few years back, although the first to fall for its charms was surrealist André Breton: 'Saint-Cirq appeared to me, embraced by Bengal fires – like an impossible rose in the night… I no longer have any desire to be anywhere else.' In summer, get there early or be prepared to share St-Cirq with a crowd; in winter you may well have it all to yourself.

St-Cirq began as a Gallo-Roman villa called Pompéjac, owned by the 7th-century AD bishop of Cahors, St Didier. It was the last possession of Duke Waiofar of Aquitaine to be conquered by Pepin 'Duke of Aquitaine', and gave its name to the La Popie family who made it their bailiwick. In the 13th century, its strategic importance was such that the site was shared by the lords of Gourdon, Cardaillac and La Popie (later succeeded by the Hébrards), each of whom had their own castle, linked together at the top of the town.

Such rare co-operation failed to keep the English out in the Hundred Years' War: not once but three times in the 14th century they played the same trick on the French barons, scaling the sheer cliff and surprising them. In 1471, Louis XI ordered the contiguous castles to be destroyed to punish the Hébrards for throwing in their cap with the English. Enough castle, however, remained intact to cause trouble in the Wars of Religion, until the future Henri IV ordered the site razed to keep out the Catholics, leaving only a few crumbling romantic walls, best seen from the belvedere by the payable car park just west of St-Cirq.

Today the **church**, built in 1522–40, is the most prominent building in the village, its buttressed apse high on the bluff, it's turreted watchtower running up the side of the stout bell tower. To the left of the portal are two medieval grain measures; inside, the church incorporates a Romanesque chapel, with a carved capital of Judith beheading Holofernes. Near the church you'll find St-Cirq's most medieval and picturesque lane, **Ruelle de la Fourdonne**, and the main street, the Grand-Rue, lined with 15th- and 16th-century houses. The Château de la Gardette holds the **Musée Rignault** (✆ 05 65 31 23 22; 🕘 Apr–Sep 10.30–12.30 & 14.30–18.30 Wed–Mon; €2), former home and garden of painter and collector Emile-Joseph Rignault, with art exhibitions every summer. The names of Rue de la Pélissaria and Rue de la Payrolerie recall two formerly important trades in St-Cirq: skin-dressing and copper-cauldron-making. Another was wood-turning: from 1810 until recently the village specialised in boxwood taps for barrels.

In 1951, André Breton bought a 12th-century house opposite the museum that had once belonged to painter Henri Martin and returned every summer hosting the likes of Man Ray and Foujita, until he died in 1966. In 2016, the Association of La Rose Impossible made the **Maison André Breton** (MAB; Place du Carol; **m** 06 51 22 22 38; **w** maisonandrebreton.fr; 🕘 in season 11.00–19.00 Wed–Mon, winter 10.00–12.30 & 14.00–19.00 Mon, Thu–Fri, 10.00–12.30 Wed, Sat–Sun; free) the International Centre of Surrealism and of Citizens of the World, dedicated to Breton and Cahors Mundi (page 255), with special exhibitions, conferences, music and poetry readings.

Bouziès just downriver is the chief pleasure-boat port on the Lot. From here you can walk the remarkable **Chemin de Halage** carved in the rock below St-Cirq in 1842–47 for mules to pull the *gabarres* upstream; part of the GR36, it's decorated with a long relief carved by Toulousain sculptor Daniel Monnier. Pech Merle (page 277) is just north.

Vers This pretty village (even though the name means 'worms') has a boatman's chapel under the cliffs, **Notre-Dame-des-Velles** ('of the sails'), with a 12th-century apse decorated with modillions. Here the little River Vers ripples down from the causse, picking up enough limestone along the way to form a series of step-like *gours* (mini dams), though it often dries up in summer. The source of the Vers was favoured by those most picky of water connoisseurs, the Romans; in the cliffs 30m above Vers the village, you can trace the rock-cut aqueduct that went to Cahors, on a long-gone bridge over the Lot. You can follow it up the valley to the pretty village of **St-Martin-de-Vers** and seek out the scanty ruins of the **Oppidum de Mursens** [256 D4] signposted from Cras.

On the left bank of the Lot, **Arcambal** has a prominent castle, restored in the 19th century, and **Le Petit Musée de Christian Verdun** (180 Rue de la Résistance; **m** 06 31 69 65 68; **w** christian-verdun.com; 🕘 15.00–18.00 Sat or by appt; free) with sculptures, paintings and installations created by the artist over the past 50 years. On the right bank, **Laroque-des-Arcs** recalls the arches of the Roman aqueduct where it crossed the Lot. It resembled the Pont du Gard, but was demolished in 1370 by the consuls of Cahors to keep the English from seizing it. Nowadays Laroque's chief landmarks are its little chapel of **St-Roch** high on a bluff over the river with a *château des anglais* below, and a 13th-century **Tour de Péage**, a tower toll booth on the riverbank owned by the Gourdon family, as was the **Château de Laroque**, with a great round 13th-century donjon.

SOUTH OF CAHORS: THE CAUSSE DE LIMOGNE AND QUERCY BLANC

South of the River Lot rises the dry, sparsely populated Causse de Limogne. More wooded and less dramatic than the Causse de Gramat, its rocky emptiness is dotted with dolmens, magnificent *pigeonniers*, abandoned walls and stone huts. Lavender is grown commercially here, and most of the Lot's truffles hide out near the roots of its twisted dwarf oaks.

Quercy Blanc (which the Lot shares with Tarn-et-Garonne) shows a markedly different, drier face south of the river, with fewer villages and farms. Conspicuous in the open countryside are the slopes where the soil has been washed away to expose the pale limestone underneath (yet sunflowers, lavender and wheat thrive here); this is also used to build the characteristic houses, giving 'White Quercy' its name.

Market day in Lalbenque is Saturday, but from December to March it hosts 'the world's biggest truffle market' every Tuesday; Limogne-en-Quercy holds a smaller one on Fridays during the same months. Montcuq holds a lively Sunday morning market.

TOURIST INFORMATION All share the same website: **w** cahorsvalleedulot.com.

i Castelnau-Montratier 1 Rue Blanié; ☎ 05 65 21 84 39; 🕘 09.00–12.30 & 14.00–17.30 Mon–Sat

i Lalbenque 120 Rue du Marché aux Truffes; ☎ 05 65 31 50 08; 🕘 09.30–12.30 & 14.00–17.30 Mon–Fri

i Limogne-en-Quercy 55 Place d'Occitanie; ☎ 05 65 24 34 28; 🕘 09.00–12.30 & 14.00–18.00 Mon–Wed, Fri

i Montcuq La Promenade; ☎ 05 65 22 94 04; 🕘 09.30–12.30 & 14.30–18.00 Mon–Sat, 10.00–13.00 Sun

WHERE TO STAY

Maison Duler [256 C6] (5 rooms) Lascabanes (east of Montcuq); 05 65 31 82 51; w saint-gery.com. In 1984, Pascale & Patrick Duler inherited this 70ha farm in ruins, & have made it into one of the most remarkable properties in the Lot. Everything is obsessively handcrafted & organic here, from the soap to the linen. Patrick is famous for his charcuterie: his *porc gascon* hams won the best-in-the-world prize a few years back. The Dulers grow their own wheat, vines, truffles in a large truffle oak plantation, olives & 100 kinds of vegetable. *Table d'hôte from €110 (eves).* **€€€€€**

Four Maison d'Hôtes (4 rooms) 4 Rue de Montmartre, Montcuq; 05 65 21 23 08; w 4ruemontmartre.com. Bob & Claude have created a little designer hideaway in this 15th-century building in the centre, plus an excellent table d'hôte (€49). B/fast inc. **€€€€**

La Vayssade (5 rooms, 2 gîtes) 205 Chemin de la Vayssade, Lalbenque; 05 65 24 31 51; w lavayssade.com. In a 12ha park of truffle oaks close to the village centre, quiet rooms in a spectacular conversion of an 18th-century stone barn with a heated pool & spa, & stable if you come on horseback. Truffle packages in season. B/fast inc. **€€€**

Lou Repaou (4 rooms) Rue de la Croix Blanche, Aujols; m 06 18 32 16 19; w lourepaou-lot.com. Unwind on the edge of sweet tiny village of Aujols in big rustic chic rooms with private entrances. B/fast inc. **€€€**

La Tissandière (5 rooms) 10 Rue des Tisserands, Lalbenque; 05 65 31 66 32; w latissandiere.fr. Spacious contemporary rooms with stone walls in a handsomely restored building near the centre of truffle town. B/fast inc. **€€€–€€**

Hotel au Charme du Levat [256 D6] (9 rooms) RD 820, 2km from St-Paul-Flaugnac; 05 65 21 93 16; w hotelaucharmedulevat.fr. Cheap & cheerful hotel with a garden & games; they'll put together what you need for a picnic. **€**

Le Vinagrou [257 E6] (4 rooms) Mas de Vinagrou, Concots; 05 65 22 58 08; w vinagrou.com. Peaceful rooms, & excellent organic restaurant (**€€**). **€**

WHERE TO EAT AND DRINK

Château de Haute-Serre [256 D5] Cieurac; 05 65 20 80 20; w hauteserre.fr; closed Wed–Thu & eves Sun. In the 1970s, the late Georges Vigouroux, one of the great Cahors wine barons, revived a famous medieval vineyard. He also restored the château, where the food is superb – menus start at €36, plus a special Lalbenque truffle menu in Feb (from €78). Vegan & vegetarian menus available with advance booking. **€€€€€**

Café de France 5 Place de la République, Montcuq; 05 65 22 52 07; w cafedefrance-montcuq.com; daily. Atmospheric bar & bistro & restaurant with a great people-watching terrace under a century-old chestnut tree. Well-prepared classics, vegetarian dishes, & Thai curry. Frequent theme nights. **€€€**

L'Esprit du Causse Concots (west of Limogne); 05 65 22 37 66; w lesprit-du-causse.com; closed Wed, lunch Sat & eves Sun–Thu. Atmospheric old inn in a former posthouse. *Exceptional €14.50 lunch & €31 dinner.* **€€**

Le Vieux Quercy Rte de Lugagnac, Limogne-en-Quercy; 05 65 31 51 17; closed Sat lunch. Charming terrace in the shade of an old hackberry tree & a very warm welcome, serving the best food around. *Lunch menus from €14.50.* **€€**

Lou Bourdie Le Bourg, Bach; 05 65 31 77 46; w loubourdie.fr; lunch only, closed Wed & Sun. Legendary family auberge serving one of the most delicious satisfying lunches in the Lot. *5-course w/day menu from €20, Sun €32, plus pricier menus featuring truffles & morels.* **€€**

Chez Nadine Le Bourg, St-Matré (12km northwest of Montcuq); 05 65 31 96 01; f Restaurant-chez-Nadine; lunch only Mon–Fri. A rare old village workers' restaurant with a different menu every day – but no choice, just like eating *chez maman. 5 courses €17.* **€**

Delia 2 Rue de la Promenade, Montcuq; m 06 38 02 22 58; f deliamontcuq; closed Mon. A fine Italian grocer's & run by a French Sicilian couple; book a superb lunch at one of the few tables in the shop. **€**

SPORTS AND ACTIVITIES Float over Quercy Blanc in a hot-air balloon with **Quercy Montgolfière** (Bellecoste, Castelnau-Montratier; m 06 13 24 33 41;

w quercymontgolfiere.fr; ring for prices) or in an ultralight from the **Cahors-Lalbenque Aérodrome** [256 D6] (m 06 27 49 49 09; 20mins from €70). The 9-hole **Golf des Roucous** [256 C7] (Sauveterre, 5km west of Castelnau-Montratier, just inside the Tarn-et-Garonne; 05 63 95 83 70; w 1520342859.jimdo.com) offers a hilly challenge and also has five woodsy gîtes (**€€€**) with a pool.

LIMOGNE-EN-QUERCY AND AROUND A truffle village and capital of the southeast causse, Limogne was the site of an experiment to see how hard it is to build a dolmen – the **Dolmen Rigounenque** just north of the village is the result. The bastide **Beauregard** to the south was founded by the abbot of Marcilhac and possesses a pretty 14th-century *halle* coiffed with a *lauze* roof. There are four dolmens near Beauregard and more in lavender-growing **Laramière** to the east, including the Lot's second largest dolmen (off the D55), the **Dolmen de la Borie du Bois**. Laramière's charming 12th-century Gothic **Prieuré Notre-Dame** (m 06 80 88 13 13; usually, but ring first) was restored by the Jesuits after being damaged in the Wars of Religion. There are sculptures from the 1300s in the chapel, a room to put up pilgrims, and a chapterhouse, visited by St Louis and his wife, Blanche de Castille, in 1244.

West of Beauregard, the **Phosphatières du Cloup d'Aural** [257 E6] (Bach; 05 65 20 06 72; w phosphatieres.com; guided tours: Apr–Nov see their website; €9, students €8, ages 5–14 €6) is a lush abyss (a collapsed *gouffre*) 25m down where phosphate was mined from 1870–90, and shipped down the Lot to Bordeaux and England, until the cheaper phosphates from North Africa ran the mine out of business. Along with phosphate, it was filled with fossils going back 30 million years and makes an interesting visit.

LALBENQUE Lalbenque is a rare village that swings into gear in winter, when it celebrates the Lot's 'black gold' with special truffle events and feasts (w truffesnoires-lalbenque.com). Get there on a Tuesday after lunch to feel the anticipation and smell the pungent truffle aroma as locals line the street with their Little Red Riding Hood-style baskets of black nuggets. At 14.00 sharp the rope goes down, and all the truffles vanish, usually within the first minute. If you want to buy just one, you can in the *mairie*, past the charming bronze statue of an old truffle hunter and his trusty dog, sculpted by Elisabeth Cibot.

The rest of the year the main sights are a 15th-century altarpiece in its church, **St-Quirin**, and a strikingly naïve 18th-century wayside cross, the **Croix de Mercadiol** by the fire station. Or you might go for a picnic at the little willow-lined **Lac de Marcenac**. Just north of Lalbenque along the D6 towards Cahors, stop to visit the **Cazelle de Nouel** [256 D6], the biggest *gariotte* or *borie* of them all, built in 1850 and standing 5.45m high. The other main 'sight' in these parts is in **Aujols**, between Montcuq and St-Cirq-Lapopie, a village as lost in time as any place in the Lot. It has an exceedingly vast public washhouse (*lavoir*) lined with 20 special wedge-shaped stones known as 'butterflies' for beating the dirt out of one's sheets. Are the locals laundry-proud, we asked, or do they indulge in too many dandelion (*pissenlits*) salads? 'No, no, that's just the way it is,' a little old lady assured us. It has a curious Romanesque church, with a crenelated tower. A walking path leads to nearby **Laburgade** with its equally odd row of pre-Revolutionary covered wells.

MONTCUQ The people of the largest and liveliest village (with an idyllic *plan d'eau* just north) claim its name comes from a pre-Indo European word for summit, *cuc*. Do pronounce the *q*, unless you want to say 'my arse' and hear the French giggle; when the makers of French Monopoly held a nationwide contest for new names for the board, Montcuq was the overwhelming winner. In the recent wave of name embellishing that has hit these parts, Montcuq now calls itself Montcuq-en-Quercy-Blanc, which according to the laws of French pronunciation forces even the most ignorant Parisian to pronounce the *q*.

Montcuq's 26m landmark, visible for miles around, is the 12th-century **Tour Comtale**, all that remains of the Count of Toulouse's castle, taken by Simon de Montfort when he sacked the village, and dismantled in 1229 by Saint Louis. Montcuq's 13th–15th-century red brick church of **St-Hilaire**, with its striking octagonal bell tower, was savaged by the Protestants and only rebuilt in the 18th century. Compostela pilgrims swarm through here in the summer – the local pharmacy does a brisk trade in sore foot treatments.

The village also has a delightful English–French bookshop, **Livres, Books & Company** (11 Rue de Montmartre; m 06 08 60 70 95; w livresbooksandcompany.com), with a tearoom and garden.

In **Rouillac** 5km south there are remarkable and extremely rare frescoes from the 12th century on the subject of Original Sin in the church of **St-Pierre**.

CASTELNAU-MONTRATIER South of Montcuq, this village started out as a *castrum* that had the honour of being razed in 1214 by Simon de Montfort. Rebuilt soon after as a bastide, it has an unusual, triangular arcaded market square and a handful of white stone houses from the 15th century. Castelnau's pride is its windmill – the **Moulin de Boisse**, now a historical monument. Two centuries ago, when it was built, almost every village without a dependable river had at least one. It provided a back-up for the 17th-century watermill, the **Moulin de Brousse** [256 C7] (D104; 05 65 21 95 81; ring the miller to visit), still in operation with a 3.5m waterfall. You can also poke around the ruins of a Gallo-Roman villa among the weeds just west at **Souquet**. To the east, the St-Paul half of **St-Paul-Flaugnac** is a striking hilltop village over the valley of the Lupte; its church, partly constructed out of a castle that once stood here, has rare octagonal vaulting.

DOWN THE LOT: CAHORS TO TOUZAC

Abruptly leaving the cliffs and causse behind, the River Lot west of Cahors suddenly decides it is in no particular hurry to get to the sea, and winds in big lazy loops through the heart of the Cahors wine region, the birthplace of Malbec, the slow ripening purple grape that loves limestone. Its wines went down so well in Rome that the Italians complained about the competition, which in those pre-EU days resulted in an order from Emperor Domitian to uproot Cahors's vineyards, in AD96. The vines were restored in AD276 by a prince named Probus; they prospered, and in 1152 they were part of Eleanor of Aquitaine's dowry. François Ier planted Cahors vines at Fontainebleau, and Peter the Great planted vines in Azerbaijan along the Black Sea, which to this day produces Caorskoïe Vino. And in 1868 a Frenchman took Malbec to Argentina, and made it famous.

Knocked out in the 1870s by phylloxera, the wine's slow revival in the Lot began in the late 1940s, making wines from at least 70% Malbec, often mixed with Merlot for bouquet and roundness, and Tannat. The 21st century has seen serious young winemakers take it to new heights, figuratively and literally, replanting vines high up on the limestone hills over the river. If you want to explore, check out the listings of the **Vignerons Indépendents** (w vigneron-I-lot.com): unlike in Bordeaux, nearly all the vineyards welcome visitors who just drop in.

GETTING AROUND Several buses a day (☎ 08 05 36 06 60; w lio.laregion.fr) from Cahors station go to Luzech, Prayssac and Puy l'Évêque to the station in Monsempron-Libos (page 309).

TOURIST INFORMATION

Luzech 90 Place du Canal; ☎ 05 65 20 17 27; w cahorsvalleedulot.com; ⌚ 10.00–12.30 & 13.30–18.00 Wed, Sat

Puy-l'Évêque Place des Rampeau, on the D811; ☎ 05 65 21 37 63; w cahorsvalleedulot.com; ⌚ 09.30–13.00 & 14.00–17.30 Mon–Sat

WHERE TO STAY

Côté Lot (11 rooms) 10 Place de la Truffière, Puy-l'Évêque; ☎ 05 65 36 06 60; w cotelot.fr. Bright rooms & bewitching views over the river from the dining room (€€€€); also a €23 lunch menu. **€€€**

Le Clau del Loup (5 rooms) Métairie Haute, Anglars-Juillac; ☎ 05 65 36 76 20; w claudelloup.com. A 19th-century stone *maison de maître* in a peaceful park, with a pool – but no TVs; the bistronomic restaurant (€€€) offers good-value lunches. **€€€**

La Mouline (3 rooms) La Mouline, Labastide-du-Vert; m 06 08 32 21 32; w la-mouline-du-vert.com. Serenity & warm rustic charm in a *maison de maître* from the 18th-century, & a pool. B/fast inc. **€€€**

Château de Rouffiac [256 A4] (4 rooms) D68, Duravel; m 06 73 38 21 46; w chateau-de-rouffiac.com. Stay in a beautiful Cahors wine estate with a pool, surrounded by forests. B/fast inc. **€€€–€€**

Auberge de la Tour (8 rooms) Rte d'Agen, Sauzet, 9km south of Luzech; ☎ 05 65 36 90 05; w aubergedelatour.com. The 13th-century Château de Sauzet is now a little hotel with a pool. The excellent restaurant (€€€) is devoted to the hallowed specialities of the southwest, including cassoulet; in the summer dine under the wisteria-covered terrace. **€€–€**

Domaine de l'Ameillée (6 rooms) Rue du Commandant Poirier, Puy-l'Évêque; ☎ 05 65 22 78 38; w lameillee.com. Don't be put off by the tired street leading up to this handsome 19th-century building in a peaceful corner overlooking the church. Rooms are packed with old-fashioned charm and details. B/fast inc. **€**

Domaine de La Source Bleue–La Tour (4 rooms) Touzac; ☎ 05 65 36 56 71; w latourtouzac.wixsite.com/lasourcebleue. Idyllic place in a lovely riverside park by a spring surrounded by a bamboo forest – once owned by Marguerite Moreno (page 289). B/fast inc. **€**

Henry (16 rooms) 23 Rue du Dr Rouma, Puy-l'Evêque; ☎ 09 70 35 17 37; w hotel-restaurant-henry.fr. Now in the hands of the 6th generation, simple rooms near the bridge, & popular bar terrace & a restaurant (€€) with a pretty garden terrace out back. **€**

WHERE TO EAT AND DRINK

Les Jardins 1533 Rte du Port de l'Angle, Parnac; ☎ 05 65 23 58 24; w restaurant-lesjardins.fr; ⌚ lunch Tue–Fri & dinner Sat. A young couple run this gourmet restaurant amid the vines with a menu that changes every season; book days in advance. *Menus €29.50–€75.* **€€€€€**

Le Caillou [256 A5] Le Caillou, Vire-sur-Lot (3km south of Puy l'Évêque); ☎ 05 65 23 78 04; w lecaillau.com; ⌚ closed Tue, & eves Sun–Thu. Sit in a pretty courtyard amid the vines, or indoors by the fire. There's a frequently changing menu, as well as a café & ceramic studio. *Good value 3-course lunch menu €19.50.* **€€€€**

Auberge du Vieux Douelle (chez Malique) 19 Rue des Tonneliers, Douelle; ☎ 05 65 20 02 03; w chezmalique.com; ⌚ Oct–Apr closed Sat–Sun. Old stone inn (simple rooms; €) with relatable great food, from salads & tapas to menus from €22 to €42.50. **€€€**

Château de Chambert [256 B5] Floressas, above Grézels; ☎ 05 65 31 95 75; w chateaudechambert.com. Striking 17th-century wine château with a wine bar-bistro & panoramic terrace. **€€€**

Le Médiéval 24 Grand Rue, Puy l'Évêque; ☎ 09 86 31 80 88; w lemedieval-puyleveque.fr; ⌚ closed Sun–Mon. Pretty dishes & a seasonal contemporary cuisine, with a twist – the owners come from Burgundy. **€€€**

Le Vigne Haut 1 Av des Tonneliers, Castelfranc; 05 65 53 08 45; w lavignehaute.net; closed Wed. Excellent starters & grilled meats all well prepared, & classic French desserts. *4-course menu €27.50.* €€€

Les Mariniers Rue des Mariniers, Douelle; 05 65 20 02 06; w lamarine-douelle.com; noon–22.00 daily. Another old favourite, with seafood platters, surf & turf, tapas & plates to share; summer terrace in the back. *Menus from €11.50.* €€€

Antinéa Le Payras, Douelle; m 06 99 05 91 28; w antinea-lot.fr. New owners run this excellent restaurant-tapas/wine bar by the beach. €€

Chez Justine Place des Justes, Mauroux; 05 65 31 69 28; f ChezJustine46; closed Tue–Wed. Chalkboard menu, organic vegetables, & craft beers on tap. Cheerful service. €€

Les Dodus Y Manger & Y Boire 11 Rue Ernest Marcouly, Puy l'Évêque; 05 65 22 91 82; f restaurant-Les-Dodus; closed Sun, Mon, Thu. New owners with excellent credentials have taken over this beloved little restaurant. €€

La Guinguette 700m west of Grézels; 05 65 30 86 91; w la-guinguette-grezels.fr; daily. A lovely spot on the river with an adjacent playground serving pizzas & unfussy fare. €€

Le Pukeko 18 Bd de la Paix, Prayssac; m 06 70 51 04 76; f cafepukeko; eves Sun, Tue–Wed, all day Thu–Sat, closed Mon. New Zealand burgers, steaks, fish & chips plus homemade pavlova & great coffee. €€

Terre Gourmande 25 Av Mar Bessières, Prayssac; 05 65 21 82 69; w terregourmande.fr; lunch Mon–Sat. Combination gourmet food & wine shop & lunch room. *Menu €15.* €€

Le Pigeonnier 1 Promenade du Héron, Puy l'Évêque; 05 65 21 37 77; f Le-Pigeonnier-du-Lot-Puy-Leveque; closed winter & lunch Wed & Sat. Beautiful views of the village, cheap & cheerful steaks, mussels, salads & crêpes, & big ice creams. €€–€

Petit Biscuit 15 Rue des Capucins, Puy l'Évêque; m 06 85 58 24 67; f petitbiscuitetgourmandise; 10.30–18.30 Wed–Sun. In the medieval centre. Vegetarian lunches in this little tearoom, & lovely homemade cakes. €

Le Couvent Place du Mercadiel, Bélaye; m 07 86 53 73 75; w lecouventbarpanoramabelaye.fr; 11.00–22.00 Wed–Mon. By the big church, a tapas bar by the belvedere overlooking the valley. Hosts frequent concerts & art expos.

SPORTS AND ACTIVITIES The local cliffs enjoy the perfect updrafts for **hang-gliding**: try Fly Douelle 46 (m 07 81 46 91 29; f flydouelle); also Club du Vol Libre Cadurcien (m 06 15 08 42 61).

Copa Caïx Bana Caïx; 05 65 21 07 86. Hire a canoe, kayak, SUP or motorboat; also a bar & campsite.

Copeyre Puy l'Évêque; 05 65 20 03 25; w gabare-copeyre.com. Rent a kayak or take a trip upriver in a *gabarre*.

Entr'Anes 40 Rue de la Baronnie; Luzech; m 06 81 28 77 12; w entr-anes.com. Donkey rides for children, donkey carts, or hire a donkey to carry your bags to Compostela.

Le Lot Canoë Kayak Floiras, Anglars-Juillac; 05 65 36 27 39; w lelotcanoekayak.com. Rents canoes, motorbikes & mountain bikes.

CAHORS TO CAÏX Although the D811 is the fast route, the scenery is much prettier along the river, carpeted with vineyards. You have several options, none straightforward, but then again, neither is the river. Leave Cahors by way of **Pradines** (now a suburb but once a village in its own right) with an 11th–12th-century Romanesque church, **St-Martial**, containing a polychrome statue of the Virgin from the same period. The road then skirts the cliffs and Lot towards **Douelle** ('barrel stave'), a river port for *gabarres* in the old days, when all the cargo was loaded into enormous barrels, some of which were made here. Douelle has seen better days, but has been decidedly more colourful ever since Didier Comizo painted the 122m quay wall with a mural on the Creation, wine and humankind – which is best seen from a boat.

Cross the narrow suspension bridge in Douelle and head towards Mercuès by way of **Caillac**, passing the handsome Renaissance château **La Grézette**, which overlooks a prestigious vineyard owned by the owner of Cartier. A bit further north, the 12th-century **Château Les Bouysses** [256 C5] (05 65 30 71 86; by appt) was donated by its builder, Raymond de Lard, to the Cistercians, who made it a priory (a rather nice one with an orangery) until the Revolution, when the Count of Mosbourg purchased it and made it a wine business, and replaced the chapel with a *chai*. Caillac's Romanesque church has a four-square bell tower and 15th-century porch, with carvings, including Adam and Eve and floral motifs.

The D23 rises up the causse to Fred Flintstone's workplace, the stone quarries of **Crayssac** – in Jurassic times this was a muddy flat surrounding a shallow sea. Just over the D811 workers here in 1995 were surprised to find footprints – rare tracks of the ancestors of the first winged dinosaurs going back 150 million years, and nothing less than 'the Holy Grail of pterosaur biology', proving that the little creatures got around rather awkwardly on all fours, using their wings as legs. See them at the **Plage aux Pterosaures** [256 C4] (book a tour: 05 65 23 32 48; w plageauxpterosaures.fr; 14.30 & 16.00; €9, ages 6–14 €6, under 6 free).

Turn south here past Crayssac church to the belvedere and narrow switchback road down towards the river to **Caïx**, where you encounter a huge panoramic view over the valley and the 17th-century **Château de Caïx** [256 C4], which flies the flag of Denmark when Queen Marguerite of Denmark is in residence (she married the owner, the late Henri de Montpezat). The late prince consort's father, Comte André de Montpezat, was a rice planter in Vietnam before returning to the Lot to become a founding member of the wine co-operative in **Parnac**, the next village west. Next along the river, **St-Vincent Rive d'Olt** has a 16th-century church with many of its original fittings.

LUZECH This large village enjoys a striking setting, on a narrow isthmus where a loop of the Lot is so tight it nearly meets. Luzech began as a Gallo-Roman citadel, of which a few bits remain on the steep hill above the town at the **Oppidum de l'Impernal**. It was captured by Richard the Lionheart in 1188, then a few years later sacked by Simon de Montfort and given to Count Bishop Guillaume de Cardaillac of Cahors, who became co-seigneur with the local barons. Castles at either end successfully repelled every English siege in the Hundred Years' War.

What remains of medieval Luzech trails under the stout **Tour de l'Impernal**, all that survives of the bishops' fort. Here you'll find the **Musée Municipal Armand-Viré** (152 Rue de la Ville; 05 65 30 58 47; 10.00–noon & 14.00–18.00 Tue–Fri, 10.00–noon Sat; €3) with finds from the oppidum, including a model of Trajan's column. A second museum **Ichnospace** (€2) at the same address has a remarkable collection of ammonites.

The wide square that carries the D8 through the village was once a canal, cutting off the loop of the river. The Flamboyant Gothic church **Notre-Dame de l'Isle** on the teardrop-shaped hill was built in 1505 in the same style as the Cahors cathedral cloister. Near the hydroelectric plant (powered by the water rushing through an underground tunnel) is something unexpected: the fascinating **La Planète des Moulins** (144 Quai Emile Gironde; 05 65 31 22 59; w museelaplanetedesmoulins.fr; Jul–Aug 10.00–noon & 15.00–18.00 Mon–Fri, by appt rest of year & Sat–Sun; €6, ages 5–16 €4, under 5 free) offering scale working models of every kind of mill ever made around the world.

Albas, just west, occupies a picturesque spot on a cliff over the river and has recently stuck 'la-Jolie' at the end of its name. Lovely views over the village and valley await from its new Jardin Toscane. Next along the river is **Anglars-Juillac**, home to **L'Oeil du Silence** (w loeildusilence.com), a mime workshop and theatre run by Anne Sicco, run by the widow of the late Marcel Marceau, who died in Cahors in 2007.

LABASTIDE-DU-VERT North of river, along the D811, this village might be best known locally its orange painted stretch of road designed to shock motorists into slowing down; along it is a rare surviving shed for shoeing oxen (opposite the *tabac*). But just 100m down the lane, the scene with its poplars, little bridge and church will look familiar to anyone who has visited the Henri Martin museum in Cahors; he is buried in the village cemetery.

CASTELFRANC This austere bastide of the 13th century – die-straight streets and a central square with a modern *halle* and a spare church, typical of medieval Quercy architecture – has a popular beach; while on the banks of the Vert the village has planted a charming medieval garden, which is always open.

The long, wooded ridge to the northwest of Castelfranc was an important Neolithic site. Take the D811 west, and then the first turn sharply right, which climbs steeply up the hill past a clutch of new houses; then pick up the marked ***circuit des dolmens***. In addition to three dolmens on this walk (there's a road, but only suitable for 4x4s), you'll encounter an unusual 'double' *garriote*, a niche called 'Caesar's armchair', near an ancient well, and, at the summit, a circle of three huge menhirs amid jumbles of rocks known as 'Chaos'.

PRAYSSAC The main market village west of Cahors (with a great Friday morning market) is worth a mention for the quite unforgettable nude Venus on Venus Square, the vernal nymph in the lobby of the cinema, and the well-endowed sphinx-like creatures by the post office. Also in marble is Jean-Baptiste Bessières, the 'Duke of Istria', across from the *mairie*. One of Napoleon's henchmen, this son of Prayssac oversaw the military occupation of Moscow, and died with a cannonball in his brain at Lützen in 1814.

On the south bank, just west of Prayssac, **Pescadoires** has a fortified Romanesque church near the river, while **Bélaye** stands high on the cliffs overlooking the valley. This ancient fortified place was one of the most important towns in the area before the English *routiers* raided it – several times – during the Hundred Years' War. The ruins of its episcopal castle remain, along with a strong-looking fortified church with an altarpiece brought back by the souvenir-hunting Maréchal Bessières.

PUY-L'ÉVÊQUE The hills close in on the river again at Puy-l'Évêque, giving it an exceptional riverside setting, best seen from the bridge over the Lot. By now, you can guess to which *évêques* this *puy* ('hill') belonged. No-one remembers its name as a Cathar village, before Bishop Guillaume de Cadaillac conquered it in 1227, and soon after built a castle – only the 22m tower survives next to the *mairie*. Not long after, local nobles added their houses in its shadow – none is that impressive individually, but the whole makes a lovely ensemble. The lofty lighthouse-like tower near the river was to keep an eye on passing boats to make sure they paid a toll.

The battered Flamboyant Gothic portal of its church **St-Sauveur** (near the top of the town), was whacked by a hundred Protestant cannonballs in the Wars of Religion; one is still embedded in the wall to the right of the door. The cemetery next to it has a 15th-century cross, reminiscent of the one of St-Projet (page 292). By the tourist office just below on the D811 is a belvedere over the village and valley. A new walkway just to right of the *mairie* leads down into the heart of the medieval village. The pretty village of **Martignac** 4km to the north has a church (🕘 09.00–17.00) with 16th-century frescoes, including the *Seven Deadly Sins* (not well preserved), some Italianate chiaroscuros, and in the apse a strange, looming figure like the king on a playing card that seems to be God himself.

South of Puy-l'Évêque, in **Grézels**, the bishop of Cahors built the **Château de la Coste** in the 12th century; after keeping the English at bay during the Hundred Years' War and a sacking by the Protestants in 1580, it was rebuilt in its current four-square Renaissance style, squatting on its hill like an elegant bunker.

DURAVEL The next village west was the Roman Diolindum. In 1055 the lord of Pestillac (page 295) donated it to the great abbey of Moissac which financed the construction of the Romanesque priory of **St-Hilaire** in the village centre and sent a gift: an 11th-century sarcophagus containing 'Three Holy Bodies' (SS Hilarion, Agathon and Poemon), which had been left at the abbey by Charlemagne and which attracted thousands of pilgrims in its day. You can see the Holy Bodies once every five years on the last Sunday in October (next in 2025); at other times they are stored in the Carolingian crypt that pre-dates the church, with primitive but finely carved capitals, one showing a peacock. The capitals in the nave and chapels (scenes of misers in hell, St Michael) have been brightly painted – a bit disconcerting at first, the way the Parthenon would be in all its original Technicolor tones. Also look for a Gallo-Roman relief of – aptly for this wine village – bunches of grapes.

TOUZAC A narrow bridge crosses the Lot at Duravel; turn right here for Touzac, site of a lovely deep-blue spring, the **Source Bleue**. Actress Marguerite Moreno (1871–1948) fell in love with the area, bought a house by the spring and used to entertain her friend Colette here. In 1938, Touzac was the scene of *La Route Enchantée*, a half-baked film written and starring Charles Trenet (his debut) who played a troubadour; Moreno played the crazy countess. She is buried in Touzac's cemetery.

Up the hill south of Touzac are **Lacapelle-Cabanac** and **Mauroux** (pronounce the *x*). Between the two, to the right of the D5, is the striking Romanesque church of Cabanac, with a bell tower rebuilt in the 13th century – all that remains of the lost medieval town of Orgueil, or 'Pride' as in one of the Deadly Sins. In the 13th century its lords, sworn enemies of the bishop of Cahors, terrorised the Lot valley, burning, pillaging and raping as far south as Moissac. Orgueil sided with the English and gave nearby Puy-l'Évêque to the Duke of Derby. When the townspeople were banished, Orgueil became a robbers' den, occupied by English *routiers* until the count of Armagnac razed the pit of vipers once and for all in the mid 1300s.

NORTHWEST OF CAHORS: LA BOURIANE

Bories are drystone huts, otherwise known as *cazelles* or *gariottes*; in this most Périgourdin corner of Quercy, however, a *borie* means a farmhouse, especially a fortified country retreat of Cahors's medieval elite. Scattered farmhouses amid lush landscapes of chestnuts, pines and meadows are indeed the order of the day in the Bouriane, but there are some unexpected treats, too.

GETTING THERE AND AROUND Gourdon has a railway station with connections to Cahors, Souillac and beyond; but otherwise you're on your own.

TOURIST INFORMATION

Cazals Rue de la République; 05 65 22 88 88; w tourisme-cazals-salviac.com; Apr–Oct 10.00–noon & 14.30–17.30 Mon–Fri, Nov–Mar 15.00–17.00 Wed, 10.00–noon & 15.00–17.00 Thu–Fri

Gourdon 20 Bd des Martyrs; 05 65 27 52 50; w tourisme-gourdon.com; Jul–Aug 09.30–19.00 Mon–Sat, 10.00–13.00 Sun, Sep–Jun 09.30–noon & 14.00–17.00 Mon–Sat

Salviac 1 Place du Foirail; 05 65 37 02 63; w tourisme-cazals-salviac.com; Apr–Oct 10.00–noon & 14.00–17.00 Mon–Fri, Nov–Mar 10.00–noon & 15.00–17.00 Mon–Tue, 10.00–noon Wed

WHERE TO STAY

Hostellerie de la Bouriane (20 rooms) Place du Foirail, Gourdon; 05 65 41 16 37; w hotellabouriane.fr. A large country inn that has long been the place to stay in Gourdon; rooms are lovely, the food (€€€) – including some fish dishes – delicious. **€€€**

Le Manoir La Barrière (5 rooms, 2 gîtes) Le Vigan; m 06 08 65 83 57; w manoirlabarriere.fr. B&B in a lakeside manor of 1590, where the bedrooms are huge & beautifully furnished. Amid the tailored lawns of the park there's a pool, & a heated one indoors. Table d'hôte available & delightful hosts Corinne & José. B/fast inc. **€€€–€€**

Domaine Le Bouysset (4 rooms) St-Martin-de-Redon; 05 65 30 34 00; w bouysset.fr. A peaceful estate run by a friendly Dutch couple, complete with a restaurant (€€), pool, tennis & a quirky 9-hole golf course. **€€**

La Métairie des Songes [256 C2] (4 rooms) Flagel, Gourdon; 09 61 29 75 84; w lametairie-gourdon.com. Only 3km from Gourdon, but very peaceful & rural, this old stone farmhouse is as cosy as they come, with a relaxing garden & charming English owners Clare & Mark, & Issac the dog, & Michelin-star-level table d'hôte (€36). B/fast inc. **€€**

Le Moulin de Planiol (5 rooms) Le Vigan; 09 74 56 85 69; w le-moulin-de-planiol-46.com. Modern rooms in a stone mill in a park with heated pool, *pétanque* court, & cosy salon with board games. B/fast inc. **€€**

Hostellerie de Goujounac (5 rooms) Goujounac; m 06 09 01 59 35. Right in the centre of the pretty village, remodelled rooms, & a restaurant (€€€) with a pretty terrace & €20 lunch menu. **€**

La Promenade (10 rooms) 48 Bd Galiot de Genouilhac, Gourdon; 05 65 41 41 44; w logishotels.com. Simple hotel in the medieval centre, with a bar & restaurant (€€) that promises homemade frites. **€**

WHERE TO EAT AND DRINK

Le Gindreau [256 C4] St-Médard; 05 65 36 22 27; w legindreau.com; closed Mon–Tue (exc Jan–mid-Mar). The region's Michelin-starred haven, with a panoramic garden terrace. Here Pascal Bardet, who worked with Alain Ducasse, prepares beautiful dishes. There's a special all-truffle menu Jan–mid-Mar. *Menus from €75, dégustation from €135.* **€€€€€**

La Récréation Les Arques; 05 65 22 88 08; w la-recreation-restaurant.com; closed Wed–Thu. A lovely setting in a former schoolhouse & playground – now a romantic garden terrace. The food is delicious, with dishes for every taste; don't miss their famous *raviolis de homard. Set menus €28–€42.* **€€€€**

Aux 4 Saisons Le Bourg, Marminiac; 05 65 21 42 81; f; closed Tue & eves Mon. A gourmet surprise in the little village that gave France its national rugby coach, Fabien Galthié. Wonderful food & charming service. **€€€**

Delicatessens [256 D2] Domaine du Berthiol, Gourdon; 05 65 32 70 56; w delicatessens.fr; closed Mon & eves Sun, Nov–May also closed eves Tue–Thu. On the D704 towards Cahors, a large stone Quercy manor house in the woods, now with a chic new look, new owners & creative cuisine. *3-course bistro menu €23, evening menu from €38.* **€€€**

Le Loup Blanc Plaça dels Telhs, St-Martin-le-Redon; m 06 72 46 69 64; w leloupblanc.net; closed Sun–Mon & lunch Tue. Gourmet locavore haven (also an épicerie & 4 pretty rooms; **€**) run by chef Pascal de Ventura, with a constantly changing lunch menu. *Lunch formules €18–€22, dinner €28–€38.* **€€€**

Un Canard sous l'Olivier [256 D3] D820 in Ussel (midway between Gourdon & Cahors); 05 65 23 64 89; f; closed eves Mon & lunch Mon–Sat. Florent & Alexandre run this lovely oasis on the edge of the Bouriane & causse with a pretty semi-tropical garden, music nights on some w/ends, & tasty contemporary cuisine. **€€€**

Aux Délices de la Serpt [256 B3] D28, Frayssinet-le-Gélat; 05 65 36 66 15; Jun–Sep daily, Oct–May usually lunch Sat–Sun. A *ferme-auberge* serving some of the best *tourin*

(garlic soup) & duck magrets in the Lot. Booking essential – & be sure to arrive hungry. €€

La Poule au Pot [256 B4] Les Andrives Hautes, Goujounac; 05 65 36 65 48; f; lunch only. A *ferme-auberge* with set menus starring duck & the best sautéed potatoes in the world, wine & coffee. Book, especially on Sun. €€

Auberge de la Place Place Hugues Salel, Cazals; 05 65 22 86 96; w aubergedelaplace-cazals.fr; mid-Jun–mid-Sep closed Mon & eves Sun, mid-Sep–mid-Jun closed Mon & eves exc Sat. A local institution, with simple dishes that never disappoint, from ravioli to cèpe omelettes. *4-course menu du jour with wine €12.80.* €

Ô Grands Gourmands St-Denis-Catus; 09 86 67 77 82; f; closed Mon. Popular informal spot with a €14.50 lunch, & pizza & burgers in the eve. €

Le Bar à Trucs Le Bourg, Lherm; 05 65 22 84 66; f; 11.00–20.00 daily. A village institution, with frequent concerts & a pretty terrace.

GOURDON Harmoniously piled on a lofty bluff, the golden stone capital of the Bouriane is easily spotted from miles around. In AD961 Count Raymond I of Toulouse gave the city to the Gourdon family. The clan, and their eponymous town, were nearly wiped out in 1189 by Richard the Lionheart, who as Duke of Aquitaine was more like the Sheriff of Nottingham than the good king of the Robin Hood legends. The son who survived the massacre of Gourdon got revenge with his crossbow ten years later at the siege of Châlus, when he shot Richard fatally in the shoulder.

Gourdon in its medieval heyday had four monasteries. In the Wars of Religion the monasteries also made a juicy target for the fierce Protestant captain Duras, who spent a month razing them to the ground and slaughtering their inhabitants. Gourdon's once-mighty castle suffered a similar fate in 1651 when its lord foolishly supported the cause of Marie de' Medici over her son, Louis XIII.

Start your tour at the top, with the fortress-like Gothic church of **St-Pierre** (Place de l'Hôtel de Ville; 05 65 27 52 50) begun in 1302, its façade flanked by two 33m towers, linked by a gallery over the 14th-century rose window. More stained glass from the same period is in the apse, along with beautiful 17th-century gilded wooden reliefs sculpted by the Tournié brothers; the organ tribune dates from the 18th century. For a view from Gourdon equal to the view of Gourdon, climb up to the **esplanade** that once formed the base of the castle: you can see the Dordogne valley, the green Bouriane and every roof in town.

Near the church, the 13th-century house of the consuls was converted in the 1700s into the Hôtel de Ville, with graceful arcades on the ground floor. Narrow little streets, like **Rue Zigzag,** are lined with medieval houses; it also has one of the **Jardins de la Butte** (w vertusvertes.com) that since 2012 have added green spaces to the centre. Behind St-Pierre in Place des Marronniers, note the fine Renaissance portal of the **Maison Cavaignac**. The Cavaignacs were prominent in the Revolution and 19th century; Jean-Baptiste served on the National Convention and ended up as a counsellor of Napoleon.

The main street, **Rue du Majou**, is lined with handsome medieval houses, a fortified gate and chapel. Here the **Maison du Sénéchal** offers displays on Gourdon's history and heritage (17 Rue du Majou; m 06 43 50 41 59; ring to see if it's reopened).

On Gourdon's ring boulevard, the Gothic church of the **Cordeliers** survived the monastic destruction. Although it's not much from the outside, the honey-hued interior is lovely and has a beautiful 14th-century baptismal font carved with the figures of Christ and the apostles. A third church, **Notre-Dame-des-Neiges**, is 1km from the Hostellerie de la Bouriane (see opposite) on the site of a miraculous spring. Although only the apse survives from the Romanesque church, the whole is charming and contains an altar by Tournier, although it's usually locked.

AROUND GOURDON The two **Grottes de Cougnac** [256 C2], 3km north of Gourdon (☎ 05 65 41 47 54; w grottesdecougnac.com; ⊕ guided tours: Palm Sun–Jul & Sep 10.00–11.30 & 14.30–17.00 daily, early Jul–late Aug 10.00–17.45 daily, Oct 14.00–16.00 Mon–Sat; €9.50, ages 5–12 €6.50), offer a taste of everything speleological: the first has a spectacular décor of stalactites and stalagmites, discovered in 1949 on the advice of M. Lagarde, a clairvoyant, and the second one in 1952 after he said there was another cave nearby. Blocked millennia ago, this one has preserved black and red outlines of goats, deer, mammoths, symbols and humans, some pierced by lances, surrounded by formations that look like trees and mutant cauliflowers. Among them, palaeontological detectives have found fingerprints believed to be 20,000 years old; some of the drawings are 10,000 years older.

But even these seem young compared with the discoveries by the University of Bordeaux at the **Gisement de Piage** [256 C1]**,** 8km north of Gourdon at **Fajoles**. Here under a low cliff, they have found extremely rare 40,000-year-old signs of early nomadic reindeer-hunting *Homo Sapiens sapiens* living beside the last Neanderthals. **La Maison du Piage** (Le Bourg, Fajoles; ☎ 05 65 32 67 36; w maisondupiage.fr; ⊕ May–Aug 14.00–18.00 Wed–Sat, 10.00–noon & 14.00–18.00 Sun; in Jul–Aug archaeology workshops (book ahead) run 10.00–noon Wed–Sat; €4) explains all, with fascinating details on the current excavations.

Milhac, west of Fajoles, is a delightful medieval village and cradle of the lords of Gourdon, while the next village west, **St-Cirq-Madelon,** has a surprise in its church of **St-Georges** (☎ 05 65 41 26 98; ⊕ by appt; donation): the entire interior is covered with frescoes: early medieval figures of Christ and the Evangelists in the apse, colourful 18th-century frescoes in the nave plus a chapel painted in the Gothic style by a 19th-century priest.

Another charmer is **Masclat** further north, built around a pretty château and church, only a few kilometres from **Lamothe-Fénelon**, cradle of that famous family (page 204); its 12th-century church, **St-Sixte**, once part of a priory of the abbey at Souillac, has a strikingly unique *clocher-mur* and murals of the *Annunciation* and *Christ in Majesty*.

LE VIGAN 6km east of Gourdon, the town is built around the massive Gothic **Abbatiale Notre Dame de l'Assomption** (☎ 05 65 41 12 46; ⊕ Jul–Aug 10.30–12.30 & 15.30–18.30 daily; other times pick up the key at the *mairie*) founded by the canons of St-Sernin in Toulouse in the 13th century. Once one of the richest abbeys in the Lot, the English in the Hundred Years' War pillaged it so thoroughly that it never recovered. Further east, **St-Projet** has a pilgrims' cross near its church, in which the serpent represents evil, the heart triumphant love, the skull and crossbones unredeemed humanity; on the top a sweet Christ is crucified.

CATUS AND AROUND This, as its name suggests, is the village of the cat, one of which, they say, showed the way to the spring that now feeds its **Lac Vert**, with a popular summer beach. The village itself eventually grew up around a buttressed Gothic church with a polygonal apse, all that remains of the 10th-century **priory of St-Jean** – originally a dependency of San Michele de la Cluse 750km away near Turin. Its 12th-century chapterhouse has a dozen magnificent if somewhat worn capitals and column bases, carved by the same school as at Moissac.

North of Catus, **Uzech-les-Oules** was founded on a hill of white clay. By the 17th century 60 potters worked here, making *oules* (pots used for conserving confits) and the ornamental *épis de fitage*, the ceramic pinnacles perched on the gables of older houses. Although the last potter died in 1956, the art has since been revived;

three ceramicists now work in Uzech full time, and in late August they hold a large ceramics fair. In the meantime you can visit the **Centre d'Art Potier** (m 06 14 70 96 91; w poterie-uzech-artisanat.com; ⌚ Jul–Sep 10.00–noon & 14.00–18.00 daily, Oct–Jun 14.00–18.00 Wed–Sun; free).

LES JUNIES Just west of Labastide-du-Vert in Castelfranc (page 288) is the turn-off on the D45 for the lush valley of the Masse. In the hamlet of **La Masse** the church (key in the house to the left) has the liveliest frescoes of any Bouriane church: a parade of the *Seven Deadly Sins*, each riding a beast guided by frisky devils and goaty satyrs. A bit further north, Les Junies was a fief given by Bishop Guillaume de Cardaillac as a thank-you-for-financing-my-stomping-on-the-Cathars present to the banker, Bertrand de Jean. The de Jeans built the very picturesque 14th-century **château** in the centre and church of **St-Pierre-ès-Liens** which boast an exceptionally elaborate carved and painted 17th-century retable and rare 14th-century stained glass showing the founders, along with scenes of *Christ and St John.*

From the centre of Les Junies, a narrow road winds its way to tiny **Canourgues** and its 12th-century church of **Saint-Martin** which has some curious modillions and rather violent 16th-century frescoes of the *Crucifixion* in one of the chapels. **Lherm**, a striking ensemble in stone, was the site of an ironworks in the Middle Ages that was left so desolated after the passing of English *grandes compagnies* of routiers in the 15th century that a wolf gave birth outside the church door.

SOUTHWEST OF GOURDON More bucolic Bouriane landscapes of rolling hills, forests and meadows wait here, on and off the D673 from Gourdon to Fumel, in the Lot-et-Garonne (page 309).

Abbaye-Nouvelle de Léobard [256 C2] (8km southwest of Gourdon; w abbaye-nouvelle.fr) Now left in romantic ruins, this Cistercian abbey was founded in 1242 on a rock overlooking the valley of the Céou on lands donated by Guillaume de Gourdon-Salviac, anxious to get back into the good graces of the Inquisition after flirting with the Cathars. The Gothic church (1274–87) was damaged in the Hundred Years' War and never properly repaired, and by 1658 the abbey was abandoned. In 1950 it was dynamited (!) by its farmer owners; the once elegant stairway was dismantled for a barn. Now only the lofty, ruined walls of the church stand, originally 28m high – Abbaye-Nouvelle was the only known Cistercian church in France without a transept, and one of the few built with two storeys. These days the abbey ruins make a lovely setting for summer concerts.

Château de Lantis [256 C3] (South of Abbaye-Nouvelle, off the D51 in Dégagnac; t 05 65 41 11 47; w chateau-de-lantis.fr; ⌚ guided tours: Jul–Aug 10.00–noon & 14.00–18.00 daily, Sep–Jun closed Tue; €8, ages 7–15 €4, under 7 free) This 15th–17th-century château took 20 years to restore; the owner, who did most of the work herself, is a fascinating tour guide. **Rampoux** just south has a 12th–14th-century Benedictine priory church (pick up the key in the house nearby), decorated with some exceptionally expressive 15th-century frescoes on the *Crucifixion.*

Salviac Here we have a Renaissance château, and a Gothic church built by Jacques Duèze of Cahors (Pope John XXII), which has some original stained glass. But it's also the vortex of a mini region of mechanical obsessions. Start with the **Musée du Patrimoine Agricole et Automobile** (Pépy – take Rue des Écoles south of Salviac;

05 65 41 56 18; w musee-agricole-salviac.com; 09.00–19.00 daily; €8, under 12 €5; guided tour with demonstrations Jul–Aug 11.00, 15.00 & 16.30; €12, under 12 €5) with 250 tractors, antique cars, motorcycles, toys, etc. A bit further south waits the **Atelier-Musée des Vieilles Horloges** (Cambelève; 05 65 32 18 80; w les-vieilles-horloges-de-salviac.com; 14.00–19.00 daily; €7, under 10 free), offering a tour of clocks from the 12th to the 20th centuries.

Cazals and around Back on the D673, near a pretty *plan d'eau*, Cazals started off as castle of Gourdon, captured by Richard the Lionheart in 1189; it was later refounded as the bastide of Montolza for England in 1319. Cazals gave the world Hugues Salel (1504–53), who translated the *Iliad* for François Ier and defended Rabelais and drove Clément Marot (page 258) crazy by imitating his *blasons*, dedicated to pins and the like. On the huge main square, the **Musée du Mecanic Art** (m 06 16 24 01 35; w museemecanicart.com; Jul–Aug 09.00–19.00 daily; €5) is unique in France, featuring paintings, posters and prints of mechanical transport – from early bicycles to the Apollo 11.

Just south of Cazals, the **Atelier-Musées des Vieilles Mécaniques** (Rte de Monclĕra; 05 65 20 29 68; w vieillesmecaniques.com; Jul–Aug 09.00–18.00 Thu, 10.00–noon Sun, other times ring; free) is dedicated to repairing old tractors and other motors and every two years on the last weekend in July holds a festival dedicated to the same. **Montcléra** on the D673 has a most beguiling 15th-century fairy-tale **château** (private), best viewed when you drive north; all it needs is a Rapunzel letting down her hair. Little **Gindou**, just east, hosts a cinema festival under the stars in summer (w gindoucinema.org).

Les Arques This sleepy village south of Gindou has always had an artist or two ever since the Cubist sculptor Ossip Zadkine (1890–1967) bought a home here in 1934, after living in Caylus (page 342). Born in Belarus, he had studied art in Paris where he was friends with Modigliani and Henry Miller – who made him into the character 'Borowski' in his *Tropic of Cancer.* Zadkine won first prize at the Venice Biennale in 1950, cementing his international reputation as arguably the greatest Cubist sculptor. Some of the works left by his widow to the city of Paris have been transferred here to create a little **Musée Zadkine**; the museum director Lionel Gramont was his child assistant in Les Arques, helping him find just the right trees to sculpt (05 65 22 83 37; Apr–Oct 10.30–12.30 & 14.30–18.30 Tue–Sun, Nov–Dec & Feb–Mar 14.00–18.00 Tue–Sun; €3/€1.50). Zadkine is best known for his *Destroyed City* (1951) in Rotterdam, and in peaceful Les Arques his sculptures seem almost too searing and painful. Next to the museum is the superb 11th-century church of **St-Laurent**, which Zadkine loved; he initiated the restoration and contributed the *Christ on the Cross* (1938), similar but somehow less controversial than the one he later sculpted, now in Caylus, as well as a *Pietà* (1957). Once a priory of Marcilhac (page 276), the interior of St-Laurent has been stripped down to its yellow-ochre stone to reveal its essentials: a single nave ending in three tiny apses, divided by columns with primitive carvings and divided by little Mozarabic horseshoe arches, while below is a tiny, ancient crypt; on one of the exterior portals, note the carved Celtic spiral.

While at the museum, pick up the key for **St-André-des-Arques**, on the other side of the D45. In 1954 Zadkine discovered its 15th-century frescoes under the plaster, unfortunately damaged by the wet: *Christ in Majesty,* the *Annunciation* and the *Apostles. St Christopher* is painted on one pillar, and baby Jesus, waiting to be carried, on the other.

Frayssinet-le-Gélat and around Notable here, besides its attractive medieval church, is the monument next to it, with the inscription TO THE MARTYRS OF NAZI BARBARISM. On 21 May 1944, the SS Division Das Reich, which would later perpetuate the massacres at Tulle and Oradour-sur-Glane, marched into the village, falsely suspected of harbouring the Maquis, and rounded up the villagers and shot and hanged 14 women and men.

The golden stone village of **Goujounac** east of Frayssinet has a pretty Romanesque church with a tympanum carved with Christ and the four Evangelists. To the southwest the little bastide of **Montcabrier**, overlooking the valley of the Thèze, was founded in 1297 by and named after Guy de Caprari, the seneschal of Quercy. Its church of St-Louis with its arcaded *clocher-mur* houses an impressive provincial retable and a prize: a reliquary housing St Louis's little finger, one of the few that portray the king with a beard.

The steep wooded heights on the opposite side of the D678 once held the town of **Pestillac**, Montcabrier's bitter rival. For three centuries, the two towns fought like Kilkenny cats; Pestillac finally succumbed in the 1500s, leaving some of the most evocative ruins in Quercy. Ask the nice lady who lives in the smaller of the two houses on the site if you can walk up through her back garden, up past wild, forested jumbled ruins of walls and bastions, to the Romanesque church of Notre-Dame, still substantially intact, with an oak tree growing right through one of its windows.

St-Martin-le-Redon, the last village in the Lot, is as cute as a button and where you can pick up the scenic winding road that swoops down to the Château de Bonaguil (page 310).

13

Lot-et-Garonne

Rolling, rich, fertile and well rivered, the Lot-et-Garonne is far more agricultural than the plain old Lot to the east. Renowned for its *pruneaux d'Agen*, it produces masses of other fruit and vegetables as well; when the nightly news shows burly, bereted French farmers with attitudes dumping imported apples and tomatoes in the streets, often they are Lot-et-Garonners, a-cussing in their distinctive Gascon twang.

Département 47 has a number of distinct personalities. West towards Bordeaux, it produces fine wines. The hilly east is dotted with castles and bastides and forests, similar to the Dordogne and Lot. The third of the département on the left bank of the Garonne is part of Gascony, the stomping ground of Henri IV. Agen, the capital, has an excellent art museum. And there's a fine collection of rivers – the Lot, Baïse, Dropt – and the Garonne canal, for boating down the stream.

AGEN AND AROUND

Agen lacks big tourist magnets, but this shapeless, rather staid departmental capital does have an ace up its sleeve: one of the finest provincial art museums in France. It's at its best when the Agenais show their wild and crazy side, when their beloved rugby squad is thumping some hapless opponent. Shop windows are full of prunes, chocolate-filled prunes, prune cream… If you remember the episode in *Le Tour de Gaule d'Astérix* in which a treacherous Agenais innkeeper tries to capture Astérix and Obélix by slipping a mickey into their prunes you will be shocked to learn that this is a flagrant anachronism – they were only first recorded in 1148.

HISTORY Caesar made the first-known mention of the humble hilltop oppidum of Aginnum in his Gallic Wars. In the Pax Romana that followed, Aginnum relocated down into the Garonne valley, where it fell prey to the usual barbarian and Norman invasions. A strong castle on the cliffs at Castillon-sur-Agen, taken by Henry II in 1161, suffered the first successful siege at the hands of his son Richard in 1175; it took two months and his courage earned him the nickname Coeur de Lion. During the Hundred Years' War that followed, Agen found itself a plaything on the front lines between French and English territory, and changed hands 11 times, but it could have been worse – each new ruler would try to make the Agenais happy to see him by granting the town new privileges.

Even after becoming a commune in the 13th century, Agen was under the influence of its noble bishops. During the Renaissance many of these were Italian, and they gave the little town a jump-start in art appreciation and the humanities. A booming textile trade, begun in the 17th century, was snuffed out by the Continental Blockade. These days it owes much of its prosperity to its location midway between Bordeaux and Toulouse; transport depots, fruit-packing, an aspirin factory and bureaucracy are the things that keep the money rolling in.

GETTING THERE AND AROUND Agen has a small domestic airport in Estillac (05 53 77 00 88) with occasional seasonal flights from Paris. There are TGVs to Bordeaux, Montauban, Toulouse and Paris from the station at Place Rabelais, and several trains (or buses) a day to Monsempron-Libos, Castelsarrasin, Périgueux and Les Eyzies (w transports.nouvelle-aquitaine.fr). For a **taxi**, call 05 53 66 39 14, m 06 09 37 07 74 or m 06 81 21 11 43.

There are **parking** garages by the covered market, and two near the art museum, at 15 Rue Garonne and Place du Esquirol.

TOURIST INFORMATION Agen's excellent **tourist office** (05 53 47 36 09; w destination-agen.com; 09.00–12.30 & 14.00–18.00 Mon, Wed–Sat, 14.00–18.00 Tue) is at 38 Rue Garonne.

WHERE TO STAY *Map, page 301*

Château des Jacobins (13 rooms) 1 Place des Jacobins; 05 53 47 03 31; w chateau-des-jacobins.com. Beautiful ivy-covered *hôtel particulier*, with a charming grandmotherly atmosphere in the public rooms, plus private parking & a pretty garden. **€€€€**

Villa St Vincent (3 rooms) 21 Av de Courpian; m 06 56 83 62 30; w villasaintvincent.wixsite.com. Stay in a peaceful garden villa overlooking Agen, with lovely hosts & a summer pool. B/fast inc. **€€€–€€**

Citotel Stimotel (58 rooms) 105 Bd du Président Carnot; 05 53 47 31 23; w logishotels.com. Business-like, but fine for a night or 2; in walking distance of the art museum. Free parking under the hotel is a bonus. **€€–€**

B&B Hotel Agen (72 rooms) Rue Lespinasse; 08 92 78 80 01 (toll number); w hotel-bb.com/fr/hotel/agen. Bright, cheerful, reliable branch of the chain located just south of the centre, with family rooms & free parking. **€**

WHERE TO EAT AND DRINK *Map, page 301, unless otherwise stated*

Le Margoton 52 Rue Richard Cœur de Lion; 05 53 48 11 55; w lemargoton.com; closed Sun–Tue. Maintains high standards & inventive cuisine; only a few choices but all good, with plenty of seafood. **€€€€**

Le Nostradamus [map, page 298] 40 Rue des Nitiobriges, north of the centre; 05 53 47 01 02; w lenostradamus.com; closed Mon, & eves Wed, Sun. Creative cuisine in a rustic chic décor, with a w/day *menu marché* (€19.50) & a shady terrace. The menu names (Revelation, Prediction) recall the famous doctor/astrologer who in 1531 married a girl from Agen, moved to a nearby farm & had a son & daughter – all of whom perished in a plague in 1538. Afterwards, suspected of Protestantism, he left – & wrote his famous poems. **€€€€**

Bistrot Voltaire 45 Rue Voltaire; 05 53 47 62 42; w bistrotvoltaire.eatbu.com; closed Sun–Mon. Pretty little restaurant on a pedestrian street with elegant dishes, lovingly prepared. If you love *baba au rhum*, look no further – it's the best in town. **€€€€–€€€**

L'Imprevu 7 Rue Camille Desmoulins; 05 53 66 39 31; closed Sun–Mon. Popular spot with its own salmon smoker & a modern bistro-style menu. **€€€**

Monsieur Jeannot 18 Rue des Cornières; 05 40 40 12 24; f; closed Sun–Mon. Come here for old-fashioned dishes you don't often see in restaurants – vol au vents with chicken hearts, *civet de sanglier*, guinea fowl with chestnuts, etc. **€€€**

La Grande Brasserie 1 Place Rabelais; 05 53 67 17 37; w la-grande-brasserie-agen.fr; 06.00–22.00 daily. Agen breaks the provincial mould with its exceptional art museum & its popular railway station brasserie, a local institution. **€€€–€€**

Le Bistronome 57 Péristyle du Gravier; 05 53 67 84 70; f lebistronome47; closed Sat–Sun & eves Mon. Friendly, informal place right on the river, with typical local dishes & fish & chips. **€€**

Osaka 38 Bd Sylvain Dumon; 05 53 66 31 76; w osaka-agen.fr; closed Sun–Mon & lunch Sat. Reliable Japanese restaurant near the station with a big choice of bentos, sashimi, sushi, meats, etc. **€€**

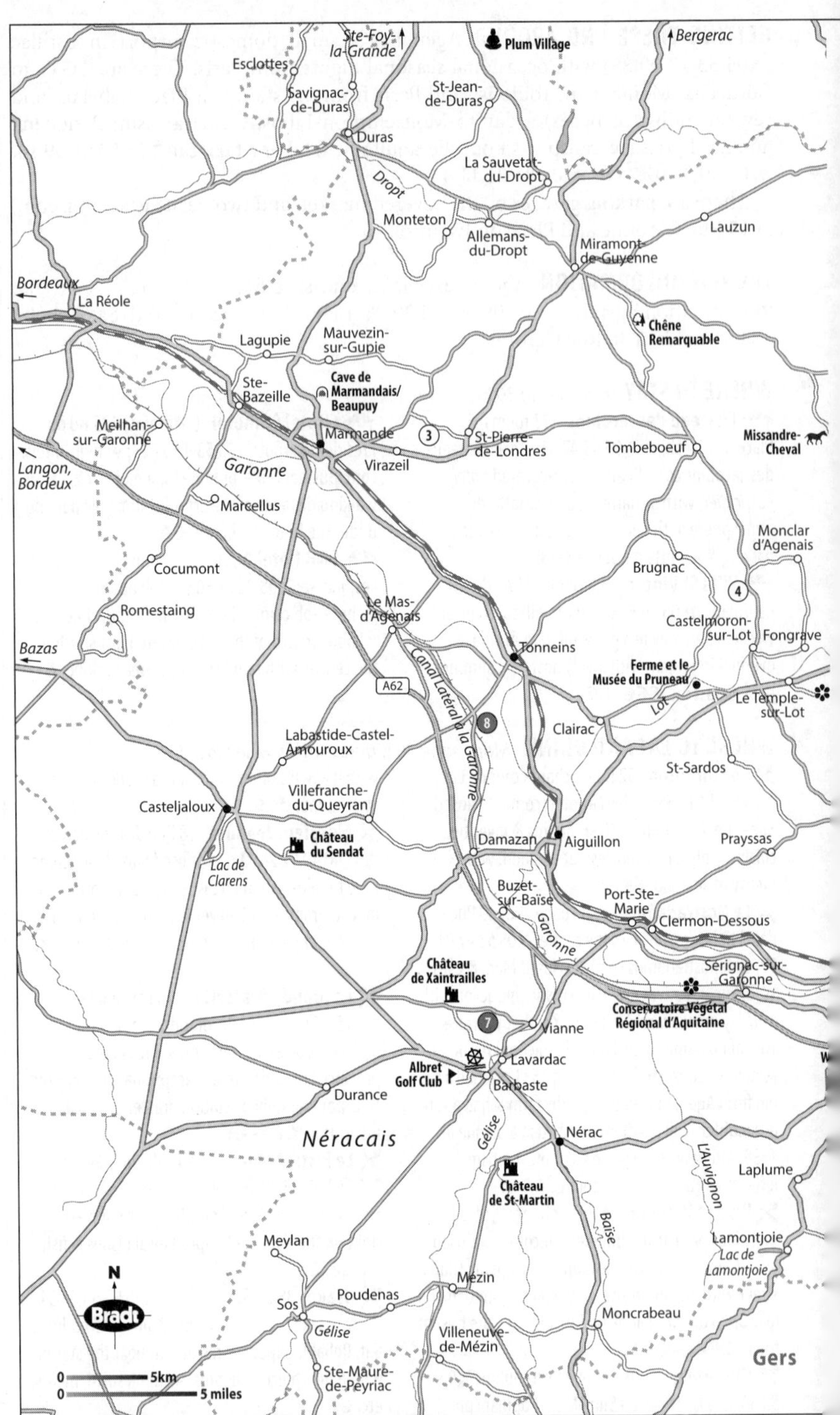
Ste-Foy-la-Grande
Plum Village
Bergerac
Esclottes
Savignac-de-Duras
St-Jean-de-Duras
Duras
La Sauvetat-du-Dropt
Dropt
Monteton
Allemans-du-Dropt
Lauzun
Miramont-de-Guyenne
Bordeaux
La Réole
Chêne Remarquable
Lagupie
Mauvezin-sur-Gupie
Ste-Bazeille
Cave de Marmandais/Beaupuy
Meilhan-sur-Garonne
Marmande
Virazeil
St-Pierre-de-Londres
Tombeboeuf
Missandre-Cheval
Langon, Bordeaux
Garonne
Marcellus
Monclar d'Agenais
Cocumont
Brugnac
Romestaing
Le Mas-d'Agenais
Castelmoron-sur-Lot
Fongrave
Bazas
Tonneins
Ferme et le Musée du Pruneau
A62
Canal Latéral à la Garonne
Le Temple-sur-Lot
Lot
Clairac
Labastide-Castel-Amouroux
St-Sardos
Villefranche-du-Queyran
Casteljaloux
Château du Sendat
Damazan
Aiguillon
Prayssas
Lac de Clarens
Buzet-sur-Baïse
Port-Ste-Marie
Clermon-Dessous
Château de Xaintrailles
Sérignac-sur-Garonne
Conservatoire Végétal Régional d'Aquitaine
Vianne
Albret Golf Club
Lavardac
Barbaste
Durance
Nérac
Néracais
Gélise
L'Auvignon
Laplume
Château de St-Martin
Baïse
Meylan
Lamontjoie
Lac de Lamontjoie
Mézin
Poudenas
Sos
Moncrabeau
Villeneuve-de-Mézin
Gers
Ste-Maure-de-Peyriac
0 5km
0 5 miles
N
Bradt

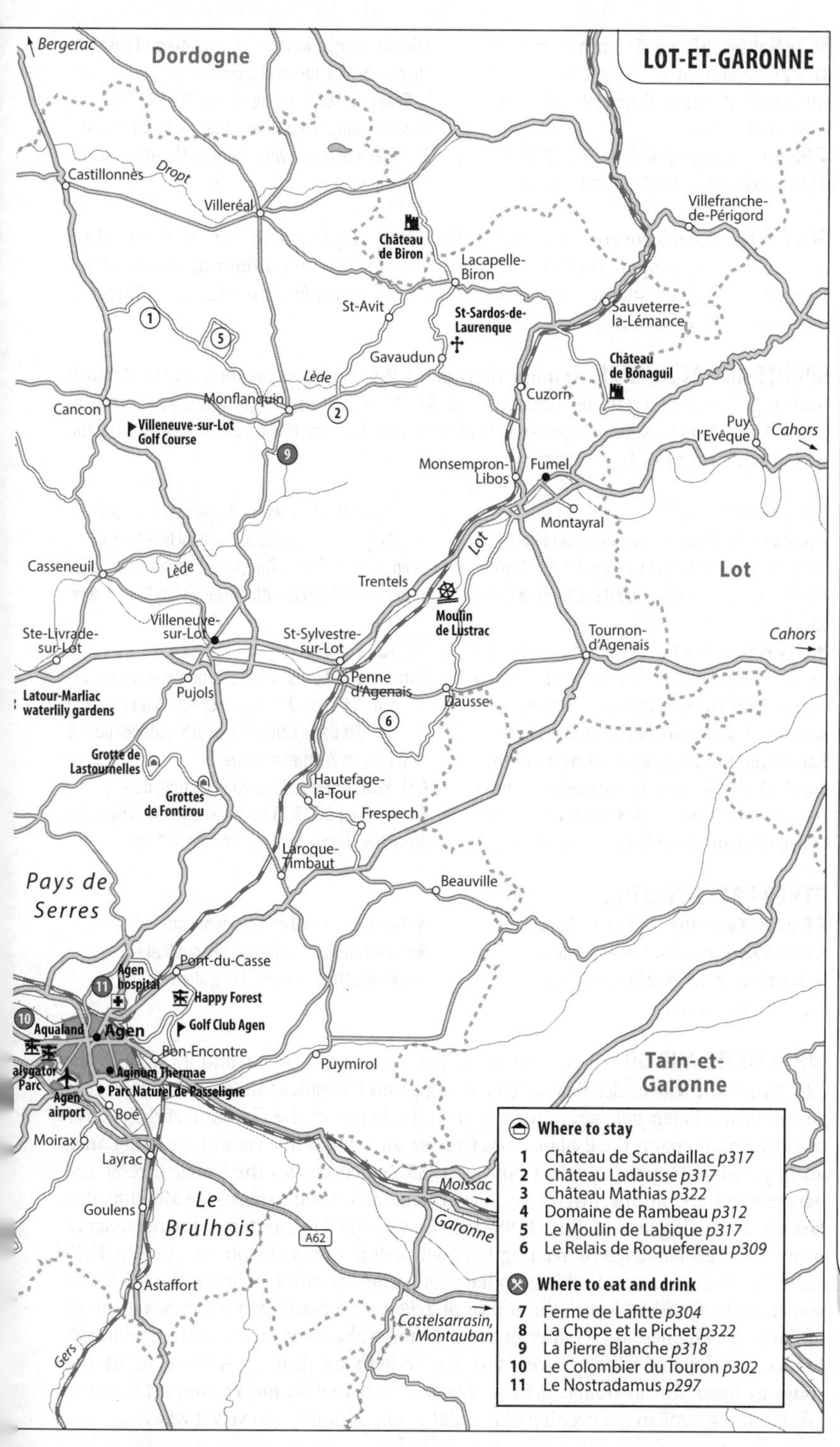

LOT-ET-GARONNE
Bergerac
Dordogne
Castillonnès
Dropt
Villeréal
Château de Biron
Lacapelle-Biron
St-Avit
St-Sardos-de-Laurenque
Gavaudun
Villefranche-de-Périgord
Sauveterre-la-Lémance
Château de Bonaguil
Cuzorn
Puy l'Evêque
Cahors
Lède
Monflanquin
Cancon
Villeneuve-sur-Lot Golf Course
Monsempron-Libos
Fumel
Montayral
Lot
Casseneuil
Trentels
Moulin de Lustrac
Villeneuve-sur-Lot
Ste-Livrade-sur-Lot
St-Sylvestre-sur-Lot
Penne d'Agenais
Tournon-d'Agenais
Dausse
Pujols
Latour-Marliac waterlily gardens
Grotte de Lastournelles
Grottes de Fontirou
Hautefage-la-Tour
Frespech
Laroque-Timbaut
Beauville
Pays de Serres
Pont-du-Casse
Agen hospital
Happy Forest
Golf Club Agen
Aqualand
Agen
Bon-Encontre
Puymirol
Walygator Parc
Aginum Thermae
Parc Naturel de Passeligne
Agen airport
Boé
Moirax
Layrac
Goulens
Le Brulhois
A62
Moissac
Garonne
Astaffort
Castelsarrasin, Montauban
Gers
Tarn-et-Garonne
Where to stay
1 Château de Scandaillac p317
2 Château Ladausse p317
3 Château Mathias p322
4 Domaine de Rambeau p312
5 Le Moulin de Labique p317
6 Le Relais de Roquefereau p309
Where to eat and drink
7 Ferme de Lafitte p304
8 La Chope et le Pichet p322
9 La Pierre Blanche p318
10 Le Colombier du Touron p302
11 Le Nostradamus p297

Ty Mat'lot 8 Rue Emile Sentini; 05 53 66 07 81; tymatlot.agen.5; closed Tue–Wed. Bijou little *crêperie* that never disappoints, with a few tables outside. €€–€

Hegoak 32 Rue Voltaire; m 07 67 27 85 23; HegoakAgen; 18.00–02.00 Wed–Sat. Friendly Basque wine bar, with platters of Basque cheeses & Andalusian charcuterie.

Seleo 2 Rue Garonne; m 06 52 81 92 23; w seleo-wine-bar.business.site; 18.00–02.00 Thu–Sat. Charming wine bar near the art museum, with good tapas.

SHOPPING Agen's **covered market** (24 Place Jean-Baptiste Durand; 07.00–13.00 & 16.00–19.30) is open Tuesday to Sunday; there's also an **outdoor market** in Place 14 Juillet on Wednesdays, Saturdays and Sunday mornings, and a Saturday farmer's market in Place Jasmin.

SPORTS AND ACTIVITIES **Aginum Thermae** (1 Rue François Neveux, in the Atrium building, ZAC de Trenque, Boé; 05 53 96 92 07; w massage-agen.fr; 10.00–19.30 Mon–Sat) is Agen's award-winning spa, inspired by the ancient Roman baths, with a wide range of treatments.

Family days out

Aqualand Château de Caudouin, Roquefort; 05 53 96 58 32; w aqualand.fr/agen; Jul 10.30–18.00 daily, Aug 10.30–19.00 daily. Offers a full day of watery fun & slides.

Happy Forest Fourtis, Pont-du-Casse; 05 53 47 25 44; w happyforest.fr; year-round, but check website for activities & hours. A forest parkour, animal park & other activities from age 3 up.

Parc Naturel de Passeligne 3km from Agen in Boé; 05 53 99 48 02; parcpasselignepelissier. Trails along the Garonne, plus a beach & play area.

Walygator Parc Roquefort, just west of Agen; 05 53 96 58 32; w walygatorparc.com; Jul–Aug daily, Jun–Nov w/ends & school hols (check calendar on website). The biggest amusement park in southwest France, with the new scary 'Dark Tower'.

Other activities

Camping St-Louis Lac de Lamontjoie, south of Agen; 05 53 99 59 38; w campingagen.fr; Apr–Oct daily. Canoeing, beach, outdoor pool & carp fishing, & other activities.

Golf Club Agen 415 Chemin du Golf, Bon-Encontre; m 06 18 78 86 50; w agen-golf.com. An attractive 9-hole course, 7km east of Agen.

OTHER PRACTICALITIES

$ **Banque Populaire** 64 Bd de la République

$ **Crédit Agricole** 204 Ave Jean Jaurès

Hospital 21 Rte de Villeneuve; 05 53 69 70 71; w ch-agen-nerac.fr

Carnot 113 Bd du Président Carnot

République 10 Bd de la République

Post office 72 Bd du Président Carnot

WHAT TO SEE AND DO There's one glorious reason to visit Agen, and it's right in the city centre: the Musée des Beaux-Arts (see opposite). Besides this, and a stroll around Agen's prune-laden *pâtisseries*, walk over to the banks of the Garonne and the city's favourite promenade, the **Esplanade du Gravier**, affording a fine view of the **Pont Canal**, an impressive 23-arch aqueduct built in 1839, which carries the Canal Latéral and barges over the Garonne. Just up Avenue du Général de Gaulle stands the **Monument to Jasmin**, honouring Jacques Boé (1798–1864), a wig-maker who started the renaissance of the Occitan language by reciting his own poems to his customers, then in 1830 published the works under his grandfather's name, Jasmin; by chance the book was picked up by Charles Nodier, the author of *Trilby*, who made Jasmin's verses the toast of Paris. Nicknamed 'the Homer of the Proletariat', he went on a lecture tour across France and donated all the proceeds to charity. Perhaps his finest lyrics were his love songs to Agen: *Me fas troubà, pel sero de ma bito/ Sourel del mèl et cami del belour…* (You found for me in the evening of my life/ A sun of honey and velvet way…).

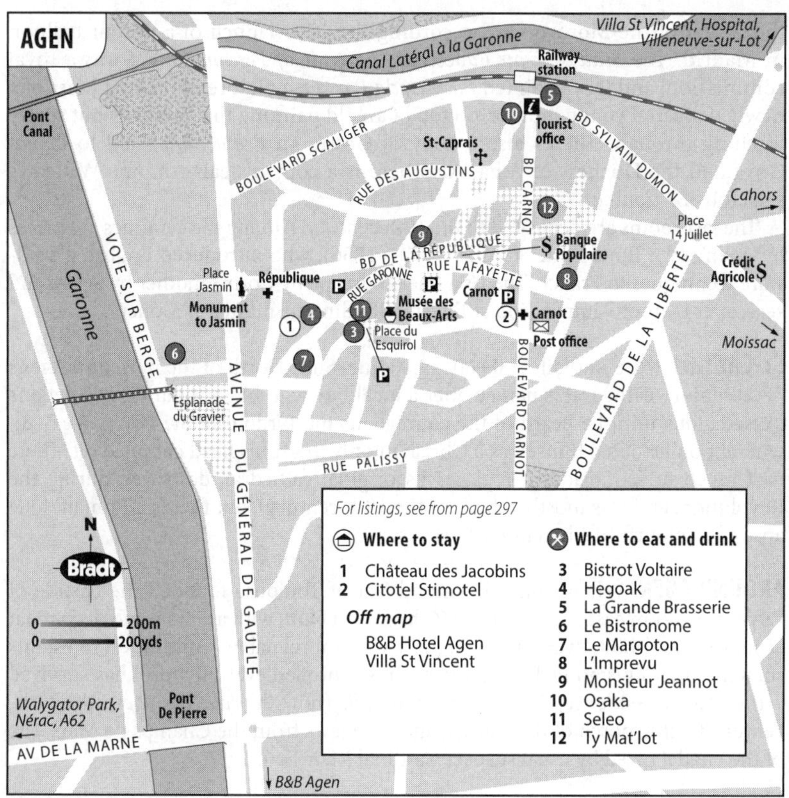

Musée des Beaux-Arts (Place du Dr Esquirol; 05 53 69 47 23; **w** musee-agen.fr; Apr–Oct 11.00–18.00 Wed–Mon, Nov–Mar 11.00–17.00 Mon, Wed–Fri, 14.00–18.00 Sat–Sun; €6, students under 26 & under 18 free) This is one of the best provincial collections of art in France, filling four beautifully restored 16th- and 17th-century *hôtels particuliers*. The star of the Gallo-Roman section is the *Vénus du Mas d'Agenais*, a 1st- or 2nd-century AD Greek marble dug up by a farmer at Mas d'Agenais in 1876, who, despite her lack of a head and part of an arm, is a Venus de Milo in her early 20s; the special lighting shows off perfectly the exceptional cut of the drapery. Don't miss the fine small bronzes – a Gaulish helmet, a Celtic horse head and a pawing horse. There are medieval tombstones and effigies, goldwork, carved Romanesque and Gothic capitals and a 16th-century tapestry of the month of March.

Up a beautiful spiral stair are the 16th- and 17th-century paintings including two striking Renaissance portraits by Corneille de Lyon, and ceramics by Bernard Palissy (page 318) and brightly coloured plates from the same period by the Italian masters. There are minor works by Tiepolo and Greuze, and *Renaud et Armide*, attributed to Domenico Tintoretto, and an unusual *Still Life with a Sparrow, Mice, Insects and Jasmin* (1712) by Jean-Baptiste Oudry.

Most famous of all are five Goyas, left to the city by Chaudordy, French ambassador to Madrid, who got them from Goya's son. There's a powerful *Self-portrait* painted by the artist in his 40s, and one of the *Caprichos*, with a donkey, elephant and bull flying over a crowd of people. Another crowd follows the ascent of the Montgolfière, recording the 1793 launch of a hot-air balloon in Madrid. The *Study for an Equestrian Portrait of Ferdinand VII* was a royal commission; and Goya painted *La Misada Parida*, a picture of the first Mass of a newly delivered young mother, on top of an old painting that is slowly but surely leaching through. There's also a copy of Goya's *La Promenade*, said to depict Goya and the Duchess of Alba. Also here is a copy of Jean-Antoine Watteau's salacious *Le Conteur.*

The last rooms are dedicated to the 19th century. Among the ceramics are pieces by Agen's own Boudon de St-Amas (1774–1856), who introduced English glazedware techniques to France. There's a fine landscape by Corot, another by Sisley, and seascapes by proto-Impressionist Eugène Boudin, the master of Monet.

St-Caprais (Rue Raspail; ⌚ 09.00–19.00 Tue–Sun) North of the museum, Agen's 12th-century cathedral is named after a local boy who hid out during Diocletian's persecutions until he heard of the courageous martyrdom of Ste Foy (page 313), whereupon he outed himself as a Christian only to get his head chopped off. There isn't much to see inside (it replaces its original cathedral, destroyed during the Revolution, and was mostly rebuilt in the 19th century), but there's a Romanesque apse and colourful 19th-century frescoes.

AROUND AGEN When Count Raymond VII of Toulouse founded the bastide of **Puymirol** (17km east of Agen) in 1246, high on a bluff, with a citadel and deep moat at its weakest point, everyone thought it was impregnable – until the Protestants shattered that illusion in 1574. Even so, much of medieval Puymirol has survived – the counts' residence, the *cornières* and *halle* (now the *salle des fêtes*), the 13th-century Gothic porch of the church, and the views from the Champs de Mars, site of the citadel razed by usual suspect Cardinal Richelieu.

Where to stay and eat

Michel Trama (L'Aubergade) (9 rooms) 52 Rue Royale, Puymirol (17km east of Agen); 05 53 95 31 46; w aubergade.com; ⌚ mid-Sep–mid-Jun closed eve Sun–noon Tue. This 13th-century residence once belonging to the Counts of Toulouse has something few one-horse towns dream of: sumptuous rooms, garden courtyard with a pool & Michelin-starred restaurant (€€€€€), founded in 1978 by self-taught master chef Michel Trama, who takes local ingredients – foie gras, cèpes, snails & so on – & combines them with the sure art & all the pretensions that only the French can muster; there's also the lovely, less pricy **L'Auberge de la Poule d'Or** (⌚ same). **€€€€€**

Le Square (12 rooms) 5 Place de la Craste, Astaffort; 05 53 47 20 40; w lesquareastaffort.fr. A big, amiable country house, with well-equipped bedrooms in that modern French taste that is hard to describe & a bar-restaurant (€€€), serving a small weekly changing menu, & Sun brunch. **€€€€**

Le Colombier du Touron [map, page 298] (11 rooms) 187 Rte des Monts-de-Marsan, Brax; 05 53 87 87 91; w logishotels.com. In a rather dreary area west of Agen, a charming oasis with a park & 18th-century *pigeonnier*. Good restaurant (€€€€) serving regional fare. **€€€€–€€€**

Le Prince Noir (24 rooms) 6 Rue De Menjoulan, Sérignac-sur-Garonne; 05 53 68 74 30; w le-prince-noir.com. In a 17th-century convent, a comfortable place to stay with traditional rooms (some for families), tennis & a pool, plus good restaurant (€€) serving a classic southwest menu. **€€–€**

La Table d'Antan (10 rooms) 41 Rue de la République, Bon-Encontre, 3km from Agen; 05 53 77 97 00; w latabledantan.com. Simple rooms in a former family house, with a good restaurant €€ in its stone walls offering quiche & home-cooked meals. **€**

L'Auberge Le Prieuré 4 Grand Rue, Moirax; 05 53 47 59 55; w aubergeleprieure.fr; ⌚ Wed–Sun. A few steps from the church of

Notre-Dame, in a handsome village house with a terrace & garden, feast on colourful & very original Michelin-star cuisine. *Lunch menu €29, dégustation €89.* €€€€€

What to see and do South of Agen, vines take over from plums in the **Brulhois**. The main town, **Layrac** grew up around a priory consecrated by Pope Urban II in 1096, itself built over a Roman villa. Its church, **St-Martin**, has an unusual elaborate marble baldachin over the altar and a 12th-century pavement mosaic on a rare theme, long-haired *Samson* wrestling with a lion. In nearby **Goulens**, the **Cellier du Brulhoise** (05 53 87 01 65; w vigneronsdubrulhois.com; 14.00–18.00 Mon, 09.00–noon & 14.00–18.00 Tue–Sat) will tell you all about the Côtes-de-Brulhois, grown here and around Donzac (page 353) – a 'black' wine from Malbec, Tannat, Cabernet Franc, Cabernet Sauvignon, Le Fer Servadou, and Merlot. A favourite tipple of the Templars and medieval English kings, it was a 'lost wine' after the phylloxera epidemic and reborn thanks to the efforts of four *vignerons* in 1964; now many of the 45 producers are organic.

Astaffort, further south, grew up as a station on a Roman road, and retains a scattering of half-timbered houses, as well as a fortified mill, and medieval churches. **Moirax** to the west of Layrac has a delightful 11th-century priory of **Notre-Dame** (10.00–18.00 daily; free). Founded by the abbey of Cluny, the great promoter of the Compostela pilgrimage, it has a pretty façade with a *clocher-mur* topped by a curious afterthought of a roof, and more than its share of fine carvings both outside and in with 130 Romanesque capitals (including a great one of Adam and Eve) – and elegant choir stalls and wooden relief panels by 17th-century master Jean Tournier.

In the centre of the Brulhois, **Laplume** was the old capital of the region and has a nice Renaissance church, with a *tour clocher*, but there's nothing feathery about it; *penn* in Celtic means hill crest (the town stands on a steep one) and the Gallo-Romans called it Penna, which was Latinised into Pluma. South, the attractive bastide of **Lamontjoie** (they've got St Louis's hand in a reliquary in the church) stands by beautiful carp-filled **Lac de Lamontjoie**.

Further west, **Sérignac-sur-Garonne** has a clutch of medieval houses around its 11th-century church of **Notre-Dame** with a dome hiding under a unique spiralling bell tower, the *clocher hélicoïdal*, built in the 16th century, knocked down in 1922 and since rebuilt. Up by the Canal Latéral you can visit the **Conservatoire Végétal Régional d'Aquitaine** (Montesquieu; 05 53 47 29 14; w conservatoirevegetal.com; Dec–Mar 08.00–noon & 13.30–17.30 Tue–Fri & Sun, 13.30–17.30 Mon, 08.00–noon Sat; Apr–Oct 09.00–noon & 13.30–17.30 Mon–Fri; €5) dedicated to biodiversity, old varieties of fruit trees, and more.

THE NÉRACAIS

This pleasant *pays*, tucked between the Armagnac and the pines of the Landes, is also often called the 'Pays d'Albret'; its long history as the feudal domain of the mighty d'Albret family has given it an identity that endures to this day. At its core is a pretty little river called the Baïse that bubbles down from the Pyrenees through rather unappreciative countryside until it gets to Nérac. This fat village counts scarcely more than 6,800 inhabitants, but its association with the d'Albrets that began in 1130, when the monks of the Abbaye de St-Pierre in Condom invited them in to protect the northern frontier of their lands, has given it the air of a little capital.

Markets are on Saturday mornings in Nérac and Fridays in Buzet-sur-Baïse.

TOURIST INFORMATION Nérac's **tourist office** (05 53 65 27 75; w albret-tourisme.com; Jul–Aug 09.00–12.30 & 13.30–18.00 Mon–Sat, 10.00–12.30 Sun, Sep–Jun 09.00–12.00 & 14.00–18.00 Tue–Sat) is at 7 Avenue Mondenard. There are **branch offices** at the Moulin in Barbaste (Apr–Oct) and Vianne (Jul–Aug).

WHERE TO STAY

Hotel Henri IV (17 rooms) 4 Place du Général Leclerc, Nérac; 05 53 65 00 63; w hotelhenriiv.fr. Charming 3-star hotel, with a little heated pool in the courtyard. **€€€–€**

Moulin des Tours (5 rooms) Chemin de la Maison Blanche, Barbaste; m 06 80 42 93 21; w chambredhotesmoulindestours.fr. Contemporary rooms in a building of 1860, with beautiful views & a pool. **€€**

The Originals City, Confluence Agen Ouest (48 rooms) 62 Av de la Confluence, Damazan; 05 53 20 38 28; w hotel-damazan-agen.com. Modern hotel, not in the prettiest setting, but convenient to the Toulouse–Bordeaux A62; also a good restaurant (€€€) & helpful staff. **€€**

La Tour De Brazalem (5 rooms) 3 Rue de l'École, Nérac; m 06 82 39 80 62; w la-tour-de-brazalem.business.site. Pleasant rooms in a 13th-century stone tower in the medieval centre; b/fast inc. **€**

WHERE TO EAT AND DRINK

Le Moulin des Saveurs 4 Rue du Moulin des Tours, Nérac; 05 53 97 06 60; w moulindessaveurs.com; closed eves Sun & Thu. Next to the famous mill in Barbaste, creative gastronomic cuisine – try the seafood cassoulet if it's on the menu, & arty desserts. *W/day lunch menu €18.50.* **€€€€**

L'Art de Vivre 7 Rue du Château, Nérac; 05 53 65 69 43; closed eves Sun–Mon. Contemporary setting & fresh market dishes, including some vegetarian. *Lunch menu €14.90, dinner €26.50.* **€€€**

Le Goujon qui Frétille 39 Blvd de la République, Buzet-sur-Baïse; 05 53 84 26 51. 'The Wiggling Gudgeon' serves superb food in a bucolic setting by the canal, including scallops, oysters & succulent beef. Lovely service & Buzet's excellent wines. **€€€**

Le Phare de Jeanne Place du Barry, Moncrabeau; 05 53 65 21 46; f; closed Wed & eves Sun, Tue. At this century-old restaurant, new owners prepare delicious seafood on the garden terrace. **€€€**

Les Contes d'Albret Comptes, Nérac; 05 53 65 18 73; w contesdalbret.fr; Jul–Aug closed eves Sun & lunch Mon, Sep–Jun Sat–Sun only. Superb *ferme auberge comme il faut*, with red-checked tablecloths, a massive terrace overlooking the dreamy countryside, & excellent duck & lamb. They also have 2 rooms (€) & camping on the farm. Booking essential. *Menus €19–€26.* **€€€**

Le Saint Romain Rte de Nérac, Lavardac; 05 53 97 03 84; w le-saint-romain.eatbu.com; 09.00–23.00 Tue–Sun. Informal bar-bistro by a supermarket but with an attractive woodsy décor, & perfectly cooked steaks & scallops. **€€€–€€**

Ferme de Lafitte [map, page 298] Montgaillard (just west of Vianne); 05 53 97 20 04; w fermedelafitte.com; closed Sun. Booking essential. *Menus from €19 inc wine.* **€€**

L'Entrepont 3 Rue Séderie, Nérac; m 06 61 69 39 75; f; closed Wed–Thu. Lively bistro with good food in an idyllic setting on the banks of the Baïse; also wine bar, shop, & bike & e-bike hire. **€€**

Café des Marronniers Place des Marronniers, Vianne; 05 53 97 35 43; w cafe-marronniers.com; daily. Simple southwest cuisine here. *3-course lunch €12, all-duck menu €17.* **€**

SPORTS AND ACTIVITIES Bring out your inner Viking, hurtling axes at the bulls-eye, then sleep in a clear bubble in the woods at **Hache IV** (Château de St-Martin, off the D656, Nérac; m 06 64 98 85 88; w hache4.fr, chrysalide-st-martin.fr). The waterpark **Lud'O Park** (Av Plaisance, Nérac; 05 53 65 77 50; w ludoparc.eu) has pools, slides and more for all ages.

IN NÉRAC WITH THE MARGUERITE OF MARGUERITES

...an asylum sweeter than freedom

Clément Marot

It was no accident that the d'Albret family came into such spectacular prominence in the 15th and 16th centuries – they were agents of the French Crown. Their loyalty assured Paris an important ally in a Gascony that had few natural ties to France. In return, the French kings showered every sort of prize on the family. With their help, Henri d'Albret became king of Navarre, at which point King François Ier found him a fitting match for his sister, Marguerite d'Angoulême (1492–1549).

Already a widow at 35, it was Marguerite's second go. Everyone at the time counted her the most eligible lady of France – not just for being the king's sister, but for a wit, charm and intelligence that stood out even in Renaissance courts. Marguerite turned their favoured residence of Nérac into a brilliant court where poetry and the new humanistic learning were the order of the day. Though they never converted themselves, Henri and Marguerite welcomed many of the new Protestant thinkers to Nérac, including John Calvin. Among the poets who enjoyed Marguerite's favour was Clément Marot (page 258), who wrote some fulsome lines in her honour. Marguerite had literary ambitions of her own. Best known among her works was the *Heptameron*, a collection of stories with a frame tale of travellers snowbound in the Pyrenees, inspired by Boccaccio's *Decameron*.

Marguerite and Henri had a cute little daughter, known to everyone in France as Mignonne, the nickname her uncle, King François, had given her. Sitting at her parents' table, Jeanne was much more impressed with the fiery preachers than the poets. She grew up to be the redoubtable Jeanne d'Albret – 'nothing in her of a woman but the sex' – a dour, intolerant Protestant who contributed as much as anyone in keeping the flames of the religious wars burning. As evidence for the argument that traits skip generations, consider Jeanne's son, the fellow who was brought up a good Protestant and fought across France for the cause, but finally found a way to use good sense and tolerance to put an end to the troubles – he was King Henri IV.

Albret Golf Club Barbaste; ☎ 05 53 65 30 30; w golf-albret.fr. Handsome 18 holes.
Canoë-Kayak du Val d'Albret Rue du Port, Lavardac; m 06 52 00 76 39; canoes, kayaks & SUPs.
Cap Cauderoue Pin, Barbaste; ☎ 05 53 65 52 74; w cap-cauderoue.com. Adventure park with 10 routes, pony & horseriding, canoeing, mountain bikes & e-scooters.
Cycles Sudouest 58 Bd de la République, Buzet-sur-Baïse; m 07 52 05 90 48; w cyclessudouest.com. Hire a bike or e-bike.
Ferme du Boué Ste-Maure-de-Peyriac, southwest of Nérac; ☎ 05 53 65 63 94; w fermeduboue.fr. Equestrian centre; with 5 gîtes (**€€**).

NÉRAC Waiting to greet you as you enter Nérac along the Allées d'Albret is the obligatory **statue of 'Our Henry'** – Henri IV, with a twinkle in his bronze eye. Henri spent much of his time in Nérac after the St Bartholomew's Day massacre until he became king. Even then the common people were fond of him, and it didn't bother Henri to learn that everybody in town called him Grand-Nas ('Big Nose'). The statue may not do it justice.

On a height over the Baïse, the **Château** is quite the most elegant thing in Nérac – at least the magnificent Renaissance courtyard built by Henri d'Albret's grandfather Alain that survived the vengeful demolitions ordered by Richelieu in 1621. The side that remains has a lovely loggia of twisted columns. Inside, the **Musée Henri IV** (05 53 65 21 11; w chateau-nerac.fr; Jun–mid-Sep 10.00–18.00 Wed–Sun, noon–18.00 Mon; €4, students & over 60 €3, under 12 free) is largely devoted to explanatory exhibits of the town in its heyday, with models of the château.

A walk from here around the old centre of Nérac won't take long. Rue de l'École was the old main street; on it you can see the 17th-century (former) town hall and a fine Renaissance palace, the **Maison des Conférences**. Nérac's church of **St-Nicolas**, like most French churches of the 18th century, hardly rates a notice in most books, but this one is a cut above the norm, with a restrained Neoclassical 'Greek' façade that is probably the better off for never having been able to afford the statuary that was intended for it, and a clean, airy interior with some 19th-century stained glass that impresses in the way such windows are supposed to impress: it tells the whole story, from Abel and Noah up to Jesus himself behind the altar.

From the back of the château, an elegant stair descends to the Baïse, leading to the Pont Neuf and Nérac's cross-river faubourg, **Petit Nérac**. Henri's father, Antoine de Bourbon, laid out a royal park here for his family, called **La Garenne**, stretching for over a mile along the riverfront, where everyone in Nérac comes in the afternoon. The park's **Fontaine de Fleurette** recalls the gardener's daughter, Henri's first love and the origin they say of the old expression *conter fleurette*, 'say sweet nothings' – the origin of our word 'to flirt'. You may take La Garenne as the setting for *Love's Labour's Lost*; most of the action of Shakespeare's play takes place in 'the king's park at Navarre'.

Petit Nérac's streets are as old as the town centre; the best part is along the river, picturesque **Rue Séderie**, site of the tanneries that were Nérac's main business. Around the corner on Rue Sully is the 16th-century **Vieux Pont**, and the **Maison de Sully**, a 16th-century house where Henri IV's great minister stayed when Henri was in Nérac.

NORTH OF NÉRAC In **Barbaste** just north of Nérac, the **Moulin des Tours d'Henri IV** is the largest fortified mill in France (Rue du Moulin des Tours; 05 53 65 09 37; w moulindestours.com; early Jul–Aug 09.30–12.30 & 13.30–18.00, 13.30–18.00 Sun–Mon; €2, under 18 free). If it looks more like a castle, it is that too; fortified mills are not uncommon in France, built in feudal times when grain was precious and there were plenty of enemies ready to try to grab it. This one, along with the medieval **bridge**, is from the 1200s. It made a fortune for the locals, who could ship the flour down to Bordeaux and beyond. In later times it belonged to the d'Albrets, and to Henri IV, who liked being called the 'Miller of Barbaste', at least, better than he liked being called 'Big Nose'. To the west, on the D665, **Durance** is a 13th-century bastide surrounded by forests that were the hunting preserve of the d'Albrets and King Henri; the village has ruins of the castle they used for their hunting lodge.

Vianne Down the Baïse, this walled English bastide was founded in 1284 by Jourdain de l'Isle, seneschal of Edward I, and named after his aunt, Vianne Gontaud-Biron – apparently it's the only bastide named after a woman. Its handsome Romanesque church of **St-Christophe** has a curious engraving of a wolf on the apse. By the Porte Romane rare Carolingian-era tombs survive; bodies would be placed in the top 'floor' until they decomposed and the bones could be moved to the bottom, freeing up the space. In the 20th century, there were still 900 people employed in the local glassworks. Today one last glassmaker, Dino Diaconescu, carries on the tradition at Dino Glass (Bd de la Gare; m 07 86 88 80 50; w dinoglass.com; 09.30–noon & 14.00–19.30 Tue–Sat, 14.00–19.30 Sun–Mon). Jean Poton de Xaintrailles, military governor of Aquitaine and a companion of Joan of Arc, built the **Château de Xaintrailles** in the hills above Vianne, where you can stroll around the park (05 53 65 51 49; Apr–11 Nov 09.30–18.30). There are occasional guided tours inside – check with the tourist office.

Buzet-sur-Baïse Further down the Baïse, where a lock separates the river from the Canal Latéral à la Garonne, pastel-tinted Buzet-sur-Baïse is an important pleasure port and wine town that gave its name to one of the best-loved up-country wines, renowned in the Middle Ages. It's dominated by the **Château de Buzet**, built by the Dukes of Gascony and sacked by the English in 1292, which led Philip the Fair to confiscate Guyenne and set off the War of Two Kingdoms (1294–1303) – the prelude to the Hundred Years' War. It was restored in the early 16th century and hosted the court of Charles IX, with Catherine de' Medici and the future Henri IV. The **Vignerons de Buzet** (Av des Côtes de Buzet; 05 53 84 17 16; w nouslesvigneronsdebuzet.fr; 10.00–12.30 & 14.00–18.00 Mon–Sat; book guided tours of the château (Jul–Aug) online; from €5, under 12 free), the co-operative that revived Buzet in the 1950s, purchased and restored the château, its park and *fabriques* (outbuildings).

SOUTH OF NÉRAC **Mézin** was the home of Armand Fallières, president of France in 1906–13. Fallières, who was also a vintner, used his office to define the Armagnac growing area from Agen almost to the Pyrenees, although in practice it's mostly produced in the Gers to the south. The firewater of the southwest, Armagnac is the oldest known *eau-de-vie* distilled from grapes, used to wet the lips of the newborn Henri IV to make sure he'd grow into a proper Gascon. The finest are aged for up to 40 years in oak barrels.

Beginning in the 18th century, the town owed its prosperity to an essential element of Aquitaine's empire of booze: cork. The **Musée du Liège et du Bouchon** (Rue du Puits St-Côme; 05 53 65 68 16; Apr–May & Oct 14.00–17.00 Tue–Fri, Jun–Sep 10.00–12.30 & 14.00–18.00 Tue–Fri, 14.00–18.00 Sat–Mon; free) has lively displays on how they make corks, and cork's new uses at Aérospatial in Toulouse.

Mézin grew up around an important Cluniac abbey on a major Compostela route, but only the church of **St-Jean-Baptiste** survives – Romanesque in the apse with some good capitals and the rest strong and graceful Gothic. On the vault over the altar, note the whimsical carving of a grimacing giant and pot of flowers. On the north door you can still (barely) make out some Revolutionary slogan about the 'Supreme Being'. The radicals in Paris were telling the peasants that it was alright to believe in God, though not necessarily the god of the Christian Church – it's a mystery, though, that so many of these inscriptions survive.

You could get lost for a long time in the lush, delightful countryside around Mézin and never mind it. On the stretch of the D656 that follows the valley of the Gélise, you'll pass plenty of farmers' signs hung out to sell you asparagus and cèpes, foie gras, and Floc de Gascogne, the 'Flower of Gascony' – the sweet apéritif wine made since the 1500s and revived uniquely for France, almost exclusively by women, the Dames du Floc de Gascogne.

Poudenas has a handsome old bridge and a fine Italianate **Château de Poudenas**. Built in the 13th century by vassals of Edward I, it was given its elegant Italian touches in the 17th century (it's now a wedding venue; w poudenas.com). There is a good Romanesque church at **Sos** and a fortified church – one of the most fortified of them all, with traces of frescoes from the 1200s – off the D5 at **Villeneuve-de-Mézin**, south of Mézin.

West, just inside the pine forest of the Landes, tiny **Meylan** village seems to consist of a swing set, a *mairie* in a shed, a picnic table and a war memorial, yet it contains so many curiosities that the Meylanais have created a little itinerary, posted in front of the *mairie*. The circuit includes the château (inhabited by the *hadettes*, fairies, who hang their chemises to dry by moonlight), the Romanesque church of **St-Pau**, a small cromlech hidden in the pines called **Las Naous Peyros** ('nine stones'), the vortex for legends of druids and witchy black sabbaths, and the little **Lac Sans-fond**, which they say swallowed up a church one Sunday (actually it's 6m deep and was probably an early iron mine).

Or you could head south of Nérac to swap some lies with the experts at **Moncrabeau**. So many locals spent so much time in the *halle* telling whoppers that in 1748, a jolly monk helped them found the **Académie des Menteurs** (**w** academiedesmenteurs.fr), and ever since its 40 members (just like the Académie Française) have met every year on the first Sunday in August for the International Festival of Liars to choose a new pretender to the throne of the King of Liars under the 'stone of truth' on the Grand Rue. Academy members judge each liar by adding grains of salt to a burlap bag – whosever bag is the heaviest wins.

DOWN THE LOT

FROM FUMEL TO VILLENEUVE-SUR-LOT At Fumel the Lot moves into the 21st century, meeting flatter country en route to its confluence with the Garonne. From the valley road the scenery might seem unexciting, but take a short detour anywhere to the south and you'll find rank upon rank of flat-topped mesas cut out of the limestone by little streams over the past few million years – the northern extremity of the Agenais Pays des Serres. However dramatic, it is still a green and pleasant land, especially in the spring when its orchards burst into blossom. Tucked in the wooded hills near the Lot border where no-one can ever find it, is one of the finest castles in the southwest, the Château de Bonaguil outside Fumel.

Libos sees a huge food and everything ***marché*** on Thursday mornings.

Getting there and around The little train and bus station at Monsempron-Libos (just outside Fumel) has a few trains a day to Les Eyzies, Périgueux, Penne d'Agenais and Agen. There are buses to Villeneuve-sur-Lot (**w** transports.nouvelle-aquitaine.fr) and several (**w** lio.laregion.fr) a day up the Lot valley as far as Cahors. An 86km bikeway stretches along the Lot from Bonaguil to Aiguillon, where you could pick up the path along the Canal Latéral à la Garonne.

Tourist information

Fumel Place Georges Escandes, by the château; 05 53 71 13 70; **w** tourisme-fumel.com; 14.00–17.30 Mon, 09.30–noon & 14.00–17.30 Tue–Fri

Penne-d'Agenais 8 Place Gambetta; **m** 06 11 59 33 90; 14.00–18.00 Wed–Fri, Sun

Where to stay

Château Le Stelsia (31 rooms) Lalande, St-Sylvestre-sur-Lot; 05 53 01 14 86; **w** lestelsia.com. The founder of the GiFi chain stores in France, Philippe Ginestet, is from the area and has made this 13th–18th-century château in a 23ha park into a vortex of childlike fun & bling. He painted the château in a startling array of colours, added a fancy spa, a comic-book library, a Michelin-starred restaurant, Le Jasmin (€€€€€), & lively gastronomic bistro (€€€€), & Europe's biggest mini-golf, filled with exotic topiary. €€€€€

Le Relais de Roquefereau [map, page 298] (2 rooms, 2 gîtes, 1 yurt) Roquefereau, 5km from Penne d'Agenais; m 06 75 49 30 24; w lerelaisderoquefereau.com. Gorgeous country chic rooms in Nathalie Guigné's 13th-century house in a big park with views, a pool, & a forest yurt. Delicious table d'hôte available. Wonderful homemade b/fast inc. €€€€€–€€€

La Maison sur la Place (3 rooms) 10 Place Gambetta, Penne d'Agenais; m 06 83 49 21 28; w lamaisonsurlaplace.com. Charming Geneviève Bovy-Cazottes's chic B&B in 3 village houses near the top of Penne is a delight; kids welcome & parking easy. Delicious b/fast inc. €€€€

Les Voyageurs (8 rooms) Tournon-d'Agenais; 05 53 40 70 28; w hotel-restaurant-les-voyageurs-47.fr. Adequate rooms by the roundabout below the village. Traditional menus (€); dine either in the dining room or on the terrace. €

Where to eat and drink

Le Moulin de Dausse Av Pierre Fournier, Dausse; 05 53 41 26 00; w moulindedausse.com; dinner Thu–Sat, lunch Sun. Exceptional, lovingly prepared food in an intimate atmosphere; the €33.50 menu includes 4 hors d'oeuvres, a choice of 3 mains, & a trio of desserts. Booking essential. €€€€

Le Bistrot Chic Av de la Gare 42, Monsempron-Libos; 05 24 32 19 77; w lebistrotchic.business.site; 10.00–23.00 Tue–Sat. Stylish & enthusiastic, & some of the best food & wine in the area & a Mediterranean courtyard in the back. *Lunch menu €22*. €€€

Le Bombe Cul 10 Place Paul Froment, Penne d'Agenais; 05 53 71 11 76; w lebombecul.com; closed Mon & eves Sun. Creative cuisine from a hard-working pair of young brothers; their Grande Salade is a meal in itself. *Lunch menu €18, dinner €28*. €€€

Le Moulin 4 Rue du Port, Penne d'Agenais; 05 53 41 21 34; closed Tue–Wed. Dine right on the Lot with a simple chalkboard menu, all *fait maison*. €€€

Auberge Les Bons Enfants Bonaguil below the château; 05 53 71 23 52; w lesbonsenfants-bonaguil.net; 10.00–15.00 & eves daily. An old mill with simple food, where everyone stops before or après castle. *3-course menu €19.80*. €€

Fumel Just west of the last Cahors vineyards waits Fumel, the Lot's own rust belt or, rather, little rust garter. The barons of Fumel, first recorded in the 11th century as protectors of Moissac, were in the Wars of Religion ardent Catholics and buddies of Henri II and Catherine de' Medici; the most famous leaf on the family tree, François de Fumel, was Captain of the King's Guard and Catherine's ambassador to Constantinople, but he was so unpopular at home that in 1562 his Protestant subjects rose up and slaughtered him like a sheep in his château. Bitter reprisals and mass executions followed. Fumel only recovered in 1848 when it opened a small steel mill that made railway bearings and pipes. In the early 1960s it employed 2,700 workers, many brought in from Algeria; today it awaits a new purpose or maybe a masterpiece from architect Jean Nouvel, who was born here in 1945.

The one sight in town is the **château**. François de Fumel was responsible for converting the medieval donjon into an Italianate villa and, if you walk up the big steps to the library, there's a stucco of François over the door, his nose busted off in Fumel's proto-Revolution. Completed in the 1700s, with garden terraces overlooking the river, the château stayed in the family until 1950, when they sold it to the city to become the *mairie*.

Just west and blending into Fumel, **Monsempron-Libos** is spread around a medieval castrum on a hill with the handsome 12th-century **Prieuré St-Géraud** (usually). The exterior is decorated with perforated metopes, while the interior has innovative vaulting and a special entrance under the choir to accommodate pilgrims. The capitals in the nave (redone in the 14th century) are carved with masks and monsters.

Château de Bonaguil [256 A4] (8km from Fumel; 05 53 41 90 71; w chateau-bonaguil.com; Apr–Jun & Sep 10.00–18.00 daily, Mar, Oct & French school hols 14.00–17.30, Jul–Aug 10.00–19.00 daily; €9.50, ages 6–12 €5; there are car parks at the bottom of the village & on top by the castle entrance) 'It's so perfect that it seems ridiculous to call it a ruin,' wrote Lawrence of Arabia of Bonaguil in 1908. Of all the castles bristling across France, few are as useless or as photogenic as the great prow-shaped Château de Bonaguil, 'the swan song of feudalism', born 200 years behind the times. Begun in the 13th century by a family of knights from Fumel, it passed in the 1460s to the hunchback Brengon de Rocquefeuil, who liked to be called 'the noble, magnificent and most powerful lord' of his assorted little possessions.

Brengon was a perfect cartoon baddie, a proto-survivalist, as nasty and paranoid as he was vain. When Charles VII fined him for brutality towards his vassals, Brengon ensconced himself at Bonaguil and surrounded it with a moat and surging walls and towers, designed to deflect cannon fire from all sides (at the same time, all the other nobles of France, like the aforementioned François de Fumel, were abandoning their medieval castles or converting them into elegant residential châteaux). 'I will raise such a castle that my villainous subjects will never take it, nor the English, nor even the most powerful soldiers of the King of France,' Brengon boasted. Never mind that none of the above ever showed the least interest in Bonaguil (although the Huguenots partially wrecked it in 1563, and it was rebuilt in 1572 by another Rocquefeuil). By the 18th century Brengon's lair was such a white elephant that it once changed hands for 100 francs and a bag of walnuts. Partially demolished in the Revolution, it was purchased by the town of Fumel in 1860, which uses it for events.

Whether you approach it from Fumel or, most scenically from above, via St-Martin-le-Redon (page 295), it is as stunning as a Hollywood set; on summer nights it's illuminated until midnight. The interior can't match the exterior: there are fireplaces suspended in the void, objects found in the castle midden, graffiti (Rocquefeuil names, games, dirty doggerel and the magic square SATOR ROTAS), and lovely views from the walls. The adjacent castle chapel, **St-Michel**, has an unusual cinquefoil window but is hardly ever open.

Sauveterre-la-Lémance From Bonaguil, winding roads will eventually bring you to this village, dominated by a large, less glamorous but actually used castle, built by Edward I in the 13th century to defend the frontiers of Guyenne. Its early Mesolithic residents have lent their name to the Sauveterrian culture (7500–5000BC), ever since 1923, when local notary Laurent Coulonges excavated the finds in the little **Musée de Préhistorique** (51 Rue du Vieux Bourg; 05 53 40 73 03; w sauveterre-prehistoire.fr; Jul–Aug 13.30–18.00 Sun–Fri; €6, ages 6–12 €4). The lush little valley of the Lémance has more reminders of the armies in the Hundred Years' War that raged up and down its length at **Cuzorn**, just south; here too are relics of the Lémance's old mainstays, forges and paper mills.

Tournon-d'Agenais South of Fumel, this pretty bastide on its hill was founded by Count Raymond VII of Toulouse in 1270. The central square survives, with a handsome 17th-century belfry and lunar clock. Today it's famous for its *tourtière*, the elaborate apple tart topped by layers and layers of flaky golden pastry leaves.

Penne-d'Agenais West of Fumel along the Lot, the **Moulin de Lustrac** in Trentels is a charming spot marked by an impressive fortified mill, founded in 1296; the adjacent château was a glorified river tollbooth. Further west, the bridge at St-Sylvestre-sur-Lot crosses over to the basilica-topped hill town that you can clock for miles around: Penne-d'Agenais. On a site inhabited since prehistoric times, then by the Gauls (*penn* means hill crest in Celtic) and Romans, the medieval village grew up around a chapel of Our Lady of the Assumption built around the year 1000 – one of the oldest churches in France dedicated to the Virgin.

In 1182, Richard the Lionheart found the site inspirational in another way, and built a mighty castle here, making Penne 'the key of Guyenne'; his name is recalled in one of the medieval gates, the Porte Ricarde, and in the nearby Fontaine de Ricard. Being chosen as the key of Guyenne was a mixed blessing: the village's other nickname was Penne la Sanglante. Many inhabitants were Cathars, and in 1212 they were besieged for 50 days by the Albigensian Crusaders before they were captured and burned alive at the stake. In 1373, during the Hundred Years' War, the English set the town afire when du Guesclin was at the point of capturing it; in 1562, Blaise de Monluc captured it from the Protestants, then put them all to the sword. Shortly after, Henri IV ordered the destruction of the castle, probably to the great relief of the people: today only two towers remain, along with the prison in the cellar of the *mairie*.

The famous church at the top of Penne, **Notre-Dame-de-Peyragude** (from *pierre aiguë*, or sharp stone), was from the start an important stop along the road to Compostela. It was rebuilt for the third time in 1653, in response to a vow, after floods from the Garonne set off a plague that killed half the population of the Agenais, then again in 1842 after the Revolution sold it off piecemeal for building stone. So many pilgrims kept turning up that in 1896 the local prelates built a huge basilica in the kitschy neo-Byzantine taste of the time, but one with great views in every direction.

VILLENEUVE-SUR-LOT TO AIGUILLON This last stretch of the valley is mostly serene and agricultural. Some 65% of all French plums dried into *pruneaux d'Agen* come from the orchards here. It isn't a touristy area, but an agricultural paradise, and home to the water lily gardens that inspired Monet.

Villeneuve-sur-Lot holds **markets** on Tuesdays in Place de la Libération, an organic market on Wednesdays in Place d'Aquitaine, and on Saturdays in Place Lafayette. Laroque-Timbaut's market day is Thursday, Friday in Ste-Livrade, and Sunday in Pujols.

Getting there and around The nearest train station is in Penne d'Agenais (see above). Buses link Agen station with Villeneuve, timed to the Bordeaux–Toulouse TGV trains. Tideo buses (w transports.nouvelle-aquitaine.fr.) link Villeneuve with the train stations in Tonneins, Marmande and Monsempron-Libos five times a day. City buses go up to Pujols.

Tourist information

Aiguillon Place du 14 Juillet; 05 53 79 62 58; w tourisme-coeurlotetgaronne.fr; 09.00–13.00 & 14.00–17.00 Mon–Fri

Pujols Place St-Nicolas; 05 53 36 78 69; Jul–Aug 10.00–13.00 & 14.00–19.00 Mon–Sat, until 18.00 Sun, Oct–Apr 13.00–17.00 Tue–Sat, May–Jun & Sep 10.00–13.00 & 14.00–18.00 Tue–Sat

Villeneuve-sur-Lot Allée Federico Garcia Lorca; 05 53 36 17 30; w tourisme-villeneuvois.com; Jul–Aug 09.30–12.30 & 14.00–18.00 Mon–Sat, Sep–Jun 09.30–noon & 14.00–17.40 Mon–Sat

Where to stay

Domaine de Rambeau [map, page 298] (4 rooms) Rambeau, Castelmoron-sur-Lot; 05 53 79 38 43; w domainederambeau.com. High-ceilinged rooms in a stone farmhouse of 1784, with friendly owners, lovely views & a solar-heated pool with a gently shelving beach & dive well, & a friendly pet pig. Families welcome. B/fast inc. **€€€€**

Les Rives du Plantié (10 rooms) Route de Castelmoron, Le Temple-sur-Lot; 05 53 70 22 26; w lesrivesduplantie.com. An idyllic place to stay, in a 19th-century *maison de maître* beside the Lot, with a shady garden, terrace & pool, & a gastronomic restaurant (€€€€€). **€€€**

Mercure Villeneuve sur Lot Moulin de Madame (30 rooms) Rte de Casseneuil, Villeneuve-sur-Lot; 05 53 36 13 56; w all.accor.com. A chain hotel, but the nicest in town, overlooking the river. **€€€**

La Résidence (17 rooms) 17 Av Lazare Carnot, Villeneuve-sur-Lot; 05 53 40 17 03; w hotellaresidence47.com. Functional, with a big flowery garden & helpful owners. **€**

Les Remparts (5 rooms) 1 Rue E Marcel, Villeneuve-sur-Lot; 05 53 70 71 63; w hoteldesremparts.site-solocal.com. Decent if unexciting rooms near the centre. **€**

Ô fil de L'Ô (5 rooms) 37 Quai Gambetta, Longueville, Clairac; m 06 27 39 76 45; w o-fil-de-l-o-clairac.hotelmix.fr. Cosy rooms & lovely hosts, & a pool by the river, just over the bridge from Clairac. **€**

Where to eat and drink

When you are tired of duck, duck, goose, Villeneuve has a great selection of alternatives.

Blue Marine 6 Allée de la Fédération, Villeneuve-sur-Lot; 05 47 01 19 18; w bluemarine47.fr; closed Mon–Tue & eves Sun, Wed. Simple décor but the place to go for seafood, with a €17 w/day lunch menu, seafood platters, & duck & steak options for the haters. Good whisky list too. **€€€€**

Hostellerie du Rooy Chemin de Labourdette, just east on the D661, Villeneuve-sur-Lot; 05 53 70 48 48; w hostellerieduroy.eatbu.com; closed Mon & eves Sun. Set back from the road, attractive inn where the chef prepares seafood, mushrooms & cèpes with a deft hand that brings out their true flavour. **€€€€**

La Toque Blanche Bel-air, Pujols; 05 53 49 00 30; f latoqueblanche47; closed Sun–Mon. Classic French cuisine (even crêpes Suzette!) in a pretty setting. *Very good €17.40 lunch menu.* **€€€€**

Le Roquentin 9 Bd du 11 Novembre, Laroque-Timbaut; 05 53 95 78 78; w restaurantleroquentin-fr; lunch Sun–Fri & dinner Fri. Seriously good food next to the church, with a small terrace. *Lunch €13.50, excellent Sun lunch menu €39.* **€€€€**

Auberge Château Lacaze 281 Rte de Lacaze, Aiguillon; m 06 37 12 96 95; w chateaulacaze.fr; closed Mon–Tue. Very reasonably priced, frequently changing menus in an idyllic setting on the garden terrace of a rose-tinted château, with games for the kids. *W/day lunch menu €15.* **€€€**

La Commanderie Place des Templiers, Le Temple-sur-Lot; 05 53 01 30 66; w restaurant-la-commanderie.fr; closed Mon & eves Sun. A restored 12th-century building set among fountains & water plants; classic stop after the water lilies. **€€€**

Bombay 33 Rue des Cieutats, Villeneuve-sur-Lot; 05 53 70 43 60; lunch only daily. A rare Indian restaurant in the area, with great choices, including many vegetarian. **€€**

Escale d'Asie 8 Rue Tout y Croit, Villeneuve-sur-Lot; m 06 80 75 81 81; w escaledasie.fr; closed lunch Mon. Chinese & Thai dumplings, soups, fondues, etc. **€€**

Yuki Bento 47 Place du 4 Septembre, Villeneuve-sur-Lot; 05 24 32 48 51; w yuki-restaurant.fr; Wed–Sat. Warm welcome & a delicious Japanese cuisine. **€€**

Ze Cuiz'in 41 Rue de Penne, Villeneuve-sur-Lot; 05 53 36 08 95; f Ze-Cuizin; closed Sun–Tue. Popular tapas bar-restaurant in front of Ste-Catherine on a pedestrian street. **€€**

Sports and activities Les Croisières du Lot (m 07 78 11 16 50; w lescroisieresdulot.fr) run short or longer dinner river cruises on a big barge departing from Castelmoron or Villeneuve.

Missandre-Cheval Roche, St-Pierre de Caubel, 9km northwest of Casseneuil; m 07 84 07 93 90; w missandre.fr. Riding centre offering short or long treks.

Villeneuve-sur-Lot Golf Course La Menuisière, Castelnaud-de-Gratecambe; 05 53 01 60 19; w vslgolf.com. 18 holes, & 12 apts (€€) for total golf.

Villeneuve-sur-Lot This sprawling market town hatched out of yet another bastide, founded by Alphonse de Poitiers, Count of Toulouse, in 1264. During a tour Alphonse had found the surrounding countryside in ruin and misery after the Albigensian Crusade, and, hoping to stabilise the area, he acquired the land from the Benedictine abbey of Eysses – hence the city's first name, Villeneuve d'Eysses. Although the town now spreads every which way – it is the headquarters of GiFi, the empire of shops founded by local self-made billionaire Philippe Ginestet (page 308) – it has retained its simple bastide heart.

Enter from the south by way of the 13th-century **Porte de Pujols**, crowned with a 33m tower. The market square, **Place Lafayette,** is framed in its *cornières*, rebuilt in the 17th century after they were trashed in the Fronde uprising against Louis XIV. Nearby, the huge neo-Gothic red-brick church of **Ste-Catherine** (Rue Ste-Catherine; ⌚ usually) was completed in 1937, replacing the original which was in danger of collapse. Its strikingly odd bell tower was inspired by St-Sernin in Toulouse; inside, the nave is lined with a charming frieze of saints (1911–20) by Maurice Réalier-Dumas. The magnificent Gothic and early Renaissance stained glass of the old church was incorporated in the modern church, depicting the *Life of Christ*; St James the Greater appears three times, in honour of the many pilgrims who passed through because Villeneuve was one of the few places on the Lot with a bridge, the **Pont Vieux**. The bridge made Villeneuve's fortune when the English built it in 1282, with three fortified towers similar to those of Cahors's Pont Valentré. Unfortunately, these tumbled down when the bridge partially collapsed in a flood – hence the asymmetrical wide arch. Further evil has since been averted thanks to a dolled-up statue of Our Lady of Joy in the chapel overhanging at the north end, rebuilt in 1642.

Not far from the bridge, the **Musée de Gajac** (2 Rue des Jardins; 05 53 40 48 00; ⌚ Apr–Oct 10.00–noon & 14.00–18.00 Tue–Fri, 14.00–18.00 Sat–Sun, Nov–Mar until 17.00; €5, ages 7–25 €3) houses a permanent exhibition of 19th-century and contemporary art (notably paintings by Maurice Réalier-Dumas (1860–1928) and engravings by Piranesi), as well as temporary shows and events.

Pujols On a hill 2km from the Pont Vieux, this began as a Celtic oppidum and Roman town named Podium, 'High Place', until its allegiance to the Cathars earned it near-total obliteration in the Albigensian Crusade. It was rebuilt with the same stone by Alphonse de Poitiers, with a 14th-century castle that resembled a mini-Carcassonne (there's a model in the tourist office) that was destroyed not by the enemy, but by the town in 1880, when the town council in a silly moment sold off the stone for 1,800 francs to build the prison at Eysses.

To enter Pujols's ancient square, pass under the arch of the tower of the 15th-century Flamboyant Gothic **St-Nicolas**. The church has star vaulting, and a chapel with Gothic tombstones and a Renaissance mausoleum that originally stood in the choir. A second church in Pujols, 15th-century **Ste-Foy la Jeune,** contains some murals from the period, one showing St George and the other of St Foy of Agen, a 3rd-century AD maiden martyred on a grill. Although her cult centre is up at Conques (Aveyron), some of her relics were taken to Glastonbury and a number of English churches were named after her.

South of Villeneuve-sur-Lot A local geography teacher gets credit for naming the triangle between the Lot and Garonne the **Pays des Serres**. It is a fitting word: *serres* means an eagle's talons (the limestone looks as if it has been clawed by a huge bird, leaving gashes between its limestone 'tables'); coincidentally the word also means greenhouses, and there are plenty of these too – or more likely plastic tunnels for fruit and vegetable primeurs.

This is southwest France, so there are caves to explore: the **Grottes de Fontirou** (Castella, 10km south of Pujols; m 06 32 92 99 13; w grottesdefontirou.wordpress.com; ⌚ guided tours: May–mid-Jun 14.00–18.00 Sun, 15–30 Jun 14.30–18.00 daily, Jul–Aug 10.00–19.00 Mon–Sat, 14.00–19.00 Sun; €8, ages 3–14 €6.50), discovered in 1905 with seven rooms of limestone formations. You can make it a full day out with the animal and play park **Z'Animoland** (Rte des Grottes de Fontirou; m 06 32 92 99 13; w z-animoland.com; ⌚ school hols, see website; €11, ages 2–13 €9, combined with Fontirou €16/€14). About 7km northwest, there are more fairy formations in the **Grotte de Lastournelles** (Ste-Colombe; m 06 63 88 90 60; w grotte-de-lastournelle.fr; ⌚ Jul–Aug 10.00–18.00 daily; mid-May–Jun & Sep 11.00, 14.00 & 15.30, also school hols; €7.50, ages 4–14 €5), and a chance to see a show cave like a spelunker; many morning tours are done in the dark, using torches going in, then turning on all the lights on the way out.

Many villages in the Pays des Serres haven't changed much since the Middle Ages, places such as **Hautefage-la-Tour**, with a Flamboyant Gothic church, hexagonal Renaissance bell tower and a village *lavoir* in the centre. Nearby **Laroque-Timbaut** has a 12th-century *halle* and tiny medieval lanes, especially the Ruelle de Lô under the clock tower. According to legend, a pretty spring by the **Chapelle St-Germain** in the nearby woods cured Charlemagne's army of a contagious disease on their way to Spain in AD778.

To the northeast, **Frespech** is a delightful fortified hilltop hamlet with old gates and houses and an 11th-century church of **Notre Dame** with interesting capitals in the nave. Here you can learn all about the manna of the southwest at the Ferme de Souleilles's **Musée du Foie Gras** (☎ 05 53 41 23 24; w souleilles-foiegras.com; ⌚ 10.00–19.00 Mon–Sat, 15.00–19.00 Sun, Jan–Mar until 18.00; €5, under 12 free).

Further east lofty **Beauville** (originally Boville, or Beef Town) is a baby bastide clinging to its promontory, complete with its arcades, vestiges of walls and Gothic church of St-Jacques with a pyramidal bell tower. In summer it's filled with young thespians at the Beauville Arts (w beauvillearts.com), an English language school for the performing arts.

The most interesting part of the western Serres is around **Prayssas**, an unusual round bastide and Chasselas grape grower. South of Prayssas, medieval **Clermont-Dessous** is clustered under a handsome 11th-century fortified church and ruins of a castle, and offers superb views down the Garonne valley. Catherine de' Medici and her daughter Marguerite de Valois spent time hiding out from the Protestants at **Port-Ste-Marie**, and met Henri of Navarre there – Marguerite's future husband. Its 16th-century church of Notre-Dame was an important pilgrimage church for river men, who would pray here before braving the next particularly dangerous stretch of the Garonne. These days the village is known for its kiwis.

Back on the Lot West of Villeneuve, the first village on the Lot is medieval **Casseneuil**, a picturesque place built on a peninsula formed by the confluence of the Lot and Lède. Since good stone was lacking in this part of the Lot valley, nearly everything is made of brick, including most of Casseneuil's houses and its church, containing good 15th-century frescoes.

The same goes for **Ste-Livrade-sur-Lot**, where there is an odd brick fortification called the **Tour du Roy**, the *roi* in this case being Richard the Lionheart. The bricks of Ste-Livrade's eponymous church are half eroded away, giving the building a slightly outlandish air. This was the church of an important priory, although the ambitions of its founders far outran the resources. It has a handsome apse, and some fine (garishly painted) capitals by the altar: a mermaid and her baby, a satyr and a monster or two. Downriver, the humdrum church of **St-Léger** at **Fongrave** houses a masterpiece: a beautifully sculpted wooden altarpiece from the 1650s with a fine Rubens-inspired painting of the *Adoration of the Magi.*

Le-Temple-sur-Lot Next down the river on the south bank, Le-Temple-sur-Lot was named after the Templar headquarters that oversaw all the order's holdings in the Agenais; the red-brick commandery survives along with its chapel, now the village church. It also has the reason the Monet painted his water lilies: the gardens of **Latour-Marliac** (☎05 53 01 08 05; **w** latour-marliac.com; 🕘 mid-Apr–mid-Oct 10.00–18.00 Tue–Sun; €7, ages 6–12 €3.50); founded in 1875 by Joseph Bory Latour-Marliac, who discovered a (still mysterious!) way to hybridise the colours of tropical water lilies to the hardy European variety. In 1889 he took his flowers to the Paris Exposition Universelle, where they caused a sensation and inspired Claude Monet, who planted them in his *jardin d'eau*, or water garden at Giverny; you can see some of his orders at Latour-Marliac's small museum. British gardeners were early enthusiasts – by 1904, nearly all the firm's business was with the UK. The gardens, now owned by American Robert Sheldon, are simply gorgeous, featuring 300 varieties of lotuses, water lilies and other water-loving plants, and bamboo, which was M. Latour-Marliac's first love. There's a café-restaurant by the garden's lake, with live concerts (accompanied by the resident frogs) on Sunday evenings in July and August.

St-Sardos In the hills to the south, off the D13, this sleepy hamlet gave its name to the War of Saint-Sardos. In 1324, the king of France gave permission for the founding of a bastide here by pro-French monks connected with Sarlat, and the spot was marked with a maypole bearing the king's arms. This infuriated the pro-English contingent at Monpezat just east, and its lord, Raymond Bernard, led a gang who burned the bastide (only St-Sardos's beautiful, sculpted Romanesque church portal survived the fire), put the monks to the sword and strung up the French seneschal from the maypole. The French accused Ralph Basset, Edward II's seneschal of Gascony, of ordering the attack. Charles IV accepted Edward's apology, but not Bernard's or Basset's and sent down an army of 7,000 to confiscate Aquitaine. A peace treaty in 1327 returned Aquitaine to English rule, with the exception of the Agenais – which would be one of the main sparks igniting the Hundred Years' War a decade later.

Castelmoron-sur-Lot and around Where the D13 meets the river stands this unfortunately named but pleasant village with half-timbered houses and a popular beach on the river. The ***mairie*** occupies a curious Arabian Nights villa complete with a minaret, built by the nostalgic wife of a former ambassador to Syria, located a street up from its impressive reinforced concrete suspension bridge of 1934.

The hills north of Castelmoron are pretty, although there is little to detain you except another of Alphonse de Poitiers's bastides, hilltop **Monclar d'Agenais**, enjoying lovely views in all directions. West, at **Brugnac**, you can visit the **Chaudron Magique** (Les Perrets; ☎05 53 88 80 77; **w** chaudronmagique.fr; 🕘 09.00–noon &

14.00–18.00 Tue–Sat; from €12.80), an organic farm offering tours, where you can learn about raising angora goats, rabbits and mohair, and make your own goat's cheese and bread to take home.

Ferme et le Musée du Pruneau (Domaine de Gabach, Lafitte-sur-Lot; ☎05 53 84 00 69; **w** musee-du-pruneau.com; 🕘 Jul–Aug 09.00–19.00 daily, Sep–Jun 09.00–noon & 14.00–19.00 Mon–Sat, 14.00–18.00 Sun (exc Jan–Mar); €5, ages 6–11 €3, under 6 free) Downriver from Castelmoron, one of the valley's largest plum farms has created this tell-all museum for the curious and the constipated; a 35-minute prune video, old drying ovens, local costumes, a prune jammery and *chocolaterie*, free tastings and the plummiest shop in the hemisphere. They have also expanded to strawberries.

Clairac This village is impressive from the riverfront; from the inside, it is perhaps less so, although it has some charming medieval streets. Clairac was once synonymous with the **Abbaye de St-Pierre**, founded by Pepin the Short in AD760, and endowed with the most extensive territories in the Agenais. One of its abbots accompanied Richard the Lionheart on the Third Crusade in 1190; another, after his abbey was ravaged by the Cathars, fought with Simon de Montfort at the Battle of Muret in 1192. In 1293, Edward I gave the abbots the right to send all their produce to sell in Bordeaux without paying any tolls. Its horticultural monks successfully grew the first *prune d'Ente* trees in their orchards (the abbot himself may have brought them back from the Middle East); another roving monk brought back and planted and acclimatised the first tobacco in France.

Although gravely damaged in the Hundred Years' War, the abbey survived. A new period began in 1482, when Louis XI sent the abbey's revenues to the pope for a few years, to restore the basilica of St John Lateran, beginning an association ratified by Henri IV in 1606, attaching Clairac to St John Lateran and recalled to this day; when presidents of France visit Rome, the Pope ceremoniously confirms their title as canons of the Lateran. But things started going downhill. In the late 1600s the Vicar General sent by the Lateran was caught spending money on his mistress in Clairac and running a gaming academy in the abbey. The Revolution finished it off. It used to host a bizarre museum of monk and nun *automates*, but now they are gone, too, and at the time of writing it's for sale and looking very sad.

Its church, **St-Pierre-ès-Liens**, still has its sturdy Romanesque bell tower; inside its old walls, the 19th-century restorers lined the nave with white columns to support a new ceiling, creating a curious effect; the high altar with its portraits of Christ and the Evangelist came from the abbey of Eysses, formerly in Villeneuve.

East of Clairac on the D911, follow the old blue historic marker signs and with luck you will find the remarkable **stone fountain** from the Château de Sauveboeuf (page 181), perhaps the work of master Renaissance sculptor Jean Goujon, standing at the edge of a broad lawn (private property; ask at the house to visit).

Aiguillon The Lot meets the Garonne at a town that began its days as a Roman encampment but knew its greatest fame as the residence of the wealthy Duc d'Aiguillon. A political figure of the last days of the *ancien régime*, the duke's little court and decadent parties made Aiguillon the hotspot of the Agenais in the summer, when lots of swells (including the duke's friend Madame du Barry) came down from Versailles. It is to him that the town owes its landmark **château** (1765), a stately work of early Neoclassical architecture, now a lycée. It also has a curious stump of an ancient Roman tower, known as the Tourrasse.

BASTIDE COUNTRY

Pretty rolling hills, woodlands and meadows – Stendhal once described this landscape as the 'Tuscany of France', and it's sprinkled with a superb collection of bastides and castles, both in the Lot-et-Garonne and just over the border in the Dordogne.

Market days are Tuesdays in Castillonnès, Saturdays in Villeréal, Wednesdays in Casseneuil and Thursdays in Monflanquin.

TOURIST INFORMATION All have the same website: w coeurdebastides.com.

Castillonnès 71 Grand Rue; 05 53 36 87 44; 09.30–12.30 & 14.00–17.00 Tue–Thu

Monflanquin Place des Arcades; 05 53 36 40 19; 09.30–12.30 & 14.00–17.00 Mon, Wed–Sat, 09.30–12.30 Tue

Villeréal Place de la Halle; 05 53 36 09 65; 09.30–12.30 & 14.00–17.00 Wed–Sat

WHERE TO STAY

Château de Scandaillac [map, page 298] (10 rooms) St-Eutrope de Born, between Monflanquin & Castillonnès; 05 53 36 65 40; w scandaillac.com. Atmospheric antique-furnished rooms in a 13th-century castle with beautiful views & a heated pool. B/fast inc. **€€€€**

Le Moulin de Labique [map, page 298] (5 rooms) St-Eutrope-de-Born, 8km south of Villeréal; 05 53 01 63 90; w moulin-de-labique.fr. Set in a 20ha estate, traditional country rooms, pool & a patio under a canopy of vines surrounded by flowers & butterflies. Choose between delicious regional options at the table d'hôte. **€€€€–€€€**

Château Ladausse [map, page 298] (5 rooms) Ladausse, Monflanquin; 05 53 36 71 63; w ladausse.com. Sleek parquet-floored suites in this charming 17th-century château with a pool run by Belgian Eric & American Diane; Eric is a superb chef & offers cookery & wine workshops. Sumptuous table d'hôte meals for min 6 adults. B/fast inc. **€€€**

Les Remparts de la Bastide (5 rooms) 26 Rue de la Paix, Castillonnès; 09 62 50 52 63; w lesrempartsdelabastide.fr. Recently renovated rooms in a 19th-century house, overlooking the ramparts; lovely garden terrace around a fountain. Excellent table d'hôte; b/fast inc. **€€€–€€**

Le Moulin de Boulède (5 rooms) Monflanquin on the road to Villeréal; m 06 62 53 07 86; w le-moulin-de-boulede.com. B&B in an 18th-century mill over a stream where Guy & Rosa will make you feel at home; they are renowned for their Michelin-star-level evening table d'hôte (€35). B/fast inc. **€€**

Europe (6 rooms) Place Jean Moulin, Villeréal; 05 53 36 00 35; w europe-villereal.com. In the centre of the action, & an excellent restaurant (€€€) with a good €15 w/day lunch. **€€–€**

La Bastide des Oliviers (8 rooms) 1 Tour de Ville, Monflanquin; 05 53 36 40 01; w labastidedesoliviers.fr. Right in the centre, a friendly Logis inn in a 19th-century building, with a bar & a restaurant (€€) with a reliable *plat du jour*. **€**

WHERE TO EAT AND DRINK

L'Effet Maison 25 Place des Arcades, Monflanquin; 09 52 13 07 73; w leffetmaison.com; eves Wed–Sat, lunch Sun. A young couple runs this fine restaurant, with a small menu using only local products. Also a vegetarian plate. **€€€€**

Le Jardin 17 Place des Arcades, Monflanquin; 05 53 36 54 15; w restaurant-lejardin47.fr; daily. Excellent seafood dishes & oysters (& other things, too) on the daily chalkboard in a 15th-century half-timbered house on the main square. **€€€€–€€€**

L'Auberge Le Donjon 300m from the Château de Gavaudun; 05 53 40 82 32; lunch Mon–Fri. A local institution since 1979 for home-cooked fills (not all duck!) & a playground & *pétanque* court. *Menus from €25–€35*. **€€€**

La Dolce Vita 31 Rue du Dropt, Villeréal; 05 53 71 64 02; w restaurant-dolcevita-villereal.com; closed Sun–Mon. Seasonal dishes & popular w/day lunch on the chalkboard (€15) which changes daily. €€€

Le Bistrot du Prince Noir 45 Place des Arcades, Monflanquin; 09 74 56 40 28; w lebistrotduprincenoir.fr; closed Sun, Wed. Warm atmosphere, & a mix of British & French cuisine (fish & chips, burgers, foie gras, vegetarian dishes). €€€–€€

L'Essential Gavaudun; 05 47 99 01 60; f Le-Café-de-Gavaudun; closed Sun, Wed & eves Tue. Typical village café, now run by a young couple serving many sharing dishes, so you can try more. €€

La Pierre Blanche [map, page 298] La Sauvetat sur Lède, south of Monflanquin; 05 53 40 69 14; w restaurantlapierreblanche.fr; closed Wed & eves Tue. Simple country restaurant (they also have 2 rooms; **€**) where Marie Laure serves up a changing menu of classics. €€

Magees 2 bis Grand Rue, Castillonnès; m 06 61 31 89 86; f magees.restaurant; closed Sun–Tue. Lot-et-Garonne's only Irish–French fusion restaurant, with fish & chips, Irish-style foie gras, & plenty of Guinness & Irish craft beers. Live music some nights. €€

La Maréchalerie 1 Grand Rue, Castillonnès; 05 53 01 58 28; w restaurantlamarechalerie.eatbu.com; closed Sun–Mon. Cheap & cheerful spot in the centre with a €13.50 menu. €

MONFLANQUIN Strategically planted atop an isolated 181m hill, the bastide of Monflanquin was founded in 1256 by Alphonse de Poitiers, Count of Toulouse, as part of his brother St Louis's strategy to Frenchify the lands recently devastated by the Albigensian Crusade. Monflanquin has preserved most of its original bastide elements: its *cornières*, a fortified church still bristling behind its original façade, its grid street plan and blocks of medieval houses; the **Musée des Bastides** (in the Maison du Tourisme; 05 53 36 40 19; w monflanquin-museedesbastides.com; May–Oct 09.30–13.00 & 14.00–17.00 Tue–Fri; €4, ages 12–18 €1.50, under 12 free) will tell you all about them. Monflanquin's most recent vocation is art, welcoming artists in residence (w pollen-monflanquin.com) and it fills the summer with events, exhibitions and festivals.

VILLERÉAL Another foundation of Alphonse de Poitiers, this bastide of 1269 on the River Dropt (or Drot) is one of the liveliest bastides. The pretty shop-filled arcades of the main square overlook the 14th-century *halle*, which had an upper storey added in the 16th century. The façade of the church is framed by two towers and retains the loopholes in the apse, from where the citizens shot at the rampaging English.

LACAPELLE-BIRON The village was founded by the baron at Château de Biron (page 227) to host the Monday market that used to take place under the château – he hated to be awakened by the noise. Today most of the noise comes from the adventure park, and natural swimming pool at the **Parc-en-Ciel** (05 53 71 84 58; w parc-en-ciel.com; Jun–Aug – check schedules on website; adventure park: €21.80, ages 6–11 €18.70; pool: €8.90, ages 6–12 €6.80).

In the nearby hamlet of **St-Avit**, the **Musée Bernard Palissy** (05 53 40 98 22; w museepalissy.net; May–Jun 14.30–17.30 Sun & hols, Jul–Aug 14.00–18.30 Wed–Mon, Sep 14.00–17.30 Sun–Mon, Wed–Fri; €4, ages 12–18 €2, under 12 free) has one of the largest collections of contemporary ceramics in France, in honour of the great ceramicist and writer born here in 1510. In 1549, after years of experiments and even burning his own furniture and floorboards, Palissy finally created a glass furnace hot enough to melt the jewel-like enamels for his *rustiques figulines* – the platters covered with plants and animals, that made him famous; Catherine de'

Medici commissioned a grotto full of them (his workshop was rediscovered in the 1980s during the construction of the Grand Louvre). He just managed to escape the slaughter of the St Bartholomew's Day Massacre in 1572, only to be arrested for his Protestant faith in 1589 and thrown into the Bastille, where he soon died.

GAVAUDUN Lacapelle-Biron and St-Avit are near the head of the leafy valley and mini-gorge of the Lède, a stream that not only sounds like the mythological river of oblivion, Lethe, but really does make the cares of the world seem far away – deceptively so: St-Avit was razed by the retreating Germans in 1944 and troops marched through in the Middle Ages. A striking 12th-century 20.8m-tall donjon teetering on a limestone outcrop dominates the ruins of the **Château de Gavaudun** (☎ 05 53 40 04 16; **w** chateaudegavaudun.com; 🕘 mid-May & Oct 10.00–17.00 Wed–Sun, Jun–Sep 10.00–18.00 daily, Jul–Aug 10.00–19.00 daily, but closed in bad weather any time of the year; €5.50, students & ages 6–16 €3.50, under 6 free), entered by way of a cave (now there are steps, originally there was a ladder). Just above Gavaudun, **St-Sardos-de-Laurenque** is a pretty Romanesque church with fish and dragons carved on the portal.

CASTILLONNÈS A decade before Villeréal, Alphonse had founded this bastide on the site of a castle – hence its name. Castillonnès has conserved its *cornières* in its square and narrow medieval lanes, and, on Rue du Petit Paris, the fine 17th-century Maison de Cours de Thomazeau designed by Victor Louis of Bordeaux opera fame. The church has a 17th-century gilded retable. Unlike its neighbours, Castillonnès has remained off the tourist trail, which means many of its shops are shuttered. It seems you can't have one without the other.

LAUZUN '*Il n'était pas permis de rêver comme il a vécu*' wrote La Bruyère, on the Duc de Lauzun. Antonin Nompar de Caumont, born the younger son of an impoverished local baron in 1633, was so endowed with natural talent, good looks and charm that he quickly become Louis XIV's favourite. The Sun King promoted him to marshal and duke; one of his missions was to help James II's queen, Mary of Modena, and her son flee from England to France during the Glorious Revolution. On another occasion Lauzun hid under the king's bed to hear what Louis and his mistress were saying about him. Women adored him, including the Big Miss herself, the Grande Mademoiselle – Louis's headstrong cousin – who fell head over heels for Lauzun, much to the fury of Louis, who sent Lauzun to the Bastille. Most accounts say that he secretly married the Grande Mademoiselle anyway, then proceeded to be terribly unfaithful to her. When she died, the spunky duke married a 15-year-old (he was 62), then to her horror lived to be 90. One thing he did was add a domed pavilion to his golden half-medieval, half-Renaissance **Château de Lauzun** (23 Rue du Château; **m** 06 74 25 16 65; 🕘 guided tours: Jul–Aug 10.00–noon & 14.00–18.00; €6, under 12 €4), renowned for its magnificent fireplaces. The Gothic **church**, next to an 11th-century tower, has an elaborately carved altar, and two statues of the Virgin from the 13th and 15th centuries.

PAYS DU DURAS

The low, rolling hills of this northwest corner of the Lot-et-Garonne hold some of the department's most unusual sights, and some of its best wine. The French come here for *douceur de vie*, and the English, perhaps remembering Duras as one of the most pro-English corners of Aquitaine, have returned to buy bits of it back.

It includes a pretty stretch of the River Dropt, 'a vision of paradise' according to the 5th-century AD poet Sidonius Apollinaris, that winds 130km from its source near Monpazier to meet the Garonne by La Réole. Because it often floods into a muddy mess in winter, there are few towns and roads along its banks.

TOURIST INFORMATION The office in **Duras** (05 53 93 71 18; w tourismeduras.com; 09.30–12.30 & 14.00–17.30 Mon–Fri) is at 14 Boulevard Jean-Brisseau.

WHERE TO STAY

Hostellerie des Ducs (20 rooms) Bd Jean Brisseau, Duras; 05 53 83 74 58; w hostellerieducs-duras.com. Near the château, this is a charming family-run hotel in an early 19th-century convent, now transformed into a hotel with a pool, garden & excellent restaurant (€€€) with daily changing menu & truly exceptional desserts. **€€€**

L'Étape Gasconne (18 rooms) Place de la Mairie, Allemans-du-Dropt; 05 53 20 23 55; w letapegasconne-hotel.com. Pleasant rooms, a pool & warm welcome for the weary, & a good restaurant (€€). *Lunch menu €14.50.* **€€–€**

WHERE TO EAT AND DRINK

La Terrasse du Château de Duras 4 Place Jean Bousquet; 05 53 84 29 62; closed Wed & eves Tue. Lovely views of the castle, & crêpes, burgers, salads & fish. Simple fare, but good. **€€–€**

Auberge du Bastide 30 Av de Paris, St-Pardoux-Issac, just north of Miramont-de-Guyenne; m 06 12 71 12 80; closed eves Sun. Delicious regional cuisine & kind prices & *formules* at this roadside inn. **€**

Chai et Rasade Place du Marché, Duras; 05 53 93 20 20; daily. Wine bar with cheese & charcuterie, & a gourmet grocery; you can also book lunch.

DURAS Spread out along a spur overlooking the emerald valley of the Dropt, Duras is the only town in France that never built a Catholic church; the current one began as a Protestant temple. Having the same name as a famous French novelist hasn't hurt it (and as she would tell her Parisian friends, it's pronounced 'dur-ass' not 'dura'); nor has the reputation of its excellent wines which first became a thing during the Hundred Years' War, when the Durfort-Duras *seigneurs*, who were great allies of the English, ruled the roost and made their wine popular in the English court.

But the main reason to visit is the mighty prow-shaped **Château de Duras** (05 53 83 77 32; w chateau-de-duras.com; Apr–Jun & Sep–Oct 10.00–13.00 & 14.00–18.00 daily, Jul–Aug 10.00–19.00 Sun–Mon, Wed, Fri, 10.00–22.30 Tue, Thu, Sat, Nov–Dec & Feb–Mar 14.00–18.00 daily; €10, students & ages 13–18 €7, ages 5–12 €5). Built in the 1100s, this castle was redone in 1310 by Gaillard de Got, with cash provided by his brother, Pope Clement V. His daughter married a Durfort, and from 1325 the castle belonged to the powerful Durfort–Duras family, who so adroitly managed the shifting alliances of state and religion that they kept it until 1838 and had many moments of renown. The town purchased it in 1969 and restored the grand halls, kitchen, the 'room of secrets', the oratory, the prison and moats, and the tower with views that on a clear day stretch to the Pyrenees. And there's often something going on; check the website. Just under the château, you can find more about the town's wine at the **Maison des Vins de Duras** (130 Rte du Stade Fonratière; 05 53 94 13 48; w vins-bergeracduras.fr).

One of 20th-century France's greatest novelists, born Marguerite Donnadieu (1914–96), took the name of her father's hometown when she published her first novel, *Les Impudents*, in 1943. In the Resistance, she met lifelong friend François Mitterrand and is best known in the English-speaking world for her Oscar-winning script to Alain Resnais's film *Hiroshima, Mon Amour* (1959) and the autobiographical *L'Amant*, made into a film in 1992. The **Centre-Musée Marguerite Duras** (1 Rue du Couvent; m 06 72 76 27 69; w margueriteduras.org; ⏲ May–mid-Sep 15.00–18.00; €5) hosts exhibitions on her life, photos, novels and films.

NORTH OF DURAS There are a good Romanesque churches here: a 13th-century one at **Esclottes** (pick up the key from the *mairie*; ☎ 05 53 83 73 44; ⏲ 08.30–17.15 Mon, Thu) with skilfully carved capitals; another, St-Vincent, at **Savignac-de-Duras**, has an untranslatable Celtic inscription to the right of the door. Up in the northeast corner, in Loubes Bernac, **Plum Village** (Meynac; ☎ 05 53 58 48 58; w plumvillage.org) was founded in 1982 by the late Thich Nhat Hanh, Vietnamese Buddhist monk and peace activist who introduced 'mindfulness' to the west. Today it's the largest Buddhist monastery in Europe.

MIRAMONT-DE-GUYENNE A 13th-century bastide founded by Edward I, Miramont was so battered in the medieval wars it only retains an arcaded square and a few old houses (one was once inhabited by Jeanne d'Albret, who like George Washington seems to have slept everywhere). It made enough money from its once-famous sheepskin slippers in the 19th century to rebuild its **church** with stained glass by modern master Emile Wachter. Between here and Tombeboeuf to the south grows the **Chêne Remarquable** a stunning isolated spreading oak believed to be at least 350 years old.

ALLEMANS-DU-DROPT Supposedly named after the barbarian tribe that pushed over the Rhine and shoved its way through in the Dark Ages (and made such an impression that the French still call Germany 'Allemagne'), Allemans-du-Dropt is a pretty place with a pretty bridge and the 10th-century church of **St-Eutrope** (Rue de l'Église; m 06 83 25 89 71; ⏲ 09.00–18.00 daily; free), given a neo-Gothic facelift in the 19th century. The choir has a Mozarabic horseshoe arch, but best of all are the 15th-century frescoes, rediscovered in 1935 under the plaster by the church bell-ringer. These are lively, colourful paintings – of the Passion, Last Judgement and most memorably of the devils, one carrying off souls like a grape-picker in a basket on his back. All the damned appear to be either women or priests. Recently added is fine long-forgotten 17th-century painting of the *Entombment of Christ*.

LA SAUVETAT-DU-DROPT This pretty little village was founded in the 6th century by priors as a place of 'safety' although it singularly failed to live up to its name in 1637, when the Duc de la Valette came and brutally put down a peasant uprising by massacring 1,500 Croquants. He razed the town for good measure, except for its charming 23-arch medieval bridge (much to the delight of kayakers playing peek-a-boo), near a picturesque *pigeonnier* and the 13th-century **St-Gervais**, a church with an ornate portal and choir that survived a cyclone in 1242, and a beautiful Renaissance house on the main street.

MONTETON The delightful Romanesque **Notre-Dame** (☎ 05 53 20 20 08; ⏲ always) sits high on a terrace where the keen of eye should be able to pick out 13 bell towers on the horizon. One of the few churches to escape damage over the centuries, it has unusual interior buttresses, fine vaults, and a triumphal arch with carved capitals.

DOWN THE GARONNE VALLEY FROM AGEN

In fact, it isn't just the Garonne: you have a choice of following either the river or the Canal Latéral à la Garonne, the 19th-century waterway that parallels the river. This is wine country, producing red, white and rosé Côtes-du-Marmandais, which they promise 'will re-animate chagrined spirits and save an ordinary meal from insipidity', much of it produced by the local co-operative, but it's also famous for tomatoes and a beautiful hilltop village with a Rembrandt.

TOURIST INFORMATION

Casteljaloux 20 Place du Roy; 05 53 93 00 00; w tourisme-coteauxetlandesdegascogne.fr; 09.00–noon & 14.00–17.00 Mon–Fri

Marmande 11 Rue Toupinerie; 05 53 64 44 44; w valdegaronne.com; 09.30–12.30 & 14.00–18.00 Tue–Sat, 14.00–18.00 Mon

Tonneins 3 Bd Charles de Gaulle; 05 53 79 22 79; w valdegaronne.com; 09.30–12.30 & 14.00–18.00 Tue–Sat

WHERE TO STAY

Clos Castel (10 rooms, 12 villas) 13 Av du 8 Mai 1945, Casteljaloux; 05 64 13 76 00; w clos-castel.fr. Recently opened complex in a 19th-century mansion with contemporary rooms & self-catering villas (sleeping up to 6) with king-size beds & wooden floors. All guests have free access to the spa. Here too is the new premises of Casteljaloux's decades-old gourmet restaurant, **La Vieille Auberge** (€€€€) featuring seasonal dishes based on things other than duck, & a pretty garden terrace. **€€€€€**

Château Mathias [map, page 298] (3 rooms) Virazeil (just east of Marmande); m 06 64 95 44 03; w chateaumathias.com. *Le Figaro* called it one of the most beautiful chambres d'hôte in France, & it's hard to argue. Gorgeous rooms in a château of 1878, in a park & garden (patrolled by white peacocks), with a pool & views as far as the Pyrenees. Excellent b/fast inc. **€€€€**

La Couronne (20 rooms) 2 Place de la Couronne, Marmande; 05 53 84 54 31; w hotellacouronne47.com. Central, cheap & cheerful, near the train station. **€€**

Le Capricorne (34 rooms) 26 Av Hubert Ruffe, Marmande; 05 53 64 16 14; w lecapricorne-hotel.com. Motel with sleek black-&-red décor, a good restaurant (€€€) & pool. **€€**

WHERE TO EAT AND DRINK

Boat aux Saveurs 36–38 Av Jean Jaurès, Marmande; 05 53 64 20 35; w restaurantboatauxsaveurs.fr; lunch Wed–Sun & dinner Sat. Chef Annabelle has made this the local go-to place for gastronomic feasts. *W/day lunch menu €26, others from €45.* **€€€€€**

La Grange 13 Rue de l'Hirondelle, Marmande; 05 53 20 81 88; florent.lagrange.9; closed Sun–Mon. Reliable *cuisine de marché* on the garden terrace. *Daily lunch €16.* **€€€**

La Chope et le Pichet [map, page 298] 42 Saint Christophe, Villeton, 4km southwest of Tonneins; 05 53 83 13 49; w lachope-et-lepichet.fr; Mar–early Nov Wed–Fri, lunch Sat, dinner Sun. Pleasant restaurant with a terrace on the canal offering a change of pace, with a beefy menu including fondue & 30 kinds of Belgian beer. **€€**

Le Cassissier Place Jean Jaurès, Casteljaloux; 05 53 93 03 38; w restaurant-lecassissier.fr; closed Mon & eves Sun & Tue. Traditional Gascon cuisine, plus generous fish dishes. *Lunch menu €16.* **€€**

TONNEINS Until 2000 the enormous **Manufacture des Tabacs** in Tonneins annually produced some 10 billion Gauloises and Gitanes, smokable only by Frenchmen and masochists; current plans are to convert it into a centre for small businesses. Today the town is proudest of its *jambon de Tonneins*, ham slow baked, then cut up and mixed with a rich sauce that turns into gelatine, to be reheated in the winter with potatoes – a dish once beloved of the river boatmen and still produced at Charcuterie Carlotti (6 Place Edouard Herriot) and Charcuterie Le Petit Gascon (2 Rue du Plaisir). From the top of town there's a wonderful panorama over the Garonne valley.

LE MAS-D'AGENAIS You'll reach this village by an elegant modern suspension bridge that crosses the Garonne and the canal. Although the sign announces the village, along with a floral arrangement of Mas's coat of arms (three gold hands on a red field), not a house is to be seen. Mas is up in the clouds, a village closed into itself; it's special, and it knows it.

Known as Velenum Pompeiacum in Roman times, Mas was still important in the Middle Ages. It isn't a large village, just a few lovely streets and squares, a brick medieval gateway, a wooden market *halle* from the 1600s, and a beautiful view over the Garonne from its little park. It also has a fascinating **Collégiale St-Vincent** (Place du Marché; 05 53 89 50 37; Apr–Oct 09.00–19.00, Nov–Mar 09.00–17.00 daily) begun in 1085, replacing a church of AD440 that itself was built on the site of a Roman temple. Tinkered with over the centuries, it isn't much to look at, outside of the modillions (including a rather alarming one of nipple-biting lions). Viollet-le-Duc gave the south portal its present appearance, and at about the same time the tall steeple that loomed over it was demolished.

The interior, however, contains a wealth of remarkable sculpture, concentrated on the capitals. In the south aisle, Old Testament scenes include *Samson, David and Goliath*, *The Sacrifice of Abraham* and *Daniel in the Lions' Den*. The capitals in the north aisle and choir are mostly New Testament vignettes, along with *St Michael* and the *Martyrdom of St Vincent*, while those high up in the nave itself have some surprising subjects: one is the *Race of Atalanta* and the *Hunt of the Calydonian Boar* from the same Greek myth.

The church contains two ancient relics: a Roman cippus with a confusing inscription (possibly the base for the statue of a god) and an early Christian sarcophagus, said to be that of the obscure martyr St Vincent, hidden in the cemetery during the Norman invasions and only rediscovered in 1785. Note also the beautifully carved choir stalls, originally intended for the abbey church at La Réole. The village's greatest claim to fame, a Rembrandt no less, was donated to the church in 1873 by a wealthy family from Mas who made it big in Dunkerque. Originally, *Christ on the Cross* (1631) was part of a series of seven on the Passion for private devotion; all the rest are now in Munich (see the photographs in the church). For anyone who thinks Rembrandt painted only portraits, they are a revelation; in these intense, remarkable paintings, Jesus goes up on the cross a man and comes down a god.

CASTELJALOUX South of Mas, the D6 passes through the lovely Forest of Mas-d'Agenais, another old hunting preserve, on the way to yet another former possession of the d'Albrets; readers of *Cyrano de Bergerac* will recognise it as the base of the Cadets de Gascogne. The name sounds as if it should mean 'jealous' but really comes from *gelos*, meaning perilous, a reality confirmed by the state of the castle itself, now a ruin but once a favourite hunting and love retreat of Henri IV. There are a few 15th-century buildings around the centre, but what draws the visitors these days is its big thermal spa, **Les Bains de Casteljaloux** (4 Rue des Thermes; 05 53 20 59 00; w bains-casteljaloux.com; 07.00–20.00 daily) with a wellness and beauty centre, restaurant and rooms. For outdoor summer fun there is the pretty sand-bordered **Lac de Clarens** just southwest, with an **Aqua'fun Park** (m 06 20 80 83 32; w aquafunparkclarens.com; ⏲ late Jun–Aug; from €5) full of floaty bouncy castles if you want to do more than sit on the beach.

Just southeast of Casteljaloux down the D11, the striking multi-towered **Château du Sendat**, begun in the 12th century, is set in a French garden. Among the Romanesque churches in the area, there's a fine one at **Villefranche-du-Queyran** east on the D120, with a score of carved capitals; **Labastide-Castel-Amouroux** to the northwest has another one, with some good monsters.

MARMANDE The most important market town between Agen and Bordeaux is currently on its third name. Originally it was Marmande-la-Royale, when it received its charter in 1182 from Richard the Lionheart. After changing hands eight times in the Hundred Years' War and a few more in the Wars of Religion, it was Marmande-la-Sainte; now it's the more secular Marmande-la-Jolie, although honestly it should be Marmande-la-Tomate: the queen of big red tomatoes that thrive in the surrounding plain. In early August they are celebrated with a cycling race while members of the local tomato guild swan around like red musketeers.

Marmande's central **Place Clemenceau**, covering an underground car park, has a fountain with a bronze statue called *La Pomme d'Amour*, a kneeling nude clutching a *tomate de Marmande*, in reference to an old belief that tomatoes were an aphrodisiac. She gazes across to the larger Europa fountain, while the nearby **Musée Municipal Albert Marzelles** (15 Rue Abel Boyé, ☎ 05 53 64 42 04; f museemarzelles; ⏲ 15.00–18.00 Wed–Fri, 10.00–noon & 15.00–18.00 Sat; free) offers a hotchpotch of local items and art, especially by local Abel Boyé (1864–1933), a student of Benjamin Constant who was one of France's most popular painters of languorous ladies. Don't miss the lavish firemen's helmets, which perhaps explain why pre-Impressionist French historical paintings were called *pompiers* (firemen).

Rue Léopold Faye, lined with half-timbered houses, leads back towards the 13th-century Gothic church of **Notre-Dame** (Place du Prieuré; ⏲ 08.00–18.00 daily) where you can inspect a pretty rose window, a Baroque *Mise en tombeau*, a 16th-century retable dedicated to St Benedict and a beautiful topiary garden in the cloister of 1545. From here Rue de la Libération leads up to the Baroque **Chapelle St-Benoît** (⏲ Jul–Aug 14.30–18.00 Wed–Sun) with a fine 17th-century ceiling painted to imitate coffering, an elaborate gilded retable and paintings on the life of Christ.

The local garden centre has created the inspirational **Jardins de Beauchamp**, with land and water gardens and a tearoom (Rue des Isserts; ☎ 05 53 64 30 12; w jardineriejay.fr; ⏲ 08.00–noon & 14.00–18.00 Tue–Sat, 14.00–18.00 Mon, Oct–May also afternoons Sun; €6). The Marmandais wine co-operative, the **Cave de Marmandais** (Lieu Dit Dupuy, Beaupuy; ☎ 05 53 76 05 11; w cave-du-marmandais.fr; ⏲ 09.00–noon & 14.00–18.00 Tue–Sat; free) is just north.

Romanesque fans have little gems to seek out north of Marmande. On a small stream rightly called the Gupie, **Mauvezin-sur-Gupie** has a 13th-century church covered by a remarkable roof shaped like a ship's keel, so impressive that Viollet-le-Duc included it in his book of architecture (to visit, ring the *mairie*: ☎ 05 53 94 20 11). **Lagupie** has a 12th-century church with a sculpted tympanum; there's another, carved with *Christ and the Elders of the Apocalypse*, to the east of Marmande at **St-Pierre-de-Londres**, an English bastide project that never got further than this church. **Virazeil**, between Marmande and St-Pierre-de-Londres, has a Neoclassical château built in 1774 by Victor Louis, architect of Bordeaux's Grand Théâtre.

STE-BAZEILLE Further down the Garonne, this was a Roman town named after the daughter of a proconsul who was martyred for her faith; decapitated, her head bounced nine times, each bounce bringing forth a spring – now known as the nine fountains, *neuffonds* (St Paul suffered a similar fate in Rome, but his head, being full of weighty theology, bounced but thrice). The **Musée Archéologique de Ste-Bazeille** (Place René Sanson; **m** 06 85 23 60 52; **w** archeo-marmandais.fr; ⌚ ring ahead) has a remarkable collection of more than 700 artefacts from Gallo-Roman to medieval items (mosaic, engraved buckles, jewellery, lamps, ceramics, and iron and bronzes, including figures of gods and dogs).

South of Ste-Bazeille, **Marcellus** is the site of a handsome 16th-century château, home of the count who bought the Venus de Milo from the Greek farmer who dug her up on the island of Milos, and kept her from rival purchaser the Prince of Moldavia (the statue was ready to be placed aboard a ship for Romania just when the French vessel from Constantinople arrived; accounts say there was either some brisk bargaining, or a tussle that the French sailors won – during which she may have lost her arms and pedestal). Further downstream, **Meilhan-sur-Garonne** sits atop a natural balcony, overlooking the hills of the Entre-Deux-Mers and their famous vineyards. South of here, the wine village of **Cocumont** has a remarkable 11th-century Romanesque church built on top of a 2,000-year-old tumulus; deep below is the circular tomb of a local chieftain, never excavated. **Romestaing**'s 12th-century church of St-Christophe has more mysterious capitals.

14

Tarn-et-Garonne

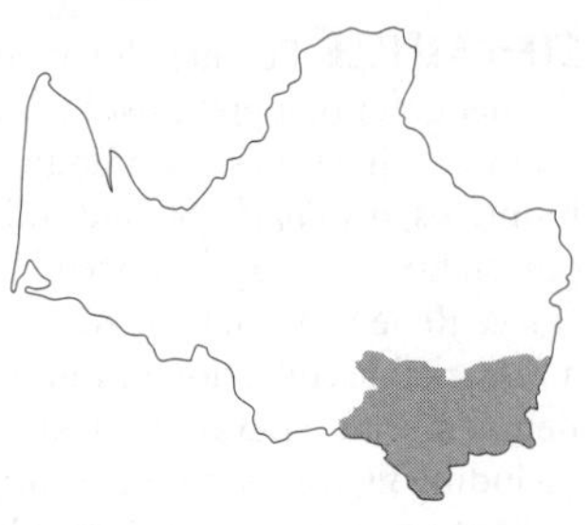

Tarn-et-Garonne was originally Bas Quercy. Although the Revolutionary bureaucrats in Paris made Quercy a single département, Montauban was mortified to find itself a mere spot on the map while rascally old Cahors got to be a capital. Montauban's indignant protests fell on deaf ears, but in 1808 the city saw its chance when Napoleon and Josephine just happened to be passing through. The city fathers rolled out the red carpet, the mayor was ever so flattering, and Napoleon, imperial ego aglow, promised to give the Montaubanais a département of their very own. He sliced off the south end of the Lot, took in the corners from several other départements, and No. 82, the Tarn-et-Garonne, was born.

The resulting mosaic of landscapes, regional architecture and allegiances, criss-crossed by the rivers Garonne, Tarn and Aveyron, contains a bit of everything, and enough fruit to have kept Carmen Miranda in hats until the end of time. Moissac is famous for its Chasselas table grapes, as well as southwest France's finest medieval art. The gorges of Aveyron supply the dramatic scenery, but there are lovely landscapes in all corners.

The Tarn-et-Garonne is said to have more dovecotes than any other département in France; if rural architecture tends to follow traditional forms, when it came to building the dovecote, or *pigeonnier*, the farmer let his imagination stray – these bird hotels come in all forms, most postdating the Revolution. Before then, only the nobility were allowed to have them, and there was nothing the peasants could do if the *seigneur*'s bird gobbled his corn. Pigeons or doves had several practical purposes: they kept down insects on the vines, they provided food for the table, but, most of all, they made a lot of guano, considered the best of all fertilisers and so precious that many a girl was married off with a dowry of pigeon poop.

MONTAUBAN

Originally covered with silvery willows, hence Mons Albanus ('white hill'), Montauban prefers to be known as 'the pinkest of the three pink cities' (pink, that is, as in brick; the other two are Toulouse and Albi). The capital of the Tarn-et-Garonne, it was cast in an original mould from its foundation, a successful medieval experiment in town planning that caught on in the 13th and 14th centuries to spawn dozens of baby Montaubans, known as the bastides. Not many of the others, however, have evolved into such pleasant medium-sized cities, or can claim a collection of art as prestigious as that of the Musée Ingres.

HISTORY Montauban may owe its origins to oversexed monks. These were the brethren of the 'Golden Hill', Montauriol, an abbey founded in AD820 by St Théobard. The monks claimed the *droit de cuissage* (the right to select bedfellows from the local population, although some argue it was the right to bake bread in their ovens). Others say it was all calumny to justify the founding of the first new town in the southwest next door to the abbey by Count Alphonse-Jourdain of Toulouse. In 1144 he laid out the grid plan of Montauban – essentially a bastide a hundred years before the others began sprouting along the battle lines of the Hundred Years' War.

The counts allowed Montauban to elect its own consuls, and gave it so many privileges that it soon sucked up all the loose people in the area; as a new town with a relatively free population it had something of the enterprising spirit of an American frontier town. By the mid 14th century Montauban was bustling with the import and export of textiles – just when the Treaty of Brétigny (1360) ceded it to England. John Chandos came in person to take it for the Black Prince, who spent many months here, plotting and fighting on the frontiers of French territory.

After the Hundred Years' War, Montauban's commerce quickly picked up again, and like other mercantile towns it was very receptive to the new doctrines of Calvin. After a good deal of simmering, the pot boiled over on 20 December 1561; the Montaubanais broke down the cathedral door, pillaged and burnt it to the ground, then did the same to all the other churches and convents in town, except for St-Jacques, which they converted into a Protestant temple. All the brick and stone of the churches immediately went into building walls, which were unusually efficient, twice repelling the concerted Catholic attacks.

The future Henri IV spent much time here, and when he became king his Edict of Nantes made Montauban a Protestant place of safety. His less tolerant and less capable son Louis XIII marched down in 1621 with an army of 25,000 and besieged Montauban for weeks, and on the advice of a sorcerer, bombarded it with 400 cannons at the same time (the origins of the French expression *faire les 400 coups*, 'to go against all reason'). And it didn't work – the Protestants held a fête instead of surrendering. Louis found them too tough and gave up. His grand vizier Richelieu, however, waited until the fall of La Rochelle in 1629, which left Montauban isolated as the last Protestant stronghold in France, and diplomatically convinced it to surrender.

No dummy, Richelieu's first act was to demolish Montauban's walls. His second was to cajole the inhabitants into not emigrating, by offering them plums – money and job-generating bureaucracies, including their own intendants. Richelieu may have been a cardinal but he knew that it was the Protestants who generated much of the nation's wealth. His plan worked so well that, by the 18th century, Montauban could proudly claim to be the third city in the southwest. Its weavers produced a wool fabric called *cadis* that sold like hot cakes in the American colonies, and merchants filled the town with impressive pink-brick *hôtels particuliers*. The intendants drew out new broad avenues and laid out the first parks.

Montauban's contribution to the Revolution was a woman 200 years ahead of her time: Olympe de Gouges, born in 1748. Defender of the rights of all people, even women, de Gouges wrote a brochure called *Les Droits de la femme et de la citoyenne*, declaring that 'if a woman has the right to mount the scaffold, she has the right to ascend to the seats of justice'. For trying to obtain political rights for women she was guillotined in 1793. But if the Revolution was blind to women's rights, the Napoleonic code that followed a few years later really put half the population of France in its place by ending rights (especially the right to buy and sell property) that even medieval women had enjoyed.

Another setback was in store – Montauban's *cadis* trade declined when France lost her colonies in Canada and Louisiana, then disappeared altogether when the new industrial mills in the north undersold the city's weavers. Napoleon's intervention,

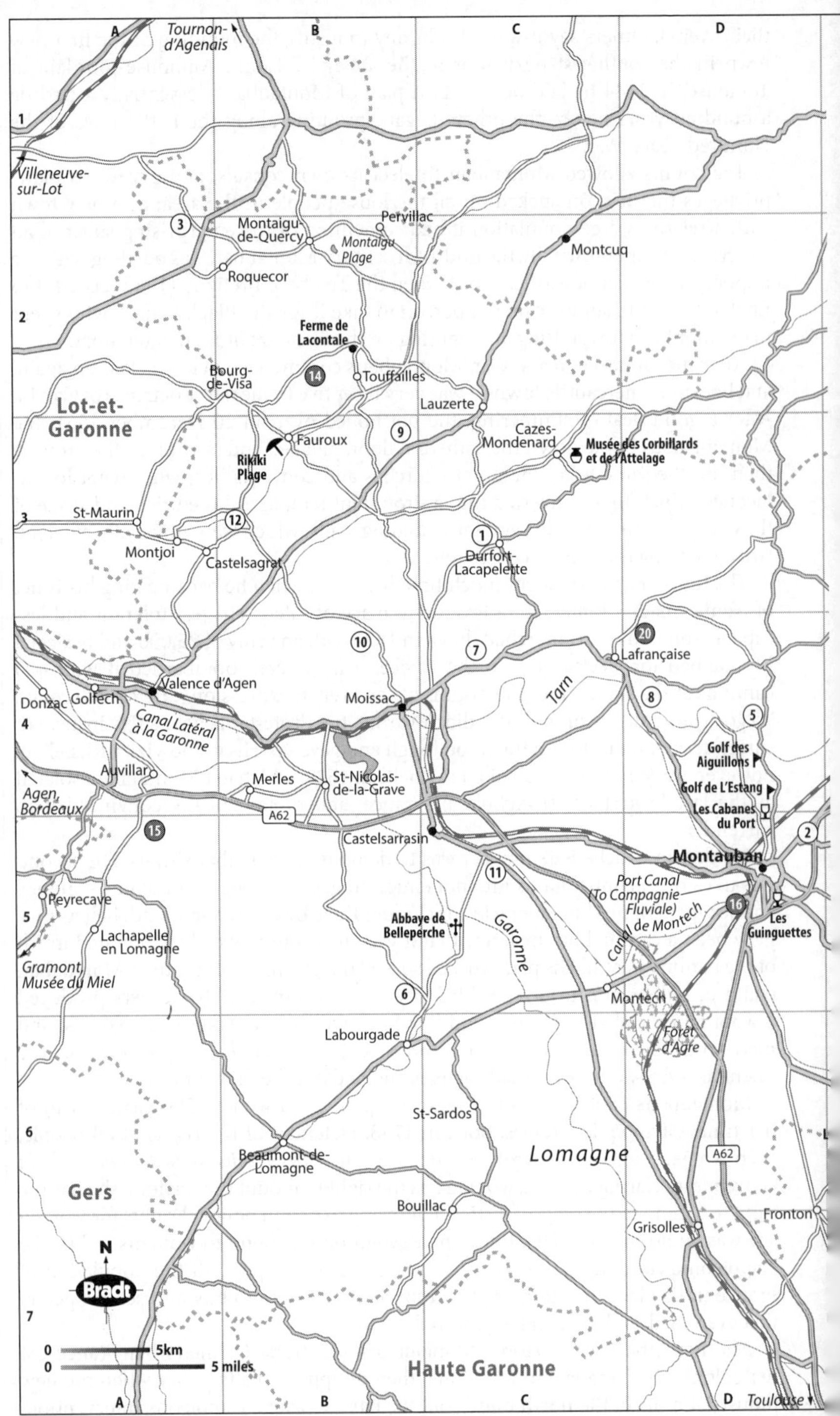

Tournon-d'Agenais
Villeneuve-sur-Lot
Montaigu-de-Quercy
Peyvillac
Montaigu Plage
Montcuq
Roquecor
Ferme de Lacontale
Bourg-de-Visa
Touffailles
Lauzerte
Lot-et-Garonne
Cazes-Mondenard
Musée des Corbillards et de l'Attelage
Fauroux
Rikiki Plage
St-Maurin
Montjoi
Castelsagrat
Durfort-Lacapelette
Lafrançaise
Valence d'Agen
Donzac
Golfech
Moissac
Tarn
Canal Latéral à la Garonne
Golf des Aiguillons
Golf de L'Estang
Les Cabanes du Port
Auvillar
Merles
St-Nicolas-de-la-Grave
Agen, Bordeaux
A62
Castelsarrasin
Montauban
Port Canal (To Compagnie Fluviale)
Canal de Montech
Les Guinguettes
Peyrecave
Abbaye de Belleperche
Garonne
Lachapelle en Lomagne
Gramont, Musée du Miel
Montech
Labourgade
Forêt d'Agre
St-Sardos
Beaumont-de-Lomagne
Lomagne
Gers
Bouillac
Grisolles
Fronton
Bradt
5km
5 miles
Haute Garonne
Toulouse

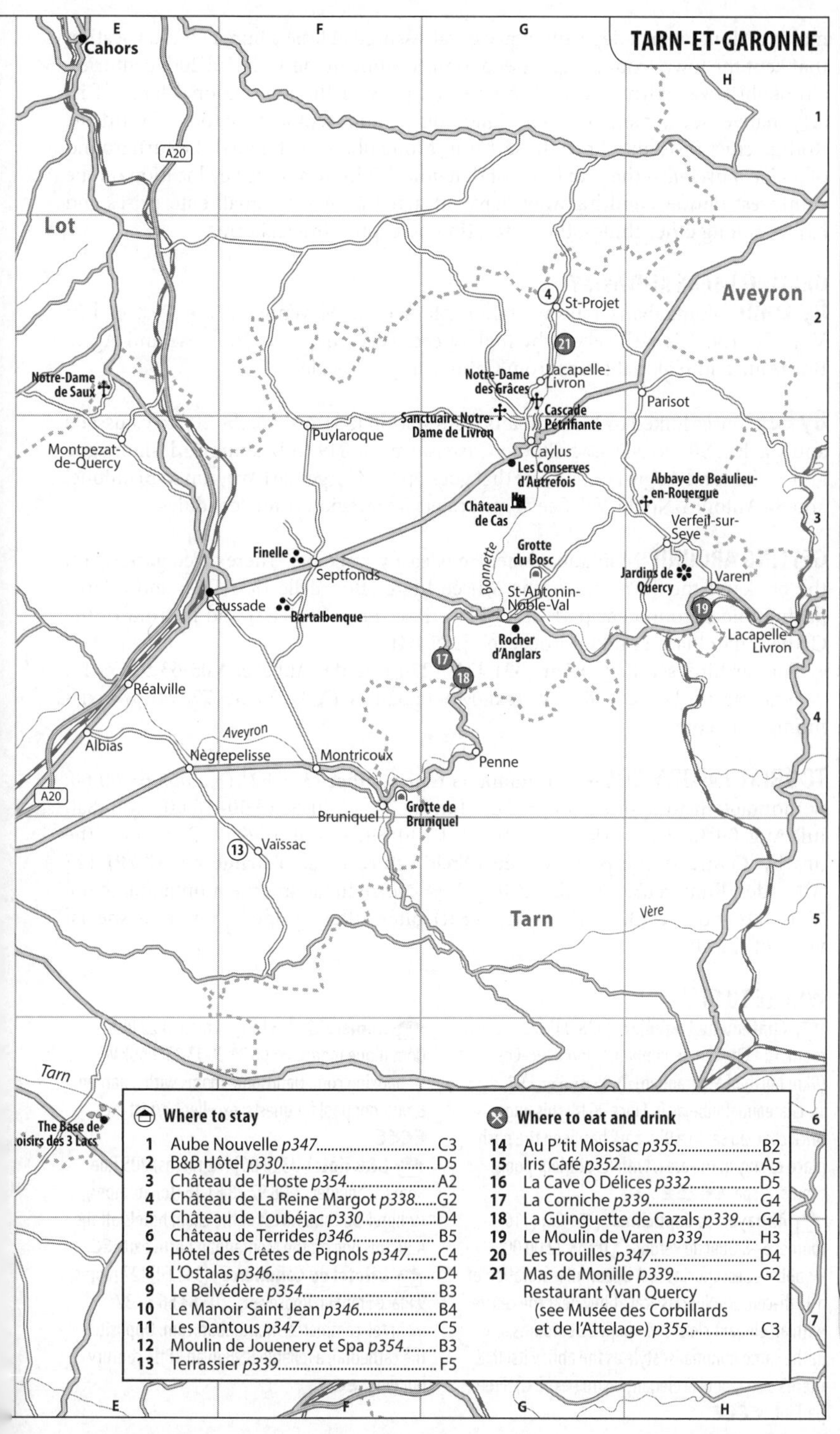
TARN-ET-GARONNE
Cahors
A20
Lot
Aveyron
St-Projet
Notre-Dame de Saux
Notre-Dame des Grâces
Lacapelle-Livron
Parisot
Sanctuaire Notre-Dame de Livron
Cascade Pétrifiante
Puylaroque
Montpezat-de-Quercy
Caylus
Les Conserves d'Autrefois
Abbaye de Beaulieu-en-Rouergue
Château de Cas
Verfeil-sur-Seye
Grotte du Bosc
Finelle
Septfonds
Bonnette
Jardins de Quercy
Varen
Caussade
Bartalbenque
St-Antonin-Noble-Val
Rocher d'Anglars
Lacapelle-Livron
Réalville
Aveyron
Albias
Nègrepelisse
Montricoux
Penne
Bruniquel
Grotte de Bruniquel
Vaïssac
Tarn
Vère
Tarn
The Base de Loisirs des 3 Lacs
Where to stay
1 Aube Nouvelle p347 C3
2 B&B Hôtel p330 D5
3 Château de l'Hoste p354 A2
4 Château de La Reine Margot p338 G2
5 Château de Loubéjac p330 D4
6 Château de Terrides p346 B5
7 Hôtel des Crêtes de Pignols p347 C4
8 L'Ostalas p346 D4
9 Le Belvédère p354 B3
10 Le Manoir Saint Jean p346 B4
11 Les Dantous p347 C5
12 Moulin de Jouenery et Spa p354 B3
13 Terrassier p339 F5
Where to eat and drink
14 Au P'tit Moissac p355 B2
15 Iris Café p352 A5
16 La Cave O Délices p332 D5
17 La Corniche p339 G4
18 La Guinguette de Cazals p339 G4
19 Le Moulin de Varen p339 H3
20 Les Trouilles p347 D4
21 Mas de Monille p339 G2
Restaurant Yvan Quercy (see Musée des Corbillards et de l'Attelage) p355 C3

making Montauban a departmental capital, assured at least a bureaucratic vocation that kept the town from complete economic decline in the 19th and 20th centuries, although it was burnished by the reflected glow of the international fame of its arty native sons, painter Dominique Ingres and sculptor Antoine Bourdelle, Rodin's chief assistant. Since the last war, Montauban has typified the turnaround of a *ville moyenne* – the proximity of dynamic Toulouse and its key location on the southwest railways and highways have attracted numerous small enterprises and led to, among other things, the restoration of its pink-brick charms.

GETTING THERE AND AWAY

By train Montauban's railway station off Avenue Mayenne, at the west end in Ville Bourbon, is well served by high-speed TGVs between Toulouse and Agen, Bordeaux and regional trains from Cahors and Caussade.

By bus Buses linked to Montauban's train station [331 A4] are the 203 to Caussade and Caylus, 801 to Moissac, 803 to Castelsarrasin, 849 to Beaumont-de-Lomagne and, in July and August only, a line that goes up the Gorges de l'Aveyron to Bruniquel and St-Antonin-Noble-Val. See w mestrajets.lio.laregion.fr for schedules.

GETTING AROUND Montauban's centre is easily walkable. There's free **parking** on the banks of the Tarn, under the Musée Ingres Bourdelle [331 D3]; and a large paying underground car park at 49 Place Prax-Paris [331 E3] and in front of the Cathedral in Place Franklin Roosevelt [331 E4].

For car hire, see **Rent a Car** [331 D4] (270 Rue de l'Abbaye; 05 63 91 33 12; w rentacar.fr). For a **taxi**, try Taxi Montalbanais (09 70 35 77 94; w taxis-montauban.com).

TOURIST INFORMATION Montauban's **tourist office** [331 E3] (05 63 63 60 60; w montauban-tourisme.com; Sep–Jun 09.30–12.30 & 13.30–18.00 Mon–Sat, Jul–Aug 09.30–18.30 Mon–Sat, 10.00–12.30 Sun) is at 1 Place Pénélope. The nearby **Centre d'Interprétation de l'Architecture et du Patrimoine (CIAP)** (25 Allée de l'Empereur; 05 63 63 03 50; w centredupatrimoine.montauban.com; 10.00–noon & 13.30–18.00 Mon–Sat) often offers guided tours and special visits of the city.

WHERE TO STAY

Château de Loubéjac [328 D4] (22 rooms) 14 Chemin de Jambau, L'Honor-de-Cos (9km north of Montauban); 05 63 65 61 03; w chateaudeloubejac.fr. Since 2018, this huge brick château set in a 9ha park has been the posh place to stay in the area, with its outdoor pools, tennis, & spa. **€€€€€**

Abbaye des Capuchins [331 C2] (116 rooms) 6–8 Quai de Verdun; 05 63 22 00 00; w abbayedescapucins.fr. A beautiful restoration of a 17th-century Neoclassical abbey near the centre, with an elegant cloister & chapel. Bedrooms are in the same minimalist style as the abbey itself, & there's a spa, pool & elegant bistro (€€€€). Free parking. **€€€€**

Numero22 [331 F1] (3 rooms) 22 Rue Dominique Ingres; m 06 31 20 13 13; book via w booking.com. Handsome rooms with a garden & outdoor pool for guests; excellent b/fast inc. **€€€€**

B&B Hôtel [328 D5] (72 rooms) 205 Rue Romy Schneider; 08 92 78 81 16 (toll number); w hotel-bb.com. Nicest of the chain hotels off the A20, this one off the Montauban north exit. **€€**

L'Hôtel du Commerce [331 E4] (27 rooms) 9 Place Franklin Roosevelt; 05 63 66 31 32; w hotel-commerce-montauban.com. Opposite the cathedral, a reliable B&B in an 18th-century building. **€€**

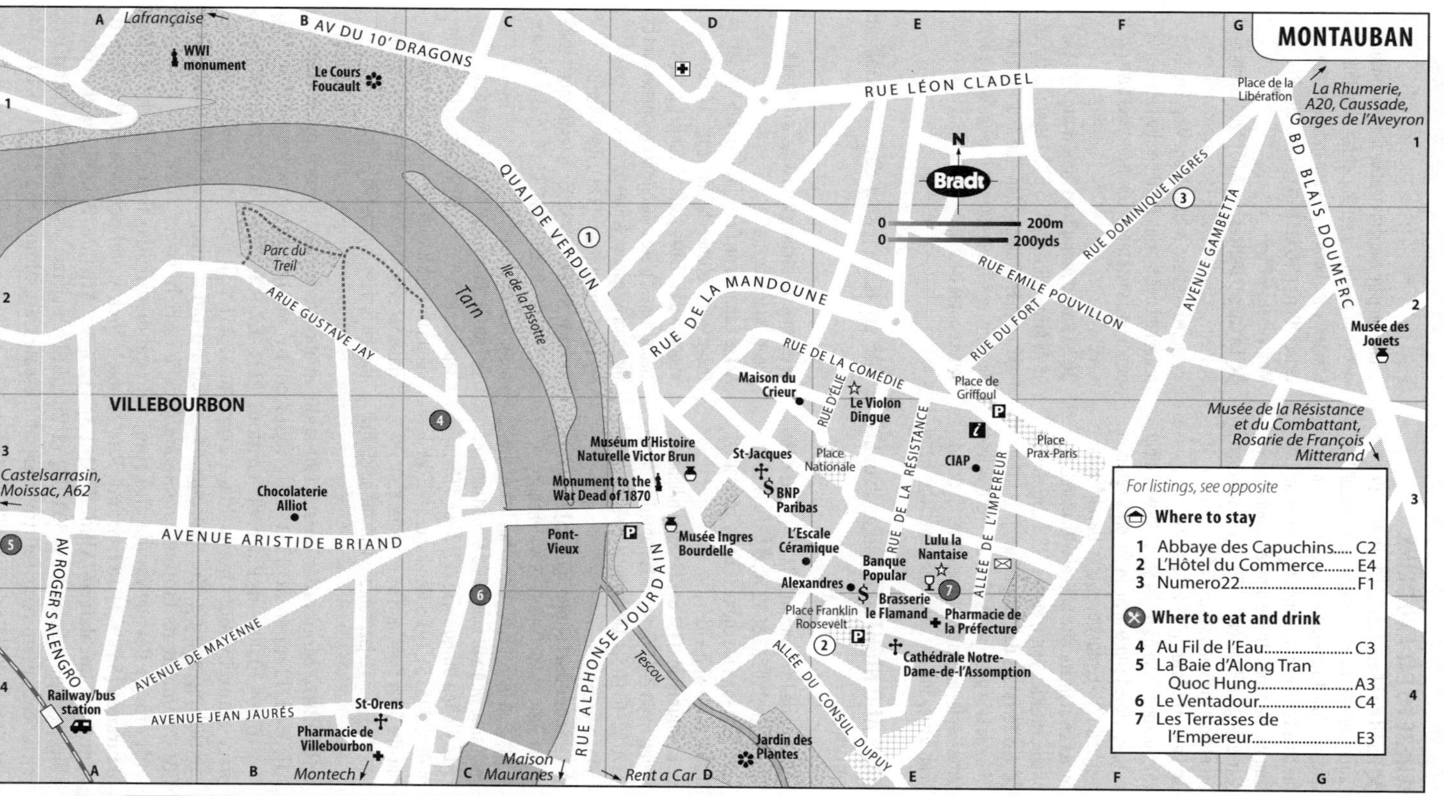
MONTAUBAN
For listings, see opposite
Where to stay
1 Abbaye des Capuchins..... C2
2 L'Hôtel du Commerce........ E4
3 Numero22.............................. F1
Where to eat and drink
4 Au Fil de l'Eau....................... C3
5 La Baie d'Along Tran Quoc Hung........................ A3
6 Le Ventadour........................ C4
7 Les Terrasses de l'Empereur........................... E3
Lafrançaise
AV DU 10' DRAGONS
WWI monument
Le Cours Foucault
RUE LÉON CLADEL
Place de la Libération
La Rhumerie, A20, Caussade, Gorges de l'Aveyron
BD BLAIS DOUMERC
Bradt
200m
200yds
QUAI DE VERDUN
Parc du Treil
Tarn
Ile de la Pissotte
RUE GUSTAVE JAY
RUE DE LA MANDOUNE
RUE EMILE POUVILLON
RUE DOMINIQUE INGRES
AVENUE GAMBETTA
RUE DU FORT
Musée des Jouets
RUE DE LA COMÉDIE
Maison du Crieur
RUE D'ELIE
Le Violon Dingue
Place de Griffoul
VILLEBOURBON
Muséum d'Histoire Naturelle Victor Brun
St-Jacques
Place Nationale
RUE DE LA RÉSISTANCE
CIAP
Place Prax-Paris
Musée de la Résistance et du Combattant, Rosarie de François Mitterand
Castelsarrasin, Moissac, A62
Chocolaterie Alliot
Monument to the War Dead of 1870
BNP Paribas
AVENUE ARISTIDE BRIAND
Pont-Vieux
Musée Ingres Bourdelle
L'Escale Céramique
Lulu la Nantaise
ALLÉE DE L'IMPEREUR
Banque Popular
Alexandres
Brasserie le Flamand
AV ROGER SALENGRO
AVENUE DE MAYENNE
RUE ALPHONSE JOURDAIN
Place Franklin Roosevelt
Pharmacie de la Préfecture
Tescou
ALLÉE DU CONSUL DUPUY
Cathédrale Notre-Dame-de-l'Assomption
Railway/bus station
AVENUE JEAN JAURÉS
St-Orens
Pharmacie de Villebourbon
Jardin des Plantes
Montech
Maison Mauranes
Rent a Car

WHERE TO EAT AND DRINK

Au Fil de l'Eau [331 C3] 14 Quai du Dr Lafforgue; 05 63 66 11 85; w aufildeleau82.com; closed Sun–Mon. In a leafy spot on the banks of the Tarn; refined regional cuisine – langoustine ravioli, truffle omelette, guinea fowl & an exceptional cassoulet (€20); good selection of wines from the southwest. €€€€

Le Ventadour [331 C4] 23 Quai Villebourbon; 05 63 63 34 58; w le-ventadour.com; closed Sun & Mon. In the brick vaults of restored 17th-century dyeworks, David Aranda serves an aromatic dish of beef with morels & other delicacies. *Lunch menus €18 & €30.* €€€€

Les Terrasses de l'Empereur [331 E3] 2 Rue de la République; 05 63 20 41 59; w les-terrasses-de-lempereur.business.site; closed Mon, & eves Sun, Tue. Michelin-starred chef Hervé Daumy prepares superb creative Mediterranean cuisine in an elegant setting with a beautiful wooden 'wine library', plus a grand panoramic terrace. Don't miss the best crème brulée in Montauban. €€€€

La Cave O Délices [328 D5] 1200 Chem. de St-Pierre; 05 63 63 69 69; w cave-o-delices.fr; closed eves Sun & lunch Mon–Wed. Excellent restaurant overlooking the Hippodrome. Creative dishes on a short menu. *Lunch formules from €19.* €€€

La Baie d'Along Tran Quoc Hung [331 A3] 18 Av Aristide Briand; 05 63 20 16 44; closed Wed, lunch Fri & dinner Mon–Tue, Thu. The best Vietnamese & Thai restaurant in town, with a big terrace at the back. €€

BARS AND NIGHTLIFE Montauban likes to kick up its heels after dark, especially in summer.

Brasserie le Flamand [331 E4] 8 Rue de la République; 05 63 66 12 20; f; 09.00–02.00 Mon–Sat. Big choice of beers, cocktails & snacks, often with a DJ.

☆ **La Rhumerie** [331 G1] 175 Rue Philippe Noiret; m 06 29 65 65 84; w larhumerie82.fr; 20.00–05.00 Sat. Lively music bar & dance club for the over 25s.

☆ **Le Nautic Bar Lounge** [328 D5] 11 Av de Toulouse; m 06 07 46 43 49; w lenautic-montauban.fr; 18.30–02.00 Thu–Sat. At the Port Canal, with a DJ from 22.00 & good mojitos.

☆ **Le Violion Dingue** [331 E2] 3 Rue d'Élie; m 06 37 90 53 51; w leviolondingue.fr; Wed–Sun. The 'Crazy Violin' puts on comedies & shows for kids, & blues & jazz concerts with the possibility of starting the evening with wine, a cocktail & cheese &/or charcuterie.

Les Cabanes du Port [328 D5] 125 Rue des Oules; w les-cabanes-du-port.com; 09.00–midnight daily. Tapas, seafood, burgers, pizza & ice cream; a great place to hang out on summer eves by the canal with music & live concerts.

☆ **Les Guinguettes** [328 D5] 993 Rue de l'Abbaye; m 06 85 33 82 06; w lesguinguettes-82.fr; 21.00–01.00, 22.30–05.00 Fri–Sat. Popular nightclub/disco.

☆ **Lulu la Nantaise** [331 E3] 6 Rue de la République; 05 63 63 00 99; f; closed Sun. Informal wine bar with a terrace & live concerts Thu & Sat eves, named after the mystery woman in the cult film *Les Tontons Flingueurs*.

SHOPPING Montauban hosts 190 stalls at its Wednesday morning **market** on Allée de l'Empereur [331 E3], followed by an organic market Wednesday (16.00–20.00) in Place de Griffoul [331 E2]; another large market takes place Saturday morning in Place Prax-Paris [331 F3]. You may find something interesting among the *brocanteurs* – second-hand shops in **Rue d'Élie** [331 E3]. Montauban's famous *mountalbane* cake (a rich, sweet yeast cake flavoured with orange flower, vanilla and rum, with candied fruits) is sold at the **Maison Mauranes** [331 C4] (82 Grand' Rue Sapiac). Pick up chocolates at the award-winning **Chocolaterie Alliot** [331 B3] (123 Av Aristide Briand; w chocolats-alliot.fr) and **Alexandres** [331 E3] (2 Rue du Dr Lacaze; w patisserie-alexandres.fr). Local ceramicists sell their art at **L'Escale Céramique** [331 D3] (14 Rue des Carmes; w potiers-terres-neuves.com).

SPORTS AND ACTIVITIES From the Port Canal, the **Compagnie Fluviale** [328 D5] (125 Rue des Oules; m 06 71 07 42 24; compagniefluviale.com; ⏲ Apr–Oct) offers a variety of cruises and excursions, including two days and a night on the Tarn in a barge. The **Base de Loisirs des 3 Lacs** [329 E6] (w basedeloisirsmonclar.com), 22km east in Monclar-de-Quercy, offers four pools (including a covered one), three lakes, a water park in the lake, little train and snack bar, etc. There are two golf courses nearby: 18-hole **Golf de L'Estang** [328 D4] (849 Rte de l'Aveyron; w golfdemontauban.fr) and the 9-hole **Golf des Aiguillons** [328 D4] (Rte de Molière; w golf-montauban-aiguillons.com).

OTHER PRACTICALITIES

$ Banque Popular [331 E4] 18 Place F. Roosevelt

$ BNP Paribas [331 D3] 60 Rue de la République

Hospital [331 D1] 100 Rue Léon Cladel; 05 63 92 82 82; w ch-montauban.fr

Pharmacie de la Préfecture [331 E4] 4 Place du Maréchal Foch

Pharmacie de Villebourbon [331 B4] 99 Av M Hamecher

Post office [331 E3] 6 Allée de l'Empereur

WHAT TO SEE AND DO

Place Nationale [331 E3] The finest gift bestowed by Alphonse Jourdain on the new town of Montauban is its central square. Although it was the prototype for the central bastide market square, none of the later squares can match its innovative, urbane sophistication. First off, it isn't even a square at all, but a more subtle, visually interesting irregular trapezoid with covered chamfered corners. The whole plan of the town echoes this slight distortion of the monotonous square grid.

Its unique 'double cloister' arcades date from 1144 and were originally built in wood; after a fire in 1614, they were slowly rebuilt exactly as they had been in warm brick, even though the style of vaulting was by then archaic (the year when each bay was completed is inscribed in the keystones of the vaults – the last reads 1708). The interior galleries functioned as covered lanes, the continuation of the streets that come into the angles of the Place Nationale; the outer galleries were given over to displays of merchandise. In the central square the Montaubanais bought their food, hanged their thieves and issued proclamations.

During the 17th-century fashion for homogenous squares, the city ordered that all the façades facing the Place Nationale should be rebuilt in the same style, with the attic storerooms lit by openings called *mirandes*. The sundial installed on the north side warns *Una tibi* ('Your hour will come!'); the metre bar set vertically in the southwest corner was put in place to instruct the locals when the Revolution standardised French measures.

Maison du Crieur [331 D3] (2 Rue Gillaque, just north of Place Nationale; ⏲ 11.00–18.00 Tue–Sat) This handsome 15th–18th-century building, used for exhibitions, is named after its figure of the town crier. Even now every Saturday, at exactly 11.44 the last town crier in France calls out the news of upcoming events in the city.

St-Jacques [331 D3] (Place Victor-Hugo; ⏲ 09.00–18.00 daily) This combination church, assembly and voting hall built by Montauban's consuls in the 13th century was erected as an expiatory church after the town's flirtation with Catharism. During the repairs following the Hundred Years' War it was given an octagonal bell tower which, like St-Sernin in Toulouse, has a curious change in design halfway up and still bears scars from Louis XIII's 400 cannonballs. The neo-Roman portal with its coloured-tile decoration dates from the 19th century; the interior is typically southern Gothic, with a large single nave. Down from St-Jacques, **Place Bourdelle** is named after Bourdelle's dramatic *Monument to the War Dead of 1870*, showing the influence of his master Rodin.

Muséum d'Histoire Naturelle Victor Brun [331 D3] (2 Place Antoine Bourdelle; 05 63 22 13 85; **w** museum.montauban.com; 10.00–noon & 14.00–18.00 Tue–Sat, 14.00–18.00 Sun; €4, over 65 €2, under 18 free) Located in the Neoclassical Tribunal de Commerce, this houses an immense collection of birds and animals, fossils (starring some unique Quercy primates from 65 million years ago), minerals, and the Orgueil meteorite that fell 15km south of Montauban in 1864, exciting much speculation about aliens from outer space; it's unique in having the exact same composition as the sun.

Pont-Vieux [331 C3] Planned by Alphonse-Jourdain, financial and technical difficulties prevented the erection of a bridge until King Philip the Fair was passing through Montauban in 1303, and the town consuls (as they would later buttonhole Napoleon) got the king to promise his assistance in raising taxes for the construction of their long-awaited bridge. Work on the 206m structure began in 1311 and was a technological *tour de force*; its seven uneven arches have stood up to the worst floods the unruly Tarn has sent down, including water so high in 1441 that it washed over the top of it. Originally the bridge resembled the Pont Valentré (page 262), but the three towers were demolished in the early 1900s to let more traffic through.

Musée Ingres Bourdelle (MIB) [331 D3] (19 Rue de l'Hôtel de Ville, 05 63 22 12 91; **w** museeingresbourdelle.com; 10.00–19.00 Tue–Sun, 10.00–21.00 Thu; €10, over 65 €5, students under 26 & under 18 free – admission includes the Muséum d'Histoire Naturelle) Recently reopened after a spectacular three-year restoration, the museum is housed in the big brick bishops' palace, built in the 1640s over the castle of the Black Prince as a symbol of the new political and religious order. After the Revolution, the building became Montauban's *mairie*, although later the mayor left the palace to serve as a monument to the city's favourite sons, painter Jean-Auguste-Dominique Ingres (1780–1867) and sculptor Antoine Bourdelle (1861–1929).

Ingres, whose donations to his hometown make up the core of the museum's collection, was tremendously popular in his time, a technical virtuoso whose icily perfect religious and mythological works fitted the mood of Napoleonic Neoclassicism; in fact many of his first paintings were kitsch propaganda pieces commissioned by the emperor. Ingres was an Academic artist from head to toe, and measured his success by the medals he won at competitions. His battles with the younger generation of Romantic painters, especially Delacroix, were legendary. The earlier paintings on display here were done when Ingres was still in the workshop of his master, the even more indigestible Jacques-Louis David.

The collection includes sketches and drawings, which show up the contrast between the Academic painter and the suppressed artist within. Ingres did much better at portraits, and also in mythological scenes such as the *Dream of Ossian*, a colossal canvas of ghostly figures in the sky, painted for Napoleon's bedroom (Ossian was the supposed medieval Scottish bard whose 'rediscovered' works, all fakes, nevertheless made a great impression on poets at the dawn of the Romantic era).

The **Salle Ingres**, the bishops' bedchamber, was partially decorated by Ingres's father, also an artist. It houses a little shrine to Ingres, with the great man's desk, his paints, a view of his studio in Rome, and his violin (he was an accomplished musician, as well as a painter). Not all the works are by Ingres. From his collection are archaeological items – an Etruscan burial urn and a black-figure Greek vase with the *Battle of Centaurs and Lapiths* which may be the best work in the museum – as well as a *Portrait of a Monk*, attributed to Van Eyck or Holbein the Younger, Raphael's *La Belle Jardinière* (with what looks like the Virgin with baby John the Baptist and Jesus, only minus the halos), a Masolino predella panel and a *Nativity* by Carpaccio, and one from Spain, a striking *St Jerome* attributed to Ribera. A flatulent historical echo is supplied by Ingres's spiritual ancestor, Charles Lebrun, the first director of the Académie: *Louis XIV in the Chariot of State*. The chilling 16th-century *Allegory of the Holy Innocents* captures the battle for hearts and minds during the Wars of Religion: baptised Catholic newborns go to heaven, but unbaptised Protestant babies must suffer eternal damnation.

Bourdelle gets a room in the first underground level with some 70 sculptures and 80 drawings donated by his family, including portrait busts of figures as diverse as Ingres himself and Krishnamurti, and a very Art Deco dance. Bourdelle's most acclaimed work, however, stands out in front of the museum on the square: the *Last Centaur Dying*, one of a dozen of his sculptures scattered around Montauban.

Down below in the **Salle du Prince Noir** (all that remains of the English castle), the museum keeps a small archaeological collection, including a Roman mosaic, and some medieval items – among them a nasty torture contraption subtly called the *banc à question*.

Cathédrale Notre-Dame-de-l'Assomption [331 E4] (20 Rue des Soubirous Bas; ☎ 05 63 63 10 23) Montauban's cathedral was rebuilt between 1692 and 1739, when Louis XIV sent down his top architect, Jules Hardouin-Mansart, to build a church worthy of the Counter-Reformation, celebrating the victory over heresy and, as always, his own glory. Unlike the warm red brick that epitomises Montauban, the cathedral shows its foreign, Parisian origins in its white stone and frostily perfect classicism. It has the tallest church door in Europe.

The vast interior is full of equally frigid 18th–19th-century furnishings, an *Entombment* (1925) by Marcel Lenoir (page 340) and one of Ingres's major works, the enormous *Vow of Louis XIII*, commissioned for the cathedral and painted in Florence. He exhibited it in the 1824 Paris salon, where it hung next to the gut-wrenching *Massacre of Chios* by Delacroix. To the Neoclassical heirs of Jacques-Louis David, Delacroix's work was 'the massacre of painting' and Ingres was declared the champion and upholder of Academic values; Delacroix sniffed that Ingres's painting was 'pure Italian', and a lifelong rivalry was born. It is certainly easy to see what Delacroix meant: the Virgin, Child and angels seem to have come straight out of Raphael's sketchbooks. Louis XIII is seen offering the Virgin his crown and sceptre, symbolising the kingdom of France. The subject could only have been suggested by a rabid Catholic (or a Parisian), as Louis XIII certainly didn't do Montauban any favours.

Le Cours Foucault [331 B1] In 1679, Montauban's Intendant Foucault initiated the greening of the pink city by planting thousands of elms on the banks of the Tarn, along the broad street that now bears his name, Cours Foucault. Enjoying a fine view of the historic centre, the Cours has been the city's most popular promenade ever since. Its focal point, closing the view between the long alleys of trees, is Bourdelle's *La France veillant sur ses morts*, a World War I monument inspired by the temples and sculpture of ancient Greece, typical of the sculptor's later career, when he moved from Rodin's romanticism to a more classical style.

Curiously, a small piece of the Cours Foucault belongs to the Osage of Oklahoma. In 1829, three members of the tribe showed up in Montauban, exhausted, starving and demoralised from a two-year tramp across Europe they had undertaken after white trappers had told them they could escape discrimination in America and become French citizens. The people of Montauban couldn't grant their wish, but they raised money to pay for their passage home. Some 160 years later contact was renewed, and a symbolic patch of France was donated to the Osage; every other year cultural exchanges take place in the summer and as of 1999 Montauban is a twin city with Pawhuska, the Osage city in Oklahoma. Learn more at the **Association Oklahoma-Occitania** (w oklahoccitania.canalblog.com).

Jardin des Plantes [331 D4] (Allées Consul Dupuy) These gardens created in 1860, have several rare species of tree, including a giant sequoia and gingko.

Musée des Jouets [331 G2] (770 Bd Blaise Doumerc; 05 63 20 27 06; w lemuseedesjouets.fr; mid-Jul–Aug 14.00–18.00 Wed–Sun, Sep–Jun 14.00–18.00 Wed, Sat–Sun; €5, ages 4–16 €3, family of 4 €15) Montauban's massive toy museum is full of fun and wonders, from model trains and dolls to the Eiffel Tower and Sagrada Familia made of Meccano, miniatures and more all donated by locals.

Musée de la Résistance et du Combattant [331 G3] (2 Edouard Herriot; 05 63 66 03 11; w museeresistance.montauban.com; 09.00–noon & 14.00–17.00 daily; closed 1st 2 weeks in Aug; free) Permanent and changing exhibitions cover the rise of Nazism to Liberation, internment camps in the region, and Free France. Next to it, thousands of roses in the **Roseraie François Mitterrand** [331 G3] explode into bloom in late May and June.

Villebourbon [331 A3] Over the Pont Vieux, Montauban's *faubourg* was named after Henri de Navarre, future Henri IV and France's first Bourbon king. A row of wealthy drapers' 17th- and 18th-century mansions, with shops and workshops on their ground floors, form a striking façade reflected in the River Tarn – the flood marker shows the horror of the 1930 flood when the river rose over 11.5m. Above all looms the tallest church tower in the department, attached to the church of **St-Orens** [331 B4], with its unusual Art Deco glass.

NORTH OF MONTAUBAN

This is the bit Napoleon gouged out of Quercy, the rolling hills that mark the transition in landscapes between the Massif Central and the Aquitaine Basin. You'll find surprises here, including a hat workshop and beautiful Flemish tapestries.

Caussade has a large **market** on Monday.

TOURIST INFORMATION

Caussade Carré des Chapeliers, Rue des Récollets; 05 63 26 04 04; w tourisme-quercy-caussadais.fr; 09.15–11.30 & 14.15–17.00 Mon–Sat, 09.15–11.30 Sun

Montpezat-de-Quercy Bd des Fossés; 05 63 02 05 55; w tourisme-quercy-caussadais.fr

WHERE TO STAY AND EAT

Auberge Le Gabachou (5 rooms) 2550 Rte de Paris, Montpezat-de-Quercy; 09 67 19 15 16; w le-gabachou.fr. Friendly roadside inn, run by Pascal, who loves motorcycles, & his partner, Évelyne, who does the cooking in the little restaurant (€€). B/fast inc. **€€**

Aux Lys d'Or (7 rooms) RN 20, Réalville; 05 63 31 04 78; w auxlysdor-restaurant.fr. Recently remodelled rooms, 5mins from Caussade. Also a sweetly old-fashioned restaurant (€€€) & bar with an €11.50 lunch menu. **€**

Eskualduna 6 Av du Gén de Gaulle, Albias (south of Caussade); 05 63 31 01 58; w eskualduna.fr; closed Mon–Tue. Now run by the 3rd generation, this informal popular Spanish Basque restaurant & grill house serves big steaks & seafood *à la plancha. Lunch menus €13.50–€35.* **€€€€**

La Table du Cardinal 3 Rue de la République, Montpezat-de-Quercy; 05 63 64 47 50; w latableducardinal.fr; closed Mon & eves Sun. The top gourmet choice here, with creative cuisine at affordable prices. *€19 menu served at lunch Tue–Sat & dinner Fri.* **€€€**

Le Regalsoupe 13 Av Dr Olive, Caussade; 05 63 63 75 77; w le-regalsoupe.fr; closed Thu & eves Wed. Minimalist décor & something different: Lyonnais cuisine (snails, quenelles, gratins Dauphinois, andouillette) by a Bocuse-trained chef. *€13.50 chalkboard lunch menu.* **€€€**

CAUSSADE The 'City of Hats' is a pleasant, bustling place with some good medieval buildings, including the *halle* and a landmark 15th-century brick bell tower in the Toulouse style. Small industries surround the town, including one that produced Maurice Chevalier's trademark straw boaters. Some of these are now in the hat museum, **L'Épopée Chapelière** (Carré des Chapeliers Rue des Récollets; 05 63 26 04 04; caussadelepopee; 09.00–11.30 & 13.30–16.00 Mon–Fri, Jul–Aug 09.00–11.30 & 13.30–16.00 daily; €4, ages 6–12 €1), along with films and history of the industry. **Hats Blocks Laforest** (see below) offers fascinating hour-long tours (mid-Jun–Oct, tours at 14.00 Mon; €4) of the hat world, in French.

Hat shops

Crambes 42 Av Mal de Lattre de Tassigny; w chapeaux-crambes.fr; 08.00–noon & 13.30–18.30 Tue–Sat. Winter & summer hats & caps.

Hats Blocks Laforest 37 Rue de la République; 05 63 26 04 04; w hatsblocks.com; 09.00–13.30 Mon, 10.30–12.30 & 14.30–19.00 Tue–Sat. For all kinds of creations, in a 13th-century building.

Willy's Paris 64 Av de Gral Leclerc; w willys-paris.com; 09.30–12.30 & 13.30–18.00 Mon–Thu, 09.30–12.30 Fri. A straw-hat specialist since 1824.

SEPTFONDS East of Caussade, Septfonds, another hat-making town, was named after its seven springs, and has some 15 dolmens from 3500–1700BC concentrated around **Finelle** [329 F3] and **Bartalbenque** [329 F3]. In 1939 the town hosted 16,000 Republican refugees from the Spanish Civil War, today marked by an austere Spanish Republican cemetery of 1939; it was re-used as an internment camp in World War II, when 295 Jews from Tarn-et-Garonne were rounded up in 1942 and sent to Auschwitz. The house of local hat-making *résistant* Raymond Peyrières is now the **Maison des Mémoires de Septfonds** (15 Rue des Déportés; 05 63 64 90 27; w septfonds-la-mouniere.com; May–Jun & Sep 14.30–18.30 Wed, Sat, Jul–Aug 14.30–18.30 Wed–Sun; other times by appt; €3) with exhibits on the camp, straw hats and local aviator Dieudonné Costes.

MONTPEZAT-DE-QUERCY This thoroughly medieval village of white stone retains its gate and arcaded square, as well as plenty of half-timbered houses. It grew up in the 10th century and in 1257, when its lord, Alphonse of Poitiers, granted it a charter as a free town, with rights to its own mill, a pigeon house and an oil press. In the 1300s, it produced a dynasty of churchmen named Des Près. Well connected at the papal court at Avignon, they brought one of the popes' architects home to build the **Collégiale St-Martin** (Rue du College; ☎ 05 63 02 05 55; ⏲ 09.00–18.00 daily; free). It makes a handsome setting for the family's Carrara marble tombs and the treasure they accumulated, including glittering medieval reliquaries and some lovely carved alabaster plaques from England. The real prize, however, is the series of tapestries hung around the apse, perfectly preserved 16th-century Flemish works commissioned by Bishop Jean Des Près of Montauban that tell the *Life of St Martin of Tours* with the colour and vivid directness of a comic strip. Woven to fit the very spot where they are displayed, each of the 16 scenes is accompanied by an Old French quatrain.

The vines growing on the limestone terraces here are destined for Vin de Coteaux-de-Quercy. They are dark, well-structured and fruity wines that can be drunk young or aged – and with some of the escalating prices of Cahors, they're a bargain, too. Find out more at the **Vignerons Du Quercy** (4555 Rte de Paris, Montpezat-de-Quercy; ☎ 05 63 02 03 50; **w** les-vignerons-du-quercy.com; ⏲ 09.00–noon Mon, 09.00–noon & 14.00–19.00 Tue–Sat).

Five kilometres northwest of Montpezat, off the D38, the 14th-century church of **Notre-Dame de Saux** [329 E2] (pick up the key at the Montpezat tourist office) has courtly 14th-century frescoes of the legends of *SS George and Catherine*, the *Childhood of Jesus* and the *Crucifixion*, discovered under the plaster in 1954.

UP THE GORGES DE L'AVEYRON

The Tarn-et-Garonne's northeast bulge, amputated out of the Rouergue and Tarn départements, has its best scenery, sliced through by the gorges of the languorous River Aveyron and its tributaries. It has the kind of unspoiled beautiful scenery and medieval villages that make this area a favourite for French film-makers, great kayaking and hiking, and perhaps more than its share of curiosities.

Markets take place in Caylus on Tuesdays and Saturdays, in Laguépie on Wednesdays and Sundays and in St-Antonin on Sundays.

GETTING THERE For summer buses, see Montauban (page 330). Regional TER trains on the Toulouse–Brive line stop at Laguépie.

TOURIST INFORMATION

Bruniquel 2 Rue de la Fraternité; ☎ 05 63 67 29 84; **w** bruniquel.fr/tourisme; ⏲ 10.00–13.00 & 14.00–18.00 daily

Caylus 20 Rue Droit; ☎ 05 63 67 00 28; **w** caylus.com; ⏲ 09.30–13.00 & 14.00–18.00 Tue–Sun

Laguépie 2 Place Henri Granier; ☎ 05 63 30 20 34; **w** tourisme-saint-antonin-noble-val.com; ⏲ Easter–Jun & Sep–Oct 10.00–12.30 & 14.00–17.30 Wed & Sat, Jul–Aug 09.30–13.00 & 14.00–18.00 daily

St-Antonin-Noble-Val 10 Rue de la Pélisserie; ☎ 05 63 30 63 47; **w** tourisme-saint-antonin-noble-val.com; ⏲ Jul–Aug 09.00–13.00 & 14.00–19.00 daily, other times shorter hours

WHERE TO STAY

La Résidence (4 rooms) 37 Rue Droite, St-Antonin; **m** 06 70 99 19 52; **w** laresidence-france.com. Charming British-owned B&B in the centre, with a little walled garden for enjoying a homemade b/fast (inc). **€€€€**

Les Gorges de l'Aveyron (5 rooms) Bruniquel; ☎ 05 63 24 50 50; **w** lesgorgesaveyron.com. Superb rustic chic hotel in a former watermill in its own private 5ha park along the Aveyron. There's an outdoor pool, & an elegant gastronomic restaurant (€€€€) with a €40 set menu. **€€€€**

Château de La Reine Margot [329 G2] (2 rooms) St-Projet, 10km north of Caylus; ☎ 05 63

65 74 85; w saint-projet.com. Rooms in the lovely castle with formal French gardens where Queen Marguerite de Valois once took refuge from the Protestants. €€€

Auberge Lion d'Or (5 rooms) 8 Rue Basse des Carmes, St-Antonin; 05 63 68 18 90; f. Charming B&B in an 18th-century inn near the centre with the original painted sign, knowledgeable hosts & a place to store bikes; b/fast inc. €€

Terrassier [329 F5] (18 rooms) Vaïssac (southwest of Montricoux); 05 63 30 94 60; w chezterrassier.com. Family-run for over 60 years, with a pool; the restaurant (€€€€) is excellent, with €14 lunch menus & duck burgers. €€

La Renaissance (9 rooms) Av Père Evariste Huc, Caylus; 05 63 67 07 26; w hotel-larenaissance-caylus.fr. A simple but tidy place to stay at in the centre of town, with a restaurant (€€) & garage (€10/night for cars or bikes). €

WHERE TO EAT AND DRINK

Le Moulin de Varen [329 H3] Rte de Laguépie, Varen; 05 63 65 45 10; w lemoulindevaren.fr; closed Wed & eves Sun. Set in a pretty old mill with a terrace overlooking the water, serving delicious meals (notably scallops) based on seasonal produce. *W/day lunch menu €25, w/ends €30.* €€€€

La Corniche [329 G4] Just off the D115 in Brousses, St-Antonin; 05 63 68 26 95; w brousses.wixsite.com/la-corniche; closed Mon & eves Wed, Thu, Sun. Tiny restaurant with lovely views from its terrace, where the chef runs a one-man show. Delicious place for a lazy lunch; bring cash. *1 menu €30.* €€€

Mas de Monille [329 G2] Loze near St-Projet; 05 63 65 76 85; w masdemonille.com; by reservation year-round. A *ferme-auberge* raising free-range black pigs (Porc Noir Gascon) in an idyllic setting, with a seasonal menu including their award-winning *boudin à la viande*. Wonderful hosts. *Set menu €28.* €€€.

La Guinguette de Cazals [329 G4] Caillol, Cazals; 05 63 68 20 84; w laguinguettedecazals.fr; May–Sep daily. Next to the beach at Cazals, in the centre of the Gorges de l'Aveyron, this place has been making locals & visitors happy since 1963. There's often live music. *Lunch menu €16.* €€

A la Table d'Antoine 5 Place Payrols, St-Antonin; 05 63 26 02 07; Jul–Aug 09.00–14.00, other times see f. Very popular with good reason for its fresh healthy food. *2 set menus only €14 & €17.* €

Brasserie Bélier Fontalès, St-Antonin; 05 81 04 86 96; f Verfeilbelier; Thu–Sun, also Wed in Jul–Aug. Lively craft brew pub with frequent concerts.

SPORTS AND ACTIVITIES The GR46 starting in St-Projet offers lovely walking all across this area; there's also an 85km bike route between Laguépie and Montauban. **Parc Aventure** (Turlande, St-Antonin; m 07 60 35 53 14; w parc-aventure-aveyron.com) has all sorts of zip lines & scary bridges; St-Antonin also has a beach and canoe and kayak rentals.

Acti Eaux Vives Marsac Bas; m 06 12 51 83 23; w actieauxvives.fr. Watersports, rock climbing & via ferrata on the Rocher d'Anglars.

Les Pieds dans l'Eau Rte de Marsac, St-Antonin; 05 63 68 24 80; w locationcanoe.com. Offers the option to paddle 10 or 17km downstream.

Nature escapade 22 Bd des Thermes, St-Antonin; 05 63 31 41 76; w nature-escapade.com. Canoe trips, SUPs & mountain bikes; also offers longer canoe journeys of up to 4 days.

Variation Chemin de la Plage, St-Antonin; 05 63 68 25 25; w variation82.eu. Offers canoes & kayaks, climbing, potholing, archery & bike rentals.

NÈGREPELISSE This bastide on the way to the gorges from Montauban is named after the blackened aprons of the charcoal burners who once worked here. It has a tragic history: in 1622, after failing to take Montauban after an 86-day siege, Louis XIII came here to pick on someone smaller; its 800 defenders were besieged, defeated, the women raped and the men all massacred, regardless of age. Today its château contains **La Cuisine, Centre d'Art et de Design** (Esplanade du Château; 05 63 67 39 74; w la-cuisine.fr; Sep–Jun 14.00–17.00 Tue–Fri, Jul–Aug 13.00–19.00 Tue–Sun; free) designed by Spain's RCR Arquitectes (winners of the Pritzker prize in 2017) dedicated to art, cuisine and design and what to do about the climate crisis, with frequent temporary exhibitions.

MONTRICOUX The gorge of the Aveyron begins (or peters out) at a town founded by the Templars. It has a 13th-century church, **St-Pierre**, topped with a 16th-century Toulouse-style bell tower; inside is a fresco from the 1920s by Marcel Lenoir. Marcel Lenoir? The name doesn't ring a bell? Then find out more in the **Musée Marcel Lenoir** (05 63 67 26 48; w marcel-lenoir.com; May–Sep 10.00–18.00 Wed–Mon; €5, ages 5–17 €2) in the Château de Montricoux. Briefly, Lenoir was born in Montauban in 1872 and died in Montricoux in 1931, but spent most of his career in the artistic whirl of Paris, where his work was admired by Braque, Matisse and Rodin. Since then, few artists have been more forgotten. Lenoir himself was partly to blame through his own stubborn integrity: he refused to accept any honours or scratch anyone's back – and the art world responded by boycotting his work. Lenoir also refused to be pinned down with an easily recognisable (and marketable) style; moving on from his early days under the Symbolist influences of Gustave Moreau and Mucha, to later experiments in Cubism, Surrealism and abstraction. He approached each new change of style with religious intensity, sometimes in religious subjects, such as his *Descent from the Cross, with Orchestra*. But there's more: the visit includes surviving frescoes and chapel of the Templar commandery that predated the château, sumptuous 18th-century rooms, and a new contemporary art museum featuring 100 paintings and sculptures by Alain Laborde (b1944; w alainlaborde.fr).

Vaïssac, 7km south, is renowned for its *cèpes* and a 1:130 scale model of Paris, located in the family garden of Gérard Brion, who spent 14 years creating **Le Petit Paris** (3225 Rte de Telarios; 05 63 64 24 80; w petitparisparc.com; May–Sep 09.30–noon & 14.00–19.00 daily, Paris by night: Jul–Aug 21.30 Tue–Thu, Oct–Apr 09.30–noon & 14.00–19.00 Sat–Sun & school hols (closed winter mornings), special lights: 15 Dec–10 Jan 17.00–19.00; €7, ages 3–18 €5, under 3 free). Apparently, it was neglected until Princess Diana's accident and all the locals came to see the Pont de l'Alma, especially after Brion added a wrecked Mercedes. Included in the admission are 50 famous monuments of France.

BRUNIQUEL A picturesque, Protestant stronghold and now an artists' colony high on the 100m cliffs at the confluence of the Aveyron and Vère, Bruniquel was founded by Queen Brunehaut (d AD613), a Visigoth, married to Siebert, the grandson of Clovis. She was as fierce as a queen on a chessboard, fighting a relentless war with the neighbouring queen Fredegunda, personally eliminating ten members of Fredegunda's family, until her own nobles tired of her cruelty and handed her over to her son, who, with a decided lack of filial devotion, tied her by the hair to a wild horse.

At the site of the Brunehauts' castle, there are now two **Châteaux de Bruniquel** (05 63 67 27 67; Mar–mid-Nov 10.00–17.00 daily, Jul–Aug 10.00–19.00 daily; €3.50, under 16 €2.50, under 5 free); the old one, home of the vicomtes of Bruniquel, dates back to the 13th century and was where the last viscountess lived until 1980, while next door is the 'new' château built in the 15th century by the vicomte's nephew after he had a quarrel with his own son, and sold the land to a cousin. The visit includes the 'Tower of Brunehaut', the kitchens, and an elegant Renaissance gallery.

The nearby **Maison des Comtes Payrol**, in Rue du Château, is a rare example of 13th-century civic architecture, with its original windows and a coffered ceiling. Two of Bruniquel's medieval gates are intact, including the picturesque **Porte de l'Horloge**, at the top of a winding lane. Below town there's an unusual 18th-century *lavoir*, built to wash horses after they worked in the nearby quarries.

In 1990 a young speleologist named Bruno Kowalczewski found the entrance to a cave overlooking the Aveyron, although the entrance was the size of a small poodle. He spent two years enlarging it so he could squeeze into the **Grotte de Bruniquel** [329 F4] where he found a vast gallery lined with animal bones left by ancient hunters and some unusual structures on the cave floor – two circles made of 400 pieces of stalactite across 112m. It made the headlines in 2016 when researchers were able to carbon-date the circles, thanks to a calcinated piece of bear bone wedged there, to 176,500 years ago, making these the oldest known work of architecture, ever, put together by the Neanderthals, perhaps for cult reasons. So many recent discoveries have shown that the Neanderthals were more sophisticated than anyone suspected even 30 years ago, but the fact that they were capable of architecture was a huge surprise. Research continues to this day.

PENNE The Aveyron cuts off a corner of the département of the Tarn, passing through a dramatic gorge; the best scenery and views are along the narrow corniche road, the D173, leading past this striking village with its insanely picturesque cadaver of a medieval **castle** (05 63 55 71 09; w chateau-penne.com; mid-Feb–Mar & Oct–mid-Nov 14.00–17.30 daily, Apr–Jun & Sep 10.00–13.00 & 14.00–18.30 daily, Jul–Aug 10.00–18.00 daily; Jul–Aug €7, ages 7–16 €5, other times €5/€3.50), once a stronghold of the Cathars, hanging with all the panache of an opera set over the cliffs. Since 2006 a family in medieval costume has been slowly restoring it, the old-fashioned way.

ST-ANTONIN-NOBLE-VAL At the confluence of the Bonnette and Aveyron, this is one of the oldest and most charming villages in southwest France. The Romans named it Nobilis Vallis; the St-Antonin of its name was tacked on when the body of the apostle of this area, Antoninus of Pamiers, floated downstream in a boat in circa AD305 in the company of two white eagles. In the 9th century an abbey was founded to house his relics; later a Cathar stronghold, it was sacked by Simon de Montfort in 1226; in the Hundred Years' War, it was occupied by the English, who left their name behind in the Rocher d'Anglars, the cliffs that loom over the village. The abbey was wiped off the face of the earth by the Protestants, who were themselves besieged in 1622 by Louis XIII. After the massacre in nearby Nègrepelisse (page 339), they paid a 100,000-livre ransom to avoid the same fate.

Because of its reliable water sources, it became wealthy from fabrics (note the drying attics on the old houses) and its tanneries. It is the only place in the southwest to be an official 'Slow City' (w cittaslow.org) dedicated to sustainability and conviviality. St-Antonin has changed so little it has been used as a film set (page 21).

Start with the lovely **Place de la Halle** and its Romanesque **Maison des Consuls** of 1125, the oldest civic building in France, latter Disneyfied by Viollet-le-Duc, who not only over-restored this rare example of Romanesque civic architecture, but added the incongruous Florentine belfry. On the first-floor gallery, note the pillar sculpted with Byzantine Emperor Justinian holding his famous Code of laws. The *halle* has a curious 15th-century Crucifixion, carved on a stone disc.

St-Antonin's labyrinthine lanes, many bearing pungent names like steep Rue Bombecul ('Show-off Buttocks Street'), have such a rare assortment of medieval houses that the town has been called an outdoor museum of secular architecture. Down by the river along the **Promenade des Moines** are the remains of the tanneries which once made St-Antonin's fortune, along with a working walnut-oil mill. Further along the river is a slate-roofed spa of 1913; the mineral spring here, the **Fontaine de Saltet**, rich in copper, has been a popular cure for urinary infections since the 18th century. Since 1990 it has been commercially bottled.

St-Antonin has plenty of boutiques and galleries, including the **Trésors d'Occitanie** (19 Place du Buoc; ⌚ 10.00–13.00 & 14.00–19.00 daily) selling the works by local artisans, and the **English Bookshop** (12 Rue Pelisserie, ☎ 05 63 68 22 66; ⌚ 10.00–12.30 & 14.30–19.00 Tue–Sat).

The well-marked paths around St-Antonin make for exceptionally fine walking, especially along the Aveyron and up to the **Rocher d'Anglars** [329 G4] with its wide-ranging belvedere over the gorge. Stalactite spotters can aim for the **Grotte du Bosc** [329 G3], 3km northeast (☎ 05 63 03 34 30; **w** grottedubosc.com; ⌚ Jun & Sep 14.00–17.00, Jul–Aug 10.00–17.30 (last tour) daily, other times 14.00–17.00 Sun & hols; €7.50, ages 13–17 €6.50, under 13 €4); there are remarkable formations and a little museum of prehistoric finds.

The D19 leads north to the **Château de Cas** [329 G3] (Espinas; ☎ 05 63 67 07 40; **w** chateaudecas.eu; ⌚ Apr–mid-Jun 14.00–18.00 Sat–Sun, mid-Jun–mid-Sep 14.00–18.00 Wed–Mon, closed some Sats for weddings; €7, ages 6–14 €5, under 6 free), a rather austere citadel that defended the Bonnette valley first built in the 9th century before becoming a Templar citadel in the 13th century, then damaged in the Revolution and World War II, and now restored to its 18th-century appearance, along with the gardens.

CAYLUS Further north, Caylus, the most important town on the Bonnette, occupies an amphitheatre at the highest point in Tarn-et-Garonne. The Counts of Toulouse built a castle here in the 1200s, and its ruins still dominate the region. It was stoutly Catholic in a surrounding sea of Protestantism; captured in 1562 by the Calvinists, 250 were put to the sword. Until the late 19th century, it was a phosphate boom town (population 5, 000, now reduced to 1,500). The medieval town is centred on the **Place du Marché**, with some arcades and a very sturdy *halle* with octagonal pillars.

The church under the mighty stone steeple is **St-Jean Baptiste**, endowed with an elegant seven-sided choir of 1470 and a naked, cross-less crucifixion, the *Christ Monumental* by Ossip Zadkine, carved in 1954 from the trunk of an elm. It caused such a scandal that in the 1960s a scarf was tied around the figure's loins, until Zadkine himself lopped off the offending member, leaving a Ken-dollish stump. It still causes controversy; in 2001, a gendarme had to be stationed in the church to protect the figure from intransigent Catholics who wanted to destroy it. Zadkine left a similar *Christ* in the church at Les Arques (page 294), but with far less controversy. Don't miss the nearby 14th-century **Maison des Loups** – as if to get back at these terrors of the Middle Ages, the wolves were made to do duty as rain spouts. Caylus is the HQ for **DRAWinternational** (**w** draw-international.com) run by artists John and Grete McNorton, who offer residencies and put on exhibits in Caylus in conjunction with les Abattoirs in Toulouse (page 387).

While in Caylus pick up patés, terrines, cassoulet, chocolates & wines at the 125-year-old firm **Les Conserves d'Autrefois** [329 G3] (Las Couchos; **w** lesconservesdautrefois.fr; ⌚ 09.00–13.00 & 14.00–18.30 Tue–Sat).

Around Caylus Two kilometres north, a geological curiosity waits just off the D97: the **Cascade Pétrifiante** [329 G3] – a waterfall so full of limestone that it now flows over a calcified spongey crust. Just west, the **Sanctuaire Notre-Dame de Livron** (1302) [329 G2], 'Our Lady of Liberation' in Occitan, was built after a pesky dragon in a nearby cave was axed by a bold knight, liberating the neighbourhood. Further north is **Lacapelle-Livron**, with another Templar commandery (rebuilt in the 1400s) with a church so fortified that it resembles a castle. For a less bristling house of God, visit the 15th-century **Notre-Dame des Grâces** [329 G2], just south, a miniature Flamboyant Gothic gem with a bird's-eye view across the causse.

Parisot, 9km east of Caylus, is a charming *village perché* with a 16th-century *halle* with intact measures, a 14th-century church of **St-Andéol** and a lofty castle still privately owned, set in a park filled with centifolia roses. In 1494 it gave birth to Jean de Valette, Grand Master of the Knights of St John, who founded Malta's capital, Valletta, and led the resistance to the great Ottoman siege of the island in 1565.

Then there's **Puylaroque**, isolated 13km west of Caylus, a beautiful 13th- and 14th-century hilltop bastide that resembles a miniature version of the famous hill town of Cordes near Albi, with a 12th-century church of St-Jacques and fine views all around.

VAREN This village's well-preserved medieval core is entered by way of a fortified gate named El-Faoure. The tiny lanes converge in the centre at a 10th-century Benedictine priory, **St-Pierre**, a barrel-vaulted, single-nave church from the late 1000s, which, unusually, has no door on its west front – originally the façade formed part of the town wall. The capitals in the choir, closed off by three mini-apses and two crypts, are among the most important from the period, decorated with sturdy knots, symmetrical face-to-face animals and biblical scenes. The adjacent 14th-century tower was the residence of the dean of the priory.

VERFEIL-SUR-SEYE A little 13th-century bastide north of Varen, Verfeil's 18th-century church of **St-Pierre-ès-Liens** houses a gilded tabernacle from Beaulieu (see below). Atop a narrow windy road just south, the **Jardins de Quercy** [329 H3] (Cambou; 05 63 64 46 22; w lesjardinsdequercy.fr; mid-May–mid-Oct 10.00–19.00 Tue–Sun; €7, ages 4–13 €3; no credit cards) offers a hectare of exquisite English gardens, complete with a box maze created by Jean Donies, member of the Royal Horticultural Society.

Three kilometres north, the **Abbaye de Beaulieu-en-Rouergue** [329 H3] (Ginals; 05 63 24 50 10; w beaulieu-en-rouergue.fr; reopening in summer 2022) is, like many Cistercian abbeys, isolated at the bottom of a wooded valley. Founded in 1144 by the bishop of Rodez, the present buildings were begun in the late 1270s after *routiers* destroyed the predecessor. In the Wars of Religion, the whole was stripped bare; the Parlement of Toulouse refurnished it in the 17th century, and the last Italianate stuccoes and marble chimneypieces were put in place just in time to be wrecked in the Revolution.

Used as a barn, the abbey was purchased in 1959 by Pierre Brache and Geneviève Bonnefoi who restored it with help from the state; today it houses their collection of contemporary art (Dubuffet, Hantaï, Viera DaSilva, etc) and annual summer art exhibitions. Because it was so often rebuilt, Beaulieu is an excellent example of the development of Cistercian architecture (and of the monks' increasing concern for physical comforts). The early 14th-century church is harmonious, with a beautiful portal and rose window. In the north crossing, a *porte des morts* survives – a door each monk went through but once in this vale of tears.

LAGUÉPIE In the very corner of the Tarn-et-Garonne, a pretty village at the junction of the rivers Aveyron and Viaur on the Conques–Toulouse route to Compostela has a romantic ruined **castle** (Jul–Aug 10.30–12.30 & 16.00–19.00

Tue–Fri, 16.00–19.00 Sat–Mon; free) and a sparkling river beach on the Viaur, with lifeguards in summer.

SOUTH AND WEST OF MONTAUBAN: THE LOMAGNE

The Tarn flows into the Garonne in a region called La Lomagne – the bit Napoleon nicked off the Gers. It's also known, after its hills, as *Gascogne bossue*, hunchbacked Gascony. This is one of the quieter corners of the département of fruit, where instead of orchards are rolling hills covered in late June with green sprouts resembling lollipops – the Lomagne has the ideal climate and soil for garlic.

GETTING THERE AND AROUND Bus 933 runs from Montauban station to Montech and Beaumont-de-Lomagne three or four times a day, but you really need your own transport to get around here.

TOURIST INFORMATION

Beaumont-de-Lomagne 1 Rue d'Église; 05 63 02 42 32; w en.tourisme.malomagne.com; 09.00–noon & 14.00–17.00 Mon–Fri, 09.00–noon Sat

WHERE TO STAY AND EAT

La Lumière de Migou (5 rooms) 38 Rue de la Font, Beaumont-de-Lomagne; m 06 74 71 77 78; book through w booking.com. Right in Beaumont's centre, rooms in an 18th-century mansion with a beautiful stone staircase. The owner offers an excellent table d'hôte for €30. **€€€**

Relais des Garrigues (33 rooms) Rte de Fronton, Grisolles; 05 63 67 31 59; w relaisdesgarrigues.fr. Modern red, grey & black hotel a 4min walk from Grisolles railway station & the Canal Latéral; the restaurant (€€€) specialises in hearty *cassoulet de canard* & other southwest standbys. **€€€–€€**

Le Saint Jean (14 rooms) 58 Av du Maréchal-Foch, Beaumont-de-Lomagne; 05 63 02 31 02; w lesaintjeanhotelrestaurant.fr. A reliable choice, with a good restaurant (closed Mon, lunch Sat & eves Sun; €) with a small but tasty menu, including frites fried in beef fat. **€€–€**

Bistrot Constant 25 Rue de l'Usine, Montech; 05 63 24 63 02; w bistrotconstant.com; daily. Superb dining on French classics in the former lock-keeper's house with a canal-side terrace, with plenty of choices on the €38 menu. **€€€€**

Auberge de la Gimone Av du Lac, Beaumont-de-Lomagne; 05 63 65 23 09; w aubergedelagimone.fr; lunch Thu–Tue, also dinner Fri–Sat. Reserve, come hungry, eat your way to duck heaven, then pop like a balloon. *Lunch formule €14*. **€€**

BEAUMONT-DE-LOMAGNE This pleasant bastide, founded in 1276 by the French, still has its original fortified church, coiffed with an octagonal 14th-century Toulousain bell tower, a handful of medieval houses and an even rarer survivor – its enormous wooden ***halle*** from the 14th century. Beaumont is famous for garlic; everyone has good clean blood, although the town dentists wear a look of continual dismay. The statue here of a 17th-century gentleman (a replica of the one the Nazis melted down) represents native son Pierre de Fermat (1607–65), a lawyer at the Parlement de Toulouse, fluent in six languages who was not only very, very smart, but was long suspected by many mathematicians of being a smart alec as well, leaving behind his famous Last Theorem (he scribbled it in a margin of a text, adding that he had the proof but it wouldn't fit in the space). Although his other theorems were proven over the centuries, it took until 1994 for British mathematician Andrew Wiles to finally discover and publish the proof. Fermat's birthplace, **La Maison Fermat**, will open as a museum in 2023 (see w fermat-science.com).

BOUILLAC Further south, lost in attractive rolling farm country, this village has a striking church of **St-Sulpice** (🕘 10.00–noon Mon–Fri) with a unique arcaded triangular *clocher-mur* – all that survived the Wars of Religion. Inside, however, in a glass case next to the choir, it has a treasure: the golden reliquaries from the 13th-century Cistercian abbey of Grand-Selve, secreted out before the abbey was smashed and burned in the Revolution – beautifully worked caskets and mini-churches of gold, filigree and precious stones from the 13th century. One, a present from Alphonse de Poitiers, contains a thorn from the Crown of Thorns purchased by his brother St Louis and installed in Paris's Sainte-Chapelle.

Just to the north begin the vines of **Saint-Sardos**, a tiny wine region famous as the only one that blends Syrah and Tannat, creating a distinctive wine that can take long aging, as well as dry and sweet white IGP wines, and Muscat rosé; try them at the **Vignerons Saint-Sardos** (2 Chemin de Naudin, St-Sardos; ☎05 63 02 52 44; **w** cave-saint-sardos.com; 🕘 Jul–Aug 09.00–13.00 & 14.00–19.00 Mon–Sat, Sep–Jun 14.00–18.00 Mon, 09.00–noon & 14.00–18.00 Thu–Fri, 09.00–noon Sat).

MONTECH On the Voie Verte 11km from Montauban, Montech was an old stronghold of the counts of Toulouse and has a fine 15th-century church with an enormous bell tower. It is in the centre of the 1,474ha **Forêt d'Agre**, which once stretched from Castelsarrasin to Toulouse. Donated by a wealthy couple to Moissac Abbey in AD680, the forest was the source of the monks' prosperity until 1361 when it was confiscated by the Crown; although now diminished and split by the railway, canal and motorway, it has shady paths to explore.

Montech is proudest these days of the world's first and only **Pente d'Eau** (1974) on the Canal Latéral, a slope where barges are hauled up by a pair of engines replacing five canal locks. Decommissioned in 2009, you can learn all about it on a discovery trail including a museum on a barge, starting at the visitor centre in a former paper mill (21 Rue de l'Usine; ☎05 63 64 16 32; **w** pentedeaudemontech.fr; 🕘 May–Sep 10.00–noon & 14.00–18.00 Tue–Sat; free; rent a canoe or kayak at CVIFS (**m** 06 70 00 63 53; **w** canoe31.fr).

Further south there is little to detain you, except perhaps a view of the canal around **Grisolles** and its charming **Musée Calbet** (15 Rue Jean de Comère; ☎05 63 02 83 06; **w** museecalbet.com; 🕘 15.00–18.00 Wed–Sat; free). Created in 1938 by local Occitan poet Théodore Calbet, this museum in a 17th-century house tells the story of sorghum straw brooms, the speciality here from 1856–1980, along with other traditional arts and crafts.

Fronton, east of Grisolles, gave its name to a vineyard dating back to the 4th century BC. Frontonnais owes its character to the Negrette grape (50–70%) brought back from Cyprus by the Crusaders. Grown on tiered terraces between the rivers Garonne and Tarn, AOP Fronton has a redcurrant fragrance, after a few years in the cellar, when it is the perfect accompaniment to cassoulet; the rosés are a fruity summer drink. Pick some up at Vinovalie, Cave de Fronton (175 Av de la Dourdenne, Fronton; ☎05 62 79 97 74; **w** vinovalie.com).

MOISSAC AND AROUND

Il n'y a rien d'aussi beau dans le Midi

Eugène Viollet-Le-Duc

There's one reason to make the trip to Moissac, but it's a solid five-star reason: the Abbaye de St-Pierre, one of the crown jewels of medieval French sculpture. The town of Moissac, washed clean of most of its character in a tragic flood in 1930 which killed more than a hundred people and destroyed more than 600 buildings in Moissac alone, led the French president to declare the first ever day of national mourning.

Less than ten years later, a house at 18 Quai du Port was used to shelter 500 Jewish children from across France and Belgium – common knowledge in Moissac, but no-one ever gave them away; when the local police got wind that a raid was planned, all the children were dispersed among the locals and never found. Ten Moissagais and the entire town were recognised as Righteous Among Nations – hence the shock in 2020 when the usual left-wing town elected a mayor accused of antisemitism from the party of Marine Le Pen, mostly through resentment over fruit pickers from Eastern Europe undercutting local wages.

Today Moissac busies itself taking care of the 15,000 pilgrims who pass through every year (from the traditional starting point at Le Puy, it's a quarter of the way to Compostela) and growing aromatic pale golden *chasselas*, 'the caviar of grapes', cultivated by the abbey in the Middle Ages and the first French fruit to attain AOC status in 1952.

GETTING THERE AND AROUND Moissac's station (Av P Chabrié) is on the regional line between Bordeaux, Agen, Montauban and Toulouse. For taxis, call m 06 32 10 63 36.

TOURIST INFORMATION

Castelsarrasin Allé de Verdun; 05 32 09 69 36; w ville-castelsarrasin.fr; 09.00–noon & 14.00–17.00 Mon–Sat

Lafrançaise 12 Place de la République; 05 63 65 91 10; w lafrancaise-tourisme.fr; 09.00–noon & 13.30–17.30 Mon–Sat

Moissac 1 Bd de Briennel; 05 32 09 69 36; w tourisme-moissac-terresdesconfluences.fr; 09.00–noon & 14.00–18.00, closed Sun Nov–Mar

WHERE TO STAY

In Moissac

Le Moulin de Moissac (36 rooms) Esplanade du Moulin; 05 63 32 88 88; w lemoulindemoissac.com. In a restored mill of 1474, this hotel offers a lively mix of old & new, with huge windows over the Tarn, a spa down in its brick vaults, a lively bar, a superb bistro-restaurant (€€€€) with riverfront terraces, & free parking. **€€€€**

Le Pont Napoléon (15 rooms) 2 Allées Montebello; 05 63 04 01 55; w le-pont-napoleon.com. Delightful old-fashioned place overlooking the Tarn bridge commissioned by Boney in 1808, who stayed here. It also has a contemporary bistro (€€). **€€€**

Le Chapon Fin (24 rooms) 3 Place des Récollets; 05 63 95 59 49; w hotelchaponfin.com. Little hotel near the abbey, with a bike garage, parking & a bar. **€€**

Around Moissac

L'Ostalas [328 D4] (12 rooms) 1080 Côte de l'Île, Lafrançaise; m 06 11 96 04 99; w domaine-lostalas.com. Eco-lodge on a 6ha farm with a pool, dojos, orchards & gardens offering yoga, qigong, meditation and more. Min stay 2 nights. B/fast & all activities inc; organic meals available, too. **€€€€€**

Château de Terrides [328 B5] (52 rooms) Labourgade, 20km south of Moissac; 05 63 95 05 20; w chateaudeterrides.fr. This handsome 13th-century brick castle has seen an extraordinary amount of often violent history, but in its retirement is a lovely atmospheric place to stay with a pool. **€€€€**

Le Manoir Saint Jean [328 B4] (10 rooms) 3619 Rte de Saint-Jean, St Paul-d'Espis; 05 63 05 02 34; w manoirsaintjean.com. Elegant Neoclassical house, 9km northwest of Moissac with a pool & spacious, bright bedrooms furnished with careful attention to detail. In summer, dine out on the restaurant's beautiful terrace, overlooking the rolling countryside (€€€€€). Continental or British b/fast available. **€€€€**

Marceillac (12 rooms) 54 Rue de l'Égalité, Castelsarrasin; 05 63 32 30 10; w hotelmarceillac.com. A delightful hotel in the centre, with 1920s-style rooms overlooking a central courtyard-garden; cyclists very welcome. **€€€**

Aube Nouvelle [328 C3] (9 rooms) 12.7km north of Moissac in Durfort-Lacapelette; 05 63 04 50 33; w aubenouvelle.chez.com. Charming little family-run inn on the Compostela route where the restaurant (€€€) serves dishes with a Flemish touch (seafood wartezoï, rabbit *à la flamande*, etc). **€€–€**

Hôtel des Crêtes de Pignols [328 C4] (12 rooms) 1167 Côte de Pignols, 4km northeast of Moissac; 05 63 04 04 04; w cretesdepignols.com. Friendly little Logis with French-American owners; there's a restaurant (€€), pool, bike garage & warm welcome. **€€–€**

Les Dantous [328 C5] (5 rooms) 1126 Chemin des Dantous, Castelsarrasin; m 06 62 61 19 91; w gitelesdantous.com. Rooms in renovated farm near the Canal Latéral, with a pool, games & boules court. The friendly owners also have a *gîte* sleeping 4. **€**

WHERE TO EAT AND DRINK

In Moissac

Le Florentin 8 Place Roger Delthil; 05 63 04 19 18; w leflorentin-bistrotgourmand.fr; closed Mon & winter. Right by the abbey, serving *foie gras de canard au Chasselas* & other delights. The same owners run the adjacent, less fancy Bistrot Gourmand, featuring *cuisine de marché* (€€). **€€€**

Le Fromage Rit 4 Place Roger Delthil; 09 67 47 28 42; f Restaurant-Le-Fromage-rit; closed Mon–Tue, lunch Wed & eves Sun. Restaurant with an international flair, & always great cheeses & wine. **€€**

Le Pigeonnier 4–6 Rue Poumel; 09 51 38 79 92; f LePigeonnierdeMoissac; daily. Laid-back place serving fresh organic food, vegetarian dishes & burgers with a concert on Sat evenings in summer. **€€**

Around Moissac

Auberge du Moulin 578 Rte de Toulouse, Castelsarrasin; 05 63 32 20 37; w lemoulindecastel.fr; closed Wed, lunch Sat & eves Sun–Tue. A great place for a guaranteed homemade dose of cassoulet, lamb, but also seafood & great desserts. *Lunch menus €16*. **€€€€**

Les Trouilles [328 D4] North of Lafrançaise on the D20, follow the signs; 05 63 65 84 46; w lestrouilles.com; booking only, closed eves Sun. Superb farm meals with plenty of duck. They also have 4 guest rooms (b/fast inc; **€€**), a pool & 4 chalets. *Set menus €30–€42, wine inc*. **€€€**

L'Art du Temps Lafrançaise; 05 63 65 80 30; w lartdutemps.com/wordpress2016; lunch daily, dinner Fri–Sat. Wine bar, restaurant & community centre with art exhibits, concerts & good food; check the weekly menu on their website. **€€**

SHOPPING Moissac's **market** takes place just south of the abbey in Place des Récollets 07.00–13.00 Sat–Sun. Visit the glass-blowing couple at **Ce Qui est en Verre** (9 Rue Jean Moura; m 06 99 81 51 46; w cequiestenverre.fr); for lovely enamel jewellery, see **Au fil d'Emaux** (2 Place Roger Delthil; m 06 73 20 94 45; w aufildemaux.com) near the cloister.

SPORTS AND ACTIVITIES Hire a bike for exploring the canal banks, or a canoe or kayak or SUP on the Garonne Rand'Eau Loisirs (220 Chemin de la Rhode; m 06 85 47 72 47; w randeau.net).

WHAT TO SEE AND DO

Moissac Abbey (Abbaye St-Pierre)

(05 63 04 01 85; w abbayemoissac.com; church 07.00–19.00 daily) The first Benedictine monastery was founded here by Clovis in AD506, commemorating his victory over the Visigoths. The battle had cost him a thousand men, whom Clovis declared would be remembered by an abbey of a thousand monks. Exactly marking the spot of such an important religious foundation being a very serious matter, Clovis, as the legend goes, climbed a hill

and hurled his trusty javelin, telling God to guide it where he saw fit. Gshshloop! went the javelin as it struck the gooey muck of a marsh. Never questioning God's peculiar choice, Clovis ordered his builders to get on with it. He had to order them three times. In the end they had to sink deep piles to support the structure. No-one knows if the story has a germ of truth in it, or if the monks made it up to explain their annoying problems with rising damp.

One of Clovis's successors, Dagobert, put the abbey under royal protection, thanks to the influential bishop of Cahors, St Didier (AD630–55), who according to some accounts was the true father of Moissac. Although royal protection was promised into the 9th century, the Merovingian and Carolingian kings proved to be too far away to be of much help when the abbey was sacked by the Arabs in AD721 and AD732 (the year of their defeat at Poitiers), then by the Normans in AD850 and by the Magyars in AD864. Fed up with royal 'protection', the abbots placed themselves under the counts of Toulouse. After a roof collapsed in 1030 and a fire in 1042, the monastery was in such spiritual and material disorder that the counts gave it to Cluny; the monks there, noting its key position along one of the main pilgrimage routes to Compostela, sent money for its restoration and a new abbot, Durand de Bredon, who was also bishop of Toulouse and who consecrated the new church on 6 November 1063.

Because of Moissac's close links with Toulouse, Simon de Montfort sacked it during the Albigensian Crusade in 1212; although Raymond VII managed to recapture the abbey in 1222, he was helpless to save the 210 Cathars burned by the Inquisition here in 1234. These human bonfires marked a turning point in the abbey's popularity; in 1466 a papal bull stripped Moissac and all its properties from Cluny and put it under absentee *abbés commanditaires*, who sucked up most of the rents due to the abbey. By 1626 the monks had been replaced by a chapter of canons. Louis XIV's finance minister, Colbert, purchased Moissac's library and moved it to Paris, and many of the abbey buildings were demolished on the eve of the Revolution, which could find no better use for the surviving monastery than as a saltpetre works, after taking care to surgically guillotine the carved figures of the greatest Romanesque cloister in France.

In 1847 Viollet-le-Duc was summoned by the then superintendent of historical monuments, Prosper Mérimée, to restore the majestic porch. He had hardly begun in 1850 when along came a cohort of philistines who made the *sans-culottes* look like schoolboys – the builders of the Bordeaux–Toulouse railway – who announced that the cloister was in the way of the line that someone in Paris had drawn for the tracks. A huge battle ensued with the preservationists, and, although the tracks were realigned at the last moment, the railway men had their evil way with the splendid refectory and kitchens.

The porch Given Moissac's record of trouble, the great abbot Ansquitil decided in 1115 to fortify the church with a tower. Sheltered underneath is the sublime porch, one of the most powerful and beautiful works of the Middle Ages; the men who commissioned it are remembered in the two statues on pilasters off on either side, Abbot Ansquitil on the left and on the right Abbot Roger (1115–35), who completed the work after Ansquitil's death.

The **tympanum**, originally vividly painted, rests on a lintel recycled from a Gallo-Roman building, decorated with eight large thistle flowers and enclosed in a cable or vine, spat out by a monster at one end and swallowed by another monster at the other. The main scene represents one of the key visions of the Apocalypse (Rev. 4: 2–8), of Christ sitting in the Judgement of Nations, with the Book of Life in his hand

('And he who sat there appeared like jasper and carnelian, and round the throne was a rainbow that looked like an emerald...and before the throne there is as it were a sea of glass, like crystal'). You might notice that this Christ has three arms, one on the book, one raised in blessing, and another on his heart, but please don't ask for an explanation: no-one's come up with a convincing one yet.

The four symbols of the Evangelists twist to surround him, and two seraphim, carrying scrolls representing the Old and New Testaments, are squeezed under the rainbow. The rest of the tympanum is occupied by the 24 Elders, no two alike, each gazing up from their thrones at Christ, 'each holding a harp, and with golden bowls full of incense, which are the prayers of the saints'. Most writers describe the fear and awe in the Elders' eyes, but in actual fact they don't look frightened at all, and in place of harps they all play the medieval proto-violin, the rebec. The whole wonderfully rhythmic composition could just as easily be an old-timers' band raising their glasses in an intermission toast to a stern but respected and beloved bandleader.

But that's not all. The central pillar of the door, the **trumeau**, is sculpted with three pairs of lions in the form of Xs, symbolically guarding the church (others prowl about the capitals of the tower). Note the scalloped edges of the doorway, a design picked up from Moorish Spain. On either side of the door are tall relief figures: St Peter with his keys, stepping on a dragon (left); Isaiah, whose scroll prophesies the coming Messiah (right); and, on the outer sides of the porch, a severe St Paul and a gentle, dreamy-eyed Jeremiah (also holding a scroll) – elongated, stylish, supple figures that sway and almost dance, most probably from the same chisel that sculpted the wonderful Isaiah at Souillac (page 252).

To the right of the portal are scenes from the life of the Virgin – the *Annunciation, Visitation* and *Adoration of the Magi*; to the left, poor Lazarus's soul is taken into the bosom of Abraham while, below, the soul of the rich, feasting Dives is carried off in the other direction. Below him, you can make out a miser with demons on his shoulder as he refuses alms to a beggar, while to the left is Lust, serpents sucking at her breasts while an amused, very Chinese demon looks on. Up above the porch on the cornice – hiding, but in plain sight – is a large figure blowing a horn, perhaps Gabriel. Few visitors ever notice him.

The church Inside the porch, the vaulted square of the narthex has some excellent Romanesque capitals, carved with voluptuous vegetation playfully metamorphosed into animals; one shows *Samson wrestling with a lion*. The church's interior had to be rebuilt in 1430 and can't begin to compete with the fireworks on the portal. You can see the foundations of the Romanesque church of 1180 (along the bottom of the Gothic nave), which like that at Cahors was crowned with a row of domes; unlike Cahors, they collapsed and have been replaced with Flamboyant Gothic vaults. Only one chapel retains its 15th-century geometrical murals, which inspired the restoration on the other walls. Some of the church's polychrome sculpture survives, especially a 12th-century *Christ* and, from the 15th century, the *Flight into Egypt* with a serious-minded donkey, the beautiful *Entombment* and a *Pietà* (the figure with the swollen head is Gaussen de la Garrigue, consul of Moissac). The Baroque organ consul bears the arms of Cardinal Mazarin, *abbé commanditaire* from 1644 to 1661 and one of the most successful grafters of all time.

The cloister (🕘 Apr–Jun & Oct 10.00–noon & 14.00–18.00 daily, Jul–Sep 10.00–19.00 daily, Nov–Mar 13.30–17.00 daily; €6.50, ages 12–18 €4.50, ages 7–12 €1, under 7 free, family with 2 children €14) Behind the church is the abbey's serenely magnificent cloister, built by abbots Durand de Bredon and Ansquitil. After Simon de Montfort sacked Moissac, the arches had to be rebuilt, and were given a gentle hint of a Gothic point (1260), but all the 76 magnificent capitals, set on alternating paired and single slender columns of various coloured marbles, come from the end of the 11th century; they are the oldest in situ in France. They also mark a major artistic turning point, away from the immobile, rather stiff, hieratical figures of the great Guilduin (as in Toulouse's St-Sernin) towards more fluid, stylised poses with a sense of movement, exquisite modelling, and a play of light and shadow hitherto unknown in Romanesque sculpture. The capitals are carved with foliage inspired by Corinthian capitals, but with luxuriant virtuosity; others have birds and animals intertwined.

Some 46 capitals tell the lives of the saints – don't miss the dynamic martyrdoms: St Lawrence burning on the grill while two Romans blow on the flames; St Martin dividing his cloak with the beggar; St John the Baptist and the feast of Herod; St Stephen being stoned; St Peter upside down on his cross next to St Paul's beheading; a capital set near a little niche that once contained some of their relics. Other scenes are rare – the *City of Jerusalem vs Unholy Babylon*, the *Story of Nebuchadnezzar*, and *Shadrach, Meshach and Abednego in the Furnace.* At the corners and in the centre of each gallery are square pillars, covered with the tops of Roman sarcophagi; the corners are carved with bas-reliefs of eight apostles, the 'pillars of the Church'; the central pillar in the east gallery has an effigy of Abbot Durand de Bredon, while on the west there's the dedication inscription: 'In the year of the Incarnation of the eternal Father 1100, this cloister was completed in the time of Lord Ansquitil, Abbot, Amen.' For more details, see Cenobium (**w** cenobium.isti.cnr.it/moissac).

Off the cloister, the 13th-century **chapel of St-Ferréol** has faint frescoes of its eponymous saint curing the ill; it now contains a museum of reliefs. Near the entrance, a narrow stair leads up to the mysterious **Upper Chapel** built of a dozen arches linked in a central oculus. This has been interpreted as a symbolic representation of heaven, or the New Jerusalem. As in similar constructions around Europe, whatever ceremonial or liturgical functions it might have had are lost in time. There are two ways to enter it, the broad door for the many, and a narrow one leading into the cloister for the monks.

Also in Moissac The **Canal Latéral** is here spanned by the **Pont St-Jacques**, one of the very last of the revolving bridges that permitted canal barges to pass. The peaceful residential 'island' created by the Tarn and the Canal offers pretty views of the river, its various mills and the wooded **Île de Beaucaire**, home of kingfishers and other birds. Upstream, the impressive 356m **Pont Canal du Cacor** takes the canal over the Tarn.

AROUND MOISSAC

Castelsarrasin Although the Arabs never built a castle here in their 8th-century thrust into France, Castelsarrasin, the Tarn-et-Garonne's second city, did have a famous six-towered 12th-century stronghold built by the counts of Toulouse, who picked up a few stylistic tips during their many journeys to the Middle East; hence Castellum Sarracenum. The castle's defenders were so terrified of Simon de Montfort in 1212 that they gave up without a fight. They were more stalwart in the Wars of Religion against the Huguenots of Montauban, only to have their exotic castle razed in the 1600s.

Castelsarrasin still has the grid plan laid out by the counts, and, more unusually, the virtuous Revolutionary names of its oldest streets, reinstated in 1876 by a mayor in the Third Republic: look for *rues* named Surveillance, Development, Peace, Friendship, Hospitality, Wisdom, Discretion and Equality, with Liberty Square in the centre. At 6 Place Lamothe-Cadillac lived the founder of Detroit, Antoine de Lamothe-Cadillac (see below). The church of **St-Sauveur** (Place de la Raison; ☎ 05 81 78 10 82; **w** eglise-st-sauveur.edan.io; ⌚ 09.00–10.30 Tue & Thu, 09.00–19.00 Sat, 10.00–noon Sun) was founded by the Moissac monks in AD961 and rebuilt in 1260 in the southern Gothic style, all in brick, its heptagonal apse added in the 15th century. It boasts magnificent Baroque woodwork, especially the elaborate organ console, crowned with wooden statues of angels and King David as conductor, carved choir stalls (39 of the original 80), the pulpit, and the pair of prayer stools, one carved with a Virgin and a unicorn, from Belleperche.

Five kilometres south, the **Abbaye de Belleperche** [328 C5] (Rte de Belleperche, Cordes-Tolosannes; ☎ 05 63 95 62 75; **w** musee-arts-de-la-table.fr; ⌚ Mar–Apr & Oct–Nov 14.00–17.00 Tue–Fri, May–Sep 10.00–18.00 Tue–Sat, 14.00–18.00 Sun; €2, under 18 free) is true to its name, prettily perched directly on the Garonne. It was founded in 1143, when local families sent a special request to the abbot of Clairvaux for permission to establish an abbey; according to legend, St Bernard himself came along to help set it up. In its glory days it had 200 monks and was noted for its magnificence; Pope Clement V and François Ier were among its guests. Nearly all was destroyed in the Wars of Religion. The church was rebuilt at the end of the 16th century, and the last work was done in 1760, just in time for it to be sold to speculators in the Revolution, who dismantled it. The enormous monastery, however, was used as a farm and survived intact, and much has been restored in the last 30 years; today it houses the **Tableware Museum**, something the French have always been good at from the Middle Ages up to the present. It is especially proud of its antique Chinese teapots.

St-Nicolas-de-la-Grave Here the swollen confluence of the big rivers makes a recreational lake, a favourite for small sailing boats as well as migratory birds. There's a **castle** with four towers built by Richard the Lionheart in the centre of town, which later belonged to the abbots of Moissac, and a church with a Toulouse-style bell tower and porch.

St-Nicolas was the birthplace of the founder of Detroit, Antoine de Lamothe-Cadillac (1658–1713), a debt Motown has acknowledged by converting his birthplace, near the centre of the village, into the **Musée Lamothe-Cadillac** (7 Rue Lamothe Cadillac; ☎ 05 63 94 82 81; **w** stnicolasdelag.online.fr/musee; ⌚ by appt; free) – the US state of Michigan's only historic site in Europe. Lamothe had gone to Canada to seek his fortune and fight the English, then founded Detroit as a commercial base linking New France (Louisiana) to Canada. 'The worst scoundrel ever to set foot in New France', according to one historian, Lamothe introduced slavery into New France and sold alcohol to native Americans; in 1717, when he returned to France, the king threw him in the Bastille…before he traded Detroit for Castelsarrasin (he may not have had a choice). He took the name 'Cadillac' from a château near Bordeaux (page 119), which General Motors also preferred to 'Lamothe', which sounds lightweight and fly-by-night to American car-buying ears.

LAFRANÇAISE By 1271, when King Philip the Bold got around to founding this hilltop bastide, they had run out of names and simply called it Villa Francese, which in 1348 must have seemed like a red flag to a bull because the English took it 13 times, although the French under the bold Aymeric de Rochechouard took it back each time. Nicknamed the Belvédère du Quercy it enjoys a grand panoramic view over the Tarn's confluence with the Aveyron, which you can inspect closer in a canoe (05 63 31 56 43; w canoe-tarnetgaronne.fr; Jul–Aug); the village also has a lake and lovely pool at the **Vallée des Loisirs**.

DOWN THE GARONNE

Heading down the big river from Moissac is melon- and wine-growing country, where you can find out all about goose quill pens, nuclear power and life in the good old days and visit a Renaissance château and a church with an opera house décor.

TOURIST INFORMATION

Auvillar Couvent des Ursulines; 05 63 39 89 82; w officedetourismedesdeuxrives.fr; Apr–Sep 10.00–12.30 & 14.00–18.00 daily, Oct–Mar 14.00–17.00 Tue–Sat

Valence-d'Agen 27 bis Rue de la République; 05 63 39 61 67; w officedetourismedesdeuxrives.fr; 09.00–noon & 14.00–18.00 Tue–Sat

WHERE TO STAY AND EAT

Hotel de l'Horloge (11 rooms) Place de l'Horloge, Auvillar; 05 63 39 91 61; w hoteldelhorlogeauvillar.com. An older hotel of character; the restaurant (€€€) uses locally sourced ingredients. **€€€–€€**

Le Tout Va Bien (21 rooms) 30 Place Sylvain Dumon, Valence d'Agen; 05 63 39 09 26; w hotel-letoutvabien.fr. 'The Everything Is Fine' says it like it is; nice rooms, nice restaurant (€€) & a nice price. **€€**

Iris Café [328 A5] Bardigues, 4km south of Auvillar; 05 63 39 05 58; w iriscafe.fr; closed Sun–Mon. In a pretty village entered through a row of plane trees, the former auberge offers good & simple food, served on the wide terrace with views. **€€**

Le Petit Palais 7 Place de l'Horloge, Auvillar; 05 63 29 13 17; ; closed Thu & eves Wed. Nothing fancy; just delicious seasonal dishes. **€€**

AUVILLAR In the heart of melon land, aim for the lovely red-brick village of Auvillar, its name derived from the Latin Alta Villa – High House. Once a fief of the Counts of Armagnac, Auvillar's strategic location on the Garonne and its important port saw it badly battered in the Hundred Years' and Religious Wars, but it recovered nicely, and in the 18th century enjoyed a little economic boom based on goose quills for pens and painted earthenware tableware (the last of the 20 little factories closed in 1909). It's a happy village that after decades in the doldrums has picked itself up by the bootstraps.

Auvillar's very fetching **Place de la Halle**, which, already defying the usual bastide geometry with its triangular shape, goes a step further in its unique circular **market**, rebuilt in 1828, with Tuscan columns, a tile roof and medieval grain measures intact and ready for use. Back then, grain was measured by the *poignée*, or fistful, the equivalent of 13kg – some fists! Next to the *poignée* measure is a 19th-century one in metal. Examples of Auvillar's earthenware, quills and objects tracing the history of river transport and life (the sailors' motto was 'I am wicked on land but a gentleman on the water') are in the **Musée du Vieil Auvillar** (05 63 39 89 82; mid-Oct–mid-Apr 14.30–17.30 Sat–Sun, summer 14.30–17.30 Wed–Mon; €3, under 12 free; guided tours of the village available as well during the same hours).

The **Promenade du Château** offers views down the Garonne. Note the alarming flood markers from 1930. Auvillar's war-scarred riverside church of **St-Pierre**, by its sheer size, hints at the town's importance in the Middle Ages, when it produced the cantankerous Marcabru (see box, below). Just to the east in **Merles**, seek out **Henri IV's oak**, 12m in circumference where the king, his wife Margot, his 44 knights and scores of courtiers stopped on a hot day in 1579 on the road from Nérac to Montauban to enjoy a picnic and to drink from the nearby spring.

VALENCE-D'AGEN This pretty town on the Garonne started as an English bastide of 1283. Today it gets on as best it can, proud of its two monumental *lavoirs* in the shadow of the steaming concrete towers of the nuclear plant at **Golfech**, producer of half of Occitanie's electricity. A new visitor's centre (☎05 63 29 39 06; w entrepriseetdecouverte.fr/visite/edf-centrale-nucleaire-de-golfech; ⏲ see their website) offers guided tours dedicated to nuclear and hydro-electricity or of the elevator built for migratory fish.

DONZAC West of Valence on the D12, Donzac has a rather ambitious museum of the 'how we used to live' kind, with its 20,000 items in the **Conservatoire de la Ruralité et des Métiers d'Autrefois** (1679 Av du Brulhoise; ☎05 63 29 21 96; w officedetourismedesdeuxrives.fr; ⏲ Apr–Jun & Sep 14.00–18.00 Wed–Sun, Jul–Aug 10.00–12.30 & 14.00–18.30 daily; €5, ages 12–17 €4, under 12 free, family €8), with, among other things, reconstructed workshops, old farm machinery, regional pottery, crafts and a boutique.

Like Layrac (page 303), it produces Côtes du Brulhois; you can visit the local winegrowers at the **Vignerons du Brulhois** (3458 Av du Brulhois; ☎05 63 39 91 92; w vigneronsdubrulhois.com).

MARCUBRU THE MISOGYNIST

The courts of love of Eleanor of Aquitaine had a role in changing attitudes towards women, which until then had been influenced by the Church's opinion that women, the daughters of Eve, were the source of Original Sin and deserved to be nothing but the property of men. With an astute mix of what we might call today 'politically correct' translations of Ovid, as well as Arthurian legend and Occitan troubadour poetry, Eleanor and her daughters (especially Marie de Champagne, her firstborn with Louis VI) formulated a startling alternative: that men were the property of women. The queen and her ladies were the judges of the new chivalric standards of behaviour of a knight towards his lady.

Auvillar's troubadour Marcabru (active c1110–50) offered the opposing view, to put it mildly. A foundling raised by Aldric d'Auvillar, he fought the Moors in Spain and had for a patron Eleanor's father, Guilhem X of Aquitaine (himself son of the first troubadour, Guilhem IX). Marcabru was a great innovator in rhymes, rhythms and metrical schemes and he used language in ways no-one had ever done before, his vocabulary ranging from the most vulgar – even obscene – realism to elegant, noble lyrics.

Of his 41 surviving poems, a few are in a tender mode, especially *A la fontana del vergier*, beautifully depicting a young girl's sorrow for her lover crusading in the Holy Land, but the majority lambast women in language unfit for travel guides. 'He was one of the first troubadours within memory …and he spoke ill of women and of love,' wrote one of his biographers, in amazement. Eleanor must have not been amused to hear his songs – or perhaps she laughed at them.

LACHAPELLE EN LOMAGNE South of Valence on the D11, lost in the middle of nowhere, this tiny village is named after an oratory that the Templars built next to one of their castles. In the 15th century it became the parish church of **St-Pierre** (m 06 12 49 23 30; w lachapelle82.fr; ⌚ Jul–Aug 10.00–12.30 & 14.00–18.30 daily, Sep–Jun 14.00–18.00 daily). In 1776, the local abbots were rolling in dough and gave the interior a surprising Venetian opera décor, complete with boxes in the arcades.

GRAMONT Further south, overlooking the hills of Gascony, Gramont is synonymous with its 12th-century **Château de Gramont** (☎ 05 63 94 05 26; w chateau-gramont.fr; ⌚ Jun–Oct 10.00–12.30 & 14.00–18.00 Tue–Sun; €6, under 18 free) built on the lands given to Simon de Montfort after the Albigensian Crusade, then morphed by later owners into a Renaissance residence in the 16th century. Now a national monument, it has a lovely 12th-century statue of the Virgin in the chapel and a 16th-century-style garden. Combine with a fascinating lesson on the bees at the **Musée du Miel** (A Mouare; ☎ 05 63 94 00 20; w lemuseedumiel.fr; ⌚ visits on the hour: Jun–Sep 10.00, 11.00, 14.00–17.00 Thu–Tue, otherwise by appt; €4, ages 7–11 €3, under 7 free; cash only).

NORTH OF MOISSAC: QUERCY BLANC

North of Moissac lies the southern half of Quercy Blanc (page 281), with lovely rolling hills of sunflowers, wheat and orchards. Attractions are few outside its lovely hill towns; if the sun isn't shining, it can be haunting, waiting for a French Thomas Hardy to do it justice.

There are lively **markets** here: Saturday morning in Lauzerte and Montaigu-de-Quercy, Sunday morning in Roquecor. In Touffailles, 10km west of Lauzerte, buy lavender essential oils, etc at the **Ferme de Lacontale** [328 B3] (☎ 05 63 95 78 12; w lavande-quercy.fr).

TOURIST INFORMATION

Lauzerte 3 Place des Cornières; ☎ 05 63 94 61 94; w quercy-sud-ouest.com; ⌚ 09.00–noon & 14.00–17.00 Mon–Sat

Montaigu-de-Quercy Place du Mercadiel; ☎ 05 63 94 48 50; w quercy-sud-ouest.com; ⌚ 09.00–noon Tue–Sat, Jul–Aug also 14.00–18.00 Mon–Sat

WHERE TO STAY

Château de l'Hoste [328 A2] (24 rooms) St-Beauzeil, 10km west of Montaigu-de-Quercy; ☎ 05 63 95 25 61; w chateaudelhoste.com. An 18th-century *gentilhommière*, with guaranteed peaceful rooms, in the midst of a large park with a pool; the pretty restaurant (€€€€) has a changing menu. Bike rentals available. **€€€€€**

Moulin de Jouenery et Spa [328 B3] (5 rooms) Jouenery, Brassac, 20km west of Lauzerte; ☎ 05 63 32 09 31; w moulindejouenery.fr. A B&B packed full of character & charm in a 17th-century mill (once owned by André Claveau, who won the Eurovision Song contest in 1958 – beating out *Volare*!). There's a laughing stream for swimming, a spa & indoor pool; table d'hôte available (from €20). B/fast inc. **€€€€€**

Le Belvédère [328 B3] (22 rooms) Martel, 5km from Lauzerte; ☎ 05 63 95 51 10; w lebelvedere-lauzerte.com. Lovely views over the Barguelonne valley in a quiet setting, with a restaurant (€€€), infinity pool, jacuzzi & sauna. **€€€€–€€€**

Hotel du Quercy (9 rooms) Rte de Cahors, Lauzerte; ☎ 05 63 94 66 36; w hotel-du-quercy.fr; ⌚ closed Nov–Mar. Simple & friendly inn outside the centre, with a good restaurant (€) & special deals for pilgrims. **€€–€**

WHERE TO EAT AND DRINK

Au P'tit Moissac [328 B2] Estripeau, Touffailles; 05 63 39 00 86; f; lunch Mon–Fri. Lovely food in a bucolic setting in a 12th-century *maison de maître*, with summer barbecues in the garden. *Weekly changing menu inc wine & coffee €26.* €€€

La Cage aux Oiseaux Place de la République, Montjoi, 16km north of Valence d'Agen; 05 63 95 26 40; w la-cage-aux-oiseaux.eatbu.com; Jul–Aug closed eves Sun, other times check the website. Delicious meat & fish dishes, & friendly staff in an out-of-the-way medieval village. €€€

L'Etincelle 6 Place des Cornières, Lauzerte; 09 82 39 02 09; f TernauxCorentin; daily, closed Oct–Mar. Fresh tasty dishes with a seasonal menu, great seafood & tables in the square. *Menus from €25.* €€€

L'Artichaut 134 Av du Stade, Montaigu-de-Quercy; 05 63 94 40 65; w l-artichaut.com; daily exc lunch Sat. A young French-English couple serves up tasty food indoors or out, on a chalkboard menu; pizza too. *€9–€14.* €€

Le Délice 87 Av du Stade, Montaigu-de-Quercy; 05 63 32 55 03; w le-delice-restaurant.eatbu.com; closed Mon. Come here for a superb lamb & prune tagine, or a vegetarian one, & other Moroccan delicacies. Friendly family atmosphere. €€

Restaurant Yvan Quercy [328 C3] Minguet, Cazes-Mondenard; 05 63 95 84 02; daily but book. This is in fact the hearse museum (see below); eating here is a pleasure, with traditional & classic menus. Entrance for museum, carriage rides & wine-tasting is separate. €€

LAUZERTE Runner-up of the 2019 France's favourite village contest, Lauzerte has always been a popular place. It was a Gaulish oppidum, renamed Lucerna 'lamp', after the way it beckons from a distance. It was refounded as a bastide in the 12th century by Raymond VI of Toulouse and nicknamed 'the Toledo of Quercy'. Once you arrive, it has a fine collection of 14th- and 15th-century houses of sun-bleached stone. Charmingly irregular *cornières* surround its central square, but one corner of the cobblestoned pavement looks as if it's been turned up like the page of a book, with coloured tiles underneath – created in 1988 by ceramicist Jacques Buchholtz, who also left a little garden of his works under the town walls.

Unusually for a bastide, the church of **St-Barthélemy** sits perpendicular to the square. One chapel is full of paintings by Joseph Ingres, père of Dominique: romantic green-blue imaginary landscapes, brought here from a fancy house in Lauzerte. On Rue de Gandillonne look up to see the curious figure of the widow, who, in 1285, noticed the occupying English garrison sneaking out to go dancing at a fair; she couldn't count so set aside a chestnut for each soldier, then took them to the First Consul, who counted them, tossed the last two Englishmen over the walls, and locked the gates; a rare occasion when it paid to go AWOL.

The village's lower church, the **Carmes,** was rebuilt in 1676 after the Wars of Religion; if it's open, pop in to see the remarkable Baroque altar (1689). All Baroque is theatrical, but the action here happens on a genuine stage, starring the Virgin handing rosaries to St Simon Stock and St Teresa of Avila, while the prophet Elijah and St John of the Cross stand by, all under God stage-managing from above.

CAZES-MONDENARD (10km southeast of Lauzerte) This village has the only museum in France dedicated to hearses, the **Musée des Corbillards et de l'Attelage** [328 C3] (on the D16; 05 63 95 84 02; ring ahead, by appt; €7, up to age 14 €2). It had to be someone's hobby to take rusting old hearses out of junkyards and lovingly restore them, and Yvan Quercy was the man. Now run by Yvan Jr, the museum has 120 of them, all horse-drawn, as well as old tractors and carriages; tastings of local produce available on request.

WEST OF LAUZERTE Rural **Bourg-de-Visa**, 18km west of Lauzerte, has a very pretty 19th-century wrought iron *halle* in the centre that is very grand for its population of 400. Just southeast at **Fauroux** (take the D43), the Romanesque church of **St-Romain** has a 2nd-century AD Gallo-Roman mosaic in the choir, suggesting it was an earlier sacred spot. Nearby you can swim in the 'tropical' lagoon of **Rikiki Plage** [328 B3], with a little white sandy beach.

Castelsagrat, south of here, was an important ancient station on the road between Lyon and Bordeaux; the Visigoths were here (a couple of tombs were found) before Alphonse of Poitiers founded it as another pretty bastide in 1270. It has a charming irregularly arcaded *place,* and a church of the **Assumption** housing a wonderfully overripe Baroque retable (1667), commissioned by the College of St-Raymond in Toulouse but relocated here after the Revolution; see if you can find wooden insects amid the foliage.

Just west on its hill, half-timbered 13th-century **Montjoi** is one of the tiniest bastides, while **St-Maurin**, further west (just inside Lot-et-Garonne), is a charming, half-timbered village near the ruins of an abbey founded in 1097 by Cluny on the site of the 6th-century AD martyrdom of St Maurin. Dismantled after the Revolution, the remaining bits (including some fascinating capitals showing the beheading of St Maurin) are currently being restored; part of it contains a little ethnographic museum put together by the villagers.

MONTAIGU-DE-QUERCY (17km northwest of Lauzerte) 'Mount Sharp', site of a 12th-century castle built by Count Raymond V of Toulouse, looks like an Italian hill town from the distance, but has a sufficiently large Brit contingent to support an English theatre company along with a pretty square with half-timbered houses, and some sharply steep streets in the centre. When it's hot, everyone heads to the artificial lake, **Montaigu Plage**, with a white sandy beach. The church at **Pervillac**, east on the D24, contains charming 16th-century frescoes long hidden under the plaster of red devils and the *Seven Deadly Sins*, *Christ in Majesty* and the *Last Supper* by the same itinerant artist who painted the churches of La Masse and Martignac in the Lot. Ten minutes to the west, the even loftier village of **Roquecor** is a sleepy, laid-back place that attracts a jovial mix of twanging locals, squires in Rollers, bikers and expats.

15

Toulouse

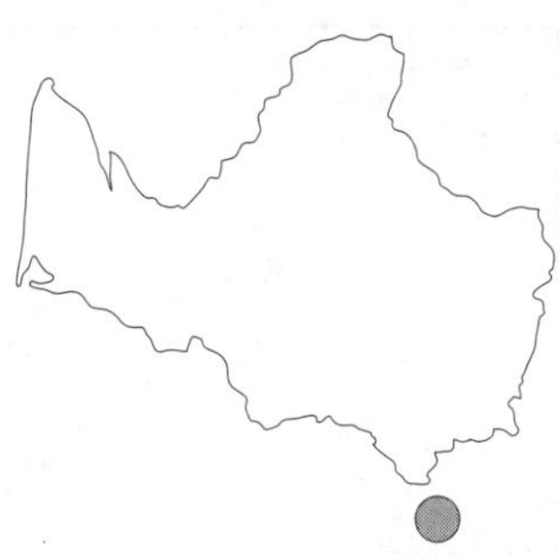

One thing that keeps the southwest from nodding off in its vats of duck fat and wine is this big pink dynamo on the Garonne. Toulouse, nicknamed La Ville Rose for its millions of pink bricks, has 1,360,000 and counting inhabitants, more than 110,000 university students, a well-preserved historic centre with the world's biggest Romanesque church, and most of the EU's aeronautics, space and related high-tech industries.

Instead of France's fourth city, Toulouse should have been the capital of a twanging, Occitan-speaking nation called Languedoc, but it was knocked out of the big leagues in the 1220s by the popes and the kings of France and their henchman Simon de Montfort. Eight centuries later, Toulouse is rediscovering its mojo as the capital of Occitanie, a *grand région* stretching from the Dordogne to the Rhône, encompassing nearly all of the former territories of the once mighty Counts of Toulouse.

Spain extends her cape here, distilling enough passion to make Toulouse *une ville d'émotion*, emotion that spills over when its beloved rugby side, the Stade Toulousain, takes to the field. The city's motto is *Per Tolosa totjorn mai* ('For Toulouse, always more'). Always more sprawl and traffic jams, but also always more for visitors to see and do, showing off its air and space technology at the Cité d'Espace and Aeroscopia – along with the cunning steampunk marvels to ride in the Halle de la Machine.

HISTORY

> The history of Toulouse is detestable, saturated with blood and perfidy.
>
> Henry James

Tolosa was founded on a hill, 10km from the modern city, at a place now called Vieille Toulouse. It was destined for big things, located by the Bazacle – a ford in the Garonne – at the centre of what ancient Greek geographer Strabo called the 'Gallic isthmus', the crossroads between the Mediterranean and the Atlantic, the Pyrenees and the Massif Central. The Gaulish inhabitants, the Volcae Tectosages, took full advantage of their location, creaming profits from the silver mines to the south and the burgeoning trade upriver with Burdigala (Bordeaux). Despite their wealth, the Tectosages ranged far and wide in search for more; in 279BC they were in Greece to help sack the treasures of Delphi. Apollo, however, put a curse on them for stealing his gold: on their return to Tolosa they all fell ill with 'distemper', until they threw their loot in a swamp.

In 125BC, Ligurian tribes in Provence asked Rome to help defend them from the pirates from Toulouse. That was all the Romans needed to muscle in: they decreed the Tectosages were an ally and sent a garrison to Toulouse to 'collaborate'. In 107BC, when the Tectosages revolted against their unwanted allies, the Senate sent

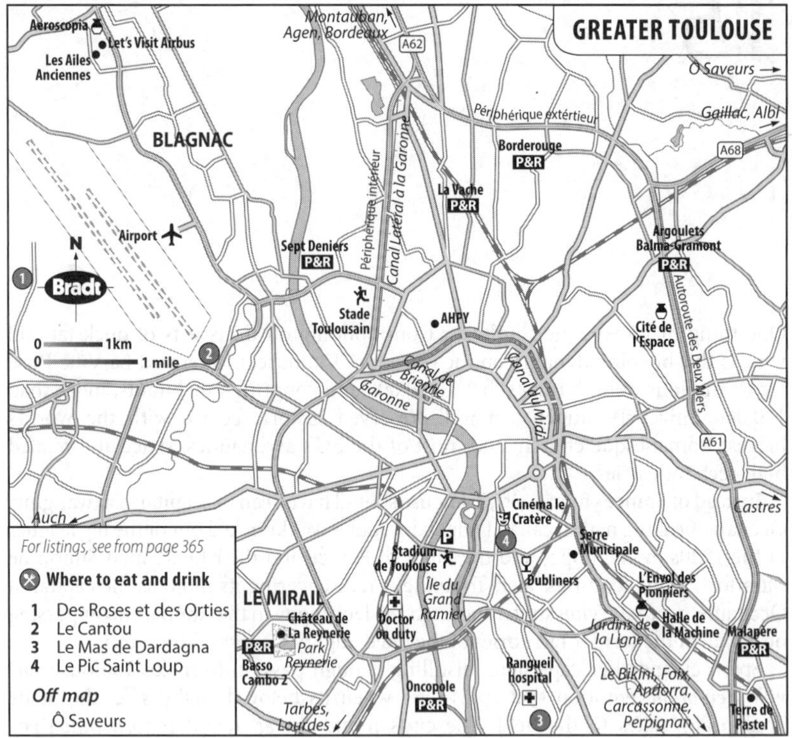

Servilius Caepio to crush them and confiscate their treasure – 50,000kg of silver and 45,400kg of gold. But only a fraction ever made it to Rome. Caepio claimed his convoy was held up by Teutones near Marseille, although the Roman Senate suspected another kind of highway robbery. Shortly afterwards Caepio was soundly defeated by Germanic tribes in the Battle of Arausio (Orange) in 105BC which left at least 70,000 legionaries dead; the Senate stripped him of all his assets and sent him into exile. And yet his descendants were fabulously wealthy – and famously unlucky – down to his great-grandson, Caesar's friend and assassin, Brutus. Hence the expression *aurum habet tolosanum* (to have the gold of Toulouse) – in other words, ill-gotten gains seldom prosper.

If Rome cleaned out Toulouse's swamp treasure, it also brought years of peace. Toulouse was refounded on the plain of the Garonne. The river city was called Palladia Tolosa after its protectress, the goddess Pallas Athena, and it was soon one of the key cities in the province of Gallia Narbonensis, with a population of around 20,000.

CAPITAL OF THE VISIGOTHS In AD410 the Visigoths under Alaric sacked Rome and took a valuable hostage – Galla Placidia, the wise and beautiful sister of Emperor Honorius. When Alaric died, Galla Placidia was inherited by his brother-in-law and new king Ataulf, who carried her off to southwest France and made Toulouse his capital. When his wife died, he married Galla Placidia. It was the love match of the Dark Ages, and her genteel Roman manners helped to tame Ataulf's uncouth Visigothic temperament. He was later killed in a palace conspiracy and Galla Placidia returned to her brother in Ravenna, where she built herself a beautiful tomb of golden mosaics which can be seen to this day.

Toulouse remained the elegant capital of the Visigoths until AD507, when Clovis, the recently baptised king of the Franks, took it upon himself to wipe out the Arian heresy – the sect of the Visigoths. After Clovis defeated Alaric II in hand-to-hand combat, the Visigoths upped sticks over the Pyrenees for Toledo, which they made their capital until they were ousted in turn by the Arabs in AD716.

Five years later these same Arab armies appeared at the gates of Toulouse. Although Clovis's successors, the Merovingian 'do-nothing kings' (*rois fainéants*), hadn't failed to neglect Toulouse, a brilliant resistance was organised by the city's Duke Eudes, who killed the emir and gave the Moors their very first taste of defeat on 9 June AD721. Every Toulousain knows this defeat was far more important than the Arabs' defeat at Poitiers in AD732, although it got all the attention because it marked the triumph of Charles Martel, whose Carolingian dynasty would replace the Merovingians in the person of his son, Pepin the Short.

Pepin, recognising the danger of a renewed Arab attack from over the Pyrenees, favoured Toulouse and spent years in the area hunting down Waiffar, the last Merovingian duke of Aquitaine, in order to establish his authority and guarantee the frontiers of the Frankish empire. Pepin's son Charlemagne continued this policy by pampering Toulouse. The most able and loyal counsellors of his sons and grandsons who inherited these marches became, in AD849, the first Counts of Toulouse, responsible for defending Languedoc – a vast territory extending from the Rhône to the Garonne and from the Pyrenees to the Dordogne.

THE COUNTS OF TOULOUSE The Counts are nicknamed the Raymondine dynasty – because nearly all were named Raymond. The first to emerge from obscurity was Raymond St-Gilles, born in 1041, younger brother of Guilhem IV. Raymond spent his youth battling the Moors in Spain with such audacity that the king of Castile gave him his daughter Elvira in marriage and put him under the wing of the great Cid himself. In 1090, when Guilhem died, he took over Toulouse as Raymond IV – where such was his reputation that in 1095 Pope Urban II came to Toulouse and asked him to lead the First Crusade.

Before leaving Toulouse, Raymond IV declared he would never return and installed his son Bertrand as Count. For his arms, he chose the 12-pointed red 'Cross of Languedoc', a symbol as old as the Visigoths. In the Holy Land, Raymond was offered the crown of Jerusalem; to everyone's amazement he modestly refused and let the honour go to Godfrey of Bouillon. Before he died in 1105 – after founding the County of Tripoli in Lebanon – he saw the birth of a fourth son, Alphonse-Jourdain, so-named for his baptism in the Jordan.

Crusading quickly became a family pastime; little Alphonse-Jourdain was shipped home to Toulouse to take Bertrand's place when the latter succumbed to the Holy Land itch. Alphonse-Jourdain stuck around long enough to found, in 1152, one of Toulouse's most enduring institutions, the Domini de Capitulo (Lords of the Chapter), or Capitouls. Each parish had its own Capitoul – in 1438 the number was fixed at eight – who were appointed each November by the count from a list of names provided by the outgoing Capitouls. At first they were in charge of administering justice; by the time of the Revolution they ran the whole city.

The next Count Raymond took over at age 14, when his father Alphonse-Jourdain headed to the Holy Land. Raymond V was a troubadour who presided over a golden age of poetry; he continued his father's administrative reforms by granting the city municipal autonomy. Another charter, in 1192, established the Moulins du Bazacle, one of the largest mills in Europe and the very first concern, anywhere, managed by shareholders; Rabelais wrote that 'they filled the ears with the infernal racket of their wheels'.

Although Raymond V is known (among non-Toulousain historians) as 'the weathervane', for his inconsistent and ambiguous diplomacy, it was all for the sake of his beloved Languedoc – a prize coveted by three great powers of the time, France, England and Barcelona. All had claims, all were ready to pounce. In 1190, the Duke of Aquitaine, Richard the Lionheart, did just that, capturing Cahors and 18 castles on the pretext of avenging attacks on pilgrims passing through the lands of Toulouse. Raymond V quietly got his revenge by asking his Mediterranean allies to refuse a safe harbour for Richard's ship on his return from the Crusades, leading directly to his capture by Leopold of Austria.

TO LOSE TOULOUSE, THROUGH LOVE When Raymond V died in 1195, his son Raymond VI had already been through three wives (the first died, the second and third were repudiated) and was ready to patch things up with the troublesome Plantagenets by wedding a fourth, Joanna, sister of Richard the Lionheart, who bore him an heir before she died.

But the scandal of Raymond VI's private life was nothing compared with the reproach heaped on him for his attitude towards the Cathars. In 1208, when one of his hot-headed vassals murdered the papal legate, Pope Innocent III demanded that the Count do penance and let himself be stripped to the waist and beaten with rods. Even this humiliation, and the fact that he had undertaken the expense of constructing a new cathedral in Toulouse, failed to convince Innocent that he sufficiently hated the heretics. And he probably didn't. Raymond VI seems to have had quite a tolerant attitude towards the Cathars: they lived honestly without harming anyone, and as their lord he considered it his job to defend them.

Innocent began recruiting in the north for what has come down in history as the Albigensian Crusade. Raymond and his barons soon enough recognised what it really was – an excuse to grab the south of France. With the pope, the Frankish barons of the north and the crusaders' fanatical leader, Simon de Montfort, lined up against him, Raymond VI summoned aid from his current brother-in-law, Pedro of Aragon, count of Barcelona. Young Pedro was fresh from a famous victory over the Moors at Las Navas de Tolosa, but he had no qualms about fighting against the pope – especially if he could combine war with a visit to his old flame, a certain Azalaïs de Boissezon. Simon de Montfort was at Muret near Toulouse when he intercepted the letter from Pedro, setting up a rendezvous with Azalaïs. 'How should I respect a king who, for a woman, marches against his God!' thundered de Montfort.

Barcelona and Toulouse had 3,000 knights against de Montfort's 1,500, but what should have been an easy victory began ominously when King Pedro turned up exhausted, barely able to sit in the saddle. One of his knights traded arms with him, hoping to conceal his identity, but from the beginning the southerners were outmanoeuvred by de Montfort. In the subsequent hand-to-hand combat, the king, fearing to be labelled a coward, revealed himself and was quickly slain. The battle of Muret (12 September 1213) turned into a rout.

In 1215, Simon de Montfort entered Toulouse, where he was made count in place of Raymond VI by the will of the pope. He ruled the city with Bishop Folquet de Marseille, a troubadour once patronised by Raymond V who in 1195 got religion and became the most rabid bigot of them all (a contemporary wrote: 'he snuffed out, in body and in soul, the lives of more than fifteen hundred people…he is more an Antichrist than a messenger of Rome').

In 1217, when young Raymond, son of the count, orchestrated an uprising in Provence, the city welcomed back Raymond VI 'as if he were the Holy Spirit', and diligently prepared against de Montfort's return and inevitable siege. It would be his last hurrah. A woman operating a homemade mini-catapult recognised de Montfort from the walls, took aim and lobbed a large rock on his skull, dashing out his brains.

Raymond VI died soon after, and was succeeded by his son, Raymond VII. His reign was a troubled one. Simon de Montfort's heir waged war on Toulouse for 17 years before he gave up and ceded his claim to Louis VIII, who embarked on another 'crusade', a fancy name for a scorched-earth campaign to crush the south once and for all.

In 1229, Raymond VII, seeing the distress of his subjects, sued for terms from the king, now Louis IX. These terms, in the Treaty of Paris, were the public submission of Count Raymond in front of Notre-Dame in Paris and his vow to round up all the remaining Cathars in his realm; then the division of his lands as booty, giving eastern Languedoc to France and the Comtat-Vénaissin to the pope (this later allowed the popes to install themselves in Avignon, and weighed in favour of Louis IX's canonisation). Jeanne, Raymond's only child, was forced to wed Alphonse de Poitiers, the king's brother. In the spirit of the times, Jeanne and Alphonse also went crusading in the East, and died childless in 1271, and Toulouse reverted to France as the chief city of the king's new province of Languedoc.

One spin-off of the Albigensian Crusade was the founding of the Dominicans (page 378). A second was the invention of the Inquisition. Raymond VII, in spite of his submission in Paris, had so little heart for persecuting the Cathars, that in 1233 Pope Gregory IX came up with the idea of creating a spiritual police force run by the Dominicans. This went down like a lead balloon in Toulouse; the Capitouls ordered an assault on their convent and forced the Grand Inquisitors to flee. Rome ordered Raymond VII to take them back, and one night a band of Cathars descended from their mountain fastness in the Pyrenees and slit their throats – an act that sealed the fate of Montségur, the Cathars' last refuge. Another side effect was the founding of the University of Toulouse: the Treaty of Paris ordered Raymond to support 14 masters of theology and canon law for a decade. They stuck around to form the second-oldest university in France.

Yet another effect of the Albigensian Crusade was a boom in the slave trade: not only were the northern French buying up recalcitrant southerners, but they now found the path to Spain clear to capture Muslims. The Capitouls found their behaviour revolting, and in 1226 struck a precocious blow for human rights by granting the right of asylum to any slave, whatever his country of origin. Despite considerable pressure from Paris, the law remained on the books until the Revolution.

The 14th century was a grim one in Toulouse, outside of the founding of the Consistori del Gay Saber, Europe's first literary society (page 384). In 1320, the northerners led a pogrom against the Jews, followed by the miseries of the Black Death and Hundred Years' War, when only Toulouse prevented total English victory after Montauban went to the Black Prince in 1360. By 1400 the population had dwindled to 19,000 souls.

A SECOND GOLDEN AGE, IN PASTEL Although the city got through the Hundred Years' War fairly intact, a fire that started in a bakery oven in 1463 destroyed 7,000 buildings in the centre, many of which had been built of wood; from then on the city would rebuild in brick, tinted pink from the iron in the local clay.

Toulouse quickly rebounded, thanks to a new cash crop – woad, or pastel (from medieval Latin *pastellum*, 'woad paste'). Cultivated with great success in the hills just southeast of Toulouse, pastel leaves were torn, steeped in hot water, then fermented in balls called *coques*, to produce a light-fast blue dye fashionable in the Renaissance. For a century so much money poured into Toulouse that it was famous as the carefree land of the *coques*, the *païs de Cocanha* or Cockaigne. Merchants from across Europe speculated and dealt in pastel credits and futures, and in 1552 these activities were centralised with the founding of Toulouse's stock exchange.

The pastel market collapsed in the 1600s with the import of cheaper indigo from India and the Caribbean – Toulouse fell into a deep economic depression and spiritual malaise. The clergy were openly corrupt, and many, especially the mercantile classes, were receptive to the preaching of Calvin. Although the Capitouls tolerated the new religion (many converted themselves), the *parlementaires* and *intendants* – representing royal power in Toulouse – stayed strictly Catholic, and conflicts were inevitable. A riot broke out in 1562 when Catholic priests stole the body of a dead Protestant woman, saying she had reconverted on her deathbed; by May it was open warfare in the streets. But the Catholics prevailed in the end, and Toulouse became one of the last cities to recognise Henri IV as king.

In 1632, with the dramatic execution of the governor of Languedoc (see box, page 376), Toulouse saw its remaining privileges slowly gobbled up by the absolute monarchy. One bright spot was the digging of the Canal du Midi, linking the Mediterranean to the Garonne and the Atlantic, planned, financed and achieved by Pierre-Paul Riquet. Louis XVI was pleased to take credit for uniting two seas and two worlds in record time (1666–81), but the cost – 3,600,000 livres – was borne by Languedoc and Riquet, who died ruined.

The new prosperity and trade brought about by 'Riquet's ditch' may have improved local morale if not local morals. The most popular entertainments in Toulouse were public executions, to the tune of three or four a month, which may be why the population grew only 10% (to around 60,000) while the rest of France shot up 40% in the 1700s.

TOULOUSE IN THE SKY WITH DIAMONDS The mid 19th century found Toulouse a mere departmental capital, a sleepy provincial backwater where the elite invested in property and farms instead of joining the Industrial Revolution. The arrival of the railway in 1856 shook things up a bit, or at least shook down branches of Paris's banks and department stores.

What proved to be the turning point for Toulouse literally fell from the sky. Clément Ader of Muret, born in 1841, gave a preview of coming events when one of his bat-winged, steam-powered *avions*, as he called them, hopped off the ground in 1873; in 1890 he flew a few dozen yards in the *Éole*, 13 years before Orville Wright's first flight at Kitty Hawk. In 1917, Pierre-Georges Latécoère founded the first aircraft factory in Toulouse – in honour of Ader, but mainly because the city was far from the front lines of World War I.

After the Armistice, Latécoère continued production, and on 12 March 1919 launched a Toulouse–Casablanca airmail route that soon extended to Dakar and eventually to South America. For this new airline, the Compagnie Générale Aéropostale, he recruited ace pilots, including Antoine de Saint-Exupéry (page 388), the 'Lord of the Sands', who immortalised his comrades in his books. A second aircraft company, founded in 1920 by Toulousain Émile Dewoitine, was nationalised in 1937 and is now Aérospatiale. Today the city is the headquarters of Airbus; CNES, the French space agency, was transferred here in 1968 along with the

French national weather service. The air and space industries have attracted scores of research centres, high-tech firms and elite schools of engineering and aviation.

The population of Toulouse has since grown apace, but not only with engineers. It was the principal centre for refugees during and after the Spanish Civil War, and, of the 360,000 or so civilians and Republican soldiers who passed through the city, a quarter stayed and became French citizens.

In 1964, when France decided to ever so slowly reverse the centralising policies of Richelieu and Louis XIV, Toulouse was made capital of the Midi-Pyrénées, encompassing the western half of its old province of Languedoc. By then Toulouse had become the fourth largest city in France. Although pink in its politics as well as its bricks for most of the 20th century, Toulouse from 1971 to 2001 was mayored by the centre-right Baudises, first Pierre, and then his son, Dominique, credited with the city's economic and cultural achievements.

21ST-CENTURY TOULOUSE Toulouse entered the new millennium with a tragic bang, when in September 2001, only ten days after 9/11 in the USA, the AZF fertiliser plant blew up, producing a massive crater with the force of a 3.4 earthquake on the Richter scale, killing 31, seriously wounding another 30 and blowing up two-thirds of the city's windows. There are suspicions that it too was a terrorist attack caused by a subcontractor killed in the explosion, although trials in 2009, 2012 and 2015 found the director and owner of the plant guilty of neglect and involuntary manslaughter. The site of the factory is marked by a simple memorial; the rest is now part of the Oncopole, dedicated to cutting-edge cancer research.

Today Toulouse, thanks to its air and space industries, its university and research facilities, is one of the fastest-growing metropolises in France, adding some 15,000 inhabitants per year. There are plans to extend the Paris–Bordeaux superfast LGV line to Toulouse in the near future and entrepreneurs have even revived its pastel industry, finding new uses for woad from beer to skin softeners to jewellery; in August 2021 the French government listed it as *Patrimoine immatériel français*.

GETTING THERE AND AWAY

BY AIR Toulouse's international airport (☎ 08 25 38 00 00; **w** toulouse.aeroport.fr) at Blagnac, 10km northwest of the centre, is one of the busiest in France.

Getting to/from the airport

The airport **bus** (☎ 05 34 60 64 00; **w** tisseo.fr; €8.50 each way) is most convenient if you have big luggage; it links Toulouse's coach station (next to the train station at Matabiau) every 20 minutes from 05.40 to 00.10 daily, with several stops in the centre (Compans-Caffarelli and Jeanne d'Arc, both on the metro B line). The ticket includes 1½ hours on the metro/tram/bus network. **Tram T2** runs from the airport to the central Place Lafourcade (€1.70, inc a bus/metro ride; get off at Arènes for the metro A line to the train/bus station).

Toulouse is the first airport offering a **car- or scooter-sharing** service (Iodines; ☎ 05 82 08 52 70; **w** iodines.fr/airport; €19 for 2hrs) from the airport. **Taxis** (airport taxi station: ☎ 05 61 30 02 54) to the centre, depending on the traffic, take around 20 minutes and cost around €30.

Car hire

All the major firms are present at the airport – see listings on the airport website. There's also car hire at Toulouse's main railway station: Enterprise (**w** enterprise.fr), Europcar (**w** europcar.fr), Hertz (**w** hertz.fr) and Sixt (**w** sixt.fr).

BY TRAIN Toulouse's main station is Matabiau [367 H2] (80 Bd Pierre Sémard; ☎3635; w sncf-connect.com). Trains from Paris-Austerlitz by way of Gourdon, Souillac, Cahors and Montauban take 6 hours 30 minutes; TGVs from Paris-Montparnasse do the same in 5 hours – by way of Bordeaux. Slow trains to Bordeaux take 2 hours 30 minutes and stop in Montauban, Castelsarrasin, Moissac, Agen and Aiguillon.

BY BUS The Gare Routière [367 G2] is next to the railway station (schedules at w lio.laregion.fr) with buses mainly to towns around Toulouse. European low-cost bus line Flixbus (w flixbus.fr) also uses the station.

BY CAR Toulouse is 2½ hours from Bordeaux on the A62 or an hour and a half from Cahors on the A62 and A20.

ORIENTATION

Within the purgatory of its octopus sprawl and hyper-busy ring roads, the centre of Toulouse is lovely, framed by the Garonne and the Canal du Midi. The historic **Centre Ville** surrounds the **Place du Capitole** and extends as far north as the great Basilica of St-Sernin; north of this is the lively **Quartier Arnaud Bernard**, first site of the university. Towards the river is the old commercial district around Place de la Bourse and the waterfront area of **La Daurade**, named after the eponymous church.

South is **Les Carmes** around the Place des Carmes, a picturesque quarter with countless little restaurants and boutiques. East, towards the **Cathédral St-Étienne**, things are more exclusive, with the elegant *hôtels particuliers* of lawyers, members of *parlement* and wealthy pastel merchants. To the south, the public parks of the **Quartier des Jardins** replace the medieval castle of the Counts. To the east are the quarters that sprang up between the old walls and the great curve of the **Canal du Midi**, including the **Allées Jean Jaurès**, the new 'Ramblas' extending to the Matabiau area and **Saint-Aubin**, an artists' district that really springs to life in the Sunday morning market.

In the Garonne is the **Île du Grand Ramier**, site of the football stadium and other sporting venues, destined to become Toulouse's Central Park, while the **St-Cyprien** district on the left bank was always the working end of the city, built up after the frequent floods ceased in the late 19th century, and now home to the city's photography and contemporary art museums.

GETTING AROUND

Toulouse has an excellent public transportation network called Tisséo (☎05 61 41 70 70; w visiteurs-tisseo.fr, in English) which you won't need for the historic centre – you can walk across it in half an hour in either direction – although it is handy for the newer attractions on the edges of town.

BY METRO, BUS AND TRAM The Tisséo website has a useful map of all the routes (the major bus routes are the Linéo lines, starting with an 'L'). There's an app to download, with the map and e-tickets to purchase.

For an overview of Toulouse, take the hop-on-hop-off **CityTour** minibus, departing from 23–27 Allées Jean Jaurès (Place d'Arménie) [367 G3], with an audio tour in English (☎05 62 07 05 04; w toulouse-welcome.com; Jun–Sep €16, students €11, under 12 €9, Oct–May €14/€10/€8). In July and August they run a shuttle from the same stop to the Cité de l'Espace and Aeroscopia.

PASS TOURISME

Visit the tourist office website to purchase a pass (24hrs €18, 48hrs €28, 72hrs €35) offering free unlimited public transport, entrance to the museums and one of the tourist office's guided tours, plus reduced admission to Cité de l'Espace, Aeroscopia and Let's Visit Airbus and reduced rates aboard the CityTour bus, boat trips and more. Tickets can be collected or purchased at the tourist office, or from the Tisséo agencies at Toulouse-Blagnac airport (Arrivals Level Gate C) or in the metro station Matabiau-SNCF station. It's especially good value if you pick it up at the airport and take the bus into the city.

BY TAXI If you can't find one cruising around or at a taxi stand, try ☎05 61 42 38 38 or ☎05 34 25 02 50.

BY CAR During the morning and afternoon rush hours, you certainly won't rush, either in the centre or on the *périphériques* (ring roads). The most convenient payable **car parks** are at Place du Capitole [373 C3], Allées Jean Jaurès [367 G3], Place Victor Hugo [373 D2] and Place St-Étienne [367 G4] (you can book a spot at Parclick: w parclick.com/parking-toulouse). Save money by leaving your car in one of the Parc Relais (P+R; see the Tisséo map) and take the tram or metro into the centre, on the condition you use a bus, tram or metro within the hour before leaving Toulouse and not leave your car for more than 24 hours.

BY BICYCLE The city's bike share scheme **Vélô Toulouse** (☎08 00 11 22 05; velo.toulouse.fr) has nearly 300 stations throughout the city. The first 30 minutes are free, then it's €1.50–€2 per hour; or a day ticket costs €1.20, a week €5.

Le Canal à Vélo [367 G1] 89 Bd Pierre Semard; ☎09 53 55 33 83. Specialises in bikes for trips along the Canal du Midi; from €10 for a half day.

Maison du Vélo [367 G2] 12 Bd Bonrepos; ☎05 34 40 64 72; w maisonduvelotoulouse.com. Rents e-bikes & folding bikes.

BY BOAT **Bateaux Toulousains** (☎05 61 80 22 26; w bateaux-toulousains.com) offers dinner cruises on the Canal du Midi and trips on the Garonne departing from the Port de la Daurade [373 A5].

TOURIST INFORMATION

Toulouse's **tourist office** [373 C3] (☎05 17 42 31 31; w toulouse-visit.com; ⏲ 09.30–18.00 daily, until 19.00 Jun–Sep) is in the picturesque Donjon du Capitole behind the Capitole in Square Charles-de-Gaulle.

WHERE TO STAY

With its many business travellers and universities, Toulouse has chain hotels and chain apartment hotels galore in the centre and out by the airport, as well as a short list of reliable independent establishments in the historic centre. Prices plunge in August.

LUXURY

La Cour des Consuls Hotel & Spa [373 B5] (32 rooms) 46 Rue des Couteliers; ☎05 67 16 19 99; w all.accor.com. Near the Pont Neuf, big contemporary rooms in a 16th–18th-century building with a peaceful courtyard, luminous

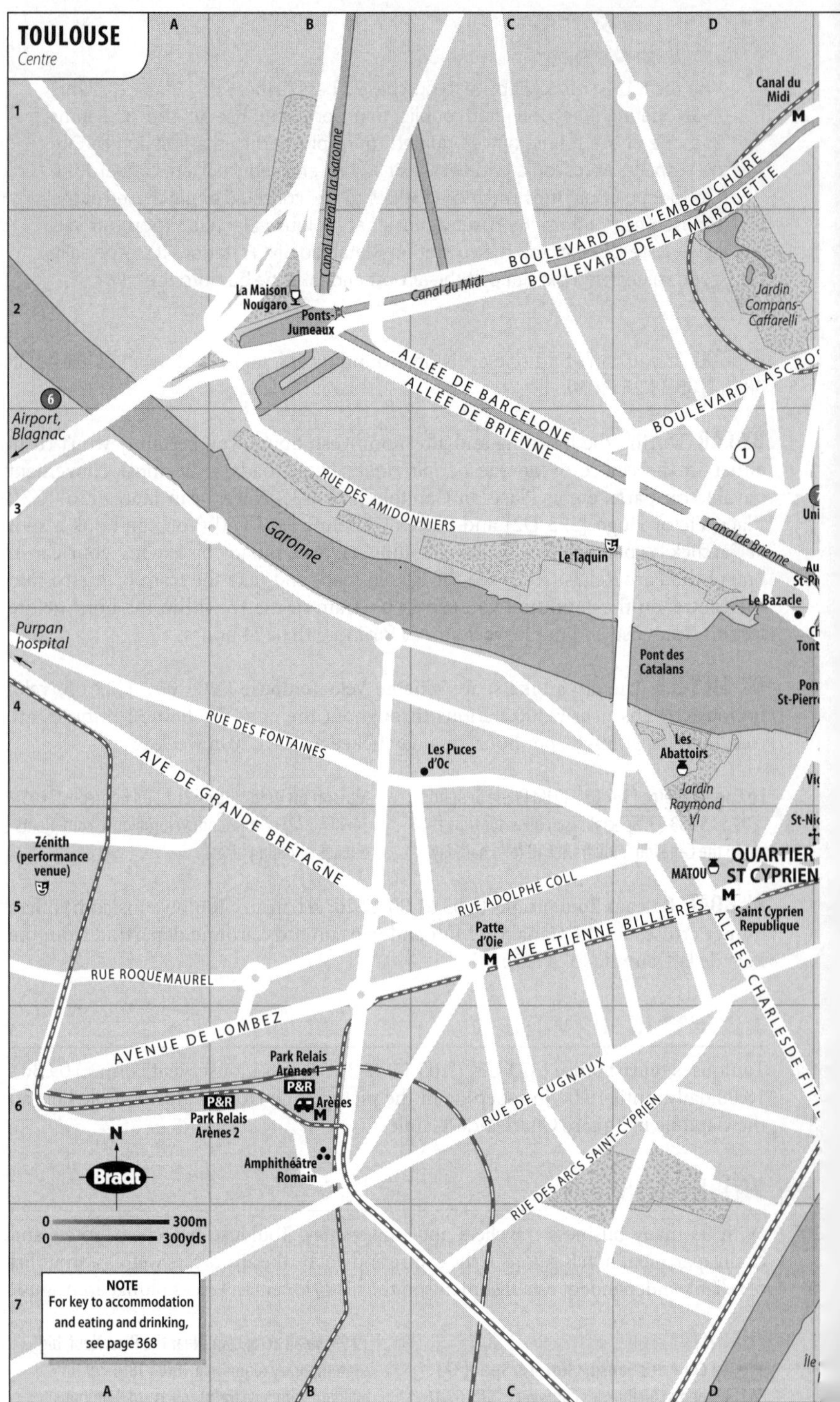

TOULOUSE
Centre
A
B
C
D
1
2
3
4
5
6
7
Canal du Midi
Canal Latéral à la Garonne
BOULEVARD DE L'EMBOUCHURE
BOULEVARD DE LA MARQUETTE
Jardin Compans-Caffarelli
La Maison Nougaro
Ponts-Jumeaux
Canal du Midi
ALLÉE DE BARCELONE
ALLÉE DE BRIENNE
BOULEVARD LASCROSSES
Airport, Blagnac
RUE DES AMIDONNIERS
Canal de Brienne
Garonne
Le Taquin
Le Bazacle
Pont des Catalans
Purpan hospital
RUE DES FONTAINES
Les Puces d'Oc
Les Abattoirs
Jardin Raymond VI
AVE DE GRANDE BRETAGNE
Zénith (performance venue)
QUARTIER ST CYPRIEN
MATOU
RUE ADOLPHE COLL
Saint Cyprien Republique
Patte d'Oie
AVE ETIENNE BILLIÈRES
ALLÉES CHARLES DE FITTE
RUE ROQUEMAUREL
AVENUE DE LOMBEZ
Park Relais Arènes 1
P&R
Arènes
Park Relais Arènes 2
RUE DE CUGNAUX
Amphithéâtre Romain
RUE DES ARCS SAINT-CYPRIEN
N
Bradt
0 300m
0 300yds
NOTE
For key to accommodation and eating and drinking, see page 368

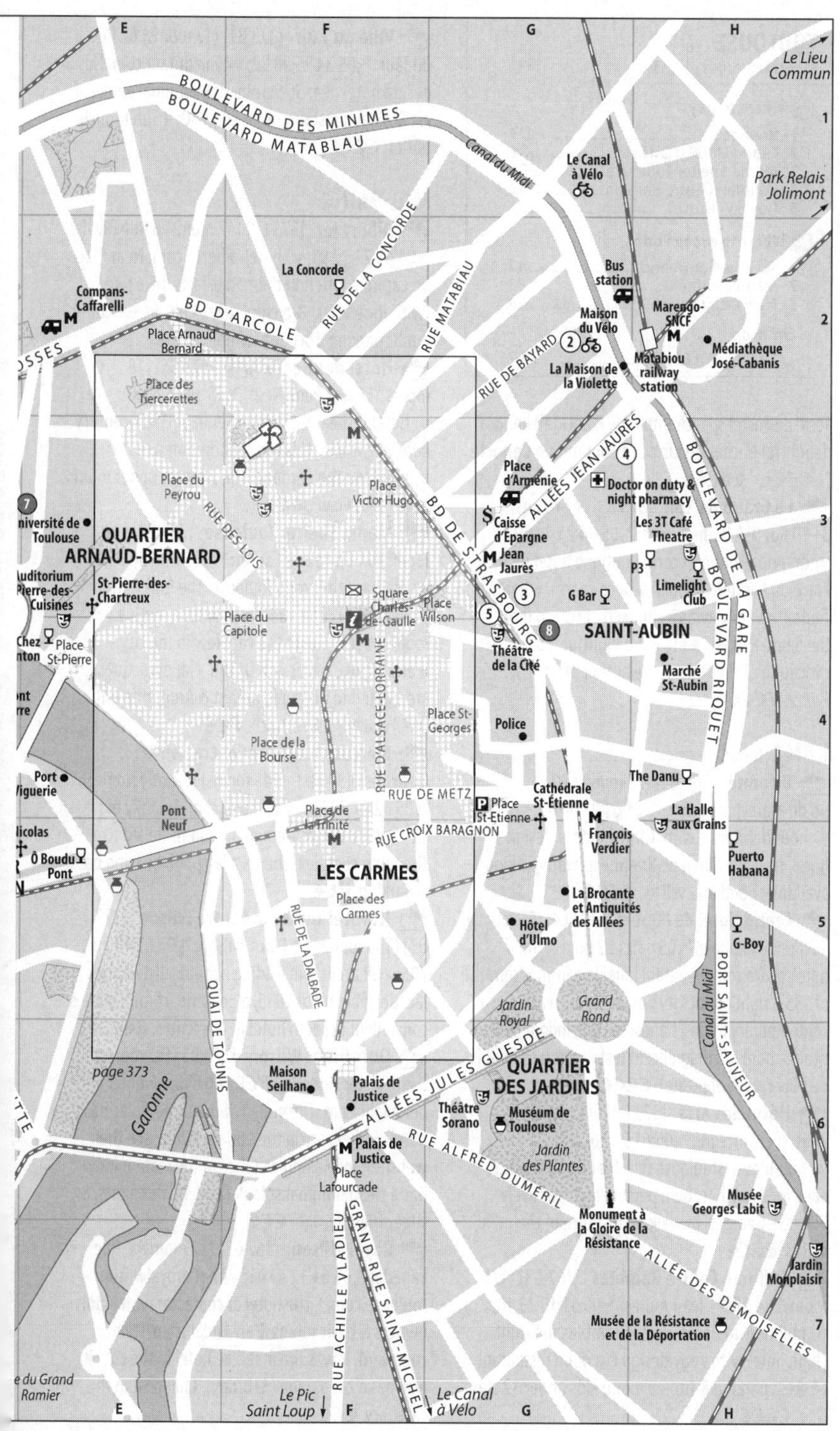

Le Lieu Commun
Park Relais Jolimont
BOULEVARD DES MINIMES
BOULEVARD MATABLAU
Canal du Midi
Le Canal à Vélo
Bus station
Maison du Vélo
Marengo-SNCF
Médiathèque José-Cabanis
Matabiou railway station
La Maison de la Violette
RUE DE BAYARD
La Concorde
RUE DE LA CONCORDE
RUE MATABIAU
Compans-Caffarelli
BD D'ARCOLE
Place Arnaud Bernard
Place des Tiercerettes
Place du Peyrou
RUE DES LOIS
Place Victor Hugo
BD DE STRASBOURG
Place d'Arménie
ALLÉES JEAN JAURÈS
Doctor on duty & night pharmacy
Caisse d'Epargne
Jean Jaurès
Les 3T Café Theatre
P3
Limelight Club
G Bar
Université de Toulouse
QUARTIER ARNAUD-BERNARD
Auditorium Pierre-des-Cuisines
St-Pierre-des-Chartreux
Square Charles-de-Gaulle
Place Wilson
Place du Capitole
Théâtre de la Cité
SAINT-AUBIN
Place St-Pierre
Marché St-Aubin
BOULEVARD DE LA GARE
BOULEVARD RIQUET
RUE D'ALSACE-LORRAINE
Place St-Georges
Police
Place de la Bourse
Port Viguerie
The Danu
Cathédrale St-Étienne
RUE DE METZ
Place St-Étienne
Pont Neuf
Place de la Trinité
RUE CROIX BARAGNON
François Verdier
La Halle aux Grains
Puerto Habana
Ô Boudu Pont
LES CARMES
La Brocante et Antiquités des Allées
Place des Carmes
RUE DE LA DALBADE
Hôtel d'Ulmo
G-Boy
Jardin Royal
Grand Rond
Canal du Midi
PORT SAINT-SAUVEUR
QUAI DE TOUNIS
page 373
Garonne
Maison Seilhan
Palais de Justice
ALLÉES JULES GUESDE
QUARTIER DES JARDINS
Théâtre Sorano
Muséum de Toulouse
Jardin des Plantes
RUE ALFRED DUMÉRIL
Palais de Justice
Place Lafourcade
Monument à la Gloire de la Résistance
Musée Georges Labit
Jardin Monplaisir
ALLÉE DES DEMOISELLES
Musée de la Résistance et de la Déportation
RUE ACHILLE VLADIEU
GRAND RUE SAINT-MICHEL
Le Pic Saint Loup
Le Canal à Vélo

TOULOUSE *Centre*
For listings, see from page 365

Where to stay

1 Brienne....D3
2 Grand Hôtel d'Orléans....G2
3 Mama Shelter Toulouse....G3
4 Pullman Centre Ramblas....G3
5 Royal Wilson....G3

Where to eat and drink

6 Au Pois Gourmand....A2
7 Michel Sarran....E3
8 New Delhi Palace....G4

Off map

Le Pic Saint Loup....F7

Terre de Pastel spa, champagne & cocktail bar & a delightful Michelin-starred restaurant, **Le Cénacle** (€€€€€). **€€€€€**

Le Grand Balcon [373 B3] (47 rooms) 8–10 Rue J-A Romiguières; 05 34 25 44 09; w grandbalconhotel.com. Boutique hotel near Place du Capitole full of Art Deco charm, where Toulouse's early aviators bunked between flights; the Saint-Exupéry suite is a delightful retro evocation of the time of the author of *Le Petit Prince*. **€€€€€**

UPMARKET

Brienne [366 D3] (77 rooms) 20 Bd du Maréchal Leclerc; 05 61 23 60 60; w hoteldebrienne.com. Ultra-modern design hotel, near the Canal de Brienne; private parking available; good for cyclists. **€€€€**

Grand Hôtel de l'Opéra [373 C4] (57 rooms) 1 Place du Capitole, 05 61 21 82 66; w grand-hotel-opera.com. Beautiful hotel in a former convent of 1359, right on the city's main square, with plush contemporary rooms, handsome bar, indoor pool, fitness room & a magnificent restaurant (Les Jardins de l'Opéra; see opposite). **€€€€**

Hôtel des Arts [373 D4] (11 rooms) 1 bis Rue Cantegril, 05 61 23 36 21; w hoteldesartstoulouse.fr. A friendly arty place, each room with its own personality near lively Place St-Georges, in walking distance of the main sights. **€€€€**

Pullman Centre Ramblas [367 G3] (125 rooms) 84 Allées Jean Jaurès; 05 61 10 23 10; w pullman-toulouse-centre-ramblas.fr. Bright chain hotel with edgy design & a good restaurant (€€€), parking & fitness room; kids under 12 stay free. **€€€€**

Villa du Taur [373 B2] (17 rooms) 62 Rue du Taur; 05 34 25 28 82; w villadutaur.com. New design hotel near St-Sernin, with original works of art & a good restaurant (€€€) with a Sun brunch buffet. **€€€€**

MID-RANGE

Albert Ier [373 C2] (47 rooms) 8 Rue Rivals, 05 61 21 17 91; w hotel-albert1.com. Near Place du Capitole, offering themed b/fasts, bike hire (with itineraries) & picnics to go. Pets are welcome; public parking discounts offered. **€€€**

Hôtel des Beaux Arts [373 B5] (18 rooms) 1 Place Pont-Neuf; 05 34 45 42 42; w hoteldesbeauxarts.com. Set in an 18th-century *hôtel particulier*, this has soundproofed rooms overlooking the Garonne. The 2 pricier upper rooms have great views. **€€€**

Mama Shelter Toulouse [367 G3] (120 rooms) 54 Bd Lazare Carnot; 05 31 50 50 05; w mamashelter.com/Toulouse. The funky, friendly chain here occupies a former cinema, with a rooftop bar – one of the very few in the city – featuring live music or a DJ Thu–Sat eves. Guests are treated to films, restaurant & Argentine grill (€€) & lively Sun brunch. **€€€**

Mercure Toulouse Centre Saint-Georges [373 D3] (148 rooms) Rue St-Jérome; 05 62 27 79 79; w all.accor.com. Swanky big city hotel with well-equipped rooms linked to a shopping complex. There's a lap pool, buzzing bar & parking. **€€€**

Novotel Toulouse Centre Wilson [373 D3] (133 rooms) 15 Place Wilson; 05 61 10 70 70; w all.accor.com. Hiding behind a listed brick façade of an inn of 1835, a peaceful, comfortable & convenient modern hotel in the centre. **€€€**

Ours Blanc Wilson [373 D2] (32 rooms) 2 Rue Victor Hugo; 05 61 21 62 40; w hotel-oursblanc.com. The queen of the three 'Polar Bear' hotels (others are in the budget range; see their website), in walking distance of the station, now has a clean minimalist look & w/end discounts, & super friendly staff. **€€€**

Royal Wilson [367 G3] (27 rooms) 6 Rue Labeda; 05 61 12 41 41; w hotelroyalwilson-toulouse.com. Little hotel of character with kindly owners & basic rooms & an Andalusian-style courtyard. It was the first bike hotel in the city; it also has a car garage (€10/day). Cheapest in this category. **€€€**

St-Sernin [373 C1] (17 rooms) 2 Rue St-Bernard; 05 61 21 73 08; w hotelstsernin.com. Opposite the big basilica, & peaceful at night; pleasant little hotel with modern rooms (the standard ones are a tad small). €€€

BUDGET

Croix-Baragnon [373 D5] (14 rooms) 17 Rue Croix-Baragnon; 05 61 52 60 10; w hotelcroixbaragnon.com. A good bet near the cathedral, with special rates at the nearby car park. €€

Grand Hôtel d'Orléans [367 G2] (55 rooms) 72 Rue de Bayard; 05 61 62 98 47; w grand-hotel-orleans.fr. Near the station, plenty of character & pink bricks, with its interior Spanish-style patio, garden & brasserie, La Ripaille (€€). €€

Le Raymond IV [373 D1] (39 rooms) 16 Rue Raymond IV; 05 61 62 89 41; w hotelraymond4toulouse.com. Art Deco building, a 5min walk from the Capitole & the train station, & parking for €17/day. Pets welcome, too. €€

WHERE TO EAT AND DRINK

Toulouse claims its cassoulet walks all over its rivals. To the base recipe of white beans, garlic, herbs, duck fat, salt bacon, pork rind, and goose or duck confits the locals often chuck in a foot or two of their renowned sausage (*saucisse de Toulouse*), shoulder of mutton, and perhaps some ham. To aid in the long and tormented cassoulet digestion, have a tipple of *eau de noix* Benoît Serres, the local walnut digestif (or Get Frères, if you like peppermint), then a good suck on a rubbery aniseed- or mint-flavoured Cachou pellet, invented in Toulouse and sold all over France in little metal tins for the past 120 years or so.

EXPENSIVE

Au Pois Gourmand [366 A2] 3 Rue Emile Heybrard (10mins from the Tram 1 Casselardit stop); 05 34 36 42 00; w pois-gourmand.fr; closed Sun & lunch Sat. A handsome 19th-century manor house with wooden galleries & a terrace overlooking the Garonne is the perfect atmosphere for the refined dishes such as red mullet grilled in fig leaves. *W/day menu €29, gourmet vegetarian menu €49.* €€€€€

Des Roses et des Orties [map, page 358] Chemin de Gramont, Colombiers (exit 3 off the *périphérique*); 05 61 15 55 55; w desrosesetdesorties.com; closed Mon. The short drive west of the airport is worth the trip to 'Roses & Nettles' set in a park overlooking Airbus. Chef Yannick Delpech will take you on a veritable culinary voyage, concentrating on local ingredients. *W/day lunch menu €29, dinner €61.* €€€€€

Emile [373 D4] 13 Place St-Georges; 05 61 21 05 56; w restaurant-emile.com; closed Sun–Mon. An institution, offering some of the very finest seafood in Toulouse or their famous cassoulet, plus a delightful alfresco terrace. *W/day lunch menu €22, dinner €45.* €€€€€

Le Cantou [map, page 358] 98 Rue Vélasquez; 05 61 49 20 21; w cantou.fr; closed Sat–Sun. An oasis of verdant tranquillity awaits in this beloved ivy-covered farmhouse, home to some of the very best regional cuisine in Toulouse. Offers an enormous southwest wine list. *Menus €38–€70.* €€€€€

Le PY-R [373 B5] 19 Descente de la Halle aux Poissons; 05 61 25 51 52; w py-r.com; closed Sat–Sun & lunch Mon, Thu. Here the bricks are painted white, the better to show off Chef Pierre Lambinon's exquisite 2-Michelin-starred seafood. €€€€€

Les Jardins de l'Opéra [373 C4] 1 Place du Capitole; 05 61 23 07 76; w lesjardinsdelopera.fr; closed Sun–Mon. Glass-covered oasis completely redecorated during the Covid lockdown. The food – dishes such as *foie gras de canard poché, aux huîtres dans un bouillon onctueux citronnelle-gingembre* – is orchestrated by Michelin-starred Stéphane Tournié. (There are cocktails & a shorter menu at the bar, the **Côté Comptoir**; same hours; €€€). *W/day lunch menu €35, 4 courses €75.* €€€€€

Michel Sarran [367 E3] 21 Bd Armand Duportal; 05 61 12 32 32; w michel-sarran.com; closed Sat–Sun & lunch Wed. For 2 decades the top 2-Michelin-star gastronomic experience in

Toulouse, offering unforgettable synthesis of sun-soaked southwest & Provençal cuisines. Superb food in an arty elegant town house, & charming service too. Valet parking. *W/day lunch menu €65.* €€€€€

Ô Saveurs [map, page 358] 8 Place Ormeaux, Rouffiac Tolosan; 05 34 27 10 11; w o-saveurs.com; closed Mon, lunch Sat & eves Sun. Just out of the city off the N88 to Albi, but on a sunny day there is no better place to have lunch than sitting outside this charming restaurant in the delightful square, enjoying light & lovely food. *W/day menu marché €30, dégustation €98.* €€€€€

Sept [373 B1] 7 Place St-Sernin; 05 62 30 05 30; w restaurant-sept.fr; Sat lunch & eves Tue–Sat. A large ivy-covered house opposite the basilica with a chic dining room, where Michelin-starred chef Guillaume Momboisse delights with his elegant culinary art. *Sat lunch €78, dinner €120.* €€€€€

ABOVE AVERAGE

Brasserie Les Beaux-Arts [373 B5] 1 Quai Daurade; 05 61 21 12 12; w brasserielesbeauxarts.fr; daily. On the Garonne, this belle époque brasserie specialises in seafood platters & oysters but they also do steak & cassoulet. *3-course lunch €25, menu €44.* €€€€

HITO [373 C7] 26 Rue de la Fonderie; 05 61 22 42 92; f restaurantHITO; closed Sat–Sun & lunch Wed. Superb Japanese–French fusion by Japanese chef Hitoshi Araki. One of the best in Toulouse. *Lunch menu only €18.* €€€€

Le Mas de Dardagna [map, page 358] 1 Chemin de Dardagna; 05 61 14 09 80; w masdedardagna.com; closed Sat–Sun. South of the centre, modern French cuisine in a red-brick barn with lovely features & a garden terrasse in a bucolic setting; dishes are almost too pretty to eat here. *Lunch menu from €25, tasting menus from €45.* €€€€

Les Caves de la Maréchale [373 C4] 3 Rue Jules-Chalande; 05 61 23 89 88; w lescavesdelamarechale.com; closed Sun–Mon. In the immense brick cellar of a 13th-century Dominican priory off Rue St-Rome, & populated with copies of classical statues. The menu features slow-cooked lamb, vegetarian dishes & lovely seafood, too. Live piano Fri evenings. *W/day lunch menu €22, dinner €42.* €€€

MODERATE

Le Colombier [373 D1] 14 Rue Bayard; 05 61 62 40 05; w restaurant-lecolombier.com; closed Sun & lunch Sat. In business since 1883, & frequent top contender in the 'best cassoulet in Toulouse' contest, plus other southwest dishes if you're not up to the mighty beans. *W/day lunch from €18; cassoulet €32 with dessert* (you won't miss a starter!) €€€

Le Pic Saint Loup [map, page 358] 7 Rue St-Léon; 05 61 53 81 51; w restaurantlepicsaintloup.com; closed Sun–Mon. Near metro St-Michel, excellent 'semi-gastro' cuisine, plus a great selection of wines from the Pic Saint-Loup recommended by the sommelier. There's a nice shaded terrasse out the back. *Weekly changing lunch menu from €17, dinner menu €32.* €€€

New Delhi Palace [367 G4] 42 Bd Carnot; 05 62 80 95 29; w newdelhi-palace.fr; closed Mon. Elegant restaurant with great service, delicious cocktails & wide choice of lovely Indian classics & organic wines. *Express w/day lunch menu €15, Sun brunch €20.* €€€

CHEAP AND CHEERFUL

Le Bibent [373 C3] 5 Place du Capitole; m 06 48 71 73 65; w lebibent.com; 08.00–02.00 daily. One of the most beautiful brasseries in Toulouse, founded in 1843, with a grand dining room last remodelled in the Roaring 20s, & a terrace; excellent shellfish selection & southwest favourites. €€

Le Florida [373 C3] Place du Capitole; 05 61 23 94 61; w leflorida-capitole.fr; 07.30–01.00 daily. Traditional brasserie from 1874 with an Art Deco interior lined with big mirrors & painted panels. Great place to sit out and watch the world go by. International menu, great ice cream, & 1940s roof lounge bar. €€

ROCK BOTTOM

L'Entrecôte [373 D2] 15 Bd de Strasbourg; 05 61 21 87 18; w entrecote.fr; noon–14.00 & 19.00–22.30 daily. Since 1959, a Toulouse institution. No reservations & only 1 menu, walnut salad, & all-you-can-eat grilled *faux filet* steak with the secret sauce & frites, & vacherin or profiteroles for dessert. Be prepared to queue. *€20; drinks extra*. €

La Faim des Haricots [373 C4] 2 bis Rue du Puits-Vert; 05 61 22 49 25; w lafaimdesharicots.fr; daily. One of few vegetarian restaurants in Toulouse, & good-quality buffet-style all-you-can-eat. *€12–€17.50*. €

Les Boulistes [373 D3] 5 Rue Labeda; 05 61 52 77 18; boulistestls; noon–02.00 Tue–Sat. Burgers, tapas, salads (choose your own ingredients) with a terrace & Toulouse's only indoor pétanque court. €

Marché Victor Hugo [373 D2] (page 375) The 1st floor of the market is chock-a-block with little beaneries that attract Toulousains of every ilk for lunch (exc Mon). €

ENTERTAINMENT AND NIGHTLIFE

Toulouse comes to life after dark. Check website listings at w toulousemagazine.com, w actu.fr/toulouse, w clutchmag.fr or in *La Dépêche du Midi*.

BARS AND CLUBS

Au Père Louis [373 C5] 45 Rue des Tourneurs; 05 61 21 33 45; 10.00–14.30 & 18.00–22.30 Tue–Sat. The most traditional bar in Toulouse has drawn local *quinquina* drinkers for over a century. Good choice of wines.

Chez Tonton [367 E4] 16 Place St-Pierre; 05 61 21 89 54; cheztontontoulouse; 07.00–02.00 daily. The most famous student bar in town, renowned for its '*mètre de Ricard*' – 10 Ricards served at once!

The Danu [367 H4] 9 Rue du Pont Guilheméry; 05 61 62 58 79; w thedanu.fr; 17.00–01.00 daily. Traditional Irish pub founded in 2004 with good music & with sports screens; great place to go to watch a rugby match & down pints with pub grub.

Dubliners [map, page 358] 46 Av Marcel-Langer; 05 61 14 23 16; w dubliners.fr; 18.00–02.00 Mon–Sat. Toulouse's oldest Irish bar features live music 3 nights a week.

L'Ancienne Belgique [373 C5] 16 Rue de la Trinité; 05 61 52 63 79; 16.00–02.00 daily. Try a glass or 6 of Belgian beer from their wide-ranging selection; nice atmosphere.

La Concorde [367 F2] 17 Rue de la Concorde; 05 67 76 36 01; Le-café-de-la-concorde; 07.15–23.30, 09.00–15.00 Sun. Atmospheric bar, dating back to the mid 19th century, with a listed façade.

La Guinguette de Chouchou [373 B6] 37 Quai de Tounis; 05 31 61 56 17; 16.00–midnight daily in summer. Great place for a relaxing drink on a pontoon with views on the Garonne.

FESTIVALS

There's always something happening in the Pink Town. In April it brings out its Spanish flair in the **Festival Flamenco** (w festival-flamenco-toulouse.fr). In mid-June **¡Rio Loco!** features concerts, each year from a different country or continent at the Prairie des Filtres; in late June and early July it's time to tango at the **Festival Tangopostale** (w tangopostale.com). Local folk music and dance, etc take over for **Le Grand Fénétra** (w fenetra.free.fr) the first weekend in July; from mid-July to August Toulouse Plage beaches set up along the Garonne (Bazacle, Prairie des Filtres and Port Viguerie) with snack bars and concerts. **Le Printemps de Septembre** (w printempsdeseptembre.com; mid-Sep–mid-Oct, even numbered years) is the city's biggest arts and entertainment festival, with scores of concerts, exhibitions, installations, shows and films of all kinds. Also, during the first half of September, the cloister of the Jacobins hosts the **Festival International Piano aux Jacobins** (w pianojacobins.com; book tickets early), followed in October by the prestigious international organ festival **Toulouse Les Orgues** (w toulouse-les-orgues.org).

La Maison Nougaro [366 B2] Péniche Sanctanox, Ponts-Jumeaux; 09 73 67 89 04; w maison-nougaro.fr; 14.00–23.30 Thu–Sat. New York had Sinatra, but Toulouse had native son Claude Nougaro singing its glories. This canal barge has exhibitions on his life & the Café Barbarbare has snacks, & hosts concerts & poetry readings in the evening with meals serving some of the singer's favourite dishes (bookings essential).

La Tantina de Burgos [373 B7] 27 Av de la Garonnette; 05 61 55 59 29; w la-tantina-de-burgos-bodega.com; 20.00–02.00 Tue–Sat. Zesty tapas bar with lots of sherry, sangria, beers & Spanish wines.

☆ **Le Bikini** [map, page 358] Parc Technologique du Canal, Rue Théodore Monod, Ramonville-Saint-Agne (exit 19 off the A61, or metro B Ramonville, then bus 111 to Hermès & walk 15mins); 05 62 24 09 50; w lebikini.com. Since 1983, famous venue with live music most w/ends, featuring French & international DJs & bands, boasting the best sound system in Occitanie. In summer, it has a restaurant (€€) & pool, where the signature dish is a whole melon stabbed with skewers of dried meat.

☆ **Le Filochard** [373 B5] 8 Place du Pont; w lefilochard.fr; 16.00–02.00 daily. Whacky bar with excellent music (live or not). The staff always end up joining the party. Take your drink over the road & admire the sunset over the dome of St-Joseph de la Grave.

☆ **Le Taquin** [366 C3] 23 Rue des Amidonniers; 05 61 21 80 84; w le-taquin.fr; noon–14.00 Mon–Tue, noon–02.00 Wed–Fri, 17.00–03.00 Sat, 17.00–02.00 Sun. Cool, intimate jazz bar with snacks; also w/day lunch.

No 5 Wine Bar [373 B5] 5 Rue de la Bourse; 05 61 38 44 51; w n5winebar.com; 18.00–midnight Tue–Sat. Awarded best wine bar in the world in 2017, 2018 & 2019 by the World Fine Wine Review, with more than 4,000 bottles, many to serve yourself with the pre-paid *carte de dégustation*; also tapas & evening meals (menu €40, vegetarian €30).

☆ **Ô Boudu Pont** [367 E5] 1 Rue de la République; 09 53 88 49 60; f oboudu; 15.00–02.00 daily, 15.00–03.00 Sat. Cultural bar with comedy acts or live music most nights of the week.

☆ **Puerto Habana** [367 H5] 12 Port St-Étienne, 05 61 54 45 61; w puerto-habana.com; 20.00–02.00 Tue–Fri, 20.00–04.00 Sat. Tapas bar for a lively night out *à la cubana*, offering salsa & bachata lessons (€8, see website for schedule) & dancing Tue–Sat.

LGBTQ+ BARS AND CLUBS

G Bar [367 G3] 11 Rue Thionville; 05 61 62 71 26; w g-boy.fr/g-bar; 18.00–02.00 Tue–Sat. Friendly gay bar with a retro décor; same owners run the gay-friendly club **G-Boy** [367 H5] (56 Port St Sauveur; midnight–07.00 Fri–Sat).

Limelight Club [367 H3] 23 bis Bd Riquet; 05 61 47 65 54; w limelight-club.com; 18.00–07.00 daily. Gay- & lesbian-friendly disco & lounge.

Moloko [373 C6] 6 Rue Joutx Aigues; 05 62 17 96 61; f LeMolokoBar; 18.00–02.00 Mon–Sat. Great cocktails, dancing & often live music.

P3 [367 H3] 28 Rue Gabriel Péri; 05 62 80 24 15; w barp3toulouse.com; 17.00–03.00 daily. Cocktail bar where everyone is welcome.

TOULOUSE *Historic centre*
For listings, see from page 365

Where to stay

1 Albert Ier....C2
2 Croix-Baragnon....D5
3 Grand Hôtel de l'Opéra....C4
4 Hôtel des Arts....D4
5 Hôtel des Beaux Arts....B5
6 La Cour des Consuls Hotel & Spa....B5
7 Le Grand Balcon....B3
8 Le Raymond IV....D1
9 Mercure Toulouse Centre Saint-Georges....D3
10 Novotel Toulouse Centre Wilson....D3
11 Ours Blanc Wilson....D2
12 St-Sernin....C1
13 Villa du Taur....B2

Where to eat and drink

14 Brasserie Les Beaux-Arts....B5
15 Emile....D4
16 HITO....C7
17 L'Entrecôte....D2
18 La Faim des Haricots....C4
19 Le Bibent....C3
20 Le Colombier....D1
21 Le Florida....C3
22 Le PY-R....B5
23 Les Boulistes....D3
24 Les Caves de la Maréchale....C4
Les Jardins de l'Opéra....(see 3)
Marché Victor Hugo (see Halle Victor Hugo)....D2
25 Sept....B1

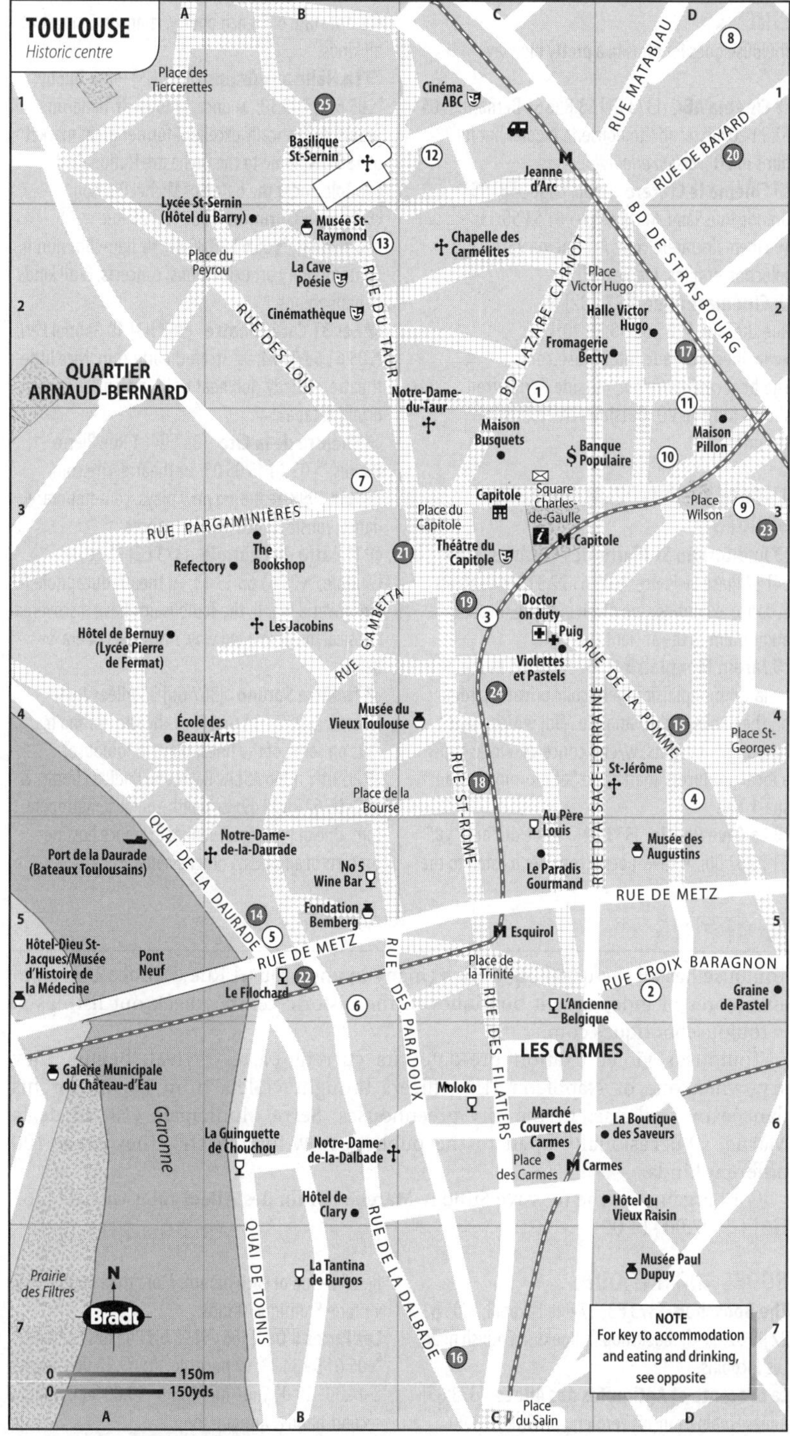
TOULOUSE
Historic centre
Place des Tiercerettes
Cinéma ABC
Basilique St-Sernin
Jeanne d'Arc
RUE MATABIAU
RUE DE BAYARD
BD DE STRASBOURG
Lycée St-Sernin (Hôtel du Barry)
Musée St-Raymond
Chapelle des Carmélites
Place du Peyrou
La Cave Poésie
Place Victor Hugo
BD LAZARE CARNOT
Cinémathèque
Halle Victor Hugo
Fromagerie Betty
RUE DES LOIS
RUE DU TAUR
QUARTIER ARNAUD-BERNARD
Notre-Dame-du-Taur
Maison Busquets
Banque Populaire
Maison Pillon
Capitole
Square Charles-de-Gaulle
Place du Capitole
Place Wilson
RUE PARGAMINIÈRES
The Bookshop
Refectory
Théâtre du Capitole
Capitole
Doctor on duty
Puig
Hôtel de Bernuy (Lycée Pierre de Fermat)
Les Jacobins
RUE GAMBETTA
RUE DE LA POMME
Violettes et Pastels
Musée du Vieux Toulouse
École des Beaux-Arts
RUE D'ALSACE-LORRAINE
Place St-Georges
St-Jérôme
RUE ST-ROME
Place de la Bourse
Au Père Louis
Notre-Dame-de-la-Daurade
Musée des Augustins
Port de la Daurade (Bateaux Toulousains)
QUAI DE LA DAURADE
No 5 Wine Bar
Le Paradis Gourmand
RUE DE METZ
Fondation Bemberg
Esquirol
Hôtel-Dieu St-Jacques/Musée d'Histoire de la Médecine
Pont Neuf
RUE DE METZ
Place de la Trinité
RUE CROIX BARAGNON
Le Filochard
Graine de Pastel
L'Ancienne Belgique
RUE DES PARADOUX
RUE DES FILATIERS
LES CARMES
Galerie Municipale du Château-d'Eau
Garonne
Moloko
Marché Couvert des Carmes
La Boutique des Saveurs
La Guinguette de Chouchou
Notre-Dame-de-la-Dalbade
Place des Carmes
Carmes
Hôtel de Clary
Hôtel du Vieux Raisin
QUAI DE TOUNIS
RUE DE LA DALBADE
La Tantina de Burgos
Musée Paul Dupuy
Prairie des Filtres
N
Bradt
NOTE
For key to accommodation and eating and drinking, see opposite
0 150m
0 150yds
Place du Salin

CINEMAS

Toulouse goes for films in a pretty big way.

Cinéma ABC [373 C1] 13 Rue St-Bernard; 05 61 21 20 46; w abc-toulouse.fr. A good bet for films in VO (*version originale*).

Cinéma le Cratère [map, page 358] 95 Grande Rue Saint-Michel; 05 61 53 50 53; w cinemalecratere.com. Art cinema with a big selection of films, many in VO.

Cinémathèque [373 B2] 69 Rue du Taur; 05 62 30 30 10; w lacinemathequedetoulouse.com. The best *cinémathèque* outside Paris often shows films in VO. Outside screenings in summer.

THEATRES AND PERFORMANCE VENUES

Auditorium St-Pierre-des-Cuisines [367 E4] 12 Place St-Pierre; 05 61 22 31 05. Concerts & dance exhibitions are given in the renovated auditorium of the ancient church.

Jardin Monplaisir [367 H7] 1 Bd Monplaisir; w jardinmonplaisir.fr. A bucolic private garden on the banks of the Canal du Midi which hosts a full range of events, w/end concerts, workshops, a local producers' market on Sat mornings, & a snack bar.

La Cave Poésie [373 B2] 71 Rue du Taur, 05 61 23 62 00; w cave-poesie.com. For a listen to the current state of French poetry, chanson & music of all kinds.

La Halle aux Grains [367 H5] Place Dupuy; 05 62 27 49 30; w onct.toulouse.fr/halle-aux-grains. Acoustically excellent former grain market of 1864, & home to the Orchestre Nationale du Capitole under the baton of Michel Plasson.

Le Lieu Commun [367 H1] 25 Rue d'Armagnac; 05 61 23 80 57; w lieu-commun.fr. Contemporary art exhibitions, concerts, & all kinds of happenings.

Les 3T Café Theatre [367 H3] 40 Gabriel Peri; 05 61 63 00 74; w 3tcafetheatre.com. Nice little theatre/comedy club near train station serving drinks & tapas.

Théâtre de la Cité [367 G4] 1 Rue Pierre Baudis; 05 34 45 05 05; w theatre-cite.com. Built in 1998, featuring new plays, contemporary dance, music & circus performances.

Théâtre du Capitole [373 C3] Place du Capitole; 05 61 63 13 13; w theatreducapitole.fr. Since World War II, the Toulousains have discovered classical music in a big way. Also hosts opera & ballets.

Théâtre Sorano [367 G6] 35 Allées Jules-Guesde; 05 34 31 67 16; w theatre-sorano.fr. Puts on some of the finest plays in Toulouse.

Zénith [366 A5] Av Raymond Badiou (Tram 1 & 2); 05 62 74 49 49; w zenith-toulousemetropole.com. One of the largest venues in France hosting concerts of all kinds & other events.

SHOPPING

Toulouse has all the usual big chains (many in and around Rue d'Alsace Lorraine) and scores of independent boutiques in the historic centre: check out listings at w toulouseboutiques.com.

Toulouse's violet fixation pre-dates its current pastel revival, begun, they say, when one of Napoleon III's officers brought violets from Parma for his fiancée in Toulouse. In the city greenhouses, Serre Municipale (18 Bd de la Marne; occasionally open to the public; see w toulouse.fr), they grow 100 different kinds.

For bargains try the massive Sunday **Marché Forain des Allées Jules Guesde** [367 G6] (07.00–14.00).

BOOKS AND ANTIQUES

The Bookshop [373 B3] 17 Rue Lakanal; 05 61 22 99 92; w thebookshop.fr. Books in English near Les Jacobins.

La Brocante et Antiquités des Allées [373 G5] Allées Forain-François Verdier; 09.00–18.00 first Fri–Sun of each month. More than 100 vintage & antique stands.

Les Puces d'Oc [366 C4] 98 bis Rue des Fontanes; 05 61 59 34 33; w pucesdoc.fr; 10.00–noon & 14.30–19.00 Thu–Tue, 14.30–19.00 Sun. Huge second-hand & antique shop.

FOOD AND DRINK

Shops

Fromagerie Betty [373 D2] 21 Place Victor Hugo; w fromagerie-betty.com. You smell it from 50 paces: there are 200 different types from across France, some of them quite special, such as the Vieux Salers, made in just one village in the Cantal & aged for a minimum of a year.

La Boutique des Saveurs [373 D6] 1 Rue Ozenne; 05 61 53 75 21; w laboutiquedessaveurs.com. Superb wine & liqueur shop.

Le Paradis Gourmand [373 C5] 45 Rue des Tourneurs; 05 61 22 05 77; w leparadisgourmand.fr. Old-fashioned sweets & nuts of all kinds.

Maison Busquets [373 C3] 21 Place Victor Hugo; 05 61 21 46 22; w maisonbusquets.com. Since 1919, wines, spirits & luxury groceries.

Maison Pillon [373 D3] 2 Rue Ozenne; 05 61 55 03 08; w maison-pillon.fr. Prize-winning handmade chocolates & pastries.

Markets

Halle Victor Hugo [373 D2] Place Victor Hugo; 06.00–13.00 Tue–Sun. 'The stomach of Toulouse' is full of goodies & cheap lunches upstairs.

Marché Couvert des Carmes [373 C6] Place des Carmes; 07.00–13.30 Tue–Sun. Very smart market, with plenty to choose from.

Marché du Cristal [373 D2] Boulevard de Strasbourg; 06.00–13.45 Tue–Sun. Huge market that takes place outdoors, all along the boulevard.

Marché St-Aubin [367 H4] Place St-Aubin; 07.00–14.00 Sun. Lively & full of crafts & fresh food to make into brunch.

Square Charles-de-Gaulle [373 C3] Tue & Sat mornings. Organic farmers' market.

PASTEL AND VIOLETS

AHPY [map, page 358] 89 Rue du Caillou Gris; 05 62 79 17 91; w ahpy.eu. Organic fabrics, clothes & more dyed in pastel.

Graine de Pastel [373 D5] 4 Place Saint-Étienne; 05 82 75 32 83; w grainedepastel.com. All kinds of pastel-based cosmetics & skin products.

La Maison de la Violette [367 G2] On a canal barge, facing 3 Bd Bonrepos; 05 61 80 75 02; w lamaisondelaviolette.com. Charming shop selling everything violet, from soaps to confits.

Terre de Pastel [map, page 358] 629 Rue Max Planck, Labège (*périphérique* exit 19 or metro to Rangueil, then Bus 80 to Grande-Borde); 08 00 94 01 67; w terredepastel.com; 10.00–12.30 & 13.30–17.00 Mon, 10.00–12.30 & 13.30–18.00 Tue–Sat. Boutique, workshops, museum & spa. Also a boutique in the Fondation Bemberg (page 383).

Violettes et Pastels [373 C4] 10 Rue St-Panteléon; 05 61 22 14 22; w violettesetpastels.fr. Cosmetics, perfumes & more.

SPORTS AND ACTIVITIES

At the time of writing, the violet-clad **Toulouse Football Club** (TFC pronounced *tay-eff-say*; w toulousefc.com) play in France's second division, but the city's heart lies with its rugby team, the **Stade Toulousain** (w stadetoulousain.fr), over a hundred years old, clad in the red and black of the city's medieval Capitouls, and frequent champions of France and Europe. Both have schedules and ticketing on their websites.

OTHER PRACTICALITIES

$ **Banque Populaire** [373 C3] 47 Rue d'Alsace Lorraine

$ **Caisse d'Épargne** [367 G3] 27 Allées Jean Jaurès

Doctor on duty [367 G3] 76 Allées Jean Jaurès; ring first 05 61 33 00 00; w sosmedecins31.org; until midnight

Hospital Purpan [366 A4] Place du Dr-Baylac; 05 61 77 22 33; w chu-toulouse.fr

Hospital Rangueil [map, page 358] Av Jean-Poulhes; 05 61 32 25 33

Puig [373 C4] 51 Rue de la Pomme

Night pharmacy [373 G3] 70 Allées Jean Jaurès; 05 61 62 38 05; 20.00–08.00 daily

Post office [373 C3] 9 Rue Lafayette

Police [367 G4] 17 Rue du Rem Saint-Étienne; 05 61 12 81 97

WHAT TO SEE AND DO

CAPITOLE AND CENTRE VILLE The heart of Toulouse owes its current charms to early 19th-century municipal architect Jacques-Pascal Virebent. Charged with 'regularising' the medieval city streets, he configured or laid out its squares, including the Place du Capitole and Place Wilson and the broad Allées Jean-Jaurès, linking the Old Town to the Canal du Midi.

Place du Capitole Toulouse's front parlour dates from 1850, after a 200-year-long campaign to rid it of excess buildings. As a permanent memorial to the southern kingdom of nevermore, the centre of the pavement is marked by an enormous Cross of Languedoc, complete with symbols of the Zodiac added in 1993, by Raymond Moretti, who also decorated the ceilings of the square's porticoes with scenes from the city's history. This same golden cross on a red background hangs proudly from Toulouse's city hall, the **Capitole** [373 C3], or *capitolium* as it reads on the façade, bowing to a 16th-century story

A CONSPIRACY'S MARTYR

Henri IV's companion-in-arms, Henri Duke of Montmorency, First Peer of the Realm and Governor of Languedoc, was succeeded in these titles by his son, Henri II, a beloved court favourite and brave warrior, a Grand Admiral and Marshal of France, a governor of Languedoc dedicated to the welfare of his people. Cardinal Richelieu, whose plans for creating an absolute monarchy for Louis XIII necessitated tripping up France's mightiest barons, choked Languedoc with taxes until it was at the point of insurrection. Montmorency's hatred of Richelieu attracted the attention of Monsieur, the king's brother, who with his scheming mother, Marie de' Medici, was always ready to befriend an enemy of the cardinal. Monsieur offered to send down troops to liberate Languedoc from the cardinal. After much soul-searching, Montmorency cast his lot with Monsieur.

Richelieu must have rubbed his hands with glee. With the king in tow he led an army south to snuff out the revolt. The promised military aid from Monsieur failed to materialise, and Montmorency, realising he had made a terrible mistake, tried unsuccessfully to surrender, hoping to avoid battle. Richelieu refused. His troops surprised the hapless duke while he was reconnoitring the lines. Montmorency, fighting singlehandedly, was wounded 17 times. Richelieu was careful to keep him alive, knowing he could make a much more memorable example *pour encourager les autres* by persuading the king to sentence the duke to death.

Montmorency's fate quickly became a *cause célèbre* across Europe – Charles I of England, the pope, the Republic of Venice and most of the nobles of France pleaded for mercy. Louis XIII turned a deaf ear, but graciously allowed the duke to be executed in private in the Capitole courtyard. On 30 October 1632, in spite of his wounds, Montmorency walked alone to the chopping block (a slab in the pavement marks the spot), his eyes falling on the statue of Henri IV. 'He was a great and generous prince, and I had the honour to be his godson,' Montmorency said, before giving the order to the executioner '*Frappe hardiment!*' He was buried in St-Sernin, the first non-saint to receive such a high honour.

claiming that ancient Rome got its Capitol idea from Toulouse's temple of Capitoline Jupiter.

Jupiter Poopiter! Everyone knows this Capitole is really named after the Capitouls. In 1750, flush with money brought in by the Canal du Midi, these worthies decided to transform their higgledy-piggledy medieval buildings into a proper Hôtel de Ville. Parts of the original complex were saved, as much as could be masked by the Neoclassical façade designed by Guillaume Cammas, who imported stone and marble to alternate with the homemade brick of Toulouse. Other critics have had trouble with the Capitole's height. '*C'est beau mais c'est bas*' was the only comment of Napoleon, an expert on the subject.

The portal on the right belongs to the **Théâtre du Capitole**, while over the central door eight pink marble columns represent the eight Capitouls. Pedestrians can cut through the magnificent gateway into the inner **Cour Henri IV**, with a statue of said king, who in 1602 gave his permission for the construction of the courtyard. Henri would have said *non!* had he known what was going to happen on this spot 30 years later, thanks to the jealous rivalries and schemes of his two neurotic sons, Louis XIII and Gaston d'Orléans ('Monsieur' for short), and the prime minister and arch-puppeteer Cardinal Richelieu (see box, opposite).

The **grand** stair leads to the delightful **public rooms** (🕘 08.30–19.00 Mon–Fri, 10.00–18.00 Sat–Sun; free), decorated between the mid 19th century and into the 1920s with monumental picture book illustrations of the history of Toulouse. It starts on the stair with the massive *Seven Troubadors Founding the Jeux Floraux* (page 384) by Jean-Paul Laurens. The **Salle de Marriage** has winsome *Allegories of Love* (at ages 20, 40 and 60) by Paul Gervais, while the **Salle Henri Martin** features paintings by Henri Martin, of the seasons and of the great Socialist leader from nearby Castres, Jean Jaurès, strolling on the banks of the Garonne. The vast **Salle des Illustres** is lined with paintings of Toulouse's moments of glory, including the stupendous *Pope Urban II Entering Toulouse in 1095 to Summon Raymond IV to the First Crusade* by Benjamin Constant and the *Victory over Simon de Montfort* by Laurens, complete with the *Apotheosis of the Woman Who Killed Simon de Montfort* on the ceiling, honouring the city's anonymous heroine.

Behind, through the back door of Cour Henri IV is the **Square Charles de Gaulle** [373 C3] and handsome **Donjon** of 1525, where the Capitouls kept their archives. The building, made more medievally better than ever with a lofty Flemish-style roof and tower by Viollet-le-Duc, now houses the city tourist office.

East of the Capitole Virebent's elliptical **Place Wilson** [373 D3] is one of the city's most urbane showcases. Virebent also laid out the broad **Allées Jean-Jaurès** that feed into the square, recently prettified as the city's demi-pedestrian 'Ramblas' with a view closed off by the large glassy arch of the **Médiathèque José-Cabanis** [367 H2], the city library. But there are plans soon to plant something much larger nearby: Toulouse's first skyscraper, the 150m curvaceous glass **Tour Occitanie**, with a spiral of forests 'inspired by the Canal du Midi' designed by Daniel Libeskind and Khardam Cardete Huet.

From Place Wilson, Rue St-Antoine-de-T (named after the tau symbol on the robes of the monks of St Anthony) leads to **Place St-Georges** [373 D4], once the main venue for Toulouse's popular pre-rugby spectator sport, executions, as it could hold the biggest crowds in the days before Place du Capitole was enlarged. Nowadays the many spectators dawdling in the cafés mainly look at one another.

St-Jérôme [373 D4] (2 Rue du Lieut-Col Pélissier; ☎05 61 12 29 08; ⌚ 08.00–19.00 Mon–Sat, 08.00–noon & 17.00–19.00 Sun) This church, completed in 1629 by the Pénitents Bleus, a lay confraternity dedicated to absolving the sins of the Protestants, combines an oval and circle to create a theatrical setting, decorated in Neoclassical white and gold.

Musée des Augustins [373 D5] (21 Rue de Metz; ☎05 61 22 21 82; w augustins.org; ⌚ closed for renovations until 2023) Housed in a 14th-century Augustinian convent, this treasure chest of art owes its founding to Alexandre Dumège, the self-taught medieval-art-loving son of a Dutch actor. During the Revolution, as the Ville Rose went about gaily smashing up its fabulous architectural heritage as ordered in 1790 by the Convention, 'to leave standing no monument that hinted of slavery', Dumège defiantly and singlehandedly rescued most of the contents of this museum, then opened its doors in 1794.

The Romanesque and Gothic sculptures, especially the capitals from long-gone cloisters, steal the show. The most beautiful come from St-Étienne – a delicate, almost fluid scene of the dance of Salome and the beheading of John the Baptist. There are scenes from a 14th-century retable, the *Group of Three Persons, One of Whom is Strangled by a Monster*, and a crooning choir of gargoyles; there's a sarcophagus with a web-footed bird carved in the side, believed to belong to the Visigoth Queen Ranachilde – *la reine Pédauque*, the goose-foot, who was said to paddle around Toulouse in aqueducts. There are reliefs by Nicolas Bachelier, and portraits of Capitouls; one of their oldest prerogatives was the *droit d'image* – the right to have their portraits painted, a rare honour in the 13th and 14th centuries. There's an extremely unpleasant *Apollo Flaying Marsyas* by Guido Reni, and paintings are by Van Dyck, Rubens, Murillo, Rigaud, Simon Vouet, Delacroix, Ingres, Manet, Morisot, Vuillard, Maurice Denis and Toulouse-Lautrec.

Musée du Vieux Toulouse [373 C4] (7 Rue du May; ☎05 62 27 11 50; w toulousainsdetoulouse.fr; ⌚ mid-Apr–Nov 14.00–18.00 Mon–Sat; €4/€2, under 10 free) The 16th-century Hôtel Dumay houses this fascinating collection from the city's history, historic costumes, porcelains, paintings and etchings.

Rue du May gives on to **Rue St-Rome**, the Roman Decumanus, lined with 16th-century mansions built by the Capitouls. At its south end don't miss the triangular **Place de la Trinité**, with a 19th-century fountain supported by bronze mermaids.

Les Jacobins [373 B4] (Place des Jacobins; ☎05 61 22 23 82; w jacobins.toulouse.fr; ⌚ 10.00–18.00 Tue–Sun; €5/€3, guided tours in English €3) Just west of Place du Capitole stands the great Dominican mother church, Les Jacobins, one of the masterpieces of southern French Gothic. The Spanish priest Domingo de Guzmán or Dominic had tried to convert the Cathars before the Albigensian Crusade, although the persuasive powers of one man, even a saint, proved negligible in the face of an intellectual revolt against the openly corrupt clergy. By 1206 Domingo had converted enough women to found a convent, which became the germ of his Order of Preaching Friars, established in Toulouse in 1215. Confirmed by the pope in 1216, the new Dominican order quickly found adherents across Europe.

In 1230, the Dominicans erected this, their third convent in Toulouse, which took the name of the Jacobins from the Dominicans' Paris address, in Rue St-Jacques (where the fanatical party of Robespierre would later meet, hence the Jacobins of the French Revolution). The Jacobins in Toulouse so impressed the popes that they made it the last resting place of the greatest Dominican, St Thomas Aquinas (d1274).

Confiscated in the Revolution, the church and convent were requisitioned by Napoleon as a barracks. When Prosper Mérimée, inspector of historic monuments, visited Toulouse in 1845, he found the mutilated complex occupied by 500 horses and cannoneers. In 1865 the army was finally convinced to donate the Jacobins to Toulouse, which spent a hundred years on its restoration.

The church is the perfect expression of the 13th-century reaction to Rome's love of luxury. Gargoyles are the only exterior sculpture in this immense but harmonious brick pile of buttresses, alternating with Flamboyant windows; its octagonal bell tower of brick and stone crowned with baby towers is a landmark of the Toulouse skyline. The interior is breathtakingly light and spacious, consisting of twin naves divided by seven huge columns, at 28m the tallest in any Gothic church, anywhere, criss-crossed by a fantastic interweaving of ribs in the vault, reaching an epiphany in the massive Flamboyant palmier in the apse. The painted decoration dates from the 13th to the 16th century, but only the glass of the rose windows on the west side is original. The 19th-century gilded reliquary shrine of St Thomas Aquinas was returned to the high altar in 1974.

A small door leads out into the lovely garden **cloister** (1309), with brick arcades and twinned columns in grey marble. The east gallery gives on to the chapterhouse, supported by a pair of slender marble columns. The walls of the Chapelle St-Antonin, the funerary chapel, were painted in the early 1300s with scenes from the *Life of St Antonin*, while the ceiling is decorated with southwest France's favourite vision from the Apocalypse: the *24 Elders and Angels Glorifying Christ*. In Rue Pargaminières, the **Refectory** (🕘 same hours) houses temporary exhibitions on historical and cultural themes.

Hôtel de Bernuy [373 A4] (Place des Jacobins; 🕘 guided tours from the tourist office) This was one of the city's most splendid residences, built in 1504 by a pastel merchant from Burgos, Don Juan de Bernuy, a Spanish Jew who became a citizen – and Capitoul – of Toulouse. Although Gothic on the outside, architect Loys Privat designed an eclectic courtyard, a mix of Gothic, Plateresque and Loire château, topped by a lofty tower rivalling those of all the other pastel nabobs. De Bernuy had a chance to repay France for the fortune he made when François Ier was captured at the battle of Pavia by Charles V and imprisoned in Madrid; the king fell gravely ill, but no-one could afford the ransom of 1,200,000 gold *écus* demanded by the emperor – until de Bernuy bailed him out. In his distress the king had promised an ex-voto to St Sernin if he survived, and in the ambulatory there you can see the black marble statue he donated when he came in 1533 to thank the saint and de Bernuy. Not long after de Bernuy's time, the Jesuits took over his mansion and made it into a college, now the prestigious **Lycée Pierre de Fermat**, named after its star pupil (page 344).

NORTH OF THE CAPITOL AND ST-SERNIN

Notre-Dame-du-Taur [373 C3] (12 Rue du Taur; 🕘 daily) This striking 14th-century church is just north of Place du Capitole. The Taur in its name means 'bull', which features in the life of the city's first saint, Sernin, who died here in the AD240s. Sernin (Saturnin) was a Greek 'apostle to the Gauls' who preached in Pamplona and Toulouse. One day, runs the legend, he happened by the temple of Capitoline Jupiter, where preparations were under way for the sacrifice of a bull to Mithras. The priests ordered him to kneel before the pagan idol, and, when Sernin refused, a sudden gust of wind blew over the statue of Mithras, breaking it to bits.

In fury, the crowd demanded the sacrifice of Sernin instead. He was tied to the bull and dragged by the maddened animal to the city gate, now Matabiou (in later hagiographies, he morphed into Pamplona's St Fermin, where he is celebrated each year by the running of the bulls). Two pious women secretly buried Sernin where this church now stands. The current church replaces an oratory built over Sernin's tomb in AD360. Its startling 40m *clocher-mur* looks like a false front in a Wild West town; the nave is surprisingly wide, and has a faded 14th-century fresco of the Tree of Jesse along the right wall.

Basilique de St-Sernin [373 B1] (☎05 61 21 80 45; **w** basilique-saint-sernin.fr; ⏱ Apr–Sep 08.30–19.00 Mon–Sat, Oct–May 08.30–18.00 daily; crypts closed 15min earlier exc Sun when they open at 14.00; free) Sernin's tomb at Notre-Dame-du-Taur attracted so many pilgrims and Christians who desired to be buried near him that in AD403 a martyrium was built 300m to the north. The saint's remains were relocated here; Charlemagne, who always seemed to travel with a trunk of sacred bones, donated a pile, and it wasn't long before tombs lined the length of Rue du Taur. In 1075, just as the Compostela pilgrimage was picking up steam, it was decided by the canons of St Sernin that they needed something far grander to deal with the pious throngs. The construction of a new basilica was of such import that in 1096 Pope Urban II consecrated its marble altar while recruiting Count Raymond IV as the leader of the First Crusade.

In 1220, St-Sernin was finished. At 115m long, with a 46m transept, it's the largest surviving Romanesque church in the world (only Cluny, destroyed in the Revolution, was bigger). It was begun at the same time, and has the same plan as the basilica of St James at Compostela, designed to accommodate crowds of pilgrims: a cross, ending in a majestic semi-circular apse with five radiating chapels. In the 19th century the abbey and cloister were demolished, and in 1860 Viollet-le-Duc was summoned to restore the basilica. He spent 20 years on the project – and botched the roof so badly that a century later it was in danger of collapse, hence a pricey 'de-restoration' project to undo Viollet-le-Duc's mischief. Today it's a UNESCO World Heritage Site as part of the Camino de Santiago de Compostela.

The exterior The apse of St-Sernin (seen from Rue St-Bernard) is a fascinating play of white stone and red brick, a crescendo culminating in the octagonal bell tower that is Toulouse's landmark. New York had its war of skyscrapers in the 1930s; 13th-century Toulouse had its war of bell towers: St-Sernin's original three storeys of arcades were increased to five for the sole purpose of upstaging the Jacobins.

The most elaborate of the basilica's portals is an odd, asymmetrical one on the south side, the **Porte Miège-ville** facing Rue du Taur; a street, called Miège-ville or 'mid-city', ran through here before the basilica was built. Devotees of medieval Toulousain arcana – a bottomless subject – say that this portal is the cornerstone of the Languedoc that the 11th-century counts were trying to create, that it's the centre of a geomantic construction, with 12 lines radiating from here across the county, connecting various chapels and villages and forming – what else? – the Cross of Languedoc.

The **tympanum** was carved by the 11th-century master Bernard Gilduin, showing the *Ascension of Christ*, a rare scene in medieval art, and one of the most choreographic: Christ surrounded by dancing angels, watched by the Apostles on the lintel. On the brackets are figures of David and others riding on lions; the magnificent capitals tell the story of the Redemption (Original Sin, Massacre of the Innocents, Annunciation). The north transept door, now walled up, was the royal door; the south transept door, the **Porte des Comtes**, is named after the several 11th-century counts who lie in the early Christian sarcophagi nearby.

The eight **capitals** here, also by Gilduin (c1080), are the oldest known Romanesque works to show the torments of hell, most alarmingly a man having his testicles crushed and a woman whose breasts are being devoured by serpents, both paying the price for Lust.

The interior Begun in 1969, the 'de-restoration' revealed some fine 12th-century frescoes, especially the serene angel of the Resurrection in the third bay of the **north transept**, which also has some of the best capitals. Here you can enter the **ambulatory** and **crypts** to make 'the Circuit of Holy Bodies'; after St Peter's in Rome, St-Sernin has more relics than any other church in Christendom. Look up to see the wooden model of this very church, a votive offering from the city to its saint for delivering it from plague in 1528. Opposite the central chapel are seven magnificent marble bas-reliefs of 1096, carved and signed by Bernard Gilduin. The *Christ in Majesty* set in a mandorla is as serene, pot-bellied and beardless as a Buddha, surrounded by the four Evangelists; the others show a seraph, a cherub, two apostles and a pair of hierarchic, extremely well-coiffed angels – scholars guess these were modelled after a Roman statue of Orpheus.

The Holy Bodies circuit continues into the **upper crypt**, with the silver shrine of St Honoratus (1517) and the 13th-century reliquaries of the Holy Cross and of St Sernin. The **lower crypt** contains, among other relics, two Holy Thorns (a present from St Louis), 13th-century gloves and mitres, and six 16th-century polychrome statues of the apostles.

Up in the **choir** an 18th-century baldachin shelters **St Sernin's tomb**, remade in 1746 and supported by a pair of bronze bulls. In the south transept, note the big feet sticking out of a pillar, all that remains of a shallow relief of St Christopher effaced by the hands of centuries of pilgrims. In the **south transept**, the shrine of St Jude, the patron saint of lost causes, blazes with candlelight in July – when French students take their exams.

Chapelle des Carmélites [373 C2] (1 Rue du Périgord; ☎ 05 34 44 92 05; ⌚ noon–19.00 Wed–Sun) From the outside this is an atavistic southern Gothic church (1643) founded by the pious Anne of Austria, wife of Louis XIII, who laid the foundation stone on the day that she learned of the canonisation of St Theresa. Inside, it's a Baroque Sistine Chapel, its walls and vaults covered with 17th-century paintings by Jean-Pierre Rivals and Jean-Baptiste Despax, featuring an allegory on the *Glory of Carmel* by Jean-Baptiste Despax.

Lycée St-Sernin [373 B2] (3 Place St-Sernin) This high school occupies the Hôtel du Barry, built by Louis XV's pimp, the Roué du Barry. Du Barry married his charming lover, Jeanne de Bécu, to his older brother in order to give her a title and then in 1759 introduced her to the king. His pandering earned him the money to build this mansion in 1777; it would later earn him and the Comtesse du Barry the guillotine. (The word *roué*, incidentally, was invented in the 1720s, to describe the bawdy companions of the Duke of Orléans by a disapproving soul who thought they deserved to be broken on the wheel.)

Musée St-Raymond [373 B2] (1 Place St Sernin; ☎ 05 61 22 31 44; w saintraymond.toulouse.fr; ⌚ 10.00–18.00 Tue–Sun; €5/€3, under 18 free) First to stand here was a pilgrims' hostel, founded in the 1070s by a chanter of St Sernin named Raymond Gayard, who was canonised for his charity to the poor; it later became the Collège of St Raymond (1505) for poor university students. It now holds the rich archaeological collections of Toulouse. The top floors concentrate on finds from the

Roman region of Narbonnaise (the predecessor of Languedoc) and Tolosa; there's a superb ephebe, a bronze Jupiter, and a relief depicting two Amazons in combat, one clearly getting the upper hand over a man. The first floor is dominated by spectacular series of imperial portrait busts and high reliefs depicting the Labours of Hercules from the enormous 1st–4th century AD Imperial Villa de Chiragan on the banks of the Garonne in Martres-Tolosane. Excavations in the basement have revealed a Christian necropolis dating from the 4th century AD and a large, circular 5th-century lime kiln. Follow your visit with a drink in the museum's shady garden Café des Antiques.

Quartier Arnaud-Bernard [373 A2] The medieval neighbourhood north of St-Sernin has been the city's Latin Quarter since 1229, when the **University of Toulouse** [367 E3] was founded in Rue des Lois. Although forced down Toulouse's throat by Paris (page 361), the university enjoyed a certain prestige in the Middle Ages; among its alumni were three popes and Michel de Montaigne. Rabelais came and 'well learned to dance and to play at swords with two hands', but he quickly got out because its regents were still burning freethinkers at the stake. 'It didn't please God that I linger,' Rabelais continued, 'me with my nature already rather parched, and not in need of any more heat.' The three principal squares of the quarter – Place du Peyrou, Place des Tiercerettes and Place Arnaud Bernard – became the centre of immigrant life in the 19th century and are still lively today.

ALONG THE GARONNE: PONT NEUF AND NORTH

Pont Neuf [373 A5] As in Paris, Toulouse's oldest span is rather confusingly called the new bridge. Begun by François Ier in 1544, this Pont Neuf harked back to Roman models, with its seven unequal arches of brick and stone and holes (*oculi*), that let flood waters flow through it without damaging its structure, allowing it to survive the 1875 floods that destroyed every other bridge in Toulouse.

Basilique Notre-Dame-de-la-Daurade [373 B5] (Place de la Daurade; 🕘 15.00–17.00 Mon, Thu, 09.00–noon & 15.00–17.00 Sat–Sun; free) Only the name recalls what was for centuries one of the wonders of Toulouse, the ten-sided, domed, 5th-century palatine chapel of the Visigothic kings, called the Daurade ('the golden one') after its shimmering mosaics. Similar to the churches of Ravenna, it was destroyed in 1761, when the nitwit monks who owned it decided to replace it with a reproduction of St Peter's. Plans for the new church collided with the Revolution and the building was only completed in the mid 19th century. The paintings in the choir are by Ingres's master, Roques; the black Virgin de la Daurade in her chapel is the official protectress of Toulouse. Just down the quay stands the **École des Beaux-Arts** [373 A4], its façade larded with allegorical figures (1895); hidden under all the sculptural icing is a 17th-century U-shaped Daurade monastery.

Place St-Pierre [367 E4] The street-lamp lined metal bridge, the **Pont St-Pierre** [367 E4], meets the wide leafy Place St-Pierre near two churches dedicated to St Peter. **St-Pierre-des-Cuisines** (to arrange a visit, contact the Musée St-Raymond, page 381), a little Romanesque priory associated with Moissac, is named after its kitchens, where one's bread could be baked at cheaper rates than at the counts' ovens. It was used as a warehouse after the Revolution until 1965, when archaeologists discovered that it was built on a 4th-century Gallo-Roman necropolis; today it's used as an auditorium. **St-Pierre-des-Chartreux** [367 E3]

(Rue Valade; ⌚ 09.00–20.00 daily; free) was founded in the 17th century by Cistercians fleeing the Huguenots and has some fine Baroque work: a grand organ (1686) originally in Les Jacobins, sculpted wood panels, stuccoes and murals from the 1680s.

Le Bazacle [366 D4] (11 Quai St-Pierre; ☎ 05 34 39 88 70; ⌚ 1hr guided tours: 16.00 Sat–Sun; free) Toulouse grew up on this spot because back in the day you could cross the Garonne here on stepping stones (the name comes from the Latin vadaculum or little ford). Later it hosted the grumbling massive 12th-century mills that so annoyed Rabelais; today enough hydroelectric watts are produced to light the bulbs of 12,000 people. The tour includes fish passages (the salmon swim by between April and June), a photo exhibition, and a fine view of Toulouse.

Canal de Brienne [366 D3] This pretty canal lined with plane trees was dug in the 18th century to link the Canal du Midi to the Garonne at the Bazacle. Inland, where it meets the Canal du Midi and Canal Latéral à la Garonne, are the monumental white marble **Ponts-Jumeaux** [366 B2], the twin bridges that mark the three-way intersection, decorated with allegorical reliefs of Languedoc imperiously pointing the Canal du Midi towards the river god Garonne.

Jardin Compans-Caffarelli [366 D2] (Bd Lascrosses; ⌚ 08.00–20.00 daily) One of the prettiest corners of Toulouse is east of the Ponts-Jumeaux along the Canal du Midi. This park was laid out in 1982 and has a great playground, an enormous metal dragon in a pond, and an exquisite Zen **Japanese garden** named after former mayor Pierre Baudis, who loved the art and culture of the far east.

LES CARMES

Place des Carmes [373 C6] In the heart of this atmospheric old neighbourhood is a market with a Tower-of-Babylon-style car park plonked on top. All around are the distinguished *hôtel particuliers* of the Languedoc parliamentarians, lawyers and merchants who once convened in Place du Parlement. Among the standouts in this mesh of narrow lanes is the sumptuously ornate **Hôtel du Vieux Raisin** (1515) [373 D6], just off the Place des Carmes at 36 Rue du Languedoc, built by a wealthy Capitoul in love with Italy.

Musée Paul Dupuy [373 D7] (13 Rue de la Pleau; ☎ 05 61 14 65 50; w ampdupuy.fr; ⌚ 10.00–18.00 Wed–Mon; €5, reduced €3) Another handsome *hôtel* houses this museum named after the obsessive collector/hoarder – every city seems to have one – who left to Toulouse his hoard of watches, automata, guns, coins, fans, faïence, pharmaceutical jars and gems like the 11th-century 'horn of Roland' and other exquisite medieval ivories, as well as a silver marigold from the Jeux Floraux of 1762.

In Rue Ninau the 16th-century **Hôtel d'Ulmo** [367 G5] (with the marble baldachin in the courtyard) was built by Jean de Ulmo, president of the Parlement, whose motto *Durum patientia frango* ('my constancy breaks adversity') hid a scoundrel to the core; caught selling every favour his office had to dispense, he was flogged, stripped of his possessions and sent off to prison, where he was given the task of keeping the accounts of the prison governor – which he falsified to his own advantage before he was hanged.

Fondation Bemberg [373 B5] (Place d'Assézat; ☎ 05 61 12 06 89; w fondation-bemberg.fr; ⌚ 10.00–12.30 & 13.30–18.00 Tue–Sun; €10, ages 8–26 €8, under 8 free)

The finest private residence, however, is north of the Place des Carmes, just off Rue de Metz: the Hôtel d'Assézat was begun in 1555 by Pierre d'Assézat, who had a near monopoly on the pastel market in northern Europe and later served as a Capitoul. Designed by Nicolas Bachelier, Toulouse's master architect-sculptor-engineer, it consists of two buildings around a large square court, and a tower crowned with an octagonal lantern and dome that served as an observation post over the Garonne, enabling d'Assézat to keep an eye on his fleet. The decoration, a rhythmic composition of Ionic, Doric and Corinthian columns, is so similar to that on the old Louvre that Bachelier was long thought to have copied the idea, although the records prove that both went up at the same time. Facing the street, an Italianate loggia has seven brackets decorated with pastel pods.

Today it holds the art collection of Georges Bemberg, heir of a German beer dynasty in Argentina who was raised in France and as a student at Harvard started buying up art he liked from the Italian Renaissance to the 20th century. It nicely picks up where the Musée des Augustins leaves off, with works by Tintoretto, Guardí, Veronese and Giambologna on the first floor; upstairs it's Signac, Monet, Marquet, Matisse, Vlaminck, Sisley, and a remarkable, glowing clutch of 35 Pierre Bonnards, all in one room; also drawings by Toulouse-Lautrec, Cézanne, Gaugin, Degas and Modigliani.

Since the 19th century, the Hôtel d'Assézat has also been the seat of the **Académie des Jeux Floraux** (📞05 61 21 22 85; w jeuxfloraux.fr), the world's oldest literary society, founded in November 1323, by seven burghers known as the 'Seven Troubadours', who regretted that poetry in their town had died out with the independence of Toulouse. To inspire new verse, they invited all the bards of Languedoc to gather on 3 May with a new poem to compete for a violet made of gold. A big crowd showed up, and ever since then Toulouse has hosted the Jeux Floraux every 3 May. Over the portico is a statue of Dame Clémence Isaure, the legendary patroness of the Floral Games.

Notre-Dame-la-Dalbade [373 B6] (30 Rue de la Dalbade; 📞05 61 25 58 05; 🕘 08.00–19.00 daily; free) 'Our Lady the Whitened' was named after its medieval whitewash, in contrast to the Daurade (page 382), although today it's as pink as the rest of the city. It has taken some hard knocks in its history; burned in the great fire of 1442, it was rebuilt in the Renaissance even taller than before, with a 91m bell tower, higher than St-Sernin's. This was chopped down in the Revolution, and rebuilt in the 1880s, using such cheap materials that it fell through the roof in 1926. The church has a rich Renaissance door and a ceramic reproduction of Fra Angelico's *Coronation of the Virgin* (1874); the interior is lofty, white and peaceful. One of the finest views of the Pont Neuf and riverfront is just west along the **Quai de Tounis**.

Rue de la Dalbade The was a chic address for the nobility; among its many *hôtels particuliers*, the standout is the **Hôtel de Clary** (no. 25) [373 B6], which, extravagantly for the Ville Rose, is made of stone. In 1538, Nicolas Bachelier designed the façades around the courtyard, the doorway, framed by statues of old men, and the monumental chimney. In the early 17th century, when the next owner, a president of the *parlement*, married a pastel heiress, he added the grandiose Baroque façade in imitation of one he saw in Italy.

At the south end of Rue de la Dalbade, in **Place du Salin** [373 C7], stood the castle of the Counts, the Château Narbonnais; in 1443 it became the site of the *parlement*. The whole complex was demolished in the 19th century for the **Palais de Justice**, with only the square brick tower of the royal treasury (converted into a

Protestant church) as a memory of days of yore. In the adjacent Place du Parlement, **Maison Seilhan** (no. 7) [367 F6] was built on the Roman wall. It became the cradle of the Dominican Order when its owner offered it to Domingo Guzmán for his new preaching order; it was later converted to the use inscribed over the door: 'Maison de l'Inquisition'. If it's reopened, you can pop inside to see seven 18th-century paintings on the life of St Dominic.

CATHEDRAL AND QUARTIER DU JARDIN

Cathédrale St-Étienne [367 G5] (Place St-Étienne; ☎ 05 61 52 03 82; w paroissescathedraletoulouse.fr; ⏲ 08.00–19.00 daily) Toulouse's oldest fountain (1546) splashes in the long square that shows off its cathedral in all its quirky glory. Begun in the 11th century by Raymond IV and completed only in the 17th century, fashions and finances rose and fell during the three major building campaigns, none of which ever got along with the other. In the centre of the façade rises a massive brick bell tower, over a Romanesque base. To the right is a worn Gothic façade, where the portal and rose window are off-centre; to the left extends the bulge of the chapel of Notre-Dame, a small church in itself.

It's even tipsier inside. In 1211, Raymond VI, keen to prove his pious credentials, threw money at it and inserted the oldest known representation of the Cross of Languedoc as the key in one of the vaults. Work continued in 1215, when Bishop Folquet rebuilt most of Raymond VI's church in the form of a single nave 19m high and 19m wide, with ogival crossings, a style that went on to become the model for southern Gothic.

In 1275, just after Toulouse was swallowed up by Paris, Bishop Bertrand de l'Isle-Jourdain decided Bishop Folquet's bit was on the puny side and came up with a plan based on northern Gothic that involved realigning the axis of the church. The fine Flamboyant **choir** was built, with beautiful 14th-century **stained glass** on the west side, but the vaults, designed to be 40m high, were cut short at 28m due to limited funds. Money and energy ran out completely when Bishop Bertrand died, leaving a curious dogleg where his choir meets Raymond VI and Bishop Folquet's nave, marked by the massive **Pilier d'Orléans**, one of four intended to support the never-built transept; it bears a plaque marking the **tomb of Pierre-Paul Riquet**, father of the Canal du Midi.

Although many of the cathedral's best decorations (especially the capitals from its cloister) are now in the Musée des Augustins, there are 15th–16th-century tapestries, faded into negatives of themselves, and some interesting grotesques in the choir. The remarkable early 17th-century **organ** was at the point of collapsing in the 1970s when it was restored and firmly bolted on its wall bracket like an elephant in a flower vase.

Rue Croix Baragnon, opposite the cathedral, has two beautiful Gothic houses, especially no. 15, decorated with a band of stone carvings.

Le Grand Rond and around When Toulouse demolished its walls in 1752 (replaced here by the Allées Jules Guesde), Louis de Londran designed the Grand Rond as a pleasure garden with a fountain to lure wealthy families back to Toulouse; its other name is Jardin du Boulingrin ('Bowling Green') after the fashionable sport imported from Britain. The bandstand is a rare relic of Toulouse's little-known 1887 International Exposition. Overhead passages link it to the **Jardin Royal** with a statue of Antoine de Saint-Exupéry and his Little Prince, and to the beautiful **Jardin des Plantes**, established in 1794 for medical students to plant their healing herbs. The 16th–17th-century **portal** on Allée Frédéric-Mistral was salvaged from the original Capitole. It was near here that Simon de Montfort was brained.

Muséum de Toulouse [367 G6] (35 Allées Jules Guesde; ☎ 05 67 73 84 84; w museum.toulouse.fr; ⏲ 10.00–18.00 Tue–Sun; €9/€7, under 6 free) The excellent Muséum de Toulouse was founded in 1796 when Philippe Picot de Lapeyrouse, director of the Jardin des Plantes, put his cabinet of curiosities on display. The first museum with a section dedicated to prehistoric humans (1872), housing 2.5 million items, it's now high-tech, with 3D exhibits, all telling the story of life on earth to the present; one highlight is the skeleton of a *quetzacoatlus*, the largest flying reptile of all time.

Musée de la Résistance et de la Déportation [367 H7] (52 Allées des Demoiselles; ☎ 05 34 33 17 40; w musee-resistance.haute-garonne.fr; ⏲ 10.00–12.30 & 13.30–18.00 Tue–Sat; free) Reopened in 2020, this museum has a fascinating and moving collection donated by veterans and deportees. The nearby **Monument à la Gloire de la Résistance** (Allées Frédéric-Mistral; ⏲ 08.30–12.30 & 14.00–17.00 Mon–Fri; free) has a crypt aligned to be illuminated by the sun's rays on 19 August, the anniversary of the Liberation of Toulouse.

Musée Georges Labit [367 H6] (17 Rue du Japon; ☎ 05 31 22 99 80; w museegeorgeslabit.fr; ⏲ 10.00–18.00 Wed–Mon; €5/€3, under 18 free) Labit was a 19th-century traveller with plenty of money and a good eye who accumulated a choice collection of Egyptian, Indian and Far Eastern Art in his striking neo-Moorish villa. It's considered the best in France after the Musée Guimet in Paris.

TOULOUSE'S LEFT BANK: QUARTIER ST CYPRIEN Each of France's four great rivers has a nickname, and the Garonne is 'the Laughing'. Often the joke was on Toulouse. Although the Left 'Gascon' Bank was settled in the Middle Ages, the periodic rampages of the river (the floods in 1875 killed more than 200) dampened property values until the late 1800s when flood control projects were completed. Cyprien was the patron saint of fishers and other folk who lived off the river, and to this day this is a popular quarter. The riverside meadow to the south, the **Prairie des Filtres** [373 A7], recalls the tanks where in the 18th century the river water was filtered and cleaned before being distributed to the city.

Galerie Municipale du Château-d'Eau [366 A6] (1 Place Laganne; ☎ 05 34 24 52 35; w galeriechateaudeau.org; ⏲ 13.00–19.00 Tue–Sun; €4/€2.50) In 1823 this handsome brick water tower was built to pump up the filtered water into the tank before it fed the city's fountains, putting all the water carriers out of work. The hydraulic machinery is still intact on the bottom level, while upstairs you can visit France's first, and one of Europe's top, photography galleries – over and over again; exhibits change 15 times a year and include both world-famous names and surprises – who knew, for instance, that Zola was an excellent photographer. An annexe has been installed in a dry arch of the Pont Neuf.

Hôtel-Dieu St-Jacques/Musée d'Histoire de la Médecine [373 A5] (2 Rue Charles-Viguerie; ☎ 05 61 77 84 25; w musee-medecine.com; ⏲ 11.00–17.00 Thu, Fri, Sun; free) One of the few old buildings to survive the floods, this enormous hospital served Compostela pilgrims since the 12th century (hence its World Heritage status). Much rebuilt in the 17th century, it also served the locals, who could drop unwanted babies through a hatch by the double stair. The hospital now houses a museum of medicine, complete with a 19th-century pharmacy and dentist's office, and a reconstruction of a medieval hospital bed that could sleep up to five (putting the most feverish patient in the middle kept everyone warm). Here too is the **Musée des Instruments de Médecine** (⌚ same hours) with historic surgical tools, wax models, etc.

Behind the hospital, **Port Viguerie** [367 E4] is a popular summer hang-out, with a Ferris wheel and *guinguette*.

St-Nicolas [366 D5] (1 Rue St Subra; ⌚ 09.00–19.00) St Cyprien, the original dedicatee of the Left Bank's parish church, proved to wield so little celestial influence over the water that when his church was rebuilt in 1300 he was sacked in favour of Nicolas, patron of sailors and protector of the flooded. The church is a small version of Les Jacobins, with another St-Sernin-style bell tower. It has a charming, colourful interior, redone in the 19th century after the last floods, along with an 18th-century altar by local painter Jean-Baptiste Despax.

Les Abattoirs [366 D4] (76 Allée Charles de Fitte; ☎ 05 34 51 10 60; **w** lesabattoirs.org; ⌚ noon–20.00 Tue–Sun; €8, over 65 €6, students & ages 13–17 €5, under 13 free, free 1st Sun of the month) In 1988 Toulouse was the last large city in France to banish its slaughterhouse from the centre, leaving this grand airy building of 1831 for a new purpose: modern and contemporary art. Before it opened, a large underground room was excavated to create space for a gift from Picasso: his enormous stage curtain from the play *Le 14 Juillet* by Romain Rolland, the *Corpse of a Minotaur in the Costume of a Harlequin* (1936), copied from the great man's gouache – although part of the year it's covered up to protect it. The permanent collection, so large that exhibits are constantly rotated, covers all the main movements from the 1950s into the 21st century. Many prize pieces were donated by Daniel Cordier, the secretary of the great Resistance hero Jean Moulin, who owned a contemporary art gallery in Nice. The many temporary exhibitions are often exceptional. In the adjacent **Jardin Raymond VI** [366 D4], you can take a spin on a seahorse or rhino on **Le Beau Manège** (**m** 06 12 22 41 62; **f**) carousel, created by François Delarozière, a preview of the delights in the Halle de la Machine (page 389).

Musée de l'Affiche de Toulouse (MATOU) [366 D5] (58 Allées Charles de Fitte; ☎ 05 81 91 79 17; ⌚ 10.00–18.00 Tue–Sun; €4/€2) More visual arts, this time in the form of graphics, posters, adverts and postcards from the 17th century to the present.

Amphithéâtre Romain [366 B6] (Rue de Purpan (Tram 1, Arènes); ☎ 05 61 22 31 44; **w** saintraymond.toulouse.fr; ⌚ 10.00 Sun for guided tours; €3, reserve via the website) Tolosa's 1st-century AD amphitheatre where gladiatorial battles took place doesn't approach the splendour of the amphitheatre at Nîmes but enough remains in situ to let your imagination fill in the rest, especially on the guided tour, which includes the nearby baths.

Le Mirail: Toulouse's Shadow Utopia [map, page 358] (South of St-Cyprien) Le Mirail was envisaged in 1960 as a Toulouse *bis*, a futurist self-contained white-collar utopia for 100,000 people. The city's then Socialist government chose as its master builder George Chandalis, who had worked with Le Corbusier on the Cité Radieuse project in Marseille. Chandalis planned a star-shaped city of five separate neighbourhoods of 20,000 inhabitants, each with its own shopping, social and cultural services, with a communal centre in the middle. Cars were banished to vast underground car parks under the large central squares so children could play safely. Each apartment was designed to have a view over the square, the ideal centre of urban life, and a view over the gardens at the back. Chandalis meant his 13-storey blocks or 'tripods' to be residential co-operatives, linked by long concourses (*coursives*) or suspended streets with shops that people would stroll past daily en route to the centralised lifts.

Two of Chandalis's five neighbourhoods were built as planned by 1971, when Pierre Baudis became mayor and radically changed the project to fit into a more traditional style. It turned out Toulouse's white-collar workers didn't care to live in co-operatives, but instead bought bungalows in suburban dreamland leaving Le Mirail to become the home to the last-off-the-boat. It does have a nice park in the centre, the **Park Reynerie** a short walk from the Mirail metro, with its centrepiece, the beautiful pink brick **Château de La Reynerie**, a '*folie*' modelled after Renaissance Italian villas. It was built in 1783 by Guillaume du Barry, the 'husband' of Madame du Barry (page 381), with some of the profits from his marital arrangement; unlike his older brother and wife he escaped the guillotine and died here. In 2019 the city completed the château's restoration; at the time of writing it hosts events.

OUTSIDE THE CENTRE

Cité de l'Espace [map, page 358] (Av Jean-Gonord (*périphérique* exit 17); ☎ 05 67 22 23 24; **w** cite-espace.com; ⌚ 10.00–17.00 daily, later on some summer days – see website, Sep–Mar closed Mon, closed Jan; book cheaper date-stamped tickets online (prices vary according to activities & season) for €21.50–€24.50, ages 5–18 €16–€18, discounts available for groups of 4 or more, for summer night, for 2 days, etc) Built to showcase the city's role as Europe's leader in the space race, there's a day's worth of discoveries here in both the latest tech and astronomy, including a giant high-tech planetarium, 3D Imax film, a life-size model of Ariane 5, the space station, the Terradome and all sorts of interactive exhibits, simulations and futuristic high-tech displays, including plenty for 4–8-year-olds, plus three restaurants.

Getting there Take the metro Jolimont or Ramonville, then bus 37. In July and August, there's a shuttle from the Place Arménie (page 364).

L'Envol des Pionniers [map, page 358] (6 Rue Jacqueline Auriol (*périphérique* exit 20); ☎ 05 67 22 23 24; **w** lenvol-des-pionniers.com; ⌚ 10.00–18.00 Tue–Sun; €8, ages 6–18 €5; combination tickets available with the Halle de la Machine) This museum opened in 2017 in the former Montaudran workshops of Air France, a hundred years after the first flight from the airstrip to Barcelona. It celebrates France's aviation pioneers, including Pierre-Georges Latécoère, the industrialist ordered in 1917 to produce 1,000 airplanes for World War I, delivering the first one in 1918 – just a few months before Armistice. The excess planes were put to use delivering the post, and Lignes Aériennes Latécoère (later Aéropostale) was born, eventually linking Toulouse – to Santiago, Chile. Exhibits honour the dauntless (and doomed) pilots who flew from here, the 'Archangel' Jean Mermoz, Henri Guillaumet and Antoine de Saint-Exupéry, complete with a flight simulator of the latter's 1924 Breget XIV biplane. The Montaudran airstrip has been transformed into **Les Jardins de la Ligne**, planted with trees from Europe, South America and Africa, the three continents served by Aéropostale. Today the museum is the centrepiece of a new neighbourhood called **La Piste des Géants**.

Getting there Take bus L8 from Matabiou or the metro Marengo to La Piste de Géants.

Halle de la Machine [map, page 358] (3 Av de l'Aérodrome de Montaudran (same directions as L'Envol, see opposite); ☎05 32 10 89 07; w halledelamachine.fr; ⏲ 10.00–18.00 Tue–Sun; €9.50, ages 13–17 €7, ages 6–12 €4.50, same price for a 40min ride on the Minotaur, combined visit & ride €16/€11.50/€8, carousel rides €3.50) The endlessly imaginative steampunk elves from Nantes have opened a stable in Toulouse to create a new range of extraordinary, whimsical articulated creations, including a Bread Catapult, L'Arraignée (a mechanical spider with legs stretching 20m), the 47m giant winged Minotaur, and the Carré Sénart carousel with all its hybrid creatures. Bilingual machinists will explain what they're creating (the current project is the Dragon du Calais).

Aeroscopia [map, page 358] (1 Allee André Turcat, Blagnac; ☎05 34 39 42 00; w aeroscopia.fr; ⏲ 09.30–18.00 daily; €14, ages 6–18 & over 62 €11, €3.50 extra for a tour of military jets, €3.50 to tour the 2 Concordes, combination tickets with Airbus tour and Ailes Anciennes available) The whole history of aviation here, from a life-size model of the *Biériot XI*, the first plane to cross the English Channel in 1909, to the enormous A380 and *Super Guppy* cargo plane, designed to bring huge plane parts to Toulouse.

Getting there Take metro Arènes, then the tram to Beauzelle-Aeroscopia, then walk 1km. In July and August there's a shuttle from Place Arménie.

Let's Visit Airbus [map, page 358] (See Aeroscopia; ☎05 34 39 42 00; ⏲ 08.00–19.00 Mon–Sat 90min tours, reservations only (English spoken) via e reservation@manatour.fr; non-EU visitors must book at least 2 working days in advance for security checks; €16, ages 6–18 €13, Airbus XL (2hrs) €20/€17, under 5 free – bring your passport) Take a bus tour through the 700ha facility, with visits to the assembly line of the latest model; the XL tour includes a presentation of test flights and a preview of the next Airbus model.

Les Ailes Anciennes [map, page 358] (4 Rue Roger Beteille, Blagnac, opposite Aeroscopia; ☎05 62 13 78 10; w aatlse.org; ⏲ 14.00–17.30 Tue–Fri, 10.00–17.30 Sat; €6, under 6 free) This is where the lucky planes and helicopters go at the end of their days – to an association of volunteers who fix them up.

Appendix 1

LANGUAGE

A working knowledge of French will make your holiday more enjoyable, but is hardly essential in the cities, where you can always find someone who speaks at least rudimentary English. Venturing into the less-travelled hinterlands may well require an effort to recall your school French; a small travel phrase book can come in handy. Even if your French is brilliant, the soupy southern twang may throw you. Any word with a nasal *in* or *en* becomes something like *aing* (*vaing* for *vin*). The last vowel or, in place names, consonants in many words that are silent in the north get to express themselves in the south (Montcuq, famously, is pronounced 'Montcuke' to avoid saying 'my bum'). What remains the same as anywhere else in France is the level of courtesy: use *monsieur*, *madame* or *mademoiselle* when speaking to anyone, from your first *bonjour* to your last *au revoir*.

For food words, see page 34.

PRONUNCIATION

Vowels

a, à, â	between *a* in 'bat' and 'part'
é, er, ez	at end of word as *a* in 'plate' but a bit shorter
e	at end of word not pronounced; at end of syllable or in one-syllable word pronounced weakly, like *er* in 'mother'
i	as *ee* in 'bee'
o	as *o* in 'pot'
ô	as *o* in 'go'
u, û	between *oo* in 'boot' and *ee* in 'bee'

Vowel combinations

ai	as *a* in 'plate'
aî	as *e* in 'bet'
ail	as *i* in 'kite'
au, eau	as *o* in 'go'
ei	as *e* in 'bet'
eu, œu	as *er* in 'mother'
oi	between *wa* in 'swam' and *u* in 'swum'
oy	in middle of words as 'why', otherwise as '*oi*', above
ui	as *wee* in 'twee'

Nasal vowels Vowels followed by an *n* or *m* have a nasal sound, especially in the southwest.

an, en	as *o* in 'pot' + nasal sound
ain, ein, in	as *a* in 'bat' + nasal sound
on	as *aw* in 'paw' + nasal sound
un	as *u* in 'nut' + nasal sound

Consonants Many French consonants are pronounced as in English, but there are some exceptions:

c	followed by *e*, *i* or *y* and *ç* as *s* in 'sit'
c	followed by *a*, *o* or *u* as *c* in 'cat'
g	followed by *e*, *i* or *y* as *s* in 'pleasure'
gn	as *ni* in 'opinion'
j	as *s* in 'pleasure'
ll	as *y* in 'yes'
qu	as *k* in 'kite'
s	between vowels as *z* in 'zebra', otherwise as *s* in 'sit'
x	at end of word as *s* in 'sit'; otherwise as *x* in 'six'

USEFUL WORDS AND PHRASES

General

hello	*bonjour*
good evening	*bonsoir*
good night	*bonne nuit*
goodbye	*au revoir*
please	*s'il vous plaît*
thank you (very much)	*merci (beaucoup)*
yes	*oui*
no	*non*
good	*bon (bonne)*
bad	*mauvais*
excuse me	*pardon, excusez-moi*
My name is…	*Je m'appelle…*
What is your name?	*Comment vous appelez-vous?*
How are you?	*Comment allez-vous?*
Fine	*Ça va bien*
I don't understand	*Je ne comprends pas*
I don't know	*Je ne sais pas*
Could you speak more slowly?	*Pourriez-vous parler plus lentement?*
How do you say…in French?	*Comment dit-on…en français?*
Can you help me?	*Pourriez-vous m'aider?*
Help!	*Au secours!*
WC	*toilettes* (men: *hommes*; ladies: *dames* or *femmes*)
water	*eau*
non-drinking water	*eau non potable*
doctor	*médecin*
hospital	*hôpital*
emergency room/A&E	*salle des urgences*
police station	*commissariat de police* or *gendarmerie*
tourist information office	*office de tourisme*

Shopping and sightseeing

Do you have…?	*Est-ce que vous avez…?*
I would like…	*Je voudrais…*
Where is/are…?	*Où est/sont…?*
How much is it?	*C'est combien?*
It's too expensive	*C'est trop cher*
entrance	*entrée*
exit	*sortie*
open	*ouvert(e)*
closed	*fermé(e)*
push	*poussez*
pull	*tirez*
bank	*banque*
money (cash)	*argent (liquide)*
credit card	*carte bancaire* (CB)
post office	*la poste*
shop	*magasin*
tobacconist	*tabac*
pharmacy	*pharmacie*
aspirin	*aspirine*
condoms	*préservatifs*
mosquito repellent	*produit anti-moustique*
suncream	*crème solaire*
box office	*bureau de location*
museum	*musée*
sea	*mer*

Transport

aeroplane	*avion*
go on foot	*aller à pied*
bicycle	*bicyclette/vélo*
mountain bike	*vélo tout terrain, VTT*
bus	*autobus*
bus stop	*arrêt d'autobus*
platform	*quai/voie*
date-stamp machine	*composter billet*
timetable	*horaire*
ticket office	*guichet*
ticket	*billet*
single to…	*un aller simple pour…*
return/round trip to…	*un aller et retour pour…*
I want to go to...	*Je voudrais aller à…*
When is the next...?	*Quel est le prochain…?*
What time does the...leave?	*A quelle heure part…?*
From where does it leave?	*D'où part-il?*
Do you stop at…?	*Passez-vous par…?*
delayed	*en retard*
on time	*à l'heure*
Where is (the railway station)?	*Où se trouve (la gare)?*
Is it far?	*C'est loin?*
left	*à gauche*

right	*à droite*
straight on	*tout droit*

Driving

breakdown	*panne*
car	*voiture*
diesel	*gazole/gasoil*
driver	*chauffeur*
electric car recharging station	*bourne de recharge*
give way/yield	*céder le passage*
hire	*louer*
(international) driving licence	*permis de conduire (international)*
motorbike/moped	*moto*
no parking	*stationnement interdit*
petrol (unleaded)	*sans plomb*
This doesn't work	*Ça ne marche pas*

Accommodation See also page 33.

single room	*chambre pour une personne*
twin room	*chambre à deux lits*
double room	*chambre pour deux personnes /chambre double*
bed	*lit*
blanket	*couverture*
cot (child's bed)	*lit d'enfant*
pillow	*oreiller*
soap	*savon*
towel	*serviette*
booking	*réservation*
Do you have a room?	*Avez-vous une chambre?*
I would like to book a room	*Je voudrais réserver une chambre*

Time

What time is it?	*Quelle heure est-il?*	evening	*soir*
		night	*nuit*
month	*mois*	today	*aujourd'hui*
week	*semaine*	yesterday	*hier*
day	*jour/journée*	tomorrow	*demain*
morning	*matin*	day before yesterday	*avant-hier*
afternoon	*après-midi*	day after tomorrow	*après-demain*

Months

January	*janvier*	July	*juillet*
February	*février*	August	*août*
March	*mars*	September	*septembre*
April	*avril*	October	*octobre*
May	*mai*	November	*novembre*
June	*juin*	December	*décembre*

Days

Monday	*lundi*	Friday	*vendredi*
Tuesday	*mardi*	Saturday	*samedi*
Wednesday	*mercredi*	Sunday	*dimanche*
Thursday	*jeudi*		

Numbers

one	*un, une*	eighteen	*dix-huit*
two	*deux*	nineteen	*dix-neuf*
three	*trois*	twenty	*vingt*
four	*quatre*	twenty-one	*vingt et un*
five	*cinq*	twenty-two	*vingt-deux*
six	*six*	thirty	*trente*
seven	*sept*	forty	*quarante*
eight	*huit*	fifty	*cinquante*
nine	*neuf*	sixty	*soixante*
ten	*dix*	seventy	*soixante-dix*
eleven	*onze*	seventy-one	*soixante et onze*
twelve	*douze*	eighty	*quatre-vingts*
thirteen	*treize*	eighty-one	*quatre-vingt-un*
fourteen	*quatorze*	ninety	*quatre-vingt-dix*
fifteen	*quinze*	hundred	*cent*
sixteen	*seize*	two hundred	*deux cents*
seventeen	*dix-sept*	thousand	*mille*

Appendix 2

GLOSSARY

abri	shelter, including prehistoric ones
auberge	inn
aven	natural well
bastide	a fortified medieval new town founded in the Middle Ages: usually rectangular, with grid of streets and a porticoed central square
beffroi	abbey
cabane	wooden hut, often with a bar or restaurant
cardo	a north–south street in Roman castrum
castrum	a rectangular Roman army camp, which often grew into a permanent settlement; often used as a village that grew up around a *seigneur*'s castle
causse	limestone plateau
cave	cellar
chai	wine or spirit storehouse
château	mansion, manor house, palace, wine estate. A strictly military castle is a *château forte*
château des anglais	a cave fortress embedded in the cliffs of the Lot or Dordogne, first built by the English in the Hundred Years' War
chemin	path
cingle	oxbow bend in a meandering river, such as the Dordogne and Lot
clocher-mur	the west front of a church that rises high above the roofline for its entire width to make a bell tower – common feature in Romanesque churches in southwest France
cloître	cloister
commanderie	local headquarters of the Knights Templar or Knights Hospitallers of St John usually to look after the order's lands and properties in an area, or attached to a pilgrims' hostel
commune	in the Middle Ages, the government of a free town or city; today the smallest unit of local government, encompassing a town or village
cornière	an arched portico surrounding the main square of a bastide
couvent	convent or monastery

croquant	('teeth-grinder') a peasant guerrilla, especially from the Dordogne, in the anti-French revolts of the 17th and 18th centuries
decumanus	east–west street in a Roman castrum
écluse	canal lock
église	church
enfeu	niche in a church wall for a tomb
étang	pond or small lake
gabarre	traditional flat-bottomed river boat used for transporting merchandise
gare (routière)	station (bus station)
gariotte	small, round drystone building with a corbelled dome for a roof. Many were built as shepherd's huts, others as refuges for villagers in times of plague. Also called *bories*, *castelles* or *cabannes*.
gentilhommière	a small country château belonging to a member of the nobility
gisement	prehistoric rock shelter
gîte	shelter (or holiday home); *gîte d'étape* basic shelter for walkers
gouffre	karstic chasm or sinkhole
grotte	cave
halle	covered market
hôtel	originally the town residence of the nobility; by the 18th century, the word became used for any large residence or public building; an *hôtel de ville* is a town hall.
lanterne des morts	('lantern of the dead') a tall or short round tower nearly always near a cemetery
lauze	heavy, flat, black stones used for tiling often steep roofs in the Dordogne and Lot. The rare *lauze* roofer these days manages to do about a square metre a day.
lavoir	communal washbasin, usually covered with a roof
lieu-dit	a place name, often a small hamlet
mairie	town hall
maison de maître	mansion or manor house
marché	market
mas	(from the Latin *mansio*) a large farmhouse, or manor or hamlet
mascaron	an ornamental mask, usually one carved on the keystone of an arch
modillion	a sculpted corbel projecting from the cornice of a church
oppidum	pre-Roman fortified settlement, usually on a height
parlement	a juridical body, with members appointed by the king. By the late *ancien régime*, *parlements* exercised a great deal of influence over political affairs.
pays	a region or country
pech	hill
pigeonnier	a dovecot, often set on stilts or attached like a tower to a house
place	square
plage	beach

plan d'eau	artificial lake
pont	bridge
puy	hill
randonnée	walk; Grande Randonnée (GR), a major hiking trail
retable	a carved and/or painted altarpiece, usually consisting of a number of scenes
routiers	English mercenaries in the Hundred Years' War
sauveterre	a village or town founded under a guarantee against violence in wartime, agreed to by the Church and local barons. Their boundaries are often marked by crosses on all the roads leading to them.
soleiho	top storey of a Quercy townhouse with an open loggia
tour	tower
trumeau	the column between the twin doors of a church portal, often carved with reliefs
tympanum	semi-circular panel over a church door, often the occasion for the most ambitious ensembles of medieval sculpture
vieille ville	historic centre

Appendix 3

FURTHER INFORMATION

BOOKS

History

Ashdown, Paddy *A Brilliant Little Operation: The Cockleshell Heroes and the Most Courageous Raid of World War 2* Aurum, 2012

Baker, Jean Claude and Chase, Chris *Josephine: The Hungry Heart* Random House, 2001. Written by one of Josephine's dozen children.

Caravantes, Peggy *The Many Faces of Josephine Baker: Dancer, Singer, Activist, Spy* Chicago Review Press, 2015. Part of a series on influential women.

Clode, Danielle *In Search of the Woman Who Sailed the World* Picador Australia, 2020. The adventurous life of the late-18th-century Jeanne Baret (page 156).

Clottes, Jean *What Is Paleolithic Art?: Cave Paintings and the Dawn of Human Creativity* University of Chicago Press, 2016. Clottes is one of the leading French authorities on Palaeolithic art.

Curtis, Gregory *The Cave Painters: Probing the Mysteries of the World's First Artists* Anchor, 2007. Good introduction.

Holt, Mack P *The French Wars of Religion, 1562–1629* Cambridge University Press, 2005

Kelly, Amy *Eleanor of Aquitaine and the Four Kings* Harvard University Press, 1991. A classic.

Knecht, Robert Jean *The French Religious Wars 1562–1598: Essential Histories* Osprey Publishing, 2002

Lucas Phillips, C E *Cockleshell Heroes* William Heinemann, 1956; reprinted by Pan, 2000. The book made into the film.

Lyman, Robert *Operation Suicide: The Remarkable Story of the Cockleshell Raid* Quercus, 2013

Pitts, Vincent J *Henri IV of France* Johns Hopkins University Press, 2012. A biography of France's best-loved king, who spent much of his time in our area.

Seward, Desmond *The First Bourbon: Henry IV of France & Navarre* Thistle Publishing, 2013

Sumption, Jonathan *The Hundred Years War* University of Pennsylvania Press, 1999–2017. Four-volume definitive history of the monumental conflict between England and France.

Literature

Duras, Marguerite *The Impudent Ones* (translated by Kelsey L Haskett) The New Press, 2021. First English translation of the first novel (1943) by the author of *The Lover* and *Hiroshima, Mon Amour*.

Fénelon, François *The Adventures of Telemachus, the Son of Ulysses* Gale Ecco, 2018. Reprint of the 18th-century classic, with a lively translation by Tobias Smollett.

Kehew, Robert and Pound, Ezra, translators *Lark in the Morning: The Verse of the Troubadours, a Bilingual Edition* University of Chicago Press, 2005. Excellent Occitan/English translation.

La Boétie, Étienne de *The Politics of Obedience: The Discourse of Voluntary Servitude* Ludwig von Mises Institute, 2015. The essay that sparked the Enlightenment.

Mauriac, François *Thérèse Desqueyroux* (translated by Raymond MacKenzie) Rowman & Littlefield, 2005. Portrait of an unhappily married woman in the Bordeaux countryside; also his *Vipers' Tangle (Le Noeud des Viperes),* many editions in English, considered by many the best book by Bordeaux's Nobel-prize laureate.

May, Peter *The Enzo Files* Quercus, 2014–21. Peter May lives in the Lot and his Scottish forensic expert Enzo Macleod is based in Cahors while solving cold cases all across France.

Merwin, W S *The Lost Upland: Stories of Southwestern France* Counterpoint; reissue edition, 2016. Charming tales of the American poet's stay in Loubressac.

Merwin, W S *The Mays of Ventadorn* Copper Canyon Press; reprint edition, 2019. Inspiring account of origins of western poetry through the troubadours.

Montaigne, Michel de *The Complete Essays* (translated by M A Screech) Penguin Classics, 1993

Moody, Mary *Au Revoir* Pan Macmillan, 2004. On her 50th birthday, the Australian celebrity author escapes family and career and ends up in Frayssinet-le-Gélat in the Lot.

Paterson, Linda M *The World of the Troubadours* Cambridge University Press, 1995. History of the medieval society that gave birth to modern Europe's first vernacular literature.

Sanders, Michael *From Here, You Can't See Paris: Seasons of a French Village and Its Restaurant* Harper Perennial; reprint, 2003. An American family spends a year in tiny Les Arques in the Lot, where La Récréation restaurant is still going strong (but under new owners).

Silvester, Ruth *A House in the Sunflowers* Allison & Busby, 1991. The first of three books about an English family buying a holiday home in the Lot-et-Garonne.

Stuart, Julia *The Matchmaker of Périgord* Harper Perennial, 2008. Charming tale of a barber matchmaker in rural France.

Walker, Martin *Bruno, Death in the Dordogne* Quercus, 2009. The first in the series of Walker's Périgourdin mysteries starring Bruno Courrèges, police chief of the imaginary village of St-Denis.

White, Freda *Three Rivers of France* Faber & Faber, 1984. Reprint of the 1950s classic of British travel literature on the rivers Dordogne, Lot and Tarn.

Food and wine

Brood, Stephen *The Complete Bordeaux* Mitchell Beazley, 2017

Chouet, Dany and Hobbs, Trish *So French* Murdoch Books, 2010. The story of the godmothers of gourmet cuisine in Australia and their retirement to Chouet's native Dordogne, with stunning photos and southwest French recipes.

Clarke, Oz *Bordeaux: the Wines, the Vineyards, the Winemakers* Sterling Epicure, 2012

Echikson, William *Noble Rot: A Bordeaux Wine Revolution* W W Norton, 2004. Covering the business side and personalities of the market, although a bit dated now.

Johnson, Hugh *Bordeaux Grands Crus Classés 1855: Wine Châteaux of the Médoc and Sauternes* Flammarion, 2018

Keevil, Susan (ed) *On Bordeaux: Tales of the Unexpected from the World's Greatest Wine Region* Academie Du Vin Library, 2021. Full of fun stories.

Kladstrup, Donald and Kladstrup, Petie *Wine and War: The French, the Nazis, and the Battle for France's Greatest Treasure* Crown, 2002

Strang, Paul *South-West France: The Wines and Winemakers* University of California Press, 2009

Wolfert, Paula *Cooking of South West France* Houghton Mifflin Harcourt, 1983; reprinted, 2005

Travel

Lyons, Declan *Cycling the Canal de la Garonne from Bordeaux to Toulouse* Cicerone, 2019

Norton, Janette *Walking in the Dordogne: Over 30 Walks in Southwest France* Cicerone, 2015

Cinema

The Cockleshell Heroes Directed by José Ferrer, 1955. A British film based on Operation Frankton (page 90), starring Trevor Howard, Anthony Newley, Christopher Lee, David Lodge and José Ferrer.

Red Obsession Directed by Warwick Ross and David Roach, 2013. Award-winning Australian documentary about the Chinese wine bubble in Bordeaux.

WEBSITES

w **about-france.com** General and practical information on France.

w **france-voyage.com** Good updated site in English full of practical information.

w **hominides.com** Excellent site dedicated to human evolution with photos of all the palaeolithic finds in the area.

w **les-plus-beaux-villages-de-france.org** There are so many members of the most beautiful villages club here we didn't ID them in this guide. But this site is full of interesting titbits about them.

w **megalithic.co.uk** Prehistoric art and monuments. Go to their map of France to find all the sites in the southwest region.

w **romanes.com** Romanesque art and architecture.

w **viamichelin.com** Plan routes and keep up with Michelin's latest restaurant reviews.

w **vide-greniers.org** Keeps track of all the flea markets and 'attic-emptiers' (car boot sales).

Index

Page numbers in **bold** indicate major entries; those in *italics* indicate maps.